Some Important Events in U.S. History

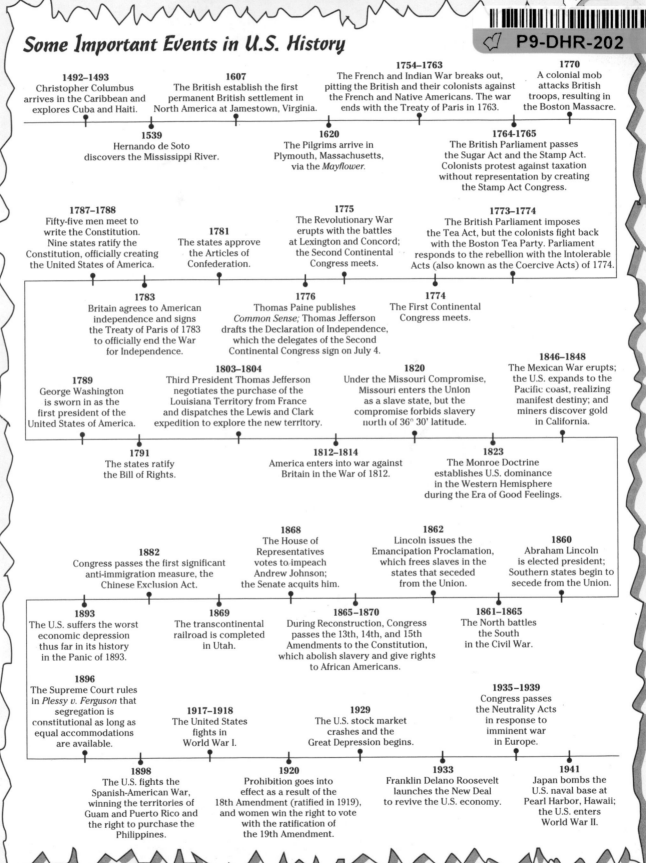

1492–1493
Christopher Columbus arrives in the Caribbean and explores Cuba and Haiti.

1607
The British establish the first permanent British settlement in North America at Jamestown, Virginia.

1754–1763
The French and Indian War breaks out, pitting the British and their colonists against the French and Native Americans. The war ends with the Treaty of Paris in 1763.

1770
A colonial mob attacks British troops, resulting in the Boston Massacre.

1539
Hernando de Soto discovers the Mississippi River.

1620
The Pilgrims arrive in Plymouth, Massachusetts, via the *Mayflower*.

1764-1765
The British Parliament passes the Sugar Act and the Stamp Act. Colonists protest against taxation without representation by creating the Stamp Act Congress.

1787–1788
Fifty-five men meet to write the Constitution. Nine states ratify the Constitution, officially creating the United States of America.

1781
The states approve the Articles of Confederation.

1775
The Revolutionary War erupts with the battles at Lexington and Concord; the Second Continental Congress meets.

1773–1774
The British Parliament imposes the Tea Act, but the colonists fight back with the Boston Tea Party. Parliament responds to the rebellion with the Intolerable Acts (also known as the Coercive Acts) of 1774.

1783
Britain agrees to American independence and signs the Treaty of Paris of 1783 to officially end the War for Independence.

1776
Thomas Paine publishes *Common Sense;* Thomas Jefferson drafts the Declaration of Independence, which the delegates of the Second Continental Congress sign on July 4.

1774
The First Continental Congress meets.

1789
George Washington is sworn in as the first president of the United States of America.

1803–1804
Third President Thomas Jefferson negotiates the purchase of the Louisiana Territory from France and dispatches the Lewis and Clark expedition to explore the new territory.

1820
Under the Missouri Compromise, Missouri enters the Union as a slave state, but the compromise forbids slavery north of 36° 30' latitude.

1846–1848
The Mexican War erupts; the U.S. expands to the Pacific coast, realizing manifest destiny; and miners discover gold in California.

1791
The states ratify the Bill of Rights.

1812–1814
America enters into war against Britain in the War of 1812.

1823
The Monroe Doctrine establishes U.S. dominance in the Western Hemisphere during the Era of Good Feelings.

1882
Congress passes the first significant anti-immigration measure, the Chinese Exclusion Act.

1868
The House of Representatives votes to impeach Andrew Johnson; the Senate acquits him.

1862
Lincoln issues the Emancipation Proclamation, which frees slaves in the states that seceded from the Union.

1860
Abraham Lincoln is elected president; Southern states begin to secede from the Union.

1893
The U.S. suffers the worst economic depression thus far in its history in the Panic of 1893.

1869
The transcontinental railroad is completed in Utah.

1865–1870
During Reconstruction, Congress passes the 13th, 14th, and 15th Amendments to the Constitution, which abolish slavery and give rights to African Americans.

1861–1865
The North battles the South in the Civil War.

1896
The Supreme Court rules in *Plessy v. Ferguson* that segregation is constitutional as long as equal accommodations are available.

1917–1918
The United States fights in World War I.

1929
The U.S. stock market crashes and the Great Depression begins.

1935–1939
Congress passes the Neutrality Acts in response to imminent war in Europe.

1898
The U.S. fights the Spanish-American War, winning the territories of Guam and Puerto Rico and the right to purchase the Philippines.

1920
Prohibition goes into effect as a result of the 18th Amendment (ratified in 1919), and women win the right to vote with the ratification of the 19th Amendment.

1933
Franklin Delano Roosevelt launches the New Deal to revive the U.S. economy.

1941
Japan bombs the U.S. naval base at Pearl Harbor, Hawaii; the U.S. enters World War II.

SAT II U.S. History
For Dummies®

Cheat Sheet

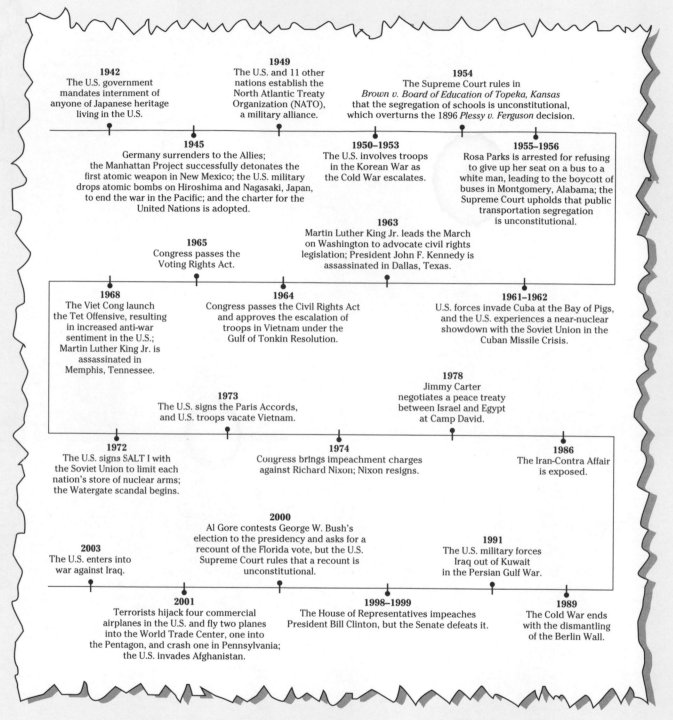

1942
The U.S. government mandates internment of anyone of Japanese heritage living in the U.S.

1949
The U.S. and 11 other nations establish the North Atlantic Treaty Organization (NATO), a military alliance.

1954
The Supreme Court rules in *Brown v. Board of Education of Topeka, Kansas* that the segregation of schools is unconstitutional, which overturns the 1896 *Plessy v. Ferguson* decision.

1945
Germany surrenders to the Allies; the Manhattan Project successfully detonates the first atomic weapon in New Mexico; the U.S. military drops atomic bombs on Hiroshima and Nagasaki, Japan, to end the war in the Pacific; and the charter for the United Nations is adopted.

1950–1953
The U.S. involves troops in the Korean War as the Cold War escalates.

1955–1956
Rosa Parks is arrested for refusing to give up her seat on a bus to a white man, leading to the boycott of buses in Montgomery, Alabama; the Supreme Court upholds that public transportation segregation is unconstitutional.

1963
Martin Luther King Jr. leads the March on Washington to advocate civil rights legislation; President John F. Kennedy is assassinated in Dallas, Texas.

1965
Congress passes the Voting Rights Act.

1968
The Viet Cong launch the Tet Offensive, resulting in increased anti-war sentiment in the U.S.; Martin Luther King Jr. is assassinated in Memphis, Tennessee.

1964
Congress passes the Civil Rights Act and approves the escalation of troops in Vietnam under the Gulf of Tonkin Resolution.

1961–1962
U.S. forces invade Cuba at the Bay of Pigs, and the U.S. experiences a near-nuclear showdown with the Soviet Union in the Cuban Missile Crisis.

1978
Jimmy Carter negotiates a peace treaty between Israel and Egypt at Camp David.

1973
The U.S. signs the Paris Accords, and U.S. troops vacate Vietnam.

1972
The U.S. signs SALT I with the Soviet Union to limit each nation's store of nuclear arms; the Watergate scandal begins.

1974
Congress brings impeachment charges against Richard Nixon; Nixon resigns.

1986
The Iran-Contra Affair is exposed.

2000
Al Gore contests George W. Bush's election to the presidency and asks for a recount of the Florida vote, but the U.S. Supreme Court rules that a recount is unconstitutional.

1991
The U.S. military forces Iraq out of Kuwait in the Persian Gulf War.

2003
The U.S. enters into war against Iraq.

2001
Terrorists hijack four commercial airplanes in the U.S. and fly two planes into the World Trade Center, one into the Pentagon, and crash one in Pennsylvania; the U.S. invades Afghanistan.

1998–1999
The House of Representatives impeaches President Bill Clinton, but the Senate defeats it.

1989
The Cold War ends with the dismantling of the Berlin Wall.

For Dummies: Bestselling Book Series for Beginners

*SAT II U.S. History FOR DUMMIES®

by Scott Hatch, JD, and
Lisa Zimmer Hatch, MA

WILEY

Wiley Publishing, Inc.

*SAT II U.S. History For Dummies®

Published by
Wiley Publishing, Inc.
111 River St.
Hoboken, NJ 07030-5774
www.wiley.com

For general information on our other products and services, please contact our Customer Care Department within the U.S. at 800-762-2974, outside the U.S. at 317-572-3993, or fax 317-572-4002.

For technical support, please visit www.wiley.com/techsupport.

Wiley also publishes its books in a variety of electronic formats. Some content that appears in print may not be available in electronic books.

Library of Congress Control Number: 2005921461

ISBN-13: 978-0-7645-7843-4
ISBN-10: 0-7645-7843-X

Manufactured in the United States of America

10 9 8 7 6 5 4 3 2 1

1B/SR/QT/QV/IN

*SAT is a registered trademark of the College Board, which was not involved in the production of, and does not endorse, this product.

WILEY

About the Authors

Scott and Lisa Hatch have been preparing students for college entrance exams for more than 25 years. While in law school in the late '70s, Scott taught LSAT preparation courses throughout southern California to pay for his education. He was so good at it that after graduation, he went out on his own. Using materials he developed himself, he prepared thousands of anxious test-takers for the SAT, ACT, PSAT, LSAT, GRE, GMAT, and even the unassuming Miller's Analogy Test (MAT).

Scott and Lisa have a special place in their hearts for standardized tests; they kindled their romance in the classroom. Lisa took one of Scott's LSAT preparation courses at the University of Colorado and improved her love life as well as her LSAT score. Lisa's love for instructing and writing meant that she fit right in with Scott's lifestyle of teaching courses and preparing course materials. They married shortly thereafter.

Since then, Scott and Lisa have been teaching test-preparation courses to students worldwide. More than 300 universities and colleges currently offer their courses through live lectures and the Internet, and the couple has written the curriculum for both formats. The company they've built, The Center for Legal Studies, not only provides standardized test-preparation courses, but it also provides courses for those who desire careers in the field of law, including paralegals, legal secretaries, legal investigators, victim advocates, and legal nurse consultants.

Scott has been presenting standardized test-preparation courses since 1979. He's listed in *Who's Who in California* and *Who's Who Among Students in American Colleges and Universities* and was named one of the Outstanding Young Men of America by the United States Jaycees. He served as a contributing editor to *The Judicial Profiler* (McGraw-Hill) and the *Colorado Law Annotated* (West/Lawyers Co-op) series and editor of several award-winning publications.

Lisa has been teaching legal certificate and standardized test-preparation courses since 1987. She graduated with honors in English from the University of Puget Sound and received her master's degree in 2000 from California State University. She and Scott have co-authored numerous law and standardized test texts, including *Paralegal Procedures and Practices* (Thomson/West Publishing), *A Paralegal Primer* (The Center for Legal Studies), and *Preparing for the SAT, Preparing for the ACT, Preparing for the LSAT, Preparing for the GRE,* and *Preparing for the GMAT.* Courses are available online at www.legalstudies.com.

Dedication

We dedicate our *For Dummies* series books to Alison, Andrew, Zachary, and Zoe Hatch. Rather than filing missing persons reports for their parents with the local law enforcement agency, they demonstrated extreme patience, understanding, and assistance while we wrote these books, which made this innovative, comprehensive, informative, and entertaining standardized test-preparation series possible.

Authors' Acknowledgments

This book would not have been possible without the extensive research and writing contributions of standardized test-prep and U.S. history experts Lindsey Mann, Mark J. Sunderman, Eric J. Morgan, and Steve Mallory. Their efforts greatly enhanced our writing, editing, and organization, and we are deeply grateful to them. We also thank the staff at The Center for Legal Studies for working diligently to execute a smooth process in the administrative tasks that were necessary to bring about this book.

We also need to acknowledge the input of the thousands of high school students and other college applicants who've completed our test-preparation courses over the last 25 years. The classroom and online contributions these eager learners have offered have provided us with lots of information about which areas require the greatest amount of preparation. Their input is the reason we're able to produce accurate and up-to-date test preparation. Many of our students, like Zach Hatch and Tyler Polhill, have also taken the sample tests that we set forth in this book and have assisted us in perfecting the questions and answer choices.

Our meticulous scholarship and attempts at wit were greatly facilitated by the editing professionals at Wiley Publishing. Our thanks go out to Georgette Beatty for her unflagging support and encouragement, to Michelle Dzurny for her attention to detail, to David Rodgers for his keen insights, and to Tracy Boggier for initiating us to the process and being available whenever we had questions.

Finally, we wish to acknowledge our literary agents Bill Gladstone and Margo Maley Hutchinson at Waterside Productions in Cardiff for introducing us to the innovative *For Dummies* series.

We commend Wiley Publishing for its pioneering efforts to make preparing for compulsory entrance exams fun. We thrive on positive reinforcement and feedback from our students and encourage our readers to provide comments and critiques at feedback@legalstudies.com.

Publisher's Acknowledgments

We're proud of this book; please send us your comments through our Dummies online registration form located at www.dummies.com/register/.

Some of the people who helped bring this book to market include the following:

Acquisitions, Editorial, and Media Development

Project Editor: Georgette Beatty

Acquisitions Editor: Tracy Boggier

Copy Editor: Michelle Dzurny

Technical Editor: David Rodgers

Senior Editorial Manager: Jennifer Ehrlich

Editorial Assistants: Hanna Scott, Nadine Bell

Cartoons: Rich Tennant (www.the5thwave.com)

Composition Services

Project Coordinator: Nancee Reeves

Layout and Graphics: Carrie A. Foster, Denny Hager

Proofreaders: Laura Albert, Cindy Ballew

Indexer: Rebecca R. Plunkett

Publishing and Editorial for Consumer Dummies

Diane Graves Steele, Vice President and Publisher, Consumer Dummies

Joyce Pepple, Acquisitions Director, Consumer Dummies

Kristin A. Cocks, Product Development Director, Consumer Dummies

Michael Spring, Vice President and Publisher, Travel

Kelly Regan, Editorial Director, Travel

Publishing for Technology Dummies

Andy Cummings, Vice President and Publisher, Dummies Technology/General User

Composition Services

Gerry Fahey, Vice President of Production Services

Debbie Stailey, Director of Composition Services

Contents at a Glance

Table of Contents

Introduction

You're merrily skimming through the admissions requirements for your favorite college when all of a sudden you're dealt a shocking blow: Your absolute top-choice college requires not only the SAT I and the ACT but also the SAT II. Indeed, yet another set of tests exists for which you'll need to sharpen more number-two pencils and awaken at the crack of dawn on an otherwise sleepy Saturday.

The SAT II U.S. History test is just one of many possible SAT II subject tests that you can take to meet the admissions requirements for many colleges and universities. Most students who take a subject test in social sciences take the U.S. history test, so you'll be in good company on test day. For this exam, you and your fellow SAT II test-takers will examine political cartoons and evaluate the characteristics of each era in American history.

You know you have to get ready for the challenge, but what should you do to prepare? Get out your spiral notebook from your last history class and sift through a year's worth of doodles? You know that you recorded the year that the War of 1812 started somewhere, but even if you could read your handwriting, your little brother's dirty handprint is concealing the date.

Clearly, you need a readable, more concisely structured resource. Well, you've come to the right place. *SAT II U.S. History For Dummies* puts everything you need to know to conquer the SAT II U.S. History test right at your fingertips. We give you a complete review of the U.S. history concepts that the exam tests and provide you with insights on how to avoid the pitfalls that the SAT II creators want you to fall into. Plus, we make preparing for the exam as enjoyable as a book devoted to treaties and political philosophy can be.

About This Book

We suspect that you aren't eagerly anticipating sitting through the SAT II, and you're probably not looking forward to studying for it, either. Chances are your parents or some other well-meaning authority figure bought this book for you for your own good, and we know just how much students enjoy doing things that are good for them!

Therefore, we attempt to make the study process as painless as possible by giving you clearly written advice in an easy-to-swallow, casual tone. We realize that you have a bunch of stuff you'd rather be doing, so we broke the information into easily digestible bites. If you have an extra hour before basketball practice or clarinet lessons, you can devour a chapter of your choice or even a particular section within a chapter. (If these eating metaphors are making you hungry, feel free to take a snack break.)

We pepper this history review with plenty of sample questions so you can see just how the SAT II tests a particular concept. Our sample questions read like the actual test questions so you get comfortable with how the SAT II phrases questions and expresses answer choices. To further enhance your comfort with the test questions, this book contains two practice tests (and their answers). Ultimately, the best way to prepare for any standardized test is to practice lots of test questions, and this book has more than 200 of them scattered throughout the review chapters and the two practice tests.

In this book, you also find time-tested techniques for improving your score. We show you how to quickly eliminate incorrect answer choices and make educated guesses, and you find out how to manage your time wisely. Additionally, we give you suggestions to create a relaxation routine that you can use if you start to panic during the test. Have no fear: We include all kinds of information to help you do your best on the SAT II.

Conventions Used in This Book

You'll find this book easily accessible, but a couple of things require brief explanation.

- ✔ **Boldfaced** text indicates the main items in bulleted lists.
- ✔ *Cascade font* highlights important vocabulary words, concepts, events, and names that you can use to develop vocabulary lists.

What You're Not to Read

Some of the chapters contain sidebars (text in a shaded box). Sidebars contain quirky bits of information that may interest you, but the info isn't essential to know for the SAT II. If you're trying to save time, you can skip the sidebars.

Foolish Assumptions

Although we guess you could've picked up this book just because you have an insatiable love for U.S. history, we're betting it's more likely that you're reading this book because you have to take the SAT II U.S. History test. (We've been praised for our startling ability to recognize the obvious!) And because we're pretty astute, we figure that you're applying to undergraduate programs that require you to take the test for admissions purposes or suggest that you take it for a variety of other reasons.

Generally, the schools that require the SAT II are highly selective, so we're thinking that you're a pretty motivated student because you have your sights set on these competitive institutions of higher learning. You probably know a lot about history already, and you've probably taken at least a year of it in high school. Some of you may have even taken advanced history classes in high school. If you have, you should do very well on the SAT II.

Your history classes may still be fresh in your mind, so you may only need to know what to expect when you arrive at the test site. This book has that information for you. Others of you may have been out of high school for a while, and your history knowledge may have left for parts unknown. This book provides you with all the basics as well as the advanced concepts necessary to give you a comprehensive foundation for the SAT II.

How This Book Is Organized

The first part of this book introduces you to the nature of the SAT II beast and advises you on how to tame it. The comprehensive history review is next and spans several more parts of the book. When you feel ready, take the two practice tests that come after the history review and find out your score.

Part 1: Putting the SAT II U.S. History in Perspective

Read this part of the book if you want to know more about the SAT II U.S. History test in general (such as when to take it and scoring considerations) and how you can handle it using surefire test-taking techniques.

Part II: The Birth of a Nation

Some of the questions on the SAT II U.S. History test deal with America's early years, from its discovery to the 18th century. The chapters in this part cover the early exploration and colonization of the New World, provide the factors that led to America's struggle for independence from Great Britain, and give you insight into the formation of the new government of the independent nation.

Part III: America's Childhood Years

This part explores the first half of the 19th century, when the United States continued to solidify its government and its identity as a nation. Chapters in this part take you from Thomas Jefferson's presidency through Abraham Lincoln's and include the important events of the era that you need to know for the SAT II.

Part IV: America as a Young Adult

Quite a few SAT II U.S. History questions concern the period after the Civil War when the United States was trying to put itself back together. During the second half of the 19th century, America expanded its borders and its level of industry. In this part, you find out how imperialism and the Industrial Revolution propelled the United States from a fledgling country to an increasingly powerful nation.

Part V: America Becomes a Grown-Up

In the first half of the 20th century, America experienced a wave of Progressivism, a devastating economic depression, and two world wars. You can bet that the SAT II will test you heavily on the information this part contains.

Part VI: America in Middle Age

This part contains information that may be more familiar to you because you've actually lived through some of the events. In addition to covering modern times, the chapters in this part review the important events that occurred in the second half of the 20th century, like the Cold War, the civil rights movement, and the Vietnam War.

Part VII: Practice Makes Perfect: Full-Length Practice Tests

When you feel comfortable with your history knowledge, you can practice on the two full-length tests in this part. Each 90-question test has a scoring guide and explanatory answers to help you figure out which eras of U.S. history you know the most about and which ones you need to brush up on.

Part VIII: The Part of Tens

This part contains a summary of ten important leaders and ten crucial presidencies in U.S. history that you should pay particular attention to for the SAT II.

Icons Used in This Book

The icons are an exciting feature of this book used to highlight especially significant information in the text. These little pictures appear in the margins and alert you to areas that you should pay particularly close attention to.

This icon means you get to practice a particular area of instruction with a question like one you may see on the test. Our examples include detailed explanations of how to most efficiently answer SAT II questions and avoid common pitfalls.

The Tip icon highlights ways that you can enhance your performance on the SAT II. These tips give you juicy timesavers and point out especially relevant concepts to remember for the test.

This icon points out the little traps that the testmakers use to tempt you to choose the wrong answer. Don't worry, though: We provide tricks you can use to avoid those traps and outsmart the SAT II.

Your world won't fall apart if you ignore our Warning icons, but your score may suffer. Heed these cautionary words of advice to avoid making careless mistakes that can cost you points.

Where to Go from Here

We know that everyone who uses this book has different strengths and weaknesses, so we designed this book so you can read it in the way that best suits you. If you're a history whiz who only needs to brush up on a few areas, you can go right to the chapters and sections that cover those areas.

We suggest that you take a more thorough approach, however. Familiarize yourself with the general test-taking process in the first two chapters and then work through the complete history review. You can skim through sections that you know a lot about by just reading the Tips, Warnings, and Traps and Tricks and working through the Example questions.

Some students like taking a diagnostic test before they study. A diagnostic test is just a fancy way of saying that they take one of the practice tests in Part VII before they read the rest of the book to find out which questions they seem to cruise through and which areas need more work. After you read the history review, you can take another practice test and compare your score to the one you received on the first test. This way, you can see just how much you improved with practice. Or, if you prefer, you can take both tests after you finish your review, using the first to point out your strengths and weaknesses and the second to see how much you improve with further review — the choice is yours.

Part I
Putting the SAT II U.S. History in Perspective

The 5th Wave   By Rich Tennant

"My SAT II scores? Why would you want my SAT II scores?"

In this part . . .

The day you've been working toward your whole life (or at least the last few days) will be here before you know it: SAT II U.S. History test day, of course. Although the SAT II U.S. History exam is important, it probably isn't very important in the big scheme of your life. Your birth, prom, first day of college, wedding day, the birth of your first born, and so on, may be more important landmarks. Unfortunately, the college admissions officers who you're desperately trying to impress think that how you perform on this test is one of the few most important things in your life.

Before you start to review U.S. history, spend a few minutes looking over this part to find out how the test is organized, what subjects it may cover, when to take it, and how it'll be scored. To help relieve some pressure, we also share guessing strategies, time-management tips, and study techniques to make your test experience less painful than a root canal.

Chapter 1

Getting the Lowdown on the SAT II

*I*f you're reading this book, you're probably planning to go to college in the very near future. Deciding where you're going to get your college education (and spend four years of your life) is one of the most exciting choices you'll make. You're going to strike out on your own, meet new people, see new places, and learn about stuff you never knew existed. But there's just one catch: The school you want to attend has to accept you first. And the SAT II is one tool that some colleges consider when deciding whether or not to accept you. Because you bought this book, we're guessing that at least one of the colleges you want to get into requires you to take the SAT II subject tests, probably U.S. history (either that or you're really into the history of your homeland).

In this chapter, you find out why some colleges want you to take the SAT II and what the SAT II U.S. History test is all about.

Justification: How Colleges Use the SAT II

How colleges and universities evaluate your SAT II U.S. History score really depends on the particular institution. Check out the following sections for the scoop.

The SAT II as an admissions requirement

Before you fill out your college application form, research the admissions requirements of your top schools. You can usually find the most up-to-date information on the college's Web site, but you can also get information from your high school counselor or request colleges to mail their brochures to you. Read the admissions requirements carefully to find out how the school applies the information it gets from your SAT II scores. Some colleges

- ✔ Don't consider your SAT II score when they decide whether or not to admit you. (They may use your score as a placement tool, though; see the next section.)
- ✔ Give your SAT II score the same weight as your SAT or ACT score and your grade point average.
- ✔ May not emphasize your SAT II score like they do your other standardized tests and grade point average but use it for additional consideration, like they would your extracurricular activities when they compare you to other applicants.

Find out how your college choices evaluate your SAT II score. If you're confused by the information that they provide, call the admissions office. Knowing just what's at stake when you walk into the testing site is a good idea.

The SAT II as a placement tool

Colleges that use your SAT II score as an admissions requirement as well as those that don't *may* consider it for placement purposes. Many colleges and universities allow first-year students to "test out" of core course requirements if they score well on the SAT II. For example, if you do really well on the SAT II U.S. History test, you may not have to take a freshman-level U.S. history course.

Another way colleges may use SAT II test scores is to place students in appropriate class levels. For example, if you score high on the SAT II Spanish exam, a college knows that you're ready for Spanish II instead of Spanish I.

College Web sites don't usually spell out the specifics on how the college uses the SAT II for placement purposes, so call the admissions office directly if you need more information about whether your SAT II score can get you out of taking one of those huge freshman lectures with 500 other students.

Decisions, Decisions: Determining Which Subject Test (or Tests) You Should Take

Deciding which SAT II subject tests you needed to take was a little easier before the SAT I changed in spring 2005. Most colleges that required the SAT II made you take the SAT II Math, the old SAT II Writing, and one other exam. The only decisions your overworked brain had to make were whether to take Level I or Level II for the math exam and which of the other subjects would provide the least amount of torture for your third choice.

But, alas, things have changed. Students entering college in fall 2006 must take a new SAT I that incorporates the old SAT II Writing test and some of the elements of the Level IC Math test. The result is that most colleges probably will no longer require particular subject tests, like math and English, and you'll have to decide which tests are best for you.

The following sections give you the scoop on the SAT II test options that you have and help you select which tests are best for you.

Checking out your subject area choices

Each SAT II subject test falls into one of five general categories. Knowing these categories is important because some colleges won't accept two tests from the same category. The five categories are

- **English:** As of spring 2005, only the SAT II Literature exam is offered.
- **History and Social Studies:** Two history tests make up this category: the SAT II U.S. History and the SAT II World History.
- **Science:** The SAT II Biology Ecological/Molecular (fondly known as SAT II Biology E/M), the SAT II Chemistry, and the SAT II Physics are all considered science tests. Go figure!
- **Mathematics:** Two separate math tests are offered: the Level IC and the more advanced Level IIC.
- **Languages:** The SAT II has 13 language tests. Some of the languages also have separate one-hour listening tests in addition to the hour-long written tests.

Figuring out the right subject area tests for you

To determine which of the 21 different subject tests are best for you, consider your strengths. Ignore what your friends are doing and choose the subjects that you do best in and that you know the most about. If you can recite the Declaration of Independence in your sleep, the SAT II U.S. History exam is probably a good bet. (And you're sure to enjoy this book!) Usually, you test better on subjects you're interested in, and the bottom line is that you want to take the SAT II exams where you'll score highest.

Admissions committees often suggest that you show your range of knowledge by taking as broad of a mix of subjects as you feel comfortable with. So even if you're a history buff, you probably shouldn't take both the SAT II U.S. History and the SAT II World History. Choose the history exam that tests the area you know more about, and then choose another SAT II exam in another subject that's comfortable for you. (To determine which SAT II tests are in the same subject areas, see "Checking out your subject area choices" earlier in this chapter.)

 If you're really conflicted about which tests to take, you may feel better knowing that you can decide which tests you're taking on test day. Nevertheless, we *highly* suggest that you decide which tests you want to take *before* you step into the testing room; that way, you can concentrate on preparing for only the tests you plan to take on test day.

It's All in the Timing: When to Take the SAT II (and What to Bring)

After you figure out which subject tests are best for you, you need to determine when the best time to take them is and what you should bring with you to the test.

The best time to take and register for the SAT II

Most SAT II subject tests are offered in January, May, June, October, November, and December on select Saturday mornings beginning at 8:15 a.m. (or the following Sunday morning, if you can't take tests on Saturday for religious reasons). Exactly when you decide to take a particular subject test really depends on what the subject test covers. You're best off taking SAT II subject tests as soon as possible after you complete specific courses. For example, if you take U.S. history and biology during your sophomore year, you'd be wise to take the SAT II U.S. History and SAT II Biology tests after you complete your sophomore year on either the May or June test date or at least in the fall of your junior year.

Obviously, the scheduling for these exams is much earlier than you'd normally take other admissions tests. Most students don't take the regular SAT or ACT until the end of their junior years. But you don't have to know exactly which colleges you want to go to when you take the SAT II exams. You can request that the College Board (the folks who administer the SAT II) send out your scores to additional colleges even after you take the SAT II. They'll hold onto your SAT II scores in their computer system for one year after you graduate from high school, and then they archive them. But they'll even send out archived scores if you decide to take a year off and apply to colleges later. If you find out you need to take SAT II tests and a year or so has passed since you've taken high school U.S. history, don't worry about being unprepared — that's what this book is for!

On the other hand, the math, literature, and foreign language subject tests cover information that you acquire over a span of several years of courses. In these cases, you're more likely to score higher on the subject exams if you wait until you've taken at least two or three years of your high school courses. In most cases, you can take these subject tests at the end of your junior year or even in the fall of your senior year.

You can take up to three SAT II subject tests in one day or you can take only one or two in one day. Whatever works best for you. So, you could take one of your tests in May, another in June, and the third one in October. Some people like to get all of them over with at one time. Others like to be able to concentrate on just one subject when they prepare, so they take just one test at a time. You're less likely to suffer burnout if you take only one or two tests on any one testing day.

When you settle on the date for your SAT II, you need to register. The deadline is usually a little over a month before the test date. You can find everything you need to know about registering for the SAT II in the *Registration Bulletin* published by the College Board. The bulletin has the test dates, instructions, registration deadlines, fees, test center codes, and other related information. You can get the bulletin from your school counselor or you can get the same information and register online at the College Board's Web site, www.collegeboard.com.

Things to take to the SAT II (and things to leave at home)

Regardless of when you take the SAT II and how many subject tests you take in one day, you need to take certain stuff with you. The absolute essentials for the SAT II U.S. History exam include

- ✔ **Your admission ticket:** When you register for the SAT II, the College Board sends you a form that you must bring to the test. This ticket proves that you registered for the exam.
- ✔ **A photo ID:** You have to prove that you're really you, not your neighbor with the borderline-genius IQ and former Teen Jeopardy champion credential coming in to take the test for you. Any form of identification that doesn't have your picture on it is unacceptable, so bring along one of the following:
  - • A driver's license
  - • A government or state-issued identification card

- A school identification card

- A valid passport

- A school identification form prepared by your school counselor (if you don't have any of the other forms of ID)

✔ **Several number-two pencils with a big eraser and a little pencil sharpener:** Carry a bunch of pencils with you and a pencil sharpener, just in case all your pencil lead breaks. A large eraser comes in handy, too, especially if you need to make clean erasures on your answer sheet.

✔ **A quiet watch:** Chapter 2 relates the importance of having your own watch with you during the test. Just make sure that your watch doesn't make any sounds.

If you plan to take more than one test, bring in a quick, light snack (like a power bar) to eat during the short break between tests. You'll need energy for the other tests.

Don't expect to be able to eat or drink during the test. Keep your snack in your pocket for later. Also, don't eat anything too heavy before a test. You want the blood pumping to your brain, not your stomach!

Don't bring any scratch paper, highlighters, protractors, or books with you. Pretty much anything we didn't list in this section isn't allowed. As nice as tuning out your neighbor's hacking cough with your CD player would be, listening and recording devices are taboo (unless you're taking a language listening test).

First Impressions: The Format and Content of the SAT II U.S. History Test

The SAT II U.S. History exam usually contains about 90 questions that you have to answer in one hour. The questions *tend* to get harder as you move through the test (question 90 is usually more difficult than question 1). Still, the test has easy and more difficult questions dispersed throughout it, so when managing your time, don't assume that question 60 will necessarily be more difficult than question 30. Whether a U.S. history question is easy or difficult usually depends on how comfortable you are with the question's subject. For instance, if you're a Civil War buff, you don't want to spend a bunch of time trying to answer a tough World War II question early on in the test because you may not get to an easier Civil War question later on. (For more details on managing your time, see Chapter 2.)

In the following sections, we cover the formatting of the answer sheet and the different question types and content that you can expect on the big day.

Managing the answer sheet

The answer sheets for the SAT II U.S. History test have bubbles for 100 questions, but you mark answers for only 90 because the test usually has only 90 questions. (Honestly, the SAT II answer sheet is like every other standardized test answer sheet. No surprises here!)

Before you start answering questions, find out how many questions you have and put a little pencil mark under the last question on your answer sheet. If, for some reason, you fill in an answer after your pencil mark or don't fill in enough answers to reach that mark, you know you've done something wrong. Be sure to erase the pencil mark before you turn in your answer sheet. (For more test-taking strategies, see Chapter 2.)

Looking at question types and subject matter

In this book, we provide many examples of sample questions as well as two full-length practice tests, so you'll have a solid idea of what to expect question-wise on the real thing. The SAT II U.S. History exam asks questions in a couple of ways. Included in the standard-issue, five-answer, multiple-choice questions are

- **Questions that ask you about direct facts and concepts:** The SAT II U.S. History exam rarely requires you to recall dates and other specifics, like how many soldiers died at Gettysburg. But you do need to know the major events and overall characteristics of each era in U.S. history and how the events relate to one another. You can often eliminate an answer choice because you know that it doesn't belong in the era that the question is testing you on. (For more about eliminating answer choices, see Chapter 2.)

- **Questions that ask you to find the exception:** Many questions on the SAT II U.S. History exam ask you to find which answer choice *isn't* right. These questions often end with a capitalized EXCEPT. For instance, "All the following SAT II U.S. History exam questions are designed to make you pull your hair out EXCEPT".

So you don't get confused about which type of answer you're looking for, rephrase the question in a positive way before you look at the answer choices. You could change our sample question to "Which of the following SAT II U.S. History exam questions are designed to help you hang on to your hair?"

- **Questions that ask you to interpret charts, maps, and cartoons:** These questions are sometimes easier than the other types because most of the information you need to answer the question is in the question booklet — you just need to know how to analyze it. The most important point to remember about analyzing charts and graphs is to make sure you know exactly what the data refers to. For instance, if you had to compare information in a graph that charts family income, you may need to know that the female head of household category differs from the single-parent household category.

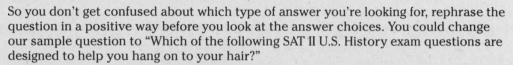

The only drawback to interpretation questions is that they can sometimes be time-consuming, so make sure you don't spend too much time analyzing a map or picture. (For more test-taking techniques, see Chapter 2.)

The SAT II U.S. History test can cover any material related to U.S. history from the year 1100 on, but about 80 percent of the test questions deal with history after 1790.

The test contains questions regarding all aspects of American history but focuses primarily on U.S. politics, economics, and society. A few questions deal with the cultural aspects of different eras and U.S. foreign policy. You can pretty much expect a little bit of something from each era of the United States' relatively short history.

Where You Stand: Scoring Considerations

So you know what colleges are looking for, but you're probably most concerned about your final score, or the number the colleges see when they get your report. Don't worry; we help you understand how the College Board figures and reports your SAT II score.

How the SAT II testers figure out your score

Each multiple-choice question has five possible answer choices. If you pick the correct answer, you get one full point for that question. If you pick the wrong answer, the SAT II deducts ¼ point from your raw score. So, one right answer covers four wrong answers.

If you skip a question, you don't get any points but you also don't lose any points. If you can eliminate at least one answer choice, you're still better off guessing because you increase the odds that you'll guess correctly from 20 percent to 25 percent, and you can't score points for questions that you skip. (For more on guessing strategies, see Chapter 2.)

To determine your raw score:

1. **Take the total number of questions you answered incorrectly times ¼.**

2. **Subtract that number from the total number of questions you answered correctly.**

For example, say you got 60 questions right, 20 wrong, and skipped 10. To find your score, you'd multiply 20 by ¼ to get your total penalty of 5. Subtract 5 from 60, and your raw score is 55 (which is great!).

Just for fun, say that instead of skipping those 10 questions, you guessed on all of them. Odds are you'd get at least two of them right even if you weren't able to eliminate any answer choices. If you do the math, you find out that guessing didn't lower your score at all ($10 - 2 = 8$; $8 \times ¼ = 2$; and $2 - 2 = 0$). And if you were lucky enough to guess right on 3 out of the 10 questions, you'd have gained 1.25 points by guessing ($10 - 3 = 7$; $7 \times ¼ = 1.75$; and $3 - 1.75 = 1.25$).

But the SAT II doesn't stop there. To try to make every test measure students equally, the SAT II develops a scale for each test. Where your raw score lands on the scale determines your final score — the one that the college admissions people see. In the case of the last example, a raw score of 55 usually translates to an awesome scaled score of around 650.

Every SAT II subject test has a final score value from 200 to 800 points. You get 200 points for knowing your name and recording it correctly on your answer sheet, but colleges aren't going to be satisfied with a 200, so you're going to have to work harder than that. Generally, if you answer at least 60 percent of the questions on the test correctly, you get a score of around 600.

Check with the schools you want to get into about acceptable SAT II scores; you'll find that most of the more selective schools look for numbers in the upper 600s and beyond.

Need more info? We provide you with complete instructions on how to score the practice exams in Chapters 23 and 25.

How the SAT II testers report your score

Unless you choose to cancel your score within three days of taking the SAT II, the College Board will report your score to the colleges you choose. If you take more than one SAT II subject test, the College Board reports all the scores at the same time. The colleges get to see them all and, usually, they choose your top subject test scores to use in their admissions' calculations. For instance, if the college requires two SAT II subject test scores and you've taken four tests in four different subject areas (because you're crazy about filling in answer bubbles), the college will probably use the scores of the two tests you did best on when they evaluate you.

About three weeks after you take the test, the College Board mails your scores to you, your high school (if you're in high school), and the colleges you requested. You can get your scores over the phone after two weeks for a fee, or you can register on the College Board Web site (www.collegeboard.com) to view your scores online after two weeks for free.

Why you should (almost) never cancel your SAT II score

The fine folks at the College Board allow you to cancel your SAT II score on the test day itself or in writing by the Wednesday following the test. Here are some reasons why you should never take them up on that offer:

- You can't know what your score is if you cancel it. Knowing how well you've done on an exam when you're in the middle of it is really difficult, plus you can miss a fair amount of questions and still do well on the SAT II. So, even though you may think you messed up, you may have really shined.

- If you cancel one SAT II test score, the scores for all the other SAT II tests you took on that day get cancelled, too.

- If you prepared well for the SAT II, you probably won't score overwhelmingly better on one administration of an SAT II exam over another. Only unusual circumstances — like getting the stomach flu in the middle of a test — cause you to perform drastically differently on an SAT II test.

- Most colleges and universities consider only your top scores, so even if you do have an unusually bad day and perform pretty poorly on one test, you can retake it (see the next section). The College Board reports the yucky score with the others, but most schools ignore it in favor of the good one.

Canceling a score is a good idea in only a few circumstances. The flu scenario previously mentioned is one. The others involve mechanical failures. If your calculator malfunctions on the math test or your cassette player fails on a language listening test, you can cancel your score on that particular test without canceling the scores for the other tests you took that day. Be prepared and have a backup calculator or cassette player with you, just in case you run into this problem.

All Over Again: Retaking the SAT II

Because most colleges consider only your top scores, retaking a subject test may be in your best interest if you aren't happy with your first score, especially if you didn't prepare for the test before you took it. The SAT II administrators let you take a test as many as six times if you want (that's pretty big of them considering you have to pay for it every time). The College Board reports scores for up to six administrations of the same test to colleges, but we don't suggest taking the same test six times. If you do retake the test, make sure you take it seriously. You want to show improvement. A college is much more impressed with a rising score than a falling one. And most colleges are turned off when they see that you've taken one particular subject test more than two or three times. The key is to prepare to do your best on the first try and, obviously, that's your goal because you've chosen to read this book!

Chapter 2

Maximizing Your Score on the SAT II

. . . .

In This Chapter

▶ Getting good at guessing

▶ Taking advantage of what you know to eliminate wrong answer choices

▶ Using your precious time wisely

▶ Escaping some of the pitfalls of standardized tests

▶ Playing it cool with some relaxation techniques

. . . .

You could've been sleeping in but instead you have to give up a cozy down comforter and fluffy pillows for a claustrophobic classroom, a bundle of number-two pencils, and a neighbor with a chronic cough. If you have to endure this agony, you may as well reward yourself with the best SAT II score you can get.

This chapter contains the tools you need to put together a winning strategy. Using what you know to your full advantage and avoiding common test-taking hazards can help you almost as much as brushing up on your U.S. history can.

Knowing When to Skip: Guessing Strategies

You may be surprised that we mention guessing at all, given that the SAT II penalizes you at ¼ point for every wrong answer (see Chapter 1). The SAT II folks created that penalty to keep you from using your test hour to fabricate fantastic artwork on your answer sheet with random sweeps of your number-two pencil rather than methodically reading through questions and answer choices. But don't let that punitive point deduction keep you from guessing. You get points only when you fill in your bubbles; and if you mark an answer only when you're absolutely sure that you're right, you may not have enough bubbles filled in to get the score you want. Our smart guessing strategies, which we cover in the following sections, will help you fill out your answer sheet quickly and confidently.

Get the lead out

How do you know when to mark your best guess and when to skip a question? As a general rule, if you can eliminate one answer, you should guess (see the upcoming sections for more details on guessing).

One of the biggest favors you can do yourself when taking a multiple-choice test is to cross out the wrong answers in the test booklet. Crossing out wrong answers serves several purposes:

✔ You don't waste time rereading a wrong answer choice. You have a limited amount of time to answer questions, so you don't want to spend it reading answers you've already decided are wrong.

✔ Crossing out answers gives you a psychological boost. When you look at the question, you don't see five possible answer choices anymore. Now, you've made your test booklet look more manageable.

✔ Determining whether or not you've eliminated enough choices to mark a bubble on your answer sheet becomes much easier.

Now, you may think that all that crossing out takes up too much of your precious time. Or maybe you're concerned about a shortage of pencil lead. These are lame excuses. You can push your pencil through a line of text in less than a second. And if you're concerned about your pencil supply, take in a bundle with you. Arrive at the test with at least ten finely sharpened number-two pencils at your service (or two number-two mechanical pencils that are fully loaded with lead). Heck, you should even take a pencil sharpener with you, just in case. Just make sure it's a manual model and not some noisy battery-operated machinery to make the proctor scowl.

If crossing out answer choices doesn't come naturally to you, practice at home. Use the practice tests in Chapters 23 and 25 to not only hone your knowledge but also to train yourself to mark through your question booklet. Feel free to mark up this book as much as you want. We take satisfaction in knowing that it's being well used.

X marks the spot

After you master the fine art of lead spreading, you can use it to determine whether you should go one step further with your pencil and fill in a bubble for a question on your answer sheet. Here's a little system that helps you decide when you should guess, and it provides a code to let you know which questions are best to return to if you have time at the end of the test. The approach we outline here helps you be a better test-taker because you'll be thinking and writing while most people are just thinking.

1. **Read the question quickly but carefully.**

2. **Examine each answer choice (once again, quickly but carefully).**

3. **Use your pencil to cross out answer choices that are obviously incorrect.** We know that you've heard this advice before, but repetition is a powerful learning tool! See the next section for great tips on eliminating wrong answer choices.

4. **If you can eliminate four answer choices (and therefore, know the correct answer), fill in the appropriate bubble on your answer sheet.** Mark a big *X* next to the question in your test booklet, and go on to the next question.

5. **If you can eliminate at least three of the five answer choices, choose one of the remaining answer choices and fill in its bubble on the answer sheet.** Put a big *X* next to this question in your test booklet and go on to the next question.

6. **If you can eliminate only two of the five answer choices, choose one of the remaining answer choices and fill in its bubble on the answer sheet.** Write a large "3" next to the question and go on.

7. **If you can cross out only one of the five answer choices, write a big "4" next to the question in your test booklet.** Leave the answer bubbles blank for this question. Go on to the next question.

8. **If you can't cross out any of the five answer choices, put a big "5" next to the question in your test booklet and leave the answer bubbles blank.** Don't worry about the question and go on.

9. **If you finish before the proctor calls time, you know which questions in the section you should take another look at.** First, go to the questions with 3s by them; then those with 4s; and, only as a last resort and if you have lots of time, the 5s.

10. **When you read through a question again, you may find that you can eliminate more answer choices because you've seen something in a later question that helps you with an earlier one or your brain continues to work on the question even as you continue to answer other questions.** Mark a new answer if you left the question blank or change the one you previously marked if you're pretty sure another answer is better.

Remember that this list provides a technique. Just like when learning any other technique, it may be awkward at first. Applying it to the practice tests in Chapters 23 and 25, though, can make it become your greatest asset.

Eliminating Choices: How to Recognize Wrong Answers

You know what to do when you determine that an answer choice is wrong, but how do you know when an answer is incorrect? With a little know-how, you can master the art of answer elimination, even if you're unsure about the information that a question tests.

Keep in mind that the following elimination techniques get you to think your way through to the best answer choice. We don't guarantee that these techniques will work in every situation, but they do provide you with positive steps toward choosing the right answers.

Use common sense

Eliminate answer choices that don't make sense. Senseless answer choices are the easiest ones to spot, if you read carefully. Most likely, you'll be able to eliminate choices because they don't fit with the era that the question asks you about. For instance, consider the following question drawn from Chapter 9.

The Republican Party was founded in 1854 as

(A) A party that was against slavery based on only moral reasons

(B) A new party opposed to slavery and supportive of freedom of expression

(C) The reconstituted American Party

(D) A successor to John Adams's Republican Party

(E) One of the first political parties of the new nation

Even if you're not sure why the Republican Party was founded, you can eliminate choices based on common sense. The question tells you that the party was founded in 1854. By 1854, the country was over 70 years old, so it couldn't have been one of the first political parties.

Even if you know very little about the origins of the Republican Party, you can eliminate (E) with very little thought.

When you study for the SAT II U.S. History exam, concentrate on the events and philosophies that define each era. If you know a lot about each era, you can more easily eliminate answer choices that don't fit in the era specified by the question.

Rely on what you know

If you come across a subject that you don't know anything about, don't panic. Read the answer choices to see if one deals with a subject that you're familiar with. For instance, in the sample question in the previous section, you may not know a thing about the Republican Party, but you may know a little about John Adams. Enough to know that he wasn't a member of the Republican Party. Therefore, you can eliminate (D). Using common sense and the information that you *do* know, you can eliminate two answer choices about a topic that is unfamiliar to you.

Avoid choices with debatable words

Another way you can weed out answer choices is to cross out the ones that contain debatable words. *Debatable words* are words that leave no room for exception and, therefore, could provoke debate. Some examples of debatable words are *all*, *always*, *only*, *complete*, *never*, *must*, *every*, and *none*.

Take a look at the earlier sample question again. Choice (A) contains the word *only*, stating that the party's opposition to slavery was only morally motivated. Most members of the Republican Party did oppose slavery because they found it morally reprehensible; however, the presence of the word *only* leaves answer choice (A) up for debate. The party also included Free-Soilers, who had economic reasons for being against slavery: They didn't want slaves to take away their jobs. Because the validity of answer choice (A) is debatable, you can eliminate it as a correct answer. Eliminating the answer choice with a debatable word leaves two answer choices.

Don't avoid choices with debatable words indiscriminately. Here are two occasions when you absolutely should not eliminate an answer choice based on the presence of a debatable word:

- ✔ If the presence of the debatable word makes the answer choice correct because the debatable word is not debatable, you can't eliminate it. Huh? Okay, for example, if the sample question contained a choice that read, "A party that only came into existence in the 1850s," you couldn't eliminate the choice because this *only* isn't a matter for debate. The Republican Party did not exist before 1854.

- ✔ If the question asks you to choose an answer that is *not* true, a choice that contains a debatable word may be just the ticket. For example, if the sample question asked you to choose the answer that was *not* true about the early Republican Party, the choice that states that the party supported slavery only for moral reasons could be the right answer.

Go for the more specific choice

When you've narrowed the answer choices to two seemingly reasonable options and you can't decide between them, the more specific choice is *usually* the best answer. Take a look at the earlier sample question one more time. Using process of elimination, you've reduced your options to (B) and (C). You may have known that the Republican Party was founded based on opposition to slavery and a penchant for free speech, but even if you didn't, you're probably safer choosing the more specific of the two remaining choices. Answer (B) reveals a special characteristic of the party and, therefore, is more specific than (C), which provides a more general concept.

Please note that choosing the more specific answer often works after you've narrowed your options to two. *Choosing the most specific answer of all the answers provided isn't wise* because the most specific answer of the five may not address the question topic.

Be politically correct

Although the history test most likely won't contain answer choices that violate political suitability (the SAT II testmakers are very careful to remain politically correct), we'll mention the point, just in case. If an answer choice ever suggests racial, gender, or cultural bias on the SAT II U.S. History exam, you can confidently eliminate it. These types of answers are never right.

Winning the Race against the Clock: Wise Time Management

Unlike the questions on the SAT I and even other SAT II subjects, the questions on the SAT II U.S. History exam don't necessarily increase in difficulty as you move through the test. Generally, the first ten questions are easier than the last ten, but the difference in difficulty isn't as drastic. For this reason, managing your time wisely on the history test is even more important than it is on other standardized tests. Check out the following sections for the best strategies.

Pace yourself

Chances are, you're taking three different subject tests in one morning, so you need a plan to help you stay focused throughout each test. Each subject test lasts for exactly one hour, and the history test has about 90 or so questions. If you do the math, you realize that you have about ⅔ of a minute to spend on each question. Now, before you panic, go get your watch with the second hand. Take a deep breath and hold it for 40 seconds. Unless you're an underwater distance swimmer or a tuba player, you probably had a pretty hard time holding your breath that long. Suddenly, ⅔ of a minute seems like a pretty long time. Plus, some questions are easy to answer in less than 40 seconds, so you'll have more time to spend on the tougher ones.

When taking the test, you need to keep track of your timing but you don't want to continually waste precious seconds glancing at your watch. So go in with a game plan. With 90 questions, check your time every 30 questions or so. At question 30, you should be about 20 minutes into the exam and, at question 60, you should be about 40 minutes into it.

If at any time, you find yourself significantly off this pace, say by five or more questions in either direction, you need to adjust your pace.

- ✔ If you're behind, you're probably spending too much time on hard questions. You need to encourage yourself to move on. (For helpful tips, check out "Don't waste your time on hard questions" later in this chapter.)
- ✔ If you're ahead, you may be moving through questions too quickly at the risk of reading carelessly.

You're much less likely to find yourself in either of these positions if you experiment with your time on the practice tests in Chapters 23 and 25.

Use your own timepiece

Here's a story for you. One of our students took the test in a room that had two clocks. The two clocks looked exactly alike except that they displayed different times. The proctor timed from the clock propped up on the table, and the other clock hung on the wall. Our student noted the time when the proctor began the test, but when she checked her pace at question 30, she couldn't remember which clock she'd started timing from and wasn't sure how much time had gone by.

You can avoid this same frustration by ignoring the clocks in the testing room. Instead, get a watch with a sweep second hand or a silent stopwatch component that you can take with you to the test, and use your watch rather than the clock provided to time yourself during the test. At the beginning of the test, set your watch to the top of the hour, any hour. You don't care about the actual time, just the passing of one hour. Remembering that your test started when the big hand was on the 12 is much easier than remembering that it started at exactly 9:17 and 32 seconds. You have enough to remember for the SAT II without having to keep in mind what time it was when the proctor said, "Go." If you set your watch for noon, you know that you need to be finished by 1 p.m. (even if the time is really 8:43 and 11 seconds).

Playing It Smart: A Few Things You Shouldn't Do When Taking the Test

The majority of this chapter focuses on the things you should do to perform your best on test day. But here we discuss a few equally helpful *don'ts* that you should know about to make sure you get your best score. Check out the following sections for the full scoop.

Don't lose your focus

You may be surprised that one hour of U.S. history may get a little boring. Don't use test boredom as an excuse to let your mind wander. The test is too important to get distracted daydreaming about what it'd be like to share a piece of chocolate mousse cake with the hottie sitting in front of you. Keep your perspective, focus on the task at hand, and promise yourself that you'll get the hottie's number when the test is over.

Don't stew about how you performed on another test

Each SAT II subject test that you take on test day is a separate entity. Keep it that way. Don't let what you think may have been a poor performance on an earlier subject test affect how you do on the history test. Every subject test has its own score, and the next test is a chance to start fresh.

Don't judge your performance by looking around at others

Sometimes in the frenzy of the exam you forget that not everyone in the room is taking the test that you are; some may be taking the chemistry exam, others may be plugging away on the literature test. So, seeing others put down their pencils while you're still slaving away can be disconcerting. If you compare yourself to those around you, you can really psych yourself into thinking that you're a loser, and feeling like a loser doesn't do much for your test score. Keep your eyes on the test and your watch until the proctor signals that time's up.

Don't waste your time on hard questions

You've probably heard this one before, but we're going to say it again: An easy question is worth the same amount of points as a hard question. In the classroom, your teacher may reward you for knowing the answers to the hard questions, you don't get more Brownie buttons for answering a hard question on the SAT II. So, discipline yourself to know when to give it up. As tempting as pondering a question until you see the light can be, you can't afford that luxury. You may miss out on a simple question at the end of the test because you've been stubbornly trying to answer a hard one. If you need to spend more than 1½ minutes on any one question, you probably won't get it right anyway. Skip it and go on.

Don't read questions at lightning speed

At the same time, you shouldn't be so concerned about answering 90 or so questions in one hour that you fly through the test. You don't get points if you don't answer questions correctly, and you have to read the questions carefully to answer questions correctly. Speed reading doesn't usually allow you to take in the specific information you need to fully process what the question is all about. You have a whopping 40 seconds to spend on each question, so make sure you use it wisely. You can always use your speed-reading skills later in college when you put off reading your 1,000-page biology text until the night before the final exam.

Don't lose track of the numbers on your answer grid

Skipping questions is normal on the SAT II. Just be really careful that if you do skip question 5, you make sure that you mark the answer to question 6 in the correct bubble, not the bubble for question 5. If you mark your answer incorrectly, you can mess up your answer sheet from that point forward. And if you don't notice until the end of the test . . . Yikes!

All that hard work for nothing! You could cancel your score (what a waste!) or try to change your answers before the proctor calls time (make sure you have a big eraser!), but the best plan is to avoid the problem altogether by doing a periodic check.

Get in the habit of checking your answer grid every fifth question to make sure you're marking the right answer in the proper spot. And always circle the right answer in your question booklet before you grid in the answer sheet. That way, if you do discover that you mess up your answer sheet, you won't have to reread the questions to figure out the right answers.

Don't fail to use extra time at the end of the test

You may finish before the testing time is up. Use those last few minutes wisely. You've already marked your test booklet so you know which questions to return to to double-check your answers. Go back to the questions with 3s next to them and double-check your answers. Why, you ask? Well, you may have discovered something from the questions you answered later in the test that will help you with the questions you had trouble with earlier. Or you may have an "Aha" moment where the answer suddenly becomes clear to you. Or you may catch a careless error. So, use your extra time to pick up additional points.

Don't cheat

Cheating isn't the right thing to do, and it's also just plain illogical. Your hand simply isn't big enough to hold all the information you need to master the history test, and the person next to you is probably working on the Chinese language test, so peeking at his or her test won't help you, either. This book gives you everything you need to do your best on the exam, so don't take such a risk.

Curbing a Case of Nerves: Relaxation Techniques

If all this talk about what you should and shouldn't do during the test is making you nervous — relax! After you've read this book, you'll be plenty prepared for whatever the SAT II U.S. History exam dishes out. You may feel nervous on test day, but that feeling is normal and even a little beneficial. The extra shot of adrenaline keeps you alert. But too much anxiety isn't good for you or your test performance; sometimes a frustrating question can paralyze you, so arrive at the testing site with a practiced relaxation plan in case you get caught with a major case of nerves.

You may be joyfully filling in answer bubbles when all of a sudden a monstrous question rears its ugly head. You know your stuff, so you're probably just missing something. But the question makes you so tense, you can't think. At the first sign of freaking, take a quick time out. The trick is to forget about that nasty question long enough so that when you go back to it, you'll have that "Aha!" experience and suddenly see the right answer. Or you'll get enough perspective to realize that it's just one little test question that's not worth your anguish, so you can merrily skip it and leave it for later. Just don't let one or two yucky questions ruin you for the rest of the test.

Inhale deeply

When you stress out, you tighten up and take quick breaths, which doesn't do much for your oxygen intake. Stressing out restricts the oxygen flow to your brain, and you need to do something about it because your brain needs oxygen to think straight. Fortunately, the solution is easy: breathe. Deeply. Feel the air go all the way down to your toes. Hold it. Then let it all out slowly and do it again several times. (Just don't blow out your air too loudly — you don't want to attract the proctor's attention or disturb your fellow test-takers.)

Stretch a little

Anxiety causes tension. Your muscles get all tied up in knots, and untying them helps. While breathing deeply, focus on reducing your muscle tension. Most people feel stress in their necks and shoulders, so do a few stretches in these areas to get the blood flowing.

- Shrug your shoulders toward your ears; hold this position for a few seconds and then release.
- Roll your head from front to back and from side to side.
- With your hands together, stretch your arms straight over your head as high as you can. Relax. Then do it again.
- Stretch your legs out in front of you. Move your ankles up and down (but don't kick the person in front of you!)
- Shake your hands vigorously as if you just washed your hands in a public restroom with no paper towels.
- Open your mouth wide as if to say "Ahhh." (But don't actually say it out loud.) Close your mouth quickly to avoid catching flies.

These quick stretches shouldn't take you more than ten seconds, so don't invest in a full workout. You need to get back to work!

Give yourself a mini massage

If you still feel tense after all that stretching, give yourself a little rub down. Rub your right shoulder with your left hand and your left shoulder with your right hand. Use both hands to massage your neck. Then move up your neck to your scalp.

Don't get carried away, though. This massage should take only about ten seconds out of your testing time. (Let's see . . . At today's going rate for a masseuse, you'll owe yourself about 30 cents.)

Think positive thoughts

Give yourself a break. Realize that the SAT II test is tough and you probably won't feel comfortable about every question. But don't beat yourself up about it because that's a sure path to disaster. If you've tried other relaxation efforts and you still feel frustrated about a particular question, fill in your best guess or just skip it. Mark the question in case you have time to review it at the end, but don't think about it until then. Put your full effort into answering the remaining questions.

Focus on the positive. Congratulate yourself for the answers you do feel confident about and force yourself to leave the others behind.

Take a little vacation

If other relaxation methods aren't working, have a place in your imagination that makes you feel calm and comfortable ready. Maybe you like the beach. Or perhaps a ski slope. Wherever your relaxation zone, sit back in your chair, close your eyes, and visit your happy place for a few seconds to get away from the question that's bugging you. Just make sure you come back!

Don't use this technique unless you're really tense. You can stay longer in "la la" land when the test is over.

Part II
The Birth of a Nation

The 5th Wave   By Rich Tennant

"Help me out here. Are these guys Pilgrims or Puritans? I can never tell them apart."

In this part . . .

This part covers 700 years (from 1100 to 1800, to be exact) of American history. Approximately 20 percent of the questions on the SAT II U.S. History test come from this time period so, unfortunately, you can't really skip this part if you find "ancient" history dull. But don't worry, this section moves quickly from North American native tribes to the first non-native settlements of North America, to the formation of the colonies, to the Revolutionary War, to the end of the Federalist Era (and more) in a mere three chapters. This early period is actually a pretty interesting time to study because it sets the foundation for the character of the country.

We know that you have other things going on besides this test, so we crammed a lot of information in this part because we definitely don't want to waste your time with too much fluff. We also threw in a few jokes — we wouldn't want you to fall asleep and start drooling all over this book.

Chapter 3

Land Ho! Mastering the Age of Exploration, 1100s–Early 1600s

In This Chapter

▶ Getting acquainted with Native American cultures

▶ Discovering early explorers of the New World

▶ Finding out about early American settlements

About 4 percent of the questions you encounter on the SAT II U.S. History exam deal with the period *before* European colonization. You don't have to be a genius to figure out that you probably won't be spending much of your studies on this time period, so we try not to waste your precious time and brain space with too many useless facts and figures. But the material for the exploration age is vast, and most students have trouble answering questions from it; so, knowing some key concepts from this early age can boost your score. You probably won't see questions based on strict fact from this time period. If we were betting people, we'd wager that the exam won't ask you to choose what year Christopher Columbus landed in the New World.

Instead, you're more likely to encounter questions that ask about the driving forces behind exploration. Something more along the lines of "Which of the following best describes the primary motivation for the European explorations that resulted in the discovery of the New World?" So, we're going to do a little exploration of our own about the movement that inspired Europeans to happen upon a new land, the cultures they found when they got there, and the settlements that they ultimately established. (Oh, and by the way, the answer is 1492.)

We Were Here First: Before Europeans Set Sail

Before the United States was even a twinkle in George Washington's eye, the forests and plains, lakes and rivers, and mountains and valleys that formed the foundation of the 13 original colonies and the countries to the south were home to non-European inhabitants. Strong evidence shows that long ago (exactly when is arguable, so the test won't ask you about it) North America's earliest inhabitants wandered from Asia across a land bridge to the area that's now Alaska. By at least 10,000 B.C., groups had moved into most of North and Central America and were headed into South America. Over the years, these groups developed civilizations and highly sophisticated cultures that populated North, Central, and South America. Some of the more well-known, and therefore, more likely to be tested, Native American groups include

✔ **The *Mayans* and *Aztecs*:** These two groups lived in Central America, also known as *Mesoamerica*.

✔ **The *Incas*:** This group lived in South America.

✔ ***Other Native American nations:*** These groups extended across North America from the East Coast to the West Coast.

When studying these early cultures, keep in mind that the makers of the SAT II root for the underdog. In an attempt to conform to political correctness, SAT II questions regarding *indigenous* (which is a fancy way of saying "native") cultures tend to be complimentary, focusing on their accomplishments. Conquering nations fare less favorably on the pages of the exam. The SAT II usually focuses on the materialistic motivations of conquering cultures; so for questions that ask about the motivations of European explorers, choose answers that suggest a desire for the acquisition of riches.

Perhaps to emphasize the greed of European conquerors in the Americas (and because high school U.S. history texts cover early Central and South American civilizations), the SAT II incorporates early Central and South American history into at least one or two of its U.S. history questions. And, for this reason, we begin our examination of early American cultures with an overview of Mesoamerican and South American peoples.

In addition, the SAT II probably won't ask you a direct question about the characteristics of early Native American cultures, but it may ask you to compare the general traits of Native American cultures with societies in Central and South America as they were before Columbus arrived.

Pre-Columbian culture of the New World: That's pre-Columbus, not pre-coffee

Some of the most advanced cultures in the world existed in the Americas before European adventurers conquered them. Two such cultures were the Mayan and Aztec civilizations. The Mayan and the Aztec civilizations were part of Mesoamerican culture. (*Meso* means middle, and *american* means, well, American; so, these civilizations existed in the middle of the Americas.) Another advanced civilization was the Incas, who populated parts of South America. For the SAT II, you don't need to know too much about early Central and South American cultures except that they existed and were advanced thinkers.

✔ Take the Mayans, for instance. They populated the Yucatan Peninsula (a region in southern Mexico) and Central America. They developed a written language and a highly accurate calendar. They were also pretty good at math. (They would have made great SAT-takers!) Unfortunately, the Mayan civilization didn't live to see the arrival of the Europeans, let alone the invasion of the College Board.

✔ The Aztecs, however, were still around when ships sailed in from Europe. The Aztecs themselves were conquerors who ruled central Mexico from their capital, Tenochtitlán, where Mexico City is now. This civilization's claim to fame included written language, a calendar so precise that it might put modern astronomers to shame, and sophisticated architecture.

✔ Farther south, in what's now South America, the Incan society reigned. Linked by an extensive road system, this feudal empire stretched about 2,000 miles along the Pacific Coast of South America. The Incans developed a fancy irrigation system and became successful farmers. Here's a little-known fact: The Incans cultivated the white potato. (The SAT II probably won't ask you about this cultural tidbit, but hey, we thought it was interesting!)

One divided into many: Native peoples in North America

Native American peoples of North America were primarily nomadic, which means they wandered as needed for survival. Communities relied on the environment for sustenance, using plants for medicines and animal products for shelter and protection. Members within each nation helped each other out, but despite the existence of the *Iroquois Confederacy* (a loosely organized confederation of five nations), nations weren't closely associated with the others. A lack of unity among the Native American peoples may have contributed to their takeover by the Europeans.

What caused this lack of unity was the diversity among nations. Each nation developed a distinct culture based primarily on the type of land that it inhabited. Here's a list, according to region, of some of the widely-known nations (and therefore, the more widely-tested nations on the SAT II) that existed when the Europeans first arrived in North America:

✔ **The Eastern Woodland Native Americans:** These farmers and hunters lived along the eastern seaboard and greeted the first British settlers in the early 1600s. These groups lived on fish, deer, and other woodland animals. They cultivated corn, beans, and squash with sophisticated farming techniques like crop rotation, using fish heads as fertilizer, and supporting bean vines with cornstalks. They lived in domed structures and created extensive villages larger than many European villages of the 1500s. The Iroquois became the most powerful group living in the Eastern Woodland region, forming an alliance of five nations known as the Iroquois Confederacy to protect themselves from the Algonquin, another powerful group in this region.

✔ **The Southeastern Native Americans:** Native Americans living in the Southeast led lifestyles similar to their neighbors to the north. They hunted and gathered and lived in wooden houses. These groups included the Cherokee, Chickasaw, Creek, and Seminole.

✔ **Native Americans of the Great Plains:** The native groups of the Great Plains relied on buffalo for their livelihood. Buffalo provided food, clothing, and portable housing in the form of teepees. The Blackfoot, Crow, Cheyenne, Comanche, and Sioux lived nomadically, following the buffalo across central North America.

✔ **The Southwestern Native Americans:** Native Americans of the Southwest were farmers who made the most of their arid environment by constructing apartment-like buildings out of clay and forming advanced irrigation systems. Better-known groups include the Apache, Hopi, Navajo, and Zuni.

✔ **Native Americans of the Northwest Coast:** Native groups living on the northwest coast had abundant resources that allowed them to develop permanent communities. Villages along the coastal shore supported fishing and farming for wealthy groups, which included the Coast Salish, Chinook, Tillamook, and Tlingit.

This info on Native American nations is all very well and good, but what does it have to do with me, you say? Well, the SAT II probably won't ask you specific questions about Native American linguistics or yearly Incan potato consumption, but you are expected to know the general whereabouts, accomplishments, and characteristics of regional North American communities as well as early Central And South American civilizations. You may see a question like the following:

Which Mesoamerican civilization existed when the Europeans landed in the New World?

(A) Mayan

(B) Iroquois Confederacy

(C) Aztec

(D) Hopi

(E) Incan

The key to answering this question correctly is knowing the definition of *Mesoamerican* and a little about its early cultures. First, eliminate all groups that lived somewhere other than Mesoamerica. A swift glance through the list of Native American nations provides you with the information you need to eliminate answers (B), (D), and (E). The Hopi and nations of the Iroquois Confederacy occupied North America. Incans hung out in South America. So that leaves the Aztecs and the Mayans. Both groups made their homes in Central America, which is also known as Mesoamerica. How do you choose between the two? The other element of the question asks you to determine who was around at the time of Columbus. You know that Mayan culture disappeared before the explorers landed in the New World. Therefore, you can confidently choose (C), Aztec.

Hello, Columbus: Early Explorers from Ericson to La Salle

The 15th and 16th centuries ushered in the Age of Exploration and a wave, so to speak, of Portuguese and Spanish navigators took to the seas in search of more efficient trade routes to the Far East for its coveted supply of spices, jewels, precious metals, and other luxuries. After almost 1,000 years of poverty and decline in the Dark Ages, Europe was ready for an extended shopping spree.

Turning over a new Leif: The Vikings in North America

Rome fell around 500 A.D. and, for the next 1,000 years, European civilization stagnated and accomplished very little. This period is known as the Dark Ages. Although Europeans languished, their Norse neighbors (better known as the *Vikings*) set out to sea from what is now Scandinavia. As early as A.D. 1000, Norse Captain *Leif Ericson* sailed west from Greenland and landed in Labrador (now Newfoundland) and again in Nova Scotia.

When taking the SAT II, keep in mind that the Vikings (or Norsemen) get the credit for first landing on North American soil.

Making advances: Portuguese innovation and exploration

In the 1400s, the Portuguese invented the magnetic compass (or *quadrant*) and a faster, sleeker sailing vessel called a *caravel,* which made long ocean voyages possible. The SAT II may ask you which innovations made the European discovery of the New World possible, so remember the compass and the caravel (sounds like a good title for a Gothic mystery, doesn't it?).

These two navigational improvements led Portuguese scholar *Prince Henry the Navigator* to finance an exploration of Africa's west coast until he died in 1460. Based on the knowledge gained from these explorations, *Bartholomeu Diaz* reached the southern tip of Africa in 1488 and discovered the eastward sea route to India. Ten years later, his fellow countryman, *Vasco da Gama,* actually made the voyage to India by sailing around Africa.

A controversial figure with an important name

Amerigo Vespucci was an Italian citizen who sailed for Spain during the 1490s and for Portugal in 1501. Controversy surrounds this explorer and whether or not he was the first explorer to officially discover the Americas. Because questions remain about his voyages and whether or not he was even on them, the SAT II probably won't ask you questions about him. Vespucci does have one genuine claim to fame, however: America got its name from Amerigo.

In 1494, Portugal and Spain signed the *Treaty of Tordesillas,* which established a north-south line that cut through the Atlantic Ocean and the bulge of South America where Brazil is now. Spain could explore lands west of this line, and Portugal could explore lands east of it. Spain and Portugal stuck to this treaty, which is why the Spanish explored the Western Hemisphere and the Portuguese explored Africa, the Far East, and Brazil (but not the rest of South America).

Conquering the world: Ten Spanish conquistadors

Because Spanish explorers paved the way for discoveries of future U.S. territory, the SAT II may ask you about them. In 1492, under the rule of Ferdinand and Isabella, Spain eliminated the Moorish occupation of Granada. Feeling pretty good about themselves, Spaniards were ready to tackle the rest of the world. And tackle they did.

Justified by the system of *encomienda* — the concept that explorers could make the native inhabitants of the New World do just about anything they wanted them to (like slave labor) as long as the explorers tried converting the Native Americans to Christianity — Spanish conquistadors raped, pillaged, and otherwise subjugated their ways through the New World. They brought tobacco and new foods like corn, potatoes, beans, and tomatoes back to Europe. They introduced cattle, horses, and small pox to the New World and enslaved the natives who lived there. Later, the conquistadors established *repartimiento,* a slave-labor system where Native American adult males rotated working on Spanish farms, ranches, mines, and factories. The Spanish were in the New World to stay. They established settlements and intermingled with the native population, which resulted in the formation of a new race, known as the *mestizos.*

The SAT II sometimes likes to throw foreign words like *mestizo, repartimiento,* and *encomienda* into its questions to check your vocabulary. If you're creating flashcards, include these gems.

Here are ten Spanish explorers the SAT II may ask you about. We listed them in chronological order of their explorations:

- ✔ **Christopher Columbus:** The first Spanish explorer wasn't actually Spanish. Italian-born Christopher Columbus had the travel bug, so he asked the king of Portugal to finance a trip across the Atlantic Ocean to reach "the Indies." Rejected by Portugal, Columbus garnered support from Ferdie and Izzy of Spain and set sail with a fleet of three ships in August of 1492. Columbus is widely acknowledged as being the first-documented European to arrive in the Americas, but because of the controversial competition with the Vikings, Amerigo Vespucci (see the sidebar "A controversial figure with an important name" earlier in this chapter), and others for this honor, the SAT II probably won't ask you about it.

- ✔ **Juan Ponce de Leon:** His explorations led him to the east coast of Florida. In 1513, he became the first European to set foot on the North American mainland.

✔ **Vasco Nuñez del Balboa:** In 1513, Balboa cut his way through the jungles of Panama and discovered the Pacific Ocean when he came out on the other side. He claimed all the land that touched the Pacific for Spain.

✔ **Hernán Cortés:** In 1519, Cortés, a true Spanish conquistador, arrived in Mexico with his army. Between 1519 and 1521, he took over the Aztec empire in Mexico and its immense riches by befriending the Aztec ruler Montezuma, imprisoning him, and then ruling through him.

✔ **Ferdinand Magellan:** Spain got a good idea of just how big the earth was when Portuguese-born Magellan led a Spanish expedition that circled the globe. The voyage took three years, lasting from 1519 to1521.

✔ **Francisco Pizarro:** Like Cortés before him, Pizarro accumulated still more treasure for Spain. In the early 1530s, he subdued the Inca Empire in what is now Peru.

✔ **Hernando de Soto:** By 1539, the Spaniards had made their way into North America, and de Soto explored the Mississippi River.

✔ **Francisco Vasquez de Coronado:** A year after de Soto came upon the Mississippi River, de Coronado led an exploration as far north as present-day Kansas and as far west as the Grand Canyon.

✔ **Juan Rodriguez Cabrillo:** The desire to convert the native population to Christianity drove Spanish explorers further west. Well, that and a lust for gold, power, adventure, and the land of milk and honey. In 1542, Cabrillo explored the coast of what is now California. His encounters with the Native Americans along the coastline were primarily peaceful, involving trade rather than invasion.

✔ **Don Juan de Onate:** In 1542, the same year that Cabrillo explored the California coast, de Onate explored northern Mexico and made his way up the Rio Grande Valley. Like Cabrillo's, de Onate's dealings with the Native Americans were mostly friendly.

How does the SAT II test this information? You probably won't encounter a question asking about a simple name, date, or place, like this one: "In 1542, Juan Rodriguez Cabrillo explored what is now which of the following U.S. states?"

Test questions that cover exploration are more likely to incorporate more than one explorer and focus on concepts rather than specific details. For instance, the following sample question tests your knowledge about the system of encomienda using the deeds of several explorers.

Which of the following is the best example of the Spanish system of encomienda?

(A) Vasco da Gama's travels to the southern tip of Africa

(B) Vasco Balboa's travels through the jungles of Panama

(C) Ferdinand Magellan's circumnavigation of the world

(D) Juan Rodriguez Cabrillo's exploration of the coast of California

(E) The invasion of Mexico by Hernán Cortés

This clever question expects you to know the definition of encomienda. Of course, having a smattering of information about the exploits of the explorers helps, too. Even if you forgot the meaning of encomienda, you could eliminate (A) because a Portuguese explorer probably wouldn't exemplify a Spanish system. But if you haven't forgotten the meaning of encomienda, you can use what you know about Spanish explorers to pick the best answer. Notice the vocabulary each of the answer choices uses: "Travels," "*circumnavigation*" (a fancy way of saying "globe circling"), and "exploration" don't immediately conjure up notions of exploitation for the sake of conversion. The answer that makes the most sense contains the word "invasion," which is the word that best relates to exploitation, so the answer is (E).

You may have wanted to choose (D) because one of the goals of Cabrillo's expedition was to convert Native Americans. But be careful. Remember that the definition of encomienda includes using conversion attempts as a justification for conquering a people. When comparing Cabrillo's exploration to Cortés's invasion, consider the full meaning of encomienda. Although both explorers may have intended to win religious converts, Cortés used it as a validation for trouncing the civilizations of Mexico; Cabrillo didn't exploit the Native Americans on the California coast. The SAT II will often ask you to make subtle distinctions when you weigh your answer choices.

Late bloomers: Explorations of the British and French

Except for **John Cabot's** explorations of the Canadian coastline in 1497 for Britain, the Spaniards had been exploring Central and North America for almost 100 years before other nations got involved. Lured by the wealth the Spaniards were enjoying, British exploration began when Elizabeth I ascended the throne in 1558. British exploration concentrated on the northeastern part of the United States.

French explorers were close by in Canada. French exploration began as a search for a *Northwest Passage* that would cut across the North American continent to the Pacific Ocean. French explorers **Giovanni de Verrazano** in 1524 and **Jacques Cartier** in 1534 investigated the northeast coast of what is now the United States looking for such a passageway. Cartier navigated the St. Lawrence River and established relations with the Iroquois nation. De Verrazano explored the North Atlantic coast and the Hudson River. He found no passage to the Pacific, but that didn't stop him from getting rich. De Verrazano was one of several French *corsairs* (a fancy French name for buccaneer) who raided the silver- and gold-laden Spanish ships traveling "from the New World to Europe. Yo, ho, ho, ho, a pirate's life for me!

More than a century later (in the early 1680s), **Robert La Salle** navigated the length of the Mississippi River from the Great Lakes to the Gulf of Mexico, claiming all the land along the river's shores for France. This expedition made him the first European to travel the entire stretch of the Mississippi River.

You most likely won't see any questions about early French and British explorers on the SAT II, but you never know what the College Board will throw your way. Focus on the countries' motivations. The more northern countries of France and Britain sent out expeditions that landed in the northern territory of the New World — modern-day New England and Canada. Their primary motivation was monetary: Both countries wanted to find that all-important quick-water route to Asia so they could beat the others to the goodies that the Eastern hemisphere offered. When they couldn't find a water route to the Pacific, some French seamen settled for trading with the Native Americans, and others traded illegally with (okay, robbed) the sailing vessels of other countries. Bottom line: These guys sought to get rich in any way that they could.

Exploiting foreign aid: The beginning of African slavery in the Americas

Some of the first Africans to land in the Americas came as explorers, serving on the crews of the likes of Hernán Cortés. Spanish mining, farming, and ranching in South and Central America were labor-intensive; as the enslaved natives succumbed to the unfamiliar diseases brought over by the Europeans, the conquerors needed a new source of labor. They found it in the African slave trade. The Spaniards rationalized their actions by promoting a myth that Africans were inferior, and they packed African men, women, and children like cargo onto slave ships en route to the Spanish colonies in the New World. Although slavery had existed for centuries, Spanish colonization marked the first time that slaves had no rights and no way of escaping enslavement because it passed down to future generations. It didn't take long for the British to adopt the practice of the African slave trade, and it eventually made its way into North America, which significantly shaped the culture of the United States for generations to come.

For the SAT II, remember that the discovery of new land led to widespread slavery. To realize their dreams of immense riches, the conquerors first enslaved the Native Americans; then they forced millions of Africans to leave their homelands and embark on a transatlantic journey to permanent toil and degradation.

That Settles It: Early Communities in the New World

Once the adventurers opened up the route to the New World, the path had been set for European attempts to settle the foreign space. Spanish and French settlements were primarily business ventures or missions, but the British rationale for settling also included more complex factors, such as escape from religious persecution. A few hardy souls from all three countries ventured across the ocean to form communities in the land that later became the United States.

Considering the plights of the early colonists sort of puts the whole SAT II thing into perspective. Hours of relentless questioning about the Magna Carta and Watergate can cause an almost-permanent migraine, but it probably pales in comparison to facing a New England winter without central heating. Despite the lack of these modern amenities, the settlements endured. And, as the 17th century progressed, civilizations in the New World flourished.

As you've probably gathered by now, the SAT II is all about motivations. So, in this section, we explain some of the reasons why Europeans risked their lives to board an uncomfortable ship and ride across a tumultuous sea to settle in an unknown land.

St. Augustine: The first European settlement in the U.S.

Although the SAT II probably won't ask you a direct question like "Which of the following was the first European settlement in the United States?", you may find St. Augustine included in an answer choice or generalized in a question about other settlements. Or the test may ask you why the Spanish decided to put down roots in Florida. So, here's a little background about the predecessor to Florida's retirement communities and Disney World.

Arghh . . . Spain's early attempts to civilize and inhabit the New World were met by the physical resistance of the corsairs, who were the famed privateers of the Barbary Coast of North Africa. Governments authorized the privateers to attack the shipping of Christian countries, so they grabbed ships and their crews while at sea and sold the sailors into slavery. Privateers successfully raided and plundered Spanish galleons bearing silver and gold. These patch-eyed pillagers were such a powerful powder keg to Spanish ships that Spain built a fort in 1565 at

St. Augustine, located on the east coast of what is now Florida, to protect its profits. In addition to protecting loot, one of the primary purposes of the fort was to protect the passageway to the Caribbean Sea. As the inaugural fort in Florida, St. Augustine became the first European settlement in what would become the United States.

It's a trade-off: French activity in North America

The French were involved in settling the New World, too. Early French explorers sought a trade route to Asia and concentrated their efforts in the regions that are now the northeastern United States and southeastern Canada. When French explorers found no trade route to Asia and no cities of gold, they concentrated on trading with the Native Americans. For this reason, French settlements primarily existed around maintaining trading posts and their relationships with Native Americans.

Among the settlements that the French established in North America were Port Royal in Nova Scotia in 1605, Quebec in 1608, and New France in 1663.

The time is right: British motivations for colonizing the New World

The Spanish settled in St. Augustine to protect their trading interests. Likewise, the French sent over a few settlers to manage their trading posts and perhaps convert a few souls. But the British had more complex reasons for settling the land to the north. Unlike the Spanish and French settlements, British settlements involved many more people — families — who intended to make the new land their permanent home. The motivations for these otherwise sane men and women to make a perilous journey across the Atlantic in search of a better way of life lie in the religious and economic climate of Britain in the 1600s.

Faith of our fathers: Religious factors

Subjects seeking religious freedom made up a significant portion of the newcomers to the young American colonies. At the time of colonization, many Protestants, Puritans, and Catholics found Britain extremely hostile toward their religious beliefs. King James (the one after whom the King James version of the Bible was named) dictated that British citizens must observe the practices of the Church of England, and any group who did not abide by the Church of England in the late 1500s and early 1600s was unable to practice its religion without persecution. Bloody battles between Catholics and Protestants made life unbearable for many citizens. Puritans and other religious sects sought a place where they could practice their faith without harassment.

Money matters: Economic factors

The discovery of new lands steered the European economy in a new direction. Spanish silver imported from the Americas flooded the European market, which caused prices to inflate. The European population was also growing at this time. In Britain, the combination of these two events increased the amount of money that landowners had to pay to maintain their land and increased competition for goods and services. The result was the *dispossession* of small landowners (in non-SAT II words: They lost their land). Crime and poverty in Britain were at an all-time high.

Merchants saw the potential for huge profits in the New World. The new colonies that explorers founded existed solely for the benefit of the mother country. The colonies provided raw products for the mother country and then paid her for her exports; it's the classic win-win situation, at least for the country controlling the trade. For the SAT II, remember this convenient practice as *mercantilism.*

Mercantilism (or the pursuit of trade) was the driving force behind the discovery and settlement of the New World. Countries' desires to find more efficient trade routes to known markets resulted in exploration. With the discovery of new lands, an entirely new trade market developed, and the founding nations capitalized on these new markets through colonization. In Britain, privately financed venturers wanted a piece of the action. The result was the creation of the *joint-stock company.* In a joint-stock company, a group of investors financed exploration and settlement expeditions to the New World. Individual investors would receive a share of any profits the expeditions made based on how much stock they had in the company. Through the joint-stock company, settling the New World became a somewhat attractive source of British investment.

Some people fled Britain's security for opportunities in the new land. Unemployed folks came to the American colonies to find jobs and sustenance. Still others were the second sons of British country gentry who had no chance of inheriting their father's possessions because under the British probate system, all property legally reverted to the eldest son. And the list of disgruntled subjects seemed to go on and on.

The SAT II may ask you to define the motivating factors of the Spanish, French, and British who settled the New World. Because very few questions on the SAT II deal with the early settlement and colonization of North America, you're most likely to encounter questions that test your general knowledge of these topics.

Jamestown in 1607: The first permanent British settlement in the U.S.

You probably won't see a specific question about the Jamestown settlement on the SAT II, but you may see it as an answer choice. With a little bit of background, you can determine whether or not you can eliminate it as an answer choice, if it shows up.

In the late 14th century, the British made two attempts at colonizing North America. Sir Humphrey Gilbert tried to set up a society in the Newfoundland area in 1585, but it didn't work. *Sir Walter Raleigh* established a colony at Roanoke off the coast of Virginia in 1591, but the colony disappeared without any explanation. Then, joint-stock companies provided the money that spurred the first successful British settlements in North America. These companies issued stock to a group of investors, who benefited from any profits gained by New World exploration and risked only the percentage of their investment.

In 1606, King James I of England granted exploration petitions to two companies: the Virginia Company of London and the Virginia Company of Plymouth. The king gave the Virginia Company of London the southern half of the Atlantic seaboard to explore, and he gave the Virginia Company of Plymouth the northern half. The speculative nature of these two companies became apparent when the Plymouth Company (not to be confused with the Plymouth Colony) failed after landing in what is present-day Maine, where they endured a torrid winter. Most of the voyagers who'd left Britain were unprepared for the harsh climate and nearly frozen tundra.

The London Company was more successful, notwithstanding the loss of ⅚ of the trippers and spending at least seven million dollars. Stamina, in the face of daily decimation and the loss of much autonomy to the King of England, ultimately led to sustenance when the settlers realized that their company, which landed in 1607, was in a very fertile agricultural area. The king had granted the London Company the geographical region known as the Southern Tidewater, which they later named Jamestown and would later become part of Virginia.

The semitropical environment was conducive to growing many diverse crops, but the newcomers lacked the leadership and persistence necessary to successfully plant and harvest produce, trap and consume wildlife, and fish the plentiful rivers and Chesapeake Bay. Unfortunately, many of the London Company settlers starved to death amid a cornucopia of natural resources, and their lack of proper hygiene and sanitation caused the rampant spread of disease. When reinforcements from Britain finally arrived in 1608, only 38 of the original 144 mostly male settlers were still alive.

The next winter was more prosperous, mostly due to the leadership of John Smith, who mandated that the settlers do some work. Those of you who've seen Disney's version of *Pocahontas* are familiar with John Smith. Despite his strong leadership (or maybe because of it), Smith was shipped back to Britain. But his example let the king know that a strong governor was essential to the survival of the colonies.

John Smith's friendship with Pocahontas, a Native American princess of the Powhatan nation, was instrumental in easing some of the tensions between the Powhatan, a Native American group that lived nearby, and the Jamestown settlers. Pocahontas eventually married British colonist John Rolfe, but the struggle between the Powhatan nation and the settlers didn't go away. The two groups fought two Anglo-Powhatan Wars; the first occurred in 1622 and the second in 1644. By the end of these wars, the Powhatan nation gave up their land to the settlers, and the two groups refrained from future interaction. By the end of the 17th century, the Powhatan nation practically ceased to exist.

The Pilgrims' progress: Plymouth Colony

When you think of the early colonization of the U.S., you probably think of the *Plymouth Colony* that the Puritans set up. The *Pilgrims,* also known as *Separtist Puritans,* were a religious group that was displeased with King James's efforts to control their religious practices. In 1608, the group moved to Holland, but they felt that they'd have greater religious autonomy if they began a community of their own. So, in 1620, after contracting with the Virginia Company of London, 102 men, women, and children set sail aboard the *Mayflower* seeking religious freedom. The London Company financed the trip and, in return, the freedom-seekers agreed to set up a colony under the company's jurisdiction. The Pilgrims' colonization attempt was more successful than the one made by the Jamestown settlers.

Before the Pilgrims landed off the New England coast, they drew up the *Mayflower Compact* to ensure that all members of the group would obey the rules the group established. Like the Jamestown settlers, many colonists died during the first year — about half the group. With the help of the Native Americans, the Pilgrims planted and harvested crops and adjusted to the environment. Under the initial rule of William Bradford and later, others, the colony continued until 1691, when the larger Massachusetts Bay Colony, which had grown up around it, absorbed the colony. (For more on the Massachusetts Bay Colony, check out Chapter 4.)

The SAT II may ask you about early colonization in general. You may have to compare or contrast the Jamestown settlement with the Plymouth settlement. The Jamestown members consisted of men seeking financial opportunity, whereas the Plymouth members were primarily families fleeing religious persecution. The London Company backed both groups, and both groups endured heavy casualties and intense hardship. The Plymouth community, however, overcame adversity to successfully establish itself much more permanently than those of Jamestown did.

Which of the following best describes the Virginia Company of London in the early 17th century?

(A) The Virginia Company of London established the system of indentured servitude, whereby a person with little money would agree to work for a patron for a specified number of years in exchange for payment of the indentured servant's passage to the New World.

(B) This joint-stock company provided the market for goods exported from British settlements in the New World.

(C) The Virginia Company of London was instrumental in founding the first European settlement in what is now the United States.

(D) This company invested in early exploration of the New World through funds provided by many investors.

(E) This joint-stock company invested in African slave-trade exportation to the colony of Virginia.

Even though the Virginia Company of London was a joint-stock company, don't be lulled into choosing (B) or (E) just because they have this term in their choices. The Virginia Company of London was not involved in slave trade in the early 17th century, and its primary focus was not providing a market for colonial goods.

You know that Spain established the first European settlement (St. Augustine), so (C) is wrong. Indentured servitude was a common practice in the 17th century, but the Virginia Company of London didn't establish it, so you can eliminate (A), which leaves (D) as the correct answer. The primary focus of the Virginia Company of London was pooling investments to fund exploration of the New World and benefit from any resulting profits.

Chapter 4

Everything Old Is New Again: Life in the Colonies, 1620–1760

....

In This Chapter

▶ Defining the characteristics of the British colonies

▶ Understanding the role of religion, culture, and politics during this period

▶ Discovering how domestic and international conflict shaped American identity

....

Spain, France, and Britain put down roots in the new land that was to become the United States, but Britain sent her subjects over in the largest quantities. Between 1600 and 1660, about 160,000 colonists left jolly ole Britain to re-create British life along the Atlantic coast of North America.

The colonists seemed to like everything about Britain except being there. British men and women imported their religious, cultural, economic, and political philosophies and formed a mini-Britain along the Atlantic seaboard — but especially along the northern coast. Although these Anglophile (that's British-loving) communities shared a common heritage, the differences in climate and resources shaped the unique regional differences that developed among the New England, Middle, and Southern populations. Sometimes these disparities caused conflict among the members of distinct colonies, but the colonists experienced more grief dealing with the Motherland than they did dealing with each other.

The SAT II focuses mostly on history after 1790, so the amount of test questions coming from the time period before the American Revolution (and hence, from this chapter) is minimal. But you can never tell what the psychometricians (a fancy name for the test developers) at the College Board will come up with for your test, so this chapter gives you a general sense of what life was like in the American colonies. We cover the characteristics of the New England, Southern, and Middle Colonies. We also touch on the roles that religion, culture, politics, and warfare played in shaping the colonies.

North, South, and Everywhere in the Middle: The Characteristics of the Colonies

The British colonization of America began with the first permanent British colony at *Jamestown,* Virginia, established by the *London Company* in 1607. Shortly thereafter, the *Pilgrims* established a more northern second colony at *Plymouth,* Massachusetts, in 1620. You can find out more information about these two settlements in Chapter 3.

Figure 4-1 shows a timeline with some of the better-known early colonies established in North America by Britain and other countries. (In this chapter, we focus on the British colonies because Britain established most of the North American colonies.) The SAT II probably won't test you specifically on the dates that the colonies started, but you should have a general idea about when colonies formed in relation to one another.

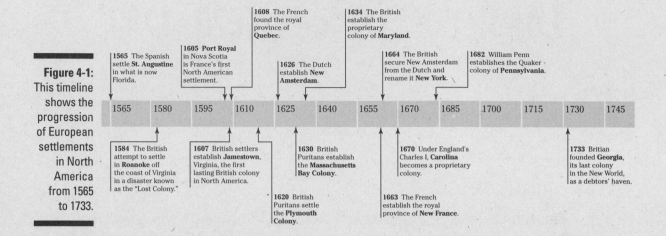

Figure 4-1:
This timeline shows the progression of European settlements in North America from 1565 to 1733.

1565 The Spanish settle **St. Augustine** in what is now Florida.

1605 Port Royal in Nova Scotia is France's first North American settlement.

1608 The French found the royal province of **Quebec.**

1626 The Dutch establish **New Amsterdam.**

1634 The British establish the proprietary colony of **Maryland**.

1664 The British secure New Amsterdam from the Dutch and rename it **New York**.

1682 William Penn establishes the Quaker colony of **Pennsylvania.**

| 1565 | 1580 | 1595 | 1610 | 1625 | 1640 | 1655 | 1670 | 1685 | 1700 | 1715 | 1730 | 1745 |

1584 The British attempt to settle in **Roanoke** off the coast of Virginia in a disaster known as the "Lost Colony."

1607 British settlers establish **Jamestown,** Virginia, the first lasting British colony in North America.

1630 British Puritans establish the **Massachusetts Bay Colony.**

1670 Under England's Charles I, **Carolina** becomes a proprietary colony.

1733 Britian founded **Georgia,** its last colony in the New World, as a debtors' haven.

1620 British Puritans settle the **Plymouth Colony.**

1663 The French establish the royal province of **New France.**

The communities that developed around the *Plymouth Colony* were almost exclusively British, so they became known as the *New England Colonies.* Settlers established communities in New England primarily to escape religious persecution. The *Southern Colonies* sprang up around the Jamestown settlement and drew fortune seekers mainly from Britain and northern Europe. The name *Middle Colonies* not only describes the colonies' location between New England and the South, but it also characterizes the personality of their inhabitants. These middle-of-the-roaders immigrated from Britain and other northern European countries, seeking both religious freedom and economic prosperity without being particularly overzealous about either pursuit.

The New England Colonies: The Puritan ethic

After the Pilgrims settled Plymouth, the *Puritans,* another religious group seeking freedom, arrived to settle the same general area. The Puritans didn't completely break with the *Anglican Church* (the Church of England), but the Pilgrims (also known as *Separatist Puritans*) did. (Both refused to conform to the authority of the Catholic Church.) The Puritans who came to America were still Anglicans, but they had a desire to establish a church "purer" than any other Christian church. And, with that goal in mind, they held to several steadfast beliefs:

- Puritan communities must be made up of pure Christians who have made a covenant with God to bring about His will on earth.

- Humankind is essentially sinful and can be saved only by the grace of God.

- Everyone must strive to do God's work and avoid temptation.

- Every person needs to be able to read the Bible.

These strict beliefs, known as the *New England Way,* shaped the community life of New England. Puritan efforts to maintain a pure society caused them to exclude people from countries other than Britain or from other faiths, so New England communities were almost exclusively British.

Devotion to hard work and temperance provided Puritans with economic success. Settlers looked to land and sea for food and wealth and developed an economy based on fishing, lumbering, shipbuilding, wool production, trading with local Native Americans for beaver pelts, and limited farming. Because reading the Bible was so important, Puritans highly valued education and set up institutions of higher learning to train young men for the ministry. (So, essentially you have the Puritans to blame for the fact that you have to sit here reading this book right now. If they hadn't constructed universities here, you wouldn't have to go through the process of trying to get into them!) Puritans also initiated publicly funded education. In 1647, *selectmen* (male church members appointed to vote) instituted a law that required towns of more than 50 residents to provide public education.

From the original settlement in Plymouth, New England communities grew to include other colonies in Massachusetts, Rhode Island, Connecticut, and New Hampshire. Religion and the freedom to practice it freely provided the incentive for establishing almost all of them; religion was also a factor in uniting them.

When you think of the New England colonies for the SAT II, remember these points:

- ✔ Puritans established colonies in New England to promote and practice a pure Christianity.

- ✔ Puritans were innovators in education and government.

- ✔ Hard-working Puritans built a thriving economy despite the harsh New England climate.

Massachusetts Bay Colony

The big daddy of New England was the *Massachusetts Bay Colony* (or the "Bay Colony," for short). The Massachusetts Bay Company, a joint-stock venture that obtained a royal grant to land in the New World, established the Bay Colony in Salem, Massachusetts, in 1630. Its members wasted no time settling in. A year later, the colonists established the city of Boston and, to advance religion and train ministers, the Puritans founded the first North American institution of higher learning, *Harvard College,* in 1636.

Stockholders of the company chose *John Winthrop* as governor of the colony. Wise, practical, and deeply religious, Winthrop preferred to use negotiation and persuasion to achieve his goals. Recognizing that a handful of men (the governing elite) were unlikely to effectively govern the colony without popular support, Winthrop proposed permitting about 100 adult male settlers of the commonwealth, called *freemen* (another way of saying "selectmen"), to participate in political affairs. This type of government was a modified form of *theocracy,* or a church-state. Winthrop attained extraordinary independence from Britain for the colony to make its own rules. By the 1690s, mainly due to its swift population growth, the Bay Colony had absorbed the Plymouth Colony.

For the SAT II, keep the Bay Colony's dedication to education and its theocratic type of government in mind.

Rhode Island

The settlement of Rhode Island was established as a colony for religious dissenters. Roger Williams, a minister from Salem in the Bay Colony, was a religious zealot — even by Puritan standards. Because of Williams's sympathy for native peoples and his staunch advocacy of the separation of church and state, Puritan leaders viewed him as a troublemaker and banished him from the Bay Colony. With the aid of friendly natives, Williams took refuge in an unsettled area south of Salem in 1636. Later, his settlement helped form the colony of Rhode Island, a haven for those seeking religious freedom — this time from other Puritans rather than from Britain.

Connecticut and New Hampshire

Partially because of population growth and partially because the Bay Colony banished more residents, the Bay Colony's success transferred to other areas of New England. The Reverend Thomas Hooker of Boston founded Hartford, Connecticut, in 1635 and, in 1638, disillusioned Puritans from the Massachusetts Bay Colony founded New Haven. Hooker was influential in drafting the *Fundamental Orders of Connecticut* in 1639, which was the first written constitution to create a government in the New World and was a model for the federal Constitution adopted by the United States 150 years later.

A royal charter established New Hampshire in 1679, but the colony came under the jurisdiction of Massachusetts in 1698. New Hampshire's economy thrived on fishing and trading fur.

All for one: Colonial unity in New England

Despite the religious intolerance that often segregated the New England colonies, their members came from very similar backgrounds and ideologies, and widespread religious persecution among the colonies was short-lived. Governor John Winthrop came to regret the widespread banishment perpetrated by the Bay Colony and, in 1649, he refused to sign another banishment order for religious dissension.

Increased population and the development of the Fundamental Orders of Connecticut initiated a change in New England's government during the 1640s. The written code of law weakened the governing elite's power because they could no longer establish laws based on Biblical interpretation. Instead, each colony had a two-house legislature that created each colony's laws, which were based on British common law. Gradually, the principle of the separation of church and state emerged, making New England's form of government a pre-cursor to the U.S. Constitution.

To protect their interests from Native Americans and French and Dutch settlers, and to maintain community as the population grew and dispersed, New England colonies (except Rhode Island) established the *New England Confederation* in 1643. This intercolonial alliance marked the first of its kind in the New World. The confederation's purpose was to coordinate defense and settle boundary disputes, but it was most useful to the colonists during *King Philip's War* in 1675. In this war, a leader of the Wampanoag nation named Metacom, who the colonists called King Philip, retaliated against the colonists' attempts to control his people. Metacom attacked New England villages, from Connecticut to New Hampshire. The unified colonial forces eventually defeated and killed Metacom and forced the nearby native populations to adapt some of their culture to that of the colonists.

Economics held the New England colonies together. Although many areas farmed standard grain crops, like wheat, barley, and oats, Europe had little demand for those products. But New England's shallow and fast-flowing rivers powered water wheels, making them good for manufacturing. During the harsh winters, many settlers manufactured goods such as bone buttons, hemp-string bags, and textiles. The colonists had surpluses of goods from local manufacturing and sea trade, so they concluded that they must seek out foreign markets. Getting goods to a foreign market required building a merchant fleet. Fortunately, the colonists had an abundance of fine timber and deep ports. As a result, many of the coastal settlements of the New England colonies became centers of shipbuilding.

And you thought your school lunch was bad!

Cooking in the colonies required some ingenuity. Sparse resources made for some, uh, unusual recipes. Here are some instructions for a colonial treat that's sure to please: Cow-heel Pudding.

Take a large cow-heel and cut off all the meat except the black toes. Save the toes for something else and mince the rest of the heel into small bits. Shred the bits with

¾ pound of beef-suet. Add cloves, mace, nutmeg, sugar, and a little salt. Mix in some sack (colonial liquor) and rose water, and combine with six beaten eggs. Butter a cloth and put it in the mix, too; boil for about two hours. To make the sauce, mix melted butter, sack, and sugar.

Yum!

The Southern Colonies: Life on the plantation

In contrast to their New England neighbors, southern colonists' prime motivation for settling was not religious but economic. The original gold-seekers who established Jamestown in Virginia in 1607 soon discovered that the stories of gold were fictitious tales, but tobacco was real. The only problem with the *cash crops* (so called because people used the actual crop to pay for taxes, goods, and services) of the South was that bringing them to harvest was extremely labor intensive.

Agriculture (accommodated by a warm climate and rich soil) provided security for the Southern Colonies of Virginia, Maryland, the Carolinas, and Georgia. Rural settlements fanned out thinly along tributaries, so southern communities, unlike those in the north, suffered from isolation. Additionally, the gap between the rich and poor grew as wealthy plantation owners prospered at the expense of poor workers.

When you consider the Southern Colonies for the SAT II, keep these facts in mind:

- ✔ Southern colonists concerned themselves primarily with building fortunes.

- ✔ The southern climate and resources provided the necessary elements to raise cash crops, such as tobacco, rice, and indigo.

- ✔ The Southern Colonies had a plantation economy, which resulted in great wealth for the plantation owners and grueling living conditions for the plantation workers.

- ✔ Eventually, the use of indentured servants to work the fields dwindled, and African slaves supplied almost all the plantation labor.

Virginia

One of the biggest problems confronting Virginia colonists was the lack of a viable economic basis. The Jamestown settlers tried to produce all sorts of commodities but had little success. (See Chapter 3 for more about the Jamestown settlement.) But that problem changed in 1613 when John Rolfe, husband of Pocahontas, introduced a certain type of tobacco. Despite the warnings of King James I that smoking was a horrible and unhealthy habit, British smokers and partakers of snuff smoked and snuffed away. And with that, Virginia colonists had themselves a profitable cash crop.

To make a profit, the London Company needed cheap labor to work the land. The first colonists, such as the ones who settled Jamestown, were employees of the London Company who usually agreed to work without pay in exchange for a share of the profits. When the contracts expired, the colonial government gave colonists 50 acres of land for each "head" whose passage they paid for to enter the colony. This *headright system* authorized the holder to take any unoccupied 50-acre tract and required him to mark boundaries, plant a crop, and construct some sort of home. So, colonists who could afford to pay for another person's passage received large amounts of land. This system, which originated in Virginia, though other Southern colonies used it, too, encouraged landless Europeans to migrate to America.

Often the "heads" brought into the colonies through the headright system arrived as *indentured servants.* In return for their passage, indentured servants contracted to work for a period of time under the strict control of their *patrons* (the person who financed the servant's passage) and without compensation beyond room and board, usually having the promise of eventual freedom and a parcel of land. Indentured servants often endured intolerable living conditions, and few ever actually became landholders, as they had been promised, because the patron would find excuses, such as punishment for rowdiness, to prolong the contract.

In 1676, Nathaniel Bacon, a freed indentured servant, led other freedmen in a protest known as *Bacon's Rebellion.* Bacon's "beef" was that Virginia Governor William Berkeley was too lenient with the Native Americans in the area, and Bacon blamed the freedmen's inability to conduct fur trade on the Native Americans. For almost six months, Bacon and his followers raided Native American villages and murdered their leaders, violating the governor's orders. The rebellion ended when Bacon died of (yikes!) lice infestation. But Bacon's Rebellion caused Virginians to fear indentured servants.

Past SAT II tests have included questions about indentured servants, so be sure you understand the system and how it came about.

Maryland

Like Virginia, Maryland prospered as a tobacco exporter and maintained a plantation economy, but Maryland was founded in a unique way. In 1634, King Charles I issued George Calvert, also known as Lord Baltimore, land in the form of *proprietary grants* (estates that, in theory, were personal property). Rather than invest their own funds in such estates, proprietors usually granted land to settlers for rent.

Lord Baltimore wanted Maryland to be exclusively Catholic, but the large Protestant population resisted. Lord Baltimore reluctantly accepted the *Maryland Toleration Act* in 1649, which guaranteed freedom of religion to anyone who declared a belief in Jesus Christ. Tolerance didn't extend to nonbelievers who professed their disbeliefs, however; they received the death penalty!

Carolina

Founded in 1670, Carolina was a proprietary colony originally intended to provide food and supplies to Britain and the sugar plantations in Barbados. In Carolina, proprietors attempted to create a feudal system (a hierarchy system of lords and tenants, complete with a hereditary nobility) just like England's to convince men with capital that they could make fortunes in Carolina rivaling those of English lords. Promoters sought to attract capital and settlers, and investors came from all over. Carolina produced tobacco, rice, and indigo, and the city of Charleston became the top port in the Southern Colonies. African slavery grew so much that by 1750, more African slaves lived in Carolina than free whites did. In 1696, Carolina adopted the *Barbados Slave Codes,* which instituted the foundation of slaves as *chattel,* or personal property, and paved the way for their brutal treatment. In 1712, small farmers in the northern part of the colony formed a separate colony called North Carolina.

Georgia

Georgia, the last of the colonial proprietary grants in America, entered the North American colonial scene late (1733) as a haven for Britain's debtors. James Oglethorpe, who was concerned about the plight of honest British men imprisoned for debt, petitioned for a grant of land in America. King George II granted Oglethorpe a charter south of Carolina and provided him with additional funds to establish a buffer between the Carolinas and the hostile Spanish in Florida and the French in Louisiana.

The growth of the African slave trade

By the end of the 17th century, colonial America seeped with African slavery. On southern plantations, labor was in high demand. Due to poor living conditions and high death rates in the colonies and an improved British economy, the supply of indentured servants from Britain dwindled. Slaves proved to be an extremely reliable, inexpensive, and profitable source of labor, particularly in colonies that depended on large-scale agriculture (namely, the Southern Colonies).

The colonies legalized slavery in 1660, and all colonies benefited economically. African slaves toiled in northern homes as agricultural laborers, domestic servants, and artisans; wealthy shipbuilders made their fortunes carrying human cargo; and wheat farmers in the Middle Colonies supplied food to slaves in the West Indies. But the Southern Colonies' agricultural economy especially depended on slave labor. Additionally, slavery lessened the class struggle between rich and poor whites in the South because the two groups now shared their disdain for African slaves.

The Middle Colonies: America's breadbasket

The Middle Colonies blended traits of both the northern and southern regions to form their own personalities. Like colonists in the New England Colonies, many people living in the Middle Colonies sought a place to practice their religion freely, but they lacked the zeal for the purity that their Puritan neighbors exhibited. Land in the Middle Colonies provided a good environment for raising beef, pork, and grain crops, such as wheat, barley, and oats but not for the South's cash crops, like rice, tobacco, and indigo. Farms in the Middle Colonies didn't reach the vastness of Southern plantations because their crops weren't as profitable. However, Middle colonists relied on indentured servants to supply labor for their farms and businesses (see "The Southern Colonies: Life on the plantation" earlier in this chapter for more about indentured servants).

The fertile farmland attracted immigrants from all over northern Europe. These immigrants settled in the Middle Colonies of New York, New Jersey, Delaware, and Pennsylvania. Unlike the Puritans, settlers in the Middle Colonies didn't discourage immigration from countries other than Britain. Middle colonists used the abundance of fine timber to build a merchant fleet to take advantage of selling their goods in foreign markets. As a result, the coastal settlements of the Middle Colonies grew into shipbuilding hubs.

When you think of the Middle Colonies for the SAT II, think a little more tolerant than New England and a little less materialistic than the South.

New York

Before the tall buildings and honking cabs, Manhattan Island was home to Native Americans. In the 1620s, the Dutch struck a deal with the Native Americans: $24 worth of goods for the entire island, which they named *New Amsterdam*. Not a bad deal for the Dutch — that is, until the British came into the picture. In 1664, King Charles II of Britain granted his brother James, the Duke of York, the entire area between Connecticut and Maryland (kings could just do that). British forces captured New Amsterdam from the Dutch within the year and renamed the settlement New York.

Pennsylvania and Delaware

King Charles II owed a debt to William Penn's dad, so to settle that debt, the king granted William Penn the expanse of land that included what is now Pennsylvania and part of Delaware in 1681. William Penn, a *Quaker* (someone whose religion supports peaceful and compassionate ways to bring about change), and his followers colonized the land grant in 1682 to escape religious persecution in Britain. His colony, called Pennsylvania, drew a diverse group of settlers. In 1682, Penn obtained another land grant that he called Delaware, which remained under the control of Pennsylvania until 1776.

Penn considered the colonies a "holy experiment" — a place where he and others could practice their beliefs of human equality and *pacifism* (opposition to using force to achieve a goal). Therefore, Pennsylvania became a haven for settlers of all faiths, including Quakers, Mennonites, Lutherans, the Dutch Reformed Church, Baptists, Anglicans, Presbyterians, Catholics, and Jews.

In a 1682 treaty, Penn wrote, "No advantage is to be taken on either side, but all is to be openness, brotherhood, and love." True to his devotion to "brotherly love" (think Philadelphia, the "City of Brotherly Love"), Penn maintained good relations with the Native Americans by buying a title to their lands and advocating that other settlers deal with them fairly.

New Jersey

In 1664 — even before the British capture of New Amsterdam — the Duke of York gave the land that would become New Jersey to several proprietors, who were a group of his friends. To attract settlers, the proprietors offered land with easy terms and assurances of freedom of religion and local governance.

Tying it all together: A sample question looks at the American colonies

We've given you a bunch of information about the characteristics of America's original colonies. For the test, you don't need to remember a lot of the specifics, like the exact dates that the colonies were founded (we've provided them so you can keep track of the flow of the time period). But you need to have a general idea about the traits of the three main regions: the New England Colonies, the Southern Colonies, and the Middle Colonies. You also need to know the factors that made them the way they were, such as what their land resources were and who settled them.

Which of the following describes the motivating force behind the establishment of the first institutions of higher learning in the British colonies of America?

(A) The Puritan desire to establish literacy and train ministers

(B) The wish of wealthy plantation owners to better the lives of their workers

(C) The Quaker aspiration to create an environment that fostered pacifism and religious tolerance

(D) The Puritan needs to train their members to construct a thriving economy based on agriculture and trade

(E) New Englanders' wish to produce political leaders devoted to the maintenance of a theocratic government

If all you know for this question is that Harvard College in Boston was the first institution of higher learning in the United States, you're ahead of the SAT II game. Boston is in Massachusetts, and Massachusetts was a New England colony, so you can eliminate the answer choices that don't have to do with New England colonists. New England wasn't home to too many wealthy plantation owners (and besides, you don't get the impression that most plantation owners were all too concerned about the welfare of their labor force), so you can easily eliminate (B). Quakers settled in Pennsylvania, so they probably wouldn't have traveled to Boston to establish a college, so you can cut (C).

On to (A), (D), and (E). The Puritan settlers of New England wanted to make sure that everyone in the community could read the Bible, and they needed trained ministers to perpetuate their religious beliefs. Higher learning provided the training grounds for ministers, and reading paved the way for college. So, literacy and minister training were the primary considerations for establishing Harvard College. Answers (D) and (E) are close to being right answers: A thriving economy based on hard work and a theocratic government was important to New Englanders, but it wasn't as important as perpetuating the Puritan religion. Answer (A) is a better answer than (D) or (E).

Notice that answer choices (C), (D), and (E) all contain elements of truth. Quakers were devoted to pacifism and tolerance; Puritans did thrive on agriculture and trade; and early Puritan leaders established theocratic governments. But these truths weren't why Puritans created a college. The SAT II tries to catch you when you're not reading carefully. If you see a true statement in an answer choice, you may be tempted to choose it. Don't be so easily fooled. Before you dedicate yourself to an answer choice, make sure that every element of it is true and that it's the best way to answer the question.

The Great Awakening and Other Eye Openers: Religion, Culture, and Politics in the Colonies

In the 1730s and 1740s, *revivalism* — a movement that placed more importance on personal spiritual experience than on church doctrine — spread throughout the colonies. This movement, also known as the *Great Awakening,* greatly impacted colonial religion. At the same time, the *Enlightenment,* a movement that encouraged using logic and reasoning to find truth, influenced colonial culture. The same independence that caused colonists to question their religious and cultural traditions also caused them to examine their government and the authority of the British government.

As you read this section, pay attention to the ways that the colonists transformed from British citizens creating an extension of the mother country in a new land to a people with independent notions on the brink of forming a new country.

The Great Awakening and the impact of religion

Puritanism permeated every aspect of early New England life. (See "The New England Colonies: The Puritan ethic" earlier in this chapter for more information). Puritans believed that God's blessings were material as well as spiritual. Thus, the accumulation of goods was likely an indication of salvation. Hard work, thriftiness, and strict attention to business were cultivated as the traits of those who enter heaven.

Ties between the church and civil government were extremely close as well. Accordingly, Puritanism contributed enormously to the development of American political institutions by its stress on *limited government* (the sinful nature of man precludes entrusting him with much authority over others), *self-government* (consider compulsory church attendance), *individualism* (every man must read and interpret the Bible for himself), and the right of every community to govern its members for the benefit of the whole. To maintain the purity of their church (known as the Congregationalist Church by the 18th century), Puritans didn't tolerate anyone whose beliefs didn't fit their own. They particularly targeted Catholics, who Puritans had broken with in the first place, and Quakers, whose faith didn't allow them to pay tithes to the Congregationalist or Anglican churches or make oaths to the government.

The Anglican Church, the official church of Britain, was less strict than the Congregationalist Church and dominated what religious life there was in Virginia. By the beginning of the 18th century, neither the Puritans in New England nor the Anglicans in Virginia had a large membership, probably because people were so spread out and because the independent colonial spirit wasn't too keen on intolerance. But the colonies' religious culture changed in the 1730s with a mass revival movement known as the Great Awakening.

An American theologian named *Jonathan Edwards* epitomized the spirit of the Great Awakening. Edwards espoused a personal, emotional approach to salvation instead of the traditional Puritan reliance on church leaders' guidance or the more rational, scientific approach that Enlightenment philosophers proposed (see the next section). He also called for unity rather than intolerance among Christian believers. Edwards preached for nearly ten years to mass audiences throughout New England. At his pinnacle, he delivered his famous sermon "Sinners in the Hands of an Angry God" in Connecticut in 1741. The sermon pointed out the sovereignty of God and the vulnerability of humans. Edwards preached that God provided salvation and empowered believers to resist evil, which contradicted the Puritan philosophy that humans could achieve salvation through their own good works. His words must have struck a chord, because many converted when they heard him speak.

Others joined the revival circuit. *George Whitefield,* a British minister who moved to Georgia known as the "Great Itinerant," eventually surpassed Edwards, making a number of tours in North America and Europe between 1740 and 1770. This time, a movement initiated in America spread to Europe rather than the other way around; the teachings of Edwards and Whitefield rocked the European religious world.

The Great Awakening sparked widespread discussion about religion. Anglicans separated into the Old Lights and the New Lights. The *Old Lights* stuck to the old church traditions, and the *New Lights* embraced the revival and established universities, such as Princeton, Brown, Rutgers, and Dartmouth, to train ministers. New denominations embraced greater religious tolerance. As the first truly national event in colonial history, the Great Awakening helped break down barriers between colonies and heighten the power of the individual.

On the day of the test, keep in mind the following significant effects that the Great Awakening had on the American colonies. It

- ✔ Promoted individual religious experience over church doctrine and decreased the importance of the Anglican clergy.

- ✔ Spread the word of the Great Awakening throughout the colonies and unified them in a way that no other movement had done before.

- ✔ Emphasized the power of the individual, which resulted in the creation of new denominations.

The influence of the Enlightenment: Art, science, and education

The Great Awakening (see the preceding section) promoted growing interrelationships among the 13 colonies, which gradually fused them together. Intercolonial trade grew and became more important. But despite stirrings of a national conscious, Europe's influence in the colonies remained significant — particularly the ideas of the 18th-century Enlightenment, which was spurred by the ideas of scientist and mathematician Sir Isaac Newton and philosopher John Locke.

The *Enlightenment,* also known as the *Age of Reason,* marked a new understanding of the natural world and a new way of thinking. Men began seeing the universe based on scientific laws governing all matter rather than seeing it as merely responding to the impulses of some almighty power. Discovery by abstract philosophizing (deduction) gave way to the methodical collection and study of facts (induction). Thus, human reasoning became the key to knowledge, not God's revelations. By understanding the laws of nature, man could master his surroundings and improve himself.

Although many thinkers of the time recognized that men weren't completely rational and that a complete understanding of the natural world was highly unlikely, readers of their works ignored the limitations and focused on the possibilities. A wave of 18th-century intellectuals responded eagerly to this new world view. These intellectuals were confident in the power of human reason and certain that no mystery could long evade the search for truth. Although many of the "laws" inducted during this period eventually proved less than perfect, they still added greatly to human knowledge.

The Enlightenment may have influenced American colonial culture even more than the Great Awakening did. Here are some of the major imprints that the Enlightenment left on colonial American culture:

- **Deism.** *Deism* was a secular theology that pictured God as being uninvolved in the lives of humans — a clockmaker who built his intricate machine and then sat back to watch it tick. Benjamin Franklin, Thomas Jefferson (see Chapter 6), and many others embraced this theology.

- **Confidence in humans' ability to control their world led to innovations in scientific discovery.** For instance, Benjamin Franklin invented the Franklin stove, bifocals, the lightning rod, and a long arm for getting groceries off of high shelves. He also made great strides in physics with his experiments in electricity.

- **Literature played a practical role in society by offering advice and instruction.** Benjamin Franklin made the majority of contributions to colonial literature. He published *Poor Richard's Almanack,* a collection of proverbs and an autobiography. But no one made a living as a writer in America during the 1700s. Religious literature, written by Jonathan Edwards and other preachers, comprised most of the colonial reading material.

- **A penchant for the practical and a pride for manual labor characterized American visual arts.** Artist John Singleton Copley painted Americans in the act of working. Craftsmen fashioned beautiful and useful objects from brass, copper, wood, and silver.

- **A new dedication to education spread through the colonies.** Although New England dominated education, the Middle Colonies and the Southern Colonies began establishing secular public schools and building secular colleges. The colonists' dedication to quality education for the majority of people, not just the elite, created an American citizenry that was better educated than the general populations of Britain and the rest of Europe.

When you study the Enlightenment for the SAT II, remember that its philosophy glorified the ability of humans to use their minds to learn about truth. "Enlightened" philosophers focused on the power of reason and intellect rather than emotion and feelings, so the arts served practical purposes and education was extremely important.

The question of authority: Colonial politics

By the 18th century, each colony (except Rhode Island and Connecticut) had an elected governor. Those governors had authority much like those of the king in England. Governors had veto power, commanded the militia, and appointed officials, like sheriffs, judges, and justices. Each colony also had a legislature, which usually consisted of two houses: one elected by the people, and the other appointed by the king.

Nevertheless, the colonies were property of the Crown. Although the British government was responsible for establishing colonial policy, it did so on an *ad hoc* basis, meaning that it treated each situation as it arose. Policy was seldom general and often decentralized. In fact, the British government's failure to ever develop an effective centralized government in the American colonies probably best explains the federal system and the sovereignty of state governments that the United States eventually adopted.

Colonists had no strong government to turn to to object to government practices, yet they were at the whim of a country across the sea. Colonists complained about trade practices and navigation laws, perceiving them as Britain's abuse of its authority. Western European thinking of the 16th, 17th, and 18th centuries considered colonies important to the mother country for economic reasons. In Chapter 3, we discuss the theory of *mercantilism* (in which the mother country profited twice from her colonies: first by using the colonies' raw products to produce finished goods and second by selling these goods back to the colonies) as a driving force for colonization.

The *Navigation Acts* were a series of laws Britain enacted over a period of a half-century or more (from 1650 on) to uphold mercantilism. Britain designed these laws to develop a merchant fleet that channeled the flow of raw materials into Britain and, at the same time, kept foreign goods and ships out of colonial ports.

The Navigation Act of 1660 reserved all colonial trade for British ships and required that captains and ¾ of all crews be British. Several years later, the British government added that virtually all European products bound for the British colonies in America must be brought to Britain first. These laws followed a design: British mercantilists saw the colonies as part of an economic unit, with Britain specializing in manufacturing and the colonies providing the raw materials. The result was that Britain became the colonies' main customer for raw materials and its main supplier of manufactured goods.

Gradually, American colonists began to resent British exploitation and their dependence on a largely inattentive British government. This resentment paved the way for the final break with the mother country. At first, Britain didn't actively enforce the Navigation Acts, so colonists could smuggle goods without too many consequences. After the French and Indian War ended in 1763 (covered later in this chapter), Britain started cracking down on colonists who violated the Navigation Acts; this unexpected crackdown contributed greatly to the colonists' quest for independence.

Although the SAT II doesn't often ask about the details of colonial government, it's very fond of questions about mercantilism, so don't be surprised if you see a question about it.

You Wanna Piece of Me? How Conflict Shaped America's Identity

Even though the British colonies in America were isolated from the Old World, they were still affected by events in the Old World as well as the New World. In the New World, subtle conflicts arose among colonies over issues like border disputes and who had the right to trade with Native Americans. More severe strains occurred among the settlers and Native Americans, like King Philip's War (see "The New England Colonies: The Puritan ethic" section earlier in this chapter) and Bacon's Rebellion (see "The Southern Colonies: Life on the plantation" earlier in this chapter). In the Old World, fierce competition for markets and raw materials among Western Europeans encouraged conflicts between Britain and other countries, which played out in the American colonies. Consequently, conflict was virtually a permanent predicament of 17th- and 18th-century colonial American life.

You're more likely to see questions pertaining to the major conflicts between Britain and other countries, but you never know what the SAT II will dish out, so make sure you have an idea about the smaller conflicts as well.

Domestic dissension: Strife among the colonies

Opportunities for wealth existed in the American colonies, and the social distinctions there were far less rigid than the ones in Europe. And inevitably, with the struggle for wealth came conflict among settlements and colonies.

The Crown bound the 13 separate colonies indirectly, more by accident than by design. Vast, open lands made travel in the colonies slow, uncomfortable, and expensive. Few people had knowledge of areas other than their own. Settlers often felt that having much in common with people of distant regions was inconceivable.

Furthermore, the royal bureaucracy prevented colonists from thinking of themselves in national terms. "American" remained an unpopular term in the mid-18th century. Instead, colonists thought of themselves as Virginians, New Yorkers, and so on; and, for a time, they thought of themselves as subjects of the king. Tension was especially evident between the northern and southern colonies, and between easterners and westerners. As we discuss in later chapters, this tension continued even after these diverse groups formed a nation.

For the SAT II, remember that differences in regional climates, economics, and attitudes caused misunderstandings and dissension among the American colonies. We discuss these points of contention in the upcoming sections.

Sober northerners versus fiery southerners

Temperament caused friction between the northern and southern colonists. To speak in sweeping generalities, people with strict religious beliefs founded the Northern Colonies. People who desired to increase their fortunes founded the Southern Colonies. Thus, the temperaments associated with these distinct goals were often incompatible. New Englanders couldn't relate to the traditionally passionate southerners any more than southerners could relate to their staid and solemn neighbors to the north.

Economic factors also divided the two groups. As we describe in "North, South, and Everywhere in the Middle: The Characteristics of the Colonies," the lifestyles of the agricultural South and its dependence on slavery differed greatly from that of the North, which relied on trade.

Eastern city dwellers versus frontier westerners

Clashes over economic interests flared up mostly between westerners and easterners. Within the same colonies, easterners lived in cities along the Atlantic Coast, but westerners inhabited the less-populated territory on the western borders. Westerners usually advocated rapid westward expansion, whereas easterners usually objected to opening up new lands for fear that the land would depress the value of established holdings. Westerners sought public funds for building roads west, because access to and from the frontier was critical for trade.

Easterners, on the other hand, usually objected to such expenditures. Westerners perceived the Native Americans as a perpetual threat, but eastern colonists, who were removed from the dangers along the frontier, pressed for restraint because warfare was expensive and risky.

Conflict also arose when the newer western counties didn't receive equal representation in provincial legislatures. As a result, western settlers often lacked the appropriate political force to ensure a political voice.

Trouble abroad: Three French and British wars

By the end of the 17th century, the Dutch lacked the resources to maintain a large empire, and Spain was in decline. Britain and France "owned" North America. Over the next 125 years, European alliances shifted dramatically, but Britain and France were always on opposite sides. Their greed for more territory and wealth churned the engines of war.

Conflicts between the British and French reminded American colonists that they were British subjects because war extended to the colonies. Victories in the colonies were usually indecisive because the scattered and dissimilar colonists had difficulty uniting and raising a militia.

For the SAT II, keep in mind that Britain's conflicts with other European countries forced the colonies into conflict as well.

King William's War

After Protestants removed Britain's King James II, a Catholic, they replaced him in 1689 with King William III, a Protestant. The French king, Louis XIV, a Catholic, was livid, and a war, known as King William's War, broke out and lasted until 1697.

French and British colonists played a minor role in King William's War. French forces entered New York, utilizing hit-and-run tactics that we know today as "guerilla" fighting. The British retaliated against various settlements in Nova Scotia, Quebec, and Montreal. The war ended in a stalemate, and all captured territory in America was restored to its original owner. King William's War pitted Protestant British colonists against Catholic French settlers and strengthened America's Protestant identity, which probably didn't make the British Catholics in the colonies feel too good.

Queen Anne's War

The next struggle occurred only four years after King William's War (in other words, 1701). The conflict was the War of the Spanish Succession, known in America as *Queen Anne's War.* Basically, Britain's Queen Anne, who succeeded William III, sought to prevent France's King Louis XIV from putting his grandson on the throne of Spain.

In the American colonies, this war was much like King William's War. A few battles occurred, various tribal allies were involved, and lots of raids and counter-raids took place. The major difference was that the British colonies were fighting the Spanish in the south and the French in the north. In 1713, the war ended. King Louis XIV put his grandson on the throne of Spain and, in exchange, Britain received Nova Scotia, Newfoundland, and the Hudson River Valley.

King George's War

The third war of the period, the War of Austrian Succession, also called *King George's War,* started in 1740. But fighting didn't start in the American colonies until 1744. Once again, few battles occurred in the colonies, a lot of raiding took place, and tribal alliances were used.

For the SAT II, all you need to know about these three conflicts is that the British wars forced the American colonists to fight, that the lack of unity in the colonies hindered their ability to battle effectively, and that the three wars led up to the great war between the French and the British, the French and Indian War.

A contest for the Ohio Valley: The French and Indian War

By 1750, conflicts between the British and French settlers north and south of the St. Lawrence River in what is now northeastern Canada were at a peak. British colonists were suspicious of the French because of their Catholic religion and blamed them for conflicts British colonists had with Native Americans in the area. Conflicting land claims also made matters worst, particularly the French's insistence that the Ohio Valley was theirs.

The French had established a chain of forts and trading posts to keep communication and supply lines open between Canada and Louisiana. By the 1740s, however, fur traders and land speculators had claimed nearly 500,000 acres in the Ohio Valley. Before this time, an area of wilderness had usually served as a buffer zone between the French and British colonists in America. But with expanding colonization, the two powers collided in the Ohio Valley. *The French and Indian War* (also called the Seven Years' War in Europe) broke out in 1754. One of the first American colonists to serve was a tall, 22-year-old Virginia militia captain named George Washington. (You can find out more about him in later chapters.)

The SAT II is more concerned with the outcome of the French and Indian War than it is with the details of the actual war. For the test, all you need to know about the war is that British forces (and their American counterparts) battled the French and their Native American allies for control of the Ohio Valley.

The *Treaty of Paris* ended the conflict in 1763. British money and soldiers provided the victory over the French. France abandoned all its claims in North America except two islands in the St. Lawrence River. Britain took over Canada and the eastern half of the Mississippi Valley, both formerly French claims. And, in a separate treaty as payment from France for Spain's alliance, Spain received the area west of the Mississippi River and New Orleans.

The outcome of the French and Indian War impacted America in more ways than the transfer of land ownership. The French and Indian War

- **Marked the end of the French colonial empire in North America.** After the war ended, France had no real holdings in North America, and British interests dominated the North American continent east of the Mississippi River.

- **Caused the British to become more involved in the American colonies.** Until the war, Britain had pretty much ignored the colonial governments and was fairly lax about enforcing laws in the colonies. While fighting the French, the British perceived that the colonists weren't really dedicated to helping out their forces. The Brits noticed that colonial merchants engaged in illegal trade with France and sensed a lack of loyalty in the colonial government. These concerns caused Britain to strengthen its presence in the American colonies.

- **Made the colonists aware of the threat of the permanent presence of the British army in America.** Even though the outcome of the war heightened colonists' pride in being a part of the British Empire, others became aware of how much Britain's presence in the colonies threatened their independence. Eventually, colonists increased their resolve to actively resist British control and seek an identity as a separate nation.

The following question asks you to make some assumptions using what you know about the French and Indian War.

All the following are effects of the French and Indian War EXCEPT

(A) Florida was controlled by the British.

(B) Spain was granted land west of the Mississippi River.

(C) American colonial desire for independence was curbed.

(D) Britain controlled the land north of the Great Lakes.

(E) France's possessions in North America were limited to a couple of islands.

Rephrase the question so that the EXCEPT doesn't throw you: "Which of the following is not an effect of the French and Indian War?" You can clearly eliminate (B), because an unambiguous effect of the war was Spain's control of land west of the Mississippi River. Likewise for (E), France's North American holdings were limited to two islands in the St. Lawrence Valley.

Now you're left with (A), (C), and (D) as choices. You know that Britain gained the land east of the Mississippi River. Florida is east of the Mississippi, so (A) must be an effect of the war; you can eliminate it as a correct answer. You also know that Britain controlled Canada. Canada is north of the Great Lakes, so (D) must be an effect of the war; you can eliminate it from contention.

Now you're left with (C). Even though colonial pride in being part of the British Empire increased right after the war, the most dominant effect of the war was that colonists began to distrust the British presence in America. The war actually ended up strengthening the colonists' desire for independence. Answer (C) is the best answer.

Chapter 5

We the People: The Fight for Independence, 1763–1800

∙∙

In This Chapter

▶ Understanding how colonists declared war and won the revolution against Britain

▶ Seeing how the founding fathers created the United States of America and its institutions

▶ Discovering the experimental republic in its formative years

∙∙

About 20 percent of the SAT II U.S. History exam covers the period from 1763 to 1800. The majority of exam questions from this time period focus on political and economic history. Social, intellectual, cultural, and foreign policy issues take a backseat to questions about power and money. Most likely, you'll see questions dealing with the American colonists' motivations for rebellion and the decisions the founding fathers made after the new nation gained independence. Remember, during this time period, the American colonies and the ensuing United States were still experiments.

Throughout the revolutionary period, you see attempts by various people and groups to control and rebel. Some of these trial administrations worked, and some didn't. But the important point is that the American colonies ended up creating an entirely new and unprecedented system of government that continues to survive today.

Untying the Apron Strings: A Prelude to Independence

The great experiment that was the American colonies became quite messy in the early 1760s. After defeating the French in the French and Indian War, the colonists and the British appeared united. Over the next decade, however, tensions mounted between the two groups. As the British became increasingly oppressive in their rule over the colonies, crisis after crisis foreshadowed the revolution.

The Proclamation of 1763

Three months after the Treaty of Paris ended the French and Indian War, Pontiac, chief of the Ottawa tribe, attacked a garrison of British soldiers at Fort Detroit. (To find out more about the French and Indian War, see Chapter 4.) Although the British defeated Pontiac after several months of fighting, King George III worried about future conflicts with the Native Americans. As a consequence of this conflict, known as *Pontiac's Rebellion*, the British government issued the *Proclamation of 1763*, which prohibited colonists from settling west of an imaginary line that followed the Appalachians from Canada to Georgia. This line was meant to protect Native Americans, colonists, and the fur trade, but many colonists had already moved beyond this boundary (or chose to ignore it). To protect their interests in uncertain times, Britain kept a large amount of soldiers stationed in the American colonies. This move, though seemingly innocent, would eventually lead to numerous confrontations between the British government and the American colonists.

Acting up: British attempts to raise revenue

Britain's debt from the French and Indian War amounted to a whopping £123 million (that's more than $220 million in U.S. dollars, and imagine if that amount were adjusted for 250 years worth of inflation!). As you can guess, the British government needed a solution to its massive debt problem. But where to get money . . . where to get the money . . . ? George Grenville, King George III's chief minister, had an answer: The British government could raise the money by taxing the American colonies, of course! And several parliamentary acts followed to attempt to ease the war debt. The British government felt these taxes were fair because its troops were stationed in the colonies to protect the colonists. To assist in collecting the taxes, in 1760, Britain began issuing *Writs of Assistance* in the colonies; these open-ended writs had no expiration dates and allowed the officer who possessed them to search and seize, especially in cases of customs inspections.

Colonists didn't accept taxation too well. Great Britain had pretty much left the colonists alone (a policy called *benign neglect*) in the decades before the French and Indian War. Now that Britain was paying more attention to the colonies, the colonists weren't used to being controlled. They didn't think they needed a standing British army in the colonies because they had their own militias to protect their interests. They also resented being taxed without having any say in the matter. The colonists had no elected officials in the British Parliament to represent their point of view when decisions to tax them were being made; the colonists had to endure British "taxation without representation." Here are some of the important tax measures and how colonists reacted to them:

- ✔ **Sugar Act of 1764:** The *Sugar Act* increased the duty (import tax) on molasses from the French West Indies and increased the penalties for smuggling sugar (which colonists did to avoid paying duties) to force the colonists to buy more expensive molasses from the British West Indies. Colonists resented this type of control over a basic commodity and became hostile toward the British government.

- ✔ **Stamp Act of 1765:** This measure imposed a tax on paper used for all sorts of colonial documents (like contracts, marriage certificates, and even decks of cards) and required colonists to place a special stamp on the paper to prove that the tax had been paid. Colonists already paid taxes to their local governments, which were made up of elected representatives. Thus, to the colonists, the *Stamp Act* represented a breach of autonomy. Even though the tax was miniscule — perhaps a cent or so — it was more than citizens living in Britain had to pay, and that seemed unfair to the colonists. They resented the control the British government exerted on their lives without their having any say in the matter.

  One of the most important results of the Stamp Act was the creation of the *Stamp Act Congress,* which met in New York City in October 1765 to write a petition to the king and to Parliament that essentially stated that colonists had the same rights as other British citizens and that no taxes should be imposed upon them by any government other than their local legislatures made up of elected representatives. The congress brought the disparate colonies together for the first time, setting a precedent for later action on the road to revolution. Parliament repealed the act in 1766, but more because it was hard to enforce than because of the colonial petitions against it.

✔ **The Townshend Duties of 1767:** The *Townshend Duties* placed taxes on common items like lead, paper, paint, glass, and tea. Once again colonists were angered about being taxed without having representation in Parliament. Colonial women were primarily affected by the tea tax, so they got involved in the protests, too.

Tensions over the acts mounted and, in Boston in March 1770, a small crowd began harassing British soldiers, and a bloody confrontation ensued. Colonists threw snow-balls and rocks at the soldiers, and the soldiers fired into the crowd, wounding 11 and killing five. Revolutionary *Samuel Adams* called the event the *Boston Massacre* and adver-tised it for anti-British propaganda purposes, and many Bostonians demanded that Britain remove the troops from their city. In 1770, the British government repealed the duties, except for the tax on tea. But colonists had seen the writing on the wall and, in 1772, Samuel Adams set up *Committees of Correspondence* to establish networks of com-munication among the colonies in order to organize resistance to British policies.

✔ **Tea Act of 1773:** Because the tax on tea remained in place, protestors like merchant John Hancock ordered a boycott on tea sold by the British East India Company, and colonial merchants and smugglers profited. This boycott displeased the East India Company, and it turned to the British government for help. In response, Parliament enacted the *Tea Act,* which lifted the tax on the East India Company's tea so it could undercut the colonial merchants' (and smugglers') prices. Most colonial ports turned away the East India ships in protest, but the British army planned to assist the East India Company so it could land its ships in Boston. *The Sons of Liberty,* a group of protes-tors that had been active since the Stamp Act crisis, thwarted the delivery by dumping the tea into the harbor to show their distaste for the Tea Act. The 150 protestors — many dressed as Native Americans — dumped the tea overboard as thousands of supporters watched from land. This incident became known as the *Boston Tea Party.*

✔ **Coercive or Intolerable Acts:** As a result of the Boston Tea Party, the British govern-ment passed the *Coercive Acts* in 1774 (which the colonists called the *Intolerable Acts*). The Coercive Acts was a series of oppressive acts intended to punish Boston, which was the heart of the rebellion. These acts closed Boston Harbor to trade; suspended the Massachusetts charter, essentially abolishing the local judicial system; allowed the quartering of soldiers in civilian homes; and gave control of present-day Ohio, where many colonists had been living, to the Canadian governors of Quebec. These acts affected all aspects of everyday life in Boston and caused fear among colonists outside of Boston, turning even the most ordinary British colonists into revolutionaries.

Colonial leaders decided to meet in the fall of 1774 in Philadelphia at the *First Continental Congress* to address the abuses of the British government.

So many acts to remember! But don't fear. The SAT II is unlikely to ask you about the details of any one act. Remember, history is *causal* — events cause other events, and so on. Understanding the causes of major events is much more important than recalling the details of individual acts on their own. You're more likely to see a question like the following:

What inspired colonists to meet in Philadelphia to hold the First Continental Congress?

(A) Wars with Native Americans

(B) Trade problems with Britain

(C) The Coercive Acts

(D) Taxation without representation

(E) The Proclamation of 1763

Upon first examination, answers, (B), (C), and (D) look plausible. However, after thinking about it for a moment, you see that taxation without representation *caused* trade problems with Britain (such as the Boston Tea Party), which in turn *caused* the Coercive Acts. Thus, the only correct answer is (C). Remembering that history is heavily influenced by momentum will help you on the SAT II.

The First Continental Congress

The First Continental Congress met in Philadelphia, Pennsylvania, in September 1774. Every colony except Georgia sent delegates. The main goals of the congress were to decide what rights the colonists wanted as British subjects and to address the Coercive Acts. After seven weeks of debate, the congress wrote a declaration of rights, which asked "only for peace, liberty, and security. We wish no diminution of royal prerogatives, we demand no new rights." The delegates also agreed on a limited boycott of imports.

In October, the delegates left the convention feeling that they had done all that they could to deal with the growing problem. But the British government did not recognize the Continental Congress and continued to enforce the Coercive Acts. Colonists across America began to realize that only drastic measures would preserve their rights.

The heat in the kitchen was rising. By the winter of 1774 to 1775, tension between the colonies and Britain had reached a fever pitch. Something big was about to happen. How and why did the colonists decide to go to war to preserve their liberties? And, most importantly, how did they defeat a vastly superior British army? You will see.

Lexington, Concord, and Bunker Hill

The boycotts of the First Continental Congress continued throughout the winter of 1774 to 1775. Many colonists were optimistic that the boycotts would influence the British government to end the Coercive Acts (see "Acting up: British attempts to raise revenue" earlier in this chapter) and return life to the status quo. Others, however, were far less enthusiastic about the possibility of compromise. In Massachusetts, militias stored gunpowder and bullets in small towns across the countryside, and local militia, known as *minutemen,* were prepared to defend their communities at a moment's notice.

Thomas Gage, the new British military commander of the colonies, knew that the possibility of an insurrection existed and decided to take action. In mid-April 1775, Gage ordered his soldiers to confiscate the stockpiles of ammunitions at Lexington and Concord and to arrest the troublemakers. In the middle of the night on April 18, the British troops crossed the Charles River, approaching the town of Lexington. In his famous ride, Paul Revere (and two others) rode on horseback through the towns to alert the minutemen that the British troops were coming.

Battling at Lexington

In Lexington, 70 armed militiamen blocked the path of the British soldiers as they marched into the town. The British commander told the militiamen to put down their arms and disperse, and some of them did. However, a shot rang out — nobody knows from where — and fighting followed. Eight colonists died and ten were wounded in the confusion.

Conflict in Concord

A similar scene occurred in Concord, a town five miles west of Lexington. Three colonists died as well as three British soldiers. Here the British soldiers became frustrated and ultimately failed in their mission because they couldn't find the ammunition stockpiles. As the British troops began their long march back to Boston, colonists shot at them from hiding places along the road. Still, blood had been spilled on both sides, and the armed struggle would only continue.

The Battle of Bunker Hill

Two months after Lexington and Concord, on June 16, the colonists and British soldiers fought one of the bloodiest battles that has ever been fought on American soil. At Breed's Hill and Bunker Hill, just north of Boston, British General William Howe decided to send his troops across water and up a steep hill toward the rebel forces in a frontal assault. After three bloody attempts to take the hill, the British were finally victorious. But the victory was costly: The British lost 226 soldiers (many of them officers) and more than 800 others were wounded. The Americans lost 140 men, and 271 were wounded. The British learned that the war against the American rebels would not be easy or won in a single battle. War had begun.

The Declaration of Independence

The fighting in Lexington and Concord prompted the Americans to call a formal assembly. On May 10, 1775, the *Second Continental Congress* met in Philadelphia with two goals: to find a reconciliation with Britain and to build an army to combat the British if reconciliation didn't work out. Most of the delegates weren't prepared yet to break from Britain, but a new piece of literature would soon help change their sentiments.

Thomas Paine's pamphlet, *"Common Sense,"* circulated in the colonies in early 1776. In simple language, Paine, a scholar, liberal thinker, and writer, argued that the British monarchy had become despotic and must be overthrown. In its place, Paine argued, the colonists should install a republican government based on the rule of the people. Paine's writings greatly influenced many Americans and, by the summer, a resolution from the Virginia delegates to the Second Continental Congress called for independence.

The battles raging between the British forces and American militias across the American countryside along with Paine's work pushed the delegates over the edge. On July 2, every state except New York voted for independence. Virginian Thomas Jefferson and his committee received the credit for drafting the document the *Declaration of Independence,* which included ideological statements about the rights of man, consent of the governed, and equality, as well as the colonists' grievances against the king and reasons for declaring war against and independence from Britain. The congress debated the grievances in the document and the contentious issue of slavery for two days before finally adopting the declaration on July 4. The Declaration of Independence included these famous and, at the time, quite radical lines: "We hold these truths to be self-evident, that all men are created equal; that they are endowed by their Creator with certain unalienable rights; that among these are life, liberty, and the pursuit of happiness."

Revolutionary battles and the Treaty of Paris

The American Revolution (also known as the Revolutionary War) was a difficult affair for both sides. The Americans had to only outlast the British; they did not have to defeat them outright. On the other hand, the British had to win a complete, forceful victory over the Americans, which was fairly hard to do, despite its superior army. The British had the arduous task of destroying the rebellion, in both substance and spirit, and restoring the British colonial government to power. This last task proved tricky because the Continental Congress moved from city to city, and the British hesitated to destroy cities or food supplies that they viewed as part of their empire. Keep in mind that the Revolutionary War was in many ways a civil war. The colonies were part of Great Britain, and the colonists were its citizens, so the rebels were fighting against their own countrymen. Deciding whether to remain loyal to British rule or to side with the rebellion was a very complicated decision for many colonists.

The British forces

At the time of the American Revolution, the British army was the largest, strongest, and most well-trained army in the world. The troops Britain sent to America were mostly professional soldiers with little vested interest in the American colonies. Basically, these men were in America doing their jobs, which was a great disadvantage for the British because they were up against Americans who were extremely committed to their cause.

But not all Americans favored revolution, and the British troops received assistance from many colonists who remained loyal British subjects. *Loyalists,* as they were called, made up between 20 and 30 percent of the colonial population. Loyalists had strong ties to the British government and the Anglican Church (the Church of England) and believed that the prosperity of the American colonies depended on a close relationship with the British Empire. Many Loyalists were merchants and lawyers who saw the rebellion against authority as a sign of chaos and anarchy. About 50 British military units during the war were made up of Loyalists.

In addition, many Native American tribes gravitated toward supporting the British. Many American colonists had encroached on Native American lands in Ohio and elsewhere, despite the Proclamation of 1763 (covered earlier in this chapter), and Native Americans feared for their futures. As a result, tribes such as the Senecas, Onondagas, and the powerful Mohawks joined the British effort, hoping that a British victory would preserve their ways of life.

In early 1776, King George III hired more than 1,000 German mercenaries (also known as *Hessians* because so many of them came from the Hesse-Kassel area of Germany) to fight the American rebels. The German soldiers weren't typical mercenaries fighting for their own profit. They were mostly debtors who received low pay (sometimes only daily food rations) for their efforts; the bulk of British payments for their services went directly to German royalty, which meant that these soldiers weren't emotionally or monetarily motivated in the war effort. German soldiers made up almost ⅓ of British troops.

The American forces

Colonists who supported the revolution, called *Patriots,* joined together to produce a military to take on the British forces. Before the war with Britain, the heart of the American military was the militia. Every able man over the age of 16 participated in the militia to help protect the colonies during their early years. But militias were best in local conflicts and didn't make for a strong national army in a war against a superior military foe. So the Continental Congress implemented a program to establish a national army, called the *Continental Army* (see "The first time around: The Articles of Confederation" later in this chapter). It required soldiers to enlist for at least three years and offered those who served for the entire war effort a bonus of 100 acres of land. Most Patriots enlisted in the Continental Army because they were personally dedicated to the revolution and were determined to win, much more determined than those who fought for the British army. Their commander-in-chief was George Washington, a competent, determined, and skilled leader who had served in the British army during the French and Indian War (see Chapter 4 for details on this war).

African Americans didn't serve in the war initially, but as manpower became more and more important, northern colonies allowed blacks to serve. In the South, some colonies allowed blacks to fight if they had their owner's permission. Women, too, served in the war against the British, usually as cooks or nurses.

One alliance in particular proved vital and ultimately a key to an American victory. After the Americans achieved a decisive victory at Saratoga in late 1777 (see the next section), France recognized America as an independent nation and provided arms, military advisors, and naval support to the Americans because the French felt the Continental Army had a chance at winning the war. After the Americans gained the French as allies, many British citizens questioned whether Britain could win the war. Spain declared war on Britain in 1779 and provided Americans with assistance in capturing British outposts on the Mississippi. Holland also supported the American Revolution, and Britain attacked the Netherlands in 1780, in part, to prevent Holland from assisting the Americans.

In the theater of war . . .

In August 1776, General William Howe, who had led the British advance at Bunker Hill (see the "The Battle of Bunker Hill" earlier in this chapter), attacked Long Island, where General George Washington and his troops had amassed. Howe was victorious, but Washington and his troops escaped because Howe did not press forward. Howe chased Washington across New Jersey and into Pennsylvania but didn't achieve a complete victory. His inability or unwillingness to deliver a knockout punch to Washington and his troops proved costly to the British because a few months later, Washington and his troops obtained several significant victories and the war continued.

On Christmas, Washington crossed the Delaware River and defeated German troops (see "The British forces" earlier in this chapter) at Trenton, New Jersey. The victory gave the American soldiers a needed boost in morale, and Washington continued on, winning several more skirmishes. Over the next three years, battles between the British and Americans raged across North America. A turning point for the Americans came in the battle they fought at *Saratoga* in New York in October 1777. American forces soundly defeated the British, which fueled American optimism and encouraged France to assist the Continental Army against the British.

The British army gave up on New England, which had proved impossible to control. Instead, the British forces headed south with a new plan. The new plan was to capture the South, perhaps disrupting the Continental Congress and the morale of the American army, and then return north. In December 1778, Georgia fell easily and South Carolina followed. General Charles Cornwallis, who now commanded the British troops, moved into North Carolina and, eventually, Virginia.

Cornwallis seemed to think he was in control of the war until he arrived in Yorktown, Virginia, to resupply. While at Yorktown, the French fleet met Cornwallis on the banks of the Atlantic Ocean. French ships bombarded the British fort and, on land, a combined French and American force that numbered more than 16,000 surrounded Cornwallis's 7,500 men and blocked them from getting necessary supplies and reinforcements. Cornwallis's southern strategy had failed, and the British general surrendered on October 19, 1781. At this point, the war was essentially over. After hearing about the surrender at Yorktown, British Prime Minister Lord North resigned. In April 1782, the British House of Commons voted to end the war with America. The war officially ended in September 1783 with the signing of the Treaty of Paris.

The Treaty of Paris

On September 2, 1783, the Americans, British, and French signed the *Treaty of Paris,* which acknowledged the complete autonomy and independence of the United States, created new boundaries, and settled debts. The British agreed to remove all soldiers from America (although it didn't, which would be part of the cause for another conflict a generation later, the War of 1812, which we cover in Chapter 6).

Ultimately, the British had not been prepared for a long-term war with the Americans. The Americans had employed guerilla tactics and Washington's sound leadership to overcome a stalemate with the British. The British had underestimated the Patriots' resolve and the effectiveness of the Continental Congress, which had been in place only since 1775, to create a powerful army capable of defeating British forces. Additionally, the alliances Americans formed with France and Spain thwarted the British efforts. After years of bloody fighting, Americans finally won their independence. Now it was up to the new leadership, including the victorious General George Washington, to decide what to do with the newfound freedom they had won.

Tying it all together: A sample question looks at the Revolutionary War

A potential question is a "big idea" question, which is a question that sums up an enormous topic in one sentence. Don't forget to note the NOT in the prompt. This tactic can be confusing, but the SAT II may use it to trick you.

Which of the following is NOT an explanation for the American victory over the British in the Revolutionary War?

(A) American forces outnumbered British troops.

(B) America formed an alliance with the French.

(C) The Continental Army engaged in guerilla warfare.

(D) The British were unable to win complete victories.

(E) Americans formed an organized, effective Continental Congress and rebellion network.

When you first read the question, you may think that all the answers are reasons why the Americans defeated the British. But it's a trick. Look at answer (A). You might assume that the Americans had more troops because it was their country that they were defending. But remember that the British had the largest, strongest, and most well-trained army in the world at the time of the American Revolution, and it vastly outnumbered the American troops. So (A) is the correct answer.

Meeting of the Minds: Establishing the U.S. Government

After the Americans won the Revolutionary War, American leaders had the difficult task of deciding what kind of government the new nation would have and what kinds of rights its citizens would have. The leaders had to decide who would govern, what the new laws would be, and who could take part in the entire process, among other issues. Simply put, American leaders struggled to define who, exactly, was an American. For nearly a decade after the end of the war, the great experiment would continue in various forms before leaders would establish the modern federal system and the Constitution. And so the American kitchen had indeed baked itself a pie, but no one was quite sure yet how, exactly, it would taste.

Surveying social issues in the new nation

While Americans were still fighting for their independence, American leaders had to consider what direction they wanted their new country to go in once they obtained their freedom. During and after the war, American leaders debated crucial social issues, such as how the new government would deal with property, education, religion, and slavery.

Property

In the Declaration of Independence, Thomas Jefferson borrowed the "life, liberty, and the pursuit of happiness" adage from philosopher *John Locke,* a philosopher who wrote about the inalienable human rights of "life, liberty, and property." American leaders were devoted to an individual's right to own property and used property ownership as a way to define voting rights and participation in government.

Nearly all states required that candidates running for government office own a significant amount of property, which disenfranchised a large portion of the population — particularly those men who didn't own land. Although these laws caused dissent, leaders did little to pacify non-landholders, The founding fathers realized that if rights were given to one group (such as non-landholding males), more and more groups would demand rights as well. And so the first American leaders held firm with their belief that property defined the right to run for government office. As a result, only the elite were able to take part in the early governments of America.

Education

To many elites, an educated population was the key to a successful and prosperous new nation. Numerous universities were established during this era, including Brown University, Rutgers University, Dartmouth College, the University of Pennsylvania, and Columbia University. Women, too, became important targets of education efforts. Female education received particular attention during the 1790s because many American elites believed that women were the rightful teachers of liberty and government to their sons. This belief became known as *Republican Motherhood,* and it argued that women had the duty to raise solid American citizens. Women were expected to be educated for the sakes of their families and their country and to help create an intelligent, loyal American population.

Religion

Many of the nation's founders had arrived in America because they objected to having a state religion. Therefore, defining the relationship between church and government in the new nation was important. Leaders heavily debated the issue of church and state during the drafting of the U.S. Constitution.

Slavery

The issue of slavery, debated during the writing of the Declaration of Independence but ultimately abandoned at the time, surfaced in the wake of the Revolutionary War as an important issue for the new nation. The Declaration of Independence stated that "all men are created equal," yet did this phrase really mean *all* men?

To most Americans at the time, it did not. After the end of the war, Americans' views on slavery varied widely from region to region and state to state. In the South, plantation farming was the backbone of the economy, and life without slaves to work the cotton and tobacco fields was impossible to many Southerners. In the North, *emancipation* — the freeing of slaves — gained momentum. Massachusetts banned slavery in 1776, Pennsylvania granted gradual emancipation to slaves in 1780, and Connecticut followed suit in 1784. New York and New Jersey would do the same several years later. But in the South, emancipation bills were rarely taken seriously and always were defeated. Efforts for emancipation in Virginia, Delaware, and Maryland all failed and, in the Deep South, few whites could fathom the idea of freeing their large labor force. But slavery did not mesh with the ideals of the Declaration of Independence, and Americans would continue to debate this issue as the nation developed.

The first time around: The Articles of Confederation

Members of the Second Continental Congress realized that a written constitution was necessary to clarify the powers of the new government. As Congress attempted to form a new nation out of many independent states, it grappled with questions about what kind of government to create and who should have power in the new society. Congress drafted the nation's new government under the Articles of Confederation, which was ratified in 1781 before the war ended.

The powers of the Articles of Confederation

Delegates of the Second Continental Congress agreed nearly unanimously on the power of the new government to regulate trade, pursue foreign relations, run a postal service, and regulate war and peace. However, the Congress agreed on little else.

In November 1777, after a year of debate, the Continental Congress passed the *Articles of Confederation*, which established the new nation as a loose confederation of states. Americans were wary of giving up freedoms to a strong central government, so leaders gave almost all powers to the states. Because Congress established the confederation during wartime, its first priority was defense, so the central government formed a national army (the Continental Army).

Under the Articles of Confederation, the only governing body of the central government was Congress, which was made up of representatives from each state. No executive or judicial branches of government existed. Congress (the central government) could declare war, set unified weights and measures (including those for coins), and settle disputes between states. All other powers, including the power to tax, were left to the states.

Problems with the Articles of Confederation

Many American elites got exactly the type of government that they wanted: a weak central government that gave the states more power. But the Articles were a weak form of government that ultimately failed. The Articles loosely governed the individual states for about a decade, but problems existed. Congress often had fewer members than necessary to vote on issues, and state legislatures were terribly slow in selecting their representatives to Congress. Also, Congress didn't have a permanent residence. Although its mobility helped in winning the war against Britain, it didn't help with its effectiveness. During its short history, Congress had moved a lot — from Philadelphia, to Lancaster, to York, to Baltimore, to Trenton, to Princeton, to Annapolis, and finally to New York City.

After the war, the nation no longer needed a large army, so Congress's main function was obsolete. It did establish two important land ordinances. *The Land Ordinance of 1785* set up the land survey and ownership provisions for subsequent expansion into new territory. In 1787, Congress established the *Northwest Ordinance,* in which the original states gave up claims to western lands and allowed them to be used for new states. Other than putting together these two ordinances, however, the central government had no real purpose. The country was more like 13 independent republics than a true confederation.

The biggest problem facing the new government involved taxation. Wary of duplicating the taxation abuses they had suffered under British rule, the Articles didn't give Congress the power to tax. Instead, Congress had to get money from the states, which weren't keen on handing over their funds to the federal government. Lack of funds left Congress with considerable war debts. So, after the war, Congress thrust nearly $500 million in paper currency (rather than currency backed by actual gold or silver) into the economy, which caused steep inflation. Without a central bank or body to govern currency, the economic state of the confederation was near chaos.

Further evidence of the crisis created by a weak central government occurred in the winter of 1786 to 1787. The government debt had trickled down to consumers and hit farmers especially hard because they'd borrowed money to produce for the war effort and couldn't pay back their loans after the war. Farmers protested the use of appointed officials (rather than elected ones) to determine debtors' cases and eventually tried to shut down debtors' courts by storming courthouses. In 1787, a group of 2,500 armed farmers, led by Daniel Shays, attacked courthouses throughout the state. Massachusetts Governor James Bowdoin sent a small army to put down the rebellion, which ended in a handful of deaths on both sides. Ultimately, Bowdoin's forces won, and the farmers were banned from having a political voice in their communities and in the state. In the aftermath of *Shays's Rebellion,* many Americans wondered if the loose confederation of states would be capable of handling future domestic disturbances. This situation, coupled with the monetary crisis, caused American elites to decide that a serious discussion on the state of the nation and its weak government was direly needed.

An exercise in compromise: Writing the Constitution

Led by *James Madison,* the Virginia delegates convinced members of Congress to hold a meeting of delegates in Annapolis, Maryland, in September 1786 to amend the Articles of Confederation. Only five states showed up; however, Madison and other concerned delegates recommended that Congress hold another meeting in Philadelphia in May 1787. One of the greatest proponents of a meeting to discuss the state of the Articles of Confederation was *Alexander Hamilton,* who hoped the meeting would create a more central, or federal, government. In May 1787, 55 men met in Philadelphia for the *Constitutional Convention,* including Hamilton, Madison, Benjamin Franklin, and George Washington. Working in secret, the delegation created several plans for a new government.

Structuring the government: The Great Compromise

Delegates at the Constitutional Convention needed to come up with a way to structure the government. James Madison put forth the *Virginia Plan* for a federal government with three branches: a judicial branch, an executive branch, and a legislative branch with a *bi-cameral* (two-house) legislature. Madison believed that the government should be run by people, not states. He wanted to *federalize* the government, or give increased authority to the three branches that he proposed. Under the Virginia Plan, the number of representatives a state would have in the federal government would be based on the state's population, which would give larger states (such as Virginia) more power in the new government.

William Paterson of the small state of New Jersey offered the *New Jersey Plan* as an alternative to Madison's idea. This plan created one house of Congress and a weak presidency, which would actually consist of three men. This plan closely resembled the Articles of Confederation because its philosophy was that states, not the people, should run the government. The New Jersey Plan advocated equal representation in the federal government for each of the states, regardless of population. Thus, the debate on the future of the nation was set: Should it be a strong central government or a government based on the rule of states (similar to the Articles of Confederation)?

The debate over the two plans lasted for weeks. Populous southern states favored the Virginia Plan because they would be able to send more representatives to the federal government, which meant having more say in governing. Less populated northern states favored the New Jersey Plan because it didn't base representation on how many people lived in a state but gave every state an equal voice.

At one point, the convention appeared to be at an impasse. But a compromise, known as the *Great Compromise* (or the Connecticut Compromise), saved the convention and helped create the modern American government. The Great Compromise proposed keeping the Virginia Plan's bi-cameral legislature. The number of state representatives in the lower house, or the House of Representatives, would be based on a state's population, so the states with larger populations would have more representatives than the less-populated states. The upper house, or Senate, would have an equal number of representatives from each state, just like the New Jersey Plan proposed. Sounds simple, right? Well, not at the time, because the idea of citizenship and population was a tricky thing: Who was the population? Only white males? Landholders? Women? Children? Slaves?

Ultimately, the Great Compromise was also known as the *Three-Fifths Compromise* because it decided that all free persons plus ⅗ of all other persons (meaning slaves, who comprised a significant amount of the population in southern states) would determine a state's population for its representation in the House. This compromise assured southerners that slaves would be considered in their populations for purposes of determining how many representatives they could send to the House and gave northerners proportionately more representation than they would have had, had slaves been 100 percent included in the population.

A matter of principles: The main points of the Constitution

The following principles of the U.S. Constitution emerged from the battles among the convention delegates:

- The U.S. government has three main branches: the legislative (Congress), the executive (president), and judicial (Supreme Court).

- The three branches are distinct and separate from each other.

- The powers of the three branches are balanced, meaning that no branch has more power than another, and each branch has the power to check the powers of the others to make sure that one branch doesn't become too powerful. This system is known as *checks and balances.*

- The United States is federal, meaning that the Constitution contains the powers given to the federal government, and other powers belong to the states.

- The Constitution has precedent over all other laws in the nation.

- All people and all states in the nation are equal and are due equal protection under the Constitution.

- Like the federal government, state governments must be based on a *republic,* which means that the people participate in government by electing individuals to represent them.

- The Constitution may be changed through an amendment process.

The convention delegates established that 9 of the 13 states had to ratify the Constitution for it to go into effect. The ratification process was not easy.

Ratification wrangle: Federalists versus Antifederalists

Two competing forces emerged in the ratification battle: the *Federalists* (who were different from the Federalist Party, see Chapter 6) and the *Antifederalists.* Federalists advocated the ratification of the Constitution and its proposed central government that would be stronger than the one established by the Articles of Confederation. Federalists included George Washington, Alexander Hamilton, John Jay, James Madison, and Thomas Jefferson. The Antifederalists, like Patrick Henry, thought the Constitution gave the central government too much power and that the president would become like a king. Antifederalists didn't necessarily want to hang on to the old government designated by the Articles of Confederation, but they knew they didn't like the proposed Constitution.

Undaunted by the Antifederalist challenge, the Federalists moved quickly to ratify the Constitution. Led by Alexander Hamilton, they targeted states that were vulnerable to the bullying of larger neighbors. New Jersey, Delaware, Georgia, Maryland, South Carolina, and Connecticut quickly joined the Federalist camp, giving the Federalists six of the nine states they needed to ratify the Constitution. In May 1788, Massachusetts narrowly voted to approve the Constitution, leaving the Federalists only one state short of victory. One month later, the small state of New Hampshire ratified the Constitution.

By the end of the summer of 1788, four states — Virginia, New York, North Carolina, and Rhode Island — had yet to ratify the Constitution. Virginia ratified the Constitution after the

Federalists agreed to consider specific amendments advocated by Virginia leaders (see the next section). New York appeared to be a challenge, but the publication of *The Federalist Papers* by Alexander Hamilton, John Jay, and James Madison, which convincingly argued the case for Federalism and the failures of the Articles of Confederation, along with the news of Virginia's ratification, tipped the balance. North Carolina soon followed and, although Rhode Island held out until 1790, the new U.S. government finally had the support of all 13 states.

This mention will not be the last time you hear about Federalist-Antifederalist debate. A question on the conflicting beliefs between Federalists and Antifederalist is a good possibility for the exam.

Which of the following best defines a Federalist during the ratification of the U.S. Constitution?

(A) One who advocated a confederation of states with no central government.

(B) One who supported a strong central government with separate branches.

(C) One who wanted one congress to loosely regulate state affairs.

(D) A member of a council of learned, elite citizens who created laws and governed the country.

(E) One who wanted one powerful ruler to run the government, like a monarchy.

This question should not be a problem if you know that Federalists supported the Constitution proposed by the Constitutional Convention. Because the Constitution was eventually ratified, you can pick the answer that describes a supporter of the type of government the U.S. has today.

This realization eliminates answer (A); the U.S. has a central government. You can also eliminate choice (C) because one congress loosely regulating state affairs doesn't describe the U.S. government. Answer (D) may throw you off if you consider the general characteristics of the delegates of the convention, but "Federalist" doesn't refer to personal characteristics. Answer (E) seems unlikely; American government isn't a monarchy. Remember, Federalists wanted a stronger central government with several different branches. So the correct answer, of course, is (B).

An addendum: The Bill of Rights

Many states, especially those that leaned toward Antifederalist ideology, ratified the U.S. Constitution based on the promise that leaders would add amendments to protect individual liberties and states' rights soon after the ratification battle was over. In 1789, to pacify growing concerns over this issue, James Madison wrote the first ten amendments to the Constitution, which came to be known as the *Bill of Rights.* In September, the House of Representatives and the Senate (which made up the new U.S. Congress) passed the ten amendments and sent them to the states for ratification (which took an additional two years).

For the SAT II, you may want to memorize the Bill of Rights because it created the first set of liberties and rights in the United States. Plus, these amendments became the source of debate and court cases for the next 200 years (and indeed still remain so) of American history. Here are the first ten amendments:

✔ **First Amendment:** Provides freedom of speech, religion, the press, assembly, and the right to petition the government for redress of grievances.

✔ **Second Amendment:** Gives the right to bear arms and form militias.

✔ **Third Amendment:** Prevents the forced quartering of soldiers.

✔ **Fourth Amendment:** Offers protection against unreasonable searches and seizures.

✔ **Fifth Amendment:** Provides the right to due process in the prosecution of criminal offenses, no double jeopardy cases (meaning that you cannot be tried for the same crime twice), as well as the protection from testifying against yourself in a court of law.

✔ **Sixth Amendment:** Grants the right to a speedy and public trial by one's peers.

✔ **Seventh Amendment:** Guarantees the right to a trial in a civil case by a jury of one's peers.

✔ **Eighth Amendment:** Prevents excessive bail or fines and offers protection from cruel or unusual punishment.

✔ **Ninth Amendment:** States that just because a right isn't specifically mentioned in the Bill of Rights doesn't mean that citizens don't have that right.

✔ **Tenth Amendment:** Declares that powers not delegated to the United States by the Constitution are reserved to the states or the people.

The First Presidents: Washington and Adams

The first pie out of the great experimental American kitchen, the Articles of Confederation, didn't taste very good. Although we know that the second experiment — the U.S. Constitution — has lasted more than 200 years, at the time, Americans didn't know how well it would work. You can trace much of the success of the early republic to one individual — a man who was deeply respected by almost every American of the time and still is by most Americans. That man, of course, is George Washington, the first president of the United States of America. Washington's presidency was followed by that of a fellow delegate to the Constitutional Convention, John Adams, whose presidency was more controversial than Washington's.

George Washington's administration

In modern America, most citizens take the party system that dominates politics and the government in the United States for granted. However, in the early years of the nation, no party system existed. The first presidential election occurred in February 1789, and George Washington ran unopposed because of the nearly unanimous respect and support that Americans had for him. Washington had tremendous and untested power in the chief executive office of the United States. How Washington used that power set a precedent for future administrations and for how the new republic would function. For instance, although the Constitution didn't set a limit for the number of terms that a president could serve, Washington felt that two four-year terms was sufficient for any president and voluntarily retired after two terms. His action set a precedent for other presidents; no president served more than two terms except for Franklin Roosevelt. (In 1951, the 22nd amendment made the two-term limit for presidents a law.)

Establishing the authority of the new government

Washington's first responsibility was to create a *cabinet* of advisors. Washington chose men he trusted for the top positions in the new government and met regularly with them, heeding their advice and expertise. He selected Alexander Hamilton as his secretary of the treasury, Henry Knox as his secretary of war, Thomas Jefferson as his secretary of state, and Edmund Randolph as his attorney general. Washington appointed John Jay, an ardent Federalist, Chief Justice of the Supreme Court.

Unlike America during the Articles of Confederation, the new government had a true center of power and several departments to carry on the affairs of the state. Perhaps the most crucial department during this tenuous period was the department of the treasury, led by the strong-willed Hamilton.

Understanding Alexander Hamilton's fiscal policy

New economic opportunities arose in the 1790s that helped stabilize the American economy. Infrastructure improvements, such as new roads that connected major centers of trade, provided an increase in commerce between different regions. The cotton trade experienced a boom during this time, largely due to Eli Whitney's invention of the *cotton gin,* which made cotton production more efficient and profitable. Also, the European population was expanding during the 1790s, and its demand for wheat and other food products helped boost the American economy.

When Washington took office in 1789, he appointed Alexander Hamilton secretary of the National Treasury, a newly created entity. As secretary of the treasury, Hamilton was an effective administrator and a foresighted economic planner. To persuade investors to devote their assets to America, the government would have to convince them that it would pay every debt in full. At the time, the United States' government owed more than $50 million to its citizens and more than $11 million to foreigners. Hamilton decided to fund the debt at face value, which meant that he had to collect all outstanding securities (America's IOUs) and issue new bonds for the same value as the old. Hamilton made sure that the U.S. had an untouchable fund from which debt principal and interest payments were automatically made when they came due. Perhaps the most controversial aspect of this national debt plan was Hamilton's intent to provide a special advantage to the rich who had the financial means to purchase the national securities. He allowed the wealthy to purchase national securities at a fraction of their face value, which meant they would make a big profit when the securities came due. Although Hamilton didn't personally benefit from the incentives, he felt the government would get stronger with the debt support of the wealthy. Congress passed Hamilton's plan, and it was quite successful. Foreign investments poured into the U.S. Hamilton had transformed the economic framework of the U.S. and prepared the nation for an economic revolution.

To fund the federal government and to help out American business, Hamilton instituted protective tariffs on imports of foreign manufactured goods. The tariffs made money for the federal government and promoted American businesses by making their products less expensive than foreign imports. Hamilton also convinced Congress to pass a 25 percent excise tax on whiskey, which raised a significant sum of money for the government (and the anger of farmers; see "Curbing domestic unrest" later in this chapter).

Hamilton's next move was to create the first *Bank of the United States* in 1791, which the U.S. government would partially fund and private investors would fund the rest. The bank stabilized the economy by establishing a national currency and by controlling credit, the value of currency, and interest rates. Hamilton learned from the mistake of the Articles of Confederation era that strong control over the national economy was necessary for the nation to experience stability and prosperity. The bank, which lasted for 20 years until its charter ran out, created controversy among those who believed that the Constitution didn't give the federal government the power to establish a national bank.

Maintaining foreign affairs

The new government faced several challenges in foreign relations during its formative years. In France, the bloody French Revolution began the same year that Washington assumed the presidency. Many Americans supported the French Revolution because it reminded them of their own efforts to break the chains of an oppressive monarchy. However, after the French beheaded King Louis XVI, Americans' sentiment for the French Revolution changed because they feared that the efforts had gone too far. The ensuing Reign of Terror in France continued to temper American support for the revolution and its consequences.

In 1793, Britain and France went to war, and Washington issued a *Neutrality Proclamation,* which stated that America took neither side in the conflict (which violated the alliance America had with France from the American Revolution). Despite the Neutrality Proclamation, American ships still traded with the French West Indies and France, which angered the British. Consequently, the British seized hundreds of American ships in the Caribbean region, which greatly angered Washington and other American leaders. Washington sent John Jay, the Chief Justice of the Supreme Court, to negotiate with the British. The treaty Jay signed (known as the *Jay Treaty*) angered many Americans because it didn't address the seized ships, pressed farmers to pay back debts to the British immediately, and allowed the British a year and a half to leave their forts in North America. Hamilton supported the treaty but Jefferson opposed it. The Senate ratified the treaty despite protests, but a clear divide emerged between Hamilton's followers and Jefferson's.

To test a point, the SAT II may insert a picture like the one in Figure 5-1, which conveys a political or social sentiment of the represented time period. Then, the exam will ask you a question that requires you to use information from the picture to answer. For instance, the SAT II may ask you the following question about Figure 5-1: "This picture shows how angry Americans felt about what event in early American politics?" You would choose the answer that suggested that Americans were upset about Jay's negotiations with the British.

Figure 5-1:
Burning Jay
in effigy.

Courtesy of Eric Zimmer

In Haiti, a revolution of slaves against their white colonists raged from 1790 to 1804. The U.S. government stayed out of the conflict, but Americans watched the revolution with great interest. African Americans were interested in the revolution's outcome because it was the first successful revolution of slaves against whites in a Western colony. The Haitian Revolution frightened many Americans, especially Southerners. Those opposed to slavery believed the revolution foreshadowed things to come in the U.S. if the government continued to deny liberties to a large portion of the population.

Curbing domestic unrest

Hamilton's excise tax on whiskey created a wave of discontent throughout the American countryside. Farmers produced the grain to make whiskey, and the whiskey tax cut into their profits. Farmers in Pennsylvania, Maryland, Virginia, and Kentucky expressed their displeasure to Congress, which resulted in small modifications to the policy. But these measures weren't enough to pacify their concerns, and dissent mounted. Many farmers refused to pay the taxes, and some burned effigies of tax collectors in protest. In Pennsylvania, a tax collector's home was burned to the ground and then an angry mob of 7,000 farmers marched to Pittsburgh to protest the whiskey tax.

President Washington, faced with his first domestic crisis, put the control of the Pennsylvania militia in the hands of the federal government and, along with Secretary of the Treasury Alexander Hamilton, rode with an army of 15,000 soldiers to quell the rebellion (imagine a modern president riding into battle!). Washington showed the members of the *Whiskey Rebellion* — and the nation — that the federal government's laws would be enforced and that resistance to those laws would be met with swift and severe consequences. Washington's actions were not autocratic — Congress, which was representative of the people, had passed the whiskey tax. Ultimately, the Whiskey Rebellion became a symbol of the continuing struggle between majority rule and minority rights.

Washington's administration also had to deal with the struggles between Native Americans and settlers in the *Northwest Territories,* which included present-day Ohio, Michigan, Indiana, Illinois, and Wisconsin. Native Americans raided American military outposts in Ohio and other Northwest Territories, hoping to push the Americans off their land. At Fort Washington, located in western Ohio, General Arthur St. Clair battled the Miami and Shawnee tribes for control of the region. St. Clair lost, which sent a poignant message about the power and resolve of the Native Americans to Washington. In response, Washington doubled the number of troops in Ohio and appointed a new general, Anthony Wayne, to defend American bases and settlements. In August 1794 at the Battle of Fallen Timbers, Wayne engaged the Delaware and Shawnee in a decisive battle. The Native Americans attacked first but were defeated by the better armed and trained American forces. As a result of the territory battles, the U.S. government signed the *Treaty of Greenville* with a dozen Native American tribes, which gave the Native Americans cash in return for the American rights to Ohio. Although the treaty did bring peace, it set a precedent that the Native American lands and pride could be bought.

Tying it all together: A sample question looks at the George Washington era

The experimental years of the Washington administration were extremely important to the development of the United States. Be prepared for at least one question from this era on the exam. The following question asks you to find the answer that doesn't fit with the others. These questions can be tricky, but don't be deceived.

All the statements about the United States in the 1790s are true EXCEPT

(A) The United States faced civil unrest from farmers and Native Americans.

(B) A weak economy forced the government to heavily tax all its citizens and procure loans from Europe.

(C) The government created a national banking system.

(D) The United States stayed relatively neutral during European conflicts.

(E) The United States expanded by purchasing land in the Northwest Territories from Native Americans.

Look carefully at the question. It asks you to find the answer that does NOT describe the United States in the 1790s. Now look at the answers. Answer (A) is certainly true — remember the Whiskey Rebellion and the battles between Native Americans and settlers in Ohio and elsewhere? What about (B)? Congress did raise taxes on whiskey, but was it because of a weak economy? Hold off on that one. Answer (C) is a fact: Hamilton created the National Bank of America as part of his new fiscal policies. If you recall, the United States stayed out of the problems in Europe, so (D) is also true. And (E) is true as well because the United States defeated the Native American forces and bought their land in Ohio. So, answer (B) must be correct.

Remember, the American economy was quite strong during the Washington administration. The whiskey tax affected only a small portion of the population, and the government certainly didn't seek loans from European nations, many of which were at war with one another. So (B) is your answer.

The election of 1796

Although America's first president was above party politics, a clear political division had grown in Congress and the nation. And so the United States' first true political battle was waged to determine who would succeed Washington and lead the future of the young nation.

The emergence of political parties

Americans had little idea what party politics would come to look like. Political divisions existed, of course, but traditionally, these divisions were based on ties such as marriage, family, or similar economic interests. These traditions would change, though, because the American Revolution had created an important ideology based on the idea of people and liberty. The Federalists of the 1790s weren't the same as the Federalists who supported the Constitution. The new Federalists gained power and created a strong central government in agreement with Hamilton's policies. They supported funding the national debt, the Bank of the United States, tariffs to stimulate economic growth, neutrality in the French and British conflicts, and a strong military. Their opponents, known as Democratic Republicans (like Thomas Jefferson), continued to worry about states' rights and individual liberties.

The Democratic Republicans

Jefferson emerged as the leader of the *Democratic Republicans,* a political party that opposed elite rule and the Federalists' strong central government. Democratic Republicans supported a *strict interpretation* of the Constitution, which meant they didn't want to give the federal government more power than the Constitution granted it. They advocated the defense of the Bill of Rights and maintained the ideals of the revolution and a "free" government.

Jefferson was a highly educated man, who was well read in history, science, agriculture, diplomacy, and political theory. He believed in personal and social independence and advocated a nation centered around farming, which he believed would improve the moral character of Americans. Having seen the urban wastelands of Britain, Jefferson wanted to expand America to the west to give Americans a chance to own land and pursue happiness on their own terms. Jefferson's ideals were attractive to many Americans, and he became the best opportunity for the Democratic Republicans to win the presidency. The Democratic Republicans selected Aaron Burr of New York as their other candidate.

The Federalists

John Adams, Washington's vice president, emerged as the leader of the Federalists. Federalists interpreted the Constitution more loosely than the Democratic Republicans did and used the *loose interpretation* (that the powers of government do not have to be explicitly stated in the Constitution) to justify a powerful central government. The Federalists wanted Thomas Pinckney of South Carolina to serve as Adams's vice president.

The Electoral College

To fully appreciate what happened next, you need to know how the original Electoral College was set up. The Constitution set up the *Electoral College* as a system of electing the president. Each state had as many electors as it had representatives in the Senate and in the House. Each elector voted for two presidential candidates. The candidate with the most votes became president, and the second-place winner became vice president. If no one won by a majority of electoral votes or if the vote was a tie, the House of Representatives would choose the winner. The system was designed to be fair and was supposed to work without political parties. But the U.S. Constitution wasn't prepared to deal with the new challenge of political parties, which was evident during the election of 1796 when the winner of the presidency and the winner of the vice-presidency came from two different parties.

Thomas Jefferson versus John Adams

The emergence of political parties made the election of president and vice-president tricky. If electors didn't vote carefully, the country could end up with a president and vice-president from opposing parties.

Adams received the most electoral votes with 71, followed closely by Jefferson with 68 votes. Pinckney received 59 votes, and Burr received 30. Adams won the presidency, and Jefferson won the vice-presidency, which established a divided executive branch.

John Adams's administration

John Adams, the United States' second president, promised to heed George Washington's advice to avoid entangling alliances, which meant staying out of European affairs. Adams also kept a Federalist cabinet — a fact that upset Democratic Republican Thomas Jefferson. Even though Jefferson and Adams had been close friends, Adams didn't actively seek out Jefferson's help or advice, and so Jefferson did little during his tenure as vice-president.

The *XYZ Affair* dominated the Adams administration. In response to the Jay Treaty of 1793 (see "Maintaining foreign affairs" earlier in this chapter), France ended its alliance with the United States, which had existed since the Revolutionary War. Because the friendly relations between the two nations ended, armed French vessels, owned privately and known as *privateers,* began to seize American ships. French privateers took complete control of the crews and cargo of more than 300 American ships, so Adams sent three ambassadors to France to negotiate and to stave off a possible war between the two nations.

Charles Maurice de Talleyrand, the French minister of foreign affairs, refused to see the American delegates but eventually sent three unnamed delegates of his own, known only as X, Y, and Z, to speak with the Americans. X, Y, and Z told the Americans that a $12 million loan to the French, along with a cash payment of $250,000, would help the diplomatic process move along more smoothly. Americans were appalled at the events of the XYZ Affair, and many argued for war against France. Even Democratic Republicans, who largely supported strong relations with France, were astounded at France's actions. In response to the XYZ Affair, the Adams administration repealed all treaties with the French, prepared troops for battle, and sent American ships to engage in an undeclared naval war with the French, based mainly in the Caribbean Sea.

Despite American sentiment in favor of going to war with France, large opposition — mainly from Democratic Republicans — protested the actions of Congress and the Adams administration. To quell the dissent, Congress passed the *Sedition Act in 1798,* which allowed the government to jail Americans involved in conspiracies against or defamation of the U.S. government. Congress also passed two *Alien Acts,* which extended the amount of time it took for an alien to become an American citizen (from five to fourteen years) and allowed the president to deport or imprison aliens during a time of war. Republicans were furious over the Alien and Sedition Acts, which they believed were counter to the ideals of Bill of Rights. Crisis seemed imminent but, in 1799, the French offered peace, which essentially ended the conflict. However, Adams's acceptance of the French peace lost him support from his own party, and he would soon become America's first one-term president.

Focusing on Federalist accomplishments

The Federalists dominated American politics and government from 1789 to 1800, but they also helped create a deep division among Americans by often refusing to compromise with Democratic Republicans. As a result, the Democratic Republican minority emerged as a powerful and attractive alternative to the Federalists, who many Americans believed had become too powerful and a threat to individual liberties. Yet the Federalists accomplished a lot in their 12 years in office.

✔ Under the leadership of Alexander Hamilton, the Federalists stabilized the American economy and created a national banking system, which helped the nation prosper economically.

✔ The Federalists also avoided major confrontations with European powers by staying out of European affairs, for the most part. The XYZ Affair under John Adams challenged George Washington's pleas to avoid such confrontations but, ultimately, America didn't go to war and peace endured.

✔ The Federalists' most important accomplishment was their ability to run an efficient government, keeping the nation together and making it stronger in its most tenuous and challenging years. Under the leadership of Washington, Hamilton, Adams, and others, the U.S. Constitution and government became stable and permanent institutions of American life.

The great American experiment, though often challenged and criticized, had finally produced a pie that was worth eating; one whose recipe Americans would tinker with for the next 200 years. But the basic recipe of republican democracy and liberty remained the same, becoming the cornerstones of the United States of America.

Part III
America's Childhood Years

The 5th Wave — By Rich Tennant

"Mr. President, the Confederate Army is massing in Virginia, several more of our officers have defected to the South, oh, and bad news — Mrs. Lincoln's redesigned tea setting won't be here until Friday."

In this part . . .

Ahh, childhood . . . ice cream cones, bicycles, no homework, ten hours of sleep every night, pajamas with feet, Saturday morning cartoons, and a blissful ignorance of college admissions exams. The United States had a childhood, too, but we bet it wasn't as fun as yours!

In this part, we take a look at a few of the main figures in America's childhood years: Thomas Jefferson, Lewis and Clark, John Marshall, and Andrew Jackson, among others. You also find out about the development of American art and literature, manifest destiny, the First Industrial Revolution, reform movements, the building tensions between the North and the South, Abraham Lincoln, and the Civil War.

The years from 1800 to 1865 make up one of the most dynamic periods in U.S. history. Although the United States experiences some growing pains during this time (don't we all?), these years are when the nation really begins to develop a personality and to grow a great deal in size. On the SAT II U.S. History test, about 20 percent of the questions deal with this time period. Okay, now get crackin'!

Chapter 6

Jeffersonian Democracy and Nationalism, 1800–1824

- -

In This Chapter

▶ Understanding how Jeffersonian democracy changed the United States

▶ Exploring how the young nation survived, thrived, and expanded

▶ Examining how the judicial branch developed during Jeffersonian America

- -

The influence of Thomas Jefferson, whose presidency lasted from 1801 to 1809, reaches far beyond his years in the White House and, thus, this chapter is an important one for you to review. Jefferson radically altered the political and literal landscape of the United States by championing a political philosophy that vastly differed from federalism and by expanding the continental United States by leaps and bounds, which would have important consequences later in American history.

The majority of questions on the SAT II that deal with Jeffersonian democracy focus on political and economic history; social, intellectual, and cultural issues take a backseat to questions about power and money. Foreign policy, as you'll see, was an important factor during this period in American history as well. So this chapter focuses almost exclusively on politics. On the exam, you'll most likely see questions on what Jefferson and his ideals did to change the face of the United States.

"The Revolution of 1800": Thomas Jefferson's Administration

Less than 20 years after helping America win the Revolutionary War against Great Britain, Thomas Jefferson declared another revolution in 1800. The Federalists (who supported a strong federal government) had been in power for about 20 years and, in the election of 1800, Jefferson, the vice president, challenged the incumbent, Federalist President John Adams.

You may recall that Adams and Jefferson ran against each other in the nation's presidential election in 1796 and, in 1800, they were once again competing for the presidency. Jefferson was the candidate for the Democratic Republican Party (see Chapter 5). Unlike the Federalists, Democratic Republicans feared that the Constitution allowed the president to act as king, and they favored the rights granted to individuals by the Bill of Rights. Jefferson's running mate was fellow Democratic Republican Aaron Burr, a senator from New York. The Federalist Party nominated President John Adams and Charles Pinckney from South Carolina.

During the election, Jefferson received the same number of votes in the Electoral College as his vice presidential candidate, Burr, did. (For more information on the Electoral College, see Chapter 5.) Both candidates won 73 electoral votes, and the total of their combined votes narrowly defeated Adams and Pinckney. It was common knowledge that Jefferson was the presidential candidate and Burr was the vice-presidential candidate, but Burr, an ambitious and proud man, refused to concede the election to Jefferson because he had tied him (and you thought modern elections were complicated!), so the decision went to the House of Representatives. After a hard-fought struggle in the House, Jefferson won the presidency with the help of Alexander Hamilton, a Federalist, who argued that Burr would be far more dangerous in the nation's highest office than Jefferson would be. (We talk more about Burr's problematic personality in the sidebar "The duel of Aaron Burr and Alexander Hamilton" later in this chapter.) So amid great controversy, Jefferson became the third president of the United States, and the Democratic Republicans took control of the executive and legislative branches of government, ushering in a new era in American history.

Making changes on the domestic front

Jefferson, a wealthy planter from Virginia, former secretary of state under George Washington, and author of the Declaration of Independence, was a strong supporter of the Constitution. However, Jefferson wanted to steer the country in a different direction than the one the Federalists had taken in the past 20 or so years — one that emphasized the rights of individuals rather than the power of the federal government. On inauguration day in March 1801, which was the first time the ceremony was held in the new American capital of Washington, D.C., Jefferson dressed informally, setting the tone that his administration would strive for simplicity and frugality.

Implementing new policies

Once in office, Jefferson moved swiftly to implement new policies to break away from the reign of the Federalists. He

- **Limited government.** Jefferson kept the executive branch small — only 130 employees throughout the various departments, including the Department of State, which employed only eight, including Secretary of State James Madison.

- **Cut the budget.** Jefferson immediately cut the federal budget and pared down the lavish building plans for the new capital.

- **Reduced the military.** He cut the size of the army by 30 percent and limited the American navy to seven ships.

- **Shifted revenue.** With the help of Congress, Jefferson eliminated all federal whiskey taxes (which helped out the farmers; see Chapter 5 for more information on the farmers and the Whiskey Rebellion) and shifted revenue responsibilities to taxes on the sales of Western lands.

- **Diminished the debt.** Jefferson's frugality significantly reduced the debt that Hamilton's fiscal policies had incurred (see Chapter 5).

- **Emphasized the importance of education.** Jefferson strongly believed in the power of education and desired that U.S. citizens have access to free schooling at every level. He was unable to achieve his goal of free public education during his presidency but, in 1825, he founded the University of Virginia, which offered free tuition to deserving students who were too poor to pay.

Warring with the judiciary

Jefferson was remarkably successful in quickly dismantling the Federalist system in the executive branch, but the judicial branch remained a challenge. While president, John Adams appointed numerous Federalists to government positions in the weeks following his loss to Jefferson. Adams and the Federalist legislature also passed the *Judiciary Act of 1801,* which reduced the size of the Supreme Court from six to five judges, and added ten additional circuit courts with new Federalist judges presiding over them all. Adams even appointed judges just hours before Jefferson's inauguration; these appointments became known as the *midnight judges.*

The midnight appointments greatly angered Jefferson and other Democratic Republicans, and Jefferson responded to Adams's sneaky moves by canceling all the appointments made to men who didn't already have *tenure* — in other words, those men who hadn't received their appointments in person yet. One of the appointments Jefferson cancelled was for William Marbury, who sued Secretary of State James Madison for not honoring an appointment made lawfully by the president of the United States. We discuss the resulting Supreme Court case, *Marbury v. Madison,* and its decision later in this chapter.

Purchasing Louisiana and the journey of Lewis and Clark

Jefferson viewed the banking and finance professions as arenas ripe for corruption where rich men would continue to get rich at the expense of others. Jefferson envisioned a nation whose economy centered around farming and the moral strength of individuals and their families. For this reason, Jefferson sought to expand the territory of the United States to encourage farming so Americans could work for both personal wealth and the good of the country.

During the early years of colonial America, France owned most, and settled some, of the land west of the Mississippi River. When Britain defeated France in the French and Indian War (see Chapter 4), France relinquished control of this vast area to Spain. But the Spanish never pursued settlement of the territory, and Americans began to populate portions of the lower Mississippi Valley, including New Orleans.

In 1802, Jefferson received news that the Spanish government was in the process of negotiating a deal that would give Napoleon Bonaparte, the emperor of France, a large part of the Louisiana Territory. Jefferson, worried about French influence on the American continent, sent Robert Livingston, the U.S. ambassador to France, to negotiate a deal to purchase the highly desirable city of New Orleans from the French. New Orleans was a key shipping port, especially for goods traveling down the Mississippi River. The French played coy and asserted that they didn't own the city. Livingston replied that if the territory could not be bought, then the United States may simply take it by force. The French negotiator then stunned Livingston by asking him to name the United States' price for the entire Louisiana Territory. Livingston hesitated, and the French eventually lowered their original asking price of $125 million to an amazing bargain of $15 million. This deal, which occurred in 1803, was the steal of the century, even by 19th-century monetary terms.

Jefferson was thrilled with the land acquisition because it gave the U.S. more room to develop agriculture. He commissioned *Meriwether Lewis,* his personal secretary, to lead an expedition in the new territory to explore the new country, observe Native American cultures, collect plant and animal samples, and map the geography. Lewis and his expedition partner, *William Clark,* left from St. Louis in the spring of 1804 and headed west. *Sacagawea,* the teenage wife of a French fur trader who was part of the expeditionary team, aided Lewis and Clark in the new country, and they reached the Pacific Ocean in November 1805. Lewis and Clark returned home as national heroes and created a new generation of explorers and settlers.

For the test, remember that through the purchase of the Louisiana Territory, Jefferson radically expanded the size of the United States and created a new American mindset, which centered on expansion, farming, and land ownership. This land acquisition paved the way for the notion of *manifest destiny* (the concept that America had the obligation to expand its possessions to the Pacific Coast; see Chapter 8).

This question asks you to use your analytical skills to figure out a leader's motivation for making an important decision that forever changed the face of the United States. The following question is a good example of something you may see on the exam.

What was one of Thomas Jefferson's main interests in acquiring the Louisiana Territory from France?

(A) To spite the Federalists

(B) To eliminate the French influence on the continent

(C) To create more land for his ideal agrarian republic

(D) To promote industrialization

(E) To move Native American populations from the East to the West

Is the answer (A)? You've found out a lot about Jefferson in this chapter, and although he didn't support most Federalist ideals, he most likely wouldn't have spent large amounts of government dollars to spite them. Actually, the Louisiana Purchase expanded the United States, which would have been something the Federalists wanted to do anyway. So (A) is not right.

You may want to choose (B). True, Jefferson was wary of French influence on the continent, but French influence on the continent had decreased rapidly following their defeat in the French and Indian War. The only country that had a significant force in North America during the Jeffersonian era was Great Britain. So you can eliminate (B).

Answer (C) certainly seems like a possibility, so leave it while you check the last two answers. You can confidently eliminate (D); Jefferson wasn't a big fan of industrialization. On to answer (E). The Jefferson administration did not have a policy to remove Native Americans, although the Andrew Jackson administration had one a few years later (see Chapter 7). So (E) is wrong. The correct answer is (C). Jefferson envisioned the United States as an agrarian (which is an SAT II way of saying "agricultural" or "farming") republic.

The duel of Aaron Burr and Alexander Hamilton

In July 1804, Aaron Burr, Thomas Jefferson's vice president, killed Alexander Hamilton, the former secretary of the treasury and Federalist founder. Hamilton had continually thwarted Burr's political aspirations (including Burr's bid for the presidency in the controversial election of 1800), and a fed-up Burr challenged him to a duel. Hamilton accepted the challenge but lost his life. The American public was shocked to find out that its vice president had killed Hamilton, and they demanded answers. A New Jersey court indicted Burr for murder, but he fled to the South. The court eventually dropped its indictment. Under the rules of the day, which carried on until the 1820s, Burr had every right to issue a dueling challenge if someone questioned his honor. Partially due to Burr's killing of Hamilton, American sentiment about taking the law into one's own hands weakened and began leaning toward evidence, trial, and monetary compensation for wrongdoing.

Getting involved in foreign affairs

Great Britain was at war during most of Jefferson's administration, which caused problems for the United States. Most of Jefferson's international issues stemmed from warlike Britain and pesky pirates.

Yo ho ho: Dealing with Barbary pirates

Along the Barbary Coast, meaning the African nations of Tunis, Algiers, Tripoli, and Morocco, pirates, who were commissioned by their governments to take over ships, cargo, and crew, still controlled shipping. American ships used to be protected from such attacks while they sailed under the British flag, but after America gained independence, leaders of the Barbary States required payment (or tribute) of $50,000 to dissuade their pirates from taking over American ships. In 1801, the leader of Tripoli increased the amount of his tribute, and Jefferson responded by blockading Tripoli and Tunis. In 1803, pirates captured the USS *Philadelphia* and its 300 crewmembers. Jefferson retaliated with an attack on Tripoli. U.S. leaders negotiated a treaty with the leader of Tripoli, and Jefferson won the freedom of the crew and the virtual end of the tribute system, which he viewed as extortion and a direct challenge to American sovereignty.

Striking back: The Embargo Act of 1807

The United States wanted to remain neutral during the many conflicts between Britain and France in the first decade of the 19th century, but Britain and France instituted policies that prevented other countries (including the U.S.) to trade freely. Jefferson, displeased with Britain's disrespect of America's right to neutrality, attempted to boycott British goods. But the boycott didn't work, and the British began the *impressment* of American sailors, meaning they forced them into British service (which didn't impress the sailors much). From 1803 to 1811, the British impressed over 6,000 American sailors. In 1807, when the British ship *Leopard* halted the American vessel *Chesapeake,* open conflict ensued. The American captain refused to turn over any sailors, and a small cannon battle developed, leaving three Americans dead and 14 wounded. Jefferson felt that he had to do something to assert American rights; this something was the Embargo Act.

In 1807, Congress passed the *Embargo Act,* which Jefferson supported. The Embargo Act banned all exports to Britain and France, and Jefferson believed this ban would hurt the British and French economies and force them to change their commercial practices. But the act wasn't too successful because it hurt American merchants more than it hurt the British or French.

Finishing What We Started: The War of 1812

By 1812, America was on the verge of war with Britain once again. Trade issues and Britain's impressment of American sailors showed Americans that the former mother country wasn't taking the United States' independence seriously. The United States had to show its strength. The result was the War of 1812.

The election of James Madison and the rising pressure toward war

Jefferson decided not to seek a third term in 1808, which left James Madison, Jefferson's secretary of state, as the obvious candidate for the Democratic Republicans. Madison easily won the contest against the Federalists' Charles Pinckney. Madison's first priority as president was to deal with the growing tensions with Britain, whose ships continued to attack

American ships and to impress American sailors into service for the Crown (see "Striking back: The Embargo Act of 1807" earlier in this chapter). The French, too, began impressing sailors, and Madison faced a serious challenge to America's sovereignty.

In 1810, Congress responded to British and French impressments by passing a law that would allow the U.S. to trade again with the first country that stopped attacking American vessels. Napoleon Bonaparte of France agreed first to stop the attacks, and the U.S. lifted the French trade embargo, which greatly angered British leaders. But the French continued attacking American ships, and Madison reinstituted the embargo. So, the U.S. was back to square one.

Conflict in Indiana and the declaration of war

To retaliate for warfare between whites and Native Americans in the Indiana Territory (like the destruction of Shawnee villages by Americans during the Revolutionary War) *Tecumseh,* the powerful chief of the Shawnee, looked for some allies in an attack against the United States. Before he acted, though, Indiana governor William Henry Harrison attacked and destroyed Prophet's Town, a Native American settlement along the Tippecanoe River, in the Battle of Tippecanoe in 1811. The battle convinced Tecumseh that he needed to go to war, so he and his followers aligned themselves with the British forces that had gathered in lower Canada. (This event was similar to that of King Philip's War, which we discuss in Chapter 4.)

Several new Congress members, like Henry Clay and John Calhoun, were called *war hawks* because they favored an aggressive military stance, celebrated Harrison's victory, and pushed several bills through Congress that increased the war budget and strengthened the armed forces. The war hawk momentum continued and, in June 1812, Congress declared war on Great Britain, primarily because of how Britain was treating American shipping and because Britain had aligned itself with Native Americans in their attacks against white Americans. The congressional vote was close: The Southern and Western representatives favored war, and the New England and Mid-Atlantic representatives voted against it. The war hawks wanted to invade Canada and believed that victory would come in one month. But British forces, with the help of Native Americans were much stronger than the Americans expected. The Americans' failure to install a permanent naval force on the Great Lakes doomed their efforts in Canada. By the fall of 1812, the war against Britain appeared to be lost.

Here's another question for you to try. The following sample question deals with motivations for war with Great Britain, which, you should remember, about only half of Congress supported.

Which of the following provides a reason that the United States went to war with Great Britain in 1812?

(A) British impressment of American sailors

(B) Native American unrest and alliance with Great Britain

(C) British embargo against United States goods

(D) A and B only

(E) All of the above

This question gives you the option of having more than one correct answer, so don't get thrown off if you see two or more right answers.

You know that the impressment of American sailors greatly angered both the Jefferson and Madison administrations, causing several non-importation and embargo acts, so (A) seems logical. Answer (B) is also correct; Native American alliances with the British forces threatened United States' security. What about (C)? This answer may appear correct, but Americans placed embargoes on British goods, not the other way around. You can eliminate (C) and (E), so the correct answer is (D), which credits both the impressment of American sailors and the Native American alliance with Britain for the United States' war against Great Britain.

The tide turns for America

Federalists were unhappy with the war against Britain, and they demonstrated their discontent in the election of 1812. Madison won re-election, this time against the Federalist Party's DeWitt Clinton of New York, by a smaller margin than he had in 1808. But the war effort took a surprising turn for the Americans in 1813, when the Americans attacked York (modern-day Toronto) and burned the city to the ground. Several months later in the Battle of Lake Erie, Commodore Oliver Hazard Perry defeated the far superior British fleet in a decisive battle. Inspired by Perry's victory, Harrison's army moved into Canada and won the Battle of the Thames against the British and Native American forces in October of 1813.

In August 1814, the British fleet moved into Chesapeake Bay, which sent the people of Washington, D.C., into a state of chaos. Several thousand British troops stormed the capital and burned the White House, the Capitol building, and several dockyards. (The Declaration of Independence escaped destruction due to the foresight of a state department official, and so did several White House pieces — including a portrait of George Washington — thanks to First Lady Dolley Madison.)

Next, the British moved to Baltimore, where the Maryland militia gave a strong stand at the Battle of Fort McHenry and stifled the British advance. At this battle, Francis Scott Key wrote the words to "The Star-Spangled Banner," which would later become the United States' national anthem. Then the British invaded the state of New York, but poor strategy and planning thwarted their efforts, and they lost several naval battles on Lake Champlain. They retreated to Canada and realized that continued war with the United States would be expensive. General Andrew Jackson's decisive victory at the Battle of New Orleans in January 1815 (fought after the war officially ended because news traveled slowly in the days before cell phones and the Internet) secured American control of the continent.

We just gave you a lot of battle names to give you a feeling about how the two sides fought the War of 1812. You won't be expected to know the details of these battles for the SAT II. You only need to know that the U.S. started out slow but eventually came out on top.

The Treaty of Ghent

The *Treaty of Ghent,* signed in December 1814, officially ended the War of 1812. The war was pretty much a draw, so neither side declared victory or claimed new land acquisitions. The United States agreed to abandon any claims in Canada, and Britain agreed to remove its troops from western forts and to end aid to Native Americans. The most important result of the Treaty of Ghent was that the two nations established a commission to determine the specific boundary between Canada and the United States.

For the SAT II, remembering the outcome of the War of 1812 is more important than remembering the actual events of the war. Even though the War of 1812 didn't have a clear winner, the war had a significant impact on the new country. It inspired a spirit of *nationalism* (or pride in one's country) among young Americans and, as a result, continental exploration, conquest, and the discovery of new markets flourished. Out of this war, the United States established itself as a sovereign nation.

The Hartford Convention

Despite the jubilation following the end of the War of 1812, not all Americans were content with the ambiguous outcome of the war. New England Federalists, who had largely opposed the war from the beginning, convened in Hartford, Connecticut, in December 1814 to discuss the direction of the United States in the postwar world.

At the *Hartford Convention,* these radical Federalists toyed with the idea of New England secession from the United States. They also proposed the annulment of the three-fifths clause for popular representation in the House of Representatives (see Chapter 5), limiting the presidency to one term, and requiring the approval of ⅔ of Congress rather than a simple majority for the admission of new states or the declaration of war. The New England Federalists wanted to reduce the South's power because it had favored the war effort. But to most Americans, these proposals appeared far too radical and un-American during a time of high patriotism. Because of its opposition to the war, the Federalist Party's popularity suffered, pretty much ending its existence.

Feeling Groovy: The Era of Good Feelings

Following the War of 1812, the U.S. experienced a period of relative peace and prosperity. National pride and a stronger feeling of independence from Britain spurred some Americans to try to strengthen the national bond. Congressman Henry Clay advocated a system to bring the various regions of the U.S. closer together, and President James Monroe issued a doctrine designed to limit European control in the Americas.

Establishing the American System

Although Jefferson and his supporters looked down upon the federal control of state and local institutions, others believed that they could successfully mix America's agrarian and commercial economies to create a more profitable and powerful United States. Henry Clay's *American System* promoted instituting protective tariffs to encourage domestic production as well as building canals and roadways, funded by the federal government, across the nation. Clay intended the system to strengthen the U.S. economy by tying the economies of the North, South, and West together. The natural resources of the South and West would supply the raw materials used for manufacturing in the North. In accordance with the American System, the federal government carried out the following actions:

- ✔ **Chartered the Second Bank of the United States.** The First Bank of the United States had a 20-year charter that expired in 1811, so no national bank existed between 1811 and 1816. But in 1816, while James Madison was still president, Congress chartered the *Second Bank of the United States,* which promoted a strong and uniform national currency to improve trade among the regions of the United States.

- ✔ **Instituted protective tariffs.** The first protective tariff in U.S. history went into effect in 1816. This tariff sought to help American merchants compete with foreign goods. It increased duties on cotton, leather, paper, sugar, and iron products from Britain, so the tariff made British goods more expensive and encouraged Americans to buy less expensive, domestically-produced goods.

- ✔ **Improved the national transportation system.** The final part of the American System was to create a large network of canals and roadways (using federal funds) to connect the states and increase trade among the main regions of the U.S.

Although Clay was a Democratic Republican, his American System, with its heavy reliance on the federal government, seemed more like a Federalist plan. Its emphasis on manufacturing and national self-reliance was more palatable to Northerners than it was to Southerners, who had made a good living for themselves exporting their goods to other countries.

The election of James Monroe

Democratic Republican *James Monroe,* the Virginia planter and the secretary of state under Madison, demolished Federalist Rufus King, of New York, in the 1816 presidential election. Monroe won 183 electoral votes to King's 34 and ushered in an era of relative peace and prosperity for Americans. A major American newspaper proclaimed the period of Monroe's presidency as the "*Era of Good Feelings.*" Four years later in the election of 1820, despite the controversy brought on by the Missouri Compromise (which you can read about in Chapter 7), Monroe won all but one electoral vote, which essentially ended the existence of the Federalists.

Issuing the Monroe Doctrine

In 1816, General Andrew Jackson, the hero of the Battle of New Orleans during the War of 1812, invaded Spanish-owned Florida to find runaway slaves who he believed the Seminole Indians were harboring. During his raid of Florida, Jackson executed two British citizens who he believed were enemies of the United States and his mission. Executing British citizens in a Spanish territory was pretty dangerous stuff, and Jackson's foolishness distressed Monroe. As a result of Jackson's aggressions, Secretary of State John Quincy Adams negotiated the *Adams-Onis Treaty,* which ceded control of Florida to the United States in 1819.

Spain had problems with its Latin American colonies, too, as one by one, they proclaimed independence from the Spanish Empire. By the mid-1820s, Columbia, Peru, Chile, and Mexico had separated from Spain. Monroe, who wanted to prevent the Spanish from attempting to re-colonize its former holdings in Latin America, issued an important ideological declaration in 1823. The *Monroe Doctrine,* as it came to be known, stated that the American continent, including Latin America, would no longer be controlled by European colonial powers. Although the U.S. wouldn't interfere with existing European possessions, it would not tolerate any European attempts to colonize the Americas or interfere with their sovereign nations. By the end of Monroe's presidency, the French, Spanish, and British (except in Canada) were effectively thrown off the continent, and the United States was free to exert control over North America without meddling from the Europeans.

In Defense of Federal Supremacy: John Marshall's Supreme Court

In the days of the early republic, the justices on the U.S. Supreme Court had the difficult task of figuring out how the judicial branch of the government would function. The Court had to determine its boundaries, how to interpret the Constitution, and how to balance the interests of states and the federal government.

John Jay was the first Chief Justice of the Supreme Court, and two other Chief Justices served after him before John Marshall took over in 1801. Marshall, appointed during Federalist John Adams's administration, served until he died in 1835. So, during the reign of the Jeffersonian

Democratic Republicans, the Marshall Court, which protected federalism and the power of the centralized U.S. government (and thus, wasn't Jeffersonian in its ideals), ruled from the bench.

The Marshall Court did a remarkable job of defining the role of the Supreme Court and, therefore, you'll probably see a question or two on the SAT II about one of its many significant decisions. You may want to add these decisions to your notecards.

Establishing judicial review: Marbury v. Madison (1803)

William Marbury sued Secretary of State James Madison for refusing to acknowledge a legal federal judge appointment when Jefferson came to power (Marbury was one of the midnight judges mentioned in "Making changes on the domestic front" earlier in this chapter). Marbury took the case of *Marbury v. Madison* to the Supreme Court because the Judiciary Act of 1789 (enacted by Congress) gave the Court the right to order a public official to follow a legal course of action. Chief Justice John Marshall was a Federalist, so his personal position was that Marbury should be granted the appointment, but he knew that Jefferson would ignore the order, and that would compromise the power of the Supreme Court. So, the Marshall Court ruled that although Marbury's commission was valid, the Court couldn't force the sitting president to deliver the appointment. The Court decided that the law that gave the Court the right to require delivery of appointments (the Judiciary Act of 1789) exceeded the powers that the Constitution gave to the Supreme Court. Thereby, Marshall's decision established the Supreme Court's constitutional right to review acts of Congress (and by implication, acts of the president) and determine whether or not they violated the Constitution. This right is known as *judicial review*.

Defending the Bank of the United States: McCulloch v. Maryland (1819)

In 1816, Congress chartered the Second Bank of the United States, which had the power to deal with national and state banking matters. (See "Establishing the American System" earlier in this chapter for more about the bank.) Maryland bankers argued that the U.S. Bank was unconstitutional because it interfered with local concerns that the Constitution protected. In an attempt to shut down the U.S. Bank, the state of Maryland taxed the U.S. Bank on any banknotes that came from banks that weren't chartered in Maryland. When the U.S. Bank refused to pay the taxes, Maryland sued its representative, James McCulloch.

The Marshall Court, in a decision favoring federalism, decided that Congress had the right to establish the U.S. Bank (the right was implied in the Constitution even though it wasn't specifically stated) and, although it may hurt individual investors, the U.S. Bank was "necessary and proper" for the continued function of the U.S. economy and, therefore, was constitutional. The Court also determined that under the supremacy clause of the Constitution (which says state laws have to comply with the Constitution), Maryland didn't have the right to tax the U.S. Bank because the tax would eventually result in the destruction of a federal institution by a state. The *McCulloch v. Maryland* decision reinforced the supremacy of federal law over state laws.

Sanctifying contracts with two important decisions

The following Marshall Court decisions established that states did not have the authority to overrule a contract.

Dartmouth College v. Woodward (1819)

The New Hampshire legislature wanted to change the charter of Dartmouth College from a private to a public institution, which they believed would better serve the larger population. The Dartmouth trustees, who didn't want to lose control of the college, hired Daniel Webster, who later became secretary of state under President Benjamin Harrison, to defend their case. The Marshall Court decided that contracts — no matter what they entailed — had to be respected and honored in the United States and that a state could not alter them.

Sturges v. Crowninshield (1819)

This case dealt with the question of whether state bankruptcy laws could alter contracts. The Marshall Court decided that states did have the right to pass bankruptcy laws, as long as those laws didn't violate the 1st Amendment to the Constitution (which establishes limits on state and federal legislative power). In turn, this decision also affirmed the sanctity of contracts and declared that a state bankruptcy law that impaired the obligation of a contract was unconstitutional.

Surrendering state sovereignty to federalism: Cohens v. Virginia (1821)

Virginia courts convicted the Cohens of selling lottery tickets illegally, but they appealed to the U.S. Supreme Court. The Court agreed to hear the case, but the Marshall Court upheld the conviction. The actual decision in the Cohens's case wasn't such a big deal (except to the Cohens); this case was important because it established the precedent for the Supreme Court to review even the criminal case decisions of state cases. This ruling gave the Supreme Court the ultimate authority over the law, even over state criminal courts.

Regulating interstate commerce: Gibbons v. Ogden (1824)

With the invention of steam engines, travel on rivers became an important means for trade and exploration in the United States. Inevitably, disputes arose over who had sovereign control over these new modes of transportation. In *Gibbons v. Ogden*, the Marshall Court decided that under the commerce clause of the Constitution (which gives Congress the power to regulate commerce among the states), Congress had the power to regulate any travel on rivers that passed through two states. This ruling led to the demise of monopolies in the shipping business as well as improvements in transportation and opportunities for businesses and passengers alike. *Gibbons v. Ogden* established that the federal government had control over routes that involved more than one state, further promoting the power of the federal government.

Responding to the Marshall Court's decisions

The Marshall Court set several precedents during its tenure from 1801 to 1835 regarding its role and power within the U.S. government, but the Court soon realized that it was powerless to enforce its decisions. In 1832, after ruling in the case of *Worcester v. Georgia* that the Cherokee tribe was a legitimate entity and could not be forcibly removed from its land, President Andrew Jackson clearly ignored the ruling and didn't enforce the Court's decision (see Chapter 7). Thus, the Supreme Court had power only if the executive branch enforced its rulings, and federalism was struck another harsh blow.

Tying it all together: A sample question looks at the Marshall Court

Memorizing these Marshall Court decisions can be confusing, but these rulings are important to know. The following question is a good possibility for the exam.

What Supreme Court case established the precedent of judicial review?

(A) *Brown v. Board of Education of Topeka, Kansas*

(B) *Gibbons v. Ogden*

(C) *Marbury v. Madison*

(D) *McCulloch v. Maryland*

(E) *Plessy v. Ferguson*

If you hadn't just reviewed major Marshall Court decisions, this question may be intimidating. Start by determining what you do know. First, you know that the Court established judicial review early in American history, so you can eliminate any recent cases. Answers (A) and (E) weren't decisions made by the Marshall Court; *Brown v. Board of Education* was a 1954 decision (for more details, read Chapter 19), and *Plessy v. Ferguson* dealt with the establishment of "separate but equal" facilities for African Americans, beginning in the era of Jim Crow laws in the late 1890s (see Chapter 10). Although both cases are extremely important, they're obviously from different eras.

That leaves (B), (C), and (D). All are Marshall Court decisions, but the earliest is *Marbury v. Madison*. You know this because one of the parties is James Madison, Thomas Jefferson's secretary of state and the fourth American president. *Marbury v. Madison* dealt with Madison's refusal to honor John Adams's last-minute federal appointments. By saying that the Supreme Court didn't have power in this instance actually gave the Court more power — the power to say that an act of Congress was unconstitutional (or judicial review). The correct answer is (C).

Chapter 7

Strife and Controversy in the Jacksonian Era, 1820–1842

In This Chapter

▶ Looking at the Missouri Compromise of 1820

▶ Walking in his father's footsteps: John Quincy Adams

▶ Knowing the differences between national political parties

▶ Differentiating among the North, South, and West

▶ Sticking with Old Hickory: Andrew Jackson in charge

▶ Exploring the impact of Martin Van Buren and John Tyler

From 1820 to 1842, America grew up but it also grew apart. By 1820, America's population was just under 10 million. With this surge in population came increased tensions in regard to tariffs, public lands, and slavery. The three main regions of the United States — the North, South, and West — had different economies, ideologies, and ways of life. What was best for the West often hurt the North, and what was best for the North frequently hurt the South.

Following the War of 1812, the Federalist Party almost ceased to exist because its members had opposed the war. In 1820, the Democratic Republican Party nominated both presidential candidates: incumbent James Monroe and John Quincy Adams. Monroe won all the electoral votes but one.

Andrew Jackson didn't enter the presidential political arena until the next election in 1824, when he ran against Adams and lost under highly controversial circumstances. Prior to Jackson, the major contenders for the presidency had been aristocrats from the original colonies and had participated in the Revolutionary War. But the popularity of Jackson, a Westerner from Tennessee and a commoner, signified a change that underscored the country's diversity now that it was adding new land and new ideas, which is why many historians begin the *Jackson Era* in the early 1820s, when the West started coming into its own.

When you think of the Jacksonian Era for the SAT II, think of the value of the common man, a widening rift between Southerners and Northerners, the emergence of the West as a influential part of the U.S., and a break from established traditions.

The Missouri Compromise of 1820

From 1817 to 1825, pro- and antislavery factions deeply divided America. As long as an even number of states supported each side of the issue, both factions had an equal number of votes in the Senate. This balance remained steady until 1819, when Missouri petitioned to enter the Union as a slave state. Northern legislators wanted Missouri statehood on the condition that it outlaw slavery. Southern politicians weren't pleased with this arrangement.

After several tries at reaching a solution, many Americans doubted that Northern and Southern politicians could reach a peaceful solution to the Missouri issue. But Congress did reach a compromise. Kentucky Representative Henry Clay, who earned his nickname "The Great Compromiser" out of this Oscar-worthy song and dance, proposed a solution that would satisfy both sides — at least for the time being. Clay got the North and South to agree to a series of arrangements known as the *Missouri Compromise of 1820:*

- ✔ Missouri would enter the Union as a slave state (like its people wanted).

- ✔ Maine would enter the Union as a free state to maintain the balance in the Senate that adding Missouri as a slave state would cause.

- ✔ The region south of 36° 30' latitude would be open to slavery.

- ✔ The region north of 36° 30' latitude, with the exception of Missouri, would outlaw slavery.

Figure 7-1 shows the dividing line for free and slave states under the Missouri Compromise. The compromise provided the possibility for many more free states than slave states in the future. This issue would continue to pose problems as the U.S. added more states and territories.

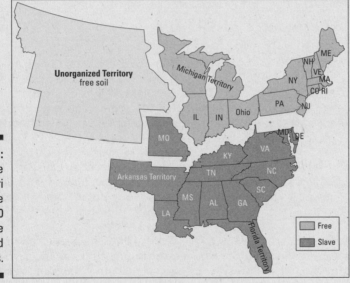

Figure 7-1:
The Missouri Compromise of 1820 divided free states and slave states.

Arguments over the Missouri Compromise emphasized the differences among the Democratic Republicans. Before the Missouri issue, Democratic Republicans were becoming more amenable to a centralized government. After the fight over the Missouri issue, many of them went back to supporting state sovereignty over a strong federal government. The supporters of states' rights would eventually make up the new *Democratic Party* and support Andrew Jackson in 1824. Those who favored a strong federal government would later form an anti-Jackson coalition that would become the *Whig Party.*

Although the SAT II may ask you about the specific elements of the Missouri Compromise, you should also be aware of its significance in the developing conflict between those who favored state sovereignty and those who supported a strong federal government.

All the following were results of the Missouri Compromise EXCEPT

(A) Missouri entered the Union as a slave state.

(B) Territorial governments in Utah and New Mexico could decide whether they wanted to allow or outlaw slavery.

(C) Members of the Democratic Republican Party united over the issue of state sovereignty.

(D) Maine entered the Union as a free state.

(E) 36° 30' latitude would mark the division between free and slave states.

Because you now know the elements of the Missouri Compromise, you can eliminate (A), (D), and (E) as obvious incorrect answer choices. These three answer choices state a direct agreement reached by northerners and southerners in 1820. The process of settling the Missouri Compromise emphasized the rift within the Democratic Republican Party between those who advocated a strong central government and those who supported state sovereignty, so answer (C) isn't right. Answer (B) sounds as if it may fit into a slavery compromise — and it does, but not the Missouri one. This answer addresses the Compromise of 1850, which considered the rights of Utah and New Mexico regarding the slavery issue (you can read about this compromise in Chapter 9). Therefore, the answer is (B).

Did the "EXCEPT" trip you up? Many SAT II test-takers have trouble keeping track of what they're looking for when confronted with an exception question. To overcome this trap, rephrase the question. In this case, think of the question as "Which of the following was not agreed upon in the Missouri Compromise"? Now when you dive into the answer choices, you know exactly what you're looking for.

The Administration of John Quincy Adams

John Quincy Adams's father, John Adams, had also been president. Both men were involved in controversial elections (see Chapter 5 for the senior Adams's scandal). In the election of 1824, the divided Democratic Republican Party nominated four candidates (Adams, Andrew Jackson, William Harris Crawford, and Henry Clay). Adams lost the popular and electoral vote to Jackson but, because none of the candidates won a majority in the Electoral College (see Chapter 5), the decision went to the House of Representatives.

According to Jackson's supporters, Adams struck a "corrupt bargain" with House representative Henry Clay, who later became Adams's secretary of state but who also sided with Adams on tariff and national improvements issues. Clay encouraged other House members to vote for Adams, and Adams won the presidency. The election widened the gap in the Democratic Republican Party between Jackson's supporters and Adams's supporters and resulted in the formation of new political parties (see the next section). The "Era of Good Feelings" (see Chapter 6) was over.

The major issue of John Quincy Adams's presidency (other than the way in which he won the presidency) also helped widen the rift within the party and between Northerners and Southerners. To understand this issue, keep in mind that the Northern economy relied on industry and the sale of manufactured goods. On the other hand, the South produced raw products (like cotton) that were used in the manufacturing process.

In 1816 and 1824, Congress passed protective tariffs on foreign manufactured goods to help out Northern industry. The tariffs made foreign goods more expensive than American goods and, therefore, increased sales for American manufacturers and kept prices high (to the dismay of Southerners, who had to pay them). In addition, high tariffs caused British manufacturers to produce fewer textiles, so they didn't buy as much Southern cotton. As a result of these tariffs, Southerners not only had to pay higher prices for manufactured goods, but they also received lower prices for their raw products.

Slaves fight back: Nat Turner's revolt and the *Amistad*

Nat Turner led America's most famous and frightening slave revolt in Virginia in 1831. Turner grew up as a slave and was deeply religious. He had visions that he interpreted as being messages from God and viewed a solar eclipse as a sign that God wanted him to prepare for rebellion. In August 1831, Turner and fellow slaves rode from house to house on horseback, killing whites and freeing slaves. During the revolt, Turner and more than 40 others killed 51 whites. Turner evaded authorities for two months. When he was caught, he was hanged. Whites killed the other African Americans who were involved in the rebellion (and some who were not). As a result, the state of Virginia severely restricted freedoms for freed and slave African Americans.

A group of slaves who rebelled on the high seas fared better than Turner did. In 1839, the *Amistad*, a Spanish slave ship, was on its way to Puerto Principe, Cuba. The enslaved Africans aboard the ship rebelled against their white captors and took over the ship by killing its cook and captain. The slaves demanded that the two slave owners onboard transport them back to Africa. The navigator deceived the slaves by steering the ship north along the U.S. coast. The U.S. Navy captured the mutinied ship off Long Island, New York, when some of the slaves went ashore to get supplies. The United States tried the slaves as mutineers and murderers, and former president John Quincy Adams represented them to the Supreme Court. In 1841, the Supreme Court decided that the original capture of the Africans was illegal and, therefore, acquitted the slaves and allowed them to return to Africa. Abolitionists formed the Amistad Committee to raise money for the slaves' defense and for their 1842 return home.

In 1828, Congress passed another tariff increase to benefit Northern manufacturers, and Adams signed it into law. Adams's vice-president, John Calhoun, was a Southerner from South Carolina. He and his supporter named it the *Tariff of Abominations* and tried to *nullify* it (void it by declaring it unconstitutional). When Adams signed the 1828 tariff, he lost credibility with his Southern supporters. He had won the presidency through suspect circumstances anyway, and the tariff issue decreased his popularity.

The Emergence of New Political Parties during the Jacksonian Era

For about ten years (about 1816–1826) the Democratic Republican Party was the only party in U.S. politics. James Monroe essentially ran unopposed in the 1820 presidential election, and all the major presidential candidates for the 1824 election were Democratic Republicans, too. After the very controversial 1824 election, though, the party system began to change (see the previous section). The election created a lot of resentment among Jackson supporters and, during Adams's presidency, the party began to split into those who supported Jackson (called the *Democrats*) and those who supported Adams and Henry Clay (called the *National Republicans*).

Adams wasn't a partisan politician. He advocated what he thought was right rather than a party platform. For this reason, the National Republican platform wasn't clearly defined. Supporters of this party tended to be Northerners from the New England states because Adams was from the North and because Southern politicians were put off by his signing the Tariff of Abominations (see "The Administration of John Quincy Adams" earlier in this chapter). National Republicans tended to favor a strong national government role in promoting economic development. Jackson and his followers liked to point out that because National Republicans were mostly aristocrats, Adams's party was one for the wealthy.

By 1828, the Democratic Republicans were also known simply as the *Democrats* and were sometimes called the "Jacksonian Democrats" because the party platform centered around

Jackson and his appeal to the common man. Being a Westerner, Jackson had a lot of support from the Western states. And because Jackson advocated states' rights over federal government involvement, he also gained the support of many Southerners as well.

The National Republican Party lasted about as long as it took to nominate John Quincy Adams as its candidate for president against Jackson in the 1828 election. When Adams lost the election (see "Facing off again: The election of 1828" later in this chapter), the party fizzled out. Later, in reaction to the way that Jackson seemed to treat the presidency (according to his opposition, as though he were the king), the party reorganized as the *Whig Party* under the leadership of Henry Clay and Senator Daniel Webster. The Whigs embraced a philosophy of *nationalism,* which was the idea that the country's strength came from states' identifying as one nation, as opposed to the Democrats' support of *sectionalism,* which was the idea that states fared better fending for themselves without a lot of federal government interference. The 1836 election was the first time that the Whigs offered presidential candidates (for more about the Whig Party and its demise, see Chapter 9).

Different Strokes for Different Folks: Sectional Politics

Sectional politics played an important role in Jacksonian America. While the North emerged industrially, the South became more dependent on slavery and the Western frontier gradually became more populated. Every issue seemed to divide the nation along geographical lines, benefiting one section of the country and hurting another. The struggle to balance the benefits and burdens of political and economic issues lasted throughout the period.

The Northern point of view and its political leaders

From 1820 to 1842, the number of Americans working in Northern factories doubled and manufacturing was its primary source of income. The North's industrial growth required markets for its products, which meant that Northerners favored protecting American markets from foreign competition. The North was influenced by the New England Protestant ethic dedicated to hard work, education, and moral fortitude. Their religious beliefs prompted quite a few Northerners to become abolitionists and reformers (see Chapter 8).

Daniel Webster, a prestigious lawyer from New Hampshire who argued cases such as *Dartmouth College v. Woodward* and *McCulloch v. Maryland* (see Chapter 6), gained stature as a great political leader from the North. As a politician and Whig leader, Webster argued for a nationalist perspective and against slavery. New Yorker Martin Van Buren served as Jackson's secretary of state. Although he was a Democrat, his positions on slavery and states' rights issues were more moderate than those of the Southern Democrats.

The Southern way of life and those in charge

During the Jacksonian era, the South's biggest crop was cotton. Growing it required large plots of land and lots of labor, so the Southern lifestyle was primarily rural and dependent on slavery. Plantations produced crops, and port cities shipped them to foreign markets.

Southern Democrats like Senator Robert Y. Hayne from South Carolina and Vice President John C. Calhoun, also from South Carolina, championed states' rights. Calhoun and Hayne played major roles in presenting and rallying support for the *nullification theory* (see the section "I said no! The nullification crisis" later in this chapter).

The Western way of life and its representatives

The idea that America had a right and obligation to expand its territories across the continent took off during the early 1800s, and many adventurous Americans packed their belongings and moved West (which referred to any land west of the 13 original states). People who settled in regions like Kentucky and Tennessee tended to be tough individualists who favored a more rustic lifestyle than those led by Southern aristocrats or New England city-dwellers. Therefore, most Westerners weren't clearly nationalists or sectionalists. They valued personal freedom, but they also needed the transportation systems and other national improvements that necessitated a strong federal government and unity with the North and South.

Great politicians came out of the Western states from both political camps. Kentucky Representative Henry Clay was a self-educated man who became a great lawyer, senator, and orator. Also known as the "Great Compromiser," Clay often negotiated understandings between the North and South; he was particularly influential during the Missouri Compromise of 1820, which we cover earlier in this chapter. Clay was the National Republican presidential candidate during the 1832 election and, later, a founder of the Whig Party. His political rival, Andrew Jackson, was also from the West. Jackson epitomized the self-made man. Although he was born in South Carolina, Jackson moved to the Tennessee Territory in his 20s.

An Era of Controversy: Andrew Jackson's Presidency

Andrew Jackson, whose presidency lasted from 1829 to 1837, polarized the American people. To friends and supporters, he was "Old Hickory," a nickname that represented his strength. To enemies (mostly members of the Whig Party), he was known as "King Andrew" because he liberally used the veto to overrule congressional legislation, which many viewed as an abuse of the checks and balances system in the Constitution (see Chapter 5).

The American people viewed Jackson as an establishment outsider, a fighter for the common man, and a hero in the War of 1812. Jackson was born into poverty and orphaned at age 14 but achieved success as a wealthy plantation owner. (Actually, a large inheritance helped Jackson quite a bit. So much for that self-made image!) Figure 7-2 portrays a royal Andrew Jackson, as opponents saw him, trampling the Constitution.

The SAT II places much significance on Jackson's presidency. You're likely to encounter a question or two that deals with the issues of his term in office.

In the following sections, we cover Jackson's ideas for the presidency and a variety of events that occurred during his time in office.

Facing off again: The election of 1828

In the election of 1828, John Quincy Adams once again faced off with Jackson for the presidency. But this time, Jackson won decidedly. In 1824, Jackson had defeated Adams in the popular and electoral votes, but because no candidate won a majority of votes in the Electoral College, the decision went to the House of Representatives, which then selected Adams. Adams had done nothing during his presidency to improve his popularity with voters. Plus, Jackson benefited from a not-so-little change in voting procedures called *mass suffrage.*

Figure 7-2:
Jackson
as "King
Andrew."

Courtesy of Eric Zimmer

Mass suffrage gave all white males, not just the ones who owned land, the right to vote. So the common man gained the right to vote just as Jackson, the "Man of the People," ran for president. Jackson's appeal to the common man inspired new voters to exercise their right. Although only 27 percent of eligible voters voted in 1824, nearly 60 percent of eligible voters went to the polls in 1828, which gave Jackson a greater edge over Adams.

Because I'm president, that's why! Jackson's concept of the presidency

Jackson, who believed in being a strong president, used every ounce of political power that the presidency gave him. His supporters championed his take-charge attitude and ability to get the job done. His opponents criticized his abuse of the powers of the office.

Thank you for your support: The spoils system

The truism "To the victor go the spoils" was coined during Jackson's presidency. Jackson made extensive use of the *spoils system.* Under this system, a president removes all government-appointed office holders affiliated with the opposite political party and replaces them with his own supporters. Jackson's opponents criticized him for making these appointments. To justify his actions, Jackson stated that replacing government workers every so often made the system more democratic.

The "Kitchen Cabinet"

Instead of using a traditional cabinet (an official advisory council to the president usually made up of high-ranking members of government), Jackson relied on a small, unofficial group of advisors. Those advisors, known as the *Kitchen Cabinet,* included only two of the official cabinet members. The Kitchen Cabinet remained intact from 1829 to 1831. In 1831, Jackson dismissed the entire official cabinet and reorganized it with his supporters.

Veto power

Until Jackson, few presidents had exercised their veto power over congressional legislation. Jackson wasn't afraid to use the veto when he felt that Congress was pushing the limits of the federal government. He vetoed the extension of the charter for the Second Bank of the United States (see "Money matters: Jackson versus the U.S. Bank" later in this chapter) and a federal public works project. Under Henry Clay's *American System* (established during James Monroe's presidency; see Chapter 6), federal funds could be used to build railroads, canals, and other transportation systems. Congress approved a federal project to build Maysville Road in Kentucky in 1830, but because Maysville Road was located exclusively in Kentucky, Jackson felt that it should be a state project rather than a federal one. His veto angered members of Congress, who didn't like having their decisions overturned.

Showing "the kindest feelings": The Indian Removal Act

Jackson signed the *Indian Removal Act* in 1830, which appropriated $500,000 for the U.S. military to force the Cherokee tribes to march from their homes in Florida and southern Georgia to Oklahoma. In 1832, the Native Americans had won a victory in the Supreme Court case *Worcester v. Georgia,* which most Northern leaders supported. The decision held that Native American nations were independent and not subject to state regulation. However, after the case, Jackson provokingly replied that Chief Justice John Marshall had made his decision and "now let's see him enforce it." Although Jackson professed to having "the kindest feelings" toward the Cherokee, his actions and subsequent statements belied his profession.

Jackson entered into treaty negotiations in 1835 with the Cherokee that ended up in their having to relinquish all their land east of the Mississippi River. Jackson gave them until the spring of 1838 to leave the area. Some left voluntarily, but most did not. Those who remained were forced by the U.S. military to walk the 1,200-mile *Trail of Tears* (enforced under President Van Buren) from Georgia to lands in Oklahoma, usually with only the clothes they were wearing. The brutal journey in 1838 to 1839 resulted in the deaths of ⅕ to ¼ of the Cherokee population from disease, starvation, exposure, and exhaustion.

Money matters: Jackson versus the U.S. Bank

Throughout his administration, Jackson challenged the Bank of the United States and its backers because he thought a federal bank violated the Constitution. In Jackson's first inauguration address, he declared his opposition to the U.S. Bank, and the bank war had begun. Bank supporters praised the stability of the economy with the bank in control. Opponents of the bank criticized it as tool that the rich used to exploit the poor.

The bank veto

Jackson had lost money in earlier dealings with banks and, therefore, he distrusted banks. In July 1832, Jackson vetoed Congress's proposal to extend the charter of the Bank of the United States, which would expire in 1836.

According to Jackson, the Bank of the United States

- Violated the Constitution
- Acted as a monopoly
- Benefited the rich and hindered the poor
- Made the United States vulnerable to foreign control by foreign stockholders

The people have spoken: The election of 1832

Jackson's opponents as well as bank supporters, like Henry Clay, Daniel Webster, and bank director Nicholas Biddle, incited the bank dispute to create a campaign issue that would defeat Jackson. Jackson said: "The bank tried to kill me, but I shall kill it." With Jackson's overwhelming election victory over Clay, he took the vote as a popular mandate against the U.S. Bank.

Cashing out: The demise of the U.S. Bank

After Jackson's reelection, he further devastated the bank by withdrawing all federal funds. Then he redeposited those federal funds into state banks where he felt that they belonged. The opposing Whig Party decried the use of Jackson's "pet banks" as more of the spoils system (see "Thank you for your support: The spoils system" earlier in this chapter). After the U.S. Bank reincorporated as a state bank, it eventually failed in 1841. Following the close of the bank, Jackson issued the *Specie Circular* in 1836, an executive order that required payments for government lands to be in hard currency because paper money was too unstable. This order devalued paper money and caused deflation and an economic depression called the *Panic of 1837,* but Jackson was safely out of office by then and President Martin Van Buren had to deal with it.

I said no! The nullification crisis

In 1828, John Calhoun tried to nullify the Tariff of Abominations (see "The Administration of John Quincy Adams" at the beginning of this chapter), which caused all kinds of sectional tension. His South Carolina Exposition and Protest of 1828 declared that states had the right to nullify federal laws that they opposed. Robert Y. Hayne took up the fight in the *Webster–Hayne Debate* of 1830. Webster, a Northern leader, argued for "liberty and union," maintaining that states had no right to attack federal laws except through Constitutional mechanisms. Hayne, a Southern leader, argued for the *Compact Theory,* which asserted that the states had ratified the Constitution and, therefore, could choose which federal laws they wanted to follow.

In 1832, Jackson passed another tariff that wasn't as strict as the 1828 tariff but that still angered Southerners. South Carolina adopted Calhoun's *Ordinance of Nullification,* which voided the tariff and prohibited the collection of tariff duties in the state. South Carolina even went so far as to threaten to secede from the Union. So Jackson passed the Force Bill in 1833, which authorized military force to collect the duties. The situation calmed when Henry Clay negotiated a compromise in which South Carolina agreed to back down in exchange for lower tariff rates. The crisis highlighted the ongoing debate among American politicians over how much power the federal government could exercise over the states.

Tying it all together: A sample question looks at Andrew Jackson's presidency

Which of the following provides the best explanation for why Andrew Jackson's presidency marked a new era in U.S. political history?

(A) It was the first time that a president was elected by the House of Representatives.

(B) It marked the first time that a president allowed a state to nullify a federal law.

(C) Jackson was the first president who did not emanate from one of the 13 original colonies.

(D) Jackson established the First Bank of the United States.

(E) Jackson's presidency did away with the spoils system instituted by prior presidencies.

Answer (A) is wrong because the House of Representatives elected Adams instead of Jackson in 1824. Jackson won in 1828 with a majority of the electoral vote. Jackson didn't allow South Carolina to nullify the tariff law, so (B) is wrong. Answer (C) is true, but look at the other choices to be sure. Jackson hated the national bank, and the first one was established during George Washington's presidency, so you can eliminate (D). Jackson used the spoils system to pad his administration with supporters, so (E) can't be right. The best answer is (C). Before Jackson, all presidents had ties to the American Revolution and all came from states formed by the 13 colonies. Jackson was a Western politician from Tennessee.

The Presidencies of Martin Van Buren and John Tyler

After the controversial but never boring presidency of Jackson, came two (actually three) forgettable presidents. The SAT II will probably forget about them, too, but just in case it doesn't, we include a few of the highlights of the terms of Martin Van Buren and John Tyler.

Martin "Barnburner" Van Buren

Martin Van Buren, a Democrat, won the 1836 election over four Whig candidates. He entered office just in time for the Panic of 1837 to hit. The panic emerged because Jackson messed with the national bank and paper currency (see "Cashing out: The demise of the U.S. Bank" earlier in this chapter) just as the price of cotton fell, which caused banks to suspend payments and to fail. Van Buren established a system of Independent Subtreasuries, financial institutions that were independent of any banks. Still, the panic continued.

Van Buren also tried to clean up some of the spoils system. But that action only got Van Buren labeled as a "barnburner," which hinted that he would burn down his own barn just to get rid of the rats. When reelection time rolled around, the Whigs chant of "Van, van is a used up man" signaled his upcoming defeat to Whig candidate William Henry Harrison in 1840.

Tippecanoe and Tyler, too

The Whig Party prospered in elections, running campaigns such as the Log Cabin and Hard Cider Campaign of 1840. In this campaign, a newspaper reporter tried to belittle presidential candidate Harrison by saying that he was best qualified for sipping cider in a frontier shack. Instead of being offended, Harrison loved being pegged as the rugged frontiersman and held rallies with hard cider in log cabins. "Tippecanoe and Tyler, too" was also a campaign slogan for the Whigs; it referenced Harrison's days as a hero in the Battle of Tippecanoe, which was fought against the Native Americans, and that John Tyler was his running mate. Harrison won the election, but the Whig Party's success wouldn't last long. The Whig Party was the first party torn apart by the slavery issue (see Chapter 9).

Harrison, an Ohio politician, didn't have much staying power. Elected in 1840, Harrison was in office only one month. He died of pneumonia, rumored to be caused by standing in the cold too long during his inauguration speech (which was the longest in history). Vice President John Tyler succeeded Harrison as president. Tyler reorganized the U.S. Navy, but his main claim to fame was that he annexed Texas during his administration.

Chapter 8

Romanticism, Revolution, and Reform, 1820–1860

. . . .

In This Chapter

▶ Looking into the roles of religion, art, and literature in the mid-1800s

▶ Super-sizing the United States with westward expansion

▶ Examining the first Industrial Revolution

▶ Reforming American society and challenging slavery

. . . .

The early to mid-19th century may be one of the most dynamic periods in American history. During this period, the land area of the United States nearly doubled because of acquisitions from Mexico and Britain, and American culture flourished, reform movements were organized, and society became polarized over the issue of slavery.

Forty percent of the questions on the SAT II U.S. History exam deal with the period from 1790 to 1898. Familiarizing yourself with the key concepts of the period from 1820 to 1860 (which is also known as the antebellum period because it came right before the Civil War) definitely will help you do well on the test. But memorizing names, dates, and obscure facts from this large body of material probably won't help you very much. Instead, concentrate on the main ideas and how everything ties together.

Romanticism: The Role of Religion, Art, and Literature

During the first half of the 19th century and, especially after 1820, religion, art, and literature began to play an important role in American society. Americans, secure and confident in their new country, wanted to create a distinct American culture that was independent of Europe. Artists and writers were free to explore and started an American renaissance of sorts, which flourished from 1812 until the Civil War. This renaissance is now referred to as the period of *American Romanticism*. Romanticism embraced

- A return to nature
- The celebration of the role of artists
- An emphasis upon the goodness of mankind and the freedom of individuals
- The glorification of the role of senses and emotions over intellect
- Patriotism

The SAT II U.S. History exam is unlikely to ask you to define romanticism. But having some concepts about what kinds of changes occurred in American society and culture in the early 19th century — especially in relation to trends in religion, art, and literature — is a good idea.

Evangelism and Transcendentalism: Two religious experiences

In the early 1800s, Americans became more secular (less religious). Many Americans, especially educated ones, began questioning aspects of Christianity and turning toward more logical views on religion. This philosophy became known as *rationalism.* Rationalists thought that people shouldn't take religious beliefs at face value and accept them without questions. Rather, rationalists questioned, investigated, and reflected upon religious beliefs.

Deists were hard-core rationalists who thought that if the Bible conflicted with reason, logic, and science, then the Bible should be ignored. Benjamin Franklin and Thomas Jefferson were two well-known deists. Rationalism also led to the rise of two other challenges to religion: *universalism* and unitarianism. Universalists upheld the importance of science, reason, and logic, had no specific creed, and felt that all souls would achieve salvation. Thomas Paine, (remember "Common Sense"?), emerged as a well-known universalist after he published his book *The Age of Reason* in the 1790s, which attacked the Bible and all organized religion.

Evangelism

Many religious types reacted to the popularity of rationalism by seeking to renew the popularity of religion in America. They did so by *evangelizing,* or preaching the gospel. Evangelists felt that organized religion ought to be more accessible to common people. Ministers encouraged followers to develop a personal and emotional relationship with God. As a result, the *Second Great Awakening* emerged by the early 1800s and continued through the 1830s. (You can read about the First Great Awakening in Chapter 4.)

As evangelism gained popularity throughout America, communities built more churches and founded many universities and colleges. Revival meetings, which began in Connecticut in the 1790s became all the rage, especially among women, Native Americans, and African Americans. These calm, quiet, and introspective revivals bore little resemblance to the riotous and frenzied revivals of the First Great Awakening. On the frontier, Methodist revivals attracted so many followers that, by 1845, Methodism was the largest Christian denomination in the U.S. Revivals inspired the creation of many reform groups and movements, such as the temperance movement, educational reform, and abolition groups. (For the scoop, see "Challenging the Status Quo: Reform Movements of the Mid-19th Century" later in this chapter.)

The transcendentalists

Transcendentalism emerged in the 1830s as another religious movement to challenge rationalism. Transcendentalists were well educated, and most of them resided in New England. They believed that people gained knowledge through truth, insight, intuition, and their senses rather than through intellect and reason. They believed in freedom for all people; they rejected materialism; they placed great importance on self-reliance; they believed in the unity of man and nature; and they sought to redefine spirituality and religion.

Two well-known transcendentalists were *Ralph Waldo Emerson* and *Henry David Thoreau,* both authors. In Emerson's well-known essays, "Nature" and "Self-Reliance," Emerson, a *Unitarian* (one who believes in the oneness of God and rejects that Jesus is God) minister, school teacher, and notable essayist, commented that trust and belief in oneself and respect for the natural world were two essential components of a fulfilling life. Thoreau advocated a simple life that was free from materialism in his book *Walden,* and he's most famous for living in a cabin in the woods for two years, free from the restraints and oppression of society and civilization. In addition to being the first American environmentalist, Thoreau was a well-known abolitionist and had strong political views. In the late 1840s, he had a short stint in jail after he refused to pay his taxes for political reasons, and it inspired him to write his essay "Civil Disobedience" in 1849.

For the SAT II keep in mind that the philosophies promoted by evangelists and transcendentalists of this period tied in well with the abolition movement and the eventual determination to end slavery in America.

Landscapes and Native Americans in art

Uniquely American art emerged by the 1820s. Artists, inspired by romanticism, painted American themes and subjects in their art. Art was also important because it was the only way to keep visual records.

Many artists began painting portraits of people and scenes of Americans in action. Beginning in 1835, the artists of the Hudson River School, including Thomas Cole and Asher Durand, painted the dramatic landscapes of the Hudson River Valley that depicted the peaceful coexistence of humans and nature. Some artists journeyed west to paint the landscapes and portraits of Native Americans. George Caitlin is a well-known artist of the 1820s and 1830s who painted and drew honest accounts of Native Americans of the West going about their daily tasks as well as their ceremonial traditions. Other artists painted and drew pictures of scientific subjects. One of the best known of these artists is John James Audubon, who in the 1820s drew and painted a large series of pictures of birds in their natural settings (as opposed to painting them dead, stuffed, and in a still-life, which many artists did at the time).

Launching the American literary canon

By 1820, America still didn't have its own literary traditions. Professors at universities, such as Harvard and Yale, began encouraging their students to become writers. Until this time, hardly any literature had American themes, American characters, or American settings. Many authors who emerged in the early to mid-1800s were inspired by the transcendentalism movement (see the earlier section "The transcendentalists" in this chapter) and/or were tired of Europeans overshadowing them culturally and, in response, developed a unique national literature.

Many famous American writers came from this period. *James Fenimore Cooper* wrote stories about the American frontier including *The Last of the Mohicans* and *The Prairie*. *Washington Irving* wrote colonial accounts that took place in the Hudson River Valley, including *The Legend of Sleepy Hollow*. Some other literary greats included *Nathaniel Hawthorne* (*The Scarlet Letter*), *Edgar Allan Poe* (*The Raven*), *Herman Melville* (*Moby-Dick*), and *Henry David Thoreau* (*Walden*). Notable poets and essayists included Walt Whitman, Henry Wadsworth Longfellow, and Ralph Waldo Emerson.

Widening Horizons: Mid-19th Century Expansion

The Louisiana Purchase (see Chapter 6) at the beginning of the 19th century was just the beginning of U.S. designs on the land west of the original colonies. After clearing up a little land matter with Britain that established Maine's state boundary in 1820, the U.S. set its sights on the West to realize what would come to be known as *manifest destiny*.

In 1845, a New York journalist coined the term "manifest destiny," which was the belief that the United States was entitled to expand west into Texas and all the way to the Pacific Ocean to be a nation that spread from coast to coast. Although the term was not used until 1845, the concept of manifest destiny had been in the works since the War of 1812 (see Chapter 6) when the warhawks declared that it was a divine mission for the United States to expand across the western frontier. Until 1845, the frontier began at the Mississippi River. In the mid-19th century, however, several different land acquisitions helped the United States expand to include what we now refer to as the "lower 48." More about manifest destiny comes up in Chapter 9, where we talk about how the expansion of the U.S. affected the slavery issue.

For the purpose of the SAT II U.S. History exam, remember that Americans felt that their desire to expand westward was an inevitable and noble endeavor. Even though Mexico and Britain held these other territories, the United States felt it was entitled to acquire them.

Defining Maine: The Webster–Ashburton Treaty

At the end of the Revolutionary War, the United States and Britain hadn't specifically defined the boundary between present-day Maine (then part of Massachusetts) and New Brunswick, Canada. After Maine achieved statehood in 1820, friction developed over this boundary. In 1842, Daniel Webster, secretary of state under President Tyler, negotiated with the British foreign minister Baron Ashburton to clearly define the northern border of Maine. In these negotiations, the U.S. gained control over approximately ⅔ of the 12,000 square miles in dispute. Furthermore, the treaty allowed the U.S. to take one of its final steps to achieve complete peace with Britain. The boundary dispute with Britain over Maine wasn't really considered a part of manifest destiny. It was more accurately a final push by the United States to push Britain out of its affairs once and for all.

Messing with Texas: Annexation

After Mexico gained independence from Spain in 1821, Americans began to move into the Mexican territory of Texas. By 1830, Americans outnumbered Mexican settlers six to one. This fact alarmed the Mexican government, which immediately placed a ban on further American settlement and strictly enforced the ban on slavery and Protestantism in the area. (Mexico had previously banned slavery in Texas, but many American farmers ignored this law and brought their slaves anyway.) Finally fed up with the oppressive Mexican rule, Texans rebelled under the leadership of General Sam Houston in 1834.

Serious fighting began with the *Battle of the Alamo* in March 1836 after a few minor battles occurred in October 1835. The decisive victory for the Texans was at the Battle of San Jacinto in April 1836. The rebels fought Mexico for eight months before they declared victory and named Texas the Lone Star Republic in 1836. Issues with slavery kept American presidents and the Senate from approving the annexation of Texas until James K. Polk won the 1844 election. Early in Polk's presidency, Congress approved the annexation of Texas under a joint resolution, making it the 28th state.

Out on the coast: Settling Oregon

The U.S and Britain each claimed possession of the Oregon Territory, which included present-day Oregon, Washington, Idaho, western Canada, and parts of Wyoming and Montana. As part of its goal to achieve manifest destiny, the U.S. desired to push westward into the Oregon territory and push Britain out.

The dispute began when the first wagon train of American settlers arrived in Oregon via the *Oregon Trail* in 1842. The following year, more than 1,000 people followed the trail west, making the difficult 2,000-mile long, six-month journey from Independence, Missouri, to start new lives in the fertile lands of Oregon's Willamette Valley. These new settlers quickly obtained political control of the territory and desired for the U.S. to officially acquire control of the territory.

In his 1844 political campaign, presidential candidate James K. Polk's campaign slogan was "Fifty-four Forty or Fight." This slogan referred to Polk's desire to take possession of the entire Oregon Territory (latitude coordinates 54 degrees longitude, and 40 degrees latitude) claimed by both the U.S. and Britain. However, when disputes erupted in Oregon in 1846, President Polk was busy with the war with Mexico (which we cover later in this chapter) and not eager to enter into another war with Great Britain, so he decided to compromise. In 1846, he signed *The Oregon Treaty* with Britain that split the Oregon Territory at the 49th parallel, which gave the U.S. everything below the 49th parallel (present-day Oregon, Washington, Idaho, and parts of Montana and Wyoming) and gave Britain everything above that line (western Canada).

What a trip! Journeys to the West

Americans wanted to move westward for many reasons. Some were after riches and wealth. Others desired fertile and plentiful land to farm. Still others desired adventure. As the population increased in the first half of the 1800s, Americans looked west for opportunities.

The road to riches: The Santa Fe Trail

Rumors of vast wealth and riches in the Spanish-ruled town of Santa Fe (in present-day New Mexico) tempted many American traders and explorers, but they were deterred by the fact that the first explorers who did go there were immediately thrown in jail because outsiders weren't welcome in the Spanish-ruled Mexican territories. Fortunately, in 1821, Mexico became free of Spanish rule. That year, William Becknell, a trader from Missouri, led an expedition from Independence, Missouri, to Santa Fe and returned — much richer, mind you — with blessings from the governor of New Mexico that American merchants and traders were welcome to come trade in the Mexican territories. Becknell returned with his men and many wagons full of goods to trade. They blazed a shortcut to Santa Fe, which they named the Cimarron Cutoff, and soon returned to Missouri with even more wealth.

When other merchants learned of Becknell's success, many followed in his footsteps, making the six-week long, 800-mile, difficult trip over the waterless desert. The traders faced many challenges, from confrontations with hostile Native Americans, to rattlesnakes, to harsh weather, to lack of water, but many still embraced the exciting adventure along the route southwest. Despite the challenges, the trail remained extremely popular from its instigation in 1821 until the railroad came to the area in 1880.

Gotta get away: The Mormons

In New York in 1820, 14-year-old Joseph Smith, claimed that he had a revelation in which God and Jesus visited him, leading him to find the buried Book of Mormon, similar to the Bible, engraved on golden tablets. He spent the next several years translating these tablets, which he published into the Book of Mormon ten years later. Within a few years of the publication of the Book of Mormon, Smith went from having six followers to thousands of followers and led these people (a majority were women) on a quest to find their "new Zion." Despite the fact that the 1st Amendment forbids religious persecution, the *Mormons,* otherwise known as the members of the Church of Jesus Christ of Latter-Day Saints, found themselves driven from New York to Ohio, to Missouri, and then to Illinois, where Smith was murdered during his campaign for president of the United States in the election of 1844.

Brigham Young, one of the Mormon apostles at the time of Smith's assassination, came to the rescue. He led the Mormons from Illinois to settle in present-day Utah, which was Mexican territory in 1847. You may wonder why the Mormons faced violent religious persecution until they settled in Utah. We'll tell you:

- Many people were suspicious of the Mormons' success at recruiting new members to the church and also didn't like them because they were very different from other Christian denominations.

✔ In addition, the Mormons practiced polygamy (in other words, it was okay for a man to have multiple wives). Non-Mormons believed that this practice was wrong.

✔ Many people were also offended by the Mormons' practice of going on missions with the goal to convert others to their religion.

✔ Finally, many people feared that the Mormons would oppose slavery, which was an extremely divisive issue at the time.

Seeking some gold: The rush to California

California faced a unique situation when American carpenter James Marshall struck gold while he was building a mill for John Sutter in 1848. Nine days after gold was discovered, the U.S. annexed California under the Treaty of Guadalupe Hidalgo (see the next section). Before too long, word got out about the gold, and the *California Gold Rush* of 1849 began. Before long, prospectors were flocking to California from all over the world to seek their fortunes (some were very successful; others went home empty-handed). Within a year, the population of California had increased by more than 100,000 people; the population of San Francisco went from 812 to 25,000 in one year. (Check out Chapter 11 for more about mining's heyday.)

With this dramatic population increase, California needed to organize a government quickly. In response, a group of Californians got together to form a government in 1849. They wrote a constitution, elected a governor, banned slavery, and requested that California be admitted to the U.S. as a free state. Within a year, under the Compromise of 1850, California was admitted to the union as the 31st state. (See Chapter 9 for more about the compromise.)

Waging the Mexican War

Mexico wasn't impressed that the U.S. had annexed Texas. Mexico's current government didn't even recognize Texas as an independent nation, even though it won its independence in 1836. Even worse, Mexico and the U.S. didn't agree on the southern border of Texas. The U.S. government thought the Rio Grande was the border, but the Mexican government thought the border was much farther north. When Mexican forces attacked U.S. troops stationed in the disputed region in 1846, the U.S. declared war on Mexico.

President James K. Polk and other Americans saw war with Mexico as an opportunity. For years, the U.S. had been trying to purchase California and the New Mexico Territory from Mexico. For two years, the U.S. fought Mexico as the fighting spread from Texas into New Mexico, California, into northern Mexico and, finally, into Mexico City, where the United States declared victory. In February 1848, the U.S. and Mexico signed the *Treaty of Guadalupe Hidalgo* and officially ended the war.

For the purposes of the SAT II, know that The Treaty of Guadalupe Hidalgo had two main points: First, it established the southern border of Texas as the Rio Grande. Second, in recognition of the U.S. victory, Mexico gave the U.S. the *Mexican Cession* — that is, California, Nevada, Utah, Arizona, and parts of Colorado, New Mexico, and Wyoming for the bargain price (even in those days) of $15 million.

The Wilmot Proviso and the election of 1848

While the Mexican War was going on, Congressman David Wilmot of Pennsylvania sensed that some trouble might ensue if the U.S. ever annexed Texas, California, and the New Mexico Territory from Mexico. In 1846, he proposed the *Wilmot Proviso,* which would prohibit slavery in any territories that the U.S. acquired from Mexico. The House easily passed the proposal, but the Senate did not. Most Southerners, of course, didn't like this proposal because they wanted all new territories to be slave-holding, whereas most Northerners agreed with Wilmot's proposal.

For the 1848 election, antislavery Whigs, abolitionists, and supporters of the Wilmot Proviso teamed up to create the *Free-Soil Party,* a political party that supported the abolition of slavery. They nominated former president Martin Van Buren (1836–1840) as their presidential candidate (see Chapter 7 for more about him). Although Van Buren didn't win any electoral votes, he won 10 percent of the popular vote. Democratic candidate Lewis Cass supported the Wilmot Proviso and advocated *popular sovereignty* (the idea that a territory could decide for itself whether or not to allow slavery) for the added territories. Zachary Taylor, a Mexican War hero and the Whig candidate, who opposed the expansion of slavery into the new territories, became president.

Tying it all together: A sample question looks at U.S expansion from 1820–1850

The SAT II may use a quote or a paraphrase of a quote to test your knowledge of philosophies and ideals. This sample question may throw you off a bit because the paraphrase comes from someone who's known for his stand on abolition, but it deals with American expansionist policy.

Abolitionist Frederick Douglass said that those who were loudly in favor of the Mexican War and heralded its violent victories with apparent glee robbed Mexico of her territory. He concluded by saying that Americans should not be rejoicing about the victory but rather should be ashamed of it. Douglass's sentiment is in direct disagreement with which of the following ideals?

(A) The Wilmot Proviso

(B) Transcendentalism

(C) Social Darwinism

(D) Manifest destiny

(E) Popular sovereignty

Before you look at the answer choices, analyze what Douglass said. He said that robbing territory from Mexico for American possession is shameful. Now look at the answer choices to determine which is most opposed to Douglass's theme.

Even though Douglass was an abolitionist, he isn't speaking about slavery in this instance, and the Wilmot Proviso opposed slavery, so answer (A) doesn't relate, nor would it disagree with Douglass's statement. Answer (B) is also wrong because transcendentalists opposed violence. Popular sovereignty was also an unrelated slavery issue that abolitionist Douglass would agree with, so (E) isn't right. That leaves social Darwinism, which essentially says that certain groups are genetically destined to dominate other groups (see Chapter 12), and manifest destiny. Answer (C) is closer to the right answer than the other three we just mentioned, and it could be right if manifest destiny wasn't an option. You always choose the best answer, and the best answer is (D), because manifest destiny deals specifically with the notion that America had the right to expand to the Pacific Ocean using any means possible, and the Mexican War was a direct means to achieving this goal.

All Business: The First Industrial Revolution

Around the same time that America was advancing westward, it also was advancing its technology. The First Industrial Revolution began in Great Britain in the 18th century, but by the 1820s, it had spread to the U.S. American enthusiasm for new philosophies and new territories also welcomed new technology (like the steam-powered printing press) that made spreading ideas across the new territory easier. Inventions that allowed for increased productivity and employment in factories changed the way that Americans made money — especially in the North — and the era of big business began.

A changing economy: The growth of industry

The first half of the 19th century brought exciting changes and developments in work systems and technology. It also saw the rise of the American corporation.

The creation of factories

During the first half of the 19th century, America transformed from a craft-based society to a manufacturing society because of advances in technology, such as the steam engine. And, out of this transformation, the American factory system was born. The first mills were built in New England, and these mills produced textiles and operated on water power, which was successful but posed geographic limitations. One of the most famous textile mills was in Lowell, Massachusetts, built in 1813, where a whole town built up to support the mill and house the workers. The workers at Lowell were mainly teenage girls from New England farm families and immigrants, called "Lowell Girls."

But factories didn't only manufacture textiles. Americans successfully transferred the factory system to many other industries, including the manufacturing of firearms, thanks to the development of a system of interchangeable parts, and the manufacture of iron and of machinery. Before the 1820s, where a factory could operate was severely limited because factories were dependent on hydropower (water power), so they had to be by a river. Later in the century, coal or steam powered many factories, which allowed factories more freedom to locate where they wanted.

Advances in technology

The first half of the 1800s welcomed many advances in technology. Americans embraced advances in transportation — such as the invention of the steamboat, the locomotive, and canals — which helped people and goods get from place to place more easily. Here are some of the accomplishments that Americans made in transportation during this era:

 ✔ **The steamboat:** Robert Fulton introduced the steamboat *Clermont,* on the Hudson River in August 1807. By the 1820s, steamboats had made their way onto the Mississippi and Missouri rivers, which led to a boom in commerce in the area and established the rivers as an important trade route. Steamboats remained a critical link between the East and the frontier until the advent of the steam railroad in the 1850s. After the 1850s, they remained crucial to transportation along the north-south routes of the Mississippi and Missouri Rivers.

 ✔ **The Erie Canal:** The Erie Canal was the first large-scale canal built in America. Finished in 1825, the Erie Canal connected the Great Lakes to the Northeast. Canals were vital at this time because they not only transported goods quickly, but they also easily transported people. By mid-century, the U.S. had built a whole network of canals connecting the Northeast to many new states in the West. It would seem slow now, but at the time, traveling to the frontier via canal was fast and relatively easy.

 ✔ **The railroad:** The first railroad operated in the United States in 1830; however, traveling by railroad at this time still wasn't very safe or reliable. In February 1854, a steam engine railroad traveled from the East Coast to Rock Island, Illinois, the first to make that long of a trip. Between 1830 and 1860, the U.S. laid 30,000 miles of railroad track and, within a few decades, railroads controlled East-West commerce in the United States. (See Chapter 11 for more details about the railroad era.)

Advances in architecture and engineering allowed contractors to build larger buildings. The first large-scale hotels, complete with bathing rooms and water closets, went up in Boston and New York in the 1830s. And New York City was home to the first department store. At the time, the idea of one store that sold almost everything was a novel concept.

Communication also improved. Newspapers gained popularity during this period. Before the widespread use of the steam-powered printing press in the 1830s, newspapers were expensive, and most Americans couldn't afford them. In 1833, publisher Benjamin Day began selling his paper *The New York Sun* for a mere penny a copy. To attract common working folks, Day published more sensational stories in his paper. Other publishers followed suit and, within eight years, nearly 1,300 more newspapers were published in the United States. To enhance communication across the growing nation, Samuel Morse patented the electric telegraph in 1844, which allowed people to send messages from one telegraph office to another one far away using codes sent over wires.

The development of corporations

Americans weren't very friendly to corporations in the early 1800s. They still favored local businesses, which were usually small, family-owned and, therefore, more approachable. Only about 200 or so corporations operated in the U.S. at that time. This changed, however, during the First Industrial Revolution when the railroads opened up markets and technology allowed for greater efficiency. Businesses grew and made greater profits, and groups of people could more effectively run large businesses than one or two private owners could. By the time the Second Industrial Revolution boomed, corporations were the preferred form of large business.

The changing face of the American worker

In the 1800s, most Americans didn't have jobs outside their homes; they worked on their farms. Even in 1850, 85 percent of Americans lived on a farm. But with the introduction of factories in America, people's work lives changed drastically. Women, children, and immigrants especially were affected by these labor changes, and with more people working outside their homes, the labor movement kicked into gear.

Women and children in the work world

Some women and children began to work outside the home as more factories opened. Not all women worked out of necessity; some just worked for the adventure of it or to earn some money before they married. Children and teens from large or poor families often worked to help support the family when there wasn't enough work for them at home.

Factory owners liked to hire women because they worked for lower wages than men. Factories also liked to hire children because they worked for even lower wages than women and were often agile, quick workers. Young children worked incredible ten- or more hour days in factories with very few breaks and no rest. Understandably, factories had many accidents — sometimes fatal — that involved workers. Think how tired you'd be if you'd been working on your feet in a factory for 12 hours! Needless to say, by today's standards, the working conditions, hours, and wages were often atrociously poor for all factory workers.

Conditions were also extremely poor in the iron mills and coal mines, where mostly men and children worked. Workers worked six days per week and up to 14 hours per day. Children often started working in the mills and mines at age nine or ten and worked there until they died. Workers at mills and mines often died prematurely due to accidents, years of back-breaking labor, and because the chemicals and dust in the air destroyed their lungs.

The role of immigrants

Immigrants also became part of the new labor force in America. Between 1847 and 1854, nearly two million Irish immigrants entered the U.S. because of the Great Potato Famine in Ireland. Large groups of immigrants also came from China, Germany, Sweden, Italy, Russia, and Greece. Approximately 80 percent of immigrants came to the U.S. from Europe. In proportion to the United States' total population, between 1845 and 1860, more immigrants entered the U.S. than at any other time in history. Until the 1880s, the U.S. government didn't restrict any ethnic groups from immigrating to the U.S.

Some immigrants came from 1820 to 1860 to try their luck at gold in California (see the section "Seeking some gold: The rush to California" earlier in this chapter) or to work on the railroads. Others came to start new lives, to escape political or religious persecution in their native countries, to seek regular work, or to seek their fortunes. Although some immigrants became farmers or headed west, many others moved to the cities to seek jobs in factories, mills, and shops. In the cities, immigrants struggled to survive and many lived in conditions of poverty because wages for immigrant workers were very low.

The birth of the labor movement

The first labor unions for *skilled workers* (those who had particular specialized training or education in their work, such as carpenters, printers, glassblowers, and so on.) appeared in the 1790s. However, *unskilled workers* didn't begin organizing labor unions until the 1820s. During this period, factory workers organized to demand a shorter work day, higher wages, and better working conditions. Throughout the 1830s and 1840s, female factory workers in Lowell, Massachusetts, went on strike numerous times without much success. Because of the influx of immigrants to the U.S. during this time and the ready labor force they created, unskilled laborers didn't have much success at labor organization until the 1860s (see Chapter 12 for more details).

Challenging the Status Quo: Reform Movements of the Mid-19th Century

Many reform movements organized in the early half of the 1800s as many Americans sought cures for the ills of society. Although some Americans organized reform movements according to the ideals of religious groups, people formed others as a reaction to the injustice, inequality, and discrimination in American society. Reformers hoped to solve the problems of society through increased public awareness and affect change in public policies.

A utopian environment: Communal living

Some groups became dissatisfied with American society and believed that they could better meet their needs by living with other like-minded people in small, self-sufficient societies. These hypothetically perfect societies became known as *utopian communities.* Although some utopian communities formed on the basis of religious beliefs, others formed based on philosophies of marriage, politics, and occupation. Many utopian communities that developed during the 1820s to the 1840s and lasted until the 1850s.

New Harmony was a utopian experiment founded in Indiana in 1825 by Robert Owen. It broke up four years later because the members quarreled so much (so much for perfection!). *Brook Farm* was a transcendentalist utopian experiment based on the concept of self-reliance that existed outside of Boston from 1841 to 1847 (for more on transcendentalism, see the section "The transcendentalists" earlier in this chapter). The only utopian community that lasted beyond the 1850s was the unconventional, perfectionist, and socially progressive *Oneida*

Commune in Oneida, New York, which didn't fizzle out until the 1880s. Here's an interesting fact that probably won't ever end up on an SAT II U.S. History exam: The Oneida commune created the company Oneida, Ltd., in 1879, one of the largest manufacturers of silver and stainless flatware in the world.

An end to playing hooky: Education reform

As a result of all free white males being able to vote in 1828, Americans began to call for education reform around the 1830s. Until that time, only New England had free public schools. Most schools, especially in rural areas, were one-room schoolhouses where children received a minimal education and, in places other than New England, people usually had to pay for education. Only half the white boys and girls in the U.S. even attended school in the early 1800s.

Education reformers called for free public education as a means to educate future voters and as a measure to prevent poverty and crime. But not everyone agreed with the reformers. Many Americans didn't want to pay additional taxes for public education because they didn't like paying taxes in the first place. Many religious groups already provided schools for their children and didn't want to pay taxes for other children to attend school, either.

When *Horace Mann* was secretary of the Massachusetts Board of Education from 1837 to 1848, he doubled the state's funding for schools and teachers' salaries. He created teacher-training programs, divided students into grades, established the use of textbooks, and required that every Massachusetts boy and girl attend school six months each year. Many other states looked at Massachusetts' education reform as an example and followed suit. By the 1850s, free public schools were commonplace in the Northern states. From the 1830s until the 1860s, the South made little progress in terms of education, mostly because the population was so spread out. Southern children were educated at home or wealthy parents sent their kids abroad or to Northern schools. In the 1820s and 1830s, Noah Webster wrote some of the first school textbooks and spelling books in America. His claim to fame: He also wrote the first American dictionary.

Second thoughts to locking up: Reforms in prisons and mental hospitals

The early to mid-1800s wasn't a good time to have a mental illness (well, not that there's ever a good time to have a mental illness . . . , but we digress). People who had mental illnesses during this time were sent to either prison alongside all sorts of criminals or to live in the poorhouse with those who couldn't pay their debts. And prisons and poorhouses provided poor living conditions and didn't provide counseling, rehabilitation, treatment, or social services for any of the inmates.

You go first: Mary Lyon and Mount Holyoke College

Mary Lyon, a young woman from Buckland, Massachusetts, loved studying and often studied up to 18 hours each day. She really wanted to go to college and was disappointed that no colleges for women existed. So, naturally, she founded the first one: Mount Holyoke College. In 1837, Mount Holyoke College opened in South Hadley, Massachusetts, to an entirely female student body of more than 100 mostly privileged female students. Mount Holyoke College is the oldest of the Seven Sisters (seven all-female colleges) and now enrolls approximately 2,100 students each year. Some famous alumni include author Emily Dickinson, Francis Perkins, the first female cabinet member, and Ella Grasso, the first female state governor.

Dorothea Dix, a social reformer, was outraged that the mentally ill were sent to prisons with no hope of treatment. This Massachusetts schoolteacher worked throughout the 1840s with other reformers to change how prisoners, the poor, and the mentally ill were treated. These reformers helped

- Open hospitals for the mentally ill
- End the physical abuse of prisoners and the mentally ill in institutions
- Keep men, women, and children in separate quarters
- Abolish the practice of imprisoning poor people who couldn't pay their debts

Ahead of their time: The women's rights movement

Women in the early to mid-1800s had few rights. They couldn't vote, hold public office, sue in court, or keep their own paychecks or property if they married. Women had no legal rights regarding their children, and they had limited access to education, though ironically, teaching was the only profession that welcomed them. This lack of rights understandably annoyed many women. They thought that men and women were created equal so they should have equal legal rights.

Three leading reformers for women's rights were *Susan B. Anthony, Elizabeth Cady Stanton,* and *Lucretia Mott.* These women organized the *Seneca Falls Convention* — a women's rights convention — in Seneca Falls, New York, in 1848. At the convention, they drafted a document modeled after the Declaration of Independence called the Declaration of Sentiments that declared women were equal to men. Unfortunately, the reformers weren't able to bring about much change as a result of this convention and their other reform approaches. Although these female reformers got the ball rolling on suffrage (that is, obtaining the right to vote for women), the results of these efforts weren't seen until 1920 (see Chapter 14 for the scoop on women's suffrage).

Everything in moderation: The temperance movement

In the early to mid-1800s, alcohol sales rose, and drinking and getting drunk was an extremely popular pastime, especially for men. Reformers, many of whom were leaders in Protestant religious communities, saw a connection between the increased use of alcohol and crime, fighting, violence, poverty, mental illness, poor job performance, increased accidents in the workplace, and spousal and child abuse. These reformers established temperance societies throughout the U.S. and petitioned state governments to make alcohol illegal.

One leader of the temperance movement was Neal Dow, a Maine businessman. Dow was disgusted with the effects that alcohol had on his community and lobbied the state government to outlaw liquor manufacturing and sales. His efforts proved to be a success when the state passed the "Maine Law" in 1851. Maine became the first state with a prohibition (no liquor sales or manufacture) law. By the 1850s, more than 5,000 temperance societies had formed, and alcohol consumption had decreased nationwide. By 1855, 13 of the 31 states had enacted laws modeled after the Maine Law.

The most explosive social evil: The antislavery movement

Southerners felt that slavery was a necessary evil. During the first half of the 19th century, cotton became an enormously profitable crop in the South because of the invention of the cotton gin and because of the growing textile industry in the North and in Britain. For these reasons, more and more southerners supported keeping slavery.

In 1808, Congress banned slave importation, but smuggling slaves was a widespread problem until the 1850s. With the country expanding westward, slavery become a hot-button issue: Would the U.S. allow slavery in new states? Abolitionists (the people against slavery) desperately wanted to stop the expansion of slavery into new territories and to outlaw it altogether. The South, however, fought back.

The plight of enslaved and free African Americans

Between 1810 and 1830, the slave population in the South had doubled. By 1850, the United States grew more than 80 percent of the world's cotton, and with the ever-increasing demand for cotton, southern plantation owners needed lots of labor to run their large cotton plantations.

More than 75 percent of slaves in the U.S. worked on these plantations, where they often lived in squalid conditions, were abused by their owners, and weren't allowed to learn to read or write. Owners expected their slaves to be completely submissive and to keep all their thoughts and opinions to themselves. Understandably, slaves were fed up with being treated badly and, by the middle of the century, the widespread oppression led to an increasing frequency of slave uprisings and escapes.

Free blacks who lived in the North didn't necessarily have a higher quality of life than the slaves in the South did. Many free blacks lived in poverty and had a hard time finding work. Blacks didn't always enjoy the same rights and privileges that whites did, such as public education, the right to vote, and land ownership, and whites often discriminated against them.

The abolitionists strive to stop slavery

Abolitionists ramped up their efforts to end slavery beginning in the 1830s. Northern abolitionists began helping slaves escape to the free states or to Canada. In fact, white abolitionists and free blacks developed the **Underground Railroad,** a secret network that helped slaves escape to freedom. **Harriet Tubman** was a notable abolitionist and former slave who escaped from a Maryland plantation in 1849. After she reached freedom, she joined the abolitionist movement and made more than two dozen trips to the South to help more than 300 slaves, including her parents, reach freedom.

Another event that helped antislavery sentiment to gather steam in the North was the publication of abolitionist Harriet Beecher Stowe's novel, *Uncle Tom's Cabin.* Published in 1852, the novel told the stories of slaves escaping to the North via the Underground Railroad. The novel added fuel to the fire of the antislavery movement and became an immediate bestseller in the North, selling more than 300,000 copies in its first year of publication.

Other famous abolitionists included **William Lloyd Garrison,** who established *The Liberator,* an abolitionist newspaper, and two antislavery organizations; **Sojourner Truth,** a freed slave who was also active in the evangelical and women's movements; and **Frederick Douglass,** a former slave who escaped to the North in 1838 and advocated equal civil rights for blacks.

Some abolitionists called for the *emancipation* (freeing) of all slaves and for the U.S. to return all blacks to Africa or the Caribbean (for more on this topic, see the next section). Other abolitionists called for the emancipation of all slaves and for the government to give all blacks complete civil rights.

The South responds

Southerners were enraged with northerners for meddling in their affairs. As a reaction to the Underground Railroad and as a way to appease southerners, Congress strengthened the Fugitive Slave Act's *Fugitive Slave Law,* which went into effect in 1850. Under this law, those who assisted a slave's escape or didn't report that one had escaped faced heavy fines and penalties. In addition, federal marshals had the authority to enter free northern states, capture escaped slaves in those free states, and return them to their owners in the South. Under the revisions, northerners were also forced to aid in the capture and return of fugitives. This enforcement stirred up resentment even among northerners who hadn't before had an opinion about slavery. Southerners applauded the measure because they saw escaped slaves as their property and felt that northerners were helping to steal their property by allowing escaped slaves to reside freely in free states. (The strengthening of the Fugitive Slave Act was a part of the Compromise of 1850; see Chapter 9.)

People in the South answered the abolitionists' efforts in several ways:

✔ Fed up with the abolitionists constantly appealing to Congress with numerous petitions calling for an end to slavery, southern Congressmen decided to take a stand. In 1836, they pushed some new *gag rules,* which were rules that prohibited the House and the Senate from discussing antislavery issues and from debating the abolitionist petitions presented to them. The gag rules remained in effect until Congress finally repealed them in 1844 due to ever-increasing pressure from northerners and abolitionists.

✔ Pro-slavery South Carolina Senator and plantation owner James Henry Hammond developed the *"mud-sill" theory* about African Americans. In a speech he gave to the Senate in 1858, Hammond suggested that all societies had a people who were the bottom of the barrel (so to speak) and were born to perform the menial and distasteful tasks of that society. Hammond suggested that blacks fit this role in American society. Those in favor of slavery used this theory as a way to rationalize the rampant discrimination against both slaves and free blacks and as a way to promote the concept of slavery as a positive good.

Tying it all together: A sample question looks at social reforms

SAT II questions about reform movements will often want you to know in what general era they occurred. This sample question asks you to place the reform movements that happened from the 1820s to the 1860s, which is the antebellum period.

Societal reforms achieved during the antebellum period in the United States included all the following EXCEPT

(A) Utopian communities.

(B) The introduction of free public education.

(C) Suffrage for women.

(D) Hospitals for the mentally ill.

(E) Temperance laws.

In this question, you have to pay close attention to the wording. "Antebellum" refers to the period prior to the Civil War. Also note the word "except." The answer is (C) Suffrage for women. Women didn't achieve suffrage in the United States until 1920 with the passage of the 19th Amendment.

Chapter 9

Sibling Rivalry: Building Up to and Waging the Civil War, 1850–1865

The SAT II U.S. History exam usually covers only a couple of questions about the period leading up to and during the Civil War. The questions primarily focus on the slave system and the causes for the strife — not on the details of the actual war. So, this chapter concentrates more on the events leading up to the Civil War than it does on the events during the Civil War. For the exam, you need to know a little about the events before the Civil War, why Abraham Lincoln was such a significant force, and what factors allowed the North to secure a decisive victory over the South.

The Gathering Storm: Events Leading Up to the Civil War

The 1850s were host to many controversies that eventually culminated in the Civil War. The hottest issue was whether or not America should expand slavery into the new states and territories — which was a touchy issue even before 1860. This issue divided the leadership of political parties and served as a great source of conflict and anxiety across the nation. (Think the Wilmot Proviso and the rise of the Free-Soil Party, both of which we cover in Chapter 8.)

Congress conveniently omitted the slavery issue from debate, essentially tabling it until the election of 1852. But ignoring the issue didn't make it go away and, ultimately, the government had to take some sort of initiative. These initiatives were the Compromise of 1850 and the Kansas–Nebraska Act, which we cover in this section. These acts addressed some of the slavery issues; however, they weren't enough to quell the growing animosities among the citizenry. And the weak leadership of Presidents Franklin Pierce and James Buchanan did little to resolve the mounting hostilities.

For the SAT II, keep in mind that during the decade of the 1850s, an ever-increasing tension between the interests of the North and South had been escalating. The two geographical areas primarily clashed on the issues of slavery and states' rights.

An uneasy balance: The Compromise of 1850

Participants of the California Gold Rush of 1849 rushed to San Francisco (see Chapter 8), and the city by the bay grew from a frumpy fishing wick to a burg of 20,000 in a matter of months. The locals petitioned President Zachary Taylor, a Whig, for immediate entrance to the Union as a free state. Because slavery was illegal under Mexican law, California was already a free territory prior to statehood. So Taylor decided to admit California as a state without going through the intermediate process of becoming a territory. Thus, he allowed the people of California to decide how they wanted their state to enter the Union.

Many Southerners abhorred Taylor's decision because it upset the balance of senators from free and slave states, which meant that the Senate would lean toward the interests of the free states. Taylor's decrees inadvertently played into Southerners' frustrations and thoughts of *secession* (separation from the Union).

So the government drafted the *Compromise of 1850* to address the California question. Kentucky Senator Henry Clay and his supporters successfully negotiated concessions from the North while appeasing the slavery interests of the South. The Compromise of 1850 stated the following five resolutions:

- California would enter the Union as a free state.

- The territorial governments in Utah and New Mexico would decide the slavery issue for themselves under the principle of *popular sovereignty.* Under popular sovereignty, the people of each territory would decide whether to permit slavery before seeking admission to the Union.

- Texas would give up its claim to a portion of New Mexico so New Mexico could become a territory and, in exchange, the United States would forgive Texas's war debt.

- Slave trade (but not slavery) would be prohibited in the District of Columbia.

- The United States would initiate a new fugitive slave law (called — you guessed it — the *Fugitive Slave Law*) that would require federal marshals to assist Southerners in capturing slaves who had escaped to the North and required citizens of free states to assist in the capture and return of any escaped slaves. (For more about the Fugitive Slave Act, see Chapter 8).

The Senate hotly debated these resolutions for months. The Northern statesman Daniel Webster surprisingly lambasted his Northern friends for their antislavery stance, and he demanded stringent enforcement of the Fugitive Slave Law. He also reminded the Senate of the ideals of states' rights and the principle of popular sovereignty in defending a state's right to choose to enter as a slave state. But the compromise the congressional windbags articulated after their debate was almost for naught, because President Taylor opposed any compromise.

Taylor didn't get the chance to put up much of a fuss, however, because he died suddenly in July 1850. His vice-president, the unremarkable Whig Millard Fillmore, became the 13th president. Under Fillmore, Democrat Stephen A. Douglas of Illinois took over from Clay as Speaker of the House and divided the compromise bill into separate pieces of legislation. Douglas worked closely with Fillmore and pushed the bundle of legislation known as the Compromise of 1850 through Congress late in 1850.

For the SAT II, remember that for the time being, the Union had addressed its growing pains constitutionally, and the citizens of both the North and South wanted to uphold the tenuous status quo as the country headed into the election of 1852. However, given the South's reliance on the slave trade and the obvious geographic sectional division between the North and South, tranquility in the Union would be difficult to maintain. Figure 9-1 gives you a picture of the balance of free and slave states after the Compromise of 1850.

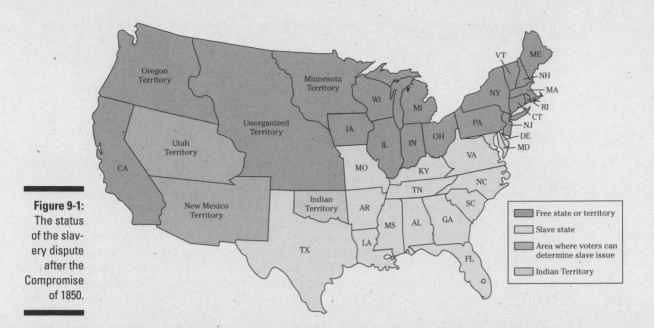

Figure 9-1:
The status
of the slav-
ery dispute
after the
Compromise
of 1850.

Franklin Pierce and increased sectionalism

In the election of 1852, Democrat Franklin Pierce crushed General Winfield Scott, the Whig candidate. After this election, the Whigs literally wigged out; that is, they never ran another candidate for the presidency again. The conflict within the party between antislavery Whigs and pro-slavery Whigs over the Compromise of 1850 provided too much division for the party to overcome, and it disintegrated. Fillmore was the last Whig president.

Once elected president, Pierce promoted the provisions of the Compromise of 1850 and, during the first two years of his presidency, peace and harmony appeared to be the general sentiment of the nation. However, lurking under this peaceful surface was an undercurrent of *sectionalism,* which is when people have an intense allegiance to local interests. (For more about sectionalism, go to Chapter 7.)

During Pierce's tenure (which lasted until 1857), industry and economy in the North boomed, and the South's plantation economy remained the same. The North's strong finances, industrial dominance, and commanding commerce caused Northerners to want Southerners to pay increased taxes for the necessary internal improvements to the Union. Southerners resented the new taxation because they felt it benefited only the Northern states, and not their interests.

The North and South battled over which route the first transcontinental railroad should take. Northerners favored a northern route to increase their profits; Southerners wanted to build the railroad in the South. To please his Southern constituents, Pierce purchased about 30,000 square miles of desert (in what is now Arizona and New Mexico) from Mexico in a transaction called the *Gadsden Purchase,* named after Southern railroad promoter James Gadsden. Pierce intended the first transcontinental railroad to take a southern route.

Additionally, an increase in abolitionist activity made the South feel both underrepresented by the U.S. government and taken advantage of. The cries against slavery were well articulated in the abolitionist movement, which featured the likes of Northerners Frederick Douglass and Harriet Beecher Stowe, who wrote and lectured against the institution of slavery. (You can read more about these characters and the abolition movement in Chapter 8.) Compounding the civil strife were a few Northern states' disregard for provisions of the fugitive slave laws, as the Compromise of 1850 stipulated them. As frustrations grew on both sides, the slippery slope to conflict became slicker.

Southerners' distaste for higher taxes, the North's continuing campaign against slavery, and the conflict over where to build the transcontinental railroad continued to divide the North and South.

Ignoring the Missouri Compromise: The Kansas–Nebraska Act and its effects

In 1854, primarily to make way for the proposed building of a transcontinental railroad along a northern route from Chicago westward, Stephen A. Douglas, submitted a bill to the Senate that would break the Union's treaties with the Native Americans and organize the land west of Missouri and Iowa into territories (the territory marked "Unorganized Territory" in Figure 9-1). The Missouri Compromise of 1820 had outlawed slavery in this territory (see Chapter 7 for more information), but to appease Southerners who opposed the railroad because it would only profit northern cities, Douglas proposed that the government allow the people of this new territory to decide whether to allow slavery there under the principle of popular sovereignty. Because cotton didn't grow in those areas anyway, Douglas didn't think slavery would be an issue.

After much debate and negotiation, this bill, known as the *Kansas–Nebraska Act,* passed with the following provisions:

✔ The government would divide the territory into two parts: Nebraska, to the west of Iowa, and Kansas, to the west of Missouri.

✔ The people of the territory would decide whether or not it would allow slavery there.

✔ The government would allow slavery north of the Missouri Compromise line (36° 30 latitude), which essentially voided the Missouri Compromise.

Kansas was more likely to become a slave state, especially because it was next to the existing slave state of Missouri, and Nebraska was likely to become a free state. See Figure 9-2 to see how the Kansas–Nebraska Act divided the territory of the United States.

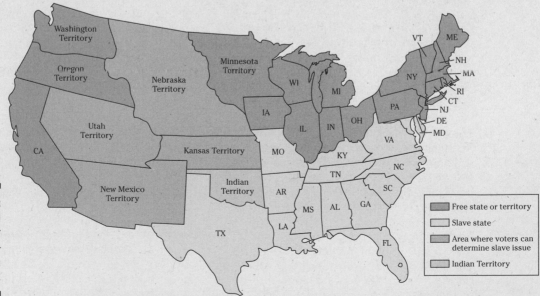

Figure 9-2: The United States after the Kansas–Nebraska Act of 1854.

Douglas thought that the popularity of his Kansas–Nebraska Act would lead him to the White House, but the new act alienated abolitionists, toppled Douglas's haughty position within the Democratic Party, and philosophically divided the Democrats over the issue of slavery. Antislavery politicians who believed that the Kansas–Nebraska Act violated the antislavery promise of the Missouri Compromise formed the Republican Party in February 1854 (for more on the Republican Party see the next section). During and immediately after the 1854 election, the territory of Kansas was a political flashpoint.

Sectional temperatures rose in the United States as a result of the Kansas–Nebraska Act and Republican successes in the election of 1854. Northern abolitionists were fanning the flames of fanaticism to ensure that the Kansas Territory became a free state. Well-heeled abolitionists sponsored trips of approximately 1,000 antislavery Northerners to inhabit the new territory. They were met by a crowd of pro-slavery Southerners.

The first election in the Kansas Territory occurred in 1855. Even though about 2,000 men — mostly Northerners — were registered to vote in the new territory, some 7,000 votes were cast. Apparently, a large number of pro-slavery Missourians, who were generally labeled "border ruffians" because they were armed to the gills, took control of the voting booths and cast four times as many ballots as there were registered voters.

Andrew Reeder, the federally appointed governor of the Kansas Territory, attempted to throw out eight of the 31 members of the new Kansas legislature on the basis of the voting irregularities. Even though Reeder was a Southern sympathizer and appointed by the feds, President Pierce capitulated to Southern demands and the new pro-slavery Kansas legislature and booted Reeder from office.

The new Kansas legislature passed outrageously harsh pro-slavery measures, which didn't seem to bother the antislavery people of Kansas because they just named their own governor and penned their own state constitution, making slavery illegal. Suddenly, Kansas had two governors and two legislatures. Yikes.

The fixed 1855 elections in Kansas focused the nation's attention on sectional, pragmatic, and philosophical tensions in the nation and the new territories. Kansas became a microcosm for the nation's growing internal frustrations. Two governors and two legislatures certainly contributed to near anarchy in Kansas in 1856, when the first of many skirmishes broke out. This first mini-war resulted in the deaths of at least 200 men and gave cause to the name "Bleeding Kansas." (The drama didn't end there; see "The ongoing saga in 'Bleeding Kansas'" later in this chapter.)

Making alliances: New political parties

In 1854, the political party scene changed quite a bit. In early American politics, two main parties existed: the Federalists, who advocated a strong central government, and the Democratic Republicans, who preferred that the federal government be less involved in individuals' lives (see Chapter 6 for more about these two parties). But the presidential election of 1816 was the last time a Federalist ran for president. In the 1824 presidential election, only one official party (the Democratic Republicans) put up candidates for president. But shortly thereafter, the Democratic Republicans split into two parties: Those who supported Andrew Jackson, the Democrats, and those who supported President John Quincy Adams, the National Republicans. The Democrats won the 1828 and 1832 elections. But the National Republican Party fell apart, and many of its members formed the Whig Party (you can read more about the Democrats, National Republicans, and Whigs in Chapter 7).

During most of the 1840s, the two main political parties were the Whigs and the Democrats, but the parties changed again in the 1850s because of anti-immigrant sentiment and the heated conflict over the expansion of slavery.

Curtailing the Catholics: The Know-Nothing movement

In the 1840s, many Irish immigrants came to the United States to escape the Great Potato Famine. Irish immigrants had strong accents and unusual traditions, and American Protestants were concerned about the influence of the Irish and other immigrant groups, like Germans, Italians, and French, that were Roman Catholic. Some feared that the Pope had a plot to take over America and wanted the U.S. to adopt anti-immigration measures to ensure that the country would remain primarily an Anglo-Saxon Protestant nation. These measures included limiting immigration from Catholic countries, requiring public school teachers to be Protestant, and instituting a 21-year waiting period before immigrants could achieve citizenship. Neither the Democrats nor the Whigs seriously considered their concerns, so people with anti-immigrant sentiments began to organize under the *Know-Nothings* because they were secretive about their organization.

Throughout the early 1850s, the Know-Nothings supported candidates from any party as long as they were sympathetic to their anti-immigrant cause. In 1854, a significant number of the candidates they supported won congressional seats and state elections. Encouraged by this success, the movement established itself as an official political party called the *American Party.* The American Party absorbed many members of the Whig Party when it crumbled and many Democrats, mostly from the North, who advocated an anti-immigrant agenda. They ran former president Millard Fillmore as their official candidate for president in 1856, but the party didn't last long. Conflicts over slavery divided members and, by 1860, the party ceased to exist.

Joining forces: The emergence of the Republican Party

Disagreement over the Compromise of 1850 split the Whig Party into two factions: those who opposed slavery and those who advocated the expansion of slavery. Quite a few anti-slavery Whigs joined the newly formed *Free-Soil Party,* which was made up of former Democrats who were abolitionists (see Chapter 8). The Free-Soil Party met with some political success, especially in gaining congressional seats, but the party didn't have enough power to make a viable run for the presidency until it merged with the newly-formed Republican Party.

The conflict produced by the Kansas–Nebraska Act disintegrated what was left of the Whig Party in 1854. The disenfranchised antislavery Whigs, Free-Soilers, and others who wanted to stop the spread of slavery joined together in February 1854 to form the *Republican Party,* which was founded with the primary platform to end the westward expansion of slavery.

In the congressional elections of 1854, the Republicans secured bunches of seats in Congress — more than the established Democratic Party and many more than the American Party. Some American Party members, who also opposed the spread of slavery, joined the Republican Party after the results of the 1854 elections.

Continuing to waffle: The James Buchanan legacy

The election of 1856 was déjà vu all over again for the Democrats, who rejected the incumbent Pierce in favor of the innocuous Pennsylvanian James Buchanan. While the violence in Kansas was going on and questions were arising about Pierce's pro-Southern foreign policy (Pierce had attempted to acquire new territories in Latin America that would enter the Union as slave territories), Buchanan was safely ensconced in Britain as America's Minister to the United Kingdom.

The Republican candidate John C. Fremont (from California) made an impressive showing for a political party with only two years under its belt as he managed to carry 11 states in the election. The American Party candidate, Millard Fillmore, managed to win eight electoral votes, but Buchanan won the election. The strong showing by a Republican candidate from a newly-formed state showed Southern Democrats that they were in danger of losing their pro-slavery, pro-states' rights voice in national politics. Though Buchanan offended few people, he proved to be just as weak as Pierce in settling the mounting conflict between the North and South.

The Dred Scott decision

Two days after Buchanan's inauguration in 1857, the U.S. Supreme Court handed down the dreaded Dred Scott decision. Dred Scott was a slave seeking emancipation from his owner, and he presented a strong case to the Court. Army doctor John Emerson owned Mr. Scott, and brought Scott with him when he moved to the free state of Illinois and then to the free territory of Wisconsin during the 1830s. During their time in Wisconsin and Illinois, both Emerson and Scott met and married their wives. In 1842, the Emersons returned to Missouri with the Scotts, and Emerson died one year later. Emerson left Scott to his widow in his will. Abolitionists encouraged Scott to sue for his freedom in the Missouri state courts, which had established a precedent that a slave who has resided in a free state or territory is automatically free. But the Missouri State Supreme Court reversed its precedent and held that Scott had to remain enslaved because he voluntarily returned to Missouri (as if slaves did anything voluntarily).

The U.S. Supreme Court heard the *Dred Scott v. Sanford* case, and Chief Justice Roger Taney wrote a majority opinion that upheld the protection of property under the 5th Amendment and established that the Missouri Compromise of 1820 (which prohibited slavery in any part of the Louisiana purchase territory) was unconstitutional, which effectively legalized slavery in new territories. The decision stated that African Americans had "no rights a white man is bound to respect" and were the personal property of whites. The Court's opinion further sectionalized an already-divided nation and served a serious blow to Northern abolitionists and the Republican Party. Ironically, even though the six Southerners on the Supreme Court thought that they were doing a great service to the South with the Dred Scott decision, the decision actually fractionalized the Democratic Party by alienating Northern Democrats who opposed the expansion of slavery into new territories.

The Dred Scott decision had such an important role in the escalating tensions between the North and the South that the SAT II is bound to ask a question (or more) about it. Check out the following example.

Which of the following is true about the Dred Scott decision?

(A) It denied a slave his freedom and declared that the federal government had the constitutional right to determine whether states entered the Union as slave states or not.

(B) It gave enslaved people who moved to a free state the right to declare their freedom.

(C) It ruled that the Missouri Compromise was unconstitutional.

(D) It granted a slave his freedom and denied the federal government the right to determine whether states entered the Union as slave states or not.

(E) It angered Northerners because it gave the federal government the constitutional right to determine whether states entered the Union as slave states or not.

Be wary of answer choices that contain more than one component. All parts of the answer must be true for the answer to be true.

The Dred Scott decision denied Scott his freedom and declared that the Missouri Compromise was unconstitutional. The decision also declared that slaves were property and, under the 5th Amendment, property was protected even in free states or territories. Therefore, you can eliminate (B). The Supreme Court definitely denied Scott his freedom, so, you can also eliminate (D). The first part of (A) seems okay, but make sure the rest of it works. The Court said that the government couldn't give a new state the right to prohibit slavery, so the last part of (A) isn't right. Likewise, (E) is wrong. The decision did anger Northerners, but not because it granted the federal government any particular rights. So you're left with (C). By denying the federal government the power to prohibit slavery, the Court essentially declared the Missouri Compromise (which designated new territory as free) unconstitutional.

The ongoing saga in "Bleeding Kansas"

Kansas continued to be a sore point during the Buchanan administration. Buchanan attempted to bring Kansas into the Union as a slave state in an attempt to solidify the support of Southern Democrats, but the antislavery Republicans controlled Kansas and would have nothing to do with legalizing slavery in their state. In 1857, a pro-slavery faction drafted four proposed constitutions that protected slavery in Kansas.

Congress didn't ratify any of the pro-slavery constitutions and establish Kansas as a slave state. Southern states threatened to secede from the Union because the impending imbalance of free and slave states threatened to diminish the South's power in Congress. After much haggling, the U.S. House of Representatives essentially gave Kansas voters the responsibility to adopt the pro-slavery constitution. Predominantly antislavery Kansans rejected the constitution and, in 1861, the territory entered the Union as a free state. But as a testimony to the conflict, the new state's constitution outlawed slavery but free blacks couldn't live there.

John Brown and the raid on Harper's Ferry

Tensions rose to an all-time high when abolitionist *John Brown* and an interracial group of 21 men attempted to ignite a slave rebellion by attacking the federal arsenal at *Harper's Ferry,* Virginia, in 1859. Brown and his men were captured in 36 hours, and not one slave joined the rebellion. But the event incited fear in the hearts of Southerners, which prompted them to strengthen their militias. Though many leaders deplored Brown's act of violence, abolitionist Northerners proclaimed Brown a hero. By the time the government hanged Brown for this insurrection, he had achieved almost godlike status in the minds of some antislavery Northerners.

The Heart of the Matter: Events Surrounding Abraham Lincoln's 1860 Election

The tensions brewing between the North and South in the 1850s eventually came to a boil. And an Illinois lawyer named Abraham Lincoln brought them to a boiling point. His actions brought about the end of sanctioned slavery in America and fended off an attempt to split the United States into two nations. The decisions Lincoln made affected the state of the U.S. forever.

Surprisingly, Lincoln doesn't appear too frequently on SAT II tests — probably because he is well known (gracing the penny and all), and the SAT II likes to test you on more obscure topics. But all topics are fair game; so as you read about Lincoln, take in his political significance. Focus specifically on how his rise to the presidency precipitated the South's secession.

The Lincoln–Douglas Debates

In the 1858 midterm elections, Abraham Lincoln, a little-known Republican politician, ran against Stephen A. Douglas, a well-known Democratic politician, for the Illinois Senate seat. In order to create a little publicity, Lincoln challenged Douglas to a series of seven open-air debates (known as the *Lincoln–Douglas Debates*) in various Illinois cities. Although the topics of the debates varied, slavery quickly became the hottest issue.

Both men quickly took the verbal offensive to make their opponent look incompetent. Douglas was the first to lash out against Lincoln. According to Douglas, Lincoln was an avid abolitionist who hoped to end slavery and make blacks and whites equal. (Thankfully, these accusations don't sound damaging these days, but in those days, they were fighting words.) Douglas tried to instill fear in the people of Illinois by claiming that if Lincoln were elected, freed black men would flock to Illinois, take jobs from white men, and marry white women. Lincoln countered Douglas by maintaining that he did want to stop the extension of slavery into the territories and asked Douglas to explain his ideas for popular sovereignty in the territories, which caused Douglas to state his *Freeport Doctrine.* In this doctrine, Douglas said that people could choose to prohibit slavery in their territories even though the Supreme Court in the Dred Scott decision forbid prohibiting slavery. The popular sovereignty issue was a tricky one for Douglas. His defense of the people's right to choose whether or not they allowed slavery alienated Southern Democrats because the position was not strongly pro-slavery. Likewise, the position turned off antislavery advocates because popular sovereignty allowed for the possibility of the spread of slavery. Lincoln made it clear that he opposed the spread of slavery but, he, in no way, intended for whites and blacks to be political or social equals. This moderate position made him acceptable to the same Northerners who Douglas was alienating.

In the end, Douglas defeated Lincoln in the Senate race, but the Lincoln–Douglas Debates propelled Lincoln into the Republican Party limelight. Two years later, Lincoln and Douglas faced off again — this time for the presidency. The Lincoln–Douglas Debates were so important to introducing good ol' Abe to the nation that the SAT II may try to sneak in a question about them. Check out the following example.

Which of the following suggests the most notable outcome of the Lincoln–Douglas Debates in 1858?

(A) Lincoln entered the political limelight.

(B) Lincoln defeated Douglas in the election of the same year.

(C) The Republican Party chose Lincoln as its presidential candidate.

(D) Douglas gained national support for his pro-slavery position.

(E) Northern Democrats rallied behind Douglas as their candidate for president.

Read the question carefully to make sure you recognize that the debates in question were the ones that preceded the Illinois Senate race rather than the presidential election. After you establish the timeframe, you can eliminate answer choices that pertain to the presidential election of 1860.

So, (C) and (E) are wrong because both deal with the presidential race. And you can pretty easily eliminate (D) because the nation was divided on the slavery issue, and no debate was going to change that. Lincoln did eventually defeat Douglas in an election, but not in 1858; so (B) is wrong. The best answer is (A) because Lincoln's debates with Douglas in the race for the Illinois Senate seat brought him from a relative political unknown to a rising star in the Republican Party and set him up for the presidential candidacy two years later.

Party splits before the election

The issue of slavery divided the Democratic Party into two factions at the Democratic Convention for the 1860 presidential election: Southern Democrats and Northern Democrats. Southern Democrats refused to endorse any presidential candidate unless he guaranteed that the rights of slave owners would be equally represented in the federal government. Northern Democrats opposed the endorsement of slavery. Due to this huge rift in the party, it actually nominated two separate Democratic presidential candidates for votes in the 1860 election. Stephen Douglas represented the Northern Democrats, and John C. Breckinridge represented the Southern Democrats. The Republicans' and their candidate Abraham Lincoln opposed the spread of slavery into the territories.

Once again Lincoln and Douglas battled for political victory, just as they had before in the 1858 Senate race. This time, the stakes were higher and, this time, Lincoln was victorious. Lincoln won the presidential election of 1860 with less than a majority of electoral votes because the Democrats split their electoral votes between Douglas for the Northern Democrats and Breckenridge for the Southern Democrats, giving Lincoln enough votes to become president. Southern states didn't even put Lincoln's name on the presidential ballot. Despite the South's sentiments, Lincoln won 40 percent of the nation's popular vote and, more notably, the electoral votes of the largest states in the West and the North.

Southern secession

Many Southerners viewed Lincoln's election as a threat to their economy and way of life. Citizens of the South pledged that they would rather secede from the Union than allow Lincoln to impede the spread of slavery. So, six weeks after Lincoln's election and before he was even inaugurated, Southern states began to secede from the Union. South Carolina was the first state to secede. Then Alabama, Florida, Mississippi, Georgia, Louisiana, and Texas soon followed. All these states produced cotton as their cash crop, and they needed the continued cheap labor of slaves to grow, harvest, and distribute it. They also needed equal representation in Congress to make sure their interests were protected, and they knew they wouldn't get it if new free states were added to the Union.

As each Southern state seceded from the Union, its leaders quit the U.S. Congress. In February 1861, men representing the secessionist states met in Montgomery, Alabama. The result of this meeting was the creation of the *Confederate States of America.* The new government of this nation maintained similarities with that of the U.S. Its Articles of Confederation were intentionally similar to the U.S.'s original Articles, but the Confederacy exhibited two distinct differences: It gave its citizens the guaranteed right to own slaves, and it granted each state independence and sovereignty. The leaders' final decision was to appoint Jefferson Davis as president of the Confederate States of America.

The Civil War: The Causes, Battles, and Conclusion

The North and South entered into civil war with different motivations and different military resources, which affected the way each side waged war. The Civil War divided a nation and pitted family members against one another. By the end of the war, nearly every person in America had experienced its impact.

Examining the war's causes

Singling out one specific cause of the Civil War is impossible to do. Today, most people attribute the cause of the Civil War to slavery. But the Civil War was the culmination of various cultural and political differences that existed between the North and the South.

The SAT II has a penchant for testing you on causes, so take a look at the main reasons that two sections of the United States decided to go to war with each other.

The Southern point of view

The Civil War began when Lincoln was elected president in 1860 and the South seceded from the Union. Here are the main reasons that the South wanted to pull away and create its own nation:

- **To prevent the threat of decreased representation in the federal government:** As the United States accumulated new territories, the government had to answer the burning question of whether or not these territories would allow slavery. Every territory that entered the Union as a free state threatened the South's position in the federal government because the population of the free states and territories kept increasing, thus increasing the representation of free states in the House of Representatives. When Lincoln became president, Southerners couldn't see how they could remain part of the Union and still have their interests equally represented.

- **To preserve slavery:** Obviously, the cotton-dependent South relied on slaves to maintain its way of life. Slavery kept production costs low, and any threat to the institution of slavery was a threat to the Southern way of life, which, for the large-plantation owning (and most politically powerful) Southerners, was pretty darn cushy.

- **To maintain states' rights:** Southerners felt that each state should be responsible for making its own decisions. Southerners didn't believe that the federal government had the right to impose laws on states, especially laws imposing tariffs and prohibiting slavery, unless the Constitution explicitly assigned the law to the federal government. Southerners felt they had the right to secede from the Union in protest over federal taxation and policies about slavery.

The Northern point of view

Northerners didn't rely on agriculture or slaves to maintain their lifestyles, so they viewed the same issues very differently.

- **Representation in the federal government:** Given Northerners' views on slavery, the North wanted new states to enter as free states. Most Northerners favored a government ban on slavery in new states.

- **Slavery:** The North was a predominately industrial society. As early as the 1780s, northern societies recognized that the institution of slavery wasn't profitable for an industrial economy. Northerners took the position a step further, looking at slavery as a threat to jobs. So, for both moral and economic reasons, the North opposed slavery.

- **States' rights:** The North supported the federal government's right to enact laws that restricted the rights of individual states. The North did not feel that a state or group of states had the right to secede from the Union in protest against federal policies.

Preparing for war: A comparison between the North and the South

As war appeared more and more inevitable, both sides prepared for battle. Each side had advantages and disadvantages that affected the eventual outcome of the war. The SAT II loves comparisons, so Table 9-1 compares the military of the Union (the North) and the Confederacy (the South). Overall, the North had the advantage in size and strength, but Southerners believed they would win because they had distinct military advantages over the North.

Table 9-1	**Union and Confederate Military Strengths and Weaknesses**	
	Union	*Confederate*
Military troops	**Strengths:** The Union army was larger than the Confederate army. The North had a population base of 22 million, including immigrants, free African Americans, and escaped slaves, from which it created a military of more than 2.1 million men. By comparison, the South had only 800,000 men in its military.	**Strengths:** The Confederate military included more experienced military leaders, including more officers who were trained at West Point and veterans of the Mexican War. Many white Southerners were members of local militias, and most lived in rural areas, and therefore, they were superior marksmen.
	Weaknesses: The military tradition in the North was not nearly as strong as it was in the South.	**Weaknesses:** The Confederate states' population of 9 million was less than half of the North's population. And, ⅓ of the South's population were slaves, who weren't allowed to fight.
Resources	**Strengths:** The industrial North produced almost all resources that were necessary for war: It had steel mills, iron mines, factories, and means of transportation. More than 70 percent of the U.S. railroads were in the North, and the North produced most ships in the U.S. The North also produced about ⅔ of the nation's food supply. The North also benefited from a stable economy, substantial food resources (Northern agriculture was dominated by food stuffs, whereas Southern agriculture was dominated by cotton, indigo, and tobacco), greater financial reserves, and better tax collection.	**Strengths:** The South was deficient in war resources, but it did produce the cotton that was necessary for British textile production, which allowed the Confederates to garner British support early on.
		Weaknesses: The South lacked the necessary natural resources, industry, and transportation for war, and it didn't have the finances to manufacture or purchase these necessities. The South also did not have substantial food resources to provide adequate food for its troops and citizenry throughout the war.
	Weaknesses: None. The Union had the upper hand in the resources department.	
Location	**Strengths:** None. The Union army fought away from home. However, fighting in the South made the North's recovery after the war easier.	**Strengths:** To make up for deficiencies in the number of troops and resources, the Confederate army waited for the North to invade them in their territory. This tactic gave them community support, familiar terrain, and proximity to the supplies that they did have.
	Weaknesses: The Union army invaded the South, so it was in unfamiliar terrain.	**Weaknesses:** Familiar territory was an advantage for the Confederate army. Picking up the pieces after the devastation of cities made postwar recovery more difficult.

Pitting brother against brother: Some important battles

At first, the Confederate army seemed like it would succeed in its desire to break away from the United States. As you know, however, Union forces eventually won.

The SAT II is unlikely to ask specific questions about Civil War battles, but review the following information to get a feeling for the general progression of the war.

Fort Sumter: The war officially begins

When the Southern states seceded from the Union after Lincoln's election in 1860, many federal installations located in the South became the property of the Confederate states. However, President Lincoln vowed to hold and occupy the few remaining installations, one of which was Fort Sumter in Charleston, South Carolina. The fort badly needed supplies, and Lincoln agreed to send them, despite the secretary of state's warning that he should evacuate the fort. Lincoln's agreement to send supplies angered Confederate President Jefferson Davis, and he instructed General Pierre G.T. Beauregard to take the fort by force, if necessary. Growing tensions between the North and South came to a head on April 12, 1861, when Confederate soldiers under the leadership of Beauregard attacked Fort Sumter — an act that marked the start of the Civil War. After two days of heavy shelling, the Confederate army had its first victory. Directly after the battle at Fort Sumter, the states of North Carolina, Tennessee, Arkansas, and Virginia joined the Confederates and seceded from the Union.

An embarrassment for the Union: The first battle for Bull Run

The first real battle of the Civil War took place in July 1861 at Bull Run, Virginia, located only 20 miles outside Washington, D.C. (This battle is known as the First Battle of Bull Run because two battles took place there.) The Union leaders thought this battle would be an easy, war-ending victory. Confederate forces saw it as an opportunity to prove their superiority on the battlefield. The outnumbered Confederate army outmaneuvered the inexperienced Union soldiers. Union troops fled the battlefield, leaving behind supplies, weapons, and men. This was a lasting psychological setback for the Union. To add insult to injury, the retreating Union troops ran right into the many Washington elites who had arrived at the battlefield to witness a quick and easy defeat of the Confederates.

The war rages on: Major battles in Tennessee and Virginia

Massive fighting in Shiloh, Tennessee, proved that the war wouldn't be a quick and easy victory for either side. In April 1862, after two days of fighting at the Battle of Shiloh, an all-out slaughter resulted in the death or wounding of more than 20,000 Union and Confederate men and boys. The brutal battle ended in a victory for the Union army.

The leaders of the Union army strategized that if they could take the Confederate capital city of Richmond, Virginia, they would win the war. In June 1862, Union and Confederate forces mounted battle after battle just outside Richmond. Union *General George McClellan* engaged in a series of clashes with Confederate *General Robert E. Lee* but refused to continue to Richmond without reinforcements. After McClellan suffered a series of defeats, Lincoln ordered him back to Washington, D.C., and gave General John Pope command of the Union army. Lee went on the offensive, and Confederate forces scored another victory at the Second Battle of Bull Run in August 1862. Confederate victories pushed the Union army out of Richmond, and Lincoln recalled General McClellan to defeat the Southern forces.

On September 17, 1862, Lee led the Confederate forces north in an attempt to break through the Union lines. What resulted was the Battle of Antietam, the bloodiest single day of battle in the entire Civil War. More than 8,000 soldiers died in action that day, and an additional 18,000 were wounded. Although, technically, the battle was a draw, it is seen as a victory for the

North because it stopped Lee and his troops from continuing northward. Lincoln responded to the Battle of Antietam with his Emancipation Proclamation (see the next section).

Lee must've been feeling pretty good about himself because he continued to go on the offensive and tried to push Union forces farther north and away from Richmond. Lee committed a daring act at Chancellorsville, Virginia, in April 1863. He split his army and surrounded Union forces. If the battle had started sooner, Lee may have captured the entire Union army. Although Lee was victorious, the battle cost the South many lives, including the life of the great Southern military leader *General Thomas "Stonewall" Jackson.* Despite the loss of men, Lee continued to push north.

The beginning of the end: Wrapping up the Civil War

In 1863, although the war was far from over, the North began to gain ground. This year was the beginning of the end for the Southern way of life.

Emancipation proclaimed

The South had fought for two years to retain its individual rights and the right to own slaves. President Lincoln issued the *Emancipation Proclamation* after the Battle of Antietam in 1862 (see the previous section), a law that freed slaves and went into effect on January 1, 1863. However, the proclamation didn't eradicate slavery in the U.S. In an attempt to appease the slave states of Maryland, Missouri, and Kentucky, which were still members of the Union, Lincoln's proclamation applied only to areas behind Confederate military lines. But the Confederate slave states had no intention of freeing slaves, so the proclamation had little actual effect on slavery. The purpose of the Emancipation Proclamation was primarily to be a symbolic gesture, but it affected real benefits for the Union cause. It reinforced the idea that the North was fighting to abolish slavery as well as to uphold the Union, which pleased Radical Republicans in Congress and won popular foreign opinion for the North. The proclamation allowed freed slaves to join the Union army, which increased Union forces by 200,000 at a time when it needed fresh troops. The proclamation also gave Northern troops a renewed sense of purpose and a much-needed morale boost.

Turning points: The Battles of Gettysburg and Vicksburg

The year 1863 would prove a decisive one in determining the outcome of the Civil War. *Lt. General Ulysses S. Grant,* general of the Union army's Western forces, began attacking the Confederate city of Vicksburg, Mississippi, in May 1863. Grant's initial frontal assault on the city resulted in too many Union casualties, so he settled for a prolonged siege on the city to starve it into surrender. Meanwhile, bolstered by his victory at Chancellorsville and hoping to divert Union forces from their attack on Vicksburg, Lee decided to invade the North again. He hoped a victory in the North would cause the North to concede altogether or at least allow Confederate troops to live off of rich Northern farms. In June 1863, Lee began to shift his armies from Fredericksburg, Virginia, and move them north toward Pennsylvania. In early July 1863, Union and Confederate armies battled outside Gettysburg, Pennsylvania, which resulted in a Confederate retreat and more than 50,000 casualties on both sides. Several months later, Lincoln dedicated the battlefield as a cemetery to honor the fallen soldiers. In his *Gettysburg Address,* Lincoln rededicated the nation to the war effort so that no soldier, from the North or the South, would have died in vain.

Coincidentally, as Lee's army was escaping south from Gettysburg, Grant's army was finally taking the city of Vicksburg. After almost two months of constant mortar attack, Grant finally captured Vicksburg on July 4, 1863, one day after the Union victory at Gettysburg. The capture of Vicksburg made Grant a national hero and gave the Union army control of the entire Mississippi River Valley, which made it one of the most important Union victories of the Civil War.

The tenacious townspeople of Vicksburg

The citizens of Vicksburg, Mississippi, didn't give up easily. When Grant laid siege to their city for two months in 1863, they fought back. They became cave dwellers after their houses were destroyed by continuous mortar fire. They fought disease, rats, lice, and despair. When food became scarce, they survived on horsemeat and dogs. They finally surrendered to the Union on July 4, 1863.

What a difference: The 1864 election

Today, Americans view Lincoln as one of our country's greatest presidents. In 1864, people predicted that he wouldn't win reelection. No president had been elected to a second term since Andrew Jackson in 1832, and no party had endorsed a presidential candidate for two terms since 1840.

More importantly, the public perception in the North was that the Civil War wasn't going very well. The battles were costly and decidedly indecisive, and Lincoln's own party was split over his nomination. Radical Republicans in Congress felt that Lincoln wasn't tough enough on slavery and that his Reconstruction plan for the South was too lenient (see Chapter 10). On the other hand, War Democrats, who had supported Lincoln, were still angry about his Emancipation Proclamation (covered earlier in this chapter), delivered in September 1862, which granted any slave in rebel-held territory their freedom. This proclamation made War Democrats think that Lincoln was fighting the war for abolition rather than for preserving the Union. Talk about damned if you do, damned if you don't.

The Republican Party changed its name to the National Union Party for the presidential election to emphasize its purpose. It nominated Lincoln with Andrew Johnson (a War Democrat) as his vice-president. The Democrats nominated General George McClellan (see "The war rages on: Major battles in Tennessee and Virginia" earlier in this chapter for more on McClellan).

The Republican and Democratic platforms of 1864 had two glaring differences (which are all you really need to know for the SAT II):

- ✔ The Republican platform endorsed an amendment to the Constitution that abolished slavery, whereas the Democratic platform denounced Lincoln's disregard for states' rights, which basically meant that they were against the ban of slavery.

- ✔ Republicans endorsed Lincoln's war policy and rejected any peace settlement except unconditional surrender by the Confederacy. The Democratic platform, written by the peace wing of the party, called for a stop to the war followed by peaceful negotiations between the Union and the Confederacy (even though McClellan rejected this plan).

Union army victories — most notably General William T. Sherman's capture of Atlanta on September 2 (see the next section) quieted Northerners' criticisms of the war and secured Lincoln's election to a second presidential term. Lincoln didn't just win, he obliterated his opponent, winning 212 electoral votes to McClellan's 21.

A new Union commander and a march to the sea

Halfway through the war, Lincoln was desperate for a bold general who would lead the Union army to victory. A review of Union campaigns gave Lincoln his man. In March 1864, Lincoln appointed Ulysses S. Grant supreme commander of all Union forces. Under Grant's direction, the Union army experienced large numbers of casualties, but it also inflicted many Southern casualties and depleted Southern resources. Grant's army continued to engage Lee's army and sent Union Generals William T. Sherman and Philip H. Sheridan to capture Atlanta. These generals used Grant's strategy at Vicksburg to take Atlanta in the summer of 1864.

During the later half of 1864, General Sherman headed to Savannah, Georgia, in what became known as his "March to the Sea." Sherman and Sheridan adopted a *scorched-earth policy* (also known as total war); that is, they ruined everything in their path. Union soldiers destroyed the Confederates' supplies of food and shelter. They burned houses and barns, killed live-stock, destroyed crops, and terrorized residents in each village, town, and city that they passed through. Sherman's response to outraged citizens was that war is hell. In December 1864, Sherman captured Savannah. The relentless March to the Sea and capture of Atlanta and Savannah destroyed Southerners' morale and crushed their ability and will to continue fighting.

Finally! Lee's surrender

The ravaged South couldn't recover from the loss of men (from death and desertion) and sup-plies. To fortify troops, the Confederate Congress authorized an act that allowed enslaved African Americans to enlist in conquered areas of the South after January 1863, but it was too late to offer too much real help.

Grant's troops continued fighting in Virginia and laid siege to the city of Petersburg for ten months (from June 1864 to April 1865) by using tactics resembling the trench warfare that would be commonly used during World War I (see Chapter 15). Grant and Sheridan finally seized Richmond in April 1865. With a total army of only 30,000, Lee was forced to surrender on April 9, 1865. Grant and Lee met at *Appomattox Courthouse* in Virginia to discuss the terms of surrender. The Civil War was over, but it resulted in the deaths of about 360,000 Union sol-diers and 260,000 Confederate soldiers. The wounded numbered 375,000.

Tying it all together: A sample question looks at the Civil War

The SAT II U.S. History exam may include a question that asks you to consider all phases and aspects of the Civil War.

Which of the following events did most to reinvigorate Northern morale during the Civil War?

(A) The Lincoln–Douglas Debates

(B) Lincoln's issuance of the Emancipation Proclamation

(C) The First Battle of Bull Run

(D) Southern secession

(E) Lee's surrender at Appomattox Courthouse

When you first read this question, you probably think the correct answer will be some Northern battle victory, so you may not recognize the answer right away.

Pay attention to time clues. The Lincoln-Douglas Debates occurred almost three years before the war began, so (A) can't be right. Lee's surrender was likely a morale booster, but because it ended the war, you can't say that it occurred during the Civil War. You can eliminate answer (E). Southern secession happened before the war began, and, besides, it was a discourage-ment to the North rather than an encouragement. So (D) isn't right.

You're left with answers (B) and (C). The First Battle of Bull Run wasn't the easy defeat that the North had expected. Instead, Union troops retreated (right into a crowd of spectators, no less). So, answer (C) isn't right; (B) must be correct. The Emancipation Proclamation rejuve-nated the cause against slavery and gave Northerners the will to keep up the fight.

Part IV
America as a Young Adult

In this part . . .

The United States experienced its angst-ridden teenage years during the eras of Reconstruction, the end of the frontier, the Second Industrial Revolution, and imperialism. Just like a typical teenager, the U.S. was generally self-centered during this time period and focused on expanding itself geographically and economically. On the SAT II U.S. History exam, around 20 to 25 percent of the questions are from this time frame. During the period covered in this part, 1865–1914, America emerged as a major world power — quite an accomplishment for a nation that came into existence a little more than 100 years before.

Chapter 10

Picking Up the Pieces: Reconstruction, 1865–1896

In This Chapter

▶ Understanding how Lincoln's plan for Reconstruction died with him

▶ Rebuilding the South with Radical Republican policies

▶ Looking at the erosion of reforms after the end of Reconstruction

Most likely, the SAT II U.S. History exam won't ask you an overwhelming amount of questions about the time period following the Civil War, known as the Reconstruction Era. However, you can be almost certain that it will include a few questions.

Oh, the dilemma! To study or not to study, that is the question. In case you're looking for a suggestion, we suggest studying this chapter anyway. It's short and undoubtedly contains all the major plot points of the Reconstruction Era that you'll need to answer any exam questions.

Abraham Lincoln and Presidential Reconstruction

The end of the Civil War did not mean that all was well in America. Immediately the United States had to go about repairing the immense financial, physical, and emotional damage caused by the war and had to admit the states that fought for the Confederacy back into the Union. President Abraham Lincoln had developed a plan for Reconstruction as early as 1863, but his opponents had their own, stricter plan to counter it, and a conflict over which plan to adopt was certain. Lincoln's assassination soon after the war ended allowed Radical Republicans in Congress more power to dictate the specifics of Reconstruction.

The SAT II U.S. History exam probably won't ask you a question on any of the details covered in the following sections, but it will expect you to know the general historical context of the turbulent years of the Reconstruction Era.

A man with a plan: Lincoln's Proclamation of Amnesty and Reconstruction

On December 8, 1863, Lincoln issued the *Proclamation of Amnesty and Reconstruction,* which applied to Confederate lands that the Union forces occupied.

For the SAT II U.S. History exam, you should know what the proclamation said. Despite the fact that the Civil War was still raging with no end in sight, Lincoln's proclamation laid out a plan to restore the Confederate states to the Union. Here's what the proclamation said:

- Lincoln would pardon almost any Confederate, with the condition that he swear allegiance to the Constitution and the Union.

- Lincoln would exclude only high-ranking civil and military leaders and anyone who committed war crimes from his pardon.

- After 10 percent of voters in a conquered Confederate state took the oath and organized a government that abolished slavery, the state could elect new congressional representatives, and Lincoln would recognize the legitimacy of the state's government. This was known as the Ten Percent Plan. Lincoln also suggested that these Confederate states provide former slaves with education.

The way Lincoln saw it (or at least played it), the Confederate states that had seceded from the Union hadn't really left because the U.S. Constitution didn't give them any means to do so. Lincoln's plan proved extremely unpopular to the radical members of his own party.

I object! The Wade–Davis Bill

In 1864, the radicals in Lincoln's party, called (what else?) the *Radical Republicans* devised a more severe alternative to Lincoln's Reconstruction plan called the *Wade–Davis Bill* (named after the bill's authors, Senator Benjamin Wade of Ohio and Congressman Henry Winter Davis of Maryland) because they believed the president was being too nice.

For the SAT II, what you need to know, in a nutshell, is that the Wade–Davis Bill was stricter than Lincoln's plan because it was intended to punish the South for its insurrection. But here are some particulars of the Wade–Davis Bill:

- It required Lincoln to appoint a provisional governor for each conquered state. This governor would reconstruct the state government according to measures that Congress laid out.

- The bill required that 50 percent of a state's voters had to swear loyalty to the Union (as opposed to Lincoln's Ten Percent Plan) before they could elect delegates to a constitutional convention and start the readmission process.

- The bill tightened restrictions on who could vote in any election, excluding all political and military officials in the Confederacy as well as "anyone who has voluntarily borne arms against the United States."

- It abolished slavery and enacted legal safeguards to protect the liberty of freed men that the federal courts would enforce.

The Wade–Davis Bill glided through Congress, passing in the House of Representatives in May and the Senate in July. The bill made its way to Lincoln's desk on July 4, where he read it and promptly pocketed it, unsigned — in effect, denying its passage and infuriating Congress. (What do you know? This action is called a "pocket veto.") Lincoln then invited the Southern states to rejoin the Union under either plan, knowing that they would choose his easier conditions. In August, the authors of the Wade–Davis Bill blasted the president in a letter to the *New York Tribune,* which history now refers to as the Wade–Davis Manifesto. The letter accused Lincoln of playing politics in an election year and of acting like a dictator with his handy-dandy pocket veto.

Although Lincoln won the battle with Radical Republicans on how to conduct the Reconstruction of the South, he wouldn't live to see his plan through (see the next section). And the Radical Republicans would decide to implement their own Reconstruction plan in the years following the Civil War (see "Rule of the Radicals: Congressional Reconstruction" later in this chapter).

The following question is a good example of what you may see on the test regarding Reconstruction Era politics. It focuses on the Radical Republican agenda.

All the following were components of the 1864 Wade–Davis Bill, EXCEPT

(A) A provisional governor was appointed for each state conquered in the Civil War.

(B) Confederate political and military officials were denied the right to vote.

(C) Slavery was no longer legal anywhere in the U.S.

(D) Before a state could elect delegates to a constitutional convention, a small percentage of a state's voters had to swear loyalty to the Union.

(E) Federal courts would act on behalf of freed men to protect their emancipation.

The "EXCEPT" can be tricky if you aren't careful. Make sure you understand what you're looking for before you dive into the answer choices.

Even if you don't remember what the Wade–Davis Bill was about, don't immediately dismiss this question and move on. You can gather clues from the question and the answer choices. The question gives you the year of the bill, 1864, so you know that it has something to do with the Civil War or Reconstruction. The answer choices here primarily deal with Reconstruction ideas, so the bill is probably a Reconstruction bill.

The SAT II will try to trick you by slipping in an element that makes an answer choice right or wrong, so you don't readily notice it. In this case, the correct answer is (D). Because the answer states that the percentage of voters is "small," (D) cannot be a component of the bill. Lincoln's Reconstruction plan called for a small percentage — 10 percent — of voters to swear loyalty, but the Radical Republicans wanted a 50 percent loyalty rate, which isn't a small percentage.

Cut short: Lincoln's assassination

Just when everything was in place for Lincoln's Reconstruction plan to go full steam ahead, a terrible turn of events occurred.

Imagine the scene: The day is Good Friday, April 14, 1865. Lincoln arrives with his wife, Mary, at the Ford Theater in Washington, D.C. to see a comedy called *Our American Cousin*. Despite the turmoil of the preceding war years (both in his political and private life) things are looking up: Robert E. Lee formally surrendered the Confederate army to Ulysses S. Grant just five days before at Appomattox Courthouse, ending the bloody, costly Civil War. Around 10:30 p.m., during the second act, a man named John Wilkes Booth enters Lincoln's box, raises a pistol, and fires a round into the back of the president's head. In the ensuing chaos, Booth stabs a Union soldier and jumps from the box onto the stage, breaking his leg but still managing to escape on horseback.

Lincoln is taken to a boarding house across the street, where he dies the following morning. He was 56 years old. A week later, Booth, an accomplished actor and Southern sympathizer, is cornered in a barn in Virginia. He was either shot or he killed himself — no one knows for sure. Many Americans saw Lincoln as a savior of the nation and a defender of a government for the people, so news of his death precipitated widespread mourning.

Rule of the Radicals: Congressional Reconstruction

When you think of Radical Reconstruction, think of it as a time of great division between the North and the South, Republican and Democrat, president and Congress. Think of it as a time of reform and a time of corruption; a time of uneasy peace and violence; a time when Congress gave legal rights to African Americans, while Southerners defiantly ignored those rights. This phase gave freedom to former slaves as well as gave birth to the Ku Klux Klan. If you remember these points and nothing else, you may still be able to guess your way through questions relating to this section on the SAT II. But taking a little time to study everything in this section is always helpful!

Andrew Johnson takes over

Andrew Johnson was sworn in as president in 1865 amidst great turmoil. The country was at the end of a long and bloody civil war, and the South was in ruins. Plantations had been burned down; fields were unplanted and overgrown; railroads and bridges had been destroyed; and disease, starvation, and lawlessness abounded. Northerners were mourning the loss of Lincoln, and some even suggested that his assassination was a conspiracy and payback, leveling accusations at the former Confederacy.

Initially, Johnson and the Radical Republicans were allies because Johnson vowed to punish Confederate leaders by confiscating their land and indicting them for treason. But the courtship didn't last. Johnson proved to be every bit the Democrat and Southerner that Republicans wished he weren't: He hated the Southern aristocracy as much as he hated Northern businessmen, and he was a committed white supremacist.

For the SAT II U.S. History exam, remember that Johnson was much more forgiving of the South than the Radical Republicans were, and therein lies his conflict with Congress, which carried on throughout his presidency.

Right off the bat, Johnson appointed provisional governors to each Confederate state and offered amnesty to all who took an oath of allegiance to the Union, with some exceptions, including everyone on the Who's Who List of the Confederacy. He stated publicly that all states had to abolish slavery, and he required Confederate states to acknowledge that seceding from the Union was wrong.

Republicans took a let's-wait-and-see approach. What happened was a little thing called *Southern defiance.* Southern states began to ignore the conditions that Johnson had set upon them. They also elected the Confederacy gang, including former Confederate Vice President Alexander Stephens, to state and federal government offices.

How did Johnson respond? As a Southern Democrat devoted to states' rights, he basically asked Southerners to be reasonable and hoped they would comply with his terms. And out of 15,000 pardon requests, Johnson granted all but 1,500. The Radical Republican Congress countered Johnson's Southern sympathies by passing federal civil rights legislation and initiating the impeachment process against him (see "Congress flexes its legislative muscles" later in this chapter).

The Black Codes and the Freedman's Bureau

Southerners decided that if slavery was illegal, then they needed a new system to control the black population. Can't you just hear the logic? "Well, we can't have slavery, so let's make up a bunch of new laws to control recently freed slaves in such a way that it will almost be like they're slaves again. And, oh, we'll call the new system the 'Black Codes.'"

The *Black Codes* were sets of laws that Southerners used to control freed slaves. These codes varied from state to state, and they did provide former slaves with some new rights, including the power to sue in court, to own property (with restrictions, of course), and to legally marry. But the negative aspects far exceeded the positive ones. The Black Codes

- ✔ Prohibited African Americans from bearing arms.

- ✔ Prohibited African Americans from working in any occupation except agriculture without a special permit.

- ✔ Put broad vagrancy laws in place; these laws greatly restricted African Americans' rights to travel and forced them to work.

- ✔ Excluded African Americans from juries.

- ✔ Set up a basis for the segregation of public facilities and banned interracial marriage.

- ✔ Made punishment for crimes more severe for African Americans.

The Black Codes lasted from 1865 until the passage of the Civil Rights Act of 1866 and the 14th Amendment (covered later in this chapter). The Black Codes actually accomplished very little, except that Northerners became aware of the fact that their Southern neighbors weren't quite willing to give up completely on the slavery thing.

In response to the Black Codes, the federal government set up the *Freedman's Bureau* in March 1865 to give freed slaves a chance that Southerners seemed unwilling to offer. The Freedman's Bureau provided African Americans (and even poor white Southerners) with a number of services until the organization disbanded in 1872.

- ✔ It provided all aid to freed men, including rations, clothing, and medicine. The bureau issued more than 150,000 rations a day and, in total, issued more than 22 million rations from 1865 to 1869.

- ✔ The bureau assumed custody of all the land that the Union army had confiscated from the Confederate states with the intent of providing the land to freed slaves and poor white Southern farmers. The land grants didn't last; former owners reclaimed most of the land when Johnson pardoned them.

- ✔ After the bureau lost its job as a land broker, it shifted its focus to negotiating better relations between freed men and plantation owners. It attempted to protect the freed men from exploitation and made sure that they honored newly signed labor agreements with the plantation owners. The bureau also oversaw a system of military courts designed to give freed men a fair day in court, unlike the highly biased, racially motivated courts of the Southern states.

- ✔ The bureau dedicated itself to assisting freed slaves in finding work. In keeping with this goal, the bureau built more than 1,000 public schools, provided teacher training, and funded some African American colleges.

The bureau was supposed to last for only one year, but Congress extended its duration in July 1866 despite Johnson's veto of the extension measure. A lack of funding caused Congress to halt all of the bureau's efforts in 1869, except those devoted to education. In 1870, Congress stopped education efforts, and the bureau officially closed in 1872.

Congress flexes its legislative muscles

President Johnson hoped to end Reconstruction in 1865, but Congress was just getting warmed up. Congress saw that the South was just as stubborn and resistant to change as ever, and clearly the region had an ally in Johnson, who was not keen on heavy federal involvement in the affairs of the states. Therefore, the Radical Republicans wasted no time in passing legislation that provided freed slaves with new rights and drastically changed the Southern way of life.

The 13th, 14th, and 15th Amendments

Passed over a span of five years and two presidencies, the 13th, 14th, and 15th Amendments represented a difficult and quarrelsome journey that Congress took to further Reconstruction efforts in the South. These amendments gave freed men the rights recognized and guaranteed by the federal government. Southern states and Democrats fought against these amendments, but Congress made their passage a condition of a state's readmission into the Union and, by doing so, slowly but surely, all three amendments became part of the Constitution by 1870.

For the SAT II, you should probably know the following about each amendment:

- **The 13th Amendment (1865):** Abolished slavery in the United States.

- **The 14th Amendment (1868):** Gave African Americans rights as citizens and prohibited states from preventing the rights of citizens or denying anyone equal protection of the law.

- **The 15th Amendment (1870):** Prohibited states from denying African Americans the right to vote based on race, color, or previous condition of servitude.

Note that the 15th Amendment gave the right to vote to freed slaves but not women. Another 50 years would pass before men would cross that bridge, kicking and screaming all the way. (Check out Chapter 14 for the scoop.)

The Civil Rights Act of 1866

Early in 1866, less than one year after the Civil War ended, Congress passed the Civil Rights Act. The act gave the rights of citizenship to freed slaves, including the right to make contracts, sue in civil court, be a witness in a court, and own personal property. Johnson vetoed the act, but Congress overrode his veto (the first time in history that Congress overrode a presidential veto).

The 1867–1868 Reconstruction Acts

Congress passed three separate Reconstruction Acts between 1867 and 1868. All passed, despite Johnson's vetoes. The *Reconstruction Act of 1867* provided the framework for the South's reconstruction according to the desires of the Radical Republican–controlled Congress. The subsequent two Reconstruction Acts reaffirmed and strengthened the agenda that Congress had laid out in the first act. The acts covered the following items:

- Congress's Reconstruction plan called for ten Southern states to divide into five military districts, and it declared the existing state governments unofficial and subject to the authority of appointed military leaders. (Tennessee wasn't included because it already had ratified the 14th Amendment and been admitted to the Union.)

- After the states accomplished this task, every state would hold a new constitutional convention and adopt a new constitution that would accept African American suffrage.

- Also, states had to ratify the 14th Amendment, giving African Americans rights as citizens.

Only when the Southern states met all these conditions would Congress allow representatives from these states to return to Congress. To Johnson, the Reconstruction Acts were fighting words, and he tried, unsuccessfully, to veto all of them. But Congress was tired of Johnson's meddling and set out to fix him good.

Johnson's impeachment trial

Because Johnson tried to thwart Congress's attempts to implement federal legislation on the Southern states, Congress decided to use the *Tenure of Office Act* to limit Johnson's presidential power. Congress had passed this act in 1867, and it prohibited the president from removing anyone whom Congress had appointed or approved from office. You may want to remember this act for the SAT II because violating it eventually led to Johnson's impeachment (surely, a topic begging to be an exam question).

Johnson violated the act by firing Secretary of War Edwin Stanton, who, coincidentally (wink, wink, nudge, nudge), was a supporter of Congress's Reconstruction policies. Johnson's defiant act gave Congress the fuel it needed to begin the impeachment process against Johnson. The House passed a resolution for his impeachment in 1868, but the Senate, after a three-month trial, did not achieve the ⅔ majority needed to remove Johnson from office (it was one vote shy). He continued his veto-happy ways, but Congress continued overriding him for the remainder of his presidency. Johnson completed his term as the first president to be impeached and the only one until Bill Clinton was impeached in 1998 (see Chapter 22).

The South's resentment grows

Taken out of the ideological halls of the Republican Congress and into the violent, chaotic, and disobedient reality that was the postwar South, Reconstruction was anything but a smooth ride. Democrats and Southerners resented Republicans and Northerners telling them what to do, and rising Southern resentment gave birth to secret societies and name-calling.

The Ku Klux Klan

The most famous secret society in the South was the *Ku Klux Klan,* formed in 1866 in Tennessee. When the Klan first began, it was a terrorist organization made up of white supremacists who decided that the way to combat Reconstruction was to intimidate and inflict death and violence on African Americans and Republican supporters.

The Klan murdered thousands of African Americans and Republican voters in the South between 1866 and 1870. The organization also burned freedman schools and prevented African Americans from voting, thus greatly diminishing the Republican voting base in the South.

Congress eventually passed legislation that enabled President Ulysses S. Grant to crack down on Klan members. (For more about Grant, see "Quite shameful: Ulysses S. Grant's presidency" later in this chapter.) With this legislation, law enforcement officials arrested and convicted hundreds of Klan members between 1871 and 1872, which led to more peaceful elections in 1872. But the Klan wouldn't go away that easily; it continued operations until later in the 19th century, when the Radical Republicans no longer imposed their civil rights agenda and the Klan was no longer needed. (However, it reorganized in the 20th century; see Chapter 16.)

Scalawags and carpetbaggers

The terms "scalawag" and "carpetbagger" were more than just bad names that Southerners called Northerners. These names were depictions of the way that Southerners viewed Northern supporters who lived in the South, and they were perceived to be extremely derogatory.

✔ *Scalawags* were Southern whites who supported the Republican Party.

✔ *Carpetbaggers* were Northerners who moved to the South following the war and also supported Republican policies.

Southerners saw scalawags as traitors and carpetbaggers as corrupt opportunists trying to take over the South and change its power structure from within. In reality, most scalawags were old Unionists or Whigs, who tended to side with Northern interests, whereas most carpetbaggers were Union army officers who decided to stay in the South after the war or businessmen who intended to invest in the South.

For purposes of the SAT II, try to remember the differences between scalawags and carpetbaggers.

Quite shameful: Ulysses S. Grant's presidency

Republicans unanimously nominated Ulysses S. Grant, the former Union general, for president in 1868. Democrats nominated former New York Governor Horatio Seymour, who was reluctant to accept it. The Republican platform supported Reconstruction, but it didn't advocate imposing African American suffrage on all states, though Congress did eventually pass the 15th Amendment in 1870 (see "The 13th, 14th, and 15th Amendments" earlier in this chapter). Democrats denounced Reconstruction as unconstitutional and called for the abolition of the Freedman's Bureau and all political endeavors designed to strengthen African American "supremacy."

Grant decidedly won the election and would win again four years later, but his presidency was marred with scandal and corruption, even though, by all accounts, Grant was an honest man who unfortunately surrounded himself with corrupt people. Reformers coined the term "Grantism" during his presidency to describe the corruption that they saw going on around them.

Grant was all for reform, but booming business, the growth of the country, and the availability of government contracts made plenty of elbow room for corruption, and temptation proved too enticing for some members of Grant's administration.

✔ The huge Credit Mobilier scandal, which occurred in 1872, involved members of Congress, the Union Pacific Railroad, and the Credit Mobilier construction company set up by the railroad to limit its liability. Congressmen received favors in exchange for granting the railroad big federal subsidies (see Chapter 11 for more about this scandal).

✔ In 1875, the attorney general and the secretary of the interior were accused of accepting bribes; both men resigned.

✔ The *Whiskey Ring* scandal rocked the nation in 1875; more than 350 government officials (mostly Republicans) and distillers were involved in a scam that cheated the government out of millions in tax revenue. The investigation implicated Grant's personal secretary, Orville Babcock, but he escaped conviction because Grant pardoned him, making Grant seem tainted to the public.

✔ In 1876, Congress impeached Grant's Secretary of War, William Belknap, for accepting bribes in return for military appointments. Grant accepted Belknap's resignation, which in turn allowed Belknap to escape conviction.

Although Grant never was involved in any of these scandals, they left a permanent stain on his reputation as president and painted the powerful Republican Congress as corrupt.

For the SAT II, remember that Grant's administration was associated with several scandals, but the test probably won't ask you any specifics about the scandals themselves.

When it wasn't dealing with scandal, Grant's administration passed some Reconstruction legislation. The federal government admitted all Southern states back into the Union by July 1870, and Grant pardoned all but 500 Confederate sympathizers when he signed the *Amnesty Act* in May 1872.

Tying it all together: A sample question looks at Radical Reconstruction

The SAT II U.S. History tests your knowledge of the general climate during Reconstruction, so you should know a little bit about the legislation that Congress passed and how the South responded to it.

Which of the following is true about Radical Reconstruction after the Civil War?

(A) Scandals marred the Grant presidency, which eventually led to Grant's impeachment.

(B) Southern scalawags joined the Ku Klux Klan to intimidate African Americans and Republican supporters.

(C) The 15th Amendment prohibited states from denying the right to vote based on race, gender, color, or previous condition of servitude.

(D) President Johnson sided with the Radical Republicans in acknowledging that slavery should be abolished.

(E) Northern states instituted Black Codes that provided freed slaves with rights that Southern citizens didn't offer.

Incorrect SAT II test answers often contain a little truth to throw you off, trying to slip the untruth right by you. Correct answers attempt to do the opposite; correct answers appear as if they're untrue, but if you read carefully, you'll find that they're right.

For instance, answer choice (A) contains a little truth: Scandal did tarnish Grant's term. But the rest of the answer is incorrect — Grant wasn't impeached. If you read the answer too quickly, you may want to pick (A), so make sure that you thoroughly read each answer choice. In (B), it's true that the Ku Klux Klan terrorized African Americans and Republicans, but scalawags didn't join them because they were Republican supporters themselves. For (C), the 15th Amendment did institute new voting rights but not based on gender. The new suffrage law didn't include females, so (C) is wrong. Answer (E) confuses Black Codes with the Freedman's Bureau. Southerners set up Black Codes and adversely affected African Americans, so you can eliminate (E). If you just read the first part of (D), you may want to eliminate it, too, because Johnson rarely sided with Radical Republicans. But despite his penchant for white supremacy, he did state publicly that slavery should be abolished, so (D) is the best answer of the five.

The End of Reconstruction and Its Aftermath

Democrats began winning back control of Southern states because of the corruption (more importantly, the inflated perception of corruption) among carpetbaggers who were holding positions of authority in state governments and because Northerners simply began losing interest and patience with the South. The North had problems of its own: a depression, declining farm markets, and wage cuts. And in the end, most Republicans just didn't care enough about the African American issue anymore.

In 1874 elections, Democrats finally won control of the House of Representatives for the first time in 18 years, and they also began to take control of Southern state governments, thanks to the Ku Klux Klan's and other white supremacist groups' widespread coercion and intimidation tactics (see the section about the Ku Klux Klan earlier in this chapter).

Reconstruction was in its death throes in the mid-1870s and fully perished in 1877, and if the Reconstruction Era was one step forward in the quest for equal rights for African Americans in the United States, the countermeasures of Southern state governments and white supremacists in the decades that followed were equal steps back.

Southern "Redemption" and the Compromise of 1877

Reconstruction brought about changes in the South that many Southerners were unwilling to accept. The presence of the military forced change, but when the federal government began pulling troops out of the South, Southerners no longer had pressure to behave. Of course, at the time, Southerners began to refer to the South's return to the good ol' days as the "Redemption" and to groups like the Ku Klux Klan as "Redeemers," which meant that African Americans began losing many of the rights they had briefly gained, and the Democratic Party once again dominated the South. The one event that really jump-started this "Redemption" and officially ended Reconstruction was the Compromise of 1877.

The *Compromise of 1877* could be called "How the Republicans Stole the Election" (see Chapter 12), but for the sake of the SAT II exam, we should probably back up a bit. In the election of 1876, Democratic presidential candidate Samuel Tilden appeared to have won over Republican Rutherford B. Hayes, but the three Republican-controlled Southern states had conflicting ballot numbers, so the election results weren't certain. Republicans and Democrats hurled accusations of fraud and coercion at each other, and the nation faced an unprecedented constitutional crisis. To settle the election, the Republican Congress set up an *electoral commission* (made up of a majority of Republicans), which awarded the election to Hayes.

Unhappy Democrats threatened the always-entertaining and draining stall tactic known as a filibuster (some even threatened to declare war), so Republicans negotiated a compromise. They offered to withdraw federal troops from the South, to appoint at least one Southerner to Hayes's cabinet, and to give the South some economic benefits. The South took the deal, and the rest is history.

The erosion of Reconstruction reforms

When studying for the SAT II U.S. History exam, remember that almost every civil rights reform that Congress enacted during the Reconstruction Era was quickly eroded through the passage of state laws in the South following the end of Reconstruction in 1877.

Southern state governments found a number of creative ways to circumvent federal laws. Laws passed from about the 1890s into the 20th century to reinforce racial discrimination were known collectively as *Jim Crow laws* (after a pre–Civil War stage character depiction of a poor, uneducated, rural African American named Jim Crow). Southerners also degraded African Americans through economic and social means. The following sections cover ways in which Southerners discriminated against African Americans in the years following Reconstruction.

Voting restrictions

The South cleverly devised ways around the 15th Amendment (ratified in 1870), which gave African Americans the right to vote, by implementing a number of laws that prevented African Americans from voting.

Here are the ones you should know for the SAT II:

- ✔ **Poll taxes:** These taxes prevented African Americans from voting because most were generally too poor to pay the tax. It also disenfranchised some poor whites.

- ✔ **Literacy tests:** This law prevented most African Americans from voting because the tests were difficult for anyone to pass, and the local white registrar determined a person's success or failure. In some cases, the tests were 20 pages long.

- ✔ **Grandfather clause:** This law stated that you could only vote if your grandfather voted in the last election. Because their grandfathers hadn't been allowed to vote, African Americans were denied the vote as well.

Legal segregation: Plessy v. Ferguson (1896)

In 1890, Louisiana passed the Separate Car Act, which segregated railroad cars. An African American man named Homer Plessy was arrested for violating this law and decided to challenge it in court. His case finally made it to the Supreme Court in 1896, where the Court ruled that the act was constitutional. This Court decision said that segregation was legal under the equal protection clause of the 14th Amendment as long as the railroad provided equal accommodations for African Americans. The "separate but equal" ruling provided the legal basis for all segregation in the South until *Brown v. The Board of Education* overturned it in 1954 (see Chapter 19).

Sharecropping

Planters still needed to plant their crops, but now they had to pay for the labor. In a cash-strapped, post–Civil War culture, paying for labor wasn't always easy. The answer: If you rented and worked a section of a planter's land, he'd pay you a percentage of the crops it yielded. He would also provide farming equipment and shelter. This is known as *sharecropping*. Many freed men and poor whites liked the idea because it gave them some sense of ownership and independence, but many fell into debt due to dropping prices of cash crops (like cotton) and because they had to purchase supplies on credit from store owners who often overcharged them. Sometimes the landowner was also the shop owner. The system was stacked against the sharecroppers, and many found themselves working harder and falling faster into debt. This system wasn't slavery, but it was certainly a close relative.

Exerting white supremacy

White supremacists not only made the wheels of Reconstruction spin in reverse, they also used legal means to take away civil rights in the South almost as fast as those rights had been given. White supremacists further degraded the rights of African Americans through threats, beatings, and murders. The Ku Klux Klan and other like-minded groups created a culture of terror in the South that took away any freedoms that African Americans had left.

Tying it all together: A sample question looks at Reconstruction's aftermath

For the SAT II, make sure that you have solid knowledge of the measures that the South took after Reconstruction to assert its beliefs after being controlled by the Radical Republican-led government. You may see a question like this one:

All the following were ways in which Southern states attempted to regain control lost in the Civil War, EXCEPT

(A) Passing the Separate Car Act

(B) Setting up an electoral commission in 1877

(C) Implementing poll taxes

(D) Imposing literacy tests for voting requirements

(E) Creating the system of sharecropping

Remember that you're looking for the answer choice that's NOT a way that the South tried to regain control.

All the answer choices involve issues about Southern "redemption," but one of them didn't directly provide a means of regaining Southern control. Passing the Separate Car Act was a means of enacting segregation, so (A) describes an attempt at regaining control. Eliminate this choice. Answers (C), (D), and (E) describe fairly obvious ways that the South tried to undermine the freedoms extended to African Americans. But (B) also seems right. Didn't the Compromise of 1877 give the South control?

Be careful with (B). Although the Compromise of 1877 did initiate concessions to the South, the electoral commission actually took away a form of Southern control. Republicans instituted the Republican-dominated commission to keep a Democrat from becoming president, so (B) is the answer that does NOT describe a way in which Southern states attempted to regain control.

Chapter 11

Reaching Boundaries: The End of the Frontier, 1860–1900

In This Chapter

▶ Surfing the wave of westward wanderers in search of gold

▶ Reliving a violent end to the Native American way of life

▶ Riding a "train" of history through western expansion

History is a funny thing; important events can take place simultaneously. Okay, we realize that you're probably not laughing about having to study for the SAT II U.S. History exam, but consider this fact: Although the Civil War (see Chapter 9) and the Reconstruction era (see Chapter 10) seem to dominate the historical landscape of the mid- to late 1800s, other significant events took place around the same time. And — you guessed it — the SAT II wants you to be aware of these events, too.

We feel compelled to warn you that SAT II History question writers don't seem to spend a whole lot of time on westward expansion, which includes topics, such as mining, cattle ranching, settlers encroaching on Native American lands and the ensuing battles, and the growth of the railroad. But all that stuff is required knowledge for high school students, so it's potential SAT II material. Just remember: An 1890 U.S. Census Bureau document stated that so many people filled in the previously "empty" areas of the West that the term "frontier line" was no longer meaningful. In other words, the West no longer had a point where civilization ended; the United States occupied the land from sea to shining sea.

The Occupation of the Far West: Gold and Cattle Fever

In the first half of the 19th century, most of America's population was on the East Coast. But in the second half of the century, some exciting stuff was going on in the West that drew many adventurous souls from established eastern cities to the wide open western spaces. For instance, the discovery of gold in western territories promised quick and easy fortunes, and the expanses of land in the western plains provided room for ranching. Government land grants enticed Americans who wanted to establish new lives. So by the end of the century, the population had spread from coast to coast.

Gold in them thar hills: Mining's heyday

In the late 1800s, gold fever was a national preoccupation. Settlers discovered gold and silver deposits throughout the West, sending thousands in waves to what are now the states of Nevada, Colorado, Idaho, Montana, the Dakotas, and Arizona. Men left their businesses, their wives, and their children for the chance to strike it rich.

Gold fever began in 1848 when a mill worker named James Marshall stumbled upon bits of yellow ore in a creek bed at Sutter's Mill in California. Word spread and, by 1849, more than 80,000 people (called "'49ers") flooded the Sacramento Valley to seek their fortunes. This migration became known as the *California Gold Rush* (see Chapter 8 for more details). By 1854, more than 300,000 people, or one in every 90 people living in the United States, had migrated to California. Boomtowns sprang up where wilderness once was, and Sacramento and San Francisco, once small villages, became thriving centers of commerce.

By the 1860s, companies mounting large-scale mining operations using heaving machinery and technology to blast holes in the earth had replaced the glory days of the lone miner panning for gold on some remote claim. Many miners went to work for these companies as wage earners, giving up their dreams of striking the "mother lode." Mining became big business, and most Western settlers made their money in this industry. By 1880, precious metal resources had dwindled and, except for a few gold and silver discoveries in Colorado in the 1890s, the mining boom had mostly faded by the end of the century.

For SAT II purposes, remember that the discovery of gold was a catalyst for the greatest westward migration in U.S. history, which, in turn, jump-started a series of changes in the West. (You find out about these changes as you read this chapter.)

Home on the range: Ranching and farming the West

Following the Civil War, Texans came home from fighting, took a look around and thought, "Well, I'll be. We sure's got a lotta cattle 'round here." In fact, around four million wild cattle roamed Texas. These cattle were descendants of animals left behind by Spanish explorers. Someone figured out that if Texans could round up the cattle and ship them east, where beef was in high demand, they could make a lot of money. So cattle ranching spread throughout the West, and the cowboy became an icon of the American West.

Cattle could graze on the open plains and, when the time came, cowboys drove them along the *Chisholm Trail* to Abilene, Kansas, to load them onto trains and ship them east. Between 1867 and 1871, 1.5 million heads of cattle passed through Abilene.

For a while, the plains were open, meaning that no one owned them. Ranchers branded their cattle and allowed them to intermingle and roam freely, knowing that they could sort out whose was whose when the time came. But things soon changed. Because ranching was profitable, it grew as an industry, which led to overgrazing and a shortage of available water. A shortage of water led to dead cattle and ranches fenced in with barbed wire. The drought of 1886 and the blizzards of 1887 wiped out about 95 percent of the cattle in one year. Oh, and one other minor detail: Because the market was flooded with beef, the price of beef dropped significantly, and many ranchers went out of business. This doomsday scenario meant that ranching was going the way of the dodo by the 1880s, which was just as well because farms began occupying the plains.

In 1862, Congress passed the *Homestead Act,* which gave 160 acres of land to anyone willing to move West on the condition that they make improvements to the land, such as adding irrigation and settling for at least five years. Thousands of Americans made the move, but this migration was just the beginning. In 1869, railroads began selling land given to them by the government so they could pay back huge loans that they'd needed to build the transcontinental railroad. Railroad companies embarked on huge advertising campaigns announcing the availability of land and describing it as a virtual Garden of Eden, which, of course, it wasn't. The advertising paid off because, between 1870 and 1890, millions took the bait. (For more about the railroads, see the section "Bridging East and West: The Railroad Era" later in this chapter.) Farming the Great Plains turned out to be extremely difficult because of the arid climate and the tough sod, which was difficult for farmers' plows to break. The result was that many farmers became destitute.

What's important to know for the SAT II is that between mining, cattle ranching, and farming, the West became less and less wild by the end the 19th century.

A Hostile Takeover: Removing the Native Americans

The tidal wave of settlers who came crashing into western lands meant progress and growth for the United States, but it meant utter destruction and ruin for the Native American tribes that called the western lands home.

The U.S. government wanted Native Americans out of settlers' ways. Nevermind that Native American tribes had signed treaties with the U.S. government that declared their rights to land that white settlers were readily helping themselves to. Native Americans were forced or tricked into signing new treaties that gave them less land; then, the government eventually broke those treaties, too. The government's ultimate goal was to remove Native Americans from the desirable lands they had occupied for centuries (and that the U.S. wished to own) and place them on reservations in less attractive locations.

Violent clashes between settlers and Native Americans were a part of life. From 1861 to 1891, more than 1,000 battles and skirmishes occurred. The U.S. government responded to this violence with military campaigns to force tribes onto reservations. The government also encouraged professional hunters to kill off the Native Americans' primary food source — the buffalo. From 1872 to 1874, these hunters killed as many as three million buffalo per year. By the early 1880s, very few buffalo were left.

In this section, we cover some of the major battles between Native Americans and U.S. soldiers and look at the problems of the Bureau of Indian Affairs.

Seen better days: Warfare and the demise of the Native American way of life

Native Americans were living in North America at least as early as 10,000 B.C. (see Chapter 3) — long before the first European settlers came. But by the late 1800s, the number of Native Americans was dwindling due to starvation, disease, and violent conflict with the white settlers who were encroaching on their land. With Native Americans' land being taken away, their way of life was coming to a forced end. Many Native Americans accepted their fate and relocated to reservation lands designated by the U.S. government, but others chose to fight.

U.S. soldiers and Native American warriors fought many battles, but for the purposes of the SAT II, we selected some of the big ones that may pop up in a question.

The Sand Creek Massacre

In the 1850s and 1860s, Colorado's population of white settlers grew, thanks to the gold and silver rushes (see "Gold in them thar hills: Mining's heyday" earlier in this chapter for more about mining). This growth angered the Cheyenne and Arapahos because white settlers overran their lands. Clashes between Native Americans and white settlers took place, and blood spilled on both sides. Colorado Governor John Evans wanted the Cheyenne and Arapaho lands open to white settlers, but the Cheyenne and Arapahos weren't having any of it. Evans ordered a militia, commanded by *Colonel John Chivington,* to attack and destroy any Native Americans in its path.

This order resulted in a bloody massacre along Sand Creek in southeastern Colorado in 1864. Chivington, a former Methodist minister who thought the only way to deal with Native Americans was to kill them, ordered his militia to attack a camp of Arapahos and Cheyenne. The Native Americans in the camp, led by Chief Black Kettle, were peaceful and believed that they had been granted sanctuary, so they weren't prepared for Chivington's attack.

Chivington's militia slaughtered hundreds of Native Americans, half of whom were women and children. Afterward, soldiers amused themselves by scalping and mutilating the dead bodies. Chivington was initially praised for his victory but eventually was court martialed for the extreme brutality of the attack on peaceful individuals. But because he no longer served in the military, he could not be punished. Evans lost his federal appointment as governor for his role in the slaughter.

The Sioux War

Once again, violence erupted when white settlers invaded Native American lands in search of gold. This time the backdrop was the Black Hills of South Dakota, a land the Sioux considered sacred. During the 1850s, the Sioux began a campaign of guerrilla warfare against mining camps, stagecoaches, and wagon trains along the Bozeman Trail, which went right through their land.

After several years of fighting, the U.S. government appeared to relent with the Fort Laramie Treaty of 1868, which acknowledged Sioux rights over the Black Hills. But in 1875, President Ulysses S. Grant informed Sioux Chief Red Cloud that the U.S. intended to buy the gold-rich Black Hills from the Sioux. When Grant realized that the Sioux would not cooperate, he sent the army after them.

On the morning of June 25, 1876, Lt. Col. *George Armstrong Custer* came upon a Sioux village along the bank of the Little Bighorn River in Montana and decided to attack it. Custer charged the village with 210 men, but he quickly discovered that he was vastly outnumbered and retreated to a nearby hilltop, which 2,500 Cheyenne and Sioux warriors led by *Chief Sitting Bull* and *Chief Crazy Horse* surrounded. This became known as *Custer's Last Stand.* In less than an hour, all 210 members of the cavalry troop were dead. The victory was short-lived, though. The U.S. Army hunted the Sioux until May 1877, when they gave up the Black Hills and agreed to settle on reservations. To escape living on a reservation, Sitting Bull led his followers to Canada.

The retreat of the Nez Perce

In spring 1877, the U.S. government decided that because white settlers were moving into Idaho, the Nez Perce bands couldn't roam the land the tribe believed it rightfully owned. Nez Perce *Chief Joseph* attempted to negotiate with Brigadier General O. O. Howard, but Howard told Joseph to leave in 30 days or else. Most Nez Perce complied, but some began conducting guerilla raids on white settlers.

On June 17, 1877, an army battalion attacked a Nez Perce camp. This struggle came to be known as the *Battle of White Bird Canyon.* The Nez Perce won the battle, but for the next four months, the army chased them for more than 1,500 miles through grueling terrain as the natives tried to make their way to Canada. The army caught up with them on September 29, 1877, in Montana. A battle ensued, followed by a standoff that lasted until October 5, when Chief Joseph surrendered with a famous speech, saying that he would fight no more.

Riddled with corruption: The Bureau of Indian Affairs

Not only did the Native Americans have their land stolen out from under them while the U.S. government looked the other way or waved guns in their faces and forced them to forfeit their lands, but to add insult to injury, the *Bureau of Indian Affairs* — the one government agency that was supposed to help them — was corrupt.

In 1849, the government transferred the bureau (which John C. Calhoun created in 1824) from the War Department to the Department of Interior and gave the bureau the responsibility of providing aid to Native Americans living on reservations, many of whom were suffering from disease and starvation. The responsibility of administering this aid went to "Indian agents," who were supposed to distribute food and supplies to the Native Americans.

By the 1860s, the system was brimming with corruption. Rather than distributing supplies to Native Americans, many Indian Bureau agents sold the goods to white settlers, making one heck of a profit. By 1869, the situation was so bad that a member of the House of Representatives said that no branch of the federal government was as corrupt as the Indian Bureau.

Government attempts to "civilize" Native Americans

In 1851, the U.S. government divided the large reservations, which President Andrew Jackson had begun in the 1830s, into smaller reservations devoted to specific Native American tribes. Government officials thought that they could better control Native Americans if they were more concentrated and on separate pieces of land.

As the century wore on, the U.S. government decreased the size of reservations to provide more land for white settlers. During the 1880s, the Native American removal policy was in jeopardy because not much land was left to remove them to. To remedy this situation, the federal government passed the *Dawes Act* in 1887. The Dawes Act divided some existing Native American reservation lands into 160-acre farms and pushed Native Americans to take up farming and take on western culture. These landholdings replaced traditional communal tribal holdings, which weakened traditional communal bonds. The government also instituted ways to "civilize" Native Americans, such as setting up schools to teach English and providing land incentives for them to change their names to more traditional English ones. Some Native Americans adapted to this cultural upheaval, but most did not.

Tying it all together: A sample question looks at policy regarding Native Americans

The SAT II U.S. History exam isn't going to try stumping you by testing your knowledge of the names of specific Native American tribes affected by western expansion or their chiefs. Nevertheless, the following question is definitely fair game because it tests what you know about the general relationship between the U.S. government and Native Americans in the second half of the 19th century.

Which of the following best describes U.S. policy regarding Native Americans during the period of western expansion, which occurred from 1860 to 1900?

(A) Peaceful renegotiation of treaties

(B) Compensation for tribal lands lost to white settlers

(C) Forceful removal of Native Americans to reservation lands

(D) Extermination of Native American tribes

(E) Encouragement of peaceful living between whites and Native Americans

Answers (A) and (B) aren't correct because, although the two groups negotiated treaties, they were often "renegotiated" at gunpoint. Native Americans often had to accept the terms "or else," and were rarely justly compensated. The terms were usually one-sided, with the U.S. government taking much more than it gave.

The question asks you for the *best* answer, which means that some answers sound kind of right but that other choices answer the question better. For instance, answer (D) is incorrect because it's too extreme. Although the U.S. Army killed a lot of Native Americans, extermination was never the official policy of the U.S. government. Correct answer choices on the SAT II are rarely fanatical; they're usually bland and safe.

Answer (E) is wrong as well; it goes to the other extreme. The U.S. government rarely punished white settlers for killing Native Americans, though it actively hunted any tribe that dared attack white settlers or refused to leave their lands quietly. The answer here is (C). When the U.S. won a battle over the Native Americans in the last half of the 19th century, it moved the defeated natives to reservations and actively pursued those tribes that resisted.

Bridging East and West: The Railroad Era

The mad dash West in the mid-1800s caused congressional leaders to rub their chins, scratch their heads, and sigh collectively. The idea to connect the Atlantic and Pacific coasts by railway wasn't new; in fact, Congress had tossed it around for years, but the growth of population and industry in the West accelerated the need. In 1862, Congress passed the *Pacific Railroad Act,* which provided the means and support to build the country's first transcontinental railroad. This job was awarded to the Union Pacific and the Central Pacific railroads.

The railroad got off to a slow start, largely because of a distraction called the Civil War, but when the war was over, the game was on. Through the hard work of labor forces made up of Chinese and Irish immigrants, the railway was completed on May 10, 1869 at Promontory Summit in present-day Utah.

Now, you may be saying that that's all fine and dandy, but do I have to know this stuff for the SAT II? And we would respond by saying, trust us, we're here to save you time, not waste it. The following information is a rundown of the major plot points regarding railroads in the late 19th century. Pay attention because, most likely, the SAT II will throw at least one question at you about railroads.

Building and routing the transcontinental railroad

The SAT II U.S. History exam is going to assume that you have some general knowledge about how the railroads were actually built. Building the first transcontinental railroad was serious business for more than one reason. The project took the Central Pacific and Union Pacific railroad companies about six years and 20,000 laborers to cover 2,000 miles of track.

Building railroads wasn't the type of job that most white Americans wanted: It was backbreaking, dangerous work. The Union Pacific relied on Irish and German immigrants, ex-slaves, and ex-Confederate soldiers for labor, and the Central Pacific relied on thousands of Chinese laborers. At first, Americans didn't believe that the Chinese could handle the work, but they proved that they were more than capable. They worked harder, complained less, and were more organized than the white laborers; they also worked for less. Throughout the 1800s, Chinese laborers made up a large percentage of the labor used to build the railroads.

Workers laid all 2,000 miles of track using pickaxes, shovels, wheelbarrows, blasting powder, and brawn and sweat. Men worked 12-hour days six days a week, living in open wilderness with very few comforts or entertainment. The Central Pacific planned a route through the Sierra Nevada Mountains, which required blasting tunnels through solid granite (sometimes progressing only several inches in a single day) and trying to avoid being killed by the explosions, avalanches, and freezing temperatures. Laborers laid the track over and through treacherous mountains, across desert sands, over canyons and rivers, and through hostile Native American territories. Thousands of workers died in the process.

The importance of railroads

Between 1860 and 1900, millions of Americans went West to seek their fortunes or to own their own stretch of land. This movement became the greatest mass migration in U.S. history, and it brought about the rapid settlement of states throughout the West and, ultimately, the end of the frontier. The migration fueled the need for railroad expansion and, in turn, the growth of railroads greatly accelerated western expansion.

Here are some key points to remember about the importance of railroads for the SAT II:

✔ The system of railroads, including a number of transcontinental lines, built in the West in the late 1800s enabled settlers to move west in greater numbers in much less time, for much less money, while being a heck of a lot safer, not to mention more comfortable, than traveling by stagecoach or wagon train.

✔ Railroads made shipping goods to markets in the East possible for farmers and ranchers, and goods and supplies from the East could easily get into the hands of Western settlers, thus, greatly increasing commerce and trade.

✔ The expansion of railroads also improved communications. Wherever a railroad track was, telegraph lines were also planted, providing transcontinental communication.

Curbing the corruption: The Interstate Commerce Act and J. P. Morgan's involvement

Despite the phenomenal growth and power of the railroad industry in the late 1800s, no referee was around to blow a whistle and toss a flag when a company committed a personal foul. In many cases, railroad companies had transportation monopolies because even though quite a few railroad companies existed, they serviced different routes. Railroad companies discriminated by charging passengers and shippers different prices in different parts of the country. Railroad companies also provided rebates to large shippers and buyers but didn't offer the same rebates to the little guy, who lacked the shipment volume necessary to obtain them. Small businesses folded because they couldn't compete, and the bigger businesses monopolized the industry and controlled prices.

One of the worst scandals to rock the railroad industry involved a company called Credit Mobilier, which stockholders of the Union Pacific Railroad set up to construct tracks. The railroad company essentially set up a system in which it awarded itself lucrative contracts financed with government money and, to make things even more convenient, the company made congressmen stockholders of the company. When a U.S. representative revealed the scandal in 1872, some politicians' reputations suffered, but no one was prosecuted.

After listening to the public, particularly farmers, complain about being ripped off by railroad companies for nearly a decade, Congress — always quick to act (that's sarcasm) — decided the time had arrived to do something. Railroads were too powerful for states to handle, so the federal government stepped in and passed the *Interstate Commerce Act* in 1887. This act

✔ Required railroads to charge "just and reasonable" rates for transporting passengers and products.

✔ Outlawed special rebates.

✔ Prohibited price discrimination against smaller businesses.

✔ Required that all railroad companies publish their rates.

✔ Most importantly, set up the *Interstate Commerce Commission* (ICC) — the first independent government regulatory agency — which was responsible for monitoring and regulating the railroad industry.

Although Congress dealt a blow to railroad corruption by instituting the Interstate Commerce Commission, reform also came from another more unlikely, source: *John Pierpont Morgan,* arguably the biggest railroad tycoon of them all. Through the banking firm Drexel, Morgan and Company, of which he was a partner (reorganized as J. P. Morgan and Company in 1895), Morgan wielded enormous power by brokering deals and investing in a wide array of industries. Most notably, he was responsible for the birth of General Electric and the U.S. Steel Company, which became America's first billion-dollar company. More importantly, at least for SAT II purposes, Morgan went to town buying up stock and gaining controlling interests (that is, 51 percent or more of a company's stock) in railroads.

Morgan began reorganizing the railroad industry in 1885 when he brokered a deal between the New York Central Railroad and the Pennsylvania Railroad (two of the largest railroads at the time). The deal minimized the destructive rate and the track-building competition that had been going on between the two companies. When the ball was rolling, Morgan began wheeling and dealing between other railroads and buying up their stocks. Through this process, Morgan consolidated and restructured many railroad companies and added his own regulations and standards to prevent the chaotic competition that was going on, which had been responsible for the rate instability. Morgan probably didn't do all this work out of a desire to help the common man; more likely, he saw an opportunity to make a lot of money. Nevertheless, his Pac-Manlike takeover of the railroad industry brought order to it. (For more about J. P. Morgan, see Chapter 12.)

The SAT II may test you on 19th-century railroad business with a question about railroad companies' corrupt practices. This question also tests what you know about the ICC.

The Interstate Commerce Act of 1887 prevented railroads from doing which of the following?

(A) Charging unfair shipping rates

(B) Segregating railway cars

(C) Transporting alcohol across state lines

(D) Neglecting safety measures

(E) All of the above

From the information we provide in this section, you get a pretty clear picture that the Interstate Commerce Act was all about regulating shipping prices, so (A) is the best answer.

The other answers seem logical and reasonable, so if you didn't know the valuable information in this chapter, you may have wanted to choose (D) or even (E). But think about the time period. The question tells you that Congress instituted the act in 1887, so you can be pretty sure that the government wasn't concerned about alcohol transportation. Now you can easily eliminate (C) and (E). Because the act is a commerce act, it probably deals with business practices. Answer (A) is the only remaining answer choice that concerns business.

Chapter 12

America's Second Industrial Revolution, 1860–1900

In This Chapter

▶ Checking out advances that jump-started industrialization

▶ Meeting the robber barons of American industry

▶ Understanding the effects of industrialization on society

▶ Finding out about politics during the Second Industrial Revolution

More than anything, the rise of big business shaped the period between 1860 and 1900, also known as the *Second Industrial Revolution.* Society's outlook changed with the emergence of the ultra rich, and industrial growth influenced several areas of American life. For instance, an increased demand for factory workers encouraged a new flood of immigration from other countries and the migration of Americans from rural areas. Urbanization brought workers closer to cities, and with the growing separation between the rich and the poor, social unrest and labor disputes emerged.

Big business wanted a government without business regulations, and the political leaders of the late 1800s wanted whatever was best for business. The boom cycle saw tremendous growth for America, but eventually the boom ended and the depression of 1893 hit.

The SAT II recognizes the important developments that occurred during the late 1800s. Therefore, understanding the main themes and events of the period are important. As you study this chapter, focus on the causes of the rise of big business, the main players, and how big business influenced society and politics.

Curious about the first Industrial Revolution in the early 1800s? See Chapter 8 for details.

Fueling the Fires of Industry: Advances That Spurred Industrialization

The dramatic increase in industrial manufacturing wouldn't have been possible without important technical advancements and the discovery of new materials. The development of steel, oil, and bituminous coal enabled industries to grow. Innovators in the late 1800s also created a remarkable number of inventions that helped industries flourish.

Steel: It sure isn't pig iron

Sir Henry Bessemer, an Englishman, discovered a cheap and easy way to purify iron in the 1850s. With purification, the new metal, called steel, was lighter, stronger, and more durable. The new process for mass producing steel was an important development in the Second Industrial Revolution. It required factory workers to blow air into the metal in order to push carbon out of standard pig iron. (Pig iron is a raw material used to produce steel.)

Steel, the new super metal, allowed for the growth of skyscrapers and bridges. For the SAT II, keep in mind that steel production made the Second Industrial Revolution possible.

Fuel for thought: Oil and bituminous coal

The late 1800s brought the advancement of fuels, which American industry needed to power industrial machines and for transportation improvements such as railroads (see Chapter 11 for the full scoop about railroads). The two major fuel advances were

- ✔ **Oil:** The first major U.S. oil well was drilled in Pennsylvania in 1859. In 1860, the U.S. produced 500,000 barrels of oil, and the number rose to 4.2 million barrels by 1870. Oil was used for heating, lighting, and the lubrication of machinery used especially in the steel industry.

- ✔ **Bituminous coal:** By the 1870s, bituminous coal, mined in Appalachia, was more prevalent in industry than anthracite (or hard) coal was. Anthracite coal was popular during the First Industrial Revolution because it was cleaner, longer-burning, and less smoky than bituminous coal was. But bituminous coal became more popular during the Second Industrial Revolution because it was more plentiful and easier to extract (and therefore cheaper), and it had a heat value comparable to anthracite coal's. Coal was required for fueling steam-powered railroads and steelmaking plants.

Lights, camera, action: New inventions

Thousands of inventions that you probably take for granted today came about in the late 1800s. Even though the SAT II won't test you on all the new-fangled inventions that cropped up during this period, you should understand the great strides that inventors made for the advancement of the country and know some of the most famous inventors and inventions. Between 1860 and 1900, the U.S. government granted 676,000 patents. The new products these patents generated along with the ones in the following list introduced a new world of manufacturing, business, and consumerism.

- ✔ **Isaac Singer:** Singer revolutionized the manufacturing sector and the garment industry with his 1851 invention of the sewing machine. His corporation, I. M. Singer and Company, was one of the first modern manufacturing corporations in the U.S.

- ✔ **Christopher L. Sholes and Carlos Glidden:** In 1868, Sholes and Glidden invented a typewriter that worked faster than a person could handwrite, significantly speeding up business correspondence.

- ✔ **Thomas Edison:** Edison was the most famous inventor of the period (and maybe of all time). Edison created a research lab to study and test new ideas and inventions in the 1870s. Among his 1,093 inventions were the phonograph, the incandescent light bulb, the motion picture, and electrical generators and power plants used to furnish electricity to homes and businesses. You might say that he's the father of MTV.

✔ **Alexander Graham Bell:** You and your significant other can talk all night without sneaking out of the house because of Bell's invention of the telephone in 1876. The telephone greatly improved communication and eventually transformed business and industry, which before the telephone's invention had relied on the tedious telegraph to get messages to distant locations.

✔ **Joel Tiffany and Gustavus Swift:** Tiffany patented the refrigerator car in 1877, which enabled Swift to create the first huge national meatpacking network in the 1880s and provide a national market for fruits and vegetables.

✔ **Georges Eastman:** Eastman (think Eastman Kodak) invented an inexpensive camera in 1879. The camera allowed individuals and businesses to document information and events with photography. We wonder how proud grandmothers showed off before Eastman . . . .

✔ **James Ritty:** Ritty helped speed up the retail sector with his invention of the cash register in 1879.

✔ **William S. Burroughs:** Burroughs made life much easier for accountants with his invention of the calculating adding machine in 1891.

Tying it all together: A sample question looks at technology and industrialization

The SAT II may ask you to identify the technology that laid the groundwork for the Second Industrial Revolution.

Which of the following advancements in technology was most instrumental in ushering in the Industrial Revolution of the late 19th century?

(A) Bessemer steel

(B) Tiffany's refrigerator car

(C) Edison's incandescent light bulb

(D) Anthracite coal

(E) The inexpensive camera

You can probably eliminate (C) and (E) right off the bat. The light bulb and the camera were important inventions, but neither was the driving force behind the Second Industrial Revolution. The refrigerator car revolutionized the meat and produce industry but not the Second Industrial Revolution in general. You can eliminate (B). All three of these answer choices refer to inventions that occurred during the Industrial Revolution, not before it.

The two forces behind the industrial revolution were improvements in steel and coal. So now you need to choose between (A) and (D).

Answer (D) throws in the distinction of "anthracite" coal. This hard coal was pretty much on the way out by 1870, so it wasn't really the coal that ushered in the industrial age. It was bituminous coal that was easier to extract, cheaper, and just as hot-burning that reigned in popularity by 1870. Don't read too quickly. And don't let the inclusion of Bessemer in choice (A) fool you. Bessemer was the inventor of the iron purification process that produced the new steel. His new process produced the most influential advancement for the Second Industrial Revolution, so (A) is the correct answer.

Winning Monopoly: The Robber Barons

Industry created growth, and growth created profits — big profits. Andrew Carnegie, J. P. Morgan, and John D. Rockefeller became the wealthiest men America had ever seen. Some people referred to them as *robber barons* because they controlled such a large percentage of American cash. These barons worked hard, made huge profits, and used their profits to create strangleholds in their industries.

How did they hang on to their industries? By creating monopolies. They formed traditional monopolies, known as *horizontal monopolies,* which means they were the only producers of a certain type of good. For example, say that the product is widgets. A savvy widget producer could form a horizontal monopoly by assimilating all the other widget manufacturers into one company. If you needed a widget, you could get it at only one place.

Using the money these businessmen gained from running horizontal monopolies, they bought up companies that manufactured the products they needed to make the goods that they sold, resulting in a *vertical monopoly.* Now the widget producer could make money not only from selling the only widgets in town, but also by owning the factories that produced the steel and other stuff used to create widgets.

By eliminating competition and controlling production within a specific industry, monopoly owners were able to effectively raise the prices of the industry's products without worrying that consumers would buy from less expensive competitors. Price increases resulted in big profits for the monopolies at the expense of consumers.

Ingenious 19th-century businessmen created powerful companies, but as you might imagine, the not-so-fortunate and more morally conscious Americans despised them for their questionable business practices, which led to the passage of the Sherman Antitrust Act.

The steel magnates: Andrew Carnegie and J. P. Morgan

Andrew Carnegie immigrated to the United States from Scotland. As a member of a poor immigrant family, Carnegie knew how to work hard. He catapulted his way up from working a 72-hour week in a cotton factory at age 12 to assisting the president of the Pennsylvania railroad when he was 17. (And he didn't even take the SAT II!)

Carnegie founded Union Iron Mills in 1863, and his revolutionary Bessemer converter and open-hearth steelmaking method allowed him to decrease labor costs. Additionally, he unified the operations of the mill to complete all stages of steel production in one integrated process. Therefore, Carnegie significantly lowered his steel prices and created a steel empire by underselling his competition. By 1901, Carnegie Steel was responsible for one quarter of all steel production in the U.S., and Carnegie eventually sold his company to J. P. Morgan for $480 million in 1901. When he joked that he should have held out for another $100 million, Morgan said he would have paid it.

Carnegie's wealth didn't make him forget his humble roots, however. He felt that with wealth came the responsibility to better society, and when he died in 1919, he had donated $350 million to charitable causes.

The purchaser of Carnegie's steel empire, J. P. Morgan, was the son of a banker and became a banker himself. He made vast profits during the Civil War and became a great financier. When he brokered the deal that bought out Carnegie Steel, he consolidated it with several other steel firms and formed the United States Steel Corporation in 1901. U.S. Steel controlled 60 percent of steel productions worldwide and became the first company in the world with an estimated worth exceeding a billion dollars ($22 billion by 1913).

The oil salesman: John D. Rockefeller

Like Carnegie, John D. Rockefeller also hailed from humble beginnings. His father was a snake oil salesman (which meant he sold bogus healing potions), but John found a much more profitable oil to sell. In the 1870s, Rockefeller purchased as many oil companies as he could to create the Standard Oil Company in Ohio. By 1882, the Standard Oil monopoly controlled as much as 85 percent of the American oil market.

Rockefeller built Standard Oil's dominance on driving competitors out of business. Standard Oil entered markets with local competition and sold its oil at a loss until the competition went out of business. After obliterating the competition, Standard Oil raised its rates. Rockefeller wasn't afraid to spy and bribe in order to achieve his goals, either. His practices made him the world's first billionaire but also caused journalists of the day to attack him.

The Sherman Antitrust Act

With large monopolies pushing out competitors, many Americans wondered where it would end. In 1890, Congress passed the *Sherman Antitrust Act* in an attempt to regulate trusts. A *trust* is any large business entity or group of businesses that come together to try to control a market. The goal of the act was to prevent the practices that create business monopolies by encouraging healthy competition in industry. It prohibited any type of trade or commerce contract between business entities and required government attorneys and district courts to investigate and prosecute trusts, if necessary. But it wasn't until Theodore Roosevelt took office in the early 1900s that the act became an effective way to control monopolies. (See Chapter 14 for more on Roosevelt and the act.)

Aftershock: Industrialization's Effects on Society

The wide separation between the haves and have nots influenced American philosophy in the late 1800s. The notion of survival of the fittest and every man for himself became ingrained in the national consciousness. Labor unions developed to organize workers victimized by impossible working conditions, and immigrants seeking work in American manufacturing arrived from different regions and changed the makeup of American culture. Meanwhile, urban areas grew, pragmatism reigned, and popular culture mirrored Americans' interest in realism.

Remember that the SAT II likes to test causes and effects with questions that require more critical analysis than straight memorization. For this reason, you should understand how industrialization affected American culture. You should also focus on the permeation of the philosophies of realism and practicality.

Social Darwinism and "The Gospel of Wealth"

Building on Charles Darwin's concept of *natural selection* (which said that in nature, only the fittest members of each species survive and the weaker members perish), English philosopher Herbert Spencer created a theory about the evolution of human society known as Social Darwinism in the 1870s. *Social Darwinism* defined individuals' progress in society using the notion of "survival of the fittest." Spencer said that competition in the marketplace created an environment in which the weak fall and the strong persevere — a sort of "may the best person win" philosophy. Many robber barons (whom we cover earlier in this chapter) used this notion to justify hostile takeovers and other aggressive business practices. Government interference with the strongest players' attempts to overcome the weak could be seen as impeding the natural course of progress. So, the rich used the theory of Social Darwinism to defend their exploitation of the poor.

However, reformers and some robber barons, like Andrew Carnegie, interpreted Social Darwinism differently. They felt that the "fittest" had an obligation to help the weak survive, too. Carnegie thought that wealth was a sign from God that you were doing okay, and he urged the rich to work on behalf of the poor in his 1889 essay titled "The Gospel of Wealth." He suggested that the wealthy should dedicate any wealth exceeding their own needs to philanthropic works.

Social Darwinism was such an important theory in the late 1800s that the SAT II is likely to ask you a question like the following.

Which of the following did robber barons of the 19th century use to justify their practices?

(A) The Sherman Antitrust Act

(B) "The Gospel of Wealth"

(C) Social Darwinism

(D) Vertical monopolies

(E) Trusts

If you didn't remember the nature of "The Gospel of Wealth," you may want to choose (B) just because of the way it sounds. A gospel of wealth seems to justify robber baron practices. But Carnegie's "Gospel of Wealth" actually encouraged the wealthy to help the underprivileged, so (B) is incorrect.

The Sherman Antitrust Act sought to curb monopolies, so it wasn't a justification for robber barons, so (A) is wrong. Business moguls used vertical monopolies and trusts to advance profits but didn't justify their practices with them; you can eliminate (D) and (E). You're left with (C). Social Darwinism and its theme of "survival of the fittest" provided robber barons with the justification big business needed to excuse its ways. Answer (C) is correct.

Riot act: A state of labor unrest

Big industry relied on lots of labor, and soon the fittest of the laborers began to fight for their survival. Laborers commonly worked a 70- to 80-hour workweek, and they often worked in polluted environments and dangerous conditions. American workers insisted on shorter hours, better education, safer working environments, an end to child labor, and a fair share of profits. Individual workers had little power to negotiate employment contracts; however, labor unions began to emerge and gave American workers a rare opportunity to make their needs known to their often indifferent employers. Unlike the earlier unions that existed during the First Industrial Revolution and included primarily skilled workers (see Chapter 8), the new crop of unions also embraced unskilled workers. The labor movement progressed slowly in the late 1800s (unions didn't become powerful until the 20th century), but here are a couple of labor unions that got their start in the last half of the 1800s:

✔ **Knights of Labor:** Uriah S. Stevens initially organized the Noble Order of the Knights of Labor in 1869. Union membership was open to all workers as long as they weren't lawyers, bankers, liquor dealers, or professional gamblers. Minorities, the skilled and unskilled, and men and women were welcome. The Knights of Labor moved into prominence and national recognition in the 1870s and 1880s under the leadership of *Terence Powderly.* By 1886, it claimed 700,000 members, but some organization and strike failures in the 1880s caused membership to shrink to only 100,000 members by 1890, and the organization failed altogether by the mid-1890s.

✔ **American Federation of Labor (AFL):** A group of representatives from craft unions founded this union in 1881 and adopted the name American Federation of Labor in 1886. *Samuel Gompers* was one of its early leaders. The AFL represented skilled laborers in craft unions in the immediate objectives of better wages, hours, and working conditions, and it was successful because of good leadership and organization. In the 1930s it was the largest union in the country (see Chapter 17).

The labor unrest developed into some major confrontations, and the amount of unrest is nearly incomprehensible. In 1894 alone, 1,400 strikes occurred that involved almost 700,000 workers. The most important labor strikes of this time period (which you should remember for the SAT II) were the Haymarket Riot, the Homestead Strike, and the Pullman Strike.

✔ **Haymarket Riot:** On May 4, 1886, labor groups organized in Chicago to support an eight-hour workday. Someone threw a bomb at police, killing one officer almost instantly, and the police fired on the crowd, killing four people. Massive hysteria ensued as the crowd fled the scene. In the end, a number of protesters were trampled to death and seven police officers later died.

✔ **Homestead Strike:** In 1892, the steelworkers union in Homestead, Pennsylvania, called a strike when the Carnegie Steel Company cut wages. The steel company hired 300 guards to protect its factories. Violent fights occurred among strikers and the guards, resulting in the deaths of three guards and seven workers. The governor of Pennsylvania ordered all of Pennsylvania's 8,000 National Guard troops to the scene to protect the strikebreakers. Unable to hold out, most strikers quit the union and went back to work for the steel company; and mill workers didn't organize again for another 40 years.

✔ **Pullman Strike:** In 1894, the Pullman Strike occurred near Chicago. The Pullman Company produced coaches for railroads, and workers often lived in company towns where the company controlled rent levels and grocery prices. So when the Pullman Company downsized its workforce from 5,500 to 3,300 and decided to cut wages by at least 25 percent and leave rents and food prices the same, workers became enraged. Labor unions led by *Eugene V. Debs* organized a national boycott of Pullman cars and equipment, severely disrupting railroad transportation between Chicago and the Pacific coast. The company responded by adding mail cars to the end of trains so that the strike caused the mail not to get through. The company also appealed to President Grover Cleveland to intervene. The federal government did intervene, using federal troops to end the strike. In two confrontations between the troops and unionists, 37 union members died.

Industrial unions faced several obstacles to their success, some external and some internal.

✔ The principal labor unions represented a small fraction of the industrial workforce in the U.S. For instance, immigrant workers, many of whom were just planning to earn some good money and then return home, did not make long-term ties and commit to labor unions.

✔ Government usually sided with employers over workers because of the wealth and power represented by corporations. Repeated government intervention thwarted many strikes.

✔ The unions themselves greatly compromised their numbers and influence. Some unions refused membership to women, minority groups, and unskilled workers and remained hostile toward integrating immigrants.

Mass movement: A new wave of immigration

American industrial growth and western expansion drew a mass of immigrants to America. Between 1880 and 1920, approximately 25 million immigrants poured into the U.S., which is even more amazing considering the fact that the U.S. population was about 50 million in 1880. In 1886, France gave the U.S. the Statue of Liberty, which was erected in New York Harbor to welcome immigrants, and in 1892, the U.S. opened Ellis Island, which transferred the control of processing immigrants from state government to the federal government.

Although America's industrial revolution offered great opportunities for immigrants, factors also existed in Europe that forced Europeans to leave their homelands. And, in most cases, America was easier to get to than other popular countries for immigrants, like Australia or Argentina. Before 1890, most immigrants came to America from northern and western Europe; they usually spoke English and practiced a Protestant faith, which most Americans accepted. (Irish immigrants were Catholic and therefore not well-accepted). However, after 1890, 80 percent of immigrants headed for America came from southern and eastern Europe — from countries like Italy, Greece, Poland, and Russia. These immigrants spoke little English and came from diverse faiths. Most settled in American cities, and, by 1920, nearly half the urban population consisted of first- or second-generation immigrants.

Although many European immigrants experienced discrimination in the land of the free, few Europeans suffered the harsh treatment that Americans reserved for Chinese immigrants. Americans victimized the Chinese, who mostly lived in the West, because their language, appearance, dress, and customs were so different, and they were often willing to work for much lower wages than whites. The U.S. government even passed the *Chinese Exclusion Act of 1882,* the first immigration law in the U.S. to target a specific ethnic group.

City life: The urbanization of America

The Second Industrial Revolution created several technologies that led to *urbanization,* or the expansion of cities. In 1860, about only 20 percent of the U.S. population lived in cities that had more than 2,500 people. By 1900, more than 40 percent of Americans dwelled in cities with populations greater than 2,500. Here are some technologies that made city dwelling more desirable:

✔ **Steam power replaced water power in the mid-1800s, so factories no longer required locations on a river.** Owners moved factories close to coal and other materials that they needed for manufacturing. The most desirable sites were on rail lines linking to water sources in cities like New York, Chicago, Cleveland, and St. Louis. Factory jobs in these cities attracted new residents from the country.

✔ **Developments in mass transportation made city dwelling more manageable.** These developments enabled Americans to begin living in suburbs and commuting to the city for work. New methods of transportation also allowed people to move about the cities more easily in the late 19th century. Here are just a few examples:

- **The elevated railway:** New York City experimented with the nation's first elevated railway in the 1870s, in which noisy and polluting steam-powered trains moved around the city raised on massive iron trellises.

- **Cable cars:** In 1873, cable car lines appeared in San Francisco. These cable cars moved passengers in a car along a cable powered by a motor at one end of the line that was strong enough to pull the cars up the city's steep hills. Chicago and New York also experimented with cable cars.

- **Bridges:** The completion in 1883 of the Brooklyn Bridge, designed by John Roebling, was one of the technological marvels of the 1800s.

- **Trolley cars:** In 1888, the folks in Richmond, Virginia, moved about in trolley cars powered by electricity from overhead cables.

- **Subways:** In 1897, Boston pioneered the country's first underground railway, or subway.

✔ **Skyscrapers and elevators made it possible to accommodate a lot of people in a small amount of space:** Modern steel engineering techniques allowed for the first skyscraper (which was actually only a ten-story building) to be built in Chicago in 1885. The development of the first electric elevator was essential to provide transportation to the top stories of those awesome buildings.

✔ **Conveniences like electricity and indoor plumbing were available in cities.** Many rural areas of the country didn't have electricity or indoor plumbing until the end of the 1930s or later, but these conveniences were readily available in cities during the late 1800s. The lure of these modern conveniences influenced some to leave their country homes and join the city life.

Urbanization also had a downside. The great influx of people to big cities produced overcrowding and increased competition for jobs. Foreign immigrants and other job seekers who came to cities with little money in their pockets found meager accommodations in teeming tenements and growing ghettos, and wealthy people moved to the suburbs to escape the crime and squalor associated with the spread of poverty in city neighborhoods. Government in this era did little to assist with domestic issues (see "All That Glitters Isn't Gold: Gilded Age Politics" later in this chapter), so private charities often provided the primary source of aid for cities' poor communities. For instance, social worker *Jane Addams* founded a settlement house called *Hull House* in Chicago in 1889. This home provided aid and services like adult education, athletics, arts and crafts, and clubs to the poor and became a center for social reform. Addams and others like her greatly assisted the large number of disinherited Americans. (See Chapter 27 for more about Addams.)

Holy cow! The Great Chicago Fire

The Great Chicago Fire in 1871 engulfed three square miles of the city in two days. It killed almost 300 people and left thousands homeless. People attributed the fire to Mrs. Catherine O'Leary and her cow. The story went that Mrs. O'Leary had lit a lantern in her barn, which her cow kicked over into the hay. The Board of Police and Fire Commissioners held an inquiry late in 1871, but they couldn't conclusively prove that O'Leary (or her cow) started the fire. The fire in Chicago and other major fires in other cities encouraged the construction of fireproof buildings, the use of modern architectural and engineering techniques in rebuilding, and the development of the professional fire department as an urban institution.

Common sense: A philosophy of Pragmatism

Industrialization glorified science and technology, so the late 19th-century philosophical movements emanated from scientific tradition. Scientists of the period devised a specific method to discern truth called the *scientific method.* This method stated that truth was most readily obtainable through observation, hypothesis, and experimentation. Essentially, seeing is believing.

The tenets of the scientific method carried over into a philosophy of *Pragmatism,* which essentially said that people can discover truth through individual experience, and that truth's relevance lies in how it affects one's life. In other words, truth depended on its practical value. No idea was valid unless experience proved it so.

Charles Saunders Peirce, a mathematician; William James, a psychologist; and John Dewey, a psychologist and education reformer, were the primary Pragmatic philosophers of the era. According to James, the test of truth lies in this question: "What, in short, is the truth's cash-value in experiential terms?"

Pragmatists maintain that pondering traditional philosophical questions like "What is real?" and "How can we know?" are unnecessary and misleading. To the Pragmatist, whether you question the existence of a green light or determine whether you experience green in the same way that someone else does doesn't matter. What's important is that when you see a green light, you can drive. Then, the green light has practical value and meaning.

Pragmatism greatly influenced education in the later half of the 1800s. In 1860 there were only 100 public high schools in the U.S., but there were 6,000 by 1900, and 31 states and territories had mandatory school attendance laws. *John Dewey,* the father of modern progressive education, believed that schools should reflect the needs of society. Dewey's schools taught chemistry and physics through practical demonstrations, such as cooking bacon and eggs for breakfast. If the SAT II test-makers would only catch on to this philosophy, test day would be much more fun and you wouldn't have to eat ahead of time!

For the SAT II, you need to know the basic theory behind Pragmatic philosophy and that it was the first philosophy exclusively developed by American thought.

Get real: An era of popular culture

Popular culture took off during the late 1800s thanks to advances in technology and industry. Newspapers and magazines were the mass media of the day, and journalists were digging up juicy stories rather than reporting boring events. Hmmm, seems kind of familiar, doesn't it? In keeping with the philosophy of Pragmatism, realism was the rage in literature and art. American literature gained greater recognition during the last half of the 19th century as authors concentrated on social commentary, and artists revoked their romantic license and depicted practical stories.

Yellow journalism

During the late 19th century, the cheap paper used for printed products had a yellow cast. Hence, the term *yellow journalism* arose to describe the kind of stories that publishers printed on this cheap, yellow paper. Yellow journalism produced lurid stories of murder, sex, and social atrocities.

William Randolph Hearst was the king of yellow journalism. His *New York Journal's* rivalry with a competing newspaper, the *New York World,* owned by *Joseph Pulitzer,* escalated yellow journalism to a frenzy before and during the Spanish-American War (see Chapter 13). From 1870 to 1910, the circulation of daily newspapers in the U.S. rose from 3 million per day in 1870 to more than 24 million per day in 1910.

Literature: Realists and regionalists

American literature came into its own in the period between 1860 and 1900. American writing focused on depicting the reality of human nature and revealing a slice of life from a variety of regions across the country. Many American classics appeared during this period.

For the SAT II, you don't have to memorize a list of names, works, and dates for every author of the period. But you should recognize some of the names and have a sense of the intent to portray regional life, both the negative and positive aspects.

To help you out, here's a list of authors of the period and their most recognizable works:

- *Horatio Alger's* popular rags-to-riches stories (like *Ragged Dick,* 1868) advance his plucky theory that with hard work, anyone could obtain wealth.

- *Louisa May Alcott's* stories, like *Little Women* (1869), provide sentimental yet realistic depictions of 19th-century domestic life in New England.

- *Mark Twain's* important classics, *The Adventures of Tom Sawyer* (1876) and *The Adventures of Huckleberry Finn* (1884), reveal life along the Mississippi River. In these works and a number of others, Twain made satirical commentary on society, poverty, class tensions, and race relations. In his 1873 book *The Gilded Age,* he commented on the social emptiness of the Industrial Revolution. This title was later used to describe the era of the Second Industrial Revolution.

- *Emily Dickinson's* unconventional poetry (which she wrote from about 1850 until her death in 1886) treated topics such as death in a matter-of-fact way.

- *Henry James* paints a realistic portrait of upper-class life in his novel *The Bostonians* (1886).

- *Edward Bellamy's* 1888 utopian novel, *Looking Backward,* depicted a new social order set in the year 2000.

- *Stephen Crane* reveals the hideousness of the Civil War in *The Red Badge of Courage* (1895). He also portrayed a realistic account of poverty and slum life in his 1893 book *Maggie: A Girl of the Streets*.

- Southern writer *Kate Chopin* wrote *The Awakening* (1899), which exposes female oppressions and reveals that women had emotional and sexual needs.

Art and architecture in the real world

Art and architecture also got an American flavor. *James Abbott McNeill Whistler's* 1872 portrait of his mother, titled *Arrangement in Gray and Black* (better known as *Whistler's Mother*), was perhaps the most famous painting to come out of the age. American realist painters like Thomas Eakins and Winslow Homer depicted their subjects as frankly as possible without idealizing them.

Residential architecture, which reflected the era's tendency to show off, demonstrated the eclectic, elaborate, and eccentric Queen Anne style, featuring spindles, towers, and wraparound porches. Churches, universities, and some residences were often constructed in the Richardsonian Romanesque style. Architect H. H. Richardson adopted Romanesque architecture into a distinctly solid and practical style with rough textures, masonry construction, geometric brickwork, and the use of the semi-circular arch for stability.

When considering the popular culture of the late 19th century for the purposes of the SAT II, focus on the permeation of the philosophies of realism and practicality.

All That Glitters Isn't Gold: Gilded Age Politics

The government of the late 19th century was unremarkable. In keeping with that whole survival of the fittest thing (see the section on Social Darwinism earlier in this chapter), the atmosphere of America at this time tended to favor big business and ignore the common man (especially farmers). America experienced major social and economic upheavals, but the political machine responded passively or not at all. As late 19th-century American society and its economy became more complex, the political leaders became more detached.

Choosing sides: Democrats and Republicans

Democrats and Republicans emerged as the two main political parties after the Civil War. The Democratic Party, which traced its roots back to Thomas Jefferson's Democratic Republican Party (see Chapter 6), traditionally sought to temper capitalism and favor social welfare programs. The Republican Party was founded in 1854 to oppose the westward expansion of slavery (see Chapter 9). Republicans traditionally favored free-market capitalism and smaller government.

Americans based their political allegiances on regional loyalties and economic issues. The South usually voted Democratic, where the Democratic Party stood for white supremacy and the South's victory over Reconstruction (see Chapter 10). Catholics, immigrants, and poor workers tended to vote Democratic because of the party's dedication to social programs. The North and the West supported the Republican Party, which had emancipated slaves and held the Union together during the Civil War. Republicans opposed slavery and advocated temperance; they supported immigration restrictions and a free-market economy because business was the foundation of the industrial North and Westerners valued freedom. Protestants leaned toward the Republican Party for its stance on smaller government.

During the late 1800s, however, the two parties shared many of the same policies and beliefs, and the elections of the last part of the 19th century were close. The Republicans tended to win the presidency, however, and the same party rarely controlled both houses of Congress and the presidency.

Great for trivia: The forgotten presidents

The presidents of the late 1800s had a lot in common: They were quite passive and little remembered. They campaigned, got elected, rewarded their supporters, refrained from implementing change, and left office.

The U.S. had a number of forgettable presidents. You should recognize most of their names, but if you forget everything else about them (like the rest of Americans), you won't suffer much on the SAT II.

Rutherford B. Hayes: The B is for boring

Rutherford B. Hayes, the Republican presidential candidate for the 1876 election, was an Ohio lawyer and politician who defeated Democrat Samuel Tilden in a election controversy. Because of allegations of election fraud, a few states reported two sets of conflicting election results, one claiming Tilden as the winner and the other claiming Hayes victorious. The matter finally ended up with an electoral commission, which awarded the victory to Hayes. When Senate Democrats threatened a filibuster (a legislative stall tactic), Republicans negotiated the Compromise of 1877 (see Chapter 10).

Ma! Ma! Where's my pa?

In the election of 1884, the country didn't have any burning political questions to help people determine who they wanted for president. The campaigning boiled down to character, and the mudslinging started. The Republicans alleged that Democrat Grover Cleveland seduced a widow, and rumor had it that the affair had produced a child. The gossip was that Cleveland had refused to marry the woman and instead paid her off. This led to the popular jeer "Ma! Ma! Where's my pa? Gone to the White House. Ha, Ha, Ha." Cleveland eventually admitted to having an illegitimate child, but he had the last laugh because he was elected.

If Hayes agreed to the Compromise of 1877 and to remove federal troops from the South, he would win the presidency. Hayes won the presidency and removed the troops from the South. The compromise marked the end of Reconstruction in the former Confederacy and impaired efforts to establish rights for African Americans. Hayes honored his promise not to seek re-election and served only one term.

James A. Garfield: With friends like that, who needs enemies?

Like Hayes, James A. Garfield hailed from Ohio, practiced law and politics, and was a Republican. His connections to the Credit Mobilier Scandal prior to his presidency, in which politicians could "buy" company shares for little or no money to keep Congress from investigating the shady dealings of the company, tainted his image (see Chapter 11). But Garfield escaped any political consequences and denied any wrongdoing.

Garfield became president in 1880. Less than a year after taking office, one of his own supporters, who was disgruntled after not receiving a patronage job, fatally shot him.

Chester A. Arthur: Reforms from a sinner

With Garfield's death in 1881, Vice President Chester A. Arthur became president. In keeping with tradition, Arthur also practiced law, but he was from New York instead of Ohio. Even though he participated in the notorious New York political machine Tammany Hall (see "Cleaning house: Attempts at political reform" later in this chapter for details) and benefited from *patronage* (getting votes for favors) for many years, Arthur attempted to end political corruption by signing civil service reform legislation. But advocating reform sealed his fate. Most Republicans didn't like Arthur's reforming ways and didn't nominate him for re-election in 1884.

Grover Cleveland: You again

Democrat Grover Cleveland won the 1884 election with the help of *Mugwumps.* Mugwumps were Republicans who voted for Cleveland (a Democrat) because, unlike other Republicans, they wanted to see some political reform. Democrat victories were rare during this period, and Cleveland was the only Democrat to serve as president from 1861 until 1913. And ironically, the Republicans were the ones who got him into office. Cleveland lost the 1888 presidential election. He won the popular vote but lost the electoral vote to Benjamin Harrison. But Cleveland won the presidency again in 1892. This unusual event gave Cleveland the distinction of being the first person to hold the office of president twice in nonconsecutive terms. Cleveland exercised a large quantity of vetoes, but he's best remembered (when he's remembered at all) for getting married while he was president and, scandalously, his bride was 28 years younger. (Well, that and he has the same name as a popular puppet character on a long-running children's television program.)

Benjamin Harrison: Taking it easy

Republican Benjamin Harrison won the 1888 election, at least in the Electoral College, where it counts (just ask Al Gore; see Chapter 22). Surprise! Harrison's term of office was uneventful. In the end, Grover Cleveland, the same person who Harrison had replaced, replaced Harrison.

Cleaning house: Attempts at political reform

The state of politics in the late 19th century was pretty dismal. The federal bureaucracy allowed rampant use of the *spoils system,* in which everyone handed out favors for favors. The number of federal employees doubled, and many worked throughout the nation rather than in Washington, D.C. The growth of local federal jobs, such as postmasters, expanded the use of kickbacks and the use of employment as a reward for political loyalty. To add insult to injury, the only guys who had the power to change the unscrupulous system were the elected politicians who benefited the most from it.

Civil service reform emerged as a major campaign issue in the early 1880s. In an attempt to end the spoils system, reforms proposed that the government select federal workers based on written examinations. In 1883, during Chester Arthur's presidency, Congress passed the *Pendleton Act,* which identified the federal jobs that were eligible to be filled by examination rather than by patronage. The examinations limited the power that government officials had to make political appointments. In addition, people hoped that this reform would promote more efficiency and honesty in government by getting the best person for the job rather than the one to whom a politician owed a favor.

Grover Cleveland, first elected in 1884, was one of the first presidents (along with James Garfield and Arthur) to try to clean up politics. Cleveland, the son of a minister, wanted an honest government and had a history of fighting corruption. For instance, he had been a leader in fighting the notorious Tammany Hall political machine.

A *political machine* was an organization designed to win votes for certain mucky-mucks by doing favors for people. In exchange for votes, a political machine made sure that compliers got jobs, some coal for the furnace, a little legal advice, and anything that they needed in order to win their support. *Tammany Hall* dominated the New York Legislature. The Tammany Bosses used favors, kickbacks, and aid to the working class to garner votes. The most notorious of the bosses were members of the Tweed Ring, led by William Marcy Tweed. As the commissioner of public works in New York City, Tweed used his power to siphon off $75 million in government funds for personal advantages. He was convicted of forgery and larceny and landed himself in jail in 1872.

For the SAT II, remember that all sorts of tricks to win votes and get in office and stay there marred the politics of the late 1800s.

Not all is golden: The plight of the farmer

Immigrant and American-born farmers rapidly developed and reorganized the West and South for agriculture, but they had a tough time during the Gilded Age. Despite advances in farm technology, such as the invention of barbed wire (to keep cattle out of crops) and advances in irrigation techniques, farmers faced a series of devastating obstacles.

Dirt farming: Hard times for farmers

Farmers took several hits in the late 19th century. Large-acreage farms and improved farming methods resulted in bumper crops. And although producing lots of crops seemed like a good thing, it actually had a negative effect on farmers. Farms produced more supply than the country or the world demanded. If you've had an economics lesson, you know that a greater supply than demand drives prices down. Many farmers had secured loans to cultivate more land and pay the high costs of transporting their crops to market. When farmers couldn't pay on these loans, bankers began to foreclose on their farms, and thousands of farmers had to abandon their farms.

To add fuel to the fire, farmers in the late 1800s experienced a series of natural disasters.

- ✔ In 1874, swarms of grasshoppers demolished crops, clothes, and even farm equipment on the Great Plains.

- ✔ During the winters of 1886–1888, devastating blizzards racked the Northeastern and Great Plains states, killing cattle, fruit trees, and people. More than 200 children died in the School Children's Storm of January 1888 on the Great Plains when they were stranded at school or heading home.

- ✔ Land and crops dried up in droughts that began in 1887 on the Great Plains.

Lonely and defeated, many farmers sought relief in industrialized cities, where a defined workweek and steady paycheck carried greater appeal than the uncertainties of farm life. The few who stayed on their farms found strength in numbers by organizing into political groups, such as the Grange and the Farmers' Alliance.

Sick and tired and not taking it anymore: Farmers unite!

To overcome the devastation they faced, farmers organized into political groups. The *Grangers* (or the Grange), founded in 1867, were the first political group made up predominately of farmers. They sought help from the government to regulate the prices that railroads charged farmers to transport their goods. The efforts of the Grange helped pass the *Interstate Commerce Act* in 1887, which set up the *Interstate Commerce Commission* to regulate railroads to ensure fair prices. However, the Granger laws, as they became known, often met dubious ends because the Supreme Court limited the government's ability to regulate the railroads.

The Grangers tended to be Western farmers, but Southern farmers also united. Forced into the old sharecropping traps, where farmers had trouble paying the rents and each year got further and further in debt, Southern farmers (and some from the Great Plains) created the *Farmers' Alliance* in 1875. The alliance was often successful in establishing *cooperatives* (or co-ops), which were legal entities owned by their members and designed to allow farmers to share production, marketing, and other costs to ease individual burdens. Railroads often suppressed the movement by refusing to handle co-op products.

Some groups became militant. Farmers called for restrictions on immigration (because farming immigrants created more competition) and for government regulation of bank loans and transportation costs. A major issue for farmers was the gold standard. Farmers preferred inflation so that the price of crops would increase each year, so they favored the use of greenbacks (printed dollars that weren't tied to any hard currency) rather than the gold standard. Many less radical politicians were willing to support the silver standard, which required a ratio of silver to back U.S. currency. (See "Let's get ready to rumble: The cause of the silverites and the election of 1896" later in this chapter for more.)

Power to the people: The emergence of the Populist Party

The *Populist* movement developed in 1890 out of Western farmers' disenchantment with the politics of big business and the failure of the Granger movement. Populists favored immigration restrictions, increased government regulation, government ownership of railroads and telephone and telegraph communications, and the abolition of national banks. They championed an income tax, rail freight controls, and free coinage of silver.

Many Populists advanced the Omaha Platform, or the OCALA platform of 1890, which called for national ownership of railroads, a secret ballot for elections, and the direct election of U.S. senators by the people rather than by representatives. The *Populist Party,* or American People's Party, ran a number of presidential candidates but was perhaps most influential when it supported Democrat William Jennings Bryan (see "Let's get ready to rumble: The cause of the silverites and the election of 1896" later in this chapter).

When taking the SAT II, remember that farmers were the main force for advancing the cause of the 19th-century common citizen in a political arena that catered to big business and cronyism.

In a slump: The depression of the 1890s

Depressions are never fun, but the one that hit in the 1890s was especially dreary. Even though farmers had been under economic duress for a number of years (see the previous section), the depression of the late 1890s took much of the nation by surprise. The depression came in with a bang; banks and railroads failed quickly in the *Panic of 1893*. Many farmers and workers (called silverites) championed the free coinage of silver as a way to stop the depression. However, President Grover Cleveland vetoed a free coinage act, and the silverites weren't able to gather enough votes to override the veto. The silver issue would become the main issue in the 1896 election between William McKinley and William Jennings Bryan, right before the economy rebounded.

The Panic of 1893

Just as President Cleveland entered his second term in office, the Philadelphia and Reading railroads failed. Soon after, the National Cordage Company failed, and the combination of three major corporate failures within two months caused the stock market to crash. The economic stability of the U.S. government itself looked like it may be in trouble. As banks and railroads failed, more Americans lost their jobs, and unemployment tripled during 1893.

The Panic of 1893 resulted in the worst depression the United States had seen up to that time. In fact, it's the second-worst depression in American history. Fallout from the economic crash was devastating. Homelessness and severe unemployment became a real problem, and many people took to riding the rails, often begging or stealing on the way. Others joined *Coxey's Army,* organized by Jacob S. Coxey to demand relief for the unemployed from the federal government. His army, which was a group of unemployed workers, marched on Washington, D.C., in 1894. The federal government ignored the demands of Coxey's Army and even arrested several of the demonstrators for trespassing on the grounds of the Capitol. Cleveland maintained that the function of government didn't include supporting the people, so he failed to pass unemployment relief and public works projects. As a result of Cleveland's *laissez-faire,* or hands off, economic policies, the depression lasted for three years.

Let's get ready to rumble: The cause of the silverites and the election of 1896

With the Panic of 1893 in full force, perhaps the largest fiscal debate in history arose. The central question was whether the United States should abandon the gold standard and allow for the coinage of silver.

The gold standard was the international standard and, according to its supporters, was sound money. The gold standard meant that every dollar the U.S. printed was backed by the availability of the same value of actual gold in the U.S. Treasury. Silver supporters, called *silverites,* wanted to coin the more ready supply of silver so that more dollars made their way into the economy. Silverites theorized that coining silver would increase the money supply and cause inflation. Inflation, in turn, would allow Americans to pay off debts more quickly and force prices up, boosting the overall economy. So naturally, Western farmers and other debtors liked the idea of coining silver, whereas Eastern bankers and industrialists preferred the gold standard. The debate came to a head in the 1896 presidential election.

The election of 1896 marked the battle between those for and against coining silver. Representing the silverites was Democrat *William Jennings Bryan.* Bryan was a popular orator and Senator from Nebraska, who delivered his famous "Cross of Gold" speech, which attacked the gold standard, at the 1896 Democratic Convention. Bryan won the Democratic nomination. Then, in an effort to get silver coinage, the growing Populist Party (covered earlier in this chapter) created a fused ticket by supporting Bryan also.

The Republicans were solidly behind gold for the election of 1896. A few Republicans, mainly from silver-mining states, walked out. But the Republican Party, the party of big business, had taken its stand to support the gold standard. The Republicans nominated William McKinley, the governor of Ohio, for president.

The campaigns of 1896 were some of the most colorful in U.S. history. Bryan represented the common person and traveled throughout the nation campaigning at train stops. McKinley mostly stayed home, working behind the scenes to solidify support. McKinley had books and pamphlets written that blasted Bryan's ideas as dangerous; he also had the support of big business, like John D. Rockefeller's Standard Oil. In the end, McKinley won the election. The election was basically a regional poll: Bryan won the South and the West but lost every state in the North and the Midwest.

Ahhh, sweet prosperity: The economic rebound

In the end, the debate over silver proved moot. The economy was set for a comeback whether the U.S. coined silver or not. In 1896, the Alaskan Gold rush hit. What was once Seward's Folly (U.S. Secretary of State William Seward's purchase of Alaska from the Russians in 1867 for $7.2 million) was now a dramatic boost for the U.S. economy. Poor crop production in India and Europe also helped the economy by creating a market for American produce. However, the growth of the economy wasn't good for everyone; without the depression to drive it, the Populist movement began to decline.

Tying it all together: A sample question looks at politics in the late 1800s

The Populist Party is a popular topic on the SAT II test, but you won't be asked for obscure facts. You'll probably just need to know general platforms.

All the following were objectives of the Populist Party, EXCEPT

(A) Government control of transportation costs

(B) Election of Democrat William Jennings Bryan to the presidency

(C) Establishment of the income tax

(D) Institution of a silver standard

(E) Cooperative ownership of individual farms

If you've read other chapters in this book, you've probably heard us say this before, but it bears repeating. When you happen upon an EXCEPT question, reword the question so the language doesn't trip you up. You can rephrase this question as "Which of the following was NOT an objective of the Populist Party?"

From reading about the Populist Party, you know that it wanted the government to step in and control big businesses, like railroads and banks. Railroads transported farm produce, so decreasing transportation costs would be a desire of the Populists, so you can cross out (A).

The insertion of "Democrat" in answer choice (B) was intended to trick you. If you didn't know about the election, you may think that Populists would vote for Populists, not Democrats. But the Populists supported Bryan in 1896, so (B) is out. Answer (C) may catch you, too. Why would anyone want to establish an income tax? But Populists supported government assistance programs for farmers, and such programs require funding. An income tax would have provided the necessary funding. Answer (C) is incorrect.

Populists sought to raise prices for their crops, and they thought that switching to a silver standard would accomplish this goal. So (D) is wrong.

Answer (E) may trick you, too. Populist farmers did form and jointly own cooperatives to sell goods and share profits but not to share ownership of individual farms. Answer (E) isn't a Populist objective; therefore, (E) is the correct answer.

Chapter 13

Imperialism at the Turn of the Century, 1890–1914

*P*lease fasten all seatbelts and put seats in their upright position, because you're about to take off on yet another chapter dealing with America in the late 1800s. No ho-hums allowed. This chapter is the last one covering material from the 19th century (we *promise!*), and because the point of this book is to prepare you for the SAT II U.S. History exam, not covering a topic bursting with potential SAT II questions would be a bad idea. The word "imperialism" may ring a distant bell in the back of your brain or maybe you're thinking "Oh, great! Another 'ism' word." Or maybe — not likely, but maybe — it triggers an avalanche of knowledge that you obtained through lively lectures, diligent note-taking, and on-the-edge-of-your-seat participation in a high school history course. Which category you fall into isn't important because, in all three cases, our recommendation is the same: Read this chapter because you can expect to answer three or four questions that deal with the era when America pushed its weight around in the world arena.

Branching Out: Reasons for American Imperialism

Imperialism describes a nation's intent to dominate other people using economic, political, or military power. In many cases, imperialism employs a combination of all three methods. Many reasons contributed to the rise of American imperialism at the end of the 1800s, all of which played their part in pushing America over the edge of isolationism (or focusing on itself) and into a new frontier of global dimensions.

Industrial progress and the search for new markets

In the late 1800s, the industrialized nations of the world were growing at a phenomenal rate. The rapid growth of industry brought on by the Second Industrial Revolution turned America into the world's leading economic power (see Chapter 12). From 1859 to 1899, the value of

American industrial goods rose from $1.8 billion to $13 billion. Vast improvements in transportation and communications made the world seem smaller and, for the first time, average Americans began to look beyond their borders. However, the growth was uneven nationally (see Chapter 12) and internationally. Entire continents, such as Africa, Latin America, and Asia, were way behind in the game, and industrialized nations like the United States began to exploit these underdeveloped continents by taking advantage of cheap labor to extract resources at a great profit.

Because of industrial growth, America was producing goods like crazy in the late 1800s, which created a problem: An overabundance of goods flooded the marketplace. This flood on the market led to huge price drops, which caused farmers to go out of business and manufacturers to lay off workers, which, in turn, led to economic hardship, strikes, and a discontent American public. Somewhere along the line, the idea of finding foreign markets to sell surplus American products developed. James G. Blaine, the U.S. secretary of state from 1889 to 1892, explained the logic well enough when he said that new foreign markets would provide new business for U.S. manufacturers, a new place for U.S. farmers to sell their products, and therefore, workers in either of these fields would have fewer reasons to strike. The need for foreign markets was not only a justification for expanding American influence to the Caribbean, Latin America, and the Far East, but it was also a means to accomplish America's imperialistic policies.

For the SAT II, remember: Although many factors contributed to American imperialism, the rapid industrialization of America in the Second Industrial Revolution really propelled American imperialism into existence. In addition, remember that America's economic power was one of its strongest tools for spreading its influence abroad.

Reign of the fittest: Applying Darwin to imperialism

British philosopher Herbert Spencer applied Charles Darwin's theory of evolution to history, creating a new theory known as *Social Darwinism.* Social Darwinism said that throughout history, nations have battled with one another for survival but only the fittest nations survive. The superior nations grow because their members have better traits for survival (like intelligence and physical stamina), whereas inferior nations eventually die off. (For more on Social Darwinism, see Chapter 12)

Social Darwinism became popular in America in the late 1800s as a means of justifying imperialism. According to this theory, America, as a superior nation, had a right and an obligation to take what it needed from "inferior" nations. This concept also tied in nicely with manifest destiny, a concept revived in America in the late 1800s that suggested that the nation's destiny was to expand beyond its borders and into foreign lands. (See Chapter 8 for more about manifest destiny.)

Social Darwinism also tied in nicely with the views of *Josiah Strong,* an influential clergyman who wrote a popular book in 1885 titled *Our Country.* In his book, Strong made the case that Americans were a God-favored people destined to lead the rest of the world. Yale Professor *William Graham Sumner* perpetuated Strong's idea in the first decade of the 1900s when he came up with the concept of *ethnocentrism,* an attitude of superiority about one's own group in comparison with others. These philosophies fostered Americans' confidence that it was their nation's duty to share its superiority with other people.

Implementing an aggressive foreign policy

During the late 1800s, America, fortified by the success of the Second Industrial Revolution, began to bare its teeth at European nations that dared to make trouble in its part of the world. In the 1880s, the U.S. came close to going to war with Germany and Great Britain. The United States also began to modernize its navy and army and became a significant military power. The U.S. justified its military power — especially its new-and-improved steel-hulled warships and its acquisition of naval bases in the Pacific Ocean and the Caribbean region — as a way to protect America's merchant ships in an ever-growing world of foreign trade. Influential men, like **Alfred Thayer Mahan,** author of *The Influence of Seapower in History,* argued that if the U.S. didn't expand, it would die. Republican leaders, such as Theodore Roosevelt and Senator Henry Cabot Lodge listened. The U.S. used its military power throughout the world to acquire territory, back its economic interests, and assert its authority over regions in its control, as you'll see in the rest of this chapter.

Protecting a Southern Neighbor: The Spanish-American War

By the late 1800s, Spain's empire was a mere shadow of its former self in the Western Hemisphere. When Mexico won its independence from Spain in 1821, Spain lost possession of land in North America. Spain still had a toehold in the Caribbean islands of Cuba and Puerto Rico, but even those colonies were slipping away. From 1868 to 1878, Cuba was in a state of revolt, and the revolt ended only because Spain promised to reform its corrupt government in Cuba. But Spain didn't keep its promise, and the Cuba Libre (free Cuba) movement turned into an all-out war in 1895. Until this point, the United States had shown only a passing interest in its southern, Spanish-ruled neighbor, but that would change dramatically.

Cuba Libre: Events leading up to the war

The brutality of the Spanish became a popular front-page topic of newspapers throughout the United States. Media barons like William Randolph Hearst and Joseph Pulitzer began to sensationalize the war in Cuba, painting a picture of Spain as an evil oppressor that committed atrocities against Cubans, who were fighting a war for their freedom. The stories were mostly true, but journalists emphasized and exaggerated them to pull at readers' heartstrings. The Spanish didn't help their image by arresting an estimated 300,000 Cubans — men, women, and children — and tossing them into concentration camps in 1896, where thousands died from disease and starvation.

This news went a long way toward changing Americans' attitudes about intervening in Cuba. Here are some other factors you should be aware of for the SAT II:

- The war decimated Cuba's economy by bringing the production of sugar — its chief export — to a screeching halt. The lack of sugar production affected American businessmen, who held substantial investments in Cuba. Their plantations and factories were literally going up in smoke, while the lives of Americans living in Cuba were being threatened by the constant warfare.

- On February 9, 1898, Hearst's *New York Journal* published a letter that someone somehow stole from a Havana post office. The letter, written by Spanish Minister Enrique Dupuy de Lome, characterized American President William McKinley as weak and eager for the admiration of the crowd. The letter also suggested Spain's intention of continuing the war in Cuba.

✔ Six days later, a U.S. ship, the USS *Maine,* exploded in Havana Harbor under questionable circumstances, killing 266 American sailors. Spain said the ship had an internal explosion, but Americans believed the culprit was a Spanish mine.

Congress approves intervention

In 1896, both houses of Congress passed resolutions acknowledging Cuba's right to revolt and right to declare independence from Spain and become its own nation. The American public echoed this sentiment, but when President McKinley stepped into office in 1897, he wasn't ready to go to war with Spain over Cuba's independence. Instead, he persuaded Spain to get rid of its military governor (the same guy responsible for the concentration camps) and the concentration camps and to accept reforms that would give Cuba limited independence. Even after the USS *Maine* exploded in 1898 and Spain had made no reforms in Cuba, McKinley once again tried diplomacy.

McKinley demanded that Spain immediately end the war and close all concentration camps. Implicit in his demands was that Spain recognize Cuba's independence. Spain complied with all of McKinley's demands except the one recognizing Cuba's independence. But to the American public, this response wasn't good enough. McKinley finally lost patience with Spain and caved in to pressure from Congress and the American public. In April 1898, he asked Congress to grant him a declaration of war. Members of Congress debated for a week before they authorized McKinley to remove Spain from Cuba by force on April 25.

On two fronts: Fighting in the Philippines and the Caribbean

Even before Americans began to fight in Cuba, a fleet of U.S. naval ships was high-tailing it to the Philippines, another Spanish colony, on the order from Assistant Secretary of the Navy Theodore Roosevelt. Commodore George Dewey commanded the U.S. fleet. Although Dewey wasn't a household name, after his success in the Philippines, he would become one.

Dewey arrived in Manila Bay on May 1, 1898, where he had a brief encounter with a decrepit Spanish fleet. Americans received word of Dewey's victory on May 7. Although Dewey's mission was to knock out Spain's Pacific fleet, U.S. officials thought, "Gee whiz, that was easy. Wonder how long it would take to take over the Philippine islands. Come to think of it, Manila Bay would make a great naval base." (Please don't quote us on that.) Shortly thereafter, more American troops arrived in the Philippines and, with the help of Filipino rebels, they gave the resident Spanish army a sound beating. The U.S. officially defeated Spain by August, but American forces still had to contend with the Filipino rebels to gain control of the Philippines (see the later section "The door to China: Acquiring the Philippines").

Meanwhile, Spain also received a thumping from American troops in the Caribbean. American troops didn't step foot in Cuba until June 22, 1898, but on July 1, American forces (among them Theodore Roosevelt and the *Rough Riders*) charged up San Juan Hill and Kettle Hill, defeating the Spanish in both battles. The U.S. Navy blockaded Cuban ports, which prevented Spanish troops from receiving supplies. On July 3, the U.S. Navy destroyed the Spanish Caribbean fleet after it waged a desperate battle to leave Santiago Harbor, and Spain surrendered Santiago on July 17. About the same time, American troops landed in Puerto Rico, where they eventually conquered half the island. By August, Spain took a look at the scoreboard and saw that it was losing on all fronts. On August 12, Spain signed an armistice.

Settling down: The Treaty of Paris

While Spain emerged from the war like a frightened turtle, America emerged as a military force to be reckoned with. American and Spanish negotiators met in Paris in December 1898 to settle the terms of peace; the brokered deal proved the adage "To the victor go the spoils."

For the SAT II U.S. History exam, remember the following points of the *Treaty of Paris:*

> ✔ Spain agreed to give Cuba its independence, which the Teller and Platt Amendments (see the section "Cuba: Dealing with the Teller and Platt Amendments" later in this chapter) later reinforced.
>
> ✔ Spain handed control of Puerto Rico and Guam to the United States.
>
> ✔ America agreed to pay Spain $20 million for the Philippines.

The "splendid little war" as Secretary of State John Hay called it, cost the lives of more than 5,400 American soldiers — 379 in combat, and the rest to yellow fever and malaria. But the benefits far exceeded the costs. With the acquisition of the Philippines, Puerto Rico, and Guam, America earned its membership in the elite club of imperialist nations.

Taking Over the Tropics: Hawaii, the Philippines, the Caribbean, and Panama

In the 1890s, the United States could be likened to a sleeping giant who awoke from a long slumber and trekked West, gobbling up frontier land until it reached the Pacific, where it cast hungry eyes at lands beyond its borders. The Spanish-American War solidified the United States as an imperialist power (see the previous section), but its appetite wasn't satisfied because other lands were still ripe for the picking.

Commandeering cane: The annexation of Hawaii and Samoa

The American presence in Hawaii dates back to 1820 when Protestant missionaries from New England sailed over to bring Christianity to the islands. Throughout the 19th century, other Americans (like the Doles of Dole pineapple fame) settled on the islands to run plantations. The Hawaiian Islands had the perfect climate for planting sugar cane, which American planters quickly grew into a thriving business. The islands also had a convenient location along the trade route to Asia and a port (Pearl Harbor) that was just begging to be an American naval station. By the 1890s, Hawaii was ripe (so to speak) for American imperialist pickings.

In 1876, Congress granted duty-free imports on Hawaiian sugar. This law translated to serious profits for the mostly American planters in Hawaii. But in the 1890s, Congress revised these tariff laws, nixing that special privilege. This change translated to profit losses for planters in the islands. Being the enterprising group that they were, they staged a revolution and over-threw the Hawaiian queen in January 1893 so the U.S. could annex the islands. The U.S. consul aided the revolution, making sure that the U.S. Navy contributed to the effort. Next, the American settlers sought annexation by the United States because they knew that if America annexed Hawaii, the planters in Hawaii would no longer have taxes on their sugar. Incoming President Grover Cleveland, who was less than thrilled with the whole affair, held up annexation but, inevitably, the U.S. annexed Hawaii five years later in 1898.

Against the crowd: The Anti-imperialist League

Not everyone in the United States wore rose-colored glasses when viewing the country's imperialistic foreign policy. Many famous and influential Americans, such as Andrew Carnegie, Jane Addams, Grover Cleveland, psychologist-philosopher William James, labor organizer Samuel Gompers, Williams Jennings Bryan, and Mark Twain, to name a few, felt that imperialism went against the American principles of justice and equal treatment for all. In 1898, they and others formed the American Anti-imperialist League to fight the U.S, annexation of the Philippines, its treatment of Cuba, and other American interests abroad, citing a gamut of reasons. The league was unsuccessful in changing American foreign policy or gathering much of a following. By the end of the Philippine resistance in 1907, the league had lost its significance and rapidly faded from the historical map.

The United States also set its sights on Samoa for many of the same reasons. These islands had a strategic port and suitable land for American businessmen to exploit. Great Britain and Germany were also interested in the islands, so in 1889 the three nations split the islands among them, unbeknownst to the Samoans. Out of the deal, the United States annexed some of the islands, including the important harbor of Pago Pago.

The door to China: Acquiring the Philippines

The end of the Spanish-American War in 1898 (see "Protecting a Southern Neighbor: The Spanish-American War" earlier in this chapter) wasn't the end of the war in the Philippines. Filipino rebels, who fought the Spanish for their independence, had a rude awakening when the U.S. took over after Spain was out. By February 1899, Filipinos had revolted against American rule, too. But occupying the Philippines gave the U.S. access to lucrative Asian markets (especially the Chinese market), raw materials, and investment opportunities, so the U.S fought against Filipino rebels to maintain control over the Philippines.

More than 4,000 American and 20,000 Filipino troops died in this little-known war, and more than 200,000 civilians died of starvation and disease. American forces put down the rebellion when they captured rebel leader Emilio Aquinaldo and forced him to announce his allegiance to the United States in 1901. The U.S. granted the Philippines limited control in 1907, but the U.S. wouldn't relinquish control of the islands until 1946.

Goodbye Cuba, hello Puerto Rico: American relations in the Caribbean

During the early 1900s, the United States used politics, economics, and its military to influence the Caribbean region. The United States saw the Caribbean as its domain and set about meddling in the affairs of everyone living there. American leaders deemed this policing necessary to protect American interests that had spread beyond its native borders. The most important interest was American financial investments in the region, which were multiplying like rabbits in spring.

Cuba: Dealing with the Teller and Platt Amendments

Following the Spanish-American War in 1898, Congress passed the *Teller Amendment* to the declaration of war on Spain to ensure that the U.S. wouldn't establish permanent control over Cuba. But this amendment didn't guarantee that the United States wouldn't maintain a controlling interest in the island country. In 1901, U.S. officials forced the Cuban government to add the *Platt Amendment* to its constitution. The Platt Amendment basically gave the U.S.

the right to intervene in Cuban affairs, both domestic and abroad. That same year, in response to their dissatisfaction with the Platt Amendment, Cubans revolted (sound familiar yet?), several times and, each time, American troops crushed the rebellions.

The U.S. presence in Cuba led to better roads, a public school system, a national army, improved sugar production, and the eradication of the dreaded yellow fever disease on the island. But Cubans resented American control, and perhaps rightly so. While America was giving Cuba an American makeover, American businesses bought up Cuban land and controlled much of the island's industry. America retained its hold on Cuba into the 1930s.

Puerto Rico: Thanks to the Foraker Act

For the two years following the Spanish-American War, the status of Puerto Rico was in limbo. The U.S. military ruled the island right after the war; on April 2, 1900, Congress passed the *Foraker Act,* which made Puerto Rico a territory of the United States. This act gave Puerto Rico its own government, which was subject to control of the U.S. federal government, and defined its inhabitants as citizens of Puerto Rico, not American citizens.

In the early 1900s, Puerto Rico became a hot spot for sugar production. American companies bought huge amounts of land, often from small, Puerto Rican farmers who simply couldn't compete. Some Puerto Ricans became dissatisfied with American authority and started an independence movement; others were dissatisfied with Puerto Rico's ambiguous political status and formed a movement to push for statehood. In 1917, President Woodrow Wilson signed the *Jones Act,* which gave Puerto Ricans U.S. citizenship and the rights that went along with it, except for the right to vote in federal elections (which many Puerto Ricans still hotly contest). Today, the island remains a U.S. territory, and the Puerto Rican population is still divided about independence and statehood.

Creating a passageway to the Pacific: Negotiating the Panama Canal

In 1901 after the assassination of President William McKinley, Theodore Roosevelt, at age 42, stepped into office as the youngest president in U.S. history. Roosevelt, who was famous for his exploits in a band of volunteer soldiers called the Rough Riders during the Spanish-American War (mostly due to favorable press), came into the presidency packing an aggressive foreign policy that was dubbed *Big Stick Diplomacy* after an adage he often recited: "Speak softly and carry a big stick; you will go far." Essentially, this concept meant that when negotiations with foreign countries broke down, the U.S. should be prepared to use military force. Roosevelt was an imperialist to the core and pushed every opportunity to expand American influence abroad. One of his interests was building the Panama Canal through Central America, which would connect the Pacific Ocean with the Atlantic Ocean.

Prior to the building of the Panama Canal, a ship that left New York bound for California had to travel all the way around the tip of South America (an additional 7,800 miles). Talk about taking the scenic route! In June 1902, Congress passed the Spooner Act, which authorized Roosevelt to build the Panama Canal. The only problem was that Colombia controlled the Panama Territory and wanted more money. In turn, Roosevelt decided to support Panama's independence with American warships and, in return (through the Hay-Bunau-Varilla Treaty ratified by the Panamanian government in 1903 and the Americans in 1904), the newly independent Panama quickly granted the United States the land it needed for the price that it was willing to pay, and the U.S began construction soon after.

The Panama Canal was completed in 1914 at a cost of $380 million and the loss of thousands of laborers to malaria. But it gave the United States power and had a revolutionary effect on worldwide shipping.

Suiting his needs: The Roosevelt Corollary to the Monroe Doctrine

Be aware; be very aware, because the Roosevelt Corollary to the Monroe Doctrine has a good shot of surfacing on the SAT II. Why, you ask? Simply stated, the *Roosevelt Corollary* said that the United States had the duty and obligation to act as an "international police power" in all Latin American affairs.

The 1823 *Monroe Doctrine* said that the United States would stay out of European affairs and expected European powers to stop throwing their weight around on the American continents (see Chapter 6). The Roosevelt Corollary carried the idea of the doctrine further by specifying that the U.S. would curtail European efforts to exert control in Latin America. Roosevelt developed his corollary to the doctrine over time, but it came about because of a specific incident. In 1902, Venezuela was in debt up to its eyeballs to European banks and decided that it couldn't pay them back. Germany, Great Britain, and Italy sent warships to blockade the Venezuelan coast, and some German ships blasted away at Venezuelan ports. Well, Roosevelt was pretty teed-off with the European nations for using force as retaliation for nonpayment of debt (a nonviolent act). He threatened to send in the U.S. Navy to defend Venezuela. The European powers, wanting to avoid war, backed off, and the Roosevelt Corollary was born.

The United States used this aggressive policing policy to justify American intervention in Cuba, Panama, Nicaragua, the Dominican Republic, Mexico, and Haiti throughout Roosevelt's presidency (and, to a lesser extent, even after that). Basically, this policy sent a message to Europe: Hands off! The affairs of Latin American countries were the interest and responsibility of the United States, and if anybody had a problem with Latin America, they had to deal with the United States first.

Tying it all together: A sample question looks at American foreign policy

The SAT II may test you on turn-of-the-century American foreign policy with a question about a specific philosophy, like the Roosevelt Corollary. To answer this sample question, you need to know about U.S. foreign policy and the corollary.

Which of the following provides the best illustration of foreign policy undertaken by the U.S. under the Roosevelt Corollary?

(A) Annexing Hawaii in 1898

(B) Building the Panama Canal

(C) Buying Honduras' debt from European banks under Dollar Diplomacy

(D) Assisting Filipino rebels in their fight for independence from Spain in 1898

(E) Passing the Teller Amendment

To answer this question, you must first consider the elements of the Roosevelt Corollary and then find the answer that satisfies them all. The main ideas of the corollary are that (1) Europe needs to stay out of Latin American affairs and that (2) the U.S. has a right to intervene in Latin American affairs if European powers do get involved. So, you're looking for an answer that shows the U.S. getting involved in stopping a European power from exerting its influence in Latin America.

Because Hawaii isn't a Latin American country, you can easily eliminate (A). Likewise, even though Spain was involved in the Filipino rebellion, the Philippines aren't in Latin America, so (D) is wrong. The Panama Canal was built in Latin America, but the U.S. wasn't involved in the project as a way to control a European power; so (B) isn't right. Now you're left with (C) and (E). The U.S. passed the Teller Amendment for its involvement in Cuba's war with Spain, but the amendment was about curbing U.S. control rather than Spain's control. Choice (E) is wrong, so (C) must be the answer.

Don't let the inclusion of Dollar Diplomacy in answer (C) fool you. Even though Dollar Diplomacy was Taft's policy, the act of rescuing the Latin American country of Honduras from control by European banks is an illustration of the Roosevelt Corollary. The U.S. exerted its influence to keep Europe out of Latin American affairs, making (E) the best answer.

Come On In: China and the Open Door Policy

Throughout the 1800s, countries such as France, Germany, Great Britain, Italy, Japan, and Russia were carving out little imperial nests for themselves in China. Each of these countries was doing business in China and had their own *spheres of influence* (foreign powers that have more rights in a foreign country than the host county has). Each country claimed exclusive trading rights, and some even claimed territory. The Chinese detested the encroachment of these "foreign devils," but what could they do? Foreign regiments with modern weapons defeated entire Chinese armies, and time and again, these nations forced emperors to grant them concessions, which only further embedded the invaders. The U.S. came into the China game late. After the Spanish-American War ended in 1898, the U.S. had acquired the Philippines, an excellent base of operations for trade in China. But China was crowded with competing imperialist nations, each claiming its own sphere of influence.

So, the United States came up with a solution called the Open Door Policy, which is a very testable subject for the SAT II. Expect to see a question or two on this policy.

Motivations for opening the door

In 1899, Secretary of State John Hay wrote letters to every nation with a controlling interest in China and asked them to consider an *Open Door Policy,* where no restrictions on trade would exist within spheres of influence. Such a policy would lessen the competition among the occupying nations for land and influence. Each nation replied with something that went like: "Sounds like a great idea, but it won't work." Undaunted, in 1899, Hay announced that because every nation agreed in principle to the policy, the United States considered the agreement "final and decisive."

The SAT II expects you to know that the U.S. wanted China badly because it had everything that a growing imperialist nation needed:

✔ **It would open trade with Asian markets.** One of the most significant reasons the United States sought to expand its imperialist powers through China was because of the economic benefits. The U.S. had just plowed its way through an industrial revolution that brought significant improvements to technology, transportation, and communication. These improvements meant that the U.S. could produce more food and more manufactured goods at a pace no nation had ever accomplished before. But this pace also led to overproduction and economic trouble. Enter China. China was a great place to dump the U.S. surplus because a lot of people lived there: Roughly 1 in 5 people in the world lived in China. Also, the enormous size of the country and its abundant natural resources meant a lot of untapped profits for American businesses. (For more about economic reasons for imperialism, see "Industrial progress and the search for new markets" earlier in this chapter.)

✔ **It would open the missionary field.** American missionaries poured into China because they viewed it as a backward culture in need of Christianity and American ideals. Missionaries built schools and hospitals and, to their credit, they fought for human rights, attempted to reform Chinese society, and cared for the poor. The problem was that reform often meant a disregard for Chinese culture in exchange for American values. Many Chinese became distrustful of missionaries and despised their efforts to change their culture.

The results of opening the door

For the SAT II, know that the Open Door Policy wasn't entirely effective. Yes, it got America trading with China, but imperialist nations competing for power and influence in China continued to compete after the U.S. initiated this policy. Other countries often ignored the Open Door Policy, sometimes with disastrous effects like the Russo-Japanese War. Additionally, the limited policy did little to help the Chinese, whose hatred of foreign influence led to the Boxer Rebellion. Still, the policy became one of the cornerstones of American diplomacy around the world. When the U.S. emerged as the dominant economic power, it used the Open Door Policy to pry open markets and dominate them.

The Boxer Rebellion

Many Chinese were angered by the invasion and exploitation of their country by foreigners. This anger led to the formation of a secret society called the Fists of Righteous Harmony, which attracted thousands of followers. Westerners nicknamed them "Boxers" because they practiced martial arts.

In 1900, in an attempt to kick out all foreigners, thousands of Boxers wreaked havoc in the countryside, slaughtering Chinese Christians and missionaries. Twenty thousand Boxers descended on the housing complex where the foreign ministers lived in Beijing. Soldiers defending the complex fought them off for two months before an international relief force from eight countries, including the United States, arrived to beat back the rebellion. America participated in the peace settlement that followed. Secretary of State John Hay called for an expanded Open Door Policy, which proposed that foreign nations allow China to preserve its territory and government and maintain open trade with other countries. All parties agreed to the terms. The Chinese government appreciated American efforts to maintain a less invasive policy and, therefore, became more agreeable to trading with the U.S.

The Russo-Japanese War

The *Russo-Japanese War* was basically a grab for land in China. In the early 1900s, Russia occupied Southern Manchuria (a region in northeast China), including Port Arthur on the Liaotang Peninsula, where it built a naval base. Japan also wanted to occupy Manchuria, but in 1903, it proposed an agreement with Russia. If Russia wouldn't mess with Japan's interest in Korea (in which Russia also had interest), then Japan wouldn't mess with Russia's interest in Manchuria. Russia refused the proposal, so on February 8, 1904, Japan launched a surprise attack on Port Arthur and blockaded Russia's damaged naval fleet. Russia surrendered in 1905 after the Japanese military had consistently beaten them on land and sea.

Theodore Roosevelt negotiated a peace settlement (for which he received the Nobel Peace Prize) between the two sides in Portsmouth, New Hampshire, in September 1905. In the treaty, Russia agreed to leave Manchuria, giving it back to China, and Japan gained the Liaotang Peninsula and Port Arthur from Russia and emerged as the first modern imperialist nation that wasn't European or American.

What's important to understand about the Russo-Japanese War for the SAT II is that it was an example of how the Open Door Policy did *not* prevent nations from competing for control of land and influence in China. In fact, both Russia and Japan clearly violated the Open Door Policy repeatedly by maintaining spheres of influence in China; the peace treaty also violated the policy by giving Japan control of land in China.

Tying it all together: A sample question looks at the Open Door Policy

On the SAT II, questions about the Open Door Policy will likely focus on its purpose and its effects. The sample question asks you to evaluate the policy and why it came about.

Which of the following describes the primary purpose of America's Open Door policy?

(A) To release free trade for the United States in China

(B) To protect China from European exploitation

(C) To modernize and reform the Chinese government

(D) To help American companies build railroads in Asia

(E) To protect American missionaries living in China

At first glance, all the answer choices may seem plausible. Each of them seems logical, and most of them contain a tidbit of truth. But you need to find the one that's the most true.

Answer (A) works well. You know that one of the prime motivations for the Open Door Policy was to open trade with China. The answer choice uses the verb "release," but open and release are similar. However, look through the other choices before you make a commitment. Answer (B) is partially right. One of the purposes was to win China over by diminishing its exploitation, but not just from European countries. Japan was involved, also. America didn't have a desire to change the Chinese government (the U.S. just wanted to do business with the Chinese), and American companies weren't building railroads in Asia. You can eliminate (C) and (D). Answer (E) may catch you. The U.S. did have an interest in sending missionaries to China, and it probably did need to protect those missionaries. But the Open Door Policy specifically helped in beginning missionary work, not in protecting missionaries who were already established. The best answer is (A).

Spreading U.S. Influence Under Taft and Wilson

The expansion of American influence continued throughout the presidencies of William Howard Taft and Woodrow Wilson. Each leader had a different take on how to implement America's foreign policy, but both vigorously employed and built upon the imperialistic policies of McKinley and Roosevelt. (For more about the Taft, Roosevelt, and Wilson presidencies, check out Chapter 14.)

Taft's Dollar Diplomacy

William Howard Taft succeeded Roosevelt as president in 1909. He shared his predecessor's desire for expanding American influence abroad, but rather than waving a big stick, Taft spread American influence through economic means. Taft's *Dollar Diplomacy* used economics to infiltrate foreign countries. Naturally, the U.S. would back up Dollar Diplomacy with the U.S. military, if necessary.

Taft encouraged American businesses to invest abroad because he believed that these investments would stimulate the economy back home and help promote American influence in Latin America and the Far East. He also believed that American influence provided foreign nations with political stability and economic growth. Basically, he believed his policy was a win-win situation for everybody.

Taft used Dollar Diplomacy to buy the debt of countries like Honduras and Nicaragua from European banks, and he persuaded American banks to refinance Haiti's national debt, all with the interest of gaining economic control of these countries. Taft also arranged for American bankers to get in on deals to finance railroads through China. Dollar Diplomacy had some successes but, overall, it flopped because it didn't have the power to counteract economic troubles and civil unrest in most countries.

Wilson in Latin America and Mexico

Woodrow Wilson stepped into office in 1913 as a man fed up with American bullying abroad. He supported a moral diplomacy policy that promoted neutrality and said that America "never again would seek one foot of territory by conquest." But Wilson's idealism quickly wore away when the economies of Nicaragua, Haiti, and the Dominican Republic became unstable and these nations suspended debt payments (from Taft's Dollar Diplomacy policy) to U.S. banks. Wilson sent American troops into these countries to ensure that they would continue paying their debts.

Wilson also had to check his idealism at the border for a situation that occurred with Mexico. American businesses were deeply entrenched in Mexico, owning 40 percent of Mexican real estate by the early 1900s. During the Mexican Revolution, which began in 1910 and continued until 1920, Wilson backed one revolutionary faction and denounced the other faction that had taken over the country's government, believing it was a threat to American businesses. The faction that Wilson backed eventually took over but rejected Wilson's guidelines for setting up a new government. So Wilson briefly considered backing another revolutionary faction led by Francisco "Pancho" Villa but ultimately decided to work with the current faction in power. Villa took Wilson's decision personally and killed a bunch of American civilians and even crossed the border to attack an American fort and nearby town, killing 14 soldiers and 10 civilians. After that episode, Wilson sent troops into Mexico to find Villa but ended up fighting soldiers who were loyal to the Mexican government, which almost led to a war. After that incident, Wilson pulled American troops from Mexico without ever finding Villa.

Part V
America Becomes a Grown-Up

In this part . . .

America's early adult years were marked by Progressive reforms, participation in two world wars, the lively and culturally rich years of the 1920s, and the devastating Great Depression of the 1930s. These challenging years prepared America for its status as the preeminent world power in the years following World War II.

To play it safe, assume that 20 percent to 25 percent of the questions on the SAT II U.S. History test cover the period of the Progressive era, World War I, the Roaring '20s, the Great Depression, and World War II. Don't stress too much because, by the time you finish reviewing this part, you're on the home stretch!

Chapter 14

Stepping Forward: The Progressive Era, 1900–1920

*P*rogressivism was a movement that emerged as a response to the ill effects of industrialization and urbanization of America in the late 1800s, such as poverty, social injustice, and ruthless business practices. Progressives represented a diverse bunch — authors, philosophers, farmers, and small-business owners, politicians, and poor urban laborers. Some Progressives were members of the social and intellectual elite, whereas others represented the urban poor, though the majority of Progressives were middle class, educated, and often female. Nevertheless, one common strand tied Progressives together: They sought to improve the quality of life for all Americans through reforms in politics, industry, business, increased government regulation, poverty relief, environmental conservation, and the expansion of the ideals of democracy.

The Progressive movement was extremely large, diverse and, at times, a haphazard movement with no true center. But with such a diverse array of issues and interests, Progressivism was limited by its own ambitions. Still, Progressivism improved the lives of millions of Americans and made an important contribution to the character and development of the United States throughout the 20th century.

About 40 percent of the SAT II U.S. History exam covers the period from 1899 to the present, of which the Progressive Era is a small, but important, subject. The majority of questions that deal with Progressivism focus on political and economic history; social, intellectual, cultural, and foreign policy issues take a backseat to questions on power and money. This chapter focuses almost exclusively on politics and the individuals involved in them. On the exam, you most likely will see questions dealing with the motivations for reform as well as on what Americans attempted to do and how successful their efforts were.

Service for All: City, State, and National Reforms

In the Progressive Era, reform began at the local level, usually in big cities, and continued at the state level before appearing on the national stage. In the 1900s and 1910s, big personalities dominated local politics, and the boldness of these big personalities was necessary to take on the daunting challenges of fighting powerful big business.

Mayors on the mend: Reforms at the city level

In Cleveland, Ohio, Mayor Tom Johnson's forceful presence brought major reforms to the Midwest city. Johnson advocated public ownership of streetcars and some utilities, wrestling power away from private corporations in an effort to curb the influence of big business. He also promoted fine arts, music, and adult education because he believed in creating an urban renaissance, which would build new and beautiful public buildings and open spaces for citizens to visit. Other mayors across America made similar efforts in cities such as Boston, Chicago, and Dallas, and experiments in Progressive reform flourished. In 1900, the municipal government proved incompetent in dealing with the aftermath of a destructive tidal wave in Galveston, Texas. The reformers in the community abolished the mayor's office and city council and replaced them with an elected, nonpartisan council of administrators. In 1907, citizens of Des Moines, Iowa, adopted their own version of this system, and many other municipalities followed suit thereafter. This system still exists today in cities and counties across the United States.

Expanding the focus: State reforms

At the state level, many individuals, such as Charles Evans Hughes, governor of New York, California governor Hiram Johnson, and Woodrow Wilson, governor of New Jersey, initiated programs to deal with the problems of industry and other social ills. Some of the state-initiated reform movements, such as women's suffrage, would be among the most important contributions of the Progressive Era. (See "The 19th Amendment: Women's suffrage" later in this chapter for more about women's right to vote.)

Robert M. La Follette, governor of Wisconsin from 1900 to 1906 (and a senator beginning in 1906), turned the state into a giant Progressive experiment and earned it the nickname the "Laboratory of Democracy." "Battling Bob" La Follette was one of America's most influential Progressives. During his tenure in various political offices, La Follette improved education throughout the state, advocated conservation, and held the first direct primary in the United States. Under Governor La Follette, Wisconsin legislators passed laws to regulate railroads, utilities, and the workplace. They passed workers' compensation legislation and dramatically increased taxes on railroads, and introduced a graduated inheritance tax.

La Follette believed in non-partisan reform efforts, which would become a major part of Progressivism, and other Progressive leaders repeated his experiments in cities across the country. Because La Follette is the most celebrated state-level reformer of the Progressive Era, he's the state-level reformer that SAT II is most likely to ask you about.

Moving to a bigger stage: National reforms

During the Progressive Era, many significant national reforms occurred. You take some of these reforms for granted now, but early in the 20th century, they were a big deal.

The 16th Amendment: Federal income tax

Prior to the Progressive Era, the federal government collected most of its money from customs duties and taxes on goods. As the rift between the wealthy and poor widened, numerous groups began to support the idea of a national *graduated income tax* (a tax that would collect a higher percentage from people who made more money) to help fund government programs and create a better balance between the rich and poor. In 1909, Congress passed the 16th Amendment, which gave the federal government the power to collect taxes from the national population. By February 1913, ¾ of the states had ratified the amendment.

The graduated income tax provided the federal government with a massive new source of income to make up for funds it lost due to substantial cuts in the protective tariff (thus, opening up U.S. markets for foreign competition to break the power of U.S. trusts and reduce the importance of big business). This first modern income tax established that individuals and corporations earning more than $4,000 per year would pay 1 percent, and rates rose according to incomes up to a maximum of 6 percent per year on incomes more than $500,000.

The 17th Amendment: Directly electing senators

Prior to 1913, state legislatures chose U.S. senators. This process took the power out of the hands of ordinary Americans, and Progressive leaders across the United States argued for a change to directly electing senators. Progressives also believed that big business held too much sway with state legislatures because it often had preferences for who it wanted to serve in the Senate — for their own interests, of course, which led to much corruption. In 1913, Progressives won this battle for reform with the passage and ratification of the 17th Amendment, which allowed the public to choose its representatives in the U.S. Senate.

The 18th Amendment: Prohibition

Progressives believed that alcohol, America's most abused drug, was a major cause of society's moral decay. *Temperance* movements (that is, those that sought to prohibit the alcohol) weren't new in America; in fact, they had been extremely popular in the 19th century (see Chapter 8). But as Progressivism attempted to make a better, more moral America, the idea of prohibiting alcohol gained popularity.

Reform groups advocated temperance by publicizing alcohol's connection to social ills, such as violence, domestic violence, abuse, poverty, unemployment, and disease. The Woman's Christian Temperance Union (WCTU), formed in 1873, led the charge for Prohibition. In 1893, the reform group, the Anti-saloon League joined the efforts of the WCTU, calling for temperance legislation at the national level.

Throughout the 1910s, a movement for *Prohibition* gained support across the United States. People in rural areas widely supported Prohibition, but immigrants and working-class voters in urban areas widely opposed it. Despite their opposition, by 1916, 19 states had passed Prohibition laws. When the U.S. entered World War I, Prohibition became more of a necessity. Prohibition of alcohol ensured a more efficient workforce with less absenteeism and allowed grain (from which alcohol is distilled) to be used for the war effort.

In 1917, Congress easily passed the *18th Amendment* to the Constitution, which banned the sale and use of alcohol. By 1919, all the states except the Catholic immigrant holdout states of Rhode Island and Connecticut had ratified the amendment. Prohibition went into effect in January 1920. Prohibition, although noble in its goals, did little to curb society's use of alcohol. Instead, it led to the proliferation of gangs led by mobsters, such as Al Capone, who managed the illegal production, shipping, and sale of alcohol. It also led to a large market for illegally and often dangerously produced alcohol and the proliferation of illegal saloons. (See Chapter 16 for more about Prohibition and Chapter 17 for more about its repeal.)

The 19th Amendment: Women's suffrage

America's entry into World War I in 1917 created an unexpected opportunity for women to prosper and make tremendous political strides. As millions of American men left to fight in Europe, women worked in factories across the country to help in the war effort.

In 1910, the movement for women's *suffrage,* or the right to vote, gained impressive momentum. The women's suffrage movement was extremely popular among middle-class women who claimed that a woman's voice would help end the violence of wars and provide a boost to the temperance movement. In 1910, Washington state extended suffrage to women. California joined in in 1911, and four other western states in 1912. In 1913, Illinois joined in the fray and, in 1917 and 1918, New York and Michigan also extended suffrage to women. By 1919, 39 states allowed women to vote in some elections, and 15 states allowed women full political participation. In June 1919, Congress passed the 19th Amendment, which gave women the right to vote. The amendment became a law in August 1920, with more than ¾ of the states ratifying it. This movement would inspire feminist and equal rights challenges that would emerge later in the century (see Chapters 20 and 21).

The movement for racial equality

African Americans also fought for equal rights during the Progressive Era. World War I provided African Americans in the South the opportunity to gain rights and a better life. As World War I raged in Europe, U.S. immigration restrictions coupled with increased industrial production created a demand in Northern factories for many new workers. In the years from 1910 to the early 1920s, nearly a million African Americans migrated from the South to northern industrial centers such as Detroit, Philadelphia, Cleveland, Chicago, and St. Louis to work in the industrial factories. In the North, African Americans earned wages that were significantly higher than what they could earn farming or sharecropping in the South. This mass movement represents the beginning of the *Great Migration,* which would continue through World War II.

But movement to the North didn't produce equality for African Americans. Many northerners had racist mindsets to rival their southern counterparts; lynchings and race riots were common in northern cities throughout the late 1910s and 1920s. Yet for all the violence associated with the migration, African Americans carved out a new world for themselves in the North's industrial centers that would have been impossible in the South.

During the Progressive Era, two African American rights reformers emerged, *Booker T. Washington* and *W.E.B. Du Bois.* Washington took a passive approach, advocating patience and further development of education and vocational skills to obtain equal treatment and rights. He founded Tuskegee University in 1881 to help execute his plan. Du Bois said that all African Americans should demand equal treatment and rights immediately. In 1909, Du Bois and a group of white reformers formed the *National Association for the Advancement of Colored People (NAACP),* calling for an end to all discrimination against African Americans. The NAACP remains a prominent organization to this day. (Read more about the NAACP in association with the civil rights movement in Chapters 19 and 20.)

Tying it all together: A sample question looks at Progressive movements

The SAT II may ask you to distinguish between Progressive movements on the local, state, and national levels.

Which of the following early 20th-century Progressive movements was initiated on the local or state level before it became a national issue?

(A) Women's suffrage

(B) The civil rights movement

(C) The Sherman Antitrust Act

(D) The Hepburn Railroad Act

(E) Prohibition of unfair trade practices

This question asks you to choose the movement that began at the local or state level before it moved to the national level. Therefore, the correct answer could be a national issue. Don't be fooled by (B); the civil rights movement began at the grassroots level, but it was a movement of the 1960s and beyond, not an early 20th-century movement.

Answers (C), (D), and (E) — which are topics we cover later in this chapter — are national movements and, therefore, are incorrect. Even if you were unfamiliar with the tenets of the Sherman Antitrust Act, the Hepburn Railroad Act, and the cessation of unfair trade practices, you may recognize that trust, railroad, and trade issues involve interstate actions and, therefore, are more likely to be regulated by the national government. Women's suffrage became a national issue because of state efforts. So, (A) is the best answer.

Progressive Presidents: Teddy Roosevelt, Taft, and Wilson

Under the administrations of Theodore Roosevelt and Woodrow Wilson, and to a lesser extent, William H. Taft, the federal government instituted wide-reaching reforms in sharp contrast to the hands-off approach that the federal government took in the late 19th century.

Teddy Roosevelt: A political maverick

No figure better represents the Progressive Era than Theodore "Teddy" Roosevelt. Born into a wealthy New York family, Roosevelt rose to national prominence rather quickly. Early in his career, Roosevelt served as commissioner of the New York City Police Department before becoming the Assistant Secretary of the Navy. In the Spanish-American War, Roosevelt gained notoriety for leading his military volunteer unit, the *Rough Riders* to victory in the Battle of San Juan Hill in Cuba (see Chapter 13 for more on the Spanish-American War). In 1900, Roosevelt became Republican William McKinley's vice-presidential candidate. After McKinley's assassination in 1901, Roosevelt became the youngest president of the United States at age 42.

"TR," as he came to be known, exuded a vibrant personality. He was intelligent, well-read, and knew a great deal about the environment, history, and naval strategy. He loved sports and competition, participating in boxing, big-game hunting, and other outdoor pursuits. His active lifestyle carried over into his presidency, which lasted from 1901 to 1909, and he became one of the most active and influential presidents in American history. Some topics he tackled were trusts, railroads, safety in the food industry, and the environment.

Roosevelt's hostility toward trusts

Roosevelt believed that the crucial question facing the United States at the dawn of the 20th century was whether the federal government had the authority to control trusts, which he believed were spiraling out of control. (*Trusts* were massive groups of American corporations that had monopolies on various industries, such as banking, steel, oil, or railroads.) Monopolies prevented healthy economic competition in the marketplace, which meant high prices for consumers. Prior to the Progressive Era, the government rarely regulated trusts, so they could do almost anything they wanted. Roosevelt was fed up with the power of trusts and wanted to eliminate corporate abuse, so he decided to take action.

In a bold move in 1902, Roosevelt utilized the 1890 Sherman Antitrust Act (an act designed to break up trusts; see Chapter 12 for more) to have the Justice Department prosecute the Northern Securities Company, a railroad monopoly in the Northwest. In 1904, the Supreme Court upheld Roosevelt's decision, determining once and for all that the U.S. government could fight against trusts. As a result of the Supreme Court's decision, the Roosevelt administration used the Sherman Antitrust Act to file antitrust suits against 40 large companies, including Standard Oil and Du Pont, from 1901 to 1909.

Roosevelt demonstrated his distaste for trusts during the coal strike crisis of 1902. More than 50,000 coal miners went on strike, demanding better working conditions and higher pay. Roosevelt intervened, inviting the union representatives and mine owners to the White House to try to find a solution. But the owners refused to speak with the union representatives. Roosevelt was infuriated by this rebuff, and he threatened to send federal troops to operate the mines. At the urging of J. P. Morgan (the renowned financier who formed the U.S. Steel Corporation), the owners backed down and gave the miners shorter workdays (9 hours) and better wages (a 10 percent increase). Roosevelt proved that he wouldn't hesitate to challenge the powers and abuses of big business.

Regulating the railroads

Railroad reform was another important contribution that Roosevelt made to the Progressive cause. At the beginning of the 20th century, railroad companies controlled the prices of their services. Roosevelt believed that this system gave private companies too much power, which ultimately hurt consumers. Thus, he supported the *Hepburn Railroad Act,* which gave the *Interstate Commerce Commission (ICC)* the power to regulate the prices of railroad rates and to audit railroad companies' financial records. Congress passed the Hepburn Railroad Act, and Roosevelt signed it into law in 1906.

The Pure Food and Drug Act, the Meat Inspection Act, and other reforms

Journalists were an important part of the Progressive Era because they uncovered abuses in industry and the urban world. In the late 1800s and early 1900s, a trend in journalism arose in which journalists directed public attention toward uncovering scandal, corruption, and injustice. These investigative journalists became known as *muckrakers* and their type of journalism was known as muckraking. They earned the nickname when Roosevelt accused one such journalist of going too far — that is, raking muck — with his essays, and the journalist (who liked the title) held onto it with pride. These muckrakers were especially influential in reforming the food industry.

In 1906, muckraking journalists reported that some companies used poisons in the production of drugs and food products, which prompted Roosevelt to urge the U.S. Senate to pass the *Pure Food and Drug Act.* Roosevelt quickly signed the act, which enacted pure food standards and regulated the sale of harmful or ineffective medicines, into law. In another journalistic exposé, a writer named Upton Sinclair described the horrors and unsanitary conditions of the meatpacking industry in his book *The Jungle* (published in 1906).

Muckrakers also influenced other reforms. *Ida Tarbell's* exposé on the Standard Oil company, *The History of Standard Oil,* derived from interviews she did with a senior director of the company, was published in 1902 as a book and also published in *McClure's* (a pioneer muckraking magazine) from 1902 to 1904. Her revelations of company corruption are credited with hastening the breakup of the Standard Oil trust in 1911. Fellow *McClure's* staff writers and muckrakers *Lincoln Steffen* and *Ray Stannard Baker* were not responsible for specific reform measures, but their articles opened Americans' eyes to societal evils. Steffen exposed government corruption in a series of articles published as *The Shame of the Cities* in 1904 and *The Struggle for Self-Government* in 1906, and Baker was one of the first prominent journalists to examine America's race issues.

Making conservation efforts

Roosevelt was an outdoorsman, sportsman, and naturalist since he was a boy. In the years before he became president, he took numerous trips West to hunt and enjoy the outdoors. He even established two cattle ranches in North Dakota and lived in North Dakota for much of the 1880s. (Here's an interesting fact that you won't need to know for the SAT II: Roosevelt was on a hiking trip with his family in the Adirondack Mountains when he received news of President McKinley's assassination and of his own succession to the presidency.)

Once in office, Roosevelt began to enact aggressive conservation policies. In 1902, he created Crater Lake National Park in Oregon. In 1902, he signed the *Newlands Reclamation Act* into law, which created 21 federal irrigation projects. In 1903, he created Pelican Island, Florida, as the nation's first federal bird reservation, and he created the first federal game preserve in Oklahoma in 1905. In 1906, Roosevelt signed the *National Monuments Act* and created Devil's Tower, the first of 18 national monuments created during the Roosevelt administration. To inventory the nation's treasures and efficiently manage their use, Roosevelt appointed a *National Conservation Commission* in 1908 and organized the North American Conservation Conference held at the White House in 1909.

In 1905, Roosevelt created the *U.S. Forest Service* and appointed Gifford Pinchot as its first director. Because he advocated a rational and efficient human use of the wilderness and forests, Pinchot was criticized by some conservationists on the left, such as *John Muir.* Muir, who founded the *Sierra Club* (an environmental protection organization) in 1892 and was its president until 1914, felt that the wilderness ought to remain untouched. But despite their differences of opinion, Roosevelt and Muir were good friends. In fact, on a memorable camping trip to Yosemite, Muir easily convinced Roosevelt to expand Yosemite National Park in California. (Yosemite had become a national park in 1890).

During his administration, Roosevelt created five national parks, 51 bird reservations, 4 federal game preserves, 18 national monuments, and preserved more than 200 million acres of land. Roosevelt also fought to regulate the lumber, cattle, and mining industries because he believed that Americans needed to use the nation's resources wisely.

Tying it all together: A sample question about TR

Teddy Roosevelt was, by far, the most visible figure of the Progressive Era and did many things during his presidency to advance the Progressive agenda. Therefore, you shouldn't be surprised if the SAT II asks you a question about Teddy and his initiatives.

The following quotation is from Theodore Roosevelt: "Our aim is not to do away with corporations. On the contrary, these big aggregations are the inevitable development of modern industrialism. We draw the line against misconduct, not against wealth."

Which of the following pieces of legislations enacted during Roosevelt's administration best relates to Roosevelt's attitude toward misconduct in industry?

(A) The 18th Amendment

(B) The Pure Food and Drug Act

(C) The Mann Act

(D) The Underwood-Simmons Tariff

(E) All of the above

What do you think of when you read Roosevelt's quote? Probably Roosevelt the "trust-buster," who wanted to regulate the misconduct of business. We'll go through the answers and see which one fits.

The 18th Amendment, which took effect in 1919 (after Roosevelt's presidency), prohibited the sale and use of alcohol. Knowing this info, you can eliminate answers (A) and (E). What about (B)? This act dealt with regulating the food and pharmaceutical industries, so it's certainly a possibility. Leave this option for consideration and move on to (C). The Mann Act of 1910, covered later in this chapter, deals with prostitution and wasn't enacted during Roosevelt's administration. So, this answer isn't correct. Finally, the Underwood-Simmons Tariff, which also takes place after Roosevelt's presidency (and which we cover later in this chapter), has to do with the lowering of the protective tariff and has little to do with trusts. So your answer is (B). Congress passed the Pure Food and Drug Act and Roosevelt signed it into law to regulate the misconduct and abuses of food and drug companies.

William H. Taft: More conservative than TR

After Roosevelt decided not to run for a second term, his handpicked successor, William Howard Taft, defeated perennial Democratic candidate William Jennings Bryan in the 1908 presidential election. Taft, a large man at more than 300 pounds, was the opposite of Roosevelt in numerous ways. Roosevelt always portrayed himself as a vigorous and sporting man, whereas Taft was an inexperienced leader (though an experienced bureaucrat) with little sense of adventure. Taft didn't appear very interested in or excited about the presidency, as Roosevelt had been, and he wasn't a very good politician. In addition, Taft had a temper and lacked the ability to compromise or deal well with crises. Taft's presidency, which lasted from 1909 to 1913, was largely a failure, although some important Progressive reforms did take place during his tenure in office.

The Payne–Aldrich Tariff

To allow more foreign trade, Taft wanted to reduce the U.S tariff, which taxed foreign goods coming into the U.S. Roosevelt had wanted to deal with the tariff issue during his presidency but knew that it'd be a political disaster. Taft, however, decided to take a chance with the issue shortly after his inauguration in 1909 and instituted the *Payne–Aldrich Tariff.*

Taft convinced the House of Representatives to reduce the tariff slightly and to make up the lost revenue by instituting a small inheritance tax. But the Senate thwarted Taft's efforts. The Senate not only defeated the inheritance tax, but it actually proposed raising the tariff. Maintaining a high tariff protected American corporations from foreign competition but did little to advance the cause of Progressivism because preventing foreign competition encouraged the proliferation of monopolies and trusts. In the end, the Payne–Aldrich Tariff reduced the tax to only 37 percent (a minimal decrease). Disagreements in Congress over the tariff created a split in the Republican Party between Progressives, who wanted to lower the tariff, and the old guard, who still wanted to advance big business. Taft didn't fight the passage of the Payne–Aldrich Tariff and even praised the bill as one of the greatest bills the Republican Party had ever passed, which made him look corrupt or foolish.

The Mann–Elkins Act

Congress passed the *Mann–Elkins Act* in 1910 in an effort to regulate the telephone and telegraph industries. As part of the act, Congress provided increased power to the Interstate Commerce Commission (originally created in 1887) to regulate the telephone, telegraph, and railroad industries. The act essentially provided the ICC with the power to control rail rates and, thus, rail competition.

Try not to confuse the Mann–Elkins Act with the *Mann Act.* Although Illinois Congressman James Robert Mann sponsored both acts (hence his name graces them both), they're very different. The *Mann Act* (sometimes known as the "white slave traffic act") also passed in 1910 and had to do with the regulation of prostitution. It made it illegal for a man to take a woman across state lines for immoral purposes. The act was primarily designed to stop the practice of bringing European immigrant women to the U.S. to work in brothels.

Woodrow Wilson: A champion of reform

Woodrow Wilson, the former president of Princeton University and governor of New Jersey, emerged in 1912 as the leading presidential candidate for the Democratic Party. Teddy Roosevelt, fed up with William Howard Taft's ineptitude, entered the race as an independent and ran as a candidate for the *"Bull Moose,"* or Progressive, Party. The Republican voters split their votes between Taft and Roosevelt. The Bull Moose Party ran the most successful third-party campaign for the presidency in U.S. history, winning 27 percent of the popular vote. Roosevelt's program of *New Nationalism* advocated allowing continued economic concentration in the form of trusts and monopolies so long as they were strictly regulated. Eugene Debs ran on the Socialist platform and also made an impressive showing by garnering 6 percent of the popular vote (or nearly one million votes).

The split between the four major parties, however, allowed Wilson to secure the presidency with only 42 percent of the popular vote. Wilson dominated the Electoral College vote, winning 435 votes to Roosevelt's 88, Taft's miniscule 8, and Deb's 0. Wilson, the son of a Presbyterian minister and a devout believer in God, wanted the United States to develop a more moral center and, to achieve that goal, he ran his presidency, which lasted from 1913 to 1921, in the spirit of Progressivism. As a presidential candidate in 1912, Wilson presented his *New Freedom,* program which advocated the destruction of all trusts and monopolies, promoted lowering tariffs, and proposed widespread banking reform.

For all of Wilson's Progressive ideals, he struggled with many movements that took place during his presidency. In the early years of his presidency, he refused to support the movement for women's suffrage. He also supported segregation in federal government agencies, which reflected his Southern background (and his desire to receive the continued support of the Southern Democrats). An astute politician, Wilson would eventually come to embrace most of these Progressive initiatives, which helped secure his political future.

The Underwood Tariff

Wilson believed that the purpose of the tariff, which taxed goods coming into the U.S. and had been greatly debated during the presidencies of Roosevelt and Taft, didn't promote effective competition. Congress, under the control of Democrats, passed the *Underwood Tariff* in 1913, which reduced tariff rates by 15 percent and encouraged competition from abroad. Wilson figured that increased competition from abroad through a reduction in the tariff would diminish the influence of trusts and big business. To make up the revenue the government lost by reducing the tariff, Congress passed a moderate income tax (see the section on the 16th Amendment earlier in this chapter). Some senators were harshly opposed to the Underwood Tariff and wanted to raise it. But Wilson appealed to the public, decrying the massive influence of big business, and with public sentiment largely favoring him, the Senate passed the tariff.

The Federal Reserve Act

Wilson was greatly concerned about the state of the economy, especially the fact that J. P. Morgan and company had a frightening monopoly over the banking industry (which had not been thwarted by Roosevelt's antitrust suits), controlling more than $22 billion in assets. (See Chapter 12 for more about J. P. Morgan.) In response to the growing power of Morgan and other conglomerates, Wilson proposed establishing a federal reserve, which would create a centralized banking system under public control and would help stabilize the economy, especially if the country faced an economic panic. The *Federal Reserve Act* of 1913 established a national banking system with 12 regional centers across the United States. The banks were privately run but supervised by a *Federal Reserve Board,* whose members would be appointed by the president. The Federal Reserve Board, or "the Fed," was put in charge of overseeing the entire banking network and the nation's fiscal policies.

The SAT II U.S. History test may ask you a question about the creation of the Federal Reserve. Remember that with the passage of the Federal Reserve Act, the federal government now had greater control over currency and credit and provided a more stable economic system for the United States. The passage of the Federal Reserve Act was one of Wilson's greatest achievements as president.

Assaulting the trusts

Unlike Roosevelt, who felt that the centralized industry in the form of a monopoly or trust was okay so long as it was heavily regulated, Wilson wanted to destroy trusts completely. In 1914, Wilson supported the *Clayton Antitrust Act,* which improved upon the Sherman Antitrust

Act (which was pretty vague and open to interpretation) by making practices such as price discrimination illegal. Congress also passed the Federal Trade Commission Act, which created a *Federal Trade Commission (FTC),* which had the power to regulate commerce and investigate unfair trade practices or violations of interstate trade regulations. The FTC also possessed the power to issue cease-and-desist orders (a government mandate to halt illegal activity) when it found a corporation guilty of violating trade regulations.

Agricultural aid and more

In 1914, Wilson supported the *Smith–Lever Act* of 1914, which provided grants to states to provide agricultural extension education. Wilson also supported pieces of legislation in 1916 that made it easier for farmers to obtain credit. His efforts to expand the role of the federal government with reform efforts in the middle years of his administration suggested that he was moving closer to Teddy Roosevelt's program of New Nationalism. In addition to legislation that supported farmers, Wilson also supported legislation against child labor in the form of the *Keating–Owen Act* of 1916 and legislation in favor of workers' compensation for federal employees so that employees injured on the job would receive medical care for their injuries.

Tying it all together: A sample question looks at presidential Progressivism

You need to commit a few pieces of legislation that passed during Roosevelt's, Taft's, and Wilson's administrations to memory because they were key to Progressive reforms. To memorize them, make flashcards of terms and people highlighted throughout this chapter.

Here's a question dealing with the Progressive Era that asks you about general agendas.

Which of the following pieces of legislation did NOT advance a Progressive agenda under President Woodrow Wilson?

(A) The Clayton Antitrust Act

(B) Keating–Owen Act

(C) The Underwood Tariff

(D) The Meat Inspection Act

(E) The Federal Reserve Act

You need to be careful here and look at the question closely. It asks you for pieces of legislation that advanced a Progressive agenda under Woodrow Wilson. Wilson was elected to office in 1912 and remained in office until 1921.

The Clayton Antitrust Act dealt with regulating trusts and was passed during Wilson's administration, so you can cross out (A) because you're looking for legislation that did *not* advance a Progressive agenda under Wilson. How about the Keating–Owen Act (B)? It had to do with eliminating child labor, and Congress passed it in 1916. That fits a Wilson Progressive agenda, so (B) is wrong. Congress passed the Underwood Tariff in 1913 to increase foreign competition in the U.S. marketplace and to break up U.S. trusts, which is a Progressive idea, so (C) isn't right. Now, look at option (E), the Federal Reserve Act. Congress passed this act in 1913 to regulate U.S. banking, so you know that (E) can't be right. By process of elimination, you're left with (D) as the correct answer. Congress passed the Meat Inspection Act under the leadership of Teddy Roosevelt in 1906.

Chapter 15

World War I and Postwar Diplomacy, 1914–1920

● ●

In This Chapter

▶ Entering the first worldwide conflict

▶ Preparing and sacrificing on the home front

▶ Fighting a new type of war at sea and on land

▶ Negotiating for peace: The Great War comes to an end

● ●

*W*orld War I, known as the Great War until World War II proved to be an even more destructive, deadly, and costly war, began in Europe in July 1914. By 1914, the major political powers in Europe were divided into two alliances: The *Triple Entente,* which consisted of Russia, France, and Great Britain, later known as the Allies, and the *Triple Alliance,* which united Germany, Italy, and the Austro-Hungarian Empire (which included parts or all of present-day Austria, Hungary, Poland, Czechoslovakia, and some of the nations of the Balkan peninsula; this region was also referred to as Austria-Hungary), later known as the Central powers.

The primary rivalry existed between Germany and Great Britain. Britain had long been a powerful imperialistic nation, and Germany wanted to be just as influential and powerful as Britain, or greater. Although the rivalry between these two big shot countries wasn't the immediate cause of the outbreak of the war, it was the source of most of the underlying tensions that led to the war.

In June 1914, a Serbian nationalist assassinated Archduke Franz Ferdinand, heir to the throne of Austria-Hungary, and his wife while they were visiting Sarajevo, the capital of Bosnia, a province of the Austro-Hungarian Empire. The Slavic people in Bosnia and Herzegovina (another province of Austria-Hungary) didn't want to be part of Austria-Hungary anymore; they wanted to be part of Serbia, an independent neighboring country. And Serbia desperately wanted to annex Bosnia and Herzegovina.

Serbia got its chance. Soon after the archduke's assassination, Austria-Hungary declared war on Serbia. Serbia had been steadily gaining power and territory for years, and Austria-Hungary wanted to quell that expansion. Austria-Hungary's declaration of war created a domino effect across Europe. Germany supported Austria-Hungary's decision to declare war on Serbia, and Serbia called on Russia for military assistance. As the Russians mobilized their army in July, the situation spiraled out of control. In early August, Germany declared war on Russia and France and invaded Belgium. One day later, to honor its alliance with France and Russia, Great Britain declared war on Germany. Within a few days, fighting broke out formally between Russia and the Austro-Hungarian Empire. By early 1915, Italy and the Ottoman Empire (present-day Turkey) had joined in the fray on the side of the Central powers. Japan and nearly 20 other nations joined the Allies. By the end of 1915, Italy had switched sides to join the Allies (in hopes of gaining land in Austria-Hungary when it lost), and the war had spread across all of Europe and parts of Asia. The United States entered the war in 1917 on the side of the Allies.

On the SAT II U.S. History exam, you're likely to run into three or four big-idea questions that deal directly with World War I. If you understand the causes and effects of World War I, you'll understand the global situation during the 1920s (see Chapter 16) and the subsequent causes of the Great Depression (see Chapter 17) and World War II (see Chapter 18).

Joining Forces: America Enters the War

For two and a half years, the United States remained neutral. President Woodrow Wilson asked Americans to remain impartial, but they didn't. Some Americans sided with the Central powers, especially those of German or Irish ancestry (Ireland had a long-standing conflict with Britain). Other Americans sided with the Allies because of the historical, cultural, and economic ties to Britain. But several events finally persuaded the U.S. to join the war on the side of the Allies.

Not our problem: American neutrality

Most Americans felt that the war in Europe had nothing to do with them, and the U.S., in its determination to remain neutral, continued trading with both sides. That is, until a British naval blockade against Germany made trading with the Central powers difficult for the U.S. As trade with the Central powers dwindled, the Allies' demand for food, clothing, monetary loans, and military supplies increased. From an economic viewpoint, heavy trading with the Allies benefited the United States, especially because Britain and France's orders for war supplies helped the U. S. economy to boom.

President Wilson believed in a peaceful, democratic world order, but he also had a personal interest in a neutral United States: 1916 was an election year, and he wanted to be reelected. By a narrow margin, the American people reelected Wilson, who ran under the campaign slogan "He kept us out of war."

Getting motivated: America joins the Allies

Germany, no match for Britain's naval power, began using newly improved submarines to sink enemy vessels. Germany resorted to this tactic to try to gain control of the Atlantic and cut the Allies off from their much-needed supplies. In early 1915, Germany warned Allied nations that German submarines (also called U-boats) would sink any enemy vessels on sight. The Germans kept their word. Off the coast of Ireland in May 1915, German submarines sank the *Lusitania,* a British passenger ship with nearly 2,000 people on board that was headed from New York to Liverpool. Over 1,200 people perished, including 128 Americans. This incident angered Americans and increased tensions between the United States and Germany. Wilson demanded that Germany stop attacking nonmilitary vessels, and Germany agreed. But in early 1916, the U.S. had another run-in with Germany. A German submarine attacked a French Steamer ship, the *Sussex,* which had several Americans on board. Wilson demanded that Germany stop its submarine warfare and, again, Germany backed down. In its *Sussex Pledge,* Germany promised not to attack merchant ships without warning.

Other U.S. interests also influenced the nation's eventual decision to enter the war. The U.S. provided food and manufactured goods to the Allies, and U.S. banks lent money to these nations. Americans worried that the Allies would never repay this money if the Central powers won the war. Also, a Central powers victory would mean that autocratic nations would take over the democratic ones in Europe.

In the early months of 1917, the following four events influenced public opinion and convinced President Wilson that the U.S. needed to go to war on the side of the Allies:

- ✔ In January, Germany resumed unrestricted submarine warfare on Allied and American ships to cut off the steady stream of supplies to Great Britain.

- ✔ In February, Britain released a telegram it had intercepted earlier from Germany's foreign minister, Arthur Zimmermann, to the Mexican government. In the telegram, Zimmermann proposed that if Mexico joined the Central powers, Germany would help Mexico get Texas, Arizona, and New Mexico back from the United States after the war. This telegram was widely publicized by the British and American media and led to an increase in public outrage against Germany.

- ✔ In March, a revolution in Russia replaced the czarist regime with a republican government, which made the United States more amenable to allying with Russia. Prior to the change in government, it would have been embarrassing for the U.S. to ally itself with an autocratic monarchy when President Wilson preached about self-determination and democracy for all nations.

- ✔ In late March, German submarines torpedoed three U.S. ships in the Atlantic. This attack was the final straw for Wilson. Two weeks later, he called for a joint session of Congress and asked for the U.S. to declare war on the Central powers. Within four days of the attack, the United States joined the Allies against the Central powers.

The SAT II may ask you about the reasons for America's entering the war.

One reason Woodrow Wilson decided to enter the war against Germany in 1917 was

(A) To gain support from the Allies for the Fourteen Points.

(B) To respond to German trade embargoes on U.S. goods.

(C) To take action for the German submarine attack on three U.S. ships in the Atlantic.

(D) To counter Mexico's allegiance with Germany and its declaration of war on the U.S.

(E) To react to the Germans sinking a British passenger ship off the coast of Ireland.

The key to correctly answering this question is to know the driving forces behind the United States' entry into World War I. Three of the four propelling events were the revolution in Russia, the Zimmermann telegram, and Germany's unrestricted submarine warfare in the Atlantic.

Don't let (D) fool you. The threat of Mexican allegiance to Germany influenced Wilson, but Mexico didn't declare war on the United States.

What about (A)? Even if you're not familiar with Wilson's Fourteen Points (which we discuss later in this chapter), you can logically surmise that gaining support for a policy wouldn't be a good reason to bring the United States out of neutrality. So, you can eliminate (A). Germany didn't initiate trade embargoes, so (B) is out. Answer (E) refers to the *Lusitania,* which the Germans sunk in 1915, so you can cross out (E). The last straw for Wilson was when German submarines attacked three U.S. ships in the Atlantic; therefore, the best answer is (C).

Over Here: The Home Front

World War I introduced many changes to the home front. Even before the United States entered the war, Wilson was preparing the country for potential involvement. In 1916, Wilson encouraged Congress to pass the *National Defense Act,* which allowed for a military buildup to prepare the country for war, also known as "preparedness." Although Wilson didn't want to bring the U.S. into the war, he felt it was better for the U.S. to be prepared if provoked into war than to be caught by surprise.

When the United States finally entered the war in 1917, President Wilson quickly organized a number of government boards to manage the sectors of the economy that were crucial to war production. He also faced the challenge of increasing the size of the military and raising money to fund the war. Meanwhile, some Americans were the target of limited civil liberties.

Easy labor: The efficiency of factories

The cooperation of U.S. industry was key because it allowed for an efficient mobilization to aid the Allies and, later, helped prepare the U.S. for full involvement in the war. In 1914, the government began offering factories government contracts to alter their production. For example, a factory that previously made corsets started making uniforms for soldiers, and a factory that made bicycles started manufacturing guns and ammunition. Competition for these coveted government contracts was fierce. By 1918, Wilson had turned over the management of the *War Industries Board* (WIB), which managed the purchase of military supplies, fixed prices, and told manufacturers what and how much to produce, to Wall Street tycoon Bernard Baruch, who ran the WIB as a tight ship. Progressives cheered for this centralized regulation of the economy, which they felt was long overdue.

As the U.S. increased its production of war goods from 1914 to 1918, factories needed more workers to keep up with the increasing production demands and to take the place of men who left the workforce to join the service. During this time, thousands of women entered the workforce, and African Americans migrated in record numbers from the South to northern cities to work in factories. (This movement is known as the Great Migration; see Chapter 14 for more on this topic.) In 1918, Wilson established the *National War Labor Board* to act as a mediator between industry and workers. While the labor board helped workers achieve many concessions (including an eight-hour work day, recognition of labor unions, fair wages and working conditions, and equal pay for women), it also demanded that workers not strike. With all these new workers in the workforce, labor union membership increased significantly (by 1.5 million Americans) between 1917 and 1919.

Under control: Passing the Lever Act

The *Lever Act,* passed in August 1917 and also known as the Food and Fuel Control Act, gave the president the authority to regulate food distribution, storage, purchase, importation, and exportation. Under the Lever Act, Wilson issued an executive order that created the United States Food Administration and the Fuel Administration. The Lever Act is significant (and fair game for the test) because it placed complete government control over private sectors of the economy to ensure that the government had everything it needed for the war, including control of key industries to distribute food and fuel quickly and efficiently.

The Food Administration

Wilson appointed Herbert Hoover head of the Food Administration. The purpose of the Food Administration was to ensure the transportation, supply, conservation, and distribution of food and to prevent hoarding of food. Basically, this organization helped the government maintain control over the food supply. The Food Administration encouraged citizens to make voluntarily sacrifices to conserve food through "meatless Tuesdays" and "wheatless Mondays." It also encouraged citizens to grow their own vegetables and eat fewer meats, fats, and sugar to secure enough food to send to U.S. troops and Allied troops abroad. By 1918, the United States exported three times as much meat, sugar, and grain to the Allies than it had prior to 1914.

The Fuel Administration

Under the direction of Harry A. Garfield, the Fuel Administration had absolute control over all the fuel supplies in the United States and regulated the production, distribution, and consumption of coal, natural gas, and petroleum. The administration encouraged citizens to conserve fuel, and Americans made do with much less fuel than they had in pre-war years.

Full support: Financing and selling the war

The United States needed a great deal of money to finance the war effort. In 1918, the government raised over $10 billion by increasing the income tax, business tax, and other taxes. The government raised another $23 billion through the sale of *war bonds,* also called "Liberty Bonds," and war savings certificates. People who purchased war bonds and war savings certificates could turn them in after the war for the face amount plus interest.

But another kind of selling was also going on — that is, the selling of the war to the American public. Wilson created the *Committee on Public Information (CPI)* in April 1917 to promote the war domestically and to publicize U.S. actions to its allies abroad. Muckraking journalist George Creel managed CPI, so it was also known as the "Creel Commission." This large-scale propaganda machine set censorship guidelines, advertised in favor of the war, and created anti-German movies, billboard posters, and pamphlets to sway the opinion of the American public.

Spying on the neighbors

During World War I, numerous citizen groups formed to find people who were disloyal to the war effort. Members of these groups watched their neighbors and targeted immigrants and minority groups. Citizen groups were particularly suspicious of Irish Americans, German Americans, and Jewish Americans.

Citizen groups targeted Irish Americans because many Irish Americans sympathized with the Germans due to Ireland's historically bad relationship with Britain. Citizens groups were suspicious of Jews because they opposed the anti-Semitic Russian government, and Russia was an American ally. In addition, many Americans perceived German Americans as a huge threat, even though most supported the Allied war effort by the time the United States entered the war. Citizens vigilantly watched their German American neighbors for anti-American activity, and all-things German became unfashionable: Libraries removed German books; schools removed German language courses; and Americans renamed sauerkraut "liberty cabbage" and the hamburger "liberty sausage." German Americans faced regular harassment, and those working in war industries regularly lost their jobs because others feared they'd sabotage production.

In addition, the CPI (see the previous section) helped pass the *Espionage Act of 1917,* which declared that making false statements intended to interfere with the success of the U.S. military was illegal, and its 1918 amendment, the *Sedition Act of 1918,* which made expressing an opinion that went against the U.S. government a crime. (See Chapter 16 for more about these acts.) The Espionage Act was put to the test in the court case *Schenck v. The United States* in 1919. During the war, Socialist Charles Schenck was arrested for distributing flyers to recently drafted men and urging them to resist conscription. He believed that mandatory military conscription conflicted with the 13th Amendment's clause on involuntary servitude, and he was convicted of violating the Espionage Act. He appealed his case until it reached the Supreme Court and argued that the act violated his 1st Amendment rights under freedom of the press.

The Supreme Court decided that Schenck's arrest was constitutional and that the 1st Amendment didn't protect against speech that encouraged mutiny during times of war. In the court's opinion, Justice Oliver Wendell Holmes stated that speech the 1st Amendment's freedom of speech clause would normally protect may be subject to prohibition when its nature and circumstances may create a "clear and present danger." Basically, the Court ruled that during times of war or national crisis, the laws governing free speech were different than they were during times of peace.

Mobilizing the military and instating the draft

Despite Wilson's preparations for war under the National Defense Act, fewer than 130,000 soldiers were in the U.S. Army when the United States entered the war. The military always had relied on volunteers but needed so many soldiers immediately that Congress passed the *Selective Service Act* in May 1917. This act required all men ages 21 to 30 (later Congress changed it to ages 18 to 45) to register for the military; over the course of the war, the act drafted three million men to serve in the war. Two million more men and women joined the military voluntarily.

During the war, nearly 400,000 African Americans volunteered to serve or were drafted into the military. The military segregated African American soldiers from white troops, but white soldiers still harassed African American soldiers. African American soldiers were usually led by white officers, and they weren't allowed to join the marines or the air force. Many African American soldiers received menial cooking and cleaning assignments instead of combat postings, and the troops who were sent to the fronts participated in some of the worst jobs, such as burying dead American soldiers and searching for bodies. The SAT II may ask you about minority troops in World War I.

Which of the following is true about African Americans who served in the United States' military during World War I?

(A) Very few African Americans served as soldiers in World War I.

(B) The United States' Marines openly welcomed African American soldiers during World War I.

(C) Most African American soldiers fought on the front lines during the war.

(D) African American troops were segregated from white troops and often led by white officers.

(E) African Americans drafted into the military during World War I were not sent to the front to fight but, instead, were sent to United States factories in northern cities to produce arms.

Right off the bat, you can eliminate (A), because nearly 400,000 African Americans served in the military during World War I. You also know that African Americans could not serve in the Marines, and most soldiers held menial jobs like cooking and cleaning. So you can eliminate (B) and (C) as options.

Answer (E) is tricky because parts of it are correct. African Americans did move to northern cities during the war to work in factories, and most didn't fight on the front during the war. But African American soldiers weren't sent to work in factories. So, (D) is the best answer because African American soldiers served in segregated units often led by white officers.

Over There: The Military Front

World War I was an entirely new kind of war for several reasons. During World War I, new technology became available that initiated changes to traditional warfare. Improvements in travel, communications, and food preservation for soldiers assisted the war effort. World War I saw the introduction of new weapons and methods of fighting, such as tanks, airplanes, poisonous gas, trench warfare, and the widespread use of barbed wire and machine guns, which made the war much more deadly.

 For the SAT II, keep in mind that World War I was the first large-scale modern war where many nations fought each other on multiple fronts scattered around the globe. More than nine million soldiers and millions of civilians lost their lives in the war, making it the most deadly war ever at that time.

When the U.S. entered the war in 1917, the Allies desperately needed help. The Central powers were wearing them down in naval battles and on the ground. The infusion of fresh American troops and supplies provided the Allies with the boost they needed to defeat Germany and its allies.

The war at sea

By the time the United States entered the war in 1917, the frequent attacks by German submarines had taken their toll on the British Navy. German subs sank one in four British ships that left Britain. Within a month of United States' entry into the war, the U.S. Navy was working with the British Navy to turn the tide of victory at sea away from the Germans. U.S. destroyers increased the campaign against the German submarines, and U.S. warships escorted Allied vessels across the Atlantic. The U.S. Navy also helped plant anti-submarine mines in the North Sea, which successfully decreased German attacks in the Atlantic. Americans hoped that only naval involvement would be required to win the war, but it was soon clear that the United States needed to send forces to the campaign on land to back up the weakening Allies.

The war on the Western front

After the Russian Revolution occurred in March 1917 and then the Bolshevik Revolution in November 1917, Russia's new leader Vladimir I. Lenin, busy with domestic issues, signed an armistice with the Central powers in December 1917, ending Russia's involvement in the war. Russia's action freed up all the German soldiers on the Eastern front to fight the Allies on the Western front. With the Allies on the verge of collapse from the miserable fighting in the trenches, the *American Expeditionary Force* (AEF) of two million fresh and eager men under the command of General John Pershing joined the Allied army in the spring of 1918. With a series of offensive campaigns (at Chateau-Thierry, Rheims, and the Argonne Forest), the AEF successfully forced the Germans to retreat. By the end of October 1918, the Allies had forced the retreating Germans back into Germany and had cut off their supply lines to the front.

When the Allies reached Germany, German leaders asked for an armistice to avoid an invasion of their country. The Allies insisted on terms for the armistice agreement that essentially made Germany surrender its military to the Allies. The Allies accepted the proposal to cease fighting and, on November 11, 1918, World War I ended on all fronts.

Disease in the trenches . . . and at home

Of the millions of American men who fought in the armed forces during World War I, 112,000 perished. Forty-nine thousand died in battle, and the remaining died of pneumonia, influenza, or other diseases that ravaged the trenches and the camps. Astonishingly, being a civilian during the war may have been just as dangerous. Civilians living in the war-ravaged countries of Europe endured shortages of food, fuel, and consumer goods along with the constant danger of enemy attack. Still, disease posed an even greater danger to European civilians and to those in America and the rest of the world. In 1918, a nasty epidemic of Spanish influenza lasted nine months and claimed the lives of more than 500,000 Americans. Worldwide, the epidemic claimed the lives of 20 million people in that same nine-month period! Some speculate that the stresses of combat combined with poisonous gas warfare may have weakened the immune systems of soldiers fighting in 1918.

Bloopers and Blunders: Wilson's Postwar Diplomacy

Although President Wilson was opposed to entering the war in the first place, he showed amazing leadership throughout the war. Under his direction, America helped bring about a quick and efficient end to the war. And the end of the war signaled the time to negotiate for "peace without victory."

Wilson in Paris: Negotiating the Treaty of Versailles

Wilson traveled to Versailles, France, in December 1918 with an American peace commission comprised of professors, Democrats, and one token Republican. (An interesting tidbit that the exam won't test you on: Wilson was the first president to travel to Europe while in office). Set in his plan and determined to negotiate with the leaders of France, Italy, and Great Britain, Wilson entered negotiations with optimism and confidence.

A man can dream, can't he? Wilson's Fourteen Points

Months before the U.S. entered World War I, Wilson had a plan for peace after the war. He presented this plan, known as the *Fourteen Points,* to Congress in January 1917. Although most Republicans opposed the plan, most of the American public supported it. Unfortunately, the other Allied leaders only partially supported or downright resisted Wilson's plan when he presented it in Versailles. The first five points of the plan reflected Wilson's ideals for a new world order:

  ✔ Open covenants rather than secret treaties among nations

  ✔ Freedom of the seas

  ✔ Free trade and removal of international trade embargoes

  ✔ Reduction of armaments

  ✔ Impartial mediation of colonial claims with regard to the interests of the natives

Points 6–13 dealt with the idea of national self-determination (the right of any national group to form its own government and independent nation) and called for the following:

- Departure of all foreign powers and military occupation from Russia
- Departure of all foreign powers and military occupation from Belgium
- That Germany return Alsace-Lorraine to France
- Adjustment of the Italian border
- Autonomy for the citizens of Austria-Hungary, Montenegro, Serbia, Romania, and the Ottoman Empire (points 10–12)
- Departure of all foreign powers and military occupation from Poland
- Establishment of the *League of Nations* (see the later section "All together now: The League of Nations" in this chapter), which would be an association of nations that would guarantee political freedom and stable territorial boundaries for both large and small countries.

Although the Allies were highly supportive of Wilson's idea to form the League of Nations, they outwardly objected to his ideas for free trade, freedom of the seas, and open covenants. Centuries of alliances and rivalries in Europe prevented European leaders from accepting these points. Wilson also faced a great deal of opposition for his idea of national self-determination for all people, which conflicted with the economic and strategic plans of the European Allies.

Gimme: European demands on Germany in the treaty

France was fed up with Germany and wanted revenge. France wanted to weaken Germany's military and to get back the land it had lost. Great Britain wanted Germany to pay for the war, and Italy wanted to expand territorially. The United States wanted to dominate and make the other nations accept the conditions in Wilson's Fourteen Points. With these desires, the *Big Four* drew up the *Treaty of Versailles*. Unfortunately, Wilson had to give in on a number of issues in order to get the other nations to accept his plan for the League of Nations. The treaty provided that

- Germany surrender all its colonies to the Allies and surrender German-occupied regions such as the Alsace-Lorraine to France, the Saar Valley to the League of Nations, and other parts of Germany to Belgium, Denmark, Poland, Czechoslovakia, and Lithuania.
- Germany disarm most of its military; ban conscription; demilitarize the Rhineland, which France would occupy for 15 years; ban all military industries; reduce its navy; and prohibit the manufacture or possession of military aircraft, tanks, poisonous gas, and submarines.
- Germany accept sole responsibility for causing the war and make reparation payments to Allied nations in the amount of $56 billion.
- Germany could not unify with Austria.

The Allies signed four separate peace treaties with the other Central power nations of Austria, Hungary, Bulgaria, and Turkey. These treaties separated Austria and Hungary, which limited the size of their militaries and forced them to make reparation payments to the Allies. The treaties also created Czechoslovakia and Yugoslavia.

All together now: The League of Nations

The Treaty of Versailles established the League of Nations, as the last of Wilson's Fourteen Points stated, and gave the United States, Britain, France, Italy, and Japan the five permanent seats on a nine-nation executive council. The goals of the League of Nations were to encourage worldwide disarmament, to settle international disputes peacefully, and to work cooperatively to solve international economic and social problems. Member nations had to assist other member nations to protect territory, borders, and political independence. The acceptance of Wilson's proposal of the League of Nations was his one victory in the peace talks.

A separate peace: Rejecting the Treaty of Versailles

When Wilson returned to the United States, he presented the Treaty of Versailles to the Senate. *Isolationists* (those who thought America shouldn't get involved with other countries) in the Senate didn't approve of the League of Nations' provision for helping other nations preserve their borders or territory because it could draw the United States into war unnecessarily, and isolationists didn't want the United States involved in the business of other nations in the first place.

Other senators thought the treaty was unfair to the Central powers. Another group of senators, led by Henry Cabot Lodge, wanted major revisions to the treaty before they would ratify it. Wilson refused to compromise and went on a cross-country campaign to gain popular support for the League of Nations. Halfway through his tour, he had a stroke and never fully recovered. The Senate refused to ratify the treaty even after Wilson presented it a second time with revisions. The United States later negotiated a separate peace treaty with Germany and never joined the League of Nations.

You may see a question like the following on the SAT II about the treaty at the end of World War I.

The Senate did not ratify the Treaty of Versailles for all of the following reasons EXCEPT

(A) A group of senators led by Henry Cabot Lodge wanted major revisions to the treaty.

(B) Ratification of the treaty would not allow the United States to join the League of Nations.

(C) Isolationists did not want to be held accountable for helping other nations in political or territorial conflicts.

(D) President Wilson refused to compromise on any aspects of the treaty.

(E) Some senators felt that the treaty was harsh and unfair to the Central powers.

Questions that ask you for the exception can be tricky because you're looking for an answer that's untrue. As you look through the choices, remind yourself that you're searching for the answer that's false.

Recall that the Treaty of Versailles ran against a brick wall in the Senate. Some senators wanted revisions, and others felt the treaty was too harsh on the Central powers. Isolationists wanted to stay out of other nations' affairs. Wilson wanted the Senate to ratify the treaty "as is" and refused to compromise. Knowing these details, you can eliminate (A), (C), (D) and (E).

The important thing to remember about the end of World War I is that although many Allied leaders widely supported Wilson's idea for a League of Nations, members of the Senate didn't like the idea of American involvement in the League of Nations. So, (B) is the untrue statement.

Chapter 16

Throwing Caution to the Wind: The Roaring '20s

In This Chapter

▶ Understanding America's problems after World War I

▶ Brushing up on the presidencies of Harding, Coolidge, and Hoover

▶ Cruising through the prosperity of the decade

*B*race yourself for a wild ride through the Roaring '20s. In this chapter, you find out about the birth of modern culture and all its subsequent growing pains. While you try to race through the important facts of this era, we advise you to slow down and absorb the material. The writers of the SAT II U.S. History exam seem to like something about this decade, and you'll undoubtedly find several questions pertaining to this era on the test. In this chapter, we cover America's transition back to normal life after World War I; the Republican presidents of the decade; and the events that shaped modern American culture.

Pride and Prejudice: Transitioning after World War I

Before the 1920s could get roaring, cultural forces collided during a short period of time following World War I. Postwar America was a scary place for Americans who resisted change. The mainstream availability of advanced technology, like the automobile; the spread of previously unfamiliar ideologies, like Communism; and increased access to communications, like movies, shaped a new, modernized American culture that pushed traditional values to the background. Small-town America resisted change, but the nation was quickly becoming an urban society. Many of the changes taking place in cities across the country filtered into the surrounding communities. The turmoil sparked clashes of ideas, and violence often resulted. But out of the chaos, a new American society emerged.

Problems with demobilization

About four million Americans participated in World War I, and almost half of them served in Europe. The horror they had seen and the terror they had experienced combined with their eye-opening travels through Europe left many Americans permanently altered. Many came home confused about their place in society, no longer desiring a life on the family farm or a return to the drudgery of factory work. Women also felt the effects. Women who had filled the workplace during the war lost their jobs to returning soldiers. Men had a hard time adjusting to the idea of women working outside the home, and women were reluctant to give up some of their newfound freedom. As a result, divorce rates skyrocketed following the war. (For more about the war, see Chapter 15.)

Another unfortunate consequence of the soldiers' return was the spread of a deadly Spanish flu epidemic. American troops had suffered almost as many deaths from the flu as they did in battle, and soldiers unknowingly brought this deadly flu home with them. From 1918 to 1919, more than 668,000 Americans died from the Spanish flu.

A lot of work: Labor issues

Without the booming war industry, the American economy was in decline, which meant hard times for American laborers. The prospect of unemployment loomed like a storm cloud. In 1919, unemployment was at 2 percent, but by 1921, it had rapidly grown to 12 percent. The war and its aftermath also drove up inflation, which sent the cost of living for Joe Factory Worker through the roof. On average, inflation rose by more than 15 percent a year in 1919 and 1920 and continued to rise at high levels through 1922. During the recession of 1920 to 1921, more than five million Americans lost their jobs, nearly 500,000 farmers lost their farms, 100,000 businesses went bankrupt, and the Gross National Product (GNP) of the U.S. dropped nearly 10 percent. The country rebounded, though, and prosperity reigned for most of the 1920s. (See "Living the good life: Postwar prosperity" later in this chapter.)

American laborers began striking all over the place. In 1919 alone, four million people participated in 3,300 strikes. Strikers walked out for all the normal reasons — better pay, shorter working days, and better working conditions. But Americans grew tired of the constant disruption, and laborers lost the support of the federal government, which they once had. The government used troops and court orders to break up strikes, and corporations began to undermine the power of unions, stealing away their members by offering pensions, profit sharing, and corporate-sponsored social and sporting events in a phenomenon later called "welfare capitalism" or "corporate welfare." Automobile tycoon Henry Ford was the industrialist who pioneered a corporate welfare program. He instituted a shorter workweek, higher wages, and paid vacations for employees of his Ford Motor Company. Because of these changes, union membership declined sharply throughout the 1920s.

No beer here: Prohibition

Consuming alcohol was always an American pastime. Founding father Benjamin Franklin once said that beer was proof that God loved people and wanted them to be happy. But by 1919, pressure from reformers of the *Temperance Movement,* greatly aided by the growth of religious fundamentalism (which we cover in "A fear of change: Protestant fundamentalism" later in this chapter), finally tipped the balance in favor of a ban on alcohol. The *18th Amendment,* which prevented the manufacture, sale, or distribution of "intoxicating liquors," took effect in 1920.

Prohibition was dubbed "the noble experiment" — but many Americans, especially those who lived in cities and urban areas — refused to take part in it. The ban on alcohol had an unintentional and unfortunate effect: It spawned a vast underground market for alcohol, which mobsters with funny names like Al "Scarface" Capone, "Machine Gun" Jack McGurn, and George "Bugs" Moran exploited. These wise guys built criminal empires on selling *bootleg liquor,* that is, alcohol they illegally imported from foreign countries or made in bathtub distilleries. Homemade liquor was often dangerous to drink and sometimes even poisonous. Prohibition also made lawbreakers out of millions of Americans, including politicians and police officers, who frequented thousands of illegal saloons called *speakeasies* across the country.

Ultimately, the noble experiment was a big fat flop. Gangsters became celebrities for their flagrant disregard for the law, and the average citizen was more tempted to drink simply because alcohol was forbidden. Congress repealed the 18th Amendment in December 1933.

Dealing with racial and ethnic unrest

The *Ku Klux Klan,* a racist group dominant in the South, reorganized in 1915 after the release of the motion picture *The Birth of a Nation,* which celebrated the early Klan in the days of Reconstruction (see Chapter 10). The Klan made a big comeback in the years following World War I. The group, which had discriminated mostly against African Americans in its previous incarnation, was concerned about Jews, Catholics, and immigrants in the 1920s. Klan members felt these groups' languages, customs, religions, habits, and values threatened their way of life.

Another reason the Klan reappeared was due to the increase in racial tensions throughout America between whites and African Americans. The *Great Migration* that began in the years before World War I and continued throughout the 1950s caused dramatic shifts in racial demographics. During the Great Migration, many African Americans left the South and settled in northern cities like Chicago and New York (see Chapter 14 for more about the Great Migration) where the standard of living was higher, wages were better, good jobs were more plentiful, and racism was less prevalent than it was in the South. But resentment arose in these cities when whites had to compete with African Americans, who were often willing to work for less pay, for factory jobs. Also, a growing movement among African Americans, especially returning war veterans, called for civil rights and respect that whites weren't willing to give them.

In what became known as the *Red Summer* in 1919 (not to be confused with the Red Scare — see the next section), race riots rocked 24 cities and towns across America. In the worst example, 38 people (both black and white) died, and more than 500 were injured when fighting between blacks and whites erupted in the streets of Chicago after a group of whites stoned a black man to death who they felt had crossed into their swimming area.

By 1924, the Ku Klux Klan had four million members, and its influence had spread well beyond the South. In 1926, the Klan published "The Klan's Fight for Americanism," a booklet that outlined the organization's credo. The new Klan was an equal-opportunity hate-monger. Gone were the days of hating blacks alone; the new Klan targeted Jews, Asians, Mexicans, Catholics, and anyone they considered "foreign."

Handling the Red Scare

When the Russian government fell to the Bolsheviks during the revolution in 1917, an irrational fear of *Communism* spread across America. This fear, tangled with American patriotism, created an atmosphere of conformity. Anyone who marched to the beat of a different drummer, such as anarchists, Socialists, pacifists, Communists, and union leaders, were suspected to be members of the Communist Party. The term "red," meaning "Communist," generally applied to all these groups, although, in truth, very few Communists were in America.

The *Red Scare* (the worry that many Americans had about a Communist plot to take over the U.S. government) started after the Russian Revolution in 1917 and reached full strength between 1919 and 1920. All told, the two Communist parties that existed in America in 1920 had a combined membership of 70,000 — not exactly revolution material.

Nevertheless, the continuous strikes and a series of attempted bombings at the homes of prominent Americans added to the general paranoia brought on by the Communist revolution. Congress passed the *Espionage Act of 1917,* which declared that making false statements that would interfere with wartime operations was illegal. The *Sedition Act of 1918* made expressing an opinion that went against the U.S. government a crime. Under the Espionage Act, the government arrested *Eugene Debs,* a labor leader and five-time presidential candidate for the Socialist Party, for an anti-war speech he made in 1918 and sentenced him to ten years in prison. After the war, more than 30 states enacted peacetime sedition (or treason) laws, and radicals became targets across the nation.

President Woodrow Wilson gave Attorney General A. Mitchell Palmer the task of rooting out the pesky Communists in America. Palmer was convinced that the flame of revolt was burning its way into the homes of American workers. To combat the blaze, Palmer set up the *Federal Bureau of Investigation* (FBI), headed by J. Edgar Hoover, to keep an eye on radicals. The FBI arrested suspected Communists and sometimes even deported them. One of the most famous incidents that occurred during the Red Scare was the case of *Sacco and Vanzetti,* two Italian immigrants who were charged with the murder of a paymaster in Massachusetts. Even though there was little evidence against them, they were convicted and sentenced to death because they were confessed anarchists. They maintained their innocence, and public support continued to grow in their favor over the years, but both were executed in 1927.

The Red Scare reached its peak in 1920 when federal agents in 33 cities arrested more than 4,000 people in what became known as the *Palmer Raids.* The FBI threw the suspected "Reds" in jail and denied their rights to representation. Most of them weren't convicted, but the government deported about 600 foreign immigrants. After the Palmer Raids, the anti-Communist madness began to die down. In 1921, President Warren Harding revoked the Espionage Act and Sedition Act and released Debs from prison. The Red Scare emerged again in full force, though, after World War II (see Chapter 19).

Locking the doors: Anti-immigration measures

The fear of foreign ideologies (like Communism) infiltrating the U.S. caused many Americans to be none too fond of foreign immigrants in the post-World War I period. Prior to 1890, most immigrants were from northern Europe, but during the early 1900s (largely to escape the ravages of World War I), a large number of immigrants came from southern Europe, which were Slavic and Asian nations. In 1924, to curtail the entry of these immigrants who seemed so different from the rest of Americans in appearance, religious beliefs, ideologies, and customs, the federal government strengthened a 1921 act of Congress that had established an immigration quota system in the U.S. (see "The policies of Harding's administration" later in this chapter). This act, known as the *National Origins Act of 1924,* banned immigration from east Asia and cut the quota on European immigrants. In 1929, Congress revised the act and allowed a maximum of 150,000 immigrants per year into the U.S.

Whenever you hear the word *Bolshevik,* equate it with Communist; the SAT II History exam may use these terms interchangeably.

A fear of change: Protestant fundamentalism

Many Americans didn't feel comfortable with the fast-paced, consumer-driven, morally loosened American culture that emerged in the postwar era. Modernist Protestants, who lived mostly in urban areas and were largely part of the middle class, adapted readily to the wonders of modern science and technological and social advances in the modern, secular society.

On the other hand, millions of provincial, mostly rural-dwelling Americans fought against the changing tides by embracing *Protestant fundamentalism,* which endorsed a rigid interpretation of the Bible, encouraged the continuation of traditional beliefs, and sought to preserve traditional faith in religion in America.

For the SAT II History exam, think of the rise of fundamentalism as a battle against modernization — the old versus the new, the secular versus the religious, the rural versus the urban. America was truly having a culture war. Case in point: the *Scopes Monkey trial.*

In the summer of 1925, a teacher by the name of John Thomas Scopes was arrested for teaching evolution in the classroom, which violated a Tennessee law. (The law said that the Bible's explanation of creation was what children should learn.) The trial attracted national attention and was the first trial ever broadcasted over the radio. Clarence Darrow, who represented Scopes, faced off against prosecutor William Jennings Bryan, the three-time presidential candidate and former secretary of state (see Chapter 12 for more about him). The jury convicted Scopes, but by all accounts, secularism won. Bryan expressed his heartfelt belief in the Bible throughout the trial and used it to back his case. Although this strategy may have convinced the jury in Dayton, Tennessee, newspapers throughout the country publicly ridiculed Bryan, making the views of fundamentalists seem outdated and foolish. Scopes was eventually fined $100, and the case was later dismissed in a higher court due to a technicality. The trial did little to resolve the conflict between fundamentalists and modernists.

The Ku Klux Klan also supported fundamentalist beliefs with their anti-immigrant and anti-urban feelings. The Klan carried out vigilante justice to anyone who didn't conform to traditional views. Klan members served as the moral police in small towns across America, using their old standby combination of intimidation and violence. But ultimately, the Klan couldn't stop the changes that were sweeping through America.

Tying it all together: A sample question looks at America after World War 1

Before you move on to the next section, try the following question, which asks you to sum up what was happening in America after the end of World War I. The SAT II often asks you to draw general conclusions about a specific period in U.S. history.

All the following describe America in the aftermath of World War I EXCEPT:

(A) Increased racial tensions

(B) Government restrictions of civil liberties

(C) Inflation and unemployment

(D) Growth of religious fundamentalism

(E) Migration of people away from cities

With this type of question, you should be thinking "Which answer doesn't belong with the others?" Remembering that the postwar years were turbulent times in America is helpful. With that in mind, (A), (B), and (C), seem to fit that description. When you think of restriction of civil liberties, think Prohibition, sedition laws, or the Palmer Raids during the Red Scare. If you remember that religious fundamentalism was a response to the changing culture in America and the fact that the Ku Klux Klan figured largely in the movement, then you can't help but conclude that (D) also fits the description. You're left with (E), which is correct. Migration occured after the war, but it was primarily to the cities, not away from them.

The Rise of the Republicans: Harding, Coolidge, and Hoover

The presidencies of three Republicans — Warren G. Harding, Calvin Coolidge, and Herbert Hoover — spanned the decade of the 1920s. With the rise of Republican power came a number of changes.

For the SAT II, what you need to understand about these Republican presidents is that they firmly believed that all levels of society benefited when big business thrived, and big business thrived (so they believed) when the government kept its intervening hands out. Harding, Coolidge, and Hoover set policies that lessened the constraints of regulation and encouraged the growth of business throughout the '20s.

"A return to normalcy": Warren G. Harding

The American public, disillusioned by the chaos of the postwar years, was looking for change by the time the election of 1920 rolled around. Woodrow Wilson wanted to run for a third term, but his poor health and declining public appeal led Democrats to choose Ohio Governor James Cox as their presidential candidate. To give the Democratic ticket a little spice, they tossed in an up-and-coming Democratic star, Franklin D. Roosevelt, as the party's vice-presidential nominee. Despite the personnel change, the Democratic campaign focused on many of Wilson's domestic and foreign policies. The topic of joining the League of Nations was a hot one, and Democrats campaigned in favor of it. But the election ultimately revealed that Americans didn't share Wilson's views on making America part of a worldwide community (see Chapter 15 for more about the League of Nations).

Instead, American citizens elected Republican Warren G. Harding, an Ohio senator and newspaper editor whose position on the League of Nations was ambiguous, as was his position on most issues. Harding won in a landslide, collecting 16.1 million popular votes to Cox's 9.1 million and winning 404 electoral votes. Cox finished a distant second with 127.

Harding's promise of "a return to normalcy" (in other words, a lack of significant conflicts abroad and a return to pre-Progressive Era domestic policies) was largely responsible for his election, and it translated into policies that removed restrictions from businesses and encouraged the accumulation of wealth — especially among the wealthy! Harding also stayed true to his word and kept America away from foreign entanglements.

The policies of Harding's administration

Many historians label Harding the worst president in American history. The reason is because of all the scandals that occurred during his three short years as president (see the next section). Despite the scandals and the fact that he died before he could finish his term, Harding's policies set a political course for the rest of the decade.

Here's a rundown of what Harding's administration did:

- ✔ It cut taxes, especially for the rich.
- ✔ It stripped the federal budget of its wartime girth.
- ✔ It raised tariffs on foreign imports to protect American businesses with the Emergency Tariff Act in 1921 and the Fordney-McCumber Tariff in 1922.
- ✔ It set higher restrictions on immigration with the Emergency Quota Act in 1921, which limited the annual number of immigrants that America would allow from any country.

Harding also supported anti-lynching legislation, approved bills that gave aid to struggling farmers, freed wartime political prisoners, and loosened many of the restrictions on civil liberties that former President Woodrow Wilson had implemented. Most importantly, he ushered in a policy of governmental cooperation with American businesses.

What a shocker: Scandals in Harding's administration

Harding himself was virtually scandal-free except for some business about gambling, alcohol, and some extra-marital relationships that became public after his death. But scandal infested his presidency because he made some very poor choices in government appointments. Take, for example, Charles Forbes, who Harding appointed to head the newly created Veteran's Bureau. A Senate investigation revealed that Forbes had looted more than $200 million from the U.S. government. In 1925, he was convicted of bribery and fraud, and he spent two years in prison.

Harry M. Daugherty was a big-time political patron of Harding's (in other words, he gave Harding money for his campaign for president) and was Harding's attorney general. Daugherty was involved with several other men in a scandal that involved a rigged sale of some government property and, in return, received some nice financial kickbacks. One of the men involved went to jail and another committed suicide, but Daugherty eventually walked free due to undecided juries in two trials.

And then there was Thomas W. Miller, who Harding appointed to the position of Alien Property Custodian (never mind what this name means — it's not important). Miller practiced fraud and spent some time in prison for it. This sort of thing happened often enough to make the American public wonder what the heck Harding was thinking.

But the mother of scandals — the *Teapot Dome Scandal* — came to light shortly after Harding's death in 1923. A congressional inquiry in 1923–1924 revealed that Albert Fall, the secretary of the interior, had accepted bribes to lease government property to private oil companies. For his role in the affair, Fall had to pay a $100,000 fine and spend a year in jail. Whether or not Harding knew about the Teapot Dome business prior to his death isn't clear, but with all these scandals, it's no wonder Harding had two major heart attacks in July 1923!

Keeping cool with Coolidge: Calvin Coolidge

Calvin Coolidge, Harding's vice president, stepped into the role of president after Harding died in 1923. Coolidge, true to his name, took a cool, businesslike approach to the presidency. If Harding was business-friendly, Coolidge was even more so. He maintained that a factory resembled a temple: It was a place of worship for the man who worked there. Coolidge said that "the business of America is business." While Coolidge reigned, business was king, and that pretty much sums up what you need to know about Coolidge for the SAT II. But here are a few more items, just in case the testmakers get fancy:

✔ **Coolidge was efficient.** Coolidge balanced the federal budget, reduced government debt, decreased income tax rates — especially for corporate businesses and the rich — and began the construction of a national highway system. (See "If you build it: Expanded construction" later in this chapter.)

✔ **Coolidge wasn't particularly farmer-friendly.** He vetoed bills designed to stabilize falling staple crop prices. This contributed to the problems during the Great Depression that you'll find out more about in Chapter 17. (Check out "An exception to the rule: Problems with income distribution and agriculture" later in this chapter.)

✔ **He was popular because of his hands-off attitude.** In his 1924 reelection bid, he beat Democrat John W. Davis by a mile (okay, he won 54 percent of the popular vote and 382 of 531 electoral votes).

"A chicken in every pot": Herbert Hoover

In 1928, Coolidge chose not to seek reelection, so the Republican Party nominated Herbert Hoover, who had served as secretary of commerce under Harding and Coolidge. Hoover was a well-known politician, a supporter of Prohibition and a respected multi-millionaire. Democrats ran New York Governor Alfred Smith, who was a Catholic with links to *Tammany Hall* (a notoriously corrupt political machine; see Chapter 12). Smith supported Progressive reform, civil rights, and was an anti-Prohibitionist, but Republicans branded him a city-slicker and a servant of the pope, successfully exploiting the biases of the American electorate.

Americans overwhelmingly voted Hoover into office at a time when the country was comfortable with the general prosperity of the 1920s and optimistic about its future. Hoover told Americans that they were closer than ever to a final triumph over poverty and vowed that each American household would be able to afford a chicken in every pot. Hoover, himself a successful businessman, entered his presidency continuing the hands-off Republican business policies that made America prosperous in the 1920s. (We discuss more about Herbert Hoover in Chapter 17.)

Tying it all together: A sample question looks at the presidents of the 1920s

Most likely, the SAT II U.S. History test won't ask you for anything specific about Harding, Coolidge, and Hoover. In the scheme of history, their administrations are fairly small fish. However, you may have to answer a general question about presidencies of the 1920s.

What best describes the approach that the presidential administrations of the 1920s took toward business?

(A) Progressive reform

(B) Increased government regulation

(C) Favor of labor over business

(D) A policy of non-interference with business

(E) Dismantling of oligopolies

Right off the bat, you can dismiss answers (A), (B), and (C) because, after reading this section, you should know that 1920s government was pro-business, and all these answers imply a less-friendly arrangement. Answer (E) may be tricky if you don't know what oligopoly means. An *oligopoly* is a few businesses that have cornered the market on a particular industry. Examples of oligopolies in the 1920s were General Electric and U.S. Steel. If you know that Harding, Coolidge, and Hoover gave business reign, you know (E) couldn't be the answer. Answer (D) is the only pro-business choice, and you should recognize the policy of non-interference as a governmental hands-off approach.

The Era of Prosperity: The Jazz Age

The 1920s were years of prosperity. What does that mean, you ask? Well, the Roaring '20s were good times for most Americans. Middle- and upper-class Americans earned decent money and even had some left over to spend on new gadgets like refrigerators, washing machines, dishwashers, radios, and automobiles. In fact, Americans were spend-crazy. This era marked the first time in U.S. history that middle-class Americans could buy things because they wanted them, not just because they needed them. Thus, the '20s ushered in the beginning of modern consumerism, promoted by a new boom in advertising. Unfortunately, the rural poor were left behind during this rise of consumerism. While middle- and upper-class incomes continued to rise in the mid- and late 1920s, the incomes of the rural poor and farmers continued to fall.)

The 1920s is the decade in which modern American culture was born. For the first time, disposable incomes allowed the average American to afford entertainment. Americans listened to jazz and went to the movies, the theater, and baseball (Babe Ruth hit his record-setting 60 homeruns in 1927) and football games in unprecedented numbers. Movie stars, sports heroes, beauty salons, and shorter skirts for women became norms.

The '20s were also an era of innovation and technology. The radio, which allowed for national communication, came of age during the 1920s. In 1920, the first commercial radio station began broadcasting and, by 1929, 12 million American households owned radio sets. Two powerhouse radio networks, CBS and NBC, arose. Americans also built millions of miles of roads and highways. Cities were booming, and the suburbs were expanding.

Living the good life: Postwar prosperity

In the 1920s, Americans had more money in their pockets and more time to spend it, thanks to modern conveniences and shorter hours at work. Average Americans spent their money on products advertisers shamelessly persuaded them that they needed, whereas corporations and wealthy people invested their money in the stock market. Throughout the decade, stock prices soared, making investors even wealthier and creating a false sense of security in the future prosperity of America. The consumer demand made making money seem easy, and completely new industries arose from that demand. For most Americans, the '20s was an era of good feeling, and no one considered that the fun would end. (That ending is an interesting story — see Chapter 17 for more.)

Cool cash: A greater real income for everyone

The economic boom of the 1920s depended on Americans' ability to spend money, and spend they did. Many Americans had more money because they earned higher wages due to increased efficiency in industry and the benefits of welfare capitalism. (for more on welfare capitalism, see "A lot of work: Labor issues" earlier in this chapter.) Additionally, products cost less because of mass production and the overall success of American industry. Much of that success came from the federal government's accommodation of big business. Republicans' policy of deregulation and bolstering business growth translated into big profits for business tycoons, but the average American also benefited by receiving an increased wage. (For more about presidents' policies regarding business, check out "The Rise of the Republicans: Harding, Coolidge, and Hoover" earlier in this chapter.)

A new ride: Automobiles and increased industrial productivity

The refinement of *mass-production* techniques (like assembly-line construction, where each worker is responsible for the completion of one small part of the entire product-assembly process) revolutionized American manufacturing and made consumer goods much more abundant and affordable. Nowhere was the refinement of mass-production techniques more apparent than in the automobile industry. In 1908, cars were a luxury plaything for the rich. In 1914, Henry Ford's Model T cost $950, but because of the efficiency of the assembly line, by 1917, the price of the Model T had dropped to $350, making it affordable for many more Americans. By 1929, a Model T cost only $290, completely defying inflation and normal price increases — since when do cars get drastically cheaper as 15 years pass? By 1923, Americans had bought more than 3.5 million automobiles, and more than 80 percent of customers bought them on credit. By 1929, one in five Americans owned a car, and the automobile industry employed one out of every 12 workers. Automobile manufacturing made up more than 12 percent of America's total output and it stimulated the growth of other industries as well, including steel, glass, rubber, and oil.

Now, you just had a lot of numbers thrown at you, but don't worry. All you need to remember for the test is that new and improved production techniques made the proliferation of cars possible, and the automobile industry was largely responsible for the boom of industry in the '20s.

What else can we buy? New industries

The growth of the average American's purchasing power ushered in a whole new batch of industries to suck money from their pockets. The rise of the automobile industry brought with it a host of new businesses that catered to the automobile enthusiast. Think of all the businesses today that revolve around owning a car: gas stations, repair shops, restaurants, and motels (called "motor inns" in the '20s). Here are several other industries that started in the '20s:

- **Advertising:** With all the new products that people were buying and companies were selling, advertising became a big business. Before the 1920s, advertisements were dull; they had no pictures, catch phrases, or sometimes not even a brand name. Advertising companies became savvier in the 1920s. They built name-brand recognition by creating memorable slogans and bombarding the public with product campaigns that prominent psychologists had designed. In addition to using print media, advertisers also used radio to promote their products. With the growth of the automobile industry and the subsequent expansion of the road system, advertisers began to use roadside billboards to advertise their goods as well.

- **Electrical appliances:** By 1930, ⅔ of American households had electricity and half had telephones. The demand for consumer products that ran on electricity led to an expansion of the electricity and telephone industries during the 1920s. New household appliances like refrigerators, washing machines, vacuum cleaners, and toasters became all the rage.

- **Movies:** Americans grew insatiable appetites for entertainment in the 1920s, and whole industries sprang up to fill that need. By 1922, movie theaters attracted 40 million viewers a week and, by 1930, that number ballooned to 100 million, which is amazing because America's population in 1930 was just over 120 million. The concept of celebrity was born on the silver screen. Americans indulged themselves in the lives of movie stars like Charlie Chaplin, Buster Keaton, Douglas Fairbanks, Mary Pickford, Lillian Gish, and Gloria Swanson. People also looked to movies to find out how to act, talk, and think.

If you build it: Expanded construction

The unbelievable rate at which Americans purchased vehicles in the '20s created a huge demand for roads. During this decade, America doubled the size of its system of roads and highways, spending more than $2 billion a year to build and maintain roads. While building the roads, Americans also needed to build bridges, tunnels, parking garages, and the first shopping centers.

Automobiles also contributed to the creation of modern suburbia. People no longer had to live in the city in order to work in the city. Automobiles made commuting to work from quiet neighborhoods surrounding the big cities possible, which fueled a boom in housing construction.

An exception to the rule: Problems with income distribution and agriculture

But the Roaring '20s weren't all wine and roses. Although many Americans experienced prosperity, the gap between the wealthy and the poor widened, and the SAT II U.S. History exam expects you to know that fact.

The government helped the rich get richer by lowering taxes on personal incomes, corporate profits, and inheritances by more than 50 percent during the 1920s, but it did little to solve the problems of the poor. In 1929, before the Great Depression hit and despite the prosperity of the 1920s, 50 percent of the American population lived at or below the poverty level. For example, Secretary of Treasury Andrew Mellon, an oil tycoon considered to be the third richest man in America, received more money back from federal tax cuts than all taxpayers in the state of Nebraska.

Farmers suffered the most because of increased overproduction, a decline in food prices, and a subsequent decline in farmers' incomes during the 1920s. During World War I, the government had encouraged farmers to beef up their crop production to feed American troops and their Allies. Gross farm income increased from $7.6 billion in 1914 to $17.7 billion in 1919. But after the war, the demand for crops substantially decreased, and the price of crops plummeted. Farm income dropped 50 percent during the '20s. In 1920, farm income represented 15 percent of the national total but, by 1929, farm income represented only 9 percent. This decrease in income caused many to give up their farms and move to cities, where they hoped to find employment. More than 3 million Americans left farming and agriculture during the 1920s.

The Lost Generation and American literature

The decade of the 1920s was also an important era for literature. Many American writers who saw through the shallowness of the postwar prosperity were disillusioned with America and settled in Paris. Writer, poet, and feminist *Gertrude Stein* called these ex-patriates (Americans who decided to live outside of the U.S.) the *Lost Generation.* One of the members, *T.S. Eliot,* portrayed the disillusionment of the Lost Generation in his lengthy poem, "The Wasteland" (1922). *Ernest Hemingway's* breakout novel *The Sun Also Rises* (1926) also recorded the postwar angst of the generation. The novels of *F. Scott Fitzgerald,* especially the American classic, The *Great Gatsby* (1925), commented on the excesses of American society in the Jazz Age. *Sinclair Lewis* offered social criticism, portrayals of strong working women, and commentary about racial concerns in novels such as *Main Street* (1920), *Babbitt* (1922), and *Arrowsmith* (1925). Another literary notable of the age was *Thornton Wilder,* who wrote *The Bridge of San Luis Rey* (1927), though he is better known for his later works, including the play *Our Town,* produced in 1938.

Jazz: A sign of the times

Jazz was the soundtrack of the 1920s, which is why people refer to the decade as the *"Jazz Age."* Jazz was a distinctive American art form played in bars and dancehalls throughout the '20s. It made unlikely stars out of African American musicians like Duke Ellington and Louis Armstrong at a time when racism was still deeply rooted in American society. The popularity of jazz helped the records of African American musicians find their ways into the homes and onto the phonographs of millions of Americans. Jazz was the first distinctly African American art form to make its way into mainstream America.

In the early 1920s, African Americans who migrated from the South during the Great Migration brought jazz with them to the North. As the population of African Americans began to swell in cities like New York and Chicago, jazz began to filter into mainstream American culture. Jazz became popular with many people — whites included — because it struck a nerve. It was urban, improvisational, and played in smoky speakeasies. It especially appealed to young, urban dwellers.

During this era, jazz greatly influenced many aspects of American culture. It inspired poetry, new writing styles, and new dances, such as the Charleston. Historians even credit jazz with influencing American painters like Georgia O'Keeffe and John Marin, composers like George Gershwin, and architects like Frank Lloyd Wright.

The popularity of jazz and the dances that went with it, like the Charleston, literally influenced 1920s women to kick up their heels. During the Jazz Age, middle-class women rejected rigid Victorian social mores and donned short *flapper* dresses and bobbed haircuts. In secular circles, women could now dance, drink, smoke, reveal their legs, use makeup, and attend raucous parties. Young, single women, especially those of the middle and working classes, embraced this liberated flapper lifestyle.

Conservative Americans with traditional and sometimes racist views found jazz to be a summation of everything wrong about the changing American culture. They attributed the corruption of American youth — the snatching away of their virginity and their ability to decipher right from wrong — to jazz.

Now, you may have a hard time believing that jazz had such an effect. For crying out loud, it's something your grandparents listen to! But, for the test, think of jazz as the rock-n-roll of the '20s. It was music for the hip, the coming-of-age, and the kids who wanted to rebel against their parents. It was also a bridge that crossed the cultural divide between blacks and whites, which was part of the reason many Americans resented it.

Jazz also inspired a remarkable growth spurt of African American intellectual culture in New York City known as the *Harlem Renaissance.* The Harlem Renaissance broadened the understanding of the black experience in America through the writings of talented African American poets, historians, essayists, playwrights, and musicians. A new attitude among African Americans emerged that rejected the idea of assimilation into white culture; instead, it exalted African Americans who were proud of their African heritage and wanted to prove to whites that their culture was worthy of respect.

A host of new African American writers emerged from the Harlem Renaissance, including *Langston Hughes,* who's well-known for his 1926 poem "I, Too," one of many poems in which he renounced racism and celebrated African American culture. Other prominent writers included Zora Neale Hurston, James Weldon Johnson, Countee Cullen, Claude McKay, and Alain Locke, who the publishing industry sought because of America's growing fascination with African American culture in Harlem (an area in New York City). In the literary movement, African American writers focused on realistically portraying African American culture. The Harlem Renaissance influenced generations of African American writers, but the white literary establishment overlooked it until very recently.

Chapter 17

Crash and Burn: The Great Depression and the New Deal of the 1930s

In This Chapter

▶ Watching as the stock market crashes and the Great Depression starts

▶ Making a fresh start with Franklin Roosevelt's New Deal

▶ Checking out American society in the 1930s

The years from 1929 to 1940 represent some of the darkest years in American history. Americans lost fortunes, and millions struggled to get by on a daily basis. President Franklin Delano Roosevelt and his New Deal policy provided America with a much-needed boost of morale. Through record-setting government spending and intervention, the Roosevelt administration helped America recover in the years between the stock market crash and World War II.

About 6 percent of the total SAT II test questions cover the period of the Great Depression. Assuming that you don't want to miss 6 percent of the test questions, you should familiarize yourself with this important and unique period of history. Concentrate on the causes of the Great Depression and the significance of the New Deal legislation.

Dude, What a Bummer: The Great Depression

From 1837 to 1929, Americans experienced five periods of severe economic downturn, or *depression*, although most of these were relatively short-lived and only the poor and disadvantaged really felt their impacts. The Great Depression, on the other hand, was different. This depression lasted nearly 12 years, and America's involvement in World War II (see Chapter 18) was really the only thing that brought the U.S. out of the Depression.

Downward spiral: The stock market crash and its causes

When Herbert Hoover became president in 1928, he had little idea of the magnitude of misfortune that he and the country would encounter in the first two years of his presidency. Unfortunately, Americans blamed him for everything, although we know now that the Depression wasn't really his fault. In the following sections, we cover the actual stock market crash and the reasons behind it.

Up and then way, way down: The stock market roller coaster

The United States was prosperous in the 1920s and, to be frank, it was a little full of itself (see Chapter 16 for the scoop on the 1920s). Investment in the stock market was at an all-time high. In the summer of 1929, the stock market absolutely boomed, and everyone seemed to play the stock market. If you didn't have a lot of money, you could buy stocks on *margin,* which is buying stocks with borrowed money and using other stocks as loan collateral. (For example, you could pay as little as $10 down, borrow $90, and receive $100 in stock. This practice is restricted today, but it was very popular in the late 1920s.) Even though people had to pay back the money they borrowed, the stocks were all increasing in price so much that they could still make a lot of money. Everyone seemed to be getting rich quickly.

In October 1929, all good things came to an end. In the middle of October, traders began to panic because two serious declines in stock prices occurred — one on October 21st and another on October 24th, and many investors began to sell their stock. The problem: They had few buyers. By the close of the market on Thursday, October 24, 1929, now called *Black Thursday,* the Dow Jones Industrial Average (which represented the stocks of the major industrials in the U.S.) fell 9 percent. For most Americans, this drop wasn't a cause to worry because the market had always recovered before, and banks helped out by purchasing $30 million of stock that flooded the market. The real fallout happened a few days later on Tuesday, October 29, now known as *Black Tuesday,* when the Dow dropped an additional 17 percent. (For the mathematically challenged, the Dow dropped a total of 36 percent in less than a week!) The sharp drop meant that the huge gains companies had made over the previous years were wiped out in a week, and thousands of companies became virtually worthless.

The Black Tuesday crash had a domino effect on businesses in the United States. Financial institutions began to call for repayment on margin loans, and everyone who'd bought on margin was required to pay back what he or she had borrowed. Unfortunately, most people weren't able to pay this money back. Even after selling everything they owned, many still faced debt. And many Americans had lost all their money in the stock market crash and hardly had enough money to buy necessities. Businesses, large and small, weren't able to sell their goods, so they lost money and had to lay off workers. Many businesses were in such deep trouble that they filed for bankruptcy and shut their doors permanently. Millions of Americans became unemployed.

The banks were in deep trouble, too. They had lent money to stockbrokers and investors. Because of the crash, stocks devalued so quickly that no one was able to pay back the banks. Banks called for borrowers to repay their loans and mortgages but ended up foreclosing on those loans and mortgages because borrowers couldn't pay. People panicked after the crash and withdrew all the money they had from the banks. Soon many banks ran out of money and had to close their doors. You probably can't imagine banks running out of money today but, at that time, most banks were not insured, so when they closed their doors, people who still had money deposited at the bank lost everything.

What just happened here? Checking out the causes of the crash

Many Americans thought that Hoover could've prevented the crash. The truth is that even the nation's top economists didn't even see it coming. Even though Americans often blame the crash on the stock market traders, the crash occurred for several important reasons — some of which were years in the making. Some of the causes of the stock market crash of October 1929 were

- **Too much stock purchased on margin.** In October 1929, Americans owed more than $7 billion for stocks that they had bought on margin. Many companies overvalued their stock to begin with, so company profits and finances didn't necessarily match up with their overinflated stock prices, which meant that stocks weren't worth what investors were paying for them.

- **Many consumers had purchased items and goods on credit.** Consumer income levels were much lower than industry production levels, which meant that companies had an excess of consumer goods available, but most Americans had very limited personal incomes with which they could purchase these goods. For this reason, 95 percent of U.S. consumers bought using credit, often overextending their finances.

✔ **America had a very unequal distribution of wealth.** In 1929, 5 percent of the population controlled most of the nation's capital and had most of the purchasing power. Well over 50 percent of the population lived very near, at, or below the poverty level.

Tax policies favored the very wealthy and contributed to the unequal distribution of wealth. As secretary of the treasury, Andrew Mellon worked to cut taxes for the rich by over 50 percent so they could invest more in business to stimulate the economy. Taxes for the poor and middle class didn't go down. As taxes for the wealthy decreased, the government cut back the already limited social services of the 1920s.

✔ **The banking system was very weak, and many banks made unstable loans.** The U.S. had many small and poorly managed banks, and ⅔ of U.S. banks weren't part of the *Federal Reserve Banking system,* which offered government protection of bank holdings (although its powers were very limited until the mid-1930s).

✔ **U.S. industry wasn't diversified enough.** A few industries, such as automobile manufacturing and construction, completely dominated the economy. The prosperity in the U.S. in the mid-1920s depended almost exclusively on the success of these few industries. When automobile manufacturing and construction began to decline in the late 1920s, newer industries weren't developed enough to pick up the slack in production and employment opportunities.

✔ **Agricultural prices were down due to extensive crop surpluses.** During World War I, and with the subsequent European dependence on U.S. exports for recovery, U.S. farmers enjoyed a high demand for U.S. farm stuffs, receiving high prices for their goods. However, as European demand waned, U.S. farmers faced much lower demands for their goods and, subsequently, much lower prices, which put them deeply in debt. By the mid-1920s, farmers couldn't pay their equipment loans, which weakened the banks holding those loans.

✔ **Depressed foreign trade.** The European economic recovery from World War I coupled with high protective tariffs designed to protect U.S. goods from foreign competition discouraged the trading of foreign goods in the U.S. and left European nations without a source of foreign exchange to repay their war debts. Because Europe didn't have the benefits of foreign trade and was unable to borrow more money from the U.S., European nations defaulted on their World War I debts to the U.S. As a result, no money was coming in on foreign debts, either.

The SAT II probably won't ask you for detailed information about the Depression. For example, "What date is associated with Black Tuesday, the beginning of the Great Depression?" More likely, test questions on the Depression era will incorporate different big ideas and concepts from the period.

The following sample question asks you to incorporate what you know about the various economic conditions in the 1920s that led to the stock market crash in 1929.

All the following were major economic conditions in the United States in the late 1920s that contributed to the stock market crash on October 29, 1929, EXCEPT

(A) High protective tariffs on European goods

(B) U.S. agricultural prices were down due to surpluses in agricultural production

(C) Industrial production far exceeded consumer ability to purchase goods

(D) Stock prices were undervalued, and only the very wealthy held stock shares

(E) The banking system was weak, partially due to bad loans and a great number of small, mismanaged banks

This question expects you to have a comprehensive understanding of the various causes of the Great Depression. As you know, more than one event caused the Great Depression.

Because this is an EXCEPT question, you're looking for the answer that's incorrect. The best answer is (D), because it's the only answer that isn't true. In the years leading up to the Great Depression, companies overvalued (not undervalued) their stock prices, and many people — rich, middle class, and poor — traded on the stock market during the late 1920s. Remember that many people without money purchased stock on margin in get-rich-quick schemes. Answer (A) is true because the U.S. did place high protective tariffs on European goods. Choices (B) and (C) are also true because U.S. agricultural prices were down due to agricultural surpluses, and industrial production in the U.S. far exceeded the consumer ability to purchase goods. Finally, (E) is true because the U.S. banking system was very weak due to mismanagement and loan defaults.

Help me, please: Hoover's efforts at relief

In the first few months following the October 1929 crash, President Hoover was optimistic that the economy would bounce back by itself. But it only got worse: Businesses failed, banks closed, and more Americans lost their jobs. The situation worsened in the spring of 1931 during an international financial panic. European nations hadn't been able to borrow money from American banks to make payments on their war debts to the U.S. since late 1929. Furthermore, European nations weren't able to trade their goods in the U.S. because of the protective tariffs. Without foreign exchange, European nations began to default on their loans with U.S. banks. As Europe experienced financial panic, the economic situation in the U.S. reached an all-time low, despite the president's and local efforts.

Examining Hoover's economic philosophy

Hoover decided that he needed to restore the public's confidence in the economy. He believed America was successful because of its *rugged individualism,* meaning that because Americans had a high level of personal liberty, they could fend for themselves. Therefore, he felt that the government should maintain only limited interference in the economy. Hoover and many economists of the time agreed that any money the government spent should be spent on business because it would help strengthen the economy, and the effects would trickle down to the people. He made a plea to businessmen to maintain employment, wages, and capital investment. This voluntary recovery program worked for a while, but by 1931, many businesses were unable to meet these requests because of falling prices and production levels, high inventories, and non-existent profits.

In 1932, in an attempt to end the depression through increased government spending, Hoover asked Congress for $423 million (a lot of money at the time) to fund public works projects, such as railroads, roads, and government buildings. Unfortunately, he didn't spend it over a long enough period of time for it to make much impact. To make matters even worse, despite his opposition to tax increases, he had to propose one in 1932 so the government would avoid a deficit. Hoover felt that the government should keep taxes low, but he was more concerned about maintaining a balanced federal budget.

Focusing on help for farmers

Farmers had a difficult time during the 1920s: Crop prices were low, and farmers' incomes were low, too. (See Chapter 16 for more on the farmers' plight.) While the rest of the nation prospered during the 1920s, the farmers surely didn't. Most farmhouses lacked indoor plumbing and electricity. Thousands of farmers, even though many were still able to feed themselves, were unable to pay their mortgages and were forced off their farms. Problems for farmers only worsened when severe droughts struck the eastern U.S. and the Great Plains in 1930 (see "What can we do? Americans in desperation" later in this chapter).

In 1929, the plight of farmers was bleak, and because farmers made up a large portion of his constituency, Hoover tried to stabilize the rapidly falling prices of agricultural goods. He ordered the newly created *Federal Farm Board* and *Grain Stabilization Corporation* (two institutions created under the Agricultural Marketing Act of 1929) to buy up the agricultural surpluses at high prices in an attempt to drive prices up. But by 1931, warehouses were full of grain, (ironic because many people at this time were literally starving), the prices started dropping again, and the Farm Board stopped purchasing the surpluses.

Looking at legislation

In an attempt to jump-start the economy, Hoover enacted a few notable but ultimately ineffective pieces of domestic legislation from 1930 to 1932.

- **Smoot–Hawley (or Hawley–Smoot) Tariff of 1930:** This act placed a protective tariff on foreign agricultural goods to protect U.S. agricultural goods from international competition. This tariff was unsuccessful because foreign markets responded by enacting their own trade restrictions, which nearly destroyed foreign trade for the U.S. In the years from 1929 to 1930, U.S. exports decreased from $5.2 billion to only $1.6 billion because of trade restrictions that other countries had imposed.

- **Emergency Committee for Unemployment:** Hoover established this committee in 1930 to help coordinate private agencies to provide relief to the unemployed. This committee was largely unsuccessful because it didn't receive sufficient federal funding. Hoover strongly opposed using federal funding for direct public relief programs because he felt this job fell to private charities.

- **Reconstruction Finance Corporation (RFC):** Hoover created this government agency in 1932 to provide federal loans to businesses, banks, and railroads and to provide public works loans to local governments. This agency only loaned $30 million out of a $300 million budget in 1932, so it didn't have much of an impact on economic recovery.

On a smaller scale: Local relief efforts

By 1932, unemployment was at 24 percent. (A "normal" unemployment rate is around 4 percent.) In some cities, like Toledo, Ohio, unemployment reached as much as 80 percent.

Members of local governments decided that they needed to do something for the poor and unemployed. In many cities, public employees took lower salaries and used the money to fund soup kitchens and other local relief efforts. Private charities provided food and clothing for poor and homeless families. Religious organizations provided aid for congregation members. Some companies began to provide aid for former employees. Other charitable organizations provided the poor with food, clothing, repayable loans, free breakfast for children, and temporary work opportunities. In 1932, soup kitchens in New York City served more than 85,000 meals each day.

What can we do? Americans in desperation

Unlike previous depressions in American history, the Great Depression affected the rich and poor alike. Some wealthy Americans lost everything (and some who did resorted to suicide rather than face the loss), and others had to drastically change their lifestyles. Newly unemployed Americans turned to all kinds of work. Former businessmen sold apples or other goods on the streets. People ate cheap food, such as rice and potatoes, and mended the holes in their clothes instead of buying new ones. Even those people who didn't lose their jobs or homes still experienced changes. Many businesses slashed wages, so even if you had a job, getting by was difficult. To make ends meet, people planted gardens, sewed their own clothes, practiced energy conservation, and only occasionally spent money on entertainment. Many Americans were unable to pay their mortgages or rent, so they moved in with relatives. Those who managed to keep their homes often took in boarders to help pay the bills.

In the early years of the Depression, thousands of urban residents became homeless. With nowhere to go and no money, many settled together in vacant lots or on the outskirts of cities, often near garbage dumps. These shantytowns were soon called *"Hoovervilles."* In Hoovervilles, the homeless and unemployed lived with their families in tents or makeshift shacks or shanties (which they built from scraps of wood, metal, paper, canvas, and boxes). The living conditions in Hoovervilles were unsanitary, and disease was rampant. They had no running water, plumbing, electricity, and little, if any, food.

These settlements were named after the president because many Americans blamed President Hoover for the economic situation in the U.S. They felt he was unsympathetic to the needs of the increasing numbers of poor, unemployed, and homeless. Hoover's efforts to improve the economy, increase jobs, and decrease poverty (see the earlier section "Help me, please: Hoover's efforts at relief" in this chapter) were largely unsuccessful.

Farmers in the Great Plains had it especially bad in the 1930s. Most of the agricultural land in the Midwest became eroded and completely infertile due to weather conditions. In 1930, severe droughts and summer heat hit the Great Plains, from Canada to Texas, and the drought continued for most of the decade. Violent winds and dust storms created blizzards of dust that only exacerbated these conditions. That along with the intense heat and even plagues of grasshoppers, farming became impossible. Hundreds of thousands of families migrated from the region dubbed the *"Dust Bowl"* to cities and agricultural regions in the West, most often California, looking for work or better farming conditions. Because many of these migrant families hailed from Oklahoma, a state that the droughts hit particularly hard, these poor migrant families came to be called "Okies."

Let's Make the New Deal

By 1932, more than 12 million people were unemployed. The Great Plains had been experiencing severe drought for two years, and Hoover hadn't been able to do anything to jump-start the economy. His policy of *laissez-faire* (no government intervention in business) wasn't working. The American people wanted a new leader; they wanted someone who understood their problems, and they wanted the government to get involved and take action to combat the Depression. They were ready for something different and drastic.

The election of Franklin D. Roosevelt

Following political precedent, the Republican Party nominated Herbert Hoover in 1932 for a second term. Considering that the public blamed the wildly unpopular Hoover personally for the Depression, it almost assured a loss for the Republicans. The Democrats nominated Franklin Delano Roosevelt (FDR), the governor of New York, as their presidential candidate.

FDR: A new optimism

In his inauguration speech on March 4, 1933, Franklin D. Roosevelt was frank with the American people. He didn't promise immediate solutions. He did express confidence in national recovery and eventual prosperity. He successfully inspired confidence in Americans in his inaugural address with his now famous words "the only thing we have to fear is fear itself."

Out of cash? Call Dad!

During the bank holiday that FDR called shortly after his inauguration, many people found themselves without any money to spend. Even the president's son Elliott was short on funds. As he drove from New York to Arizona with his wife during the bank holiday, Elliott realized that they were going to run out of money because they only had $32. He called his father from Arkansas to ask him what he should do. FDR couldn't help; he only had $8 himself. Luckily, by the time they reached Dallas, a group of Texas businessmen, wanting to make a good impression on FDR, helped the young couple out by feeding them, putting them up for the night, and sending them off with some cash for the rest of their journey.

FDR was a distant cousin of former President Teddy Roosevelt and married Teddy's niece (and FDR's distant cousin) Eleanor. FDR served on the New York state legislature and served under Woodrow Wilson as assistant secretary of the Navy during World War I. In 1921, he was stricken with polio and lost the use of his legs. From then on, he could walk only by using crutches and leg braces. He recovered enough by 1928 to run for governor and, from 1928 to 1932, he served as governor of the State of New York.

Unlike Hoover, FDR felt that the government should take whatever steps necessary to help the people and ensure their well-being. The American public viewed Hoover as cold, distant, and stiff, whereas they saw that FDR was a natural politician. He was dynamic, energetic, enthusiastic, and optimistic. In his presidential campaign, FDR promised a "new deal" for the American people.

FDR won the election by a landslide. He received nearly 58 percent of the popular vote and 472 out of 531 electoral votes, winning all but five states. Furthermore, the Democrats cleaned house in the election and won majorities in both houses of Congress. In the interim period before FDR's inauguration, a banking panic caused hundreds of more banks to close, and the number of unemployed increased to nearly 16 million people — a whopping 25 percent of the population. People optimistically welcomed FDR into office on March 4, 1933.

The "Hundred Days"

Hoover's chair in the Oval Office wasn't even cold yet when Roosevelt and his advisors started to take action. Convinced that government spending could revive the economy, FDR proposed 15 major pieces of legislation to Congress and got them passed within his first 100 days in office. The new legislation designed programs that offered relief to suffering people, recovery to the economy, and reform in the U.S. government to bring the nation out of economic devastation. FDR wasn't afraid to try new and innovative ideas to get the economy rolling again. The following sections cover the highlights of his economic recovery plan.

A pair of banking acts

Two days after his inauguration, FDR called a four-day bank holiday in response to the ongoing bank crisis. This bank holiday allowed time for a special session of Congress and meetings with banking leaders. On the fourth day, Roosevelt submitted the *Emergency Banking Relief Act* to Congress. Congress passed the legislation within a few hours.

The Emergency Banking Relief Act continued the bank holiday for four more days to allow the U.S Treasury inspections to determine which banks could reopen. The act also provided for federal assistance to banks and the reorganization of some banks. And last, the act gave the Federal Reserve Board the authority to print currency to ease the shortage. Within days, the bank panic ended and 75 percent of the Federal Reserve Banks reopened for business. As people regained confidence in the banking system, Roosevelt encouraged them to trust the banks and deposit their money back into the banks.

In June 1933, FDR and Congress also created the Federal Deposit Insurance Corporation (FDIC) under the Glass-Steagall Banking Act. The FDIC guaranteed that federal funds would back bank deposits, meaning that people wouldn't have to worry whether they'd lose their money if they entrusted it to banks again. This act further stabilized the U.S. banking system.

The Civilian Conservation Corps

Roosevelt was both very dedicated to conservation and wanted to do something to restore confidence, responsibility, and self-worth for millions of unemployed young men. Within three weeks of entering the presidency, he created the *Civilian Conservation Corps* (CCC). The men employed by the CCC lived in camps and worked on various conservation projects. They planted trees, fought forest fires, and built reservoirs, dams, forest trails, roads, parks, cabins, and campgrounds. Workers received room and board and were paid $30 each month, $25 of which the CCC automatically sent back home to their families. The CCC was one of the most successful New Deal projects because it employed more than two million out-of-work men between the ages of 17 and 25 from 1933 to 1941.

Gold standard no more

FDR issued an executive order in April 1933 that officially took the U.S. off the gold standard. Under the old gold standard system, each dollar in circulation was backed by an actual equivalent amount of gold held by the government; most countries at that time followed this financial policy. Roosevelt hoped that removing the U.S. from the gold standard would stimulate the economy, but it didn't have any immediate effects. Many European countries had recently gone off the gold standard also, which made international trade even more depressed due to unstable currency exchange rates. When Roosevelt took the U.S. off the gold standard, he set a precedent. This precedent gave the federal government the authority to raise or lower currency value in response to economic circumstances.

The Agricultural Adjustment Act

In May 1933, Congress enacted the *Agricultural Adjustment Act* (AAA) to regulate farm production, increase farmer income, and end agricultural surpluses. The AAA offered farmers monetary incentives, called subsidies, if they agreed not to plant overabundant staple crops (like cotton, wheat, corn, rice, and tobacco) on all their land. By leaving some of their land idle, farmers grew fewer crops, which reduced the crop surplus, slowing the momentum of rapidly decreasing produce prices. The AAA also offered advance payments to farmers who stored surplus crops for use in years when yields were low rather than place them on the market when crop surpluses were high. The AAA was generally successful because farmers' incomes increased, and prices of farm commodities rose in the years after 1933. However, the Supreme Court declared parts of the AAA unconstitutional in 1936, primarily because the act taxed other groups to pay for the subsidies. A revision in 1938 funded the plan through general taxation.

The Tennessee Valley Authority

Congress established the *Tennessee Valley Authority* in May 1933 to bring relief to the chronically impoverished residents along the Tennessee River Valley. Residents of the Tennessee River Valley suffered from frequent flooding, malaria, extreme poverty, and malnutrition. The valley was beautiful, but much of the farmland was unproductive. The plan to revitalize the region created controversy, however.

The project initially involved constructing five dams along the Tennessee River, which provided the region with cheap electrical power, flood control, irrigation, reforestation, soil conservation, and the production of nitrates for cheap fertilizer to help farmers increase productivity on land that was previously unproductive. The project also included social and educational programs for residents of the region. Conservatives and utility companies criticized and strongly opposed the project because it involved big government, but it virtually stopped flooding in the area, brought affordable electricity to thousands of poor families, encouraged the development of local industries, helped farmers increase their productivity, increased reforestation, and helped revitalize the region.

The National Industrial Recovery Act

In June 1933, Congress passed the *National Industrial Recovery Act (NIRA)*. This act created a new public agency called the *National Recovery Administration (NRA)*. This agency called for fighting deflation in industry through an increase in employment and consumer purchasing power. The federal government called on businesses to enact a minimum wage of 30 cents to 40 cents per hour, to place a cap on the workweek at 35 to 40 hours, and to abolish child labor.

NIRA also created the *Public Works Administration (PWA)*. The PWA provided jobs for a half million people and spent billions of federal dollars on infrastructure projects, such as constructing bridges, tunnels, ports, highways, schools, post offices, playgrounds, public swimming pools, and roads from 1933 to 1938.

A few more relief acts

The following four pieces of legislation alone had a beneficial impact on the morale of large segments of the U.S. population by offering direct and almost immediate relief.

- **Beer-Wine Revenue Act (March 1933):** This act was a very popular measure that made the sale of beer and wine legal for the first time in 13 years. It repealed Prohibition, the 18th Amendment (see Chapter 14 for more information on Prohibition).

- **Federal Emergency Relief Act (May 1933):** This act created the *Federal Emergency Relief Administration (FERA)*, which provided federal money directly to states to provide unemployment relief.

- **Emergency Farm Mortgage Act (May 1933):** This act allowed farmers to refinance existing mortgages with lower interest rates and lower monthly payments.

- **Homeowners Refinancing Act (June 1933):** This act allowed more than a million homeowners to refinance their mortgages immediately with lower interest rates and lower monthly payments.

The start of the Second New Deal

For the first two years of his presidency, FDR remained extremely popular. He was optimistic and charismatic. He worked hard to come up with innovative ways to offer relief to the American people. He connected with many Americans through his *"fireside chats,"* which were regular radio addresses to the American public in which he outlined his plans and efforts for continued recovery and relief. By using radio as a means to communicate with the American people, he was able to reach far more people on a regular basis than by traveling around the country, which was difficult for him anyway because of his disability.

The overwhelming Democratic victories in the 1934 elections proved the popularity of FDR and the New Deal. More Democrats in Congress allowed FDR to pass more New Deal programs — and meet less congressional resistance — during his Second New Deal.

Despite his popularity and efforts, no end was in sight for the Depression, and Americans were growing restless by 1935. The New Deal had many right-leaning opponents who criticized Roosevelt's policies as being dictatorial, and they called for less government intervention in business. Some liberal opponents, like Louisiana Senator Huey P. Long, felt that the

New Deal didn't do enough to address the social and financial problems of the poor and middle classes.

Members of the Roosevelt administration knew they needed to do something different to ensure FDR's reelection in 1936. Roosevelt needed to respond to the political pressure from Democrats and Republicans and take further steps to address the economic crisis that the New Deal hadn't alleviated. In spring 1935, FDR launched the *Second New Deal,* which called for a reorganization and intensification of previous relief, recovery, and reform efforts. The following sections cover the highlights of the Second New Deal.

The Emergency Relief Appropriation Act and the Works Progress Administration

Faced with the lack of economic recovery, FDR's administration decided it couldn't continue to balance the federal budget. Deficit spending was necessary to bring full economic recovery to the nation. The *Emergency Relief Appropriation Act* passed by Congress in April 1935 gave FDR $5 billion to fund relief efforts, most of which he put toward funding the *Works Progress Administration.* FDR created the WPA to employ more than two million unemployed workers. Starting in May 1935, WPA workers built schools, airports, roads, bridges, and public buildings.

The WPA also offered assistance to the artistic community. It put writers to work under the Federal Writers Project. It employed artists to paint public murals and to create sculptures under the Federal Arts Project. The Federal Music Project and the Federal Theater Project provided opportunities for unemployed musicians, actors, and directors. Partially due to the efforts of the WPA, unemployment fell 5 percent between 1935 and 1937.

Other projects included the National Youth Administration (NYA) under the WPA, which provided scholarships, part-time employment opportunities for students, and job training and employment for 16- to 25-year-olds. The Emergency Housing Division of the WPA funded public housing projects.

The National Labor Relations Act

Along with the Second New Deal and an increased desire to ensure fair wages and working conditions for workers came increased government support for organized labor. The July 1935 establishment of the National Labor Relations Act, also known as the Wagner Act, increased union rights. It gave employees the right to join and organize labor unions and to participate in bargaining. In addition, the act prevented employers from interfering with unions and required employers to enter into collective bargaining with unions.

Throughout the mid-1930s, union membership increased, and unions won increased political influence. Labor unions became big supporters of the Democratic Party (and they still are today). In 1935, the *American Federation of Labor (AFL)* was the largest organized labor group in the country, but it didn't sufficiently represent industrial workers. In 1935, industrial leaders broke off from the AFL to form the *Committee of Industrial Organizations (CIO),* a new labor union, to rival the AFL. By 1937, the CIO had more than four million members, including many women and African Americans. (You've probably heard of these unions because they merged together in the 1950s, becoming the AFL–CIO.)

The Social Security Act

The *Social Security Act,* established in 1935, provided immediate federal assistance for the retired elderly. It also achieved long-term goals; it established a pension (funded by employees and employers through a payroll tax) that would begin making payments in 1942 and would provide the elderly with income upon retirement. Employees and employers in business or industry paid payroll taxes to fund the pension system. This act also created unemployment benefits and a welfare system to aid the disabled, the elderly, and children.

Try this sample test question.

Which of the following represents the main purpose of the Social Security Act of 1935?

(A) To provide national health care for all Americans

(B) To protect workers' wages, job security, and encourage labor union membership

(C) To provide healthcare to the poor and unemployed

(D) To create a benefit program for the elderly upon retirement, welfare for the disabled, and a nationwide system of unemployment insurance

(E) To provide jobs for the unemployed during the Second New Deal

Choice (D) is the correct answer. The main purpose behind the Social Security Act of 1935 was to create a benefit program for the elderly and the disabled and to create a nationwide system of unemployment insurance, so individuals who became unemployed could collect government financial assistance for a limited time. The act didn't establish a healthcare program, so you know that (A) is wrong. Option (B) isn't right because social security was designed to aid the unemployed rather than the employed. You can cross out (C) because healthcare wasn't a part of the Social Security Act. The act provided monetary aid rather than jobs, so (E) is also wrong.

For the SAT II, remember that the Social Security Act is probably the most important achievement of the Second New Deal, if not the most crucial piece of social welfare legislation in American history. Before the implementation of the Social Security Act, Americans had to fend for themselves or have their families take care of them. The Social Security Act was a Progressive, new way for Americans to think about government assistance.

Reforming the tax system

FDR needed money to pay for his programs, and he found a solution in tax reform. The wealthy were unsurprisingly alarmed when FDR proposed a comprehensive tax reform plan in 1935, called the Revenue Act. He proposed an income tax of up to 75 percent and an inheritance tax of up to 70 percent for taxpayers in the highest tax brackets. He also proposed up to a 15 percent tax on corporations in the highest tax brackets. Those people who opposed this tax system called the tax reforms a "soak the rich" scheme. Although these tax rates were the highest in peacetime in U.S. history, in reality, the actual tax burden for most individuals and corporations rose very little.

A fight for (and the end of) the New Deal

Even though the results of the 1936 election proved FDR's popularity, the New Deal faced many political challenges during his second administration that would prevent the development of substantial New Deal legislation from 1936 to 1939.

Second time around: The election of 1936

The important legislation passed during the start of the Second New Deal in 1935 (see the earlier section in this chapter, "The start of the Second New Deal") reflected the interests of Americans who would become FDR's main supporters, known as the "Roosevelt Coalition," in the 1936 election: African Americans, women, farmers, organized labor, the poor and unemployed, and the urban working class. Many of these groups had received substantial benefits from New Deal legislation since 1933 and were strong Roosevelt supporters.

By the summer of 1936, Roosevelt seemed like he would win a second term. The economy began to revive, and Americans had regained confidence in their government and were optimistic that with FDR as president things would continue to improve. In a race against Kansas

Governor Alf M. Landon, Roosevelt won by a landslide. He won 61 percent of the popular vote, 523 of 531 electoral votes, and all states except Maine and Vermont. In the congressional races, the Democrats maintained a strong majority in both houses.

The election of 1936 was an important one for the Democrats (and an important one to remember for the SAT II) because of the development of a majority coalition for the party. The coalition emerged in 1936 with the support of the urban working class, the poor, the unemployed, farmers, traditional progressives, a group of new liberals, Catholics and, most importantly, African Americans who had traditionally voted Republican.

A fight with justices: A struggle in the Supreme Court

In 1937, frustrated by the dominance of conservative judges on the Supreme Court and the fact that the Court had struck down several pieces of New Deal legislation as unconstitutional, FDR proposed a court reform bill. He proposed to relieve the "overworked" courts by appointing six new Supreme Court justices (one for each current justice over the age of 70). The proposal was widely criticized by members of both parties because FDR clearly wanted to increase the liberal influence in the Supreme Court. They also saw it as an appeal for power on the part of FDR, and Congress soon defeated Roosevelt's "court-packing plan."

End of the line: The close of the New Deal

The late 1930s brought a round of opposition for New Deal policies. By 1937, FDR faced many challenges that were limiting the success of New Deal reform and recovery efforts. The three main obstacles that faced FDR and New Deal policy were

- The courts were constantly challenging New Deal legislation.

- Congressional opposition to New Deal policies and proposals was growing. Both houses of Congress had conservatives who wanted to cut federal spending and not allow the passage of any more Depression relief efforts.

- An economic recession began in August 1937, which proved that the New Deal programs were unable to revive the economy completely. During this recession, 5.5 million workers lost their jobs, unemployment rose, industrial output dropped 40 percent, and stock prices dropped 33 percent. Sometimes referred to as the "Roosevelt Recession," this economic downturn occurred when the federal government began reducing spending and assistance programs. It demonstrated that economic recovery relied on continued government spending.

In the years from 1937 to 1939, Congress passed some pieces of New Deal legislation. The most notable was the *Fair Labor Standards Act* of 1938, which affected many industries. The act established a 40-hour workweek and a 40 cents per hour minimum wage. It also took an important step toward abolishing child labor by making it illegal.

The end of 1939 signaled an end for the New Deal because congressional and conservative opposition kept increasing and because the president was more and more distracted by the events in Europe (see Chapter 18 for more details).

A little perspective: The significance of the New Deal

New Deal policy was significant in American history for several reasons. Keep the following in mind for the SAT II:

- **The era of the New Deal was a revolutionary time because the U.S. government broke with tradition, expanding federal powers and increasing spending to deficit levels.** American leaders successfully regulated and preserved capitalist democracy, despite an unprecedented economic crisis. Through increased regulation, some aspects of the economy, such as the banking system and the stock market, became more stable than ever before under the New Deal. Much of this type of regulation continues to this day.

✔ **Historically, the federal government refused to provide direct assistance to the poor and needy during times of economic trouble, but New Deal policies changed that precedent.** The American welfare state was born out of New Deal legislation through the numerous relief efforts that benefited the poor and needy and the advent of the Social Security system.

✔ **Individual citizens earned new rights, protections, and respect.** New Deal legislation opened doors for and supported some groups of people in an unprecedented way. For instance, women achieved public success when Francis Perkins became the first woman cabinet member ever, serving as secretary of labor. FDR appointed more than 100 women to prominent federal positions during his administration. Children, the elderly, and disabled individuals also benefited. (For more about different groups during the 1930s, see "Striving for change: Social reforms for minorities" later in this chapter.)

✔ **New Deal programs created a sizeable bureaucracy of federal agencies that had significant economic and legislative power.** These agencies resulted in a substantial increase in the number of federal employees and increased the presence of the federal government in almost every area of life.

✔ **Many New Deal programs provided the unprecedented governmental support of the arts and recreation.** It sponsored the creation and improvement of national and local parks, the construction of thousands of public buildings, and the funding of American art, theater, literature, and music.

Surveying Society in the 1930s

Despite the hardships of the Depression, American culture thrived throughout the 1930s. New Deal programs, such as the WPA (see the earlier section "The Emergency Relief Appropriation Act and the Works Progress Administration" in this chapter), funded creative folks to produce and perform their art during the years of the Depression. Minorities also benefited from some social reforms that the New Deal enacted.

Get creative: Art and photography

Through New Deal funding, the government commissioned artists to paint thousands of murals in public buildings and individual pieces of art. Many now-famous artists, including Jacob Lawrence, Mark Rothko, and Jackson Pollock, were employed as artists under the WPA. Through their art, artists helped document the feel of the Depression.

The WPA commissioned photographers to document the many problems of the Depression in order to reinforce the necessity of New Deal programs. Others photographed New Deal construction projects. Dorothea Lange, who photographed migrant farm families in California, is the best known of the Depression-era photographers. Some photographers also worked independently selling their photographs to magazines.

A surge in popularity: Movies, radio, and the printed word

Movies were very popular during the Depression years because they provided a diversion from the hardship and harsh reality of daily life. Because people needed an escape from the harsh reality of the Depression, musicals and comedies were especially popular during this era. Even though seeing a film during the Depression years was relatively inexpensive — sometimes only 5 cents — many theaters struggled to stay afloat. Theaters attracted viewers with free gifts, film serials, newsreels, and sometimes even a second movie (a double feature). Another extremely popular form of cheap entertainment was the radio. Millions of Americans listened to their favorite radio shows each night in their homes.

During the 1930s, some authors wrote about the Depression, but others avoided it. *John Steinbeck* wrote about a migrant farm worker family traveling from Oklahoma to California during the Depression in his book *The Grapes of Wrath*. Other notable authors like Ernest Hemingway and William Faulkner avoided the topic. New Deal projects, such as the Federal Writer's Project helped provide out-of-work writers with employment on various writing projects. This program also helped give rise to many African American writers, such as Richard Wright. Magazines were popular with Americans and so were comic books. Surprisingly, newspaper circulation didn't diminish during the Depression. Newspapers were cheap and allowed Americans to stay current with events in the U.S. and abroad.

Striving for change: Social reforms for minorities

Minority groups were some of the hardest hit Americans during the early years of the Depression. They were left out of New Deal programs and were often the last to receive federal aid due to enduring discrimination policies and racial barriers left over from the days of slavery. As the Depression wore on, some of their conditions improved.

✔ FDR's administration didn't do much to help African Americans directly or to eliminate discrimination. African Americans had a hard time finding work and didn't get paid equally to whites, even under New Deal programs. However, First Lady Eleanor Roosevelt was committed to racial equality and worked to ensure that African Americans weren't left out of New Deal relief programs. FDR also appointed many African Americans to significant positions within his "Black Cabinet" and tripled the number who held federal jobs.

Because African Americans were receiving some support from New Deal programs, they gradually shifted their political support toward FDR. By the 1936 and 1940 elections, ⅔ of African Americans voted for the Democratic president when, historically, the majority had voted Republican (Lincoln and those in favor of ending slavery had been Republicans in the late 1800s).

✔ The passage of the *Wheeler–Howard Indian Reorganization Act* in 1934 favored a policy of *cultural relativism,* which said that people should accept every culture equally and that no culture is more superior than any other culture. John Collier, a Progressive and the Indian affairs commissioner, encouraged Native Americans to maintain their cultures, to own tribal land collectively, and to maintain tribal governments. In the years following this act, tribal lands increased by millions of acres, and the agricultural income of Native Americans increased by millions.

✔ Because Mexican Americans held low-paying jobs, whites saw them as a drain on the economy during the Depression. The federal government deported thousands back to Mexico and strongly restricted legal Mexican American immigration to the U.S. During the Dust Bowl migration in the early and mid-1930s, Okies displaced Mexican American migrant farm workers from their jobs. Mexican Americans experienced discrimination and didn't find much relief under the New Deal.

Chapter 18

Coming Out of Our Shell: World War II, 1936–1945

In This Chapter

▶ Stirring up trouble: The events leading to World War II

▶ Isolating America

▶ Feeling the war's effects on the American home front

▶ Bringing it on: The Allies end the war in Europe

▶ Negotiating peace in Europe

▶ Concluding the war in the Pacific

World War II involved almost all of the world's nations, and fighting took place simultaneously in several different areas of the world. It was the most widespread and expensive (in terms of money spent and lives lost) war ever, and it profoundly changed the world politically, economically, and psychologically.

Despite the war's impact on the United States, you'll probably see only one or two questions on the SAT II that deal directly with World War II. However, because World War II is a major turning point in United States' history, the exam may throw in a few other questions about trends or events that started during or after World War II. So, understanding the events that led to World War II and the United States' involvement in the crucial events of World War II is important.

 Although this chapter has a lot of dates, memorizing them isn't important. Just work on understanding what events led to what, and familiarize yourself with the general progression of the war so you can put the pieces together. By the way, even though the war officially started in 1939, the United States didn't enter World War II until 1941.

The Rise of Fascism and the Start of World War II

The spread of *Fascism* (a political philosophy that emphasized the importance of the nation and the race over the individual) arose from economic hardship in European countries following World War I, especially in Germany. Germans, in desperate need of a savior, looked to Adolf Hitler to rescue them from a government and economy that were in complete disarray. German Fascism found like-mindedness in the dictatorships of Italy, Spain, and Japan. In fact, Germany, Italy, and Japan joined purposes to form the Axis powers (the Roman-Berlin-Tokyo axis). When Hitler took power in Germany, he intended to take over the whole of Europe and eventually, the world.

The SAT II U.S. History exam is a test on U.S. history (seems obvious, huh?). Therefore, you need to know what was going on in other parts of the world only in the ways that the events impacted the United States. So, even though this chapter mentions World War II events before the United States became involved for the sake of context, it doesn't go into these events in great detail.

Examining European dictatorships

Germany wasn't the only country in Europe with a Fascist dictatorship. Italy had Benito Mussolini. But Germany had the most powerful Fascist dictatorship in Europe, and it rose from the backlash of World War I.

The emergence of Adolf Hitler in Germany

The Treaty of Versailles, which had ended World War I, wasn't especially friendly toward Germany (see Chapter 15 for details). Throughout the 1920s and early 1930s, Germany had to pay reparations to the countries harmed in World War I. German industry, transportation systems, and structures suffered greatly because of the war and needed to be rebuilt. Due to inflation, war recovery, and war reparations, the German economy was in serious disarray in the 1920s, and the German people wanted a strong and powerful leader who would help solve Germany's economic problems.

In January 1933, the German Reichstag (congress) selected a new chancellor, Adolf Hitler, of the *National Socialist Party,* also known as the *Nazi Party.* Eighteen months later, Hitler became dictator. We probably don't need to tell you this tidbit, but Hitler was one scary dude. However, at first, he seemed okay: He was a powerful orator, confident, young, energetic, and dynamic. He promised the German people that he would fix the economy, convinced them that Germany was the greatest country in the world, and told them that Germany could do no wrong. He also enforced the people's belief that other countries were to blame for the outcome of World War I and for Germany's problems.

Hitler was a right-wing nationalist. He convinced the German people that the interests of Germany always came first. Hitler was also a vehement anti-Semite; he blamed the Jews for all the problems in Germany. He also hated Slavs, Catholics, homosexuals, the disabled and handicapped, gypsies, Communists, and pretty much anyone else who disagreed with him. He felt that Aryan (of white northern European descent) people were genetically superior and called for domination by the German "master race."

By 1935, Hitler and the Nazi Party had absolute authority in Germany. The Nazi Party was the only political party. It completely controlled the media and disbanded trade unions. And every German province was under the local jurisdiction of a governor appointed directly by Hitler. Those who didn't support him either left Germany or kept their mouths shut and pretended to agree with him.

You'd think that Americans would have been outraged by this behavior, but, remember, the United States was in the midst of the Great Depression. Until about 1935, Americans and the U.S. government had so many of their own problems that they weren't really paying too much attention to what was going on in Germany. Also, the U.S. still had a lot of racism itself in the 1930s. The United States had racist immigration policies, the Ku Klux Klan, and many anti-Semitic and xenophobic (anti-foreigners) people. Hitler's discrimination agenda didn't seem as horrible and outrageous to Americans in the mid-1930s as it would to Americans today.

By 1937, the financial situation in Germany had improved under Hitler. Similar to Franklin D. Roosevelt's plans, Hitler had expanded the economy through government financing of public works and industry. Industry doubled; arms and weapons manufacturing increased; and unemployment dropped. The improved economy gave the grateful German people confidence in their leader, country, and government.

Benito Mussolini: Italy's Hitler wannabe

Italy, too, felt wronged after World War I. Italy had been on the winning side but never received the land that Great Britain and France promised when the war ended. In 1919, Benito Mussolini created a following of former soldiers who agreed with his Fascist, anti-socialist, anti-trade union, and nationalistic agenda. Over the next few years, Mussolini and his Fascist supporters gained widespread support.

In 1921, the Italian people elected many Fascists to parliament, and the authoritarian, right-wing *Fascist National Party* was born later that year. Mussolini, backed by the Fascist National Party, organized a march on Rome in 1922 to establish the Fascist Party as the most important party in Italy. It must have made an impact, because when Italy's prime minister resigned that same year, King Victor Emmanuel III gave Mussolini the job. Throughout the 1920s, Fascists dominated Parliament through the use of corruption, intimidation, and violence. Unlike Hitler, Mussolini never gained *totalitarian* (complete control) power. Mussolini headed the government, but he ruled under the king in cooperation with the Catholic Church, which wasn't controlled by the Fascist party.

Japan: A rising power in Asia

After World War I, Japan faced a series of problems, including the installation of a new emperor in 1921, high inflation, labor unrest, an economic recession, and a huge earthquake in 1923 that caused severe damage all over the country. Throughout these hardships, the military remained a stable and widely supported entity. The military didn't even have to answer to the government.

Although Japan already governed Taiwan and Korea, the government also had its eye on China. Japan lacked many natural resources, like oil and rubber, and it couldn't even grow enough food to feed its own people. China was a ready market for trade and could provide an enormous supply of the natural resources that Japan needed. Japan already had troops in Manchuria (part of China) guarding Japan's economic interests there, but in 1931, the Japanese military sent more troops to occupy the territory. Without the knowledge or consent of the Japanese government, the military captured the capital of Manchuria. When the League of Nations ordered Japan out of Manchuria, Japan left the organization.

By 1935, Japan had conquered most of northern China. Two years later, Japan controlled most of the coastline, cities, and railroads in China. The members of the Japanese military, like the members of the Nazis, believed that they were superior to the Chinese, so they tortured and killed millions of Chinese civilians. Both Great Britain and the United States provided some aid to the Chinese resistance; this move alienated both nations from Japan.

Brutal force: Germany's escalating aggression

After Hitler had strengthened Germany domestically, he was ready to assert his power over other countries. Beginning in the mid-1930s, Nazi Germany initiated a series of aggressive events that led to the beginning of World War II on the European front. Here are some of the more important ones:

- ✔ **German re-arms:** In 1935, Hitler ordered military conscription and increased the manufacture of arms and weapons, which violated the provision of the Treaty of Versailles that Germany limit its military force.

- ✔ **Germany invades the Rhineland:** In March 1936, Hitler sent about 20,000 soldiers to invade and re-occupy the Rhineland, a region along the border between France and Germany that Germany had to give up to France after World War I. Hitler ordered his troops to retreat if they met French troops, but they were left alone.

✔ **Germany annexes Austria:** Although the Treaty of Versailles prohibited the union of Austria and Germany, Hitler rationalized that all German-speaking people should unite under one nation, so the Nazis invaded and quickly occupied Austria in March 1938. The invasion was pretty easy for the Nazis because Austria had instituted a Fascist government even before its unification with Germany.

✔ **Germany occupies the Sudetenland:** In the fall of 1938, Hitler planned to invade the Sudetenland, a region of Czechoslovakia inhabited by German speakers. Counting on help from the Soviet Union, Great Britain, and France, the government of Czechoslovakia refused to give in to Hitler's demands. Finally disturbed by Hitler's aggression, the British prime minister and the French premier called a meeting with Hitler and Hitler's ally, Mussolini, in Munich, Germany, and formulated the *Munich Pact*. In exchange for the Sudetenland, Hitler agreed that he would not demand any further territory.

✔ **Germany occupies Czechoslovakia:** But the Sudetenland didn't appease Hitler for long. In March 1939, Nazi troops invaded and occupied the rest of Czechoslovakia. Leaders of Great Britain and France finally realized that they couldn't trust Hitler. The two countries agreed to join a military alliance and agreed to aid Poland, Hitler's next likely target.

✔ **Germany meets with the Soviet Union:** In 1939, Hitler demanded that Poland return the parts of Poland inhabited by German-speaking people to Germany. Then Hitler set up a meeting with Joseph Stalin, the Soviet Union's dictator, to discuss how the two countries would control their border states of Poland, Estonia, Latvia, and Lithuania as spheres of influence. The two leaders signed a non-aggression pact in which they agreed to the following terms:

  • Germany wouldn't invade or attack the Soviet Union.

  • Germany gave the Soviet Union permission to annex a small part of Eastern Poland, Estonia, Latvia, and Lithuania.

Stalin reluctantly agreed to the pact with Hitler rather than creating an alliance with Great Britain to keep from fighting a war with Germany over Poland. This pact alarmed Great Britain, France, and other countries in Europe because they realized that Hitler had designs for all of Europe.

At first, Great Britain and France ignored much of these events, using a policy called *appeasement,* which means that they decided to essentially ignore Germany's acts of aggression. These countries didn't intervene because they were still psychologically and economically devastated by World War I. They feared new bombing methods, and some saw German aggression as just because they felt Germany got a raw deal in the Treaty of Versailles. Additionally, some nations viewed the Communist threat as more evil than the Nazi threat and generally dismissed the danger of Nazi Germany.

The official start: The German invasion of Poland

The Nazi forces invaded Poland on September 1, 1939. Two days later, Great Britain and France kept their word to Poland and declared war on Germany, although they didn't send troops to Poland to fight against the German forces (which caused historians to call this period the "phony war"). Poland had a very outdated and undersupplied cavalry-based military and wasn't prepared for the modern, well-equipped German military.

When the German military invaded Poland, it employed the tactic of *blitzkrieg,* which means "lightning war." Using this tactic, the German military launched rapid and massive surprise attacks from the air and from tanks on the ground. Within three weeks, the Soviet Union invaded Poland from the west, and Hitler and Stalin split up Poland as they previously had agreed. By October 1, the Nazis occupied Warsaw, the Polish capital, and a week later, all Polish resistance ceased. (See Figure 18-1 for a visual of Germany's movements.) With the invasion of Poland, World War II had officially begun.

March 1936, Rhineland
March 1938, Austria annexed
October 1938, Czechoslovak frontier regions (Sudetenland) annexed
March 1939, Memeland from Lithuania
March 1939, annexation of Bohemia and Moravia
September 1939, German occupation of Poland

Figure 18-1:
Germany's
designs on
Europe.

Germany takes over France

In May 1940, Hitler set his sights on conquering France and Great Britain. He planned to do so by attacking and quickly occupying the Low Countries — the Netherlands, Luxembourg and Belgium. French troops responded to this threat by entering Belgium. Through a series of strategically planned movements, Germany entered France and successfully separated French troops from British troops. By June 14th, German troops had captured Paris, and French troops had surrendered unconditionally. The capture of France had been all too easy, and the French troops had been none too sharp. Great Britain finally got serious and took steps to secure itself from similar capture.

Staying Out of It: The United States' Neutrality

The U.S. wasn't eager to enter a worldwide war again so soon after World War I. During the 1920s and 1930s, it had taken action to ensure that it would remain neutral should conflict again arise in Europe. In 1940 and 1941, war between Germany and Great Britain made it increasingly difficult for the U.S. to maintain a neutral stance in the Atlantic, and Japan forced the U.S. to get involved when it bombed Pearl Harbor in late 1941.

Leave well enough alone: Support for isolationism

United States' *isolationism* (the desire to stay out of foreign affairs) rose after World War I and continued through much of the 1920s and 1930s. Many events fostered the policy of isolationism in the United States:

- Many Americans thought that U.S. banks and corporations interested in protecting their interests abroad and making exorbitant profits had tricked the United States into entering World War I in 1917. The Nye Report, a report a Senate committee issued that investigated the United States' motives for entering World War I, supported this theory.

- Isolationists in Congress successfully prevented the United States from joining the World Court under the League of Nations during the successive administrations of Warren G. Harding, Calvin Coolidge, Herbert Hoover, and Franklin Roosevelt.

- Many Americans felt that the League of Nations had been somewhat of a failure because it didn't end Japanese aggression in Asia.

- In 1924, Congress passed new laws that limited immigration to the United States and fostered a spirit of nationalism in the United States.

- The Smoot–Hawley Tariff Act of 1930 (also known as the Hawley–Smoot Tariff Act) imposed protective tariffs on U.S. goods, which significantly diminished foreign trade with the United States.

- In 1934, Franklin Delano Roosevelt (FDR) signed a bill that prohibited U.S. banks from loaning money to any nation that had defaulted on outstanding debts. Foreign nations with debts were constantly increasing their debts by borrowing more money from the United States so they could make their initial debt payments.

  By 1934, Europe was in financial crisis. Without German reparation payments, which had stopped in 1931, and the ability to borrow money from American banks, the only nation that continued to make debt payments to the United States was Finland.

- When civil war broke out in Spain in 1936, Hitler and Mussolini quickly jumped in to support Franco. The United States teamed up with Great Britain and France and agreed that they would provide no assistance to either side of the Spanish conflict.

- In 1937, despite Roosevelt's concerns about Japanese aggression, most Americans didn't want to enter any conflicts and overlooked Japan's attacks on provinces in northern China as well as an attack on a U.S. gunboat on the Yangtze River in China.

In 1937, Roosevelt delivered a speech that suggested that the United States "quarantine" the aggressor nations of Germany, Italy, Spain, and Japan. This speech didn't go over well, and Roosevelt didn't receive much public support for the idea. Some even called him a warmonger. At this time, Americans weren't entirely convinced that Hitler, Francisco Franco, Mussolini, or the military-controlled nation of Japan posed a dangerous threat to the United States.

The Neutrality Acts of 1935, 1937, and 1939

In the late 1930s, the U.S. attempted to maintain its isolation from international events by passing the *Neutrality Acts.* Congress passed the Neutrality Act in 1935 and later revised it in 1937 and 1939. The Neutrality Act of 1935 had four components:

- It placed an embargo on selling arms and weapons to combatants (called "belligerents" in the act) engaged in an international war.

- It asked Americans to refrain from traveling aboard belligerents' ships.

- It prohibited American merchant ships from entering war zones.
- A 1936 amendment to the act prohibited the U.S. from making loans to belligerents.

In 1937, Congress included combatants in civil wars and added the following elements to the Neutrality Act:

- The U.S. government allowed warring nations to purchase only non-military goods.
- It banned Americans from traveling as passengers on belligerents' ships.
- Warring nations that purchased goods from the United States had to pay cash for these goods and send their own ships to pick up the goods they purchased. This policy was known as the *cash-and-carry policy.*

The 1939 revision to the Neutrality Act modified a provision of the 1937 act. The modification lifted the arms embargo and allowed the United States to sell arms and weapons to warring nations on a cash-and-carry basis.

Congress passed these acts primarily in reaction to a war between Italy and Ethiopia, the Spanish Civil War, and the Sino-Japanese War (you won't need to know about these wars for the test). These wars had a great effect on the conflict in Europe, which meant that the Neutrality Acts created controversy among United States citizens for several reasons:

- The trade policies of the Neutrality Acts didn't distinguish between victims and aggressors in a war situation, which meant that the United States could sell arms and weapons to Germany and Great Britain. Most Americans felt this policy was unjust because they saw Great Britain as a victim and Germany as an aggressor.
- When the United States placed an embargo on arms and weapons sales in the Neutrality Acts of 1935 and 1937, the policy actually favored the aggressor nations (like Germany) because they were well equipped for war and didn't need American goods as much as the weaker and less-prepared nations (like Great Britain) did. Despite Americans' desire for neutrality, most didn't favor a policy that strengthened Nazi Germany and weakened its victims.
- When the United States lifted the arms embargo in 1939, isolationist Americans thought that U.S. arms and weapons trades would benefit U.S. industry so much that big business would influence the government to enter into a war just to increase profit margins.

The Lend-Lease Act of 1941

By the end of 1940, a nearly bankrupt Britain was no longer able to meet the cash-and-carry requirements for importation under the Neutrality Acts. Roosevelt felt that it was essential to United States' national security that Great Britain continue to defend itself against the aggressive Nazi Germany. So, to get around the prohibition of arms sales instituted by the Neutrality Acts, in March 1941, Roosevelt signed the *Lend-Lease Act,* which allowed Great Britain or any other nation "vital to the defense of the United States" to lease arms from the United States under permission from the president. That way, a cash-poor Britain could "borrow" arms from the United States, as long as it promised to return them to the United States after the war.

Although the U.S. wanted to remain neutral, by 1941, Roosevelt couldn't ignore the threat of the German war machine in Europe and the possible threat it posed to the U.S. So the U.S. began to become involved in assisting Germany's victims. Under the Lend-Lease Act, Roosevelt authorized more than $50 billion in aid to Great Britain and, later, to the Soviet Union after Germany attacked it in July 1941. FDR also authorized the U.S. Navy to escort British trade ships (and their borrowed goods) part of the way back from the U.S. across the Atlantic Ocean to Great Britain and to track the location of the German submarines in the Atlantic so that British ships could avoid them.

A great benefit of the Lend-Lease Act (remember this act for the test) was that it helped mobilize U.S. industry for war production. By the time the United States officially entered the war in 1941, U.S. industry was already supplying the Allies with billions of dollars worth of arms and supplies.

Making plans: The Atlantic Charter

In August 1941, FDR met with British Foreign Secretary Winston Churchill on a British ship off the coast of northeastern Canada. FDR didn't commit to U.S. involvement in the war, but the two leaders discussed their visions for the future of the world and laid the groundwork for a future international peacekeeping organization. FDR and Churchill drafted a document that called for the destruction of "Nazi tyranny" and established the following principles:

- ✔ Neither Great Britain nor the United States wanted to gain any territory as a result of the war.
- ✔ The world should have freedom from the fear of aggression.
- ✔ All nations should abandon the use of force.
- ✔ People of all nations should have the right to choose their own form of government.
- ✔ World nations should establish a "system of general security," or an international peacekeeping organization, to prevent future large-scale wars. (Something along the same lines as the failed League of Nations.)

In 1942 (after the U.S. entered the war), FDR and Churchill met with representatives from 26 other Allied nations in Washington, D.C., and created the United Nations (the international peacekeeping organization), pledged continued support for the Atlantic Charter, and agreed not to make individual peace agreements with any of the Axis powers.

In the zone: Getting involved in the Atlantic

Despite American neutrality, the U.S. Navy became actively involved in the fight in the Atlantic when German U-boats increased hostilities against Canadian and British ships carrying weapons "borrowed" from the United States under the Lend-Lease Act in 1941. As early as October 1939, as a response to these increased hostilities, the United States had established a Pan-American Neutrality Zone, which included the entire length of the North, Central, and South American coasts and eventually extended east to Iceland. This zone gave U.S. naval ships the license to fire upon any Axis vessels within the neutrality zone.

In October 1941, a German U-boat attacked a U.S. destroyer in the neutral zone near Iceland. The destroyer sank, and 100 crewmembers died. U.S. neutrality appeared to be an impossibility after this incident, and the attack of Pearl Harbor two months later clinched America's official entrance into World War II.

A rude awakening: Pearl Harbor

While things were heating up for the U.S. in the Atlantic, trouble was also brewing in Asia. You probably won't see any of these details on the test, but we're giving them to you so you have a little background about why Japan bombed the U.S. In July 1941, Japan continued its campaign to take over surrounding regions, this time invading Vietnam. American intelligence officials knew that Japan intended to invade the Dutch and British holdings in the Pacific next. The U.S. responded to Japan's invasion of Vietnam by freezing all Japanese assets in the

United States and ending all trade with Japan, including the petroleum trade, which . high and dry on the supplies that they needed. FDR hoped that this action would con Japanese to negotiate with the U.S. rather than invade the Dutch and British territories.

For a while, the Japanese appeared willing to negotiate. But Japan stalled the negotiations while it secretly prepared for war against the United States. By the end of November 1941, American intelligence had broken Japanese code and discovered that an attack in the Pacific was imminent, but officials didn't know where the attack would occur. They didn't anticipate a direct hit on U.S. forces.

At 7:55 a.m. on Sunday, December 7, 1941, the Japanese bombed the U.S. Pacific fleet stationed at the U.S. Naval Base in Pearl Harbor, Hawaii. More bombers showed up an hour later. Because almost everyone was asleep and because the fleet had no warning, the United States didn't have much opportunity to fight back. Within two hours of the bombing, the United States lost numerous battleships, airplanes, and other vessels. More than 2,000 American soldiers and sailors died and more than 1,000 were injured in the attacks.

Japan's sneak attack forced the United States into war. On December 8, 1941, Congress voted to declare war against Japan. And because Japan was allied with the Axis powers, Germany and Italy declared war on the United States on December 11. Congress immediately voted unanimously to join the *Allied forces* of Great Britain, the Soviet Union, and other nations (also known as the Allies) and enter into war against Germany and Italy. Almost at once, the United States was at war on two fronts.

On the Home Front: Americans at Home During the War

FDR entered into an unprecedented third term in office in 1941 as world events drew the United States closer to war. After the Japanese bombed Pearl Harbor in December 1941, the United States quickly mobilized for war, and the nation was ready to help. The military prepared to fight, industry kicked into high gear for wartime production, and citizens made sacrifices for the war effort. But discrimination, especially against Japanese Americans, grew.

Preparing the military

The *Selective Service Act of 1917* gave the president the power to call for a peacetime military conscription (also known as the draft). Roosevelt used his power to institute a draft in 1940 because he worried about a foreign threat to national security, even though the U.S. wasn't yet officially involved in the war. The draft required all men between 18 and 65 to register, but between 1940 and 1943, the government called men only ages 20 to 45 to serve. As fighting escalated, the U.S. needed more troops. In 1943, the armed forces also called up 18- and 19-year-olds to serve and, from 1941 to 1945, more than 300,000 American women volunteered to serve in the military in noncombat positions, such as nursing and administrative work.

Building the economy

During the years leading up to America's involvement in World War II, the U.S. suffered a severe depression. As war escalated in Europe and the demand for U.S. industry increased, the U.S. economy gained momentum, unemployment all but disappeared, and the Great Depression ended.

Between 1940 and 1945, industrial output doubled. Before and during World War II, the United States produced more than four times as many war materials (guns, tanks, artillery, airplanes, ships, bombs, and so on) than the combined production of the Axis powers did. As the U.S. economy boomed, workers benefited. By 1945, approximately 45 percent of the population solidly landed in the middle class, based on income level. (In contrast, in 1936, only 15 percent of the population was in the middle class.) Between 1939 and 1945, wages rose nearly 45 percent, partially because labor union membership also increased dramatically during these years.

The war also had an effect on the makeup of the workforce. By the end of 1942, the United States was experiencing an acute labor shortage because able-bodied men were at war. To solve the labor shortage, the government extended the workweek, and businesses employed millions of women and allowed 14- to 17-year olds to work. By 1945, women made up 36 percent of the workforce. Extensive war propaganda, such as the well-known image of *Rosie the Riveter,* inspired women to enter the workforce in record numbers.

To deal with a lack of skilled labor, industry emphasized mass production and assembly-line techniques. This strategy allowed industry to use the scarce skilled laborers for what they did best, while the unskilled laborers completed the repetitive assembly work. Here are some of the other ways that the war affected U.S. industry.

- The government created the War Production Board (WPB), which offered businesses incentives to switch their industries to wartime production. For example, a factory that made automobiles may have changed its production to only tanks or airplanes.

- Businesses that switched to wartime production advertised their involvement in the war effort throughout the war to create a sense of national unity and to build goodwill.

- The government created a federal agency called the Office of Price Administration (OPA) to set price ceilings on wartime and consumer goods to prevent price increases and inflation. The OPA also set up a program for rationing scarce goods, like shoes, gasoline, tires, canned foods (tin was needed for war production), coffee, and sugar (the U.S. had to import both items).

Making everyday sacrifices

Most Americans were pretty fired up about the war after the attack on Pearl Harbor. They felt that the United States was doing a good deed by helping quash the evil aggressors in Europe and Asia. To fund the war, the government sold war bonds and increased taxes, and FDR encouraged individuals to make sacrifices at home to redirect needed supplies to the military and to help out the war effort. Americans saved gasoline by carpooling, bicycling, walking, or taking mass transportation. The government encouraged Americans not to hoard scarce goods like sugar, meat, and butter. Americans grew their own fruits and vegetables in "Victory Gardens" and recycled everything possible. People collected scraps of metal and even donated old cars to the war effort.

Discriminating against Japanese Americans

The American media rallied citizens with intense propaganda about the evil nature of the enemy. Italian and German non-citizens experienced some discrimination in the United States, and the government imposed some restrictions at the beginning of the war. But most Americans didn't blame German and Italian immigrants or descendants living in the United States for the actions of Hitler and Mussolini.

But the United States treated Japanese Americans more harshly. Maybe the reason was because the Japanese military had bombed the United States on its own soil or because the Japanese looked different. Or maybe the reason was because the media and political frenzy that portrayed the Japanese in America as savage and cunning people who were a threat to American security. Whatever the reason, Americans harbored a lot of hatred toward Japanese Americans in the early years of the war.

More than 65 percent of the Japanese population living in the United States were U.S. citizens. However, the War Department, military officials, and many politicians on the West Coast anticipated the threat of a West Coast invasion and believed that the Japanese living there posed a security threat. They thought they may help Japan invade the United States or that they would spy for Japan. This pressure led FDR to sign an executive order for the *internment,* or imprisonment, of the Japanese in early 1942.

With this order, the U.S. government evacuated more than 120,000 Japanese people from coastal areas and gave them the option to move to other inland states to live or be imprisoned in camps. About 10,000 moved to inland states. The government rounded up the remaining Japanese and interned them in ten bleak camps (known as War Relocation Camps) scattered throughout the West. The detainees weren't murdered or tortured, but they did endure substandard living conditions. Within a year, nearly 20,000 Japanese Americans proved that they posed no security threats and were permitted to leave the camps. Another 40,000 left in 1944. By the beginning of 1945, the camps had all but emptied.

Despite the suffering they experienced at the hands of the American government, many of the Japanese who left the camps worked in industry. Japanese American women worked as Army nurses or in the Red Cross, and Japanese American men served as soldiers, spies, or interpreters for the U.S. military intelligence.

Tying it all together: A sample question looks at the home front during World War II

On the SAT II, questions about World War II tend to focus less on the actual fighting and more on the effects of the war. For instance, the following question tests your knowledge about the war effort that Americans made at home.

During World War II, Americans did all the following to help out the war effort at home EXCEPT

(A) Millions of women entered the workforce.

(B) Citizens rationed scarce consumer goods.

(C) Men and women purchased U.S. war bonds to help the government pay for the war.

(D) Americans planted their own vegetables and recycled.

(E) Workers took lower wages due to decreased labor union bargaining.

This question is a bit tough because all the answers sound reasonable at first glance. Look closely at (E), however. Even though taking lower wages during wartime sounds very patriotic and even though labor union activity occurred less frequently during the war years than in the years after, wages actually increased substantially during the war.

Millions of women did enter the workforce, and men and women purchased war bonds and planted vegetables. So, (A), (C), and (D) are incorrect answers. You also know that citizens refrained from hoarding scarce commodities, so you know that they engaged in rationing; thus, (B) is also incorrect. Answer (E) must be the answer.

Defeating Hitler: America and the Allies Fight in Europe and Africa

During World War II, fighting took place throughout the world. In Europe, fighting occurred in Eastern and Western Europe. Battles also occurred in North Africa and the Middle East as well as across the Mediterranean Sea. Opposing forces waged war in the Pacific arena and across much of East and Southeast Asia, too (see the later section "Anything but Peaceful: America's Battle in the Pacific.")

During the Nazi invasion of France in 1940, the British military narrowly escaped the Nazi forces and returned to Britain. Without backup, France crumbled quickly. Italy joined Germany in the war and sent troops to Africa. With France secured, Germany turned its attention to Great Britain and began a massive three-month air campaign in 1941 until the Royal Air Force (RAF) sent the Nazis into retreat.

Frustrated by the British, the Nazis invaded and occupied the Balkan nations, located in southeastern Europe, and sent troops to aid Italy in Africa in 1941. Then Hitler made a crucial mistake. In June 1941, just as he had done in Poland, he ordered a *blitzkrieg* against the Soviet Union. He thought the battle would be an easy and quick victory, but the Soviet army, called the Red Army, and the Soviet winter turned out to be formidable foes. During the harsh winter of 1941–1942, the Red Army successfully halted German troops and forced the Nazis into retreat. Hitler's attack on the Soviets provoked the U.S. into including the Soviet Union in the Lend-Lease Act and officially marked the Soviet Union as one of the members of the Allies.

When the United States entered the war in December 1941, the Allies developed a plan of attack. They determined that they must concentrate their efforts on defeating Germany and Italy before focusing on Japan. U.S. involvement was the beginning of the end for Hitler.

Checking out the major battles

The SAT II probably won't ask you to remember the specific battles of World War II, but you should be familiar enough with events to know what role the United States played in defeating the German fighting machine. The following list covers the major battles that the U.S. and its Allies fought.

- **Africa:** The Allies sent troops under American *General Dwight D. Eisenhower* to French North Africa in November 1942 to defeat the Axis armies. Eisenhower ended the war there in May 1943.

- **The Soviet Union:** In early 1943, the Red Army took down 300,000 Nazi troops over six months in the Battle of Stalingrad, and the German forces surrendered. The Red Army regained lost ground and, by early 1944, had pushed Germany back to the border of Poland.

- **Italy:** In the summer of 1943, the Allies invaded Sicily and southern Italy and overthrew Mussolini and the Fascist government. Defeated, Italy surrendered unconditionally. Under German protection, Mussolini retreated to Northern Italy after the surrender, and the Italian people executed him in April 1945.

- **Eastern Europe:** In 1944, the Red Army rapidly pushed the Nazis farther west, liberating Poland, Bulgaria, Yugoslavia, Romania, Hungary, Czechoslovakia, and Austria from the Nazis.

- **Operation Overlord:** In early 1944, the Allies launched air attacks on Nazi-occupied territories. On June 6, 1944 (D-Day), in one of the most famous battles of World War II, a massive installation of more than three million Allied troops invaded France through the beaches of Normandy. The operation combined air attacks with land and sea invasions. The Nazis provided strong resistance, but the Allies successfully captured Paris and forced the Nazis to retreat.

- **Battle of the Bulge:** In December 1944, Nazi reserves put up a strong fight in the Battle of the Bulge in Belgium and Luxembourg. But one month later, the Allies were victorious.

- **Germany:** In April 1945, Allied forces entered Germany from the west and met up with the Red Army from the east. The Allies surrounded Berlin; Hitler committed suicide; and Germany surrendered unconditionally on May 8, 1945, known as V-E day (which stands for Victory in Europe Day).

The horror of the Holocaust

The *Holocaust* was the name for the Nazi campaign to persecute and exterminate the Jewish people from 1933 to 1945. Between 1933 and 1941, the German government systematically stripped Jews of most of their rights. Beginning in 1942, the Nazis began rounding up Jews (and Poles, Communists, gypsies, the disabled, homosexuals, and anyone else they didn't like) and sending them to concentration camps, making plans to methodically murder millions of people.

In as early as October 1942, reports of the horrors of Nazi concentration camps started to circulate in the U.S., and public pressure in the United States and other Allied nations grew for the governments to do something about the horror. These nations also faced significant public pressure to take in millions of Jewish refugees. Unfortunately, these nations, including the United States, did relatively little to remedy the situation. The Allied invasion of Germany in 1945 and other Nazi-held territories confirmed the horrific reports of the Holocaust as troops discovered dozens of Nazi work and concentration camps, where more than six million Jews and four million non-Jews perished under Hitler's direction. A major motivating force for U.S. troops in Europe was the obliteration of the Holocaust.

Calming the Winds of War: The Yalta Conference

Anticipating an imminent end to the war, President Roosevelt, the Soviet Union's Joseph Stalin, and Britain's Prime Minister Winston Churchill met in Yalta in the Soviet Union in February 1945. Because Stalin controlled most of Eastern Europe at this time, he had more leverage in the negotiations at the Yalta Conference. In these negotiations, the "Big Three" (FDR, Churchill, and Stalin) agreed on the following terms:

- The Allies would temporarily divide Germany into four zones of Allied military occupation, and Germany would have to pay the equivalent of billions of dollars in reparations to the Soviet Union.

- The powers declared that Europe would be free and allowed for democratic elections in all liberated areas.

- Soviet interim governments would remain in all the Soviet-occupied countries of Eastern Europe.

> ✔ The Soviet Union would have more power in the plans for an international peacekeeping organization, the United Nations, and would have veto power on the United Nations Security Council.
>
> ✔ The Soviet Union would enter the war against Japan in exchange for control of Manchuria.

The Yalta Conference was the last face-to-face meeting of the Big Three. FDR didn't live to see the end of the war. To the shock and dismay of most Americans, he died on April 12, 1945, just three months after he began his unprecedented fourth term as president. His vice president, Harry S Truman, succeeded him.

Though the SAT II probably won't ask you to name specific battles that the U.S. fought in Europe, it may ask you about the agreement the Big Three reached at the Yalta Conference to end the war in Europe.

At the Yalta Conference in 1945, the "Big Three" agreed on all the following EXCEPT

(A) Soviet involvement in the Pacific arena of World War II

(B) The permanent division of Germany into four zones of Allied military occupation

(C) Plans and voting procedures for the United Nations

(D) Designated control of Manchuria

(E) Continued Soviet occupation in Eastern Europe

Don't let the mention of the "Big Three" throw you. The Yalta Conference was a meeting of Stalin, Churchill, and FDR, so carry on.

The correct answer is (B), but you may have been caught off guard with this one. The Yalta Conference did divide Germany, so the answer seems like it may be wrong. But if you read the answer choice carefully, you see that it specifies the *permanent* division of Germany. The divisions the leaders agreed upon at Yalta were temporary. All the other answer choices were valid agreements of the Yalta Conference.

Anything but Peaceful: America's Battle in the Pacific

"Pacific" means peaceful, but the Pacific region was pretty ferocious during the first half of the 1940s. By 1941, Japan occupied much of northern and central China, and Japanese leaders hoped that the U.S. would negotiate with them to allow Japan to do what it wanted in China, but the U.S. wouldn't negotiate. During 1942, the United States and Japan battled on strategic islands in the Pacific Ocean, including major battles at the Coral Sea and Midway, both of which stopped Japan's advance. Under the command of *General Douglas MacArthur,* the U.S. military employed a strategy to "leap-frog" from island to island toward Japan. In September 1942, the Allies captured the island of Guadalcanal and handed Japan its first outright defeat in four years, which marked a turning point in the war in the Pacific. As the United States secured islands under its control, it used these islands as bases from which to conduct air raids on Japan. And, during the summer of 1944, the Allies were able to destroy the Japanese naval fleet.

In early 1945, the United States fought and won two long, bloody, high-casualty battles on the Pacific Islands of Iwo Jima and Okinawa. By spring 1945, U.S. bombing missions regularly assaulted mainland Japan. Numerous Japanese cities sat in rubble, and millions of Japanese citizens were homeless and starving. Despite enduring daily bombings and possessing no navy, the Japanese forces stubbornly refused to surrender unconditionally to the Allies. The United States needed a solution, and it found one in the atomic bomb.

In 1939, rumors reached the United States that the Nazis were developing an atomic bomb. So beginning in 1941, the U.S. government secretly provided more than $2 billion in funds for the *Manhattan Project,* a project in which scientists under a secret government contract worked in undisclosed labs around the country to develop an atomic bomb. Scientists worked quickly and had a prototype to test by July 1945. On July 16, 1945, the scientists of the project gathered to watch the first-ever atomic explosion in New Mexico. When Truman learned of the project's success (which was only after he became president), he issued Japan an ultimatum demanding that its government surrender by August 3 or face "prompt and utter destruction." Truman ordered the U.S. Air Force to use the weapon if Japan didn't surrender.

On August 4, 1945, in an attempt to warn civilians that their city was going to be destroyed, the U.S. Air Force dropped 700,000 leaflets on Hiroshima, Japan. On August 6, 1945, out of a B-29 bomber named the *Enola Gay,* the United States dropped the first atomic bomb on the Japanese industrial center of Hiroshima. When it hit, the bomb created a 4,000-degree Celsius fireball that killed more than 80,000 people, injured nearly 100,000 more, and completely flattened 4 square miles.

Two days later, the Soviet Union declared war on Japan and invaded Japanese-held Manchuria. When Japan still wouldn't surrender, the United States dropped a second atomic bomb on the industrial port city, Nagasaki, on August 9. The Nagasaki bomb killed and injured tens of thousands more. Finally, on August 15, 1945 (also known as V-J Day for "Victory in Japan"), Japan surrendered unconditionally.

You may encounter a question on the SAT II that doesn't deal directly with the fight in the Pacific. A question may ask you about the Manhattan Project.

Which of the following provides the main goal of the Manhattan Project in the 1940s?

(A) To facilitate a surprise attack on the Nazi forces at Normandy, France

(B) To cause the unconditional surrender of the Japanese

(C) To develop a new bomber plane for the U.S. Air Force

(D) To develop the world's first atomic weapon

(E) To capture Adolf Hitler as a prisoner of war

Because you just read about the Manhattan Project, you may think that this question is easy. But by the time of the exam, you may forget that the goal of the Manhattan Project was to develop an atomic weapon, which is answer (D).

Don't be fooled by (B). Although the atomic bomb was eventually used to bring about the Japanese surrender, the goal of the Manhattan Project was specifically to develop the bomb.

The goal of the Manhattan Project was to develop a bomb, not a bomber, so you can eliminate (C). The Allied attack at Normandy was called Operation Overlord, which, like (E), refers to the war in Europe; so both (A) and (E) are incorrect.

Part VI
America in Middle Age

The 5th Wave By Rich Tennant

"Our committee has determined that going into Vietnam, neutralizing the spread of Communism, and getting out again should be as easy as putting one foot in front of the other."

In this part . . .

America's middle-aged years bring you from the grand finale of World War II in 1945 to the Cold War and the Vietnam War to the present day. This period is one of great change in American society. Many of the things you take for granted came into being during the last 60-plus years: television, computers, the Internet, rock 'n' roll, environmental conservation, and civil rights for women and minorities. In this part, you get to read about how these advancements came about and how they impacted American society.

Assume that 15 to 20 percent of the questions on the SAT II U.S. History test cover the material in this part. If you feel bogged down by the information overload in your brain, you can relax because the end is in sight. You may even get your social life back one of these days!

Chapter 19

Keeping Cool: Truman, Eisenhower, and the Cold War, 1945–1960

......

......

*W*ith the close of World War II, the United States emerged as the new world power on the global stage. The increased industrialization for the war also brought an end to the Great Depression once and for all. Following World War II, the United States experienced military and ideological wars; booming babies and economies; the birth of television, rock 'n' roll, and suburbia, not to mention the civil rights movement; and presidents named Harry and Ike. In this chapter, you find useful information about this pivotal era for the SAT II History exam plus a smattering of sample questions to test your newfound knowledge.

Taking Over the Reins: The Truman Presidency

Good ol' Franklin Delano Roosevelt (FDR) was so beloved by the American people that they elected him to a fourth term in 1944. Too bad they didn't see that he wasn't fit to take office again. Old age, a Great Depression, a second world war, and three full terms in the White House didn't exactly do wonders for his health. FDR died of a cerebral hemorrhage after three months of his fourth term in 1945. Lucky for the United States, Roosevelt picked Harry S Truman as his vice president. If Truman (another Democrat) was lacking in experience, he quickly made up for it with strong leadership and decisiveness, although he was a bit over-whelmed at first. He told reporters, "I felt like the moon, the stars, and all the planets had fallen on me." Truman led the U.S. through the end of the war and difficult times after World War II and made some tough choices. Today, historians rank him as one of America's finest presidents.

Changing U.S. international policy

After World War II, the U.S. couldn't revert to the isolationist policy that it had held on to for so long during the first half of the 20th century. Japan's attack on Pearl Harbor in 1941 had let Americans know that they couldn't hide from world conflict. Plus, the threat of the spread of Communism forced the U.S. government to acknowledge that it needed to be involved in world affairs to promote and preserve democratic governments (see the section "Red Scare: America Battles the Spread of Communism" later in this chapter). For these reasons, the American government increased its involvement on the international stage, beginning with the peace negotiations of World War II.

Keep the peace: Forming the United Nations

President Roosevelt and Winston Churchill, the leaders of the United States and Great Britain, talked about forming an international peacekeeping organization as early as 1941 when they drew up the Atlantic Charter. They formalized their plan at their first meeting with Stalin in Teheran, Iran, in November 1943. In 1944, officials from Great Britain, the Soviet Union, China, and the United States met in Washington, D.C., to pound out the details of the organization. What came out of the meeting was an informal agreement for the *United Nations (UN)*. The United Nations would consist of a General Assembly, where every nation had a vote, and a Security Council (where the real power was), which had five permanent members (France, China, Great Britain, the U.S., and the Soviet Union) and ten rotating temporary members from other nations, that had the power to veto any resolution. At a conference in April 1945, delegates from 50 nations hammered out the agreements and completed the charter for the United Nations. Members from the 50 original member countries signed the charter in San Francisco on June 26, 1945.

Previously, Americans had said no to President Woodrow Wilson's attempt to form a similar international body (the failed League of Nations) following World War I (see Chapter 15). But this time around, they overwhelmingly supported the idea: The Senate ratified the charter of the United Nations on August 8, 1945, by a vote of 89 to 2. Although the goal of the UN was to promote world peace and stability, it was helpless to stop the oncoming glaciers of the *Cold War.* After all, the two biggest rivals (the U.S. and the Soviet Union) were also the strongest nations with permanent membership on the Security Council. They had the power to veto each other's resolutions (and did), making the UN virtually powerless in the Cold War, although it had success with humanitarian and economic aid.

One last time: The Potsdam Conference

The *Potsdam Conference,* held between July 17 and August 2, 1945, was the last meeting of the Big Three, although it wasn't the same ol' trio anymore. Truman had replaced Roosevelt, and Britain's new Prime Minister Clement Atlee had replaced Winston Churchill, who was defeated in his run for reelection, midway through the negotiations. The Soviet Union's Joseph Stalin was the only original member of the Big Three.

At the conference, the U.S., Great Britain, and the Soviet Union agreed to some general policies for dealing with Germany in the postwar era, such as complete German disarmament, the elimination of military-related industry, the dissolution of Nazi institutions and laws, and the prosecution of war criminals. They also reached a compromise on how Germany had to pay reparations. The leaders also agreed to divide Germany into four military zones of occupation, which the U.S., the Soviet Union, Great Britain, and France would occupy.

Although knowing all that info doesn't hurt, what's more important to know for the SAT II is that the conference signaled a new relationship between the U.S. and the Soviet Union.

Roosevelt and Truman differed greatly in their views on the Soviet Union. Roosevelt felt that Stalin was a reasonable and flexible man and open to negotiations with the U.S. Truman, like many others in U.S. government, felt that Stalin was untrustworthy and was generally suspicious of him and the Soviet Union. Roosevelt was appeasing and cooperative when he negotiated with Stalin, whereas Truman was aggressive and confrontational. Part of the reason for this change in negotiation styles had to do with different personalities, but another part of it had to do with a memo that Truman received within days of arriving at the conference. The memo informed Truman of the first successful detonation of the atomic bomb in New Mexico.

America had a new weapon, and Truman felt he no longer needed Soviet help to defeat Japan in the Pacific. (For more details about the atomic bomb and the defeat of Japan in World War II, see Chapter 18.)

By the summer of 1945, some tension occurred between the U.S. and the Soviet Union because of the Soviets' failure to live up to the promises they made at the Yalta Conference in regard to Poland, Eastern Europe, and joining the U.S. in fighting the war in the Pacific. (See Chapter 18 for more details about what went down at Yalta.) Besides, Truman knew the only thing that America had in common with the Soviet Union was the desire to defeat Germany and, with that point accomplished, they were quickly becoming enemies.

Truman's reconversion policy

World War II ended a little more quickly than expected, thanks to the atomic bomb. This shortened timeframe put a squeeze on economic planners trying to prepare the American economy for a transition from war to peace. This process was called *reconversion,* and it involved easing government controls that had been put in place during the war.

Immediate problems surfaced following the war, with unemployment being the biggest. Within a month after victory in Japan in August 1945, more than a million Americans were out of a job and hundreds of thousands filed for unemployment. Veterans returning home sought industrial jobs that mainly women and minorities had held during the war. Although some women voluntarily left the work force to return to their domestic lives, as many as 80 percent of women wanted to continue working. Nearly all of the African American and Hispanic males who had entered the industrial work force during the war wanted to continue working, too.

As part of the effort to make reconversion a smooth process, the federal government intervened. In June 1944, Congress and Roosevelt approved the Servicemen's Readjustment Act of 1944, better known as the *GI Bill of Rights.* The GI Bill provided federal aid to war veterans to help them readjust to civilian life and, as a result, expanded the economy and increased consumer spending. The GI Bill provided veterans with free college or trade school tuition and subsidized living expenses while they attended school. The bill also established veterans hospitals, offered job training, and provided low-interest mortgages to war veterans. To help spur the economy and encourage consumer spending, Congress passed a $6 billion tax cut in 1945. In early 1946, Truman established the Office of Economic Stabilization to facilitate the conversion to a peacetime economy.

Truman also asked Congress to extend unemployment compensation, to guarantee full employment, to increase the minimum wage, and to adopt permanent farm price supports and new public works projects. Congress didn't approve Truman's original proposal, but responded with the *Employment Act (1946),* which stated that the U.S. government would use its resources to achieve "maximum employment, production, and purchasing power." One thing to note here, in the spirit of the New Deal, Truman wanted Congress to approve the bill that guaranteed full employment for every American, so that every American who wanted work would be guaranteed a job to achieve zero percent unemployment. Congress changed this to "maximum employment," which stipulated that some unemployment was acceptable and that up to 6 percent unemployment would be considered normal.

With those goals accomplished, Truman still had to deal with inflation and striking workers. Americans had saved more than $140 billion in personal earnings during the war and were ready to spend their money. Most Americans had been scrimping, saving, and living frugally for more than 16 years during the Depression and the war, and they wanted to spend, spend, spend. This desire to spend led to a huge demand for consumer goods, which were scarce because of wartime production restrictions, and drove prices up. In the two years following the war, inflation hovered at around 14 to 15 percent. In the summer of 1946, inflation reached a high of 25 percent during one month when Truman vetoed a bill that would extend the authority of a wartime department, the Office of Price Administration, to continue to set price controls on consumer goods. When inflation reached 25 percent later that month, Truman gave in and signed a bill allowing price controls to continue.

Adding to Truman's headache were workers who were striking all over the country for the usual reasons, including labor unrest, a desire for higher wages (to compensate for high inflation), shorter hours, and better benefits. In 1945 and 1946, major strikes took place in the steel, automobile, and electrical industries. A major coal strike of the United Mine Workers also shut down the coal fields for 40 days, which led to widespread panic because much of the country still relied on coal power for heating and electrical power. During the strikes in 1946, 4.5 million workers walked out. Even though the American economy fared far better than it had following World War I, Americans were angered at the inconvenience of the postwar economy and blamed Truman.

The Republican-controlled Congress didn't score any points in 1947 with the passage of the Labor-Management Relations Act of 1947, better known as the *Taft–Hartley Act.* Truman vetoed the Taft–Hartley Act when it came across his desk, but the conservatives in Congress over-rode his veto and passed it anyway. The act was predominately an attack on the 1935 Wagner Act, which had provided increased federal protection and granted many powers to organized labor during the New Deal. The Taft–Hartley Act

✔ **Made closed shops illegal:** A *closed shop* is a workplace where, in order to get hired, one had to be a member of the union first.

✔ **Allowed the continued creation of union shops:** *Union shops* required employees to join the union as soon as they were hired. The Taft–Hartley Act allowed union shops but gave states the right to prohibit them by passing "right-to-work" laws. To the labor movement, this part of the act was the most controversial section, and they fought it for decades.

✔ **Established a cooling-off period:** In cases where a work shutdown could lead to endangered national health or safety, the president could call for a ten-week cooling off period prior to a strike, during which the opposing sides would try to negotiate an agreement.

Union leaders weren't impressed by the passage of the Taft–Hartley Act. Many referred to it as the "slave labor bill" and worried that it may destroy the power of the labor movement, which had made great strides since the turn of the century. The act didn't destroy the labor movement, but it did have two notable effects: It damaged the weaker unions in industries that weren't heavily organized (such as the chemical and textile industries), and it hampered the organization of workers who hadn't previously been in unions, especially in industries in the West and South.

Truman did have two notable successes with the Republican Congress during his first administration. In 1946, Congress approved the *Atomic Energy Act,* which gave the government full control over all atomic research and production in the U.S. In 1947, Congress approved the *National Security Act,* which unified the armed forces, the Army, Navy, Air Force, and Marines under the new Department of Defense. It also created the *Central Intelligence Agency (CIA),* which was responsible for collecting information, openly and covertly, and whose role would increase throughout the Cold War.

A close call: The 1948 election

By the time the 1948 election rolled around, experts predicted that Truman would lose. Time magazine said that only a miracle or an exceptional Republican folly could save the Democratic Party. What happened ended up being a bit of both. Truman was unpopular with the public. Many Americans felt that his administration was weak and incompetent. However, when Republicans took control of Congress in 1946, they seemed hell-bent on out-doing Truman in that department. They refused to enact Truman's domestic policies, which were based on popular New Deal policies (see Chapter 17) and, in 1947, they enacted (over-riding Truman's veto) the extremely unpopular Taft–Hartley Act. Although Truman remained unpopular with many voters, he maintained the support of farmers, organized labor, middle-class workers, Catholics, Jews, and immigrants.

Truman's proposed civil rights legislation didn't win him any friends with southern conserva-tives (who were still Democrats at this time).They split and created their own *States Rights Party* (or Dixiecrat Party) with conservative and segregationist South Carolina Governor Strom Thurmond as their candidate. Things worsened for Truman when the left-wing side of the Democratic Party split and formed the *Progressive Party,* which nominated Henry A. Wallace, FDR's vice president from 1940 to 1944, as its candidate. Members of the Progressive Party were dissatisfied with the Truman administration's lack of success with enacting domes-tic policies and weren't comfortable with Truman's strong-armed attitude toward the Soviet Union. Despite these setbacks, Truman trudged on, determined to win the election. In the campaign, Truman blamed the Republican-controlled Congress, sometimes referred to as the "Do-Nothing Congress" for accomplishing little, enacting legislation that hurt the workers and common people, for refusing to enact Truman's proposed domestic legislation, and for promoting high inflation.

The Republican Party nominated New York Governor Thomas E. Dewey again (FDR's oppo-nent in the 1944 election) as their candidate. Confident, popular, and competent, Dewey seemed like he would win the election. Dewey's popularity gave the Republicans a false sense of confidence, and they didn't count on Truman's fighting spirit.

Truman embarked on a 30,000-mile "whistle stop" campaign around the country, making hun-dreds of speeches to gain support. But on election night, he was still considered the under-dog. With the returns showing a lead for Dewey, the *Chicago Daily Tribune* was so confident that Dewey would win that the staff ran the headline "Dewey Defeats Truman" and began printing it for the following day's paper. Hours later, when Truman took the lead, the paper realized it had made a mistake. When all the votes had been counted, Truman surprised everyone by pulling off the greatest presidential upset in history. In this election, the Democrats also regained control of both houses of Congress.

Building on the past: Instituting the Fair Deal

Riding on the success of his victory in the 1948 election, on January 5, 1949, Truman outlined an ambitious domestic agenda before Congress in his State of the Union address. Truman's domestic philosophy was directly influenced by his predecessor, Franklin Roosevelt, whose New Deal policies expanded the role of the federal government to include the management of the economy and welfare programs for American citizens (see Chapter 17). Through Truman's updated domestic policy for the postwar era, which became known as the *Fair Deal,* he wished to address many of the nation's most pressing social problems. The Fair Deal built upon the New Deal and included

- ✔ **Expanded social security:** Congress passed the Social Security Act Amendments of 1950, which increased social security benefits. The amendments extended social secu-rity coverage to ten million more American workers, including the self-employed, state and local government employees, and agricultural and domestic workers.

- ✔ **An increased minimum wage:** In 1949, Congress passed the Fair Labor Standards Act Amendments of 1949, which raised the federal minimum wage from 40 cents to 75 cents per hour.

> ✓ **A public housing program:** Congress passed the *Housing Act of 1949,* which provided federal funds to state and local governments for urban renewal. The act also provided federal funds for housing and mortgage assistance for low-income families to provide "a decent home and suitable living environment" for all Americans.

As part of the Fair Deal, Truman also proposed economic assistance for farmers in the form of subsidies, a national health insurance plan, tax cuts for the poor, federal education funding, and civil rights legislation. Truman had mixed success pushing his domestic agenda through Congress. Congress passed some laws, like increasing the minimum wage, extending social security benefits, and providing housing for the poor, but Congress shot down national health insurance and civil rights legislation. Had it not been for the foreign policy problems that dominated the second term of Truman's presidency, he may have been able to accomplish more on the domestic scene.

Red Scare: America Battles the Spread of Communism

Americans feared the spread of Communism the way that people today fear the spread of incurable diseases. After World War II, U.S. leaders and citizens saw Communism as a great threat to the American way of life and to democracy in general. In the postwar years, the Red Scare of the post-World War I period reemerged in America (for more information on Communism and the Red Scare, see Chapter 16).

The United States and the Soviet Union emerged from World War II as the dominant world powers and as bitter political rivals. As World War II drew to a close, The U.S. became increasingly suspicious of the Soviet Union and its aggressive territorial advances in Eastern Europe. Initially, Roosevelt (and later Truman) appeased the Soviet Union, thinking that Stalin would cease his territorial advances and cooperate with the Allies — he didn't. By the end of 1945, it was apparent that the Soviet Union would not work with the U.S. and its allies to construct a modern world according to the ideals of the 1941 Atlantic Charter. The U.S. would have to take a different approach to contain Stalin's spread of Communism.

On the other hand, Stalin didn't ever want a repeat of Germany's invasions during the previous world wars. His country had been ravaged by wars and revolutions since 1914. In order to protect the Soviet Union, Stalin set up a buffer zone of nations between Western Europe and the Soviet Union. His army established pro-Soviet governments in Bulgaria, Hungary, Poland, and Romania and strengthened the existing ones in Albania and Yugoslavia. In essence, Stalin established what Churchill referred to as an *"Iron Curtain"* to separate Eastern Europe and the Soviet Union from the West.

With the two world superpowers pitted against one another ideologically, the *Cold War* was on. For the U.S. government, fighting the Cold War meant stopping the spread of Communist influence at home and abroad. Americans used a variety of methods, not all of them honorable or effective, to stop the threat of Communism. With the proliferation of nuclear weapons, armed conflict was a last resort, so Americans used sneakier, dirtier tactics, and the Soviets did the same.

The SAT II question possibilities on foreign matters and Communism during the Truman era are vast. The exam may ask you about events in the following sections, such as the Truman Doctrine, the revolution in China, or even the Berlin Airlift, so be prepared.

A few test cases: Iran, Greece, and Turkey

Conflicts between the U.S. and the Soviet Union over Iran, Greece, and Turkey initiated the Cold War. The first real instance of butting heads between the U.S. and the Soviet Union developed over the situation in Iran following the war. Great Britain and the Soviet Union had occupied Iran during the war to prevent Iran's vast oil reserves from falling into German hands. After the war, both countries agreed to withdraw by March 1946. But when that time rolled around, Soviet troops still occupied northern Iran and were supplying military aid to pro-Communist rebels there. American officials saw this continued occupation as a move to seize control of northern Iran. The Soviets countered that American and British oil interests in Iran gave them political control over the southern half of the country. The newly-formed United Nations investigated the Soviet action in Iran (which ticked off Soviet leaders), and ordered the Soviet Union to cease occupation. The Soviets refused, but after continued pressure from the United Nations Security Council, the Soviets withdrew six weeks later.

Around the time that the whole Iran business was being settled, political problems emerged in Greece and Turkey. Following World War II, Stalin decided that the Soviet Union needed Turkey to get access to vital sea lanes, and he began to put pressure on the Turks. Greece faced a different problem: Communist political forces in Greece threatened the pro-Western government in power. Britain, which maintained political and economic influence on both Greece and Turkey, was hampered by its own economic problems and couldn't continue to aid Greece and Turkey in their efforts to stave off the Communists. As a result, Britain appealed to the U.S. to take over its influence in the two countries.

Truman responded to Britain's request by asking Congress to grant $400 million in aid to Greece and Turkey to reinforce the armies of both countries and to provide economic assistance to Greece. With the U.S. aid, Turkey overcame Soviet pressures, and the Greek government defeated the Communist uprising. Truman stated in a speech before Congress that "It must be the policy of the U.S. to support free peoples who are resisting attempted subjugation by armed minorities or by outside pressures." This speech became the backbone of Truman's foreign policy, known as the *Truman Doctrine,* which established the basis of American foreign policy for the next 30 years. The U.S. accepted the Soviet Union's establishment of Communist governments in Eastern Europe but insisted that the Soviet's sphere of Communism be contained within its current boundaries.

Being firm: The U.S. containment policy and the Marshall Plan

In 1947, George Kennan, the influential American diplomat, wrote in favor of a "policy of firm containment, designed to confront the Russians with unalterable counterforce at every point where they show signs of encroaching upon the interests of a peaceful and stable world." Basically, this policy of *containment* meant that whenever or wherever Communism threatened to spread, the United States would be there to prevent it. Containment also meant that relations between Americans and Soviets would continue to deteriorate along an ideological fault line. The policy of containment along with the Truman Doctrine shaped American foreign policy throughout the Cold War.

Containment heavily involved the U.S. in European affairs. Post-World War II Europe was a train wreck, and U.S. leaders worried that Communism would creep in. After the war, the countries of Western Europe lacked the funding needed to adequately feed their citizens, let alone rebuild their war-ravished cities. Pro-Communist parties began gaining influence in many Western European countries. In order to help the Europeans get back on their feet, to prevent Western Europe from becoming an economic drain on the U.S., and to create a market for American consumer goods, the U.S. had to step in and help. In 1947, Secretary of State George C. Marshall announced the European Recovery Program, which became known as the *Marshall Plan*. The Marshall Plan provided more than $12 billion in aid to European countries in the form of food, fuel, and the rebuilding of industry between 1947 and 1951. Sixteen Western European countries participated in the program. The idea was simple enough: A strong, healthy Europe would be better able to ward off the advance of Communism, and the plan was also an investment to strengthen trade.

A question on the purpose or goal of the Marshall Plan is a good candidate for the SAT II U.S. History exam. Try out your newfound knowledge on this example.

One purpose of America's 1947 Marshall Plan was to

(A) Topple Latin American dictatorships.

(B) Give military aid to guerillas fighting Communists.

(C) Help European countries regain economic stability.

(D) Support the growth of democracy in Asia.

(E) Rebuild Japan after the bombing of Hiroshima and Nagasaki.

You should be able to toss out (A), (D), and (E), if you can remember that the Marshall Plan had to do with Europe. Now you're left with choices (B) and (C). The Marshall Plan had to do with giving economic aid, so you can eliminate answer (B), which leaves you with the correct choice, (C). When you think of the Marshall Plan, remember the two *Es:* Europe and economic aid; it can go a long way toward making the correct choice on a question like this.

Here's a pneumonic device to help you remember the Marshall Plan (as long as you're a fan of Westerns). Beware, it's a little corny. Think of the Gunfight at the O.K. Corral. The European Recovery Program, ERP, with George Marshall becomes Marshall ERP! . . . er, ah, Earp (as in Wyatt Earp?). I warned you it was corny, but it just might work for you!

Drawing the iron curtain: The Soviets in Czechoslovakia and Germany

The Soviet army had overrun most of Eastern Europe by 1944 on its way to Germany. Following the war, Soviets retained control of most of Eastern Europe because Stalin felt he needed a buffer zone to block Western influence from entering the Soviet Union and prevent the Soviet Union from being invaded again. The U.S. and Britain allowed Soviet control because Stalin promised at the Yalta Conference to hold free elections in the countries that his nation occupied, but those elections never happened. In 1945, the Soviet Union denied free elections in Poland, which directly violated the agreements at Yalta, and had set up Communist puppet governments in Romania, Bulgaria, and Hungary by 1947.

But in Czechoslovakia, it wasn't Soviet politics as usual, at least initially. The Soviets allowed free elections, and Czechoslovakia appeared as if it would become a democracy, but the Marshall Plan changed things. Czechoslovakia showed interest in receiving American aid, which the Soviet Union saw as a challenge to its authority in the region. The Soviets backed Communist rebels, who overthrew the newly elected Czechoslovakian government in a sudden coup in February 1948. The Czechoslovakian government was the last Eastern European government to fall to Communism. The fall of Czechoslovakia influenced Congress to approve the creation of the Economic Cooperation Administration, the agency that would administer the Marshall Plan. Rapid economic recovery in Europe over the next four years successfully aided the U.S. containment policy.

In 1948, an O.K. Corral-type showdown (in the spirit of Marshall ERP) occurred between the U.S. and the Soviet Union over Berlin, Germany. The Allies had divided postwar Germany and its city of Berlin into four zones of occupation; France, Britain, the United States, and the Soviet Union each controlled one zone of the country and the city, even though the city of Berlin was deep in the Soviet zone. In spring 1948, Truman decided that the recovery of Germany was essential to the recovery of Western Europe and proposed to Britain and France that the three countries merge their zones of occupation in Germany and Berlin into a new West German republic. Stalin didn't like this idea and felt threatened. He immediately cut off Western access to Berlin, hoping to force the U.S. and its allies to give up the city permanently. Stalin was playing a dangerous game that could've turned the Cold War into a hot one, but Truman decided to respond to the crisis by ignoring the blockade. British and American cargo planes, heavily laden with food and supplies, began making round-the-clock deliveries to Berlin, which became known as the *Berlin Airlift.* This aid continued until May 1949, when Stalin finally lifted the blockade, realizing that he couldn't win. In October 1949, Germany officially became two countries: the Federal Republic of Germany (West Germany) and the Democratic Republic of Germany (East Germany). Berlin was also divided into East Berlin and West Berlin. These divisions were maintained for the next 40 years.

All for one: The creation of NATO

A month before the Soviet Union lifted the Berlin Blockade in 1949, America and 11 friendly nations founded the *North Atlantic Treaty Organization (NATO),* a military alliance. In effect, an alliance already existed between the U.S. and the nations of Western Europe, but the Berlin crisis united the alliance and NATO formalized it. With the Marshall Plan, the U.S. hoped to protect Europe through an economic alliance; with NATO, the U.S. hoped to combat Communism through the might of a military alliance. The NATO countries agreed that an attack against one NATO member would be considered an attack against all members. Furthermore, NATO maintained a standing army in Europe to defend against the threat of a possible Soviet invasion. In response, the Soviet Union formed its own military alliance with the countries of Eastern Europe called the *Warsaw Pact* in 1955.

Revolution in China and recovery in Japan

Western Europe wasn't the only battleground for Communism and democracy in the late 1940s. Communist forces led by Mao Tse-tung fought U.S.-backed nationalist forces in China led by Chiang Kai-shek, but as Truman would later admit, "We picked a bad horse." Chiang's government was corrupt and inept; starvation and inflation ran unchecked; and Chiang's goons silenced any dissenters. From 1945 to 1949, the American government gave Chiang $3 billion in aid, but he misspent the money and refused American military advice. Although Truman was willing to fund Chiang, he wasn't willing to send American troops to China to help out. Mao, who by 1945 had control of 25 percent of the population, defeated Chiang in 1949 and set up the People's Republic of China. Chiang and his Nationalists were forced to flee to the island of Taiwan, just off the coast of China. Americans were shocked because with China's conversion to Communism, 40 percent of the world's population and 20 percent of its land mass were now under Communist control. The U.S. refused to recognize the Communist Chinese government until the early 1970s when President Richard Nixon traveled to China and finally opened formal diplomatic relations (see Chapter 21).

With China's fall to Communism, the U.S. decided to change its policy with Japan. Since the end of the war, Japan had been under U.S. occupation. In the years of occupation, the Japanese changed their government to a pacifist constitutional monarchy and tried to recover from the devastating war. Fearing that a weak Japan could also succumb to Communism, the federal government decided that Japan would become a pro-Western, pro-American force in

Asia. In the early 1950s, the United States encouraged economic growth and lifted restrictions on industrial development. It worked; the Japanese economy boomed and, by the end of 1952, the Japanese were experiencing pre-war standards of living.

On the inside: Communism in America

Americans saw the growing Communist threat around the world and then turned their sights inward. Communist factions had existed in America since the end of World War I but had never attracted many followers. Even still, the American public was increasingly fearful of Communist infiltration.

In the late 1930s, the federal government responded to a Communist threat by setting up an investigating committee called the *House Un-American Activities Committee (HUAC),* which was responsible for hunting down Communist conspirators in American society (and German American involvement in KKK or Nazi activities). In 1947, HUAC focused its attention on Hollywood, which resulted in the blacklisting (banning) of a number of writers and filmmakers. Truman also got in on the action by ordering government employees to undergo "loyalty" reviews to root out Communist sympathizers in government jobs. When all was said and done, 490 government workers lost their jobs, hundreds more were forced to resign or otherwise pressured to quit, and thousands had their lives and careers ruined. Congress also passed laws like the McCarran Internal Security Act in 1950, which required all Communist organizations and their members to register with the attorney general and banned them from defense-related industries.

While this shotgun approach to hunting Communists wasn't very effective in catching many real Communists, the U.S. government did strike gold a couple of times, such as in the Alger Hiss case. The focus on Communism in America also led to the power wielded by a senator named Joseph McCarthy.

The Alger Hiss case

A conservative *Time* magazine editor named Whittaker Chambers testified before Congress in 1948 that he had been part of a Communist spy ring in the late 1930s but, more importantly, he claimed that *Alger Hiss,* a former high-ranking member of the State Department in the 1930s, had also been part of the Communist spy ring. Chambers claimed that Hiss had stolen State Department documents in 1937 and 1938. Hiss dismissed the charges, but when Chambers presented irrefutable evidence (Chambers produced microfilm with State Department documents typed by Hiss's typewriter), Hiss was all but convicted in the eyes of Americans. The U.S. government couldn't charge Hiss with espionage because too much time had lapsed since the crime, but the government nailed him on perjury and sentenced him to five years in jail in January 1950. If it weren't for the relentless efforts of HUAC committee member and the freshman Republican congressman by the name of Richard Nixon (see Chapter 21) Hiss may have walked free. The hoopla surrounding the Hiss case confirmed the fears of Americans who believed that Communist spies were all around them, working in the shadows to overthrow the American government.

The rise and fall of McCarthyism

An obscure Wisconsin senator named Joseph McCarthy rose to fame (and later infamy) on the coattails of Communist conspiracy. In 1950, he announced in a speech that the State Department was "thoroughly infested with Communists" and claimed to have a list of 205 of them. McCarthy was brash and reckless, firing accusations and innuendos of Communist involvement at prominent members of society, political rivals, and organizations. For a while, people believed him, and McCarthy wielded a lot of political power.

Americans coined the term *McCarthyism* to describe his reckless style of making damning charges without having any evidence or justification and shifting attention elsewhere when those charges proved false. Americans bought what McCarthy was selling because he played on their fears, but people grew tired of his shenanigans. Eisenhower got fed up with McCarthy when McCarthy went after the Army. When the Army-McCarthy Hearings were televised, McCarthy didn't make a positive impression on the American public, who saw him as a fraud and a bully. In December 1954, McCarthy's fellow senators censured him for "conduct unbecoming a member." McCarthy died three years later in a fog of obscurity and alcoholism.

A New Conflict: The Korean War

The Cold War wasn't always chilly. In some instances, like the Korean War, things got pretty heated. When Communist North Korea invaded South Korea in 1950, U.S. leaders believed that the Soviets were making a move on pro-U.S. territory. The Soviets had less to do with the war than their Red (meaning Communist) neighbor China. The Korean War was typical of armed conflict throughout the Cold War. Rather than superpowers duking it out head-to-head, they fought each other through armed conflict in countries like China, Korea, and Vietnam (see Chapter 21).

Entering the war

At the close of World War II, Korea split into two parts along the 38th parallel. The Soviet Union would control the northern half, and the U.S. would control the southern half.

This division was a recipe for war. U.S. troops pulled out of South Korea in June 1949, leaving behind a pro-Western government and a modest South Korean army. In North Korea, the Soviets set up a Communist government with a far superior and well-supplied army. Both North and South Korea wanted to reunify, but the two countries had competing governments with competing ideologies. The 38th parallel was a line begging to be crossed, and on June 24, 1950, North Korean forces mounted a surprise attack on South Korean forces. Though seemingly inconsequential, the U.S. saw the Communist takeover of South Korea as a threat to world stability and decided to put its containment policy to work.

On June 27, 1950, Truman ordered American troops to South Korea and appealed to the UN to intervene in the situation in Korea. The UN passed a resolution condemning the actions of North Korea and requested UN member nations to take action against North Korea. Soviet representatives, who were boycotting the UN because the UN Security Council refused to recognize the new Communist government of China, weren't present at the time of the decision, allowing the American delegates to win the UN decision. General Douglas MacArthur commanded the American-led UN forces (the U.S. had committed 1.8 million troops to the war by July). By September 1950, North Korean forces had pushed American troops to the southern tip of the Korean peninsula, but when MacArthur pulled off a daring amphibious assault (a surprise invasion by water) at Inchon behind enemy lines, the tides began to change. By November, MacArthur had driven the North Koreans out of the south to the edge of the Chinese border. This effort angered the Chinese, who hated the idea of having hostile military forces so close to its border. As a result, China entered the war with overwhelming force, pushing MacArthur's forces back to the 38th parallel by the end of December 1950. The Soviet Union wasn't actively involved in the conflict but supplied the Chinese and North Korean troops with military combat advisors, aircraft pilots, and arms.

MacArthur began to argue in favor of invading China, but Truman refused. Truman didn't like that MacArthur was trying to bully him, and he thought going to war with China would be too risky. Truman preferred diplomatic negotiations with China over an invasion and felt that MacArthur was insubordinate and fired him over the matter in April 1951.

Talks to negotiate an end to the Korean War began between the opposing sides in July 1951. For two years, a stalemate existed until July 1953, when commanders from the North Korea, China, and the American-led UN forces signed an armistice (or cease-fire) agreement that restored the 38th parallel as the boundary between the North Korea and South Korea. As of this writing, North Korea and South Korea had not yet signed a peace treaty.

The Korean War is often referred to as a *limited war,* which is a war in which two superpowers fight against each other without involving all-out war or using nuclear weapons. The Korean War was the first armed conflict of the Cold War between the U.S. and the Soviet Union and the first conflict between the U.S. and the Soviets that didn't concern Europe.

Examining the consequences

All told, American forces suffered 54,000 deaths and 103,000 wounded. But the total loss was more devastating. The military and civilian casualties from Korea, China, the U.S., and the UN forces are thought to exceed 2.5 million people. The price tag for the war was $50 billion, and the U.S. had no clear victory. America didn't lose the war in Korea (they did drive the North Korean forces out of South Korea and restore the 38th parallel boundary), but America didn't exactly win, either. Truman wanted to eliminate Communism from the Korean peninsula entirely, and he had a stronger military with more advanced weaponry to do it with, yet American forces didn't decisively defeat the North Koreans. Why, you ask?

One reason was because Americans weren't used to fighting a limited war with limited goals and limited success. When MacArthur suggested taking the war to China, many applauded the idea and immediately were suspicious when Truman rejected the idea. Truman's popularity was at an all-time low, and he chose not to seek reelection in 1952, but his foreign policy carried on. Truman argued, "We are fighting in Korea, so we don't have to fight in Wichita or in Chicago or in New Orleans or on San Francisco Bay." The main impact of the Korean War was that it announced to the world that the U.S. was ready, willing, and able to fight against the spread of Communism, wherever it may occur.

Tying it all together: A sample question looks at the Korean War

The SAT II may test your knowledge of the Korean War by asking you about the political philosophy that motivated the U.S. to get involved. For instance, try the following question.

American involvement in the Korean War is an example of which of the following?

(A) Monroe Doctrine

(B) Dollar Diplomacy

(C) Containment

(D) Imperialism

(E) Atomic Diplomacy

Answer (A) has to do with Latin America (see Chapter 6), so you can cross off that choice right away, and answer (B) has to do with the spread of American influence through economic means (see Chapter 13), so you can eliminate that answer, too. Truman specifically avoided the use of atomic weapons during the Korean War, so (E) isn't the right answer. Now you're left with (C) and (D).

While you could certainly classify American actions in Korea as imperialism, answer (C) is more specific and a better choice than (D) because containment refers specifically to halting the spread of Communism to non-Communist countries.

Liking Ike: The Eisenhower Presidency

Truman's successor, Republican Dwight D. Eisenhower, was president at a time of remarkable domestic prosperity and pushed through a lot of his domestic agenda because of his moderate style. But despite the calm waters, sharks were swimming just beneath the surface. Paranoia about Communism abounded in the United States as the nation continued to combat the spread of Soviet influence abroad. Meanwhile, African Americans began to hold sit-ins, boycotts, and demonstrations in an effort to gain civil rights.

In moderation: Eisenhower's political style

Eisenhower's 1952 campaign slogan wasn't the typical slam on the opposition; instead, it had the simple phrase, "I Like Ike," which went a long way toward explaining his landslide victory. "Ike," as the American public affectionately called Eisenhower, was one of the most popular presidents in U.S. history. He earned higher approval ratings than any other 20th-century president. The armistice in Korea within seven months after he entered office definitely didn't hurt his reputation, either.

Historians have described Ike as having a winning smile and a warm, down-to-earth personality. Ike was a hero of World War II who Americans described as honest, decent, and humble. The 1950s were known as "happy days," and Americans associated Eisenhower's presidency, which lasted from 1953 through 1960, with the good times. Eisenhower was a moderate who disliked big government but also felt that government was responsible for taking care of its citizens. He worked with both Democrats and Republicans, pursuing and endorsing policies from both sides. He was a strong leader who preferred working behind closed doors and often relied on the advice of his cabinet to make decisions.

Eisenhower took a middle-of-the-road approach to politics. Ike once said that when it came to money, he was a Republican, but when it came to human beings, he was a Democrat, (what historians like to refer to as a *modern republican*). Because Ike was a Republican, Americans expected him to unravel the massive social policies that had accumulated from 20 years of Democratic presidential leadership. He eliminated some of these policies, but he left the New Deal and Fair Deal policies of Franklin Roosevelt and Harry S Truman in place. In fact, he even added to them with some progressive social policies of his own. On the other hand, he appointed rich businessmen, who pursued conservative economic policies that benefited American businesses, to his cabinet.

Eisenhower's domestic policy

Because of Ike's moderate political stance, he was able to push much of his domestic agenda through Congress, despite the fact that Democrats controlled both houses for six of the eight years that he was president.

Remember the following key points about Ike's domestic policy for the SAT II:

- ✔ Throughout his administration, Ike pursued conservative economic goals, including a balanced budget, reduced government spending, lower taxes, and lower inflation rates. He encouraged private enterprise, returned power to states, and limited federal controls of the economy.

- ✔ In 1954, Eisenhower approved an amendment to social security that raised benefits and granted coverage to 1.7 million additional workers.

- ✔ Eisenhower approved massive public works projects. The first project was the St. Lawrence Seaway Project (1954), which built a canal that connected the Great Lakes to the Atlantic Ocean with the hope of spurring economic growth in the Midwest. In 1956, Eisenhower launched the National Interstate and Defense Highways Act of 1956, the largest public works project in U.S. history. The Highway Act authorized $31 billion to be spent over 13 years to build a 41,000-mile interstate highway system. Congress approved the highway system so readily because Eisenhower promoted it as necessary in the event of a Communist attack. The highway system was designed so that in the event of a nuclear attack, mass evacuation from cities would be possible and so that one in every five miles was perfectly straight so planes could use it as an airstrip in a time of war or national emergency. But to most Americans, it was just an easier way to get around. (The next time you're driving on an interstate highway, you can thank Ike.)

- ✔ Eisenhower signed civil rights legislation into law in 1957 and 1960 (which we cover in the next section), but he sympathized with southern whites and favored a gradual civil rights process. He disagreed with the Supreme Court decision to desegregate public schools, and many historians claim that this stance was one of the major faults of his presidency.

The emergence of the civil rights movement

In August 1955, a 14-year-old boy named Emmett Till was kidnapped from his uncle's home in Mississippi. Days later, his body was found floating in a river. Allegedly, Till whistled at a white woman in a grocery store, and the woman's husband and his half-brother decided to make an example of him by beating him and then shooting him in the head. The two men were put on trial for the boy's murder, but an all-white jury acquitted them after deliberating a little over an hour and despite significant evidence that they were guilty. (A year later, the two men boasted about how they killed Emmett to a national news magazine).

Tragic injustices like this brutal event fueled the growing civil rights movement in the 1950s. African American leaders spoke out against such injustices like brutal attacks on African American, segregation, and Jim Crow laws (see Chapter 10). Young African Americans took up a call to action, employing tactics of *civil disobedience,* such as protests and sit-ins. Politicians took notice of the growing number of disenchanted African Americans voters, and media attention — accelerated by television coverage — made white America aware of African Americans' plight. Segregation was on its way out, and changes began with the public school system in 1954.

Brown v. Board of Education (1954)

The *Brown v. Board of Education* case was the result of decades of legal action against segregation in the public schools. In 1950, the **National Association for the Advancement of Colored People (NAACP),** recruited African American families in Topeka, Kansas, to take part in a class-action lawsuit against the Topeka school board. African American children in Topeka were allowed to attend only schools designated for African Americans, even though these schools were often far from the children's homes. The Brown family was one of the families that the segregation affected. Thurgood Marshall, who would later become a Supreme Court Justice, was one of the attorneys for the plaintiffs. When the case reached the Supreme Court in 1952, the Court combined five different cases from Kansas, South Carolina, Washington, D.C., Virginia, and Delaware, under the heading of *Brown v. Board of Education of Topeka.*

On May 17, 1954, the Supreme Court, led by Chief Justice Earl Warren, unanimously ruled that the segregation of blacks and whites in public schools was unconstitutional because it violated the 14th Amendment, which guaranteed all citizens "equal protection under the laws." Furthermore, the Court ruled that separate educational facilities were inherently unequal, striking down the 1896 *Plessy v. Ferguson* decision that made "separate but equal" laws legal. To make sure that the Court's decision was enforced, in 1955, the Supreme Court, in a case known as *Brown II,* provided that the desegregation of public schools should be carried out "with all deliberate speed" but didn't set specific guidelines for a desegregation timeline. Some school districts, such as those in Washington, D.C., complied quickly, whereas others (especially in the deep South) ignored the Supreme Court's ruling. Throughout the South, many schools eventually complied with the decision, but others used the Court's phrasing to delay desegregation as long as possible.

Because civil rights is an important issue generally and for the purposes of the SAT II, you're likely to see at least one question about important civil rights events. For more about the civil rights movement, see Chapter 20.

The 1954 Supreme Court decision in *Brown v. Board of Education* did which of the following?

(A) Set up a timetable for desegregation of public schools

(B) Declared that segregation of public schools was unconstitutional

(C) Upheld the *Plessy v. Ferguson* decision

(D) Declared poll taxes and literacy tests illegal

(E) Ruled that separate but equal laws were constitutional

You can eliminate (D) because it has to do with voting, and you should be looking for something that has to do with education. *Plessy v. Ferguson* was the 1896 Supreme Court case that ruled that segregation was legal if a separate but equal accommodation was provided; this decision was the legal justification for segregation for the next 58 years. If you know that the Court decided in favor of desegregation, you can rule out (C) and (E), leaving answers (A) and (B). Answer (A) is incorrect for two reasons. The Court mandated desegregation in the 1955 *Brown II* case (rather than the 1954 case), and it didn't set up a timetable for implementing desegregation. The correct answer is (B).

Rosa Parks and the Montgomery Bus Boycott

Inspired by the success of *Brown v. Board of Education of Topeka,* civil rights advocates began to challenge segregation in the South. On December 1, 1955, an African American woman named Rosa Parks was arrested in Montgomery, Alabama, for refusing to give up her seat and move to the back of a bus when a white passenger boarded. The law that required her to move to the back of the bus was one of the Jim Crow laws that still ruled much of the deep South in the 1950s.

Parks was an active and widely admired civil rights leader in Montgomery, and her arrest inspired the African American community to quickly mobilize and organize a boycott of the city's buses in an effort to demand the end of segregation on public transportation. For nearly a year, Montgomery African Americans (and some whites, too) boycotted the city buses, which was economically damaging to the bus company and the downtown merchants that the buses serviced. In late 1956, the Supreme Court ruled that segregation on public transportation was unconstitutional. The Court's ruling forced the Montgomery buses to end segregated seating, and the boycott ended.

The Civil Rights Act of 1957

Eisenhower signed the *Civil Rights Act of 1957* into law in September, making it the first piece of civil rights legislation passed since the Reconstruction Era (see Chapter 10). In theory, the Civil Rights Act of 1957 provided the federal government with the authority to investigate and prosecute cases of *disenfranchisement* (denial of the right to vote). Southern states regularly used tactics, such as literacy tests and poll taxes, set up under those ages-old Jim Crow laws to prevent African Americans from voting. The problem was that the law was a dud because it required a jury trial to determine whether a citizen had been disenfranchised. But, in the South, African Americans weren't allowed to serve on juries. This fact almost assured that no one would ever be convicted of denying an African American's voting rights. Nevertheless, the law was a symbol of hope that things could change in the South. Congress passed the law with a 72 to 14 vote, thanks to the efforts of Senate Majority Leader Lyndon B. Johnson, who became president six years later. (See Chapter 20).

In 1960, Eisenhower followed up with the *Civil Rights Act of 1960* in response to an outbreak of bombings against schools and churches in the South in 1958. The 1960 act went further than the 1957 act did to bring about social changes, but it still fell short. The 1960 act provided that anyone who prevented someone from registering to vote or actually voting would be fined. Furthermore, the act set up a permanent *Civil Rights Commission* within the Justice Department to protect African Americans' voting rights in southern states.

The Central High School crisis in Little Rock

A violent uproar in Little Rock, Arkansas, occurred in September 1957 when a federal court ordered the desegregation of Central High School. Nine African American students, known as "The Little Rock Nine," were the first admitted to the school, but Arkansas Governor Orval Faubus sent in the National Guard to block their entrance. Some white students taunted, yelled, and spat at the new nine students, and angry mobs of white Southerners rioted in the streets. Television cameras from all over the country covered the events in Little Rock and Americans across the nation viewed the events and were shocked at what they saw. The Little Rock Nine couldn't attend classes for weeks. The one day they managed to get into the school, the entire city fell into chaos, and the nine students were quickly evacuated. With the city of Little Rock essentially under siege, Eisenhower, who initially tried to stay out of the whole mess, ordered 1,100 federal paratroopers to land in Little Rock to maintain order and to protect the students. Ike also ordered National Guard troops to escort the students to school. Faubus and many others in the South resented the federal government's intrusion into what they thought was a states' rights issue.

Deep freeze: The Cold War continues

Despite the end of the conflict in Korea, the Cold War continued. It dominated many of America's domestic issues and foreign policies throughout the 1950s.

The Cold War at home

Around the same time that Eisenhower took office, Senator Joseph McCarthy was at the peak of his career, with his Communist conspiracy rants the subject of newspaper headlines across the country. Eisenhower didn't like McCarthy, who began attacking his political appointments, but he refused to confront McCarthy publicly, which historians view as one of the mistakes of his presidency. (For more about McCarthy, see "The rise and fall of McCarthyism" earlier in this chapter.)

Despite the fact that Eisenhower gave McCarthy an open hand to pursue his destructive anti-Communist inquiries, he was far from being a softy on Communism. Eisenhower expanded Truman's loyalty program and purged the State Department of employees who were suspected of Communist sympathies. In 1953, he denied Julius and Ethel Rosenberg clemency (the Rosenbergs were convicted in a plot to smuggle atomic secrets to the Soviet Union), and they were sentenced to death. He also signed the *Communist Control Act of 1954* into law, which effectively made being a member of the Communist Party illegal.

The Cold War abroad

Americans still worried about Communism around the world. In March 1953, Soviet dictator Joseph Stalin died. His successor, Nikita Khrushchev, denounced Stalin and his policies and sought "peaceful coexistence" between the Soviet Union and the U.S. Tensions lessened somewhat between the Cold War giants, but several notable conflicts occurred that ensured the continuation of the Cold War.

✓ **Coups in Iran and Guatemala:** Eisenhower authorized the Central Intelligence Agency (CIA) to carry out covert operations in foreign countries to overthrow unfriendly (Communist) governments or to protect governments that were friendly to the U.S. The CIA carried out coups in Iran (where the new Nationalist government wanted to end U.S. and British influence in Iran, which the U.S. feared would open up Iran to more Soviet influence) in 1953 and Guatemala in 1954 (which was under the control of a potentially Communist government).

✓ **The French in Indochina:** The Eisenhower administration held to the Domino Theory (that if one county fell to Communism, others around it would too; see Chapter 20 for more about this theory). So, to curb the spread of Communism in Southeast Asia, the U.S. supported the French against pro-Communist forces led by Ho Chi Minh in Indochina (made up of Cambodia, Laos, and Vietnam). By 1954, Eisenhower's administration had committed the federal government to supporting France in fighting in Indochina, paying 75 percent of the war's expenses. When France finally pulled out, the U.S. set up a non-Communist government in South Vietnam and supplied it with financial aid and military advisors. American involvement in Vietnam would lead to a costly war in the 1960s, which you can read about in Chapter 21.

✓ **Hungarian unrest:** In 1956, university students and laborers in Budapest, Hungary, began a movement to rid Hungary of Soviet domination. Hungarian officials promised free elections and denounced the Warsaw Pact (see the section "All for one: The creation of NATO" earlier in this chapter). Soviets sent in 16 army divisions and 2,000 tanks, quickly crushing the rebellion. Eisenhower didn't involve the U.S. in the conflict because he feared the risk of nuclear war was too great.

✓ **The U-2 crisis:** In 1960, a few days before an East-West summit meeting between Eisenhower and Soviet Premier Kruschev, the Soviets shot down a U-2 (a high-altitude spy plane) flying over Russian territory and took the American pilot prisoner. At first, Eisenhower denied Kruschev's accusation that the plane had been spying on the Soviet Union, but Kruschev provided proof, and Eisenhower had to admit that the plane had deliberately violated Soviet air space. Kruschev canceled the summit meeting and withdrew an invitation for Eisenhower to visit the Soviet Union. It was suspected that the Kremlin thought Kruschev was playing too nice with the U.S. and wanted him to take a harder line, and this incident gave Kruschev his opportunity.

One of the biggest sources of sleepless nights for world leaders following World War II and into Eisenhower's administration was the development and proliferation of nuclear weapons. The world witnessed the awesome and terrible power of the atomic bomb when the U.S. leveled Hiroshima and Nagasaki in 1945, but not much time passed before the Soviet Union had an atomic bomb of its own. The fear and mistrust these two countries had for each other led to a proliferation of military might that the world had never seen. This military buildup was known as the *arms race.*

Soviets and Americans competed to build bigger bombs and better ways to deliver them. In 1952, for example, the U.S. annihilated a small island in the Pacific with the first successful explosion of the hydrogen bomb (H-bomb), which packed a punch 750 times more destructive than the atomic bomb that had wiped out Hiroshima. The Soviets quickly followed with an H-bomb of their own and, following that accomplishment, they launched the first successful intercontinental missile. Of course, Americans said, "Oooh, I have to get me some of that!" And the competition continued.

While the U.S. and the Soviet Union stockpiled nuclear arms (enough to blow up the world several times over), a dangerous game of political and ideological warfare played out, and the rest of the world held its breath, fearing World War III and the very real possibility of the extinction of the human race. Each side believed that if it built a big enough arsenal, it would discourage the other from attacking. This strategy was known as *nuclear deterrence.*

The arms race broke new ground (or sky) when the Soviets launched Sputnik I, a little metal ball that beeped, into orbit in 1957. This event shocked Americans, who feared that their country was falling behind in the technology race. The U.S. government responded with the funding of a new agency called the *National Aeronautics and Space Administration* or probably known to you as NASA. And the *space race* (see Chapter 20) was on, but it didn't distract the Cold Warriors from inventing new and improved ways to blow up the world.

Life in the Burbs: American Culture in the 1950s

Ah, the fun-loving culture of the 1950s. The pop culture of the 1950s produced the TV shows *Leave it to Beaver* and *I Love Lucy;* rock legends Elvis Presley and Chuck Berry; movie stars James Dean and Marilyn Monroe; and an eclectic mix of entertainment icons, such as Ed Sullivan, *Catcher in the Rye, Playboy, Invasion of the Body Snatchers,* and Disneyland.

The list goes on and on, but unless you're studying for Trivial Pursuit, the details aren't necessary. Remembering that the 1950s were a time of pop culture explosion, with similar blasts in the growth of suburbs, the economy, and the birth rate, will help your SAT II score.

Exiting the cities: The move to the suburbs

One of the most significant changes in America was the rapid growth of the suburbs. In the 1950s, more than 13 million new homes were built, most in suburban developments. The reasons for migration to the suburbs were the wide ownership of automobiles and the nationwide push to build roads and highways. The average American was more mobile than ever and didn't need to live where he or she worked. As a result, middle-class families fled cities for the perceived utopia of the burbs, which symbolized safety, friendliness, and a sense of belonging (as long as you didn't stand out too much) to many.

Government programs, such as the Veterans Bureau and the Federal Home Loan Mortgage Administration, which offered low interest mortgages, aided the housing boom. Additionally, many middle-class Americans had a lot more money to spend because during the Eisenhower presidency, the average income increased 45 percent.

William J. Levitt was one of many developers to cash in on the housing demand. Levitt bought 1,500 acres of land on Long Island, where he built 17,000 houses using assembly-line construction techniques. This method brought building costs down, making homes more affordable.

Levittown, as his development was called, served as a model for suburban developers across the country. Although Levitt's method made houses more affordable and decreased construction time, some criticized the uniformity of suburban homes. Nevertheless, by 1960, as many Americans lived in suburbs as lived in cities.

But all this suburban development had a significant downside, too. Crime and poverty rates in the cities began to rise as the wealthy left for the outlying areas, and more federal, state, and local money went toward roads than toward expanding or maintaining public transportation in the nation's urban areas. Development also used up lots of land and, during the 1950s, the U.S. lost a lot of open space, farmlands, and forest areas.

On the fast track: Economic and baby booms

Americans had the urge to spend, spend, spend, and spend some more following World War II. Wartime scarcity meant many Americans had bulging bank accounts after the war was over. This huge demand for products caused an unprecedented economic boom. Between 1945 and 1960, the gross national product rose from $200 billion to $500 billion per year. Although inflation was initially out of whack, the economy stabilized by 1950 as America entered an era of unprecedented prosperity. Americans enjoyed higher salaries and a higher standard of living that they had never known before. They bought houses, cars, televisions, insurance policies, household appliances, and family vacations.

The end of World War II also caused a boom of another sort. Men and women coming of age in the 1940s married in record numbers. And when the war was over, it was time to have some babies — and plenty of them. Between 1946 and 1964, 75.9 million babies were born, and during the 1950s, the population grew 20 percent. People born during this time became known as the "baby boomers."

The beginnings of the women's movement

Women attended college in the 1950s in record numbers, but when they graduated, they found that many career options weren't open to them. Women could be clerks, secretaries, nurses, or any job considered beneath the abilities of a man. And they received significantly less pay for their work, which forced many single women into poverty.

On the home front, many young mothers discovered that the fulfillment they were supposed to find in taking care of their homes, husbands, and children was lacking. Something was missing from their lives, and many women began to realize that they weren't going to find it in their domestic duties. This discontentment in the home and in the work place recharged the women's movement, which grew into a force to be reckoned with in the 1960s (see Chapter 20 for more on this topic).

Good times: 1950s pop culture

By the mid-1950s, 13 million teenagers were hanging out in America, and most had money burning holes in their pockets. The affluence of American society combined with the abundance of teenagers caused a boom in the entertainment industry. Television became a phenomenon. And, lest we forget that rock 'n' roll music was born in the 1950s, making Elvis Presley one of the most widely recognized pop icons in the world.

A new craze: The emergence of television

While Americans were in buy-crazy mode, the most popular item sold was the television. In 1950, only 3.9 million households had televisions, but by the end of the decade, that number had skyrocketed to 46.3 million. Part of the reason for the increase in TV sales was the price drop from $500 to $200 per television set in the early 1950s.

The television affected every aspect of American culture. Politicians became television savvy or went the way of the dodo. Television boosted interest in professional sports, and broadcast news caused interest in newspapers and magazines to wane. But Americans were most interested in television for its entertainment value. TV brought Americans a weekly dose of the hilarious physical comedy of stars such as Lucille Ball in *I Love Lucy.* Hollywood, seeking to compete with television, produced new movie-going experiences like the drive-in and 3D.

Television revolutionized advertising; never before had such a captive and receptive audience existed for companies to market their products to. The money spent on advertising grew from $171 million in the early 1950s to $1.6 billion in 1960. Television told people what to eat, drink, smoke, wear, and how to think and live through shows and commercials. Television programming and advertising also led to the spread of mass market fads in the 1950s, like Hula Hoops, Slinkies, Frisbees, Silly Putty, and Mickey Mouse ears. Some worried about the negative effects of television but, for most Americans, its place in the household was undisputed.

Rocking and rolling

Rock 'n'roll rose to popularity in the early 1950s. This new sound, though rooted in African American rhythm and blues music, was different from traditional rhythm and blues with its youth-oriented lyrics and electric guitars. Older folks thought the music was dangerous and evil because it was loud and its stars danced provocatively, but the younger generation embraced rock 'n'roll for the same reasons. Rock 'n'roll gave them a way to rebel against the conformity of 1950s society. Some of the first rock 'n'roll stars were *Chuck Berry, Little Richard,* and *Buddy Holly.* But the king was *Elvis Presley.* To many young Americans in the late 1950s, Elvis was an idol; the sexual innuendo in his songs and his signature hip gyrations thrilled teens but shocked their parents. Each of the 14 records he produced between 1956 and 1958 sold more than a million copies.

Marching to a different drummer: The Beat Generation

Not everyone in America was comfortable with conformity during the 1950s. A small group of young poets and writers went against the grain of the 1950s suburban culture. They were known as the Beat Generation. "Beat" referred to their weariness with the popular culture and its conservative values. The Beats produced some notable writing and poetry, such as *Allen Ginsberg's* poem "Howl" (1956) and *Jack Kerouac's* novel *On the Road* (1957), but it was more than just their writing that caught the attention and adoration of America's youth in "the 1960s. It was their experimentation with sex and drugs as well as their listless wandering ways that struck a chord.

Chapter 20

A New Revolution: The Kennedy and Johnson Years, 1960–1968

- -

In This Chapter

▶ Revering Camelot: The short-lived presidency of John F. Kennedy

▶ Dreaming of a Great Society: Lyndon B. Johnson in the White House

▶ Fighting for civil rights for all Americans

▶ Rocking and rolling through the social and cultural changes of the 1960s

- -

The decade of the 1960s was a time of growth and contradiction in the United States. The decade started with John F. Kennedy's campaign concern that there was a "missile gap" between the U.S. and the Soviet Union and ended with a conclusive victory for the U.S. in the space race when Apollo 11 landed on the moon in 1969. Domestically, the civil rights movement reached its peak, and the nation's youth developed a counterculture devoted to peace and love.

The '60s were important in U.S. history, and the makers of the SAT II U.S. History exam agree. Approximately 10 percent of the test questions address issues or events from the 1960s or ask about trends over a period of time (for example, the period after World War II, the last half of the 20th century, and so on). Needless to say, to do well on the test, you need to have a solid understanding of the significance of the 1960s in relation to surrounding decades and of the major events that went on in the United States during the 1960s.

Doing for the Country: John F. Kennedy

John F. Kennedy (JFK), the grandson of an Irish immigrant and the son of Joseph P. Kennedy (a successful businessman, former U.S. Ambassador to Great Britain, and head of the Securities and Exchange Commission), had a wealthy and privileged background. JFK received his education at Harvard, was a decorated soldier in World War II, and served in the House for six years and the Senate for eight years before he became president. He was attractive, young, dynamic, energetic, warm, and engaging. And his wife, Jacqueline (Jackie), was young, beautiful, and glamorous. JFK was a charismatic leader who wanted to bring positive change to the nation.

Ready for change: The 1960 election

The political climate in the late 1950s called for change. Think of the quiet, conservative 1950s as a pot of water heating up on the stove. In the 1960s, that pot began to get really hot, simmering during the early years of the decade and boiling over by the end. In other words, the '60s was a very turbulent time, politically and socially.

By 1960, many people in the United States were frustrated with the Dwight D. Eisenhower administration. "Ike," as Eisenhower was known, was 70 years old and the oldest president ever up to that time. His dogmatic belief in decentralization and his strong support of private enterprise reduced his commitment to social welfare acts and to preserving natural resources. Needless to say, his political effectiveness was waning.

During Democratic nominee John F. Kennedy's campaign for the presidency, he successfully alleged that U.S. politics had virtually stood still for eight years. During the late 1950s, social tensions had dramatically increased: Poverty was a significant problem, the civil rights movement was about to explode, and America was dealing with urban decay, unemployment, substandard housing, and almost nonexistent healthcare. Not since the early years of the Great Depression had the citizens of the United States clamored for such significant social and economic change. (For more details about the 1950s, see Chapter 19.)

The 1960 election was one of the most closely contested presidential races in U.S. history. Eisenhower's Vice President Richard Nixon ran as the Republican candidate, and JFK was the Democratic candidate. In his campaign, Kennedy introduced a bold program of social reform called the *New Frontier.* In this trail-blazing program, Kennedy presented the American people with a set of challenges (as opposed to promises) that he requested them to undertake. The American people wanted change, and many felt that Kennedy could bring it.

However, many Democrats had doubts about Kennedy. He was only 43, which would make him the youngest elected president, and he would be the nation's first Catholic leader. No president had ever been a non-Protestant, and citizens in portions of the country — especially rural areas and the West — didn't trust Catholics and feared that a Catholic leader would subject the U.S. to papal intrusion. Southern Democrats didn't like Kennedy because he was Catholic and because of his stance on civil rights. Kennedy wouldn't compromise with any Southerners on the issue of civil rights. Kennedy's positions and principles brought him tremendous support from minority groups, organized labor, and large industrial states.

Nixon, who was also a young candidate, ran on a moderate platform. He had experience as vice president and the backing of Eisenhower, which made him a credible all-around candidate. During his campaign in 1960, Nixon promoted Ike's policies and promised to extend Ike's programs in new liberal directions. Nixon wanted to expand the forces of racial equality that Ike and his predecessors had introduced and to hasten the progress of civil rights for all Americans. Like Ike, Nixon favored the expansion of federal programs, such as the construction of schools and highways, and he wanted to expand social security coverage.

JFK's popularity was largely due to his belief in the American people and their ability to work with the government and each other to progress from "the safe mediocrity of the past." JFK's platform emphasized the importance of repairing the image of the U.S. abroad and restoring America's military supremacy by eliminating the nuclear "missile gap" between the U.S. and Russia. Feeding the fears of Americans regarding the alleged nuclear weapon inequality with the Soviet Union proved to be a strategically successful political move.

The press indicated that the presidential election of 1960 was very tight. That is, until Nixon accepted Kennedy's challenge to a series of televised political debates, which turned out to be a slick move for the Democrats. Many political commentators felt that Nixon's biggest campaign bungle was to accept this challenge. They thought that the nationally recognized V.P. Nixon was unnecessarily going out of his way to introduce the lesser-known, yet more charismatic, Kennedy to the American public. The debates provided Kennedy with national exposure that he may not have otherwise gotten prior to the 1960 election. JFK emerged on the airwaves as a talented debater who displayed youth, vigor, and a memorable smile. On the other hand, Nixon appeared swarthy and had a staid argumentative style.

The results of the election were extremely close. Kennedy won 303 electoral votes and 49.9 percent of the popular vote, and Nixon came away with only 219 electoral votes but 49.6 percent of the popular vote.

During Kennedy's inauguration, his charisma and leadership brought hope and confidence to the American people. A believer in active political action, Kennedy asked Americans, "Ask not what your country can do for you, ask what you can do for your country."

By 1960, JFK had become a beloved public figure to most Americans and to much of the free world. He quickly developed a reputation as a war hero, a freethinking liberal, a young husband, and a gracious father. He was hard-fighting and humane, and he instilled the perception of idyllic happiness in the White House in the public mind. JFK captured the nation's imagination and instilled a mood of optimism. His concern for culture and learning attracted America's intellectuals to the White House, and his supposed family values ushered in the period that commentators and the country felicitously dubbed "Camelot."

Facing a few roadblocks: The issues at home

Kennedy entered office early in 1961 during a minor economic recession, sluggish economic growth, and 6 percent unemployment. He made boosting the economy an immediate goal. But Kennedy had trouble obtaining congressional approval for much of the domestic legislation he outlined in his New Frontier program due to the political climate in Congress. Southern Democrats more often sided with Republicans than with the more liberal Democratic Party. During his nearly three years as president, JFK failed to obtain legislation for a tax cut (to help spur the economy), federal aid for K–12 education, medical care under social security for the elderly, and voting rights and equal treatment in public places for African Americans.

On the other hand, Kennedy successfully passed key legislation, such as an increase in the minimum wage and the expansion of social security benefits and coverage. He also gained congressional approval for several other important pieces of legislation, including the *Trade Expansion Act,* which enabled the president to lower tariffs to stimulate trade. JFK's legislative policies were in the spirit of FDR's New Deal (see Chapter 17) and Harry Truman's Fair Deal (see Chapter 19) because all were intended to hasten economic recovery and to provide more housing, more federally backed healthcare benefits, and higher wages. Here are the highlights of the legislation passed under Kennedy:

- ✔ **Area Redevelopment Act (1961):** This legislation provided federal funding for grants and loans to assist economically disadvantaged communities and to provide job training for their members.

- ✔ **Housing Act (1961):** The Housing Act provided nearly $5 billion in federal grants for cities to use to subsidize middle-income housing, to preserve open spaces, and to develop and implement mass transit systems.

- ✔ **Trade Expansion Act (1962):** This act lowered tariffs to help expand foreign trade.

- ✔ **Medical Education Act (1963):** This act offered student loans for medical students and funding for improved education facilities in various medical fields.

- ✔ **Mental Retardation and Health Centers Act (1963):** Through this act, the country supplied federal funding for research and treatment of mental disabilities.

- ✔ **Clean Air Act (1963):** This act required a reduction in factory and auto emissions. Rachel Carson, a scientist, wrote *Silent Spring,* a book published in 1962 that revealed the hazards that the pesticide DDT wreaked on the environment. Her work criticized the harm and overuse of pesticides and served as an excellent example of the protest literature that took hold during the Kennedy era. Carson's message was successful; within a few years, many states banned or restricted the use of DDT.

Throughout his presidency, JFK wasn't able to push through much of his proposed reform. Even though Democratic majorities existed in the House and the Senate, many of these Democrats were Southern Democrats, who were much more likely to side with Republicans than a progressive, liberal Democrat from the North. Remember, in 1960, much of the South was still heavily segregated, and the civil rights movement wasn't in full swing yet.

Around the world: The issues abroad

During his three years in the White House, JFK, as the leader of the largest free nation in the world, played an important role in international diplomacy. Perhaps in an effort to divert the nation's attention from the nuclear missile race with the Soviets, Kennedy announced *Project Apollo* in 1961; its goal was to place a person on the moon by 1970. Even though the Soviets were quicker to blast off from earth in the *space race,* JFK lived to witness American Alan Shepard's historic space voyage in May 1961 and John Glenn's three-day orbital flight around the earth in 1962. The following list summarizes JFK's accomplishments as well as a few unsuccessful efforts in the world arena.

✔ **Alliance for Progress (1961):** Members of Kennedy's administration were concerned with the deteriorating relationship between the U.S. and Latin America. Kennedy developed the Alliance for Progress, a cooperative program between the U.S. and Latin American governments, to improve relations with Latin American nations through peaceful U.S. aid in support of economic development and political stabilization.

✔ **Peace Corps (1961):** The Peace Corps provided opportunities for young American volunteers, including teachers, health workers, engineers, and others, to provide education and assistance in third-world countries. The Peace Corps also spread international goodwill on behalf of America.

✔ **Bay of Pigs invasion (1961):** Continuing a plan of containment inherited from Eisenhower, who in 1960 had sent a group of more than 2,000 members of the CIA to train and arm Cuban exiles, JFK approved a plan to have the exiles invade the island of Cuba at the *Bay of Pigs.* The perceived threat of this hostile and militant new Soviet-backed Communist satellite state, which was located only 90 miles off the American coast, represented a serious security concern.

The exiles were supposed to get American air support backup, inspire a civil uprising in Cuba, and overthrow Fidel Castro and his Communist government, which had been established in 1959. Although Kennedy approved the plan, he didn't want to involve the U.S. directly. Sensing that the mission was headed for failure, he withdrew the air support at the last minute. The Cuban people didn't stage an uprising as expected, and Fidel Castro's military forces crushed the exiles. The entire situation was an embarrassment to the U.S. and did nothing to improve the United States' already-shaky relations with the Soviet Union.

✔ **The Berlin Crisis (1961):** The international tensions created by the Cuban debacle and exacerbated by the space race (which presented underlying concerns about the placement of targeted atomic weaponry in space) caused Kennedy to call a meeting with the Soviet Union's Premier *Nikita Khrushchev* in June 1961.

At the meeting, JFK requested more open communication and more peaceful relations with the Soviets in an effort to avoid another world war. Khruschev said that Communism was spreading virtually without his control, and that the Soviets refused to discuss an end to nuclear testing or disarmament. Khrushchev also demanded that the U.S. sign a peace treaty with Germany or face the possibility of being forced out of West Berlin, which was the most vulnerable area of free Europe, locked in and surrounded by Soviet-controlled East Germany. The burgeoning West German economy and the desire for political freedom encouraged thousands of East Germans to escape from the Soviet sector to West Berlin.

Khrushchev intensified Western woes by threatening to recognize East Germany's independence by the end of 1961, thus, leaving West Berlin to the mercy of East Germany, unless the West acknowledged East Germany as a sovereign nation. The West unanimously refused, which led to even more military readiness by both sides. JFK asked Americans to build fallout shelters. As this crisis intensified, the number of refugees fleeing from East Germany to West Berlin tripled.

Surmising that the West was not going to budge in its refusal to recognize the autonomy of East Germany, the Soviets haphazardly constructed a wall from concrete, barbed wire, tank pylons, and other pieces of material to physically separate Berlin into East and West Berlin. This structure was known as the *Berlin Wall.* By October 1961, Khrushchev had withdrawn his ultimatum. The freedom of West Berlin was maintained, but the Soviets had violated the international agreement to an entirely free Berlin. On Kennedy's historic visit to West Berlin in June 1963, he suggested that the isolation that the Berliners suffered by being surrounded by a police state stood as a symbol of the need to continue the effort to maintain freedom.

✔ **Cuban Missile Crisis (1962):** In response to the U.S. placing nuclear missiles in Turkey and the Bay of Pigs invasion, the Soviet Union began constructing missile sites in Cuba in 1962 with the approval of Communist leader Fidel Castro. The Kennedy administration felt this act was direct aggression toward the U.S. and immediately placed a naval and air quarantine around Cuba and planned an air attack to destroy the missile sites. With tensions high on both sides and a worldwide fear of nuclear war, in the final hours before a U.S. attack, Khrushchev agreed to remove the missile sites from Cuba if the U.S. agreed not to invade Cuba and to remove its missiles from Turkey.

The Cuban Missile Crisis was the closest the U.S. and the Soviet Union ever came to nuclear war. JFK had shown that the Soviet leaders would back down to avoid unmitigated war. Kennedy's domestic popularity skyrocketed, and Soviet leader Khrushchev had been taught that the threat of nuclear war could not be used to intimidate the U.S.

✔ **Limited Nuclear Test Ban Treaty (1963):** The U.S., Britain, and the Soviet Union agreed to ban all above-ground and ocean testing of nuclear weapons to prevent dangerous nuclear fallout in the atmosphere. This ban marked the first move toward reducing nuclear weapons by prohibiting nuclear tests underwater, in space, and in the air.

✔ **Vietnam:** Largely out of fear of the spread of Communism, both Truman and Eisenhower had provided financial aid and equipment to French forces fighting in Vietnam. Both presidents adhered to the *domino theory* (see Chapter 19), which maintained that if one country in Southeast Asia fell to Communism, the neighboring nations would also become Communist. The French eventually withdrew from Vietnam, and when Kennedy took office, he substantially increased U.S. military aid to the South Vietnamese government to help maintain its freedom from the Communists in the North. Kennedy also sent American advisors to Vietnam and, by 1963, more than 16,000 U.S. advisors occupied Vietnam. To find out more about the Vietnam War, turn to Chapter 21.

You may see a question like the following on the SAT II U.S. History exam.

During his presidency, JFK dealt with a major international situation that almost resulted in the U.S. entering into nuclear war with the Soviet Union. Which country did this situation take place in?

(A) Vietnam

(B) Dominican Republic

(C) Turkey

(D) Cuba

(E) Venezuela

This question may confuse you if you forget about the Cuban Missile Crisis in 1962. Although the U.S. was involved in Vietnam during JFK's presidency, no threat of nuclear war existed over Vietnam during the Kennedy presidency, so you can eliminate (A). Kennedy's successor, Lyndon B. Johnson, sent troops to occupy the Dominican Republic, so (B) is also out. The U.S. had nuclear weapons in Turkey, but no international situation occurred there. So, (C) is wrong. The U.S. intervened in Venezuela in 1958, but that was before JFK's tenure; vote no on (E). Now you're left with (D). The Cuban Missile Crisis in 1962 almost sent the U.S. into nuclear war with the Soviet Union, so (D) is correct.

A dream cut short: The Kennedy assassination

On November 22, 1963, JFK and Jackie traveled to Dallas, Texas, to gain popular and political support in a politically divided state for the following year's election. Once there, the president and first lady met and traveled with the governor and his wife to a luncheon in an open car. As the presidential motorcade passed the crowds of cheering supporters, Lee Harvey Oswald, a known Marxist and former resident of Cuba and the Soviet Union, shot the president twice from an upper floor window of an old book warehouse. The motorcade rushed the president to a nearby hospital, where doctors later pronounced him dead. Police apprehended Oswald in a movie theater after he shot a Dallas police officer. Two days later, Dallas nightclub owner and supposed staunch admirer of Kennedy, Jack Ruby, shot and killed Oswald as he was being moved between jails.

The Kennedy assassination had a deep and profound effect on the American people as well as people and leaders around the world. Millions of Americans witnessed the shocking event on their televisions as news broadcasts repeatedly played the horrific incident, and activity in the nation came to a standstill. His violent death marked the end of Camelot.

Supreme Court Chief Justice Earl Warren headed a committee that conducted a ten-month investigation into the assassination of Kennedy. The commission found that Oswald acted as the lone Kennedy assassin and that Ruby acted alone in the assassination of Oswald. In the late 1970s, a congressional subcommittee disputed that the Warren Commission's findings were incomplete. To this day, some people feel that evidence supports a conspiracy theory in JFK's assassination.

Stepping into JFK's Shoes: Lyndon B. Johnson

Within two hours of JFK's assassination, Vice President Lyndon B. Johnson (LBJ) was sworn in as the new president of the United States aboard Air Force One. Johnson's background was very different than JFK's. Johnson grew up on a farm in the poor hill country of western Texas. His grandfather had been a secretary of state for Texas, and his father was a farmer who served in the Texas legislature. After working his way through college and teaching for a year, Johnson followed in his family's political footsteps. He began serving in the U.S. House at age 29 and enlisted in the Navy during World War II (he was the first Congressman to enlist in World War II). He served in the Senate from 1948 to 1960 and as Senate majority leader from 1954 to 1960. In 1960, he lost the Democratic bid for the presidency to JFK but accepted the job of vice president.

LBJ's years in the Senate taught him how to cajole, persuade, compromise, make deals, and twist arms to get what he wanted. When he unexpectedly became president in late 1963, he had a rough year ahead of him. He needed to comfort a grieving nation, figure out how to get important social legislation passed by Congress, and prepare for a presidential election that was less than a year away.

In 1964, Johnson won congressional support for many of the New Frontier programs that Kennedy had been unable to push through as president. LBJ's popularity as a devoted "New Dealer" who exuded great respect and admiration for Roosevelt's New Deal programs that aided debtor farmers and urban middle-income constituents combined with the legislative experience that LBJ gained as an effective majority leader of the Senate, facilitated passage of JFK's New Frontier programs. In the election later that year, Johnson won the largest majority ever against Barry M. Goldwater, a senator from Arizona. Johnson won 44 states, 486 of 538 electoral votes, and more than 61 percent of the popular vote. The 1964 congressional elections also increased the Democratic majority in the House and Senate.

As president, LBJ continued to break records. From 1963 to 1966, he passed more legislation through Congress than any other president since Franklin D. Roosevelt. The LBJ administration operated with the same goals as the Kennedy administration: to expand government support of, and responsibilities for, social welfare programs and to fortify the U.S. economy. Johnson took his goals a step further than Kennedy: He wanted to unleash a war on poverty. Johnson didn't just envision a new frontier, he envisioned a "Great Society." Fortunately, Johnson reached the pinnacle of the political pyramid through his ability to seek compromise and his devotion to accomplishing the political objective at hand.

In this chapter, we focus on domestic issues during LBJ's presidency. Keep in mind, though, that LBJ still had the Cold War to deal with. Under his administration, the U.S. signed the *Nuclear Non-Proliferation Treaty* in 1968, which limited the number of nuclear weapons that the U.S., Great Britain, France, the Soviet Union, and China could possess. And American involvement in Vietnam escalated quickly during LBJ's administration. For the full scoop on the Vietnam War, including LBJ's role, flip to Chapter 21.

Building a "Great Society"

From 1965 to 1966, Congress (with a huge Democratic majority) was productive and cooperative and passed an enormous amount of social legislation in an attempt to establish a *"Great Society."* Here are some significant pieces of legislation passed from 1964 to 1968:

- **Civil Rights Act (1964):** This act prohibited racial and sexual discrimination by employers and labor unions, racial discrimination in voter registration, and racial discrimination in public accommodations. This act permitted the U.S. attorney general to intervene in cases of racial discrimination and gave the federal government the right to withhold federal funding for a project if racial discrimination existed.

   Johnson's actions in the civil rights arena led to greater racial equality and increased civil rights for minorities. (For more about civil rights during the 1960s, see the section "The Civil Rights Movement Flourishes" later in this chapter.)

- **Economic Opportunity Act (1964):** LBJ wanted to end poverty altogether. With this act, Johnson launched his "War on Poverty." This act provided funding for remedial education and job training for unemployed and out-of-school young people. It also created VISTA, a domestic Peace Corps-type network of volunteers working in social work, education, and other forms of assistance in poverty-stricken areas. The Economic Opportunity Act provided funding for Project Head Start, a preschool program for underprivileged children to help them succeed in school, and a program to finance work-study opportunities for underprivileged college students.

- **Voting Rights Act (1965):** This act permitted the federal government to register voters in regions where less than 50 percent of eligible voters were registered and prohibited state laws that imposed registration restrictions, such as literacy tests and poll taxes.

This act affected most of the South and tremendously expanded African American participation in the political process. The act was also controversial because it gave the federal government a sort of veto power over state voting laws.

✔ **Health Insurance Act for the Aged (1965):** This act created Medicare and Medicaid, which provided medical insurance for the elderly under social security (Medicare) and free healthcare for people on welfare (Medicaid). Although LBJ created Medicare and Medicaid, he didn't achieve his goal of universal healthcare for all Americans.

✔ **Immigration Act (1965):** This act restricted the number of immigrants to the U.S. to 170,000 annually and eliminated the discrimination of the "national origins" structure from the 1920s immigration restriction that gave northern European immigrants preference over immigrants from other countries. Eliminating this restriction changed the makeup of the U.S. population over the next few decades and resulted in a significant increase in Asian immigrants.

✔ **Elementary and Secondary Education Act (1965):** This act provided federal funding for public schools and instructional materials for public, private, and parochial schools.

✔ **Higher Education Act (1965):** The Higher Education Act supplied federal grants for building colleges and universities and for student loans.

✔ **Clean Rivers Restoration Act (1966):** Through this act, Johnson increased protection measures to rid the nation's rivers of pollutants.

✔ **Truth in Lending Act (1968):** This act required lenders to disclose the actual costs of consumer credit.

✔ **Civil Rights Act (1968):** This second civil rights act prohibited racial discrimination in housing (real estate sales and rentals). The SAT II wants you to know that Johnson's administration passed a lot of domestic reform legislation, and it may ask you specific questions about the major reform bills like the Civil Rights Act of 1964.

A question like the following may appear on the SAT II U.S. History exam.

The Civil Rights Act of 1964 prohibited all the following EXCEPT

(A) Racial discrimination in employment on basis of race

(B) Racial discrimination in public accommodations

(C) Racial discrimination in voter registration

(D) Racial discrimination in housing

(E) Discrimination in employment on basis of sex

Because the first four answers deal with racial discrimination and the last one deals with sexual discrimination, you may be tempted to choose the answer that doesn't look like the others. Consider every answer carefully, because the exam may use this method to trick you.

During the 1950s and 1960s, Congress passed numerous civil rights acts, so confusing them is easy to do. The best strategy is to remember that the civil rights acts all build on each other, so try to think about what was going on in America in 1964. Now you should be able to eliminate (A) and (B) as pretty obvious components of the 1964 act because the 1964 act focused on discrimination in the workplace and in public places. Answer (C) may be tricky because more than one civil rights act addressed voting rights; however, the answer choice isn't specific, and the 1964 act did address voter registration — just not in much depth. Answer (E) is there to throw you off; the 1964 Civil Rights Act did address equality of sex and race in the workplace. The best answer is (D); Congress didn't legislate equal housing rights until the Civil Rights Act of 1968.

Decisions of the Warren Court

The U.S. Supreme Court handed down a number of significant decisions throughout the 1960s under the direction of the liberal Chief Justice Earl Warren. You've probably heard of many of the landmark cases passed in the 1960s. Here are some of the most notable cases that you should remember for the test:

- ✔ *Engel v. Vitale* (1962): The Court's decision prohibited prayer in public schools, upholding the principle of the separation of church and state.

- ✔ *Gideon v. Wainwright* (1963): The Court determined that any citizen accused of a crime must be represented by legal counsel; if the person cannot afford to pay for counsel, the state must pay for it.

- ✔ *Wesbery v. Sanders* (1964): Known as "one man, one vote," this case ended the pattern of representation in congressional districts (especially in the South) where (primarily white) rural voters were overrepresented while (primarily African American) urban voters were underrepresented.

- ✔ *Miranda v. Arizona* (1966): This case determined that law enforcement must inform suspects of a crime of their Constitutional rights prior to questioning. You've probably heard the "Miranda Rights" on TV cop shows: "You have the right to remain silent . . . ."

- ✔ *Loving v. Virginia* (1967): This decision ended laws that prevented interracial marriage.

The Civil Rights Movement Flourishes

The civil rights movement emerged during Dwight D. Eisenhower's administration in the 1950s. Events such as *Brown v. Board of Education* and the Civil Rights Act of 1957 (see Chapter 19 for details) took place during his presidency. The movement grew rapidly during John F. Kennedy and Lyndon B. Johnson's administrations.

In the following sections, we give you information about the prominent civil rights leader, Martin Luther King Jr., the Student Nonviolent Coordinating Committee, and the move to more violent protests in the civil rights movement.

A man with a dream: Martin Luther King Jr.

Martin Luther King Jr. was the most prominent civil rights activist in the 1950s and 1960s. Reverend King started his career during the 1954 Montgomery Bus Boycott (see Chapter 19), and then headed the *Southern Christian Leadership Conference (SCLC)*, a civil rights organization dedicated to the nonviolent civil disobedience (like sit-ins and boycotts). He was a distinguished orator and committed to nonviolent protest and resistance. In the early '60s, he helped organize numerous nonviolent demonstrations, several of which took place in the segregation stronghold of Birmingham, Alabama. In May 1963, King was arrested and jailed for participating in one of these marches. In jail, he composed his "Letter from Birmingham Jail," stating that people had the right and responsibility to disobey unjust laws.

In August 1963, more than 200,000 demonstrators marched on the mall to the Lincoln Memorial in Washington, D.C., in support of President Kennedy's proposed civil rights legislation; this march is known as the *March on Washington*. Here, King made his famous "I have a dream" speech in which he declared that he hoped for the day when all would be equal regardless of race.

In 1965, King led a series of demonstrations in Selma, Alabama, to support full voting rights for African Americans. That same year, he led another demonstration in Birmingham, Alabama. The Alabama demonstration erupted in violence as the police attacked peaceful demonstrators (the incident became known as Bloody Sunday); the violence was televised, and millions of Americans watched in horror. Not only did these demonstrations increase public support for the civil rights movement, but they also led to the passage of the Voting Rights Act in 1965 (see "Building a 'Great Society'" earlier in this chapter).

In April 1968, King traveled to Memphis to support a group of African American sanitation workers who were on strike. While standing on the balcony of his hotel, King was shot and killed by James Earl Ray, a white racist and escaped convict. Americans of all races grieved, and many African Americans became very angry. In the days following King's assassination, major riots broke out in dozens of U.S. cities, which led to nearly 50 deaths, more than 3,000 injuries, and nearly 30,000 arrests.

Group action: Students for nonviolence

In February 1960, a group of African American college students organized a sit-in at a segregated Woolworth's lunch counter in Greensboro, North Carolina. Other students followed suit and, throughout the spring and summer, African American students (and some white students, too) all over the South organized sit-ins, forcing merchants to integrate lunch counters. Large groups of white youths came into the restaurants to harass and physically abuse the students, who reacted to the cruelty without demonstrating anger or violence.

Some of the students formed the *Student Nonviolent Coordinating Committee (SNCC),* an interracial organization based on peaceful resistance. Members of the SNCC traveled around the South to educate African Americans about their rights to vote and how to get around the various voting obstacles, such as poll taxes and literacy tests. John Lewis, a leader of the march that erupted in Bloody Sunday (see the previous section), was president of the SNCC. In 1961, he and other SNCC members responded to white attacks on African American bus riders who defied segregation laws. The group rode buses into the Deep South in an act so dangerous that the Kennedy administration had to provide them with protection to avert mob violence. The protest was called the *Freedom Rides.*

The group established Freedom Schools to teach African American children to stand up for their rights and, in 1964, the group instituted the *Mississippi Freedom Summer Project* to get the Democratic Party to acknowledge Mississippi Freedom Democratic Party candidates at the Democratic Convention. Johnson gave the party two non-voting seats, a decision that alienated him from the SNCC and other civil rights leaders.

In the mid-1960s, the SNCC, under the leadership of Stokely Carmichael, turned toward more radical resistance than it or other similar organizations like the SCLC and the *National Association for the Advancement of Colored People (NAACP)* had used. After the assassination of Malcolm X in 1965, Carmichael turned toward violent resistance to carry on Malcolm X's legacy of promoting "black power." (See "The reign of Malcolm X" later in this chapter.)

Beyond peaceful protest: Violent measures

By the mid-1960s, peaceful resistance more often than not gave way to more violent demonstrations. Poor African Americans in the nation's northern urban areas were growing discontent, and many Americans were frustrated with the slow results of civil rights, which led many people to forceful approaches.

Still a threat: Actions of the Ku Klux Klan

In the 1960s, white supremacist groups took on the infamous Ku Klux Klan name and used violent means to oppose civil rights in the Deep South. Moderate whites in the South feared retaliation by the Klan. Even if someone supported civil rights, he or she usually wouldn't speak out for fear of the Klan. The Klan also supported Eugene "Bull" Connor, a white supremacist police chief in Birmingham, Alabama, who turned fire hoses and police dogs on young protesters.

In May 1963, a Klan member assassinated Medgar Evers, a civil rights activist and the NAACP's first field officer in Mississippi. And one of the most egregious acts of the Ku Klux Klan was the September 1963 bombing of the 16th Street Baptist Church in Birmingham (because churches were meeting places for protesters), which resulted in the deaths of four young girls who were attending Sunday school. Klan members were also responsible for the 1964 murders of three male volunteers (two whites and one African American) of the Freedom Summer Project's voter registration drive in Mississippi.

Terror in the streets: Riots in cities

In the mid-1960s, the continuing lack of civil rights for African Americans along with poverty and poor urban living conditions resulted in a series of race riots. A series of small riots took place in Harlem, a neighborhood in New York City, in the summer of 1964, but the first major riot happened in the summer of 1965 after a white police officer struck an African American bystander with his club during a traffic arrest in Los Angeles. The Watts Riots lasted a week, and more than 30 people were killed in the violence — most of them African Americans. The following summer of 1966, 43 notable riots occurred in various cities across the country; the worst ones took place in Cleveland and Chicago.

In the summer of 1967, eight major riots erupted, the worst of which happened in Detroit, Michigan. To stop the violence and the riots, President Johnson appointed a Commission on Civil Disorders. In 1968, the commission suggested that a huge amount of federal spending be used to improve living conditions in America's urban ghettos. Many white Americans disagreed and felt that the cities needed more police and stricter laws to quell the violence.

The reign of Malcolm X

Malcolm X, whose real name was Malcolm Little but he changed it to X to symbolize his lost African surname, had a difficult childhood. His father, a Baptist minister and civil rights activist in the 1920s, was murdered in 1931, most likely by members of a white supremacist group. A few years later, his mother was committed to a mental institution, and her children were sent to different foster homes. At age 21, Malcolm X began a six-year prison term. While in prison, he studied the works of Elijah Muhammad, the leader of the Nation of Islam. The radical Nation of Islam encouraged complete racial separation from the white devil and emphasized the Islamic faith. When Malcolm X got out of prison in 1952, he became a minister for the Nation of Islam in Boston, where he quickly became more powerful, popular, and influential than Elijah Muhammad. Malcolm X preached about black self-reliance, freedom from whites, black pride, black independence, and black power.

Malcolm X criticized the March on Washington, which he viewed as run by whites, and he intimated in a speech he gave after Kennedy's assassination that Kennedy deserved the violence he'd received because he had done too little to end the violence suffered by African Americans. In late 1963, the Nation of Islam censured Malcolm X for his statements (perhaps because some leaders were jealous of his popularity) and suspended him for six months. In 1964, Malcolm X broke from the Nation of Islam and traveled to Mecca (Islam's holy city in Saudi Arabia), where he learned about orthodox Islam and revised many of his ideas and beliefs, including his belief that the white man was the devil. In 1965, he formed the *Organization of Afro-American Unity,* based on brotherhood and cooperation among African

Americans, but Nation of Islam members (perhaps supported by the FBI) assassinated Malcolm X at a rally for that organization in February 1965. His book, *The Autobiography of Malcolm X,* is a lasting legacy and is still influential today. Though he mellowed his positions before his death, his fiery anti-racist speeches influenced leaders of the Black Power movement, like Stokely Carmichael and the *Black Panthers,* a group based in Oakland, California, whose members carried firearms. The Black Panthers organized community services in the ghettos, protected African Americans from police harassment, and called for a revolution to shake up American government and society.

Tying it all together: A sample question looks at the civil rights movement in the 1960s

The SAT II may ask you to assess the protest styles of civil rights leaders in the 1960s. This question asks you to determine which leader gave anti-racist speeches.

Which of the following 1960s civil rights leaders headed the nonviolent protest organization called the Student Nonviolent Coordinating Committee?

(A) John Lewis

(B) Malcolm X

(C) Martin Luther King Jr.

(D) Elijah Muhammad

(E) Stokely Carmichael

Because the group advocated nonviolent protest, you can eliminate (B). Malcolm X, at least in his early days, wasn't an advocate for a nonviolent response to abuse, so his is the least likely to lead the SNCC. Malcolm X's fiery anti-racist speeches inspired Stokely Carmichael (E), so he probably didn't head a nonviolent organization, either.

Martin Luther King Jr. advocated nonviolent protest, so you may be tempted to choose (C). But King wasn't a student in the 1960s, so it's unlikely that he would head an organization of students in the 1960s. Elijah Muhammad (D) was a leader of the Nation of Islam, so he probably wasn't leading the SNCC. The best answer is John Lewis (A), who was president of the SNCC during the march in Selma, the Freedom Rides, and the Mississippi Freedom Summer.

Culture Shock: Social Change in the '60s

The 1960s represented a period of great social change in America. The war in Vietnam and other events throughout the 1960s inspired young people to get involved in politics. The hippie philosophy flourished, and music in the 1960s reflected the changing times.

Political activism and organization

The 1960s brought about a new era of political awareness, activism, and organization in American society. Throughout the 1950s, a majority of Americans went with the status quo. In the 1960s, the members of the postwar Baby Boom reached young adulthood in large and powerful numbers and could make their message heard. Many Americans changed their attitudes in the '60s, which was a time of dynamic transformations.

In the '60s, many groups formed to address social problems in the United States. Groups of college students formed on campuses around the country and worked for civil rights and free speech or to protest the war in Vietnam. Women across the nation fought for equal rights and recognition and against societal repression. Mexican Americans united to form a union for farm workers.

Students for a Democratic Society

College attendance soared in the 1960s, and campuses became hubs of social reform. Many protest movements during the 1960s originated on college campuses. In the spring of 1962, students in Ann Arbor, Michigan, who were disillusioned by the complacency and indifference of society in the late 1950s and early 1960s and wanted to bring about extensive social change for the future founded the *Students for a Democratic Society (SDS)*. Their goals were to mobilize the left and support the goals of the "New Left," which included opposition to authority, restrictions, and the establishment.

Throughout the 1960s, SDS members at college campuses nationwide sponsored rallies, demonstrations, teach-ins, sit-ins, and draft-card burning ceremonies to protest the Vietnam War and to support the civil rights movement. The SDS, however, didn't fully recognize the rights of women. Despite the organization's huge influence, members didn't treat women as equals within the organization, which added fuel to the fire of the women's liberation movement on college campuses around the country in 1967.

The free speech movement

In the fall of 1964, the administration of the University of California at Berkeley, in a highly confrontational move, declared that non-university political literature could no longer be distributed on the Berkeley campus. Students felt that this decision was unfair and that it violated their rights. Students protested against the administration en masse for months until the chancellor was replaced and free speech was restored on the Berkeley campus. Some students were arrested, beaten, or even suspended for participating in the demonstrations.

The sit-ins, rallies, and demonstrations at Berkeley inspired hundreds of similar demonstrations at several universities around the nation. Colleges and universities eventually became more sympathetic and responsive to the needs of students. Student protests soon became commonplace occurrences because, at the same time the free speech movement was born in Berkeley, President Johnson was planning a massive escalation of military force in Vietnam (see Chapter 21).

Women's liberation

The women's liberation movement emerged in 1963 with the publication of *The Feminine Mystique* by Betty Friedan. Friedan encouraged women to fully develop their potential, to seek out "something more" than the drudgery of domestic life.

LBJ took a step to protect women's rights with the Civil Rights Act of 1964, which prohibited sexual (and racial) discrimination by employers. Women wanted to be treated equally to men in employment, wages, housework, childcare, and higher education. In 1966, women's rights activists (including Friedan) formed the National Organization for Women (NOW) to mobilize political pressure in favor of women's rights at a national level.

The United Farm Workers

In the early 1960s, Cesar Chavez, a Mexican American, helped form the *National Farm Workers Association,* a labor union of farm workers that helped Mexican Americans and other migrant farm workers obtain fair wages and safe working conditions. In 1965, Chavez organized a strike against grape growers in California. He later organized a march across California to raise awareness for his cause and organized a nationwide boycott of table grapes. The march made an impression on some grape growers, who signed on with the union. The organization later was renamed the United Farm Workers and became part of the national labor union, the AFL–CIO.

Right on: Understanding the hippie philosophy

By the mid-1960s, a new counterculture youth movement had developed in America. This counterculture, known as the "hippie" movement, had two geographical centers: the Haight-Ashbury neighborhood in San Francisco and the East Village in New York City. Hippies valued living life in the now and just "being." They questioned life and the established order, embraced spontaneity, rejected materialism, and refused to conform to society. The hippie philosophy valued music, freedom, protest, peace, love, ideas, respect for mankind, and respect for the earth.

Many factors embodied this new hippie lifestyle. The widespread (and almost common) social use of marijuana (and later other drugs) was one. The concept of "free love" embraced the new knowledge about and acceptance of human sexuality and fostered uninhibited views on sex. Some hippies lived in cooperative communes, and many members of the older generations thought the young, long-haired, free-spirited, colorful dressing hippies were just plain strange. Hippies didn't usually work traditional 9 to 5 jobs; some worked in the civil rights movement; some worked in political activism, helping people register to vote; and others worked to protest the Vietnam War.

By 1967, the "Summer of Love" brought the hippie lifestyle to national attention. Young people protested the war throughout the nation. In one famous demonstration at the Pentagon in Washington, D.C., some of the hippie demonstrators stuck flowers in the barrels of the rifles of the policemen who were guarding the demonstration. After this incident, Americans often used the terms "flower child" and "hippie" interchangeably.

Getting into the groove: Music of the 1960s

The 1960s brought a wider variety of popular music than ever before. The massive social change, revolution, freedom, and confidence of the '60s are reflected in the music of the era. Completely new styles of popular music emerged in the U.S., and the decade also witnessed the birth of a unique British music scene.

Motown

Named after producer Berry Gordy Jr.'s record label in Detroit, Michigan, *Motown* was the first style of African American music that had mass appeal to a white audience. During the 1960s, Motown had 110 top-ten hits and was a major force in the record industry.

Motown music usually included the use of a tambourine, rhythm and blues instrumentation, and lyrical techniques similar to gospel music. Some of the notable Motown artists during the 1960s were The Four Tops, Stevie Wonder, Smokey Robinson, The Temptations, Rick James, Gladys Knight and the Pips, Marvin Gaye, and The Supremes.

Folk singers

Folk music gained popularity in college towns around the nation in the early 1960s. By 1963, Berkeley, California, and Cambridge, Massachusetts, were two of the major folk centers. In the activist climate of the 1960s, folk singers began to create protest songs and became cultural icons of various causes. Not only did folk singers sing to protest the war in Vietnam, racial discrimination, and a variety of other issues, but the artists also traveled around the country in support of those causes.

Folk singers challenged tradition and believed that they could make a difference in the world through music. Folk music was extremely popular on college campuses and with the hippies in the early to mid-1960s, and the folk trend even caught on worldwide by the mid-1960s. By the end of the 1960s, folk music had been pushed to the back burner, but it remained a significant grassroots music trend. Some of the notable folk artists of this time period were *Joan Baez; Joni Mitchell; Bob Dylan; Odetta;* and *Peter, Paul, and Mary.*

The British Invasion: The Beatles and The Rolling Stones

When British kids heard Elvis in the 1950s, they began to create rock and roll bands of their own. The U.S. didn't hear much about them until the American success of The Beatles in 1964, which opened the door in America for an invasion of a bunch of British rock bands, like The Kinks, The Who, The Dave Clark Five, and *The Rolling Stones.* But *The Beatles* were the most successful rock band of the 20th century.

The band formed in the late 1950s in Liverpool, England, a working-class city. The Beatles couldn't believe the reception they received in America. Everywhere they went, throngs of screaming, hysterical teenage girls met them. In February 1964, The Beatles made their first appearance on the *Ed Sullivan Show,* which millions of Americans tuned in to watch. Their appearance on the show pretty much marked the official start of "Beatlemania" in the U.S.

From 1964 to 1965, The Beatles had numerous singles reach number one on the American pop charts and filmed two movies. The band stopped playing live shows because fans screamed so loudly that they couldn't hear themselves play. In late 1965, the band members began to experiment with LSD, leading to the creation and release of more psychedelically influenced albums, including *Revolver* and *Sgt. Pepper's Lonely Hearts Club Band,* both released in 1967. Tragedy hit the band in 1967 when band manager Brian Epstein died of a drug overdose. The band stayed together, even though the members had individual side projects going on throughout the 1960s, until their official breakup in January 1970.

Another British group, The Rolling Stones, formed in 1961 and rose to popularity in the United States in the mid-1960s. The Rolling Stones embodied a blues style of music. The Rolling Stones started by performing a lot of rhythm and blues classics from the 1940s and 1950s but soon wrote most of their own lyrics. The Stones displayed an irreverent, somewhat sloppy, and disheveled look that complemented the growing rebellion of youth, which helped them attract throngs of screaming teenagers to their shows.

Head trip: Eastern influences and psychedelic rock

In the mid- to late 1960s, Americans began turning to other cultures for ideas and inspiration. Elements of Eastern cultures, including Asian Art, Eastern musical techniques, fashion, and religions, such as Taoism, Buddhism, and Vedanta, all influenced American culture in the 1960s. Eastern influences were part of the counterculture movement from eating habits (increasing the number of vegetarians), to fashion (fabrics and styles), to musical trends. For example, in surf music, which emerged in southern California in the mid-1960s, artists used the Eastern musical technique of staccato picking on the guitar to obtain their desired sound. George Harrison of The Beatles played the Indian instrument called the sitar on songs they recorded in 1965.

During the 1960s, a drug culture emerged, fostered by the professor and psychologist Timothy Leary's LSD experiments. The culture influenced literature (Ken Kesey's *Electric Kool-Aid Acid Test* was a hippie favorite) and music. Psychedelic rock, inspired by the use of mind-altering drugs such as marijuana, mescaline, mushrooms, and LSD, was characterized by long instrument solos, cryptic lyrics, and trippy special effects. The psychedelic rock movement was native to the West Coast, and included bands such as The Doors, Jefferson Airplane, The Grateful Dead, and Jimi Hendrix. The trend later caught on in the United Kingdom, where bands like The Who and The Beatles embraced it. Psychedelic rock also heavily influenced start-up bands like Pink Floyd and Cream.

What a show! Woodstock

Woodstock was the largest music concert ever organized. It took place over three days in Bethel, New York, in August 1969. The organizers knew the concert would be popular but didn't expect 500,000 people to show up. Young people of all races, male and female, gay and straight, Vietnam vets and antiwar protesters, came. Despite a lack of resources for all the concertgoers and a heavy dose of rain, no rioting, looting, or fighting occurred. Most everyone got along, made do, helped each other, and enjoyed the show.

Tying it all together: A sample question looks at 1960s culture

For the SAT II, you should have a general idea of 1960s pop culture. The anti-establishment climate fostered new values that manifested themselves in music and student protests.

The American counterculture movement of the 1960s included all the following characteristics EXCEPT

(A) An embracing of Eastern culture and philosophies

(B) A return to traditional lifestyles

(C) The emergence of many new styles of music

(D) Protesting against the Vietnam War

(E) Increased political activism and organization among young people

Numerous characteristics embodied the American counterculture movement of the 1960s. The 1960s are often associated with political struggle, protest, and new ways of life (think hippies). The 1960s are also associated with the development of many new and diverse forms of music and a support for ideas from different cultures. With these factors in mind, you can eliminate (A), (C), (D), and (E). American 1960s counterculture isn't characterized by a return to traditional lifestyles, rather it's characterized by a departure from traditional lifestyles. Therefore, (B) is the best answer.

Chapter 21

Challenging Authority: Vietnam and the 1970s

- -

In This Chapter

▶ Wading into deep waters with the Vietnam War

▶ Taking a look at the policies and scandals of Richard Nixon's presidency

▶ Getting acquainted with President Jimmy Carter

- -

*B*y many accounts, the Vietnam War was a disaster, and its effects on American culture are still felt today. Much of the anger and bitterness toward war and the cynicism and distrust of the federal government that exists today stems from the Vietnam catastrophe. Maybe Americans could have recovered their faith, had it not been for a second blow called Watergate.

In this chapter, we guide you through the turbulent 1970s, giving you all the information you need to get a handle on this era for the SAT II U.S. History exam.

"Waist Deep in the Big Muddy": The Vietnam War

America became involved in Vietnam, a small Southeast Asian country, in 1954 (though, unofficially, the U.S. had been providing aid to the French in Vietnam for years leading up to 1954) to stop the spread of Communism. In 1954, President Dwight D. Eisenhower explained the *Domino Theory* in a news conference: "You have a row of dominoes set up; you knock over the first one, and what will happen to the last one is that it will go over very quickly." The idea was that if Vietnam fell to Communism, then its neighbors soon would, too. In the 1960s, Presidents Kennedy and Johnson took Eisenhower's Domino Theory to heart, using it as the reason for continuing to augment forces in Vietnam in the years 1960 to 1969.

At first, the U.S. provided only financial aid to South Vietnam. But as time progressed, America became embroiled in a full-blown war — a nasty one that government and military officials didn't know how to win. Nor did they maintain the support of the American people, who became disenchanted as the war went on with no clear victory or objectives in sight. Vietnam is truly a dark blot on the timeline of American history. Throughout the late 1960s, many artists wrote songs about the mess in Vietnam, including one well-known one entitled "Waist Deep in the Big Muddy" by Pete Seeger in 1967.

The SAT II likes to test you on consequences, so pay particular attention to the consequences of the Vietnam War. The war in Vietnam was an international embarrassment for the United States, and it ushered in a new wave of cynicism among the American public. Americans no longer viewed their country with rose-colored glasses. They distrusted the government, and their confidence in the moral superiority of American ideals was shattered.

America's growing involvement in Vietnam

The story of the Vietnam War is long; in other words, we don't have the time to cover it all here. But for the SAT II, you should know some of the back story and some of the key events that contributed to America's involvement in Vietnam.

✔ America became involved in the affairs of Southeast Asia in the late 1940s when the federal government began to dole out aid to the French, who were fighting a war to regain control over Indochina (Cambodia, Laos, and Vietnam) — its former colony — against Communist rebels led by a man named Ho Chi Minh. France, which had controlled Indochina since 1887, lost control of Indochina during World War II when the Japanese invaded and occupied the region.

✔ Ho Chi Minh's forces defeated the French in 1954, and the U.S. increased its involvement by setting up a pro-Western government eventually led by dictator Ngo Dinh Diem in the southern half of Vietnam. By the late 1950s, Communists in the south organized themselves into the National Front for the Liberation of South Vietnam (NLF), known in the U.S. as the *Viet Cong.* Ho Chi Minh's Communist government in Hanoi sent assistance to the rebels in the south.

✔ The U.S. government initially supported Diem, who was a corrupt and unpopular leader, by supplying financial aid and military advisors. By the time Eisenhower left office in 1960, more than 650 U.S. military advisors were in South Vietnam, and the U.S. was providing aid in the form of weapons and ammunition. Under John F. Kennedy's (JFK) administration, aid to South Vietnam steadily increased. Despite aid from the U.S., Diem's regime was on the brink of collapse by fall 1963. The military struggle against the Viet Cong was failing, and a religious crisis had erupted and enforced the popular resistance to the government in the South. In early November 1963, military leaders in South Vietnam who had been assured of U.S. support, staged a coup and killed Diem and his brother. By the time of Kennedy's assassination in late November 1963, the number of military advisors in Vietnam totaled 16,000.

✔ The crisis escalated during the administration of President Lyndon B. Johnson, JFK's successor. For the first several months of his administration, LBJ laid low, increasing only the number of military advisors in Vietnam by about 5,000. In August 1964, the North Vietnamese attacked the USS *Maddox* in international waters. To this day, it's a bit sketchy whether the ship was actually attacked or if the attacks were reported accurately. In response to the attack, Congress passed the *Gulf of Tonkin Resolution,* which gave Johnson the power to "take all necessary measures to repeal any armed attack against the forces of the United States and to prevent further aggression."

President Johnson (and later President Richard Nixon) used this declaration to fight an undeclared war in Vietnam without further congressional approval. Within a few months of the Gulf of Tonkin Resolution, American bombers were continuously bombing North Vietnam under U.S. order "Operation Rolling Thunder." By the end of 1965, 184,000 American ground troops were stationed in Vietnam.

✔ In 1966 and 1967, Johnson continued escalating the U.S. military presence in Vietnam. By the end of 1967, 500,000 troops were stationed in Vietnam. By the end of 1966, the U.S. had 4,000 American causalities in Vietnam. In 1966 and 1967, the U.S. also ramped up the air war in Vietnam. By the time the U.S. withdrew from Vietnam, the total tonnage of bombs dropped in Vietnam from 1954 to 1973 exceeded that of all military theaters of World War II.

> ✔ In the early morning hours of January 31, 1968, North Vietnamese and Viet Cong (South Vietnamese Communists) forces unleashed a massive attack on unsuspecting U.S. positions throughout South Vietnam. The attack was known as the *Tet Offensive;* "Tet" referred to the Vietnamese New Year on which the attack began. American forces eventually defeated the attackers, inflicting heavy casualties on enemy forces, but the attack was a blow to American morale. By this time, most Americans realized that the war wouldn't be as easily won as they had been initially led to believe, if it could be won at all.

The SAT II may require you to know about the factors that brought the United States into the Vietnam War. Check out the following question.

The Gulf of Tonkin Resolution was used to

(A) Reduce American presence in Southeast Asia.

(B) Negotiate a peace treaty with North Vietnam.

(C) Wage an undeclared war in Vietnam.

(D) Justify the use of nuclear weapons.

(E) Reinstate diplomatic ties with China.

If you remember that the Gulf of Tonkin Resolution had to do with Vietnam, you can eliminate choice (E). You're already within guessing range. If you remember that the Gulf of Tonkin Resolution escalated the war in Vietnam, you know that neither (A) nor (B) can be the answer, and (D) should seem out of place because the question of nuclear weapons didn't factor in to Vietnam. By process of elimination, the answer is (C). If you can narrow down your choices, you can increase the probability of getting the correct answer.

A new kind of enemy: Vietnam combat

When U.S. soldiers arrived in Vietnam, they stepped into an ongoing civil war that they didn't understand. After being "in country" for a while, soldiers were often confused about why they were even there. Soldiers were sent on search-and-destroy missions through dense jungles, where they engaged the enemy in sporadic firefights. Many soldiers died in ambushes laid by enemy troops, who knew the jungle much better, or were picked off by sniper fire or killed or maimed by booby traps. Tempers flared and frustration levels soared as American soldiers searched for an enemy, who typically attacked in quick bursts only to disappear into dense foliage and peasant villages. American soldiers were ordered to burn down many villages, hoping to flush out enemy soldiers, but distinguishing friend from foe was very difficult. They didn't know whether a child walking toward them had a grenade behind his back or just wanted their chocolate bars. For nearly a decade, American troops were fighting a war that they didn't understand and didn't seem able to win. For this reason, you sometimes hear the Vietnam War referred to as the "quagmire."

Soldiers killed civilians, women, and children, sometimes by accident and sometimes with cold intent. As American involvement in Vietnam grew, so did the despondency of American soldiers. Desertions and AWOLs (Absence Without Leave) abounded and so did drug use. While American bombers were bombing North Vietnam, many American soldiers were getting bombed and getting stoned, partly to cope with their situation, partly because drugs like opium, heroin, and marijuana were readily available. American soldiers had an overwhelming superiority in numbers and firepower, but the American goal to protect South Vietnam was a limited goal. The North Vietnamese were committed to winning at any cost, and the American public counted the high cost of war.

Voicing opinions: Antiwar protests

At least initially, the majority of Americans supported the war in Vietnam, but as television brought the reality of war into the living rooms of millions of homes, as the body count rose and rumors of atrocities reached American ears, and as Johnson continued a stubborn doctrine of escalation that had no clear purpose or results, millions of Americans angrily protested. Mass demonstrations became frequent, and they multiplied as the war escalated and the bad news continued.

In April 1965, 25,000 people marched to the White House. Two years later, 100,000 people marched on Washington and, by the early 1970s, hundreds of thousands protested across the country for an end to the war. Some burned American flags, others burned their draft cards. Some Americans even showed public support for the North Vietnamese.

Dodging the draft was common in the late 1960s and early 1970s. Thousands of young men faced jail time or fled the country to Canada, Sweden, or other countries. Thousands more simply didn't register, and many burned their draft cards at college campus antiwar rallies. The government estimates that at least 500,000 men committed draft violations during the war. Johnson's approval rating dropped like a stone and, in 1968, Johnson announced that he would not seek reelection.

A messy inheritance: Richard Nixon's role in the Vietnam War

Richard Nixon inherited a war that his predecessors had begun that had spiraled out of control. America couldn't win the war, but it couldn't back out because too much had been invested: lives, money, and the reputation of the United States. Nixon had pressure to end the war, but he had to find a way to do it and save face for America. Ultimately, his attempts were futile.

The turbulent election of 1968

Americans were slammed with bad news in 1968. Two assassinations occurred, one of civil rights leader, Martin Luther King, Jr. (see Chapter 20), and the other of Robert Kennedy, the front-running Democratic presidential candidate and JFK's brother and former U.S. attorney general. The *Tet Offensive* in January 1968 gave Americans little reason to remain optimistic about the war in Vietnam and many reasons to become disillusioned. Within a few weeks of the Tet Offensive, public opposition to the war more than doubled and Johnson's approval rating sunk to a mere 35 percent, (the lowest of any president since Harry Truman). Americans received even more bad news in August 1968 when, thanks to television, Americans witnessed the ugly riots at the Democratic National Convention in August, where Chicago police used teargas and billy clubs against antiwar protesters, injuring hundreds.

Without Robert Kennedy as an option, the Democrats chose Hubert Humphrey, Johnson's vice president, as their candidate. Democrats assumed that Humphrey would carry on with the policies of the Johnson administration. The Republicans chose Richard Nixon, the former vice president under Eisenhower. Nixon was in favor of ending the war in Vietnam with what he called "peace with honor." Alabama Governor George C. Wallace, a staunch segregationist, ran as an independent third-party candidate. Wallace never really had much chance of winning, but he put in a good showing. His platform called for a crackdown on antiwar protests and race riots, and he appealed to the Deep South and even some northerners with his tough stance on law and order. The election was extremely close: Wallace won 13 percent of the popular vote and split the Democrat vote, but Nixon won back the White House for the Republicans with a 500,000 popular vote victory over Humphrey.

Nixon's approach to the war abroad and at home

Nixon's strategy in Vietnam was to gradually remove the U.S. from the war and turn responsibility over to the South Vietnamese. This policy became known as *Vietnamization* (try saying that ten times fast). The U.S. began a slow process of pulling out American troops and training and arming the South Vietnamese army to take over the war. But in the spring of 1970, Nixon also stepped up bombing raids in Northern Vietnam and expanded the war into the neighboring country of Cambodia, which the North Vietnamese were suspected of using as a safe haven to launch their attacks on South Vietnam and the U.S. forces. Nixon kept the raids on Cambodia a secret from both Congress and the public. Only after the U.S. military had successfully established a pro-American regime in Cambodia did Nixon inform the American public that he was sending U.S. troops into Cambodia.

Antiwar protests in response to the Cambodia announcement literally increased overnight. On May 4, at Kent State University in Ohio, national guardsmen shot and killed four student demonstrators. On May 14, police killed two black college students at an antiwar protest at Jackson State University in Mississippi. As the antiwar fervor mounted in the media, Congress repealed the Gulf of Tonkin Resolution in December 1970, basically repealing any legal basis for the U.S. to continue involvement in the war. In February 1971, Nixon ordered the Air Force to assist the South Vietnamese in invading Laos, using the same rationale with which they invaded Cambodia. However, the Laos outing was unsuccessful, and the South Vietnamese were defeated there within a few weeks. Throughout 1971 and into 1972, the U.S. continued to bomb Vietnam and Cambodia with little success.

In June 1971, top-secret Defense Department documents that detailed governmental decision-making in Vietnam during the Johnson administration were leaked to *The New York Times*. These documents, known as the *Pentagon Papers,* proved that the U.S. government lied about how it had been conducting the war. The Pentagon Papers revealed that the U.S. government had lied about the military progress in the war and about its motives for involvement in the war. Neither of these revelations surprised the public or the media.

Throughout 1971, public support for the war sank to an all-time low. In public opinion polls, more than ⅔ of the American public supported American withdrawal from Vietnam. However, the Nixon administration remained stubborn. Nixon and his advisors were concerned that a defeat in Vietnam would take away what remained of the administration's credibility. However, with the election looming in 1972, Nixon was forced to take action or risk losing reelection. He decided that the U.S. had to pull out, regardless of the occupation of North Vietnamese troops in South Vietnam. Throughout the spring, summer, and early fall of 1972, Henry Kissinger, assistant to the president for national security affairs, met repeatedly with the North Vietnamese foreign secretary to work out the terms for a ceasefire. In late October 1972, only a few days before the election, Kissinger succeeded, temporarily.

Despite the protests and the unpopularity of the war, the American people reelected Nixon in 1972 (his opponent was antiwar Democratic candidate George McGovern). When problems erupted again in Vietnam in late November and talks were unsuccessful, Nixon promptly ordered the bombing of the North Vietnam capital, Hanoi, and other targets in North Vietnam, in December 1972. Nixon hoped the bombing would force the North Vietnamese into making concessions and ending the war.

The end of the war and its aftermath

Finally, in January 1973, the U.S. and North Vietnam returned to the negotiation table to make a deal. On January 27, 1973, they signed the *Paris Peace Accords,* which officially ended the war, ordered an immediate ceasefire, and called for the immediate release and return of all several hundred American prisoners of war. As part of the agreement, America also agreed to remove all troops from Vietnam within 60 days and to help establish a coalition government in South Vietnam that included the Viet Cong. However, no sooner had U.S. troops left than fighting broke out once again. The South Vietnamese government fell, and American officials and civilians had to escape quickly. The North and the South continued to fight until 1975 when North Vietnamese forces finally overran the South and returned peace to the war-ravaged nation.

More than 58,000 Americans died in Vietnam, and more than 150,000 were wounded. The U.S. government estimates that more than 800,000 Vietnam veterans suffered psychological trauma as a result of the war. The Vietnamese lost a whole lot more; the U.S. government estimates that two million Vietnamese died as a result of the war. Bombs decimated their countryside (remember, the U.S. dropped more bombs in Vietnam than all bombs dropped in World War II), and more than one million Vietnamese fled the country. The war cost the U.S. government $176 billion, but the numbers alone don't adequately explain the long-term emotional and psychological consequences of the war for either side.

Keeping Track of "Tricky Dick": Richard Nixon's Presidency

Richard Nixon had a long, successful career as a politician, despite his loss to John F. Kennedy in the 1960 presidential election. Nixon came back big, winning the presidential election of 1968 and slaughtering the competition in the 1972 election by winning the electoral vote of every state except Massachusetts. Nixon earned his nickname "Tricky Dick" from the media in the U.S. Senate election in 1950 because he used very effective negative campaign techniques against his opponents. His willingness to use dirty tricks and his desire to win at all costs ended up doing him in. Engulfed in scandal, Nixon became the first and only American president to ever resign his office in disgrace.

Diving into domestic issues

By the time Nixon took office in 1968, his administration had to battle inflation, unemployment, a slowing economy, and address social issues, such as the environment, civil rights, and feminism. Nixon was a pragmatic politician who used whatever means at his disposal to solve domestic problems.

Curbing inflation and unemployment

For the SAT II, note that two of Nixon's biggest problems during his presidency were domestic. The American economy was experiencing rising inflation and unemployment, which was a double whammy that economists had never seen before. A new term, *stagflation,* cropped up to describe the phenomenon.

Although stagflation stuck with Nixon throughout his presidency, the situation probably wasn't his fault. Historians blame the problem on Lyndon B. Johnson's deficit spending to cover the costs of the Vietnam War and his gigantic social programs (see Chapter 20). Nixon tried to halt stagflation through a plan he developed in 1971 called the *New Economic Policy.* This policy called for temporary wage and price freezes, tax cuts, a 10 percent import tax, and measures to devalue American currency. The economy recovered briefly, just long enough for his reelection in 1972, but was on the downturn again in 1973.

Preserving the environment

One of the many movements that sprang from the turbulent 1960s was environmentalism. By the early 1970s, the majority of Americans believed that the environment was one of the nation's most urgent problems. Nixon's administration responded to the public outcry by signing a boatload of legislation aimed at protecting air, land, and sea into law. In 1970, Congress passed a law that created the *Environmental Protection Agency (EPA)* and the National Oceanic and Atmospheric Administration (NOAA) and beefed up the *Clear Air Act* of 1967 (and changed the name to the Clean Air Act of 1970), which gave the government authority to set air-quality standards. Congress passed other laws to protect endangered species and marine mammals and to set standards for noise pollution and clean water. Acts of Congress also set aside more than 100 million acres of land for parks, wildlife refuges, and wilderness areas and passed laws to gradually ban the use of aerosol cans after studies revealed their harmful effects on the ozone layer.

Taking a softer stance on civil rights

By late 1968, the civil rights movement (see Chapter 20), overshadowed by Vietnam and U.S. domestic issues, was running out of steam. Nixon appealed to Americans who wanted a reprieve from the chaos of the 1960s. He wanted to appeal to his constituency, which was largely conservative, white, middle-class voters, who wanted a *New Federalism* with less interference by the federal government and fewer social programs. As part of Nixon's Southern strategy, he began courting Southern voters for the 1972 election by softening the federal government's support of implementing civil rights laws. During Nixon's first administration, widespread public criticism surfaced over the issue of busing children across towns and cities to integrate schools. Nixon called on Congress to ban the practice and went on television to denounce it as a radical and destructive policy. He repeatedly, and unsuccessfully, tried to get Congress to pass legislation prohibiting segregation through the use of forced busing.

Nixon also tried to appeal to his conservative constituency and the South, when he appointed four allegedly conservative Supreme Court justices: one in 1969 and 1970, and two in 1972. In his second appointments in 1970, Nixon tried to appoint two inexperienced southern federal judges, one of whom was a segregationist. Congress shot both justice nominations down, forcing Nixon to come up with more widely accomplished and moderate nominations. Although the four justices who Nixon nominated ended up in the Court, they were thought to be conservatives. But the new Court surprised everyone because its members turned out to be much more reform-minded than anyone thought.

"I am woman": Feminism takes hold

When the 19th Amendment passed in 1920, women gained the right to vote, and the women's movement took a chill pill for a few decades. The movement revived in the 1960s because more women had entered the workplace and found that they weren't exactly welcome. Some issues that women faced in the workplace included discrimination based on sex (the big one that describes all the others), limited opportunities for professional careers, unequal wages, and inadequate daycare facilities for children. (See Chapter 20 for more about the start of the women's movement.)

By the early 1970s, a new brand of feminist emerged — a more radical version that was known to burn bras in public protest over sexual inequalities. Other goals of the women's movement included making affordable contraception widely available, developing more women's health clinics, and eliminating all-male (and all female) colleges. Congress responded to the growing demands of women by approving the Equal Rights Amendment, which basically outlawed discrimination based on sex in 1972, but the amendment eventually was defeated in 1978 because not enough states ratified it. Despite this setback, women gained rights through the court system, most notably in the 1973 Supreme Court decision *Roe v. Wade,* which legalized abortion. Feminists saw this decision as a huge victory; finally, women had the right to control what was going on in their own bodies. But this decision is one of the most controversial in Supreme Court history, and Americans still dispute it on legal, moral, and political grounds today.

Focusing on foreign diplomacy

If Nixon left any mark other than the stain of Watergate (see the next section), it was on U.S. foreign relations. So, the SAT II may test your knowledge in this area, too.

Nixon and his National Security Advisor Henry Kissinger (who later became Nixon's secretary of state) acted as a dynamic duo shaping American foreign relations through a policy known as *détente,* which sought better relations with the Soviet Union and limitations on the arms race while continuing to keep Soviet expansion in check. Détente played out directly in relations between the superpowers and indirectly through conflicts in Third World countries where both powers held interests.

The following are the highlights of Nixon's foreign policy:

✔ **Beginning relations with China:** Nixon softened diplomatic relations with China and the Soviet Union, hoping to use their mutual distrust of one another to America's benefit. In 1972, Nixon made a trip to China and met with Chairman Mao Tse-Tung, Premier Chou-En-lai, and other Chinese leaders. The trip was an historic event that received lots of media attention because, after essentially ignoring China for the previous 20 years, Nixon's visit opened diplomatic relations. The trip signaled a turning point for Chinese-American relations and showed that the U.S. was ready to recognize China as a Communist nation.

✔ **SALT:** Nixon also made a historic trip to Moscow in 1972 and was the first American president to set foot in the Soviet capital. Nixon met with Soviet leader Leonid Brezhnev for the *Strategic Arms Limitation Talks (SALT),* which led to *SALT 1 (Strategic Arms Limitation Treaty.)* This treaty limited the proliferation of anti-ballistic missiles and the number of nuclear missiles that each country could have, which slowed the arms race.

✔ **Relations with Israel:** In 1973, Egypt (backed by the Soviet Union) and Syria attacked Israel, which, as a result of a middle eastern war that ended in 1967, was occupying lands that Arab nations claimed. The refugees from this territory were placing a strain on other countries, such as Jordan and Lebanon. Egypt and Syria stepped in to get control of the land back. The U.S. provided aid to Israel throughout the conflict, known as the *Yom Kippur War.* Because of the United States' involvement, the oil-producing Arab nations imposed an embargo on all oil shipments to the U.S., which caused a severe oil shortage in the U.S. Kissinger negotiated a peace settlement. The Arab nations lifted the oil embargo, and friendlier relations between the U.S. and Egypt opened up.

A trail of corruption: The Watergate scandal and Nixon's resignation

At 2:30 a.m., June 17, 1972, police arrested five men who they caught placing phone taps and sifting through files at the offices of the Democratic National Committee located in the Watergate Hotel in Washington, D.C. Four of the men were ex-Cuban nationals with ties to the Bay of Pigs invasion (see Chapter 20), and the fifth was an ex-CIA agent. All of them were working for the Committee to Re-Elect the President (CREEP), and all of them had been paid out of a secret reelection committee fund controlled by White House staff. Although Nixon denied that his administration had any involvement in the break-in, subsequent investigations revealed a trail of coverups and corruption that ran through the White House and ended with the president himself.

The Watergate scandal wasn't a single incident but a web of interrelated plots with a huge cast of characters. For the SAT II U.S. History exam, you don't need to know all the details of the Watergate scandal. The list that follows gives you all the major plots points that you need to know for the exam.

- Although the scandal officially began with the break in at the Watergate Hotel, the story actually begins a year earlier when Nixon illegally formed his own secret investigative team nicknamed "The Plumbers" to prevent information about his administration from being leaked to the press and to perform operations against antiwar protestors and Democrats. The Plumbers carried out a number of functions that basically amounted to spying on government employees. They tried to discredit the former Pentagon employee who was responsible for leaking the Pentagon Papers (see the earlier section in this chapter, "Nixon's approach to the war abroad and at home").

- Early in 1973, the Watergate burglars went on trial, and one of them told the judge that White House officials knew about the break-in and were paying the defendants to keep their mouths shut. Reporters *Bob Woodward* and *Carl Bernstein* from *The Washington Post* were present at the trial of burglar James W. McCord Jr. (the ex-CIA agent). The two reporters got interested in the scandal and began a long investigation.

- In 1973, the Senate Select Committee on Campaign Practices heard testimony from White House aides suspected of involvement. John Dean, White House counsel, dropped a bombshell when he revealed that a coverup was underway and that Nixon was involved. Another aide testified that Nixon had taped conversations in the White House, including conversations about Watergate.

- During the trials of the burglars and investigations of White House staff members, Nixon repeatedly assured the American public of his innocence.

- Obtaining information from a secret White House informant who went by the name of "Deep Throat," Woodward and Bernstein wrote a series of articles in *The Washington Post* that maintained public interest in the story and eventually led to the Nixon administration's guilt and coverup.

- Nixon tried to distance himself from the scandal by firing some of his aides who the Senate committee suspected of involvement. Archibald Cox, the special prosecutor appointed by the attorney general to investigate Watergate, took Nixon to court in October 1973 to force him to give up the tapes. Nixon sent the prosecutor packing. The attorney general and his deputy resigned in protest over this incident, and the mass exodus became known as the *Saturday Night Massacre.* Nixon's reputation with the public slid after this incident.

- Due to public outrage, Nixon appointed a new special prosecutor, Leon Jaworski, who was just as determined as Cox. He took Nixon to court over the tapes. In late 1973, Nixon's vice president, Spiro Agnew, resigned after pleading no contest to charges of bribery and tax evasion while he was governor of Maryland and vice president. Under the principles of the 25th Amendment, which had been adopted in 1967 regarding the succession of the vice presidency and presidency, Nixon appointed Gerald Ford, House Minority Leader from Michigan, to replace Agnew as vice president.

- On March 1, 1974, the grand jury in the Watergate investigation indicted seven of Nixon's top aides on charges of obstructing justice and conspiracy in hindering the investigation.

- Throughout early 1974, Nixon refused to give up the taped conversations, claiming executive privilege, so Jaworski appealed to the Supreme Court. On July 24, 1974, the Supreme Court, in a unanimous decision in *United States v. Richard M. Nixon*, ordered Nixon to release all the tapes in question to Special Prosecutor Jaworski.

- In July 1974, the House of Representatives began a formal impeachment investigation of President Nixon. The hearing, which lasted for several days in July 1974, was nationally televised. After several days of testimony, the House Judiciary Committee voted to impeach Nixon for obstruction of justice, abuse of power, and contempt of Congress.

- On August 5, Nixon finally released the remaining tapes he had, which contained incriminating evidence that Nixon had ordered the FBI to stop the Watergate investigation three days after the 1972 break-in. Three days later, on August 8, 1974, Nixon officially resigned from office, the first president ever to do so.

On August 9, 1974, Gerald Ford became president. A month after he took office, Ford granted Nixon a full pardon. Although he claimed that it was to avoid long-term litigation in association with Watergate, issuing the pardon did little for Ford's credibility in this time of disillusionment. Many Americans thought that he granted the pardon as some sort of special agreement between himself and the disgraced former president.

The Watergate scandal had many lasting effects. As you've probably figured out by now, the makers of the SAT II just love to come up with cause-and-effect questions. One of the most important effects of the Watergate scandal was that Americans became disillusioned with the federal government. For a long time after the scandal, the American public had little trust in the federal government and their leaders. Also, since Watergate, Americans have expected a higher level of personal disclosure from public officials. Furthermore, the media, following in the footsteps of Woodward and Bernstein, is now much more aggressive in reporting the activities of politicians. Because many of those involved in the Watergate scandal were lawyers, including Nixon, the legal profession underwent some changes, too. The American Bar Association strengthened its code of professional conduct for lawyers and required law students to take a course in professional responsibility.

Had enough of Nixon yet? Not so fast — now you have to put your newfound knowledge to the test!

All the following were results of the Watergate scandal EXCEPT

(A) Successive presidents were expected to fully disclose their activities.

(B) Nixon became the first president to resign from office.

(C) The 25th Amendment was put into use for the first time.

(D) U.S. involvement in the Vietnam War ended.

(E) The American public lost trust in the government.

Okay, this question may seem like a tough one, but apply what you know about Watergate.

Nixon resigned, and no other president had ever done so, so you can eliminate (B). What happened when Nixon resigned? Gerald Ford became president. Remember, Ford was *not* elected — Nixon appointed him vice president after Spiro Agnew resigned his position. Nixon appointed Ford under the 25th Amendment, which was adopted in 1967. This incident was the first use of this amendment, therefore, you can cross off (C). So, you're left with (A), (D), and (E). Naturally, Americans lost trust in their government officials after such a serious scandal, so you can confidently cross out (E). After Watergate, the public and the media became suspicious of politicians and, although it's not a law, most presidents disclose all their activities, so (A) isn't correct. By the time you take the SAT II History, you should remember that the Vietnam War really had little to do with the Watergate scandal and that the U.S. involvement in the war officially ended in January 1973, 18 months before Nixon resigned from office, so the correct answer is (D).

The Man from Georgia: Jimmy Carter's Presidency

Gerald Ford's presidency lasted only through 1976, the year of the bicentennial (America's 200th birthday). The Ford administration was unsuccessful with America's economic problems. The nation experienced a serious recession in 1974 to 1975, but the administration refused to lower interest rates, refused to cut taxes, and opposed an increase in federal spending. Inflation was out of control, reaching 11 percent in 1976. Ford also had to deal with an energy crisis and rapidly rising oil prices.

In 1976, Ford ran for reelection. He barely made it out of the primary due to a challenge from fellow Republican Ronald Reagan, who you can read more about in Chapter 22. Ford's Democratic opponent was the little-known Jimmy Carter from Georgia. Carter won the race with 50 percent of the popular vote, compared with Ford's 48 percent.

Democrat Jimmy Carter, a former governor of Georgia, was a political outsider who promised the American people that he would never lie to them. Coming off Vietnam and Watergate, this promise was music to American voters' ears. History remembers Jimmy Carter as a nice guy but a lousy president. Although he was an extremely intelligent and quick-witted, man, his intellect didn't help him much at 1600 Pennsylvania Avenue. Carter fought an uphill battle throughout his presidency because of problems that originated before his time; nevertheless, he still proved himself a poor leader who couldn't rally support from the American people. His presidency suffered from missteps at home and abroad.

Woes at home: Domestic dilemmas

Carter's presidency was marred by domestic economic troubles that most historians agree weren't his fault. Unemployment and inflation (the combination of the two occurrences is called "stagflation"; see "Curbing inflation and unemployment" earlier in this chapter) were already climbing when Carter took office. In early 1977, the unemployment rate was 7.4 percent (anything above 6 percent is bad) and was still over 7 percent when he left office in 1980. Inflation rose from 5 percent in 1970 to 14.5 percent in 1980, which basically meant that the prices of goods increased steadily and made the average American's paycheck worth less and less. Carter used a number of different approaches to try to check stagflation, but none of them worked.

Increased competition from foreign competitors and American dependence on foreign oil contributed to the United States' economic troubles. In the '70s, American oil reserves were drying up, and the Organization of Petroleum Exporting Countries (OPEC) steadily raised the price of oil. In 1974, OPEC raised oil prices 400 percent, knowing that America had to pay whatever the cartel asked. The rising cost of fuel meant that the U.S. couldn't supply as much oil as it had in the past. With a 400 percent price increase, oil simply became unafford-able and much less was available. Standing in line for gas seems unimaginable today, but in the '70s, gas stations had only so much gas to sell and, when it ran out, they wouldn't have more until the station received the next delivery.

Americans experienced long lines (and high prices) at the gas pumps. Nationwide, there were many attempts to conserve energy. People turned down their thermostats, carpooled, took public transportation, and drove their vehicles less. They also began to buy automobiles from Europe and Japan, which tended to be much more fuel efficient than big American cars. As a result, the American auto industry and related industries like steel, rubber, and glass fell on hard times. Unfortunately, OPEC didn't stop at one rate hike. In 1979, the cartel members decided to raise prices again, causing the nation's second energy shortage in a decade.

Carter initiated a number of programs to fight the rising energy costs. He encouraged devel-oping alternative energy sources and deregulating domestic oil pricing to jump-start domes-tic oil production. One of the great hopes to solve America's energy problems was nuclear power but, in 1979, a nuclear reactor melted down at Three Mile Island in Pennsylvania. Although very little radiation escaped, the incident put the brakes on the development of nuclear power plants.

Carter lacked the leadership qualities and the personality to inspire Americans' confidence. He also lacked the political skills necessary to work with Congress to accomplish his agenda of improving the economy and reforming the U.S. tax system. His administration did oversee the founding of the Department of Energy and the Department of Education, create a public works program, and enact environmental legislation, though. Despite his squeaky-clean image, scandals popped up around him, most notably when his brother Billy received $250,000 from Libya, a known terrorist state, under mysterious circumstances. Carter was unable to project a positive image in the media. For example, in July 1979, he gave what became called his "malaise speech." In this speech, he blamed many of America's problems on Americans themselves, saying that they had "a crisis of confidence." Despite his criticisms of the public, the speech was well received, but when he turned around and asked for resignations from all his cabinet officers, even his limited popularity began to fade.

An uneven record: Foreign triumphs and defeats

Unlike his predecessors, Carter's emphasis in foreign policy was not on fighting Communism; his main goal was to promote human rights around the world. When Carter took office in 1977, he promised to reduce America's military presence abroad, slow the arms race, and reduce the sale of arms. He also promised to use diplomatic means to bring peaceful solutions to world conflict. But by the end of his presidency, he had accomplished almost none of these goals. America had more troops overseas, and military spending and the sales of arms had increased. His diplomatic approach had a spotty record, at best.

Carter did have some successes in his dealings with other nations. He negotiated a peace treaty called the *Camp David Accords* between Israel and Egypt in 1978 and 1979. Israel agreed to remove its forces from the Sinai Peninsula, a territory it had occupied since 1967, and both countries agreed to recognize each other's governments. In 1977, Carter also completed negotiations on a treaty between the U.S and Panama to return the Canal Zone to the government of Panama in 1999. Unfortunately, Carter managed to screw up a number of other high-pressure international incidents.

In 1979, Carter negotiated the SALT (Strategic Arms Limitation Treaty) II arms control agreement with the Soviet Union. This treaty stipulated limitations on the number of certain kinds of weapons that each country could have. (To find out about SALT I, see the section "Focusing on foreign diplomacy" earlier in this chapter.) Initially, Carter and the Soviets agreed, but conservatives in Congress deeply opposed the treaty because they distrusted the Soviets.

In December 1979, Soviet troops invaded Afghanistan to protect the Communist government they had established there the previous year. (For those who are geographically challenged, Afghanistan is smack-dab between the former Soviet Union and Iran.) This invasion angered Carter, who saw this move by the Soviets as a way to take over the world's oil supplies in the Middle East. Carter immediately took action in an effort to force the Soviet army out of Afghanistan. He suspended grain and technology shipments to the Soviet Union, imposed other economic sanctions on the Soviet Union, withdrew SALT II from consideration by the Senate, and cancelled American participation in, and called for an international boycott of, the 1980 Summer Olympics in Moscow.

Carter also bungled the *Iran Hostage Crisis.* In 1979, the fundamentalist Islamic religious leader (and America-hater), Ayatollah Khomeini, came to power in Iran, deposing the American-friendly Shah of Iran, Mohammed Reza Pahlavi, who was dying of cancer. The U.S. admitted the Shah for medical treatment, which angered the Ayatollah and his fundamentalist followers, especially when Carter refused to turn the poor guy over to stand trial for his crimes during his years of totalitarian rule in Iran. For decades, the United States had financially backed the autocratic Shah, who had made efforts to modernize and Westernize Iran. Fundamentalist Iranians resented the Shah, though, for his repressive and authoritarian tactics during his rule.

On November 4, 1975, an angry armed mob of students stormed the U.S. embassy in Teheran, Iran, and took 66 Americans hostage. They released 13 of the hostages two weeks later (the women and African Americans) and a sick one in July 1980, but the radicals held the remaining 52 Americans hostage for more than a year and taunted the American government with them. Carter immediately applied pressure to Iran to release the hostages and, in November 1979, the U.S. stopped buying oil from Iran, froze $8 billion in Iranian assets in the U.S., expelled some Iranian immigrants from the U.S., and tried to get other countries to sanction Iran.

Carter attempted to negotiate with Iran, but attempts failed when Iran's list of demands got unreasonable. Finally, in April 1980, Carter authorized an ill-advised rescue attempt, but that mission failed when three U.S. helicopters suffered technical problems, and a fourth U.S. helicopter crashed into a U.S. transport plane (both were part of the rescue fleet) in the Iranian desert, killing eight American soldiers. It got even worse when some Iranian fundamentalists got a hold of the bodies of these soldiers and paraded them through the streets of Tehran for the benefit of international news cameras. Even worse, they also found the plan for the mission on one of the planes and publicized that to the world media, resulting in further embarrassment to the U.S.

The tide turned for the U.S. in July 1980 when the Shah died and when Iraq invaded Iran two months later. These two events made Iran much more receptive to resuming negotiations with the U.S. At the very end of his presidency, Carter was finally able to negotiate the terms of the hostages' release by releasing the billions in Iranian assets held in the U.S., which the Iranians were desperate to get their hands on in order to fund their escalating conflict with Iraq. The 52 hostages were released on Ronald Reagan's inauguration in January 1981, 444 days later. Throughout the crisis, Americans felt angry and violated. This event was the icing on the cake after more than a decade of international humiliation and defeat with the failure in Vietnam, the embarrassment of Watergate, and the essential breakdown of détente with the Soviet Union.

The SAT II may test you on Carter's presidency by asking you about his foreign diplomacy.

The Strategic Arms Limitation Treaties (SALT) between the U.S. and the Soviet Union during the Nixon and Carter administrations were attempts to

(A) Ban nuclear weapons.

(B) Slow the arms race.

(C) Bring stability to the Middle East.

(D) Increase trade between the countries.

(E) Improve relations with China

If you can remember that SALT stands for Strategic Arms Limitation Talks, you're home-free on this question.

By the title of the treaties, you can assume that they had to do with limiting arms. With that fact in mind, you can cross out (C), (D), and (E). Answers (A) and (B) look promising, but (A) sounds a little extreme. Because you've read this chapter, you know it doesn't mention banning nuclear weapons, so cross off (A).

Chapter 22

Moving Ahead: The United States at the Turn of the Century, 1980–Present

In This Chapter

▶ Making America more conservative: The Ronald Reagan years

▶ Looking at the highlights and lowlights of George H. W. Bush's presidency

▶ Meeting a controversial man: Bill Clinton and his administration

▶ Stepping into the future with George W. Bush's administration

You've now arrived at the blurry line where history meets current events. Some of the stuff in this chapter may appear on the SAT II, but it's really anyone's guess. Still, making a little more room in that already-stuffed noggin of yours won't hurt.

In this chapter, you find out about the four presidents who shaped the last decades of the 20th century and the first decade of the 21st: Ronald Reagan, George H. W. Bush, Bill Clinton, and George W. Bush. Three of these presidents were Republicans, and one was a Democrat. During these four presidencies, Americans witnessed an end to the Cold War and an escalation in the war on terrorism. Domestically, Americans experienced periods of economic uncertainty and others of nearly unprecedented economic stability. And each of the presidents had equal shares of both triumph and calamity, not unlike the administrations of prior decades.

Ronald Reagan and the Rise of Conservatism in the 1980s

Only in America could a modestly talented and moderately successful actor rise from the silver screen to the presidential podium. Republican Ronald Reagan, who defeated incumbent Democrat Jimmy Carter in the 1980 presidential election, led a revolution in the United States known as the *"Reagan Revolution."* The Reagan Revolution brought America into an era of conservatism, which the nation hadn't experienced since the 1920s.

At 69 years of age, Reagan was the oldest president ever elected to office, and he was also the only president who'd ever been divorced. Reagan had plenty of dissenters, like John Hinckley Jr., who tried to end Reagan's presidency in 1981 with an assassination attempt. But Reagan had been a former Hollywood actor, and he had a way with people and charmed the American public. He focused on the economy and instilled public confidence in America once again, which was sorely needed to heal the wounds of Vietnam and Watergate (see Chapter 21). Reagan, who served two terms, was a strong leader who stood firm against Communism and the Soviet Union, and his administration's policies arguably sped up the collapse of the Soviet Union.

Of the four presidents in this chapter, the SAT II exam is most likely to cover Ronald Reagan's administration because it is the oldest and, therefore, the most "historical" of the four.

The Reagan Revolution

In contrast to, and probably in reaction to, the free-love and anti-establishment 1970s, many Americans in the 1980s, including young people, were more conservative and materialistic. Religious groups concerned about a perceived slipping away of morals due to the 1970s sexual revolution and drug culture stepped up their political involvement. The *New Christian Right* and the *Moral Majority* were two religious political groups that helped elect Reagan to the White House. The hippies of the 1970s gave way to the *yuppies* (or Young Urban Professionals) of the 1980s, who were characterized as young men and women with graduate degrees who cared mostly about making money and moving up the corporate ladder. Yuppies favored conservative government policies that promoted the corporations that they worked for.

When Reagan entered office in 1981, the so-called Reagan Revolution wasn't just about fighting the Communists; it also involved changing the atmosphere of America. The rise of conservatism meant that Republicans had won a majority in the Senate for the first time since 1952 and, although the House had a Democratic majority, House conservatives were pretty good at persuading others to vote their way, making getting legislation approved easier for the Reagan administration.

Trickle down: Reaganomics and its effects

When Reagan entered office, the economy was in a slump. In 1980, interest rates were at an all-time high (often exceeding 20 percent!) and inflation was way up, too, averaging 10 percent. During his election campaign, Reagan promised to turn the economy around using bold economic strategies like reducing taxes and the federal budget and decreasing unemployment, inflation, and interest rates.

Reaganomics is an easy concept to remember if you think of Reagan as an anti-Robin Hood character, taking from the poor and giving to the rich. Of course, this generalization is grossly over-simplified (although Reagan-bashers would claim it as gospel), but it gets you thinking in the right direction.

Reagan thought that if he cut taxes for businesses and the wealthy while reducing government regulations on industry, the movers and shakers would turn around and invest more in the American economy. This investment, in turn, would stimulate growth, which would create more jobs. But cutting taxes meant cutting government services, especially for the poor. Reagan justified this point by saying that the benefits of a booming economy would eventually "trickle down" to the poor. This theory is also known as *supply-side economics.*

During the first eight months of 1981, Congress passed Reagan's economic legislation package, which included $40 billion in budget cuts and the largest cuts to personal and corporate income taxes in U.S. history. The Reagan administration cut billions of dollars from welfare programs like Medicare and Medicaid, food stamps, school lunches, student loans, and welfare subsidies for the working poor. The economy didn't immediately benefit from these tax and budget cuts. By 1982, the U.S. was experiencing the worst recession since the Great Depression in the 1930s and the highest level of unemployment (11 percent) in 40 years. However, by mid-1983, the economy showed signs of improvement: Unemployment fell to 8 percent, and inflation fell to 5 percent.

Cuts in domestic spending affected poor Americans the most. In the first few years of the Reagan administration, the number of homeless rose to the highest level since 1965, and that number continued to rise throughout the 1980s, partially due to major cutbacks in federal spending for low-income housing programs. During the first five years of Reagan's administration, the number of poor increased by about nine million, and the gap between the rich and the poor grew tremendously. The administration also cut programs that provided federal assistance to states and cities, which reduced what local governments could do to help the poverty crisis in their own backyards.

So, you may be wondering, was Reaganomics successful? If you were rich during the 1980s, you'd probably say yes, but if you were poor, you'd probably say no. Historians tend to say no also. Even with Reaganomics, the nation experienced two severe recessions, one from 1981 to 1983 and another from 1987 to 1989. The 1987 recession began on October 19, 1987, with the largest single-day stock market decline (20 percent) in history. (Yes, even bigger than that other dark October day, October 29, 1929). Reaganomics also helped create the second-largest federal budget deficit from a combination of increased costs of running "entitlement" programs, such as Medicare and social security (despite cuts to their budgets), increased military spending, and tax cuts.

SAT II questions about Reagan may likely test your knowledge of Reaganomics. Check out the following question.

Reagan's economic policy, known as Reaganomics, involved all the following EXCEPT

(A) Tax cuts for corporations and the wealthy

(B) Cuts in welfare programs

(C) Reduction of regulations on industry

(D) Trickle-down effects

(E) Increased government assistance for the poor

You have four correct answers and one that's incorrect which, in this case, is the one you want.

Reagan was a business-friendly president (like most Republican presidents), so you can assume that Reaganomics helped businesses. With that fact in mind, you can eliminate choices (A) and (C). If you know a little about Reaganomics and understand that in order to cut taxes, Reagan had to cut welfare programs, then you can eliminate choice (B). Answer (E) starts to look good because it's basically the opposite of (B).

However, (D) can be tricky if you don't know that trickle-down effects refer to the idea that helping the wealthy and businesses eventually benefits the poor. If you can remember that concept, eliminating (D) is easy, which leaves (E) as the correct answer. Even if you can't remember what trickle-down effects are, you'd still have a 50/50 shot of correctly answering the question.

To your health: Warnings from the Surgeon General

In 1981, the first cases of AIDS (Acquired Immune Deficiency Syndrome) began to pop up in the U.S. Because the first cases were found in homosexual men, the disease was called the "gay plague" or "gay cancer." But as the number of reported cases multiplied, it became clear that heterosexuals were not immune. Panic spread throughout the country because so little was known about the disease.

In 1986, Surgeon General C. Everett Koop released a comprehensive report on AIDS, which had a huge impact on the understanding of the disease. "Safe Sex" campaigns began to advocate the use of condoms, and frank conversations about sexual history became common between couples. The freewheeling sexual revolution was over.

Koop also worked with First Lady Nancy Reagan in her "Just Say No" to drugs and alcohol crusade. With her "Just Say No" campaign, the First Lady actively advocated for public awareness of the problems of drug and alcohol abuse and for an end to drug and alcohol abuse, particularly for young people. Koop was also responsible for issuing groundbreaking reports that confirmed that cigarette smoking created dangerous health hazards and was as highly addictive as hard drugs, such as cocaine or heroine. He required alcohol and tobacco companies to include warning labels about the health consequences of drinking alcohol and smoking cigarettes on their packages.

A conservative Court: Reagan's Supreme Court appointments

One of Reagan's goals as president was to counteract the long, steady progression of liberal social policies that the government had undertaken since the days of Franklin Roosevelt's New Deal (see Chapter 17). One of the ways Reagan attempted to change liberal policy was by appointing conservative Supreme Court justices. He appointed Sandra Day O'Connor in 1981 (the first woman ever to sit on the Supreme Court), and Antonin Scalia in 1986. The new justices were conservative appointments, and Scalia was ultra-conservative, but each received unanimous approval from the Senate.

When Chief Justice Warren Burger announced his retirement in 1986, Reagan appointed Justice William Rehnquist, the most conservative justice on the Supreme Court, to the position of Chief Justice. President Richard Nixon had appointed Rehnquist to the Supreme Court in 1972. Liberal Senators like Edward Kennedy of Massachusetts were outraged and charged that Rehnquist was a radical conservative. But despite a few protests from left field, Congress approved Rehnquist's appointment.

Where Reagan really caused a stir was when he tried to appoint a conservative federal appeals court judge named Robert Bork to the empty justice seat left by Rehnquist on the Supreme Court in 1987. Bork had impeccable credentials as a judge, but Democrats feared his appointment would shift the power balance in the Supreme Court too far to the right. Bork believed in the concept of *original intent,* which said that the Constitution should be interpreted according to the words and the intent of the founding fathers who wrote it. This belief scared the heck out of liberals, who worried that Bork may vote to overturn important Supreme Court decisions like *Roe v. Wade*. Democratic senators held up Bork's appointment by hammering him with questions; they eventually gained enough votes to shoot down his appointment. When Bork's appointment failed, Reagan nominated Justice Anthony Kennedy, another conservative, in early 1988 to take over the empty seat left by Rehnquist. In all, Reagan appointed 358 judges to federal courts, the majority of whom are still around today.

Breaking the ice: Reagan and the end of the Cold War

By the time the 1980s rolled around, the Cold War was anything but over. Reagan was a hardcore anti-Communist who viewed the Soviet Union as an "Evil Empire" that threatened America and democracy around the world. He even went a step further; in a 1983 speech, Reagan said that the Soviet Union was "the focus of evil in the modern world."

Reagan's harsh rhetoric heated up the Cold War and so did his actions. He began the largest peacetime military buildup in the nation's history and sought to undermine Communist-leaning governments around the world through direct military action and covert operations. In 1985, Reagan declared that the U.S. would openly support anti-Communist movements, including rebels fighting against Soviet-backed governments or directly against the Soviets themselves. This policy was known as the *Reagan Doctrine.*

During the Reagan administration, Congress authorized unprecedented levels of defense spending. In Reagan's first two years in office, the U.S. nuclear arsenal expanded to an alarming level. The public's dissatisfaction with the nuclear buildup in the U.S. and the Soviet Union and growing fears of the likelihood of a nuclear war led to Reagan's development of the *Strategic Defense Initiative (SDI),* also called "Star Wars." SDI was a military program that used satellites and lasers to create a sort of invisible shield to protect against any incoming nuclear missiles. The Reagan administration spent billions on SDI, but the program was never actually completed.

Despite all this anti-Communist business, at the beginning of his second term, Reagan began to lighten up a bit, mainly due to the fact that the Soviet Union had a new leader — Mikhail Gorbachev. Gorbachev came to power in 1985 and immediately enacted a series of economic reforms (under a program called *perestroika*) and social reforms (with a program called *glasnost*). Under perestroika, Gorbachev aimed to improve living standards and worker productivity and permitted private business ownership. Under glasnost, he released thousands of political prisoners and lifted restrictions on speech and the press. Reagan and Gorbachev held five summit meetings between 1985 and 1989 and, in 1988, the two leaders reached an agreement to destroy all land-based intermediate-range nuclear missiles in Europe. The treaty, the *Intermediate-Range Nuclear Forces Treaty (INF),* was the first to actually reduce (rather than just limit production of) nuclear arsenals, and it signaled the beginning of the end of the Cold War.

The fruits of Reagan's negotiation efforts with Gorbachev were realized after Reagan left office. In Germany in November 1989, the *Berlin Wall* (the physical embodiment of the "iron curtain" and the symbol of division between Communism and Democracy) came tumbling down, a symbol of the official end of the Cold War. Berliners celebrated while the world watched on television. By the end of 1989, Soviet control of Eastern Europe had collapsed, which opened the door for more democratic forms of government. By 1991, the economy of the Soviet Union had collapsed under its own weight. The Soviet Union dissolved, and the Soviet republics gained political freedom, and Gorbachev was ousted. A new Russian president, Boris Yeltsin, was elected to office in 1991.

Contra controversy: The Iran-Contra Affair

White House officials got caught with their pants down in 1986 when rumors began flying that the U.S. government was secretly selling weapons to Iran in exchange for the release of American hostages in Lebanon. This scandal was known as the *Iran-Contra Affair.* Talk about national embarrassment. Throughout his presidency, Reagan had taken a firm stance against terrorism, denounced Iran as a terrorist nation, and demanded that allied countries not trade with it. In addition, Reagan had said that the U.S. did not negotiate with terrorists. As if that part of the scandal weren't enough, the U.S. government illegally funneled the money from the sale of weapons to revolutionaries (called Contras) in Nicaragua, who were trying to overthrow the leftist Sandinista government.

An investigation ensued, and Americans speculated about Reagan's involvement in the scandal and some made comparisons to Watergate. In the end, Reagan walked away without any serious damage to his image or popularity, while an obscure Marine lieutenant colonel named Oliver North took most of the blame. For many Americans, the scandal renewed a feeling of distrust of the federal government that they hadn't experienced since Watergate in the mid-1970s.

Daddy Bush: The Presidency of George H. W. Bush

George H. W. Bush (also father of the 43rd president, George W. Bush) offered Americans a kinder, gentler nation when he ran for president in 1988. And in some ways, he delivered. Bush, who had been Reagan's vice-president, certainly wasn't the ardent cold warrior that Reagan was, but he didn't need to be. The Soviet Union was crumbling under its own weight, and Soviet-supported governments in Eastern Europe were turning over democratic leaves. But Bush was also tough when he needed to be.

For the SAT II, keep in mind that Bush's greatest accomplishment as president was the Persian Gulf War. He was able to effectively use the power of diplomacy and America's military might to deliver a sound rebuke to a tyrannical Iraqi dictator, but this victory wasn't enough to secure his reelection. The ailing economy and an eccentric Texas billionaire with big ears did him in.

The success of the Persian Gulf War

On August 2, 1990, the Iraqi army swiftly invaded and took over the tiny oil-rich nation of Kuwait. Iraq's leader, Saddam Hussein, was a dictator who wasn't opposed to using poisonous gas to murder his own people. Hussein cited some weak reasons for his invasion of Kuwait and dared anyone to do anything about it.

On August 6, President Bush, afraid that Iraq would invade Saudi Arabia next and take control of the oil supplies of the region, announced to the American people that "This aggression will not stand." But rather than going to war immediately, Bush first attempted diplomacy. He built an international coalition of nations and sought and received United Nations (UN) resolutions condemning Iraq's actions. But soon the only choice became war. (As with the Korean and Vietnam Wars, the U. S. military wasn't technically at war with Iraq in the Persian Gulf War.)

On January 16, 1991, UN coalition forces led by the United States began a massive air assault. For six weeks, coalition forces bombed Iraqi forces and military installations into oblivion. Some experts estimate that 30 percent of the Iraqi army quit before a ground assault even began, and four days after coalition forces stepped foot on the ground, Iraq called it quits. Even though Iraq had the fourth-largest army in the world, Iraqi soldiers were demoralized and shell-shocked by the bombardments.

The *Persian Gulf War,* also referred to as *Operation Desert Storm,* freed Kuwait, but the international coalition allowed Hussein to remain in power. Hussein continued to be a thorn in the side of the U.S. and the UN for another decade until a different Bush decided that enough was enough. (See "Bush II: George W. Bush's Presidency" later in this chapter.)

Domestic disenchantment

Although America received a huge morale boost from the Gulf War and President Bush received a surge in approval ratings for the way he handled it, domestic problems began to erode his popularity. His biggest problem was the economy. By 1989, the budget deficit had reached a staggering $3.2 trillion, and a recession began that would last until 1992. When Bush had campaigned for the presidency, he promised the American people no new taxes. His famous quote was, "Read my lips, no new taxes." But when confronted with mammoth budget woes, Bush reneged on his promise — which the American people definitely didn't appreciate.

The savings and loan industry was also a mess. Reagan's deregulation of the industry had led to all kinds of problems and, by the late '80s, many savings and loan companies had gone bankrupt. The federal government had to step in and spend billions to bail many of these businesses out so that people wouldn't lose their savings.

People began to make Bush the scapegoat for a lagging economy, and this perception proved too great an obstacle for him to overcome in the 1992 election. Bush also wasn't helped by the fact that billionaire Ross Perot ran as a third-party candidate and received 19 percent of the vote, most of which came out of Bush's constituency. Democrat Bill Clinton won the 1992 election.

Tying it all together: A sample question looks at George H. W. Bush's presidency

The SAT II may test you on the highlights of the first Bush's presidency.

The presidency of George H. W. Bush is best remembered for which of the following?

(A) Sound domestic policy

(B) A thriving economy

(C) Saddam Hussein's removal

(D) Rampant scandals

(E) The success of the Gulf War

Bush isn't known for his domestic policies, so you can easily eliminate (A) and (B). He didn't remove Saddam Hussein from power; his son accomplished that feat a decade later, so (C) is out. Scandals didn't mar Bush's presidency, so (D) is an obviously wrong answer. Because the Persian Gulf War was seen as an overwhelming success and was by far the highlight of Bush's administration, (E) is the correct answer.

Prosperity and Controversy: Bill Clinton's Presidency

Five-time Arkansas Governor William Jefferson Clinton became the 42nd president of the United States when he defeated George H. W. Bush in 1992. As president, Clinton had a terrific record on domestic policy, a mixed record on foreign policy, and an utterly shameful record in the personal integrity department. Despite the controversy, peace and prosperity abounded during his years in the Oval Office.

SAT II tests in past years haven't had very many questions about Clinton, but in upcoming years as his two terms become more historical and less current, you may see one or two questions appear on his administration and the political climate of the 1990s.

Examining domestic issues

Domestic issues were a big part of the 1992 election platforms, and third-party candidate and millionaire Ross Perot promised to make significant economic changes. The people responded by giving Perot almost 20 percent of the popular vote (some think that Bush would have won the election had Perot not split the Republican vote). In his 1993 inaugural address, Clinton reassured Americans that "There is nothing wrong with America that can't be fixed with what is right in America." Those were strong, confident words from a newly-elected president, who won with only 43 percent of the popular vote.

Clinton, who constantly battled Republicans in Congress during his two terms in office, failed in his attempt to modernize and reform the healthcare system. An anti-government movement and terrorist incidents also affected his presidency. To his credit, he beat down the federal deficit and signed massive welfare reform into law. Clinton also raised the minimum wage and helped the working poor and middle-class families by cutting their taxes. But what Clinton is most remembered for was the enormous economic prosperity that existed during his two terms as president. Of course, historians and political pundits debate how much Clinton actually had to do with the success of the economy.

Enjoying an expansive economy

Clinton benefited politically from a booming economy that persisted throughout his presidency. America was coming out of the economic coma it had been in when he took office in 1993. America rode a wave of prosperity, which was largely due to the booming technology industry fueled by *dot-coms* (companies that grew from the popularity of the Internet), the Clinton administration's sound economic policies, and the economic contract Congress made with America. By the time Clinton left office in 2001, the Dow Jones Industrial Average (the stock performance index of 30 of the nation's largest and most widely-held industrial companies) was triple what it had been when he was inaugurated in 1993. Businesses created more than 22 million new jobs, unemployment was the lowest it had been in 30 years, the average household income was up, home ownership was higher than it had ever been, and the government turned the largest federal budget deficit in U.S. history into a surplus.

Conflicting with the right

Clinton had a lot of success on the domestic front, and when he defeated Republican Senator Bob Dole in the 1996 election, he was the first elected Democratic president to be reelected since Franklin Roosevelt. (Presidents Harry S Truman, who we discuss in Chapter 19, and Lyndon Johnson, covered in Chapter 20, both served over one term but had entered their first terms when their predecessors died in office.) Clinton called himself a "New Democrat" and pushed his party toward the center of the political spectrum. He took conservative stances on many social issues, such as favoring the death penalty and welfare reform. Despite his moderate stances, Republicans despised him, and his presidency became one of the most controversial in U.S. history.

Throughout Clinton's presidency, conservatives attacked Clinton and his wife Hillary, partly because of scandals (see "Dealing with personal issues" later in this chapter) and partly because they were Democrats. Two years into his presidency in the 1994 midterm elections, Republicans regained control of both houses of Congress, which proved a significant obstacle for Clinton. Republicans aggressively pushed their agenda called the "Contract with America" while thwarting Clinton's. Congressional votes on issues were sharply divided along party lines, and the Republican Congress shut down the federal government twice in a political power play to push through their version of the federal budget despite Clinton's vetoes. However, the move backfired because it inconvenienced a lot of Americans, who then blamed Republicans, which ended up boosting Clinton's public image.

In 1998, the ultimate conflict between Republicans and Democrats during the Clinton administration occurred when the House of Representatives voted to impeach Clinton on charges of obstruction of justice and perjury, stemming from a sex scandal involving a White House intern (see the section "Sexual scandals" later in this chapter). Clinton was the second president in U.S. history to be impeached (Andrew Johnson was the other; see Chapter 10). As with Johnson, the House voted to impeach Clinton, but the Senate didn't have enough votes to convict him. Following the impeachment, many Americans were disgusted with Clinton's lack of moral character, but they were also appalled by the mean-spirited partisanship of Republicans.

Managing anti-government sentiment and terrorist attacks

In the 1990s, an alarming number of religious wackos, white supremacists, and other assorted right-wing nut jobs began to band together in little disillusioned pockets, forming militias and survivalist groups. By 1997, these groups existed in every state. Those groups, combined with a number of domestic terrorist incidents, made Americans fear for their safety in their own country for the first time. Here are a few of the highlights:

✔ **The World Trade Center bombing:** On February 26, 1993, a car bomb went off in a parking garage beneath the World Trade Center buildings in New York City. Six people were killed and more than 1,000 were injured. A number of radical Islamic conspirators were sentenced to life in prison.

✔ **The Waco cult:** On February 28, 1993, federal agents tried to raid the compound of a religious cult called the Branch Davidians in Waco, Texas. The agents were looking for guns and explosives, but the Davidian's leader David Koresh knew they were coming. The two sides exchanged gunfire, and four agents and two cult members died. The feds laid siege to the compound for 51 days before they decided to storm it. Somehow a fire broke out, which engulfed the building and resulted in the deaths of 82 people, including 17 children. Americans heavily criticized the federal government for the botched raid.

✔ **The Oklahoma City bombing:** On April 19, 1995, a truck bomb decimated a federal building in Oklahoma City, killing 168 people, including 19 children, in the worst act of domestic terrorism Americans had ever experienced up to that time. Two Americans, Timothy McVeigh and Terry Nichols, who were linked to an extremist militia group, perpetrated the crime. McVeigh was sentenced to death, and Nichols got a life sentence.

✔ **The Unabomber:** For 18 years, domestic terrorist Theodore Kaczynski sent mail bombs to people in an effort to fight technological progress. Kaczynski was what you might call a "mad scientist." He earned a math degree from Harvard and a PhD from the University of Michigan. He targeted university professors and graduate students, computer store owners, and advertising industry executives, among others. His bombs killed 3 people and injured 27 others. The FBI finally tracked him down when his younger brother, who recognized his handwriting on Ted's manifesto published in the New York Times, turned him in.

✔ **Centennial Olympic Park bombing:** On July 27, 1996, a bomb ripped through Centennial Olympic Park in Atlanta, Georgia, during the Summer Olympics. Two people were killed and more than 100 were injured. Two years passed before authorities pinned down a suspect — an American man named Eric Robert Rudolph, a right-wing extremist who was involved in the bombing of several abortion clinics in the South.

Looking at foreign affairs

Clinton came into office with little experience in foreign policy matters, but he had his own ideas about how the United States should relate to the rest of the world. With the Cold War over, Clinton embraced strengthening the U.S. economy through integration with the world economy. He engaged the U.S. in efforts to reduce restrictions on international trade and built coalition forces to intervene in several international crises.

The U.S. remained active abroad, but Clinton preferred America's role to be one of an umpire for the UN; that is, to make sure everyone followed the same rules of fairness. He wanted the United States to use its military power only for altruistic purposes; using it to further business and economic interests abroad became sinful, at least according to the rhetoric. Clinton had some successes in foreign policy with an equal number of failures.

Signing NAFTA

In 1993, Congress passed the *North American Free Trade Agreement (NAFTA),* which eliminated most trade barriers with Canada and Mexico. NAFTA supporters tended to be large multinational corporations that stood to make huge profits. Politicians argued that NAFTA would create new, higher-wage jobs and raise the standard of living in the U.S., Canada, and Mexico. But its detractors believed that NAFTA would send hundreds of thousands of American jobs to Mexico, where labor was dirt cheap, and threaten health and environmental standards. NAFTA is still in effect today, and the jury is still out on whether its effects have been positive or negative.

All you really need to know about NAFTA is that it was an agreement among Canada, Mexico, and the U.S. to eliminate trade barriers.

Sending troops to Somalia, Bosnia, and Kosovo

The U.S. government sent soldiers to Somalia, a country located in East Africa, in 1992 to stabilize the country. Somalia was in the midst of a civil war and a severe drought, which led to a severe famine. The nation had no functioning government, and warlords had divided the country into warring factions. UN peacekeeping efforts were failing, and President George H. W. Bush announced that the U.S. would take the lead in restoring order to the country. Clinton continued this effort when he took over in 1993, but the situation turned ugly when two American helicopters were shot down in Somalia's capital Mogadishu and a handful of American soldiers were rushed by thousands of angry Somalians, who dragged one soldier's body jubilantly through the streets. This incident was more than enough to turn American sentiment against operations in Somalia, and Clinton withdrew all American troops.

Somalia was counted as a foreign policy failure for Clinton, but he faired a little better in dealing with the war in the Balkans. The Balkan states — Bosnia–Herzegovina, Serbia, Croatia, Macedonia, Montenegro, Albania, and Slovenia — developed out of the former Yugoslavia, which began to break apart after the fall of the Soviet Union in the late 1980s. With no unifying national identity, centuries worth of ethnic hatred was rekindled among Serbs, Bosnians, and Croatians.

Serbians, led by the Yugoslav People's Army, started wars in Slovenia and Croatia in 1991 and in Bosnia in 1992 as an effort to keep Yugoslavia united. The United States led NATO air strikes that took out Serbian forces and compelled Serb leader Slobodan Milosevic to attend peace talks in November 1995. As a result of the peace talks, leaders split Bosnia among the ethnic factions, and the U.S. placed 20,000 troops in the area to ensure peace. In 1996, the country held free elections.

In 1996, conflict broke out in Kosovo, a region that Albanians and Serbians both claimed. This time the Serbs were fighting ethnic Albanians, who were fighting for their freedom. Once again, the fighting got ugly as Milosevic began "purifying" Kosovo of Albanians, a process called "ethnic cleansing." Milosevic chased Albanians out of Kosovo into neighboring countries, creating thousands of refugees, which threatened to further destablize the region. The United States, the European Union, and NATO decided something needed to be done. The U.S. organized NATO air strikes, which eventually forced Milosevic to withdraw and, in the process, the Milosevic government fell. Clinton was widely admired in the U.S. and abroad for his persistence to maintain peace in the Balkan region.

Negotiating in the Middle East

Clinton became deeply involved in trying to negotiate peace between Israel and the Palestinian Liberation Army (PLO) in the Middle East. Israelis and Palestinians have been fighting each other forever, and most of the fighting has been over two pieces of land called the West Bank and the Gaza Strip. Israel controlled these areas, but Palestinians wanted them to build their own nation. Clinton mediated peace talks between Israel and Palestine and, in

August 1993, Israeli Prime Minister Yitzhak Rabin and Palestinian leader Yasser Arafat signed the *Oslo Peace Accords* at a secret meeting in Oslo, Norway. This agreement gave Palestinians the right to establish some authority in the West Bank and Gaza Strip, and Israel promised to withdraw troops from those areas.

Neither side could agree on the details, though, and tempers flared over the next seven years. In an effort to negotiate a final agreement in accordance with the Oslo Peace Accords, Clinton organized a July 2000 peace summit between Israeli Prime Minister Ehud Barak and Palestinian leader Yasser Arafat at Camp David. The two leaders couldn't reach an agreement, and the deal was essentially off. Fighting resumed, and Clinton, who had tried more than any other U.S president to bring peace to the Israeli-Palestinian conflict, could do very little to stop it.

Dealing with personal issues

The press had a field day coming up with names for all the scandals that occurred during Clinton's presidency. There was Filegate, Travelgate, Troopergate, Pardongate, Monicagate, Chinagate — you get the picture. So many scandals and so little time. First Lady Hillary Rodham Clinton tried to blame all the scandals on a "vast right-wing conspiracy," and though conservatives were certainly jumping for joy and slapping high-fives over the Clinton administration debacles, Bill and Hillary didn't really help their own cause. No other president or first lady, for that matter, have provided so many jokes for late-night talk show hosts or graced the covers of tabloid magazines so frequently.

Whitewater

In 1993, Clinton and his wife were connected to some shady business deals that involved their investment in the Whitewater Development Corporation in Arkansas in 1978. The investment tanked, and the Clintons lost money. Their business partners, Susan and James McDougal, were later charged with a number of white-collar crimes relating to a savings and loan company that James McDougal owned.

The web of accusations against the Clintons (who eventually were cleared of any wrongdoing) and the confusing nature of the fraudulent business deals they were vaguely linked to are too confusing to bother relating here because they won't do you a darn bit of good on the SAT II. However, the *Whitewater scandal* is important because it opened the door for an intense investigation into the personal lives of the president and the first lady. Special Prosecutor Kenneth Starr hounded the Clintons for several years, looking for some evidence of impropriety. Some even claimed the Clintons had something to do with the death of a White House staff member named Vincent Foster, which was ruled a suicide. Starr eventually did dig up some credible dirt, but it had to do with Clinton's weakness with the ladies, not questionable business deals.

Sexual scandals

Bill Clinton wasn't the first president to be accused of sexual impropriety. Thomas Jefferson, Warren G. Harding, Franklin Roosevelt, John F. Kennedy, to name a few, all suffered the same fate. But let's face it, Clinton outdid his predecessors in that department.

The American public first learned of Clinton's fidelity issues when he was running for president in 1992 from a woman named Gennifer Flowers. Clinton tried to deny the affair but eventually admitted to it. Another scandal, dubbed "Troopergate" alleged that Clinton used Arkansas State Troopers to pick up women for him, although this story was never proved.

In 1994, Paula Jones, a former secretary for the State of Arkansas, filed a sexual harassment suit against Clinton. The court dismissed the case, but Jones appealed. Instead of going to court, Clinton shelled out an $850,000 settlement. During the Jones case, rumors began to circulate that Clinton was having an affair with a twenty-something White House intern named Monica Lewinsky. Monica's friend, Linda Tripp, to whom she told sordid details about the affair in phone conversations, taped the phone calls (without Lewinsky's knowledge) and turned the tapes over to attorney Kenneth Starr, who brought a case against the president. While he was under oath in an unrelated trial, Clinton denied having sex with Lewinsky, but Kenneth Starr was able to get Lewinsky to admit to having oral sex with the president in the Oval Office and procured evidence to prove it. In August 1998, Clinton appeared before a grand jury and finally came clean about the affair. The Lewinsky affair eventually led to Clinton's impeachment on charges of obstruction of justice and perjury. (For more on his impeachment, see "Conflicting with the right" earlier in this chapter).

Tying it all together: A sample question looks at Bill Clinton's presidency

The SAT II History exam may ask you a general question about Clinton's administration, such as the following.

All the following describe events that occurred in America during Clinton's administration EXCEPT

(A) Politics were sharply divided along party lines.

(B) The country experienced uninterrupted economic prosperity.

(C) There were incidents of domestic terror and antigovernment sentiment.

(D) America decreased trade with Mexico and Canada.

(E) Dot-coms fueled a booming stock market.

Clinton was politically controversial, so crossing off (A) should be easy. If Clinton's presidency is remembered for one thing, besides his sexual escapades, it was his positive effect on the economy. With that fact in mind, you can eliminate (B) and (E). Although Americans didn't begin to take terrorism seriously until 9/11 (see the section "An American tragedy: September 11, 2001" later in this chapter), domestic terror was very much a part of the 1990s, so you can cross off (C), too. Answer (D) is the correct option. When Congress passed NAFTA in November 1993, it eliminated most trade barriers with Canada and Mexico, thus increasing trade with Canada and Mexico.

Bush II: George W. Bush's Presidency

When Republican George W. Bush, the governor of Texas, won the 2000 election, he accomplished a feat that had only happened once before in American history. George W. Bush and his pa George H. W. Bush were the first father and son to be elected presidents since John Adams and John Quincy Adams, the second and sixth U.S. presidents, respectively.

During the first year of George W.'s presidency, he focused on his domestic agenda, pushing a huge tax cut and the *No Child Left Behind Act,* which called for sweeping reforms of the education system, through Congress. But Bush's presidency would be defined by his response to the September 11 attacks.

The SAT II is unlikely to test you on George W. Bush's presidency in any test offered before 2004, but after that time, you may see a question or two about the 2000 election or 9/11, so make sure you read to the end of the chapter.

The controversial election of 2000

On the eve of the 2000 presidential election, polls showed that Bush led Democratic candidate Al Gore (Clinton's former vice president), but his lead was within the statistical margin of error. In other words, the vote was too close to predict a winner. It took five weeks and a court decision to finally declare Bush the winner. Americans endured lawsuits and allegations of disenfranchisement of Florida voters, not to mention countless descriptions of confusing ballots and vote-tallying procedures.

The election came down to the votes in Florida, where Bush had an ultra-slim lead. Gore had won the popular vote, but with a win in Florida, Bush won the electoral vote. Gore challenged the vote tally in Florida in court because rumors of conspiracy spread about lost votes and faulty voting machines in a state where Bush's brother was governor. The Florida Supreme Court ruled in Gore's favor to recount the votes, but Bush appealed to the U.S. Supreme Court, which ruled 5 to 4 to overturn the decision. Florida votes weren't officially recounted, and Bush remained the winner. Following Bush's victory, news organizations paid to have the Florida votes recounted anyway. They concluded that Bush ended up winning Florida by 537 votes.

You probably won't see a question about such recent history on the SAT II, but if you do, it'll likely be about the 2000 election.

The 2000 presidential election was decided by

(A) A court-ordered recount.

(B) A ruling from the Supreme Court.

(C) The popular vote.

(D) Gore conceding defeat.

(E) A vote in Congress.

The 2000 election came down to the Supreme Court's decision because of the narrow margin of Bush's victory in Florida, so you can quickly eliminate (C), (D), or (E). The Court ruled against a recount in Florida, reversing the Florida Supreme Court's decision, so (B) is the correct answer.

Bursting the bubble: The fall of the dot-coms

In the 1990s, much of America's economic prosperity was attributed to the incredible growth of the Internet. A large group of dot-coms selling products and services related to the Internet sprang up. Investors couldn't get enough of these companies and sunk billions of dollars into dot-com stocks, which sent them soaring. But very few of these companies had proved that they could turn a profit. Their popularity was based on potential and, well, their popularity rather than anything substantive.

By March 2000, the dot-com bubble had burst. Dot-coms began to fail and laid off their high-paid employees, which created a major increase in unemployment. The prices of technology stocks fell, which negatively affected the entire stock market. All kinds of computer-related industries took hits as well, and the economy began a swift downturn. By the time George W. Bush took office in January 2001, the fall of the dot-coms had signaled the end of the uninterrupted economic growth and prosperity of the 1990s. To make matters worse for the new president, financial scandals about a number of prominent American companies, such as Enron and WorldCom, came out, which contributed to the public's growing distrust of business and its hesitancy to invest in the already-declining stock market.

An American tragedy: September 11, 2001

At 8:48 a.m. on September 11, 2001, a commercial airliner crashed into the North Tower of the World Trade Center in New York City, marking the beginning of a historic tragedy that would change America forever. As smoke and fire billowed from the tower and rescue workers arrived on scene, Americans could believe that this incident was a terrible accident. But at 9:03 a.m., a second plane crashed into the South Tower of the World Trade Center, confirming Americans fears that this was no accident.

The South Tower collapsed at 9:59 a.m., followed by the North Tower at 10:28 a.m., killing employees who were trapped inside the buildings, the rescue workers who were trying to save them, and even some pedestrians in the area. At 9:37 a.m., another plane from Dulles airport in Washington, D.C. crashed into the Pentagon. A fourth plane crashed into a rural area in Pennsylvania at 10 a.m. after passengers who'd received word of what was happening by cell phone decided to revolt against the plane's hijackers.

In response to the attacks, the government evacuated all public buildings in New York and Washington, D.C., and the Port Authority in New York and New Jersey shut down bridges and tunnels. Throughout the nation, many other federal buildings and structures were evacuated or closed, and skyscrapers such as the Sears Tower in Chicago were evacuated. The Federal Aviation Administration (FAA) grounded all flights and closed every U.S. airport, and top government officials in Washington and their families were moved to safe, top-secret locations.

About 3,000 Americans died in the deadliest act of terrorism ever on American soil. It was also the first foreign attack on the U.S. since the War of 1812. (Hawaii was not a state until 1959, thus disqualifying Pearl Harbor). The 19 hijackers, 15 of them from Saudi Arabia, had received their flight training in American flight schools. The hijackers were linked to a worldwide terrorist organization called *al-Qaeda,* which was headed by an international outlaw named Osama bin Laden.

The events of September 11 forever changed generations of Americans who hadn't experienced a nationwide tragedy like this in their lifetimes. Americans felt gratitude toward the numerous police, fire, and safety personnel who gave their lives to help in the time of crisis. And out of this terrible tragedy arose the stories of heroism and a renewed sense of unity and nationalism among Americans.

A new kind of war: The War on Terror

Following September 11, Americans began to realize that al-Qaeda had already been at war with the United States for years. U.S. authorities had linked the organization to the 1993 World Trade Center bombing, the deaths of 19 American soldiers in Saudi Arabia in 1996, the 1998 bombing of U.S. embassies in Kenya and Tanzania, and an attack on a U.S. warship in Yemen in 2000, which killed 17 U.S. sailors. Al-Qaeda resented the presence of American soldiers stationed in the Middle East and U.S. support for Israel. The organization's main goal was to drive all infidels (anyone not Muslim) from the Middle East.

Soon after the 9/11 attack, Bush declared a *War on Terror.* He not only targeted terrorist groups but also the nations that harbored them. Bush organized an international coalition to help fight the war against terrorism and received bipartisan support from Congress. Not long after 9/11, Bush issued an ultimatum to Afghanistan, which the U.S government believed to be harboring Osama bin Laden: "They will hand over the terrorists, or they will share their fate," Bush announced to the world.

Invading Afghanistan

Predictably, the *Taliban* government, the oppressive Islamic fundamentalist regime that ruled Afghanistan, did not give up bin Laden or any of the many terrorist organizations that operated freely within its borders. So on October 7, 2001, the United States led a coalition attack on Afghanistan with the help of the Northern Alliance, a group of Afghani fighters who opposed the Taliban. The attack was known as *Operation Enduring Freedom.* Taliban fighters folded like lawn chairs, and the U.S.-led strikes advanced quickly. Months passed before the U.S. defeated the Taliban and al-Qaeda forces there. Rooting out the bad guys proved difficult, and many of the Taliban and al-Qaeda leaders escaped, including bin Laden and Taliban leader Mullah Omar.

Waging the war in Iraq

Intelligence agencies around the world generally believed that Iraq had large stockpiles of biological and chemical weapons, and evidence suggested that it was trying to develop nuclear weapons or perhaps even possessed nuclear weapons. Bush saw Iraq as a threat to the United States because Iraqi leader Saddam Hussein had shown his willingness to use chemical and biological weapons (on his own people) and because American intelligence believed that Hussein had significant ties to terrorism.

In October 2002, Congress passed a resolution authorizing the president to use force if Iraq didn't hand over its weapons of mass destruction. The UN Security Council passed a unanimous vote demanding that Iraq allow weapons inspectors into Iraq and demanded that Iraq disarm immediately. Iraq let the UN inspectors into the country in November 2002 and filed a 12,000 page weapons declaration report, but both the UN and the U.S. agreed that Iraq was not disclosing all of its weapons. By March 2003, Iraq still hadn't complied with UN requests to disarm, and Bush told Hussein he had 48 hours to give up his power or face invasion.

Basically, Hussein thumbed his nose at Bush. Two days later, without the backing of the UN Security Council, the U.S., with the help of Britain and minor help from several other countries, attacked Iraq. The U.S. was at war with Iraq for the second time (see "The success of the Persian Gulf War" earlier in this chapter for details about the first war). After several weeks of fighting, U.S. forces toppled Hussein's Ba'athist Party government, and the U.S. occupation of Iraq began. U.S. forces eventually took Hussein into custody, and both his sons were killed in a bombing earlier in 2003. Bush prematurely declared an end to major combat operations in May 2003, but fighting in Iraq continued as Hussein loyalists and insurgents (Islamic fighters from other Arab nations in the region) conducted a guerilla campaign against American troops and Iraqi civilians supporting U.S. efforts.

The war in Iraq was controversial from the start at home and abroad. The cohesiveness seen among Americans during the September 11 attacks all but disappeared. Americans were fiercely divided over the war in Iraq. The weapons of mass destruction Iraq was widely purported to have never surfaced, which didn't bode well for the Bush administration. To add to that, Iraq's ties to terrorism proved murky. Some argue that the war in Iraq wasn't necessary and that it actually sidetracked the war on terror and destabilized the region. Proponents of the war point to the fact that the war removed a ruthless dictator and his repressive regime from power and that a free Iraq will pave the way for democracy and peace in the Middle East.

Despite controversy over the war in Iraq and problems with the American economy, Americans voted Bush into office again in 2004 in a close race with Democrat John Kerry. Republicans controlled the executive office once again, but Americans seemed to want to a balance between conservatives and liberals, because the 2004 election produced Democratic majorities in the House and Senate.

Part VII

Practice Makes Perfect: Full-Length Practice Tests

The 5th Wave   By Rich Tennant

Kenny didn't need the distraction, but it was just his luck that the Zorlocks' invasion of Earth would begin JUST as he opened his SAT II booklet.

In this part . . .

*W*ell, you've finally reached the pinnacle — the chance to show off all the facts you know about U.S. history. Plus, by unloading some of that information you've crammed into your brain, you'll have more room for important things like obscure song lyrics and which celebrities are dating this week.

In this part are two full-length practice SAT II U.S. History tests that have the same types of questions and that cover the same areas as the actual test. (We give you full answers and explanations, too.) Take these practice tests seriously because they're a good substitute for the real thing. Set aside uninterrupted time to take them in a quiet room. And don't forget to time yourself. Additionally, make sure you go over the answers afterward — the ones you got right and the ones you got wrong. You may discover something new that can help you on test day, or at least the next time you play Trivial Pursuit. Good luck!

Practice Test 1 Answer Sheet

Each question in this chapter is followed by five suggested answers designated (A), (B), (C), (D), and (E). Select the best answer for each question and fill in the proper oval on your answer sheet.

1. Ⓐ Ⓑ Ⓒ Ⓓ Ⓔ	46. Ⓐ Ⓑ Ⓒ Ⓓ Ⓔ
2. Ⓐ Ⓑ Ⓒ Ⓓ Ⓔ	47. Ⓐ Ⓑ Ⓒ Ⓓ Ⓔ
3. Ⓐ Ⓑ Ⓒ Ⓓ Ⓔ	48. Ⓐ Ⓑ Ⓒ Ⓓ Ⓔ
4. Ⓐ Ⓑ Ⓒ Ⓓ Ⓔ	49. Ⓐ Ⓑ Ⓒ Ⓓ Ⓔ
5. Ⓐ Ⓑ Ⓒ Ⓓ Ⓔ	50. Ⓐ Ⓑ Ⓒ Ⓓ Ⓔ
6. Ⓐ Ⓑ Ⓒ Ⓓ Ⓔ	51. Ⓐ Ⓑ Ⓒ Ⓓ Ⓔ
7. Ⓐ Ⓑ Ⓒ Ⓓ Ⓔ	52. Ⓐ Ⓑ Ⓒ Ⓓ Ⓔ
8. Ⓐ Ⓑ Ⓒ Ⓓ Ⓔ	53. Ⓐ Ⓑ Ⓒ Ⓓ Ⓔ
9. Ⓐ Ⓑ Ⓒ Ⓓ Ⓔ	54. Ⓐ Ⓑ Ⓒ Ⓓ Ⓔ
10. Ⓐ Ⓑ Ⓒ Ⓓ Ⓔ	55. Ⓐ Ⓑ Ⓒ Ⓓ Ⓔ
11. Ⓐ Ⓑ Ⓒ Ⓓ Ⓔ	56. Ⓐ Ⓑ Ⓒ Ⓓ Ⓔ
12. Ⓐ Ⓑ Ⓒ Ⓓ Ⓔ	57. Ⓐ Ⓑ Ⓒ Ⓓ Ⓔ
13. Ⓐ Ⓑ Ⓒ Ⓓ Ⓔ	58. Ⓐ Ⓑ Ⓒ Ⓓ Ⓔ
14. Ⓐ Ⓑ Ⓒ Ⓓ Ⓔ	59. Ⓐ Ⓑ Ⓒ Ⓓ Ⓔ
15. Ⓐ Ⓑ Ⓒ Ⓓ Ⓔ	60. Ⓐ Ⓑ Ⓒ Ⓓ Ⓔ
16. Ⓐ Ⓑ Ⓒ Ⓓ Ⓔ	61. Ⓐ Ⓑ Ⓒ Ⓓ Ⓔ
17. Ⓐ Ⓑ Ⓒ Ⓓ Ⓔ	62. Ⓐ Ⓑ Ⓒ Ⓓ Ⓔ
18. Ⓐ Ⓑ Ⓒ Ⓓ Ⓔ	63. Ⓐ Ⓑ Ⓒ Ⓓ Ⓔ
19. Ⓐ Ⓑ Ⓒ Ⓓ Ⓔ	64. Ⓐ Ⓑ Ⓒ Ⓓ Ⓔ
20. Ⓐ Ⓑ Ⓒ Ⓓ Ⓔ	65. Ⓐ Ⓑ Ⓒ Ⓓ Ⓔ
21. Ⓐ Ⓑ Ⓒ Ⓓ Ⓔ	66. Ⓐ Ⓑ Ⓒ Ⓓ Ⓔ
22. Ⓐ Ⓑ Ⓒ Ⓓ Ⓔ	67. Ⓐ Ⓑ Ⓒ Ⓓ Ⓔ
23. Ⓐ Ⓑ Ⓒ Ⓓ Ⓔ	68. Ⓐ Ⓑ Ⓒ Ⓓ Ⓔ
24. Ⓐ Ⓑ Ⓒ Ⓓ Ⓔ	69. Ⓐ Ⓑ Ⓒ Ⓓ Ⓔ
25. Ⓐ Ⓑ Ⓒ Ⓓ Ⓔ	70. Ⓐ Ⓑ Ⓒ Ⓓ Ⓔ
26. Ⓐ Ⓑ Ⓒ Ⓓ Ⓔ	71. Ⓐ Ⓑ Ⓒ Ⓓ Ⓔ
27. Ⓐ Ⓑ Ⓒ Ⓓ Ⓔ	72. Ⓐ Ⓑ Ⓒ Ⓓ Ⓔ
28. Ⓐ Ⓑ Ⓒ Ⓓ Ⓔ	73. Ⓐ Ⓑ Ⓒ Ⓓ Ⓔ
29. Ⓐ Ⓑ Ⓒ Ⓓ Ⓔ	74. Ⓐ Ⓑ Ⓒ Ⓓ Ⓔ
30. Ⓐ Ⓑ Ⓒ Ⓓ Ⓔ	75. Ⓐ Ⓑ Ⓒ Ⓓ Ⓔ
31. Ⓐ Ⓑ Ⓒ Ⓓ Ⓔ	76. Ⓐ Ⓑ Ⓒ Ⓓ Ⓔ
32. Ⓐ Ⓑ Ⓒ Ⓓ Ⓔ	77. Ⓐ Ⓑ Ⓒ Ⓓ Ⓔ
33. Ⓐ Ⓑ Ⓒ Ⓓ Ⓔ	78. Ⓐ Ⓑ Ⓒ Ⓓ Ⓔ
34. Ⓐ Ⓑ Ⓒ Ⓓ Ⓔ	79. Ⓐ Ⓑ Ⓒ Ⓓ Ⓔ
35. Ⓐ Ⓑ Ⓒ Ⓓ Ⓔ	80. Ⓐ Ⓑ Ⓒ Ⓓ Ⓔ
36. Ⓐ Ⓑ Ⓒ Ⓓ Ⓔ	81. Ⓐ Ⓑ Ⓒ Ⓓ Ⓔ
37. Ⓐ Ⓑ Ⓒ Ⓓ Ⓔ	82. Ⓐ Ⓑ Ⓒ Ⓓ Ⓔ
38. Ⓐ Ⓑ Ⓒ Ⓓ Ⓔ	83. Ⓐ Ⓑ Ⓒ Ⓓ Ⓔ
39. Ⓐ Ⓑ Ⓒ Ⓓ Ⓔ	84. Ⓐ Ⓑ Ⓒ Ⓓ Ⓔ
40. Ⓐ Ⓑ Ⓒ Ⓓ Ⓔ	85. Ⓐ Ⓑ Ⓒ Ⓓ Ⓔ
41. Ⓐ Ⓑ Ⓒ Ⓓ Ⓔ	86. Ⓐ Ⓑ Ⓒ Ⓓ Ⓔ
42. Ⓐ Ⓑ Ⓒ Ⓓ Ⓔ	87. Ⓐ Ⓑ Ⓒ Ⓓ Ⓔ
43. Ⓐ Ⓑ Ⓒ Ⓓ Ⓔ	88. Ⓐ Ⓑ Ⓒ Ⓓ Ⓔ
44. Ⓐ Ⓑ Ⓒ Ⓓ Ⓔ	89. Ⓐ Ⓑ Ⓒ Ⓓ Ⓔ
45. Ⓐ Ⓑ Ⓒ Ⓓ Ⓔ	90. Ⓐ Ⓑ Ⓒ Ⓓ Ⓔ

Chapter 23

Pulling It All Together, Part I: Practice Test 1

● ●

*O*kay, the time has finally come for some actual practice — yikes! The following test looks very similar to the actual test. This practice test has 90 questions, and you have 60 minutes to complete the test. If you do a little simple math, you discover that you have 45 seconds or less to answer each question. Don't let this brief time period alarm you; you should be well prepared by now. Just keep an eye on the time as you take the test so you can get through as many questions as possible. At 30 minutes, you should be at about question 45.

If you're using this practice test to get an idea of how well you'll do on the SAT II U.S. History exam, you should try to take your run-through seem as much like the real test situation as you can. To take the practice tests under actual exam conditions, do the following:

- ✔ Set a timer or alarm for an hour and stop as soon as the timer or alarm goes off.

- ✔ Take the exam in a quiet place where no one can interrupt you: your bedroom, a library, or anywhere else that's quiet.

- ✔ Remove all distractions; let your family know not to bother you, unplug the telephone, and so on.

- ✔ Use the answer grid we provide in this chapter, just like you would in the actual exam.

- ✔ If you need to use the bathroom, leave the clock running; the test proctor isn't going to stop the time during the actual test for you to make a bathroom run.

- ✔ If you finish your exam early, go back and check the answers on the ones you weren't sure about.

- ✔ Try to take at least one practice exam at the same time of day that you'll be taking the real exam. This suggestion may sound weird, but it really can help. Unfortunately, many testing centers offer these tests only on weekend mornings, and that's probably the time that you normally sleep in until noon. We know that waking up and taking a practice SAT II exam sounds like torture, but get up early one Saturday, eat a good breakfast, and take the practice test for an hour at the actual time you'll be taking it on exam day. It's good practice for the big day!

When you finish your practice exam, check your answers against the answer key at the end of this chapter. You can also figure out your score. After you take care of that business, go through the explanations of *all* the answers in Chapter 24. Of course, you want to check the ones you got wrong but, as tedious as it sounds, go through all of them. You may find some worthwhile information there, and you may find out something that can help you on test day!

Practice Test 1

1. The Native Americans who populated the American Southwest around the time of Columbus were best known for

   (A) salmon fishing and creating totem poles.

   (B) building elaborate clay dwellings and using advanced irrigation techniques.

   (C) dwelling in domed structures and implementing crop rotation.

   (D) using the buffalo extensively and living in portable housing.

   (E) hunting and gathering small mammals, seeds, and nuts.

2. "The truth of the matter is that Europe's requirements for the next three or four years of foreign food and other essential products — principally from America — are so much greater than her present ability to pay that she must have substantial additional help or face economic, social, and political deterioration of a very grave character. The remedy lies in breaking the vicious circle and restoring the confidence of the European people in the economic future of their own countries and of Europe as a whole. The manufacturer and the farmer throughout wide areas must be able and willing to exchange their products for currencies, the continuing value of which is not open to question."

   This excerpt from the 1948 Marshall Plan supports which of the following?

   (A) Military support and occupation in Germany and Italy

   (B) Reconstruction of infrastructure in the nations of Europe involved in World War II

   (C) The United States' sending food and necessities in exchange for military occupation in numerous European countries

   (D) The provision of food and other necessities to the nations of Europe, regardless of the European countries' ability to pay

   (E) A decrease in inflation and the stabilization of currency in the nations of Europe

3. The following list provides three actions, numbered I, II, and III, taken by colonial Spanish explorers. Which of the answer choices presents, in order from I–III, an account of the Spanish explorer who was responsible for each of the three actions?

   I.   Conquered the Aztecs in Mexico

   II. Explored the coast between the Mississippi River and Florida

   III. Conquered the Incas in Peru

   (A) Vespucci, de Leon, Magellan

   (B) de Soto, Pizarro, Magellan

   (C) Cortes, Coronado, Cabot

   (D) de Soto, Cartier, Vespucci

   (E) Cortes, de Soto, Pizarro

4. A policy popular in the late 1800s in which the government did not interfere with the economic marketplace and let the economy self-regulate was called

   (A) Social Darwinism.

   (B) laissez-faire politics.

   (C) The New Economic policy

   (D) Progressivism.

   (E) "The Gospel of Wealth."

5. The mass migration of people from the cities to the suburbs in the 1950s and 1960s resulted in all the following EXCEPT

   (A) Growth of housing subdivisions in the suburbs.

   (B) higher crime and poverty rates in the cities.

   (C) A decline in urban public transportation systems.

   (D) Loss of open space, farm land, and forest lands.

   (E) A rapid decline in automobile sales.

Go on to next page

Courtesy of BoondocksNet.com

6. What is the most likely interpretation of this cartoon published in February 1917?

   (A) The women want President Wilson to declare war on Germany.

   (B) The women want to take a tour of the White House.

   (C) The women want President Wilson to uphold his campaign promise to support women's suffrage.

   (D) The women are striking labor union members.

   (E) The women want President Wilson to end Prohibition.

7. Through which of the following did the United States officially acquire the present-day states of California, Nevada, Arizona, and Utah?

   (A) The Treaty of Guadalupe Hidalgo

   (B) The Treaty of Versailles

   (C) Popular sovereignty

   (D) The Adams–Onis Treaty

   (E) Manifest destiny

8. Elizabeth Cady Stanton, Lucretia Mott, and Susan B. Anthony are best known for their roles as

   (A) flappers.

   (B) women's rights activists.

   (C) abolitionists.

   (D) first ladies.

   (E) mental health workers.

Go on to next page ⟶

9. The decision in the case of *McCulloch v. Maryland* (1819) during John Marshall's term as Chief Justice of the Supreme Court was significant because

   (A) it ruled that the Indian Removal Act was unconstitutional.

   (B) the Court established the power of judicial review and the authority of the Supreme Court to declare an act of Congress unconstitutional.

   (C) it allowed for the implementation of the Monroe Doctrine.

   (D) the Court ruled that slavery was illegal in Maryland.

   (E) it ruled that states did not have the right to tax federal institutions.

10. President Andrew Jackson's advisors were called the Kitchen Cabinet because

    (A) the first official meeting of the cabinet took place in the White House kitchen.

    (B) Jackson was the first president who used the spoils system extensively.

    (C) the cabinet was diverse and comprised of men from many different backgrounds, geographic regions, and political experiences.

    (D) the unofficial cabinet was comprised of Jackson's close friends and political allies, some of whom had little experience in politics.

    (E) President Jackson came from a poor family and had little formal education.

11. *Encomienda* during the early Spanish conquests in the New World was most similar to

    (A) plantation owners' view of slaves in the American South before the Civil War.

    (B) the philosophy of industrial mill owners in the Northeast in the 1800s.

    (C) the mindset of wealthy classes who occupied holiday and summer homes in the late 1800s.

    (D) landlords' treatment of immigrants in New York tenements in the late 1800s.

    (E) large ranch owners' management of ranch hands in the American West.

12. In *The Jungle,* published in 1906, author and muckraker Upton Sinclair revealed

    (A) corruption in local politics.

    (B) the poverty of the urban slums that would only improve by implementing unfettered capitalism.

    (C) the struggles of Latin American immigrants in New York City tenements.

    (D) unsanitary conditions and abuses within the meat-packing industry.

    (E) the cut-throat business practices of the Standard Oil Company.

13. The establishment of the Massachusetts Bay Colony in the 1600s was primarily the result of

    (A) the complete separation of church and state in the Rhode Island Colony.

    (B) religious and political oppression of the Puritans in Britain.

    (C) Britain's wish to establish a haven for debtors.

    (D) the Quakers' desire for a refuge from religious persecution.

    (E) Britain's desire for a place to grow tobacco.

14. Which of the following New World settlements was founded by a group made up almost exclusively of men?

    (A) Plymouth Colony

    (B) Massachusetts Bay Colony

    (C) The settlement in New Haven, Connecticut

    (D) The Quaker settlement in Pennsylvania

    (E) The settlement at Jamestown, Virginia

Go on to next page

15. Which of the following actions taken by American colonists prior to the Revolutionary War most directly resulted in the British Parliament imposing the Intolerable Acts on the colonies?

    (A) The publication of Thomas Paine's *Common Sense*

    (B) The establishment of the Sons of Liberty

    (C) The Boston Tea Party

    (D) The Stamp Act Congress of 1765

    (E) The meeting of the First Continental Congress

16. Which of the following statements about social and cultural trends in the 1960s is INCORRECT?

    (A) Increasing numbers of women left the workforce and returned to the home.

    (B) Many young Americans became political activists.

    (C) Farm workers united to obtain better wages and safer working conditions.

    (D) College enrollment increased dramatically.

    (E) An unprecedented increase in youth counterculture movements emerged.

Go on to next page

Female-Headed Households With Children, by Race/Ethnicity, 1970–2002

Female-headed households with children as a percent of all households

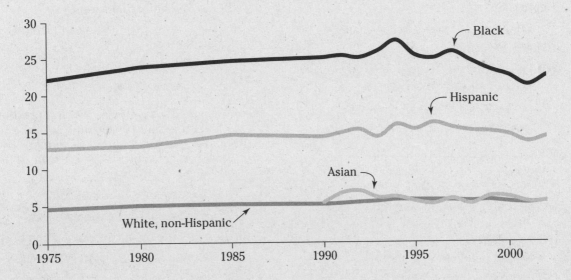

Source: AmeriStat, analysis of data from the Current Population Survey (March Supplement), various years.

Courtesy of the Population Reference Bureau

17. Which of the following statements is NOT consistent with the data presented in this graph?

   (A) The percentage of households headed by white females remained relatively constant from 1975–2000.

   (B) The percentage of households headed by black females declined roughly 2 percent from the beginning of the Clinton administration to the end of it.

   (C) The percentage of households headed by Asian females increased slightly between 1990 and 1992.

   (D) The percentage of households headed by Hispanic females has been on a steady decline since 1980.

   (E) The percentage of households headed by black females experienced a steady increase from 1975–1994.

18. Benjamin Franklin, a key figure of the Enlightenment, is known for all the following EXCEPT

   (A) embracing a secular theology called deism.

   (B) writing a book of pithy sayings.

   (C) serving as vice-president of the United States.

   (D) inventing the lightening rod.

   (E) Serving as a delegate to the Constitutional Convention.

19. Under which president did the United States almost enter into nuclear war with the Soviet Union over a conflict in Cuba?

   (A) Lyndon B. Johnson

   (B) Harry S Truman

   (C) Richard M. Nixon

   (D) Dwight D. Eisenhower

   (E) John F. Kennedy

Go on to next page

20. Which of the following was a signature method of communication used by President Franklin D. Roosevelt in his efforts to connect with the American people, rally support for his programs, and build public confidence in the economy during the Great Depression?

    (A) Frequent interviews in newspapers

    (B) "Fireside chats" on the radio

    (C) Frequent travel to meet with individuals around the country

    (D) Frequent television appearances

    (E) Monthly State of the Union addresses

21. Which characteristic of the United States today may best be considered a legacy of Thomas Jefferson's principles?

    (A) State dinners and inauguration balls at the White House

    (B) Prevalent opportunities for citizens to receive a college education

    (C) Large-scale corporate farming

    (D) A strong centralized government

    (E) A highly industrialized economy

22. As of 2004, which of the following rights was protected by an amendment to the Constitution?

    (A) The right of Congress to reinstitute the draft without presidential approval

    (B) The right of residents of Puerto Rico to vote in U.S. presidential elections

    (C) The right of citizens to obtain an expeditious trial when they're accused of a felony

    (D) The right of the Supreme Court to declare a winner in a presidential election in the case of an electoral tie

    (E) The right of homosexuals to marry other homosexuals

23. The Union had many advantages over the Confederacy at the start of the Civil War. Which of the following was NOT considered an advantage for the Union?

    (A) More experienced military leaders

    (B) Greater industrialization

    (C) More extensive funding and a more stable economy

    (D) Plentiful food resources

    (E) The size of its population

24. Theodore Roosevelt was the first president to bring the issue of land and natural resource conservation to the public forefront. During his presidency, he did all the following EXCEPT

    (A) Visit Yosemite with John Muir.

    (B) Create numerous national parks.

    (C) Create the Civilian Conservation Corps.

    (D) Strengthen the U.S. Forest Service.

    (E) Fight to regulate lumber, mining, and cattle industries.

25. Which of the following was NOT a diplomatic agreement to reduce or limit nuclear arms during the Cold War Era?

    (A) SALT I

    (B) Nuclear Non-Proliferation Treaty

    (C) Strategic Defense Initiative

    (D) SALT II

    (E) Limited Nuclear Test-Ban Treaty

26. Which president of the latter half of the 20th century was responsible for reopening the possibility of diplomatic relations between the United States and China?

    (A) John F. Kennedy

    (B) Jimmy Carter

    (C) Gerald Ford

    (D) Richard Nixon

    (E) Ronald Reagan

Go on to next page

27. Economic development among the New England, Middle, and Southern Colonies varied predominantly due to

    (A) distinctions in geography and climate.

    (B) diversity in the form of government practiced by the colonies.

    (C) differences in the countries of origin of the colonists.

    (D) distinct opportunities for higher education.

    (E) dissimilarities in the religion practiced by the majority.

Go on to next page

IMMIGRANTS ADMITTED BY TOP 15 COUNTRIES OF BIRTH IN FISCAL YEAR 1990

Country of Birth	1990
Total	656,111
Mexico	56,549
Philippines	54,907
Vietnam	48,662
Dominican Republic	32,064
Korea	29,548
China (mainland)	28,746
India	28,679
Soviet Union	25,350
Jamaica	18,828
Iran	18,031
Taiwan	13,839
United Kingdom	13,730
Canada	13,717
Poland	13,334
Haiti	11,862
Other	248,265

28. This chart does NOT support which of the following statements about immigration to the United States in 1990?

(A) In fiscal year 1990, about 650,000 legal immigrants were admitted into the United States.

(B) The largest group of immigrants in fiscal year 1990 came from Mexico.

(C) The smallest group of immigrants from one country to enter the United States came from Haiti in fiscal year 1990.

(D) In fiscal year 1990, nearly twice as many immigrants entering the United States were from the Soviet Union than were from Poland.

(E) Nearly an equal number of immigrants from Canada and the United Kingdom came to the United States in fiscal year 1990.

Go on to next page

29. Which of the following statements best reflects the sentiments behind the Sherman Antitrust Act of 1890?

    (A) The federal government should completely regulate businesses.

    (B) The federal government should prevent monopolies in business and encourage healthy competition in industry.

    (C) The federal government should limit the size of businesses and encourage the proliferation of small businesses.

    (D) Businesses should be able to expand without the government's interference.

    (E) The economy would benefit from a lack of business competition in the marketplace.

30. The post-World War II foreign policy, the Truman Doctrine, is best described as

    (A) a policy whereby the United States supplied aid to impoverished nations in Africa and Asia.

    (B) the policy in which the United States provided reconstruction loans to countries that needed to rebuild infrastructure following World War II.

    (C) a policy under which the United States increased trade with the nations of Western Europe to help those countries recover economically.

    (D) a policy under which the United States provided economic and military aid to countries threatened by Communism.

    (E) a policy under which NATO was established to collectivize security for the United States, Canada, and ten Western European nations.

Go on to next page

Courtesy of BoondocksNet.com

31. This cartoon from 1913 is most likely making which of the following points?

   (A) Businesses are forcing children to work in the factories.

   (B) Children who work do not get paid enough.

   (C) Businesses take advantage of child labor in order to reap great profits.

   (D) Working children receive low pay and are forced to work long hours.

   (E) Businesses are killing children in order to turn profits.

32. Ronald Reagan's economic program of supply-side economics, often called "Reaganomics," was characterized by

   (A) record low unemployment and a balanced federal budget.

   (B) increased spending on social programs, such as school lunches, public transportation, and federal student loan programs.

   (C) extensive government support for social programs for the impoverished.

   (D) low inflation and low interest rates.

   (E) tax cuts, a trickle-down theory, and a federal budget deficit.

33. Which of the following is true about civil rights leader Malcolm X?

   (A) He was head of the Southern Christian Leadership Conference.

   (B) He preached about African American self-reliance and freedom from whites.

   (C) He advocated non-violent protest even in response to violent acts perpetrated by whites.

   (D) He encouraged African Americans to get along with whites in an effort to promote unity between the two races.

   (E) He rejected the orthodox Islamic faith after he made a trip to Mecca.

Go on to next page →

34. Similarities between the New Deal of the 1930s and the Great Society of the 1960s include all the following EXCEPT

    (A) Both resulted in increased involvement of the federal government in the economy.

    (B) Both executed landmark legislation on civil rights issues.

    (C) Both included legislation to provide assistance to senior citizens.

    (D) Both instituted federal programs to provide employment for underprivileged youth.

    (E) Many of the goals of both policies never came about because of a shift in federal focus and funds going toward foreign policy issues.

35. John F. Kennedy and Lyndon B. Johnson augmented troops in Vietnam because of a belief in

    (A) the cause of the Viet Cong.

    (B) the Gulf of Tonkin Resolution.

    (C) Eisenhower's "Domino Theory."

    (D) the Tet Offensive

    (E) détente with the Soviet Union.

36. The Supreme Court decisions in *Brown v. Board of Education of Topeka* (1954) and *Plessy v. Ferguson* (1896) addressed which of the following issues?

    (A) Prayer in public schools

    (B) One-man, one-vote

    (C) Interracial marriage

    (D) Separate but equal facilities

    (E) Voting rights

37. French goals in the New World in the 1500s and 1700s included all the following EXCEPT

    (A) Trading with the Native Americans

    (B) Finding a Northwest Passage to Asia

    (C) Converting people to Christianity

    (D) Finding gold and diamonds

    (E) Using the New World as a refuge for debtors being kept in French prisons

38. Jane Addams is best known for

    (A) Leading the women's suffrage movement.

    (B) Social work and the establishment of the first settlement house, called Hull House.

    (C) The founding of the Young Men's Christian Association or YMCA.

    (D) The founding of the Salvation Army.

    (E) Establishment of Head Start preschool programs for impoverished children.

39. What is the significance of Henry Ford's assembly-line method of production?

    (A) It allowed workers to master many different components of the automobile manufacturing process.

    (B) It decreased productivity in his automobile plants.

    (C) It helped make the automobile a symbol of wealth and privilege in United States' society.

    (D) It was an inefficient method of mass production.

    (E) It made automobiles affordable for many Americans.

40. Which U.S. president urged the United Nations to deploy troops to the Persian Gulf in order to force Iraq out of Kuwait?

    (A) Bill Clinton

    (B) George H. W. Bush

    (C) Ronald Reagan

    (D) Jimmy Carter

    (E) George W. Bush

41. As Chief Justice of the Supreme Court, Earl Warren issued significant legal decisions on all the following EXCEPT

    (A) The segregation of schools.

    (B) The Miranda Rights and defendants' right to legal counsel.

    (C) The assassination of John F. Kennedy.

    (D) Prayer in public schools.

    (E) Interracial marriage.

Go on to next page

Courtesy of Picture History

42. Which of the following best summarizes the idea expressed in this 1898 cartoon?

    (A) The United States was unsure which nation to conquer first.

    (B) The United States wanted to go to war to gain control of Cuba, Puerto Rico, the Philippines, and the Sandwich Islands.

    (C) The United States wanted to protect economic and trade interests abroad.

    (D) President McKinley desired to demonstrate American military strength abroad.

    (E) The United States was following an imperialistic late 19th-century foreign policy.

43. From the mid-1940s until about 1990, the United States spent the largest percentage of the federal budget on

    (A) public education programs.

    (B) welfare and social programs.

    (C) scientific advancement.

    (D) national defense and security.

    (E) farm subsidies.

44. All the following represent events leading up to the passage of the Civil Rights Act of 1964 EXCEPT

    (A) The Freedom Summer.

    (B) The series of nonviolent demonstrations in Birmingham, Alabama, organized by Martin Luther King Jr.

    (C) The sit-in at Woolworth's Lunch Counter in Greensboro, South Carolina.

    (D) The March on Washington, organized and led by Martin Luther King Jr.

    (E) The Freedom Rides organized by the Congress of Racial Equality (CORE).

Go on to next page

45. The primary purpose of the first colleges and universities established in the American colonies between 1636 and 1754 was

    (A) to provide young men and women with a well-rounded education.

    (B) to provide training in medicine and law.

    (C) to prepare young men for the ministry.

    (D) to provide a broad liberal arts education for young men.

    (E) to provide training in agrarian sciences and farming techniques.

46. Which of the following was NOT a result of Alexander Hamilton's financial policies during the 1790s?

    (A) The establishment of the two-term precedent for the president of the United States

    (B) Establishment and strengthening of the credit of the new nation

    (C) The Whiskey Rebellion of 1794

    (D) The rise of two increasingly divided political parties: the Federalists and the Democratic Republicans

    (E) Formation and charter of the Bank of the United States

47. What do the following five people have in common: Jack Kerouac, Elvis Presley, Chuck Berry, Lucille Ball, and Allan Ginsberg?

    (A) All represent cultural icons of the 1920s.

    (B) All were made famous by the emergence of television in the 1960s.

    (C) All represent cultural icons of the 1950s.

    (D) All represent famous authors of the 20th century.

    (E) All represent cultural icons of the 1970s.

48. The United States entered World War II as a direct result of which of the following events?

    (A) The German invasion of the Soviet Union

    (B) The Japanese attack on Pearl Harbor

    (C) Germany's declaration of war on the United States

    (D) Japan's seizure of Hawaii

    (E) Germany's unrestricted submarine warfare on American ships

49. One similarity between William Howard Taft's "dollar diplomacy" policy (1909–1912) and John Hay's Open Door policy (1899) was that

    (A) both policies protected American economic interests abroad.

    (B) both protected U.S. allies from foreign invaders.

    (C) both policies protected American territorial interests.

    (D) both protected U.S. military bases abroad.

    (E) both policies were important to securing America's status as a world power.

50. Thomas Jefferson did all the following as president EXCEPT

    (A) Sign the Embargo Act of 1807.

    (B) Purchase the Louisiana Territory.

    (C) Reduce the size of the military and cut taxes.

    (D) Write the Declaration of Independence.

    (E) Organize the Lewis and Clark expedition.

51. Each of the following decisions impacted how slave states would be represented in Congress EXCEPT

    (A) The Three-Fifths Compromise in the Constitution.

    (B) The Compromise of 1850.

    (C) The Compromise of 1820.

    (D) The Fugitive Slave Law.

    (E) The U.S. Supreme Court decision in the Dred Scott case.

52. The United States' military intervention in Korea and Vietnam were both characterized by

    (A) total war rather than limited war.

    (B) an attempt by the United States to prevent the spread of Communism.

    (C) a strong youth anti-war movement in the United States.

    (D) direct military involvement of more than ten years.

    (E) military assistance from the United Nations.

Go on to next page

53. Which constitutional amendment established a two-term limit for U.S. presidents?

    (A) The 10th Amendment

    (B) The 19th Amendment

    (C) The 25th Amendment

    (D) The 22nd Amendment

    (E) The 18th Amendment

54. The primary motivation of the Monroe Doctrine was

    (A) to keep European powers from meddling in the affairs of the Americas.

    (B) to drive the British out of Canada.

    (C) to keep the United States out of entangling alliances.

    (D) to purchase Louisiana from France.

    (E) to give the United States the ability to promote democratic governments in Latin America.

55. Reasons for American victory in the American Revolution include all the following EXCEPT

    (A) Competent, determined, and skilled leaders led the American troops.

    (B) France, Holland, and Spain supported the colonies in the war against Britain.

    (C) British troops didn't expect the war to last as long as it did.

    (D) The colonies possessed well-trained troops and excellent military equipment.

    (E) Because the colonists were fighting for their own independence, they were more determined than the British to be victorious.

56. Which territories did Spain cede to the United States through the Treaty of Paris at the end of the Spanish-American War?

    (A) Guam, Puerto Rico, and Cuba

    (B) Hawaii, Guam, and Puerto Rico

    (C) Cuba, Puerto Rico, and Hawaii

    (D) Hawaii and the Philippines

    (E) Guam, Puerto Rico, and the Philippines

57. The Indian Removal Act of 1830 gave President Andrew Jackson the authority to

    (A) divide Native American reservation lands into 160-acre farms.

    (B) create the Bureau of Indian Affairs.

    (C) use force to move Native Americans to designated western lands.

    (D) require Native Americans to assimilate to Western culture.

    (E) create distinct reservations for each Native American tribe.

58. Abraham Lincoln was not a popular presidential candidate in the South in the election of 1860 because

    (A) Southerners wanted to secede from the Union.

    (B) Southerners supported Lincoln's opponent Stephen Douglas, who ran on a platform that favored popular sovereignty.

    (C) he opposed extending slavery to the territories.

    (D) he was a known abolitionist who had worked for many years on the Underground Railroad.

    (E) he was a member of the Free-Soil Party.

59. Why did Andrew Jackson veto the bill to recharter the U.S. National Bank?

    (A) He felt it favored wealthy Westerners.

    (B) The U.S. already had more than enough banks.

    (C) He feared too much concentration of economic power in one institution.

    (D) He wanted revenge for the election of 1824.

    (E) He thought the National Bank was unfriendly to foreign interests.

Go on to next page

60. The main reason Thomas Jefferson sought to purchase New Orleans and Louisiana was because

   (A) he was afraid Napoleon would start an invasion of the United States from New Orleans.

   (B) he wanted to stop the slave trade in New Orleans.

   (C) he wanted cities to emerge across the continent.

   (D) the purchase assured that the U.S. would have access to the Mississippi.

   (E) Lewis and Clark recommended the purchase after returning from their exploration expedition.

Go on to next page

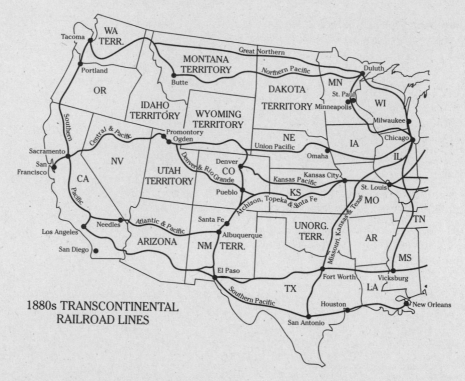

1880s TRANSCONTINENTAL
RAILROAD LINES

61. Which of the following statements is INCONSISTENT with the data provided on this map?

(A) Passengers could travel from Duluth to Tacoma on the same rail line in the 1880s.

(B) In the 1880s, people could travel from Butte to Santa Fe without passing through Chicago or California.

(C) In the 1880s, people could travel from Los Angeles to New Orleans on the Southern Pacific rail line.

(D) The shortest route from Portland to El Paso in the 1880s passed through California, Arizona, and the New Mexico Territory.

(E) To travel from the West Coast to New York, one probably had to travel through St. Louis, Chicago, or Mississippi.

62. Which of the following was a consequence of Prohibition, the 18th Amendment Congress passed in 1920?

(A) Bootleggers were highly unsuccessful in their efforts to smuggle liquor into the United States from other countries.

(B) All places that sold alcohol in the United States went out of business.

(C) Americans had devout respect for the new law.

(D) Grain's availability declined, and its price increased during the 1920s.

(E) Organized crime increased.

Go on to next page

63. Rachel Carson's 1962 book *Silent Spring* was significant because

    (A) it explained the embarrassing reasons behind the April 1961 Bay of Pigs invasion.

    (B) she wrote about declining bird populations in the American countryside.

    (C) the book alerted Americans to the dangers of the pesticide DDT and raised an awareness of the environment.

    (D) it painted a graphic picture of what Americans would experience in the aftermath of nuclear war.

    (E) it was the most comprehensive work written to date about the D-Day invasion that occurred in Spring 1944.

Go on to next page

Courtesy of Eric Zimmer

64. Which of the following statements is the most comprehensive interpretation of this cartoon depicting Herbert Hoover and Franklin Roosevelt in 1933?

(A) Herbert Hoover is sullen because he thinks the country is doomed under Franklin Roosevelt. Roosevelt is optimistic that he can quickly improve the economic situation in America.

(B) Herbert Hoover is mad because he wasn't promised a balanced federal budget.

(C) Herbert Hoover is sullen because he lost the presidential race by such a large margin, and Franklin Roosevelt is beaming because he enters his first term with a majority in the House and Senate and a convincing mandate from the people.

(D) Franklin Roosevelt is upbeat because he was thinking about the upcoming Bank Holiday.

(E) Herbert Hoover feels depressed because he was responsible for creating the Great Depression.

65. The Central Pacific Railroad, built east from California, owed its rapid and difficult completion to which of the following immigrant groups?

(A) Japanese

(B) Italians

(C) Germans

(D) Irish

(E) Chinese

66. Which of the following is a correct pairing of a U.S. president and a major piece of legislation that took place during his administration?

(A) Andrew Jackson, the Fugitive Slave Law

(B) Harry Truman, the Taft–Hartley Act

(C) Abraham Lincoln, the Sherman Antitrust Act

(D) Woodrow Wilson, the Smoot–Hawley Tariff

(E) Theodore Roosevelt, the Chinese Exclusion Act

Go on to next page

67. What did Harriet Beecher Stowe, Frederick Douglass, William Lloyd Garrison, and Harriet Tubman all have in common?

    (A) They were all journalists and authors.

    (B) They were all escaped slaves.

    (C) They were all jazz musicians.

    (D) They were all abolitionists.

    (E) They all supported the Confederacy.

68. The principle of popular sovereignty stated that

    (A) slavery would be permitted only in Southern states.

    (B) slavery would not be permitted in any new territories admitted to the Union.

    (C) Congress would decide if slavery would be legal in a territory when each territory applied for statehood.

    (D) the citizens of each territory would decide the legality of slavery before the territory would seek admission to the Union.

    (E) slavery was prohibited in any territory gained from Mexico.

69. All the following statements are true about the American colonies EXCEPT

    (A) The citizenry was comprised of people from diverse, though mainly northern European, countries and cultures.

    (B) The manufacturing and trade of finished goods with Britain and other colonies was an important component of the colonial economy.

    (C) American colonists were generally better educated than the citizenry of Europe or Britain.

    (D) Many immigrants entered the Southern Colonies as indentured servants.

    (E) Colonial government had a legislature that usually consisted of two houses.

70. Which of the following is one of the leading causes of the Great Depression?

    (A) Uneven distribution of wealth among Americans

    (B) Agricultural shortfalls and high crop prices

    (C) A firm banking system

    (D) A lack of stock-market speculation

    (E) Low trade tariffs

71. Despite the loss of millions of men to positions in the military, American industry was able to increase production during World War II predominantly due to

    (A) child labor.

    (B) tripling the hours of workers who were not called to military duty.

    (C) women entering the workforce in record numbers.

    (D) recruitment of workers from foreign countries.

    (E) the increased mechanization in factories.

72. Which of the following was NOT created as part of the New Deal under the Roosevelt administration?

    (A) The Civilian Conservation Corps

    (B) The Tennessee Valley Authority

    (C) The Federal Deposit Insurance Corporation

    (D) The Social Security Act

    (E) The Emergency Committee for Employment

73. Which of the following statements conveys the mid-19th century philosophy of manifest destiny?

    (A) The United States should impose protective tariffs on British manufactured goods.

    (B) The United States should annex Texas and California.

    (C) The United States should colonize Samoa and Midway Island.

    (D) The United States should annex Cuba.

    (E) The United States should help South Korea resist Communism.

Go on to next page

74. "A government of our own is our natural right: And when a man seriously reflects on the precariousness of human affairs, he will become convinced, that it is infinitely wiser and safer, to form a constitution of our own in a cool deliberate manner, while we have it in our power, than to trust such an interesting event to time and chance."

The author of this statement would be likely to support which of the following?

(A) The Intolerable Acts

(B) The Writs of Assistance

(C) British mercantilist laws in the colonies

(D) An overthrow of the despotic British monarchy

(E) The Proclamation of 1763

Go on to next page

Courtesy of BoondocksNet.com

75. Which of the following statements is a likely interpretation of this cartoon published in the *Chicago Daily News* in January 1917?

(A) World War I was losing steam and peace was on the horizon.

(B) The United States was making renewed efforts to stay out of the European conflict.

(C) European nations were making renewed efforts to obtain peace without the assistance of the United States.

(D) The possibility of the United States maintaining peace and staying out of World War I was fading away.

(E) In the wake of the bombing of Pearl Harbor, the United States could no longer make peace proposals and was forced to enter the war.

76. All the following represent social activist organizations formed during the 1960s EXCEPT

(A) The Black Panthers.

(B) The National Organization for Women.

(C) The Students for a Democratic Society.

(D) The Southern Christian Leadership Conference.

(E) The Student Nonviolent Coordinating Committee.

77. Which of the following were independent nations before becoming states?

(A) Texas, New Mexico, and Arizona

(B) New Mexico and Arizona

(C) Texas and Hawaii

(D) Oregon and Washington

(E) Alaska, Hawaii, and Montana

Go on to next page

78. Since the Revolutionary War, when is the only time the U.S. Army has fought foreign troops in the continental United States?

    (A) The War of 1812

    (B) World War II

    (C) The French and Indian War

    (D) The Civil War

    (E) World War I

79. Which of the following is NOT a part of the Declaration of Independence?

    (A) The Articles of Confederation

    (B) A declaration of the unalienable rights of colonists

    (C) A list of grievances King George III committed against the American colonists

    (D) The colonies' announcement of freedom from Great Britain

    (E) The statement "all men are created equal"

80. Which of the following is NOT an example of Theodore Roosevelt's foreign policy to "speak softly, but carry a big stick"?

    (A) The military occupation of Cuba

    (B) Military assistance for Panamanian independence from Columbia

    (C) The moral diplomacy policy

    (D) United States' interference in the foreign affairs of the Dominican Republic

    (E) The Roosevelt Corollary to the Monroe Doctrine

81. Joan Baez, Joni Mitchell, and Bob Dylan were creators of what popular music style that gained popularity during the 1960s?

    (A) Motown

    (B) Psychedelic rock

    (C) Rock 'n' roll

    (D) Folk music

    (E) Jazz

82. The platform of the Populist Party supported all the following EXCEPT

    (A) A graduated income tax to replace tariffs.

    (B) Restrictions on immigration.

    (C) Direct election of U.S. senators.

    (D) Maintenance of the gold standard.

    (E) Government ownership of utilities.

83. Two of the primary legislative goals behind the women's movement of the 1960s and early 1970s were

    (A) to advocate for federally-funded research into new contraception methods and laws that would allow women to run their own health clinics.

    (B) to advocate for legalized abortions and equal pay and rights in the workplace.

    (C) to gain admission for women to all-male colleges and prohibit women's colleges from admitting male students.

    (D) to show support for *The Feminine Mystique* and NOW.

    (E) to advocate free love and bra-burning.

84. Muckrakers are best described as

    (A) Southern white Republicans or moderates who favored Reconstruction.

    (B) people who illegally smuggled liquor into the United States during Prohibition.

    (C) former slaves who paid or gave a share of their crops to white landowners in exchange for a parcel of land to farm.

    (D) white opportunists from the North who relocated to the South during Reconstruction.

    (E) journalists who exposed scandal, social injustice, and corruption in the hopes of encouraging reform.

Go on to next page

85. Which of the following authors best represents the transcendentalist movement?

    (A) Henry David Thoreau, author of *Walden*

    (B) Thomas Paine, author of *The Age of Reason*

    (C) Harriet Beecher Stowe, author of *Uncle Tom's Cabin*

    (D) Edward Bellamy, author of *Looking Backward From 2000 to 1887*

    (E) Mark Twain, author of *The Adventures of Huckleberry Finn*

86. Which of the following is a reason that Southern states opposed protective tariffs imposed by Congress in 1816 and 1824?

    (A) The tariffs did not impose strict enough limitations on British merchants.

    (B) Tariffs increased the cost of raw products the South purchased from the North.

    (C) The tariffs impeded Southern trade with the Western states.

    (D) The tariffs limited the demand for Southern goods.

    (E) Southerners felt tariffs were unfair because the money they generated was used to assist British merchants rather than American concerns.

87. Progressivism surfaced in the early 1900s as a response to

    (A) yellow journalism during the Spanish-American War.

    (B) the rise of the Anti-imperialist League, which opposed American expansion abroad.

    (C) a desire for reform in industry and politics.

    (D) the United States' construction of the Panama Canal and U.S. intervention in the Dominican Republic.

    (E) the growth of organized labor and the increased frequency of labor strikes during the late 1800s.

88. Beginning in 1763, a series of British actions angered the American colonists and led them on the path to the Revolutionary War. Britain's actions included all of the following EXCEPT

    (A) The Stamp Act and the Sugar Act

    (B) The Coercive Acts

    (C) The establishment of the Committees of Correspondence

    (D) The Townshend Duties

    (E) The Proclamation of 1763

89. "No Person except a natural born Citizen, or a Citizen of the United States, at the time of the Adoption of this Constitution, shall be eligible to the Office of President; neither shall any Person be eligible to that Office who shall not have attained to the Age of thirty five Years, and been fourteen Years a Resident within the United States."

In this excerpt from The U.S. Constitution, the founding fathers

    (A) mandated that a president has to be a United States's citizen but did not have to be born in the United States.

    (B) set requirements for the succession of a president in the event of death or incapacitation.

    (C) limited the length of the service of a president to two four-year terms.

    (D) determined that under the Constitution a "citizen" was a white male.

    (E) established requirements for the eligibility of future presidents.

90. The slogan "Fifty-four forty or fight" refers to

    (A) the amount of money the U.S. demanded from Britain after the War of 1812.

    (B) the desired location of the border between the western United States and western Canada.

    (C) the land acquired from Mexico as a result of the 1853 Gadsden Purchase.

    (D) the dispute with Great Britain over the boundary of Maine.

    (E) The purchase of the Mexican Cession.

Answer Key for Practice Test 1

1. B	31. C	61. B
2. D	32. E	62. E
3. E	33. B	63. C
4. B	34. B	64. C
5. E	35. C	65. E
6. C	36. D	66. B
7. A	37. E	67. D
8. B	38. B	68. D
9. E	39. E	69. B
10. D	40. B	70. A
11. A	41. C	71. C
12. D	42. E	72. E
13. B	43. D	73. B
14. E	44. A	74. D
15. C	45. C	75. D
16. A	46. A	76. D
17. D	47. C	77. C
18. C	48. B	78. A
19. E	49. A	79. A
20. B	50. D	80. C
21. B	51. D	81. D
22. C	52. B	82. D
23. A	53. D	83. B
24. C	54. A	84. E
25. C	55. D	85. A
26. D	56. E	86. D
27. A	57. C	87. C
28. C	58. C	88. C
29. B	59. C	89. E
30. D	60. D	90. B

Scoring Practice Test 1

Okay, now you get to assess the damage. First, you determine your raw score. To do so, follow the directions in this section. Your *raw score* is based on the number of questions you answered correctly or incorrectly.

Calculating your raw score is somewhat tricky, but here's how you do it.

1. **Find the number of questions you answered correctly:** _____

2. **Find the number of questions you answered incorrectly:** _____

3. **Multiply the number you calculated in Step 2 by 0.25 (or ¼), which leaves you with:** _____

    (Remember, you lose only ¼ of a point for each wrong answer, and you aren't penalized for leaving answers blank.)

4. **Take the number you calculated in Step 3 and subtract it from your answer in Step 1:** _____

5. **Round your answer in Step 4 to the nearest whole number.** (Tip: 0.50 or greater round up, 0.49 or less, round down.) The result is your raw score: _____

Next, use your raw score to determine your three-digit scaled score. Your *scaled score* is the one that colleges and universities see (see Chapter 1 for more information on how colleges and universities use your score). To figure out your approximate scaled score, find your raw score in Table 23-1 and its corresponding scaled score. If you didn't score as well as you wanted to, figure out which questions you answered incorrectly and review the chapters that cover the information those questions tested. You should also review Chapter 2 for ways to improve your guessing strategies. Then, take the practice test in Chapter 25 to see how much you've improved.

Table 23-1		Score Conversion Chart			
Raw Scores	*Scaled Score*	*Raw Scores*	*Scaled Score*	*Raw Scores*	*Scaled Score*
82–90	800	50	620	19–20	440
79–81	790	49	610	17–18	430
77–78	780	47–48	600	15–16	420
75–76	770	45–46	590	13–14	410
73–74	760	44	580	11–12	400
72	750	42–43	570	9–10	390
70–71	740	40–41	560	7–8	380
69	730	39	550	5–6	370
67–68	720	37–38	540	3–4	360
66	710	35–36	530	2	350
64–65	700	33–34	520	0–1	340
62–63	690	31–32	510	–1	330
61	680	30	500	–2/–3	320
58–59	670	28–29	490	–4/–5	310
56–57	660	26–27	480	–6/–7	300
55	650	24–25	470	–8/–9	290
53–54	640	22–23	460	–10	280
51–52	630	21	450		

Chapter 24

Explaining the Answers to Practice Test 1

● ●

*W*ell, you've finished the test in Chapter 23, but you're not done yet. Now you have to check your answers. We strongly suggest reading through *all* the answer explanations, even the ones for questions that you answered correctly. Our reasoning is simple: You may come across information that you hadn't thought of before in an answer's explanation.

1. **B.** Because you're likely to run into at least one question on early Native American groups, make sure you know the basic characteristics of the five main American geographic regions so you know how they influenced the natives who were living there; you can read about this topic in Chapter 3. Thinking about the geography and climate of the regions is an easy way to keep the tribes straight. For example, thinking that a tribe from the desert Southwest would fish for salmon is illogical.

2. **D.** The Marshall Plan was a four-year reconstruction plan for Europe under which the United States provided more than $12 billion in aid to help economically and politically stabilize the nations of Europe. The excerpt highlights the importance of providing food and other essential products; therefore, you can eliminate answer choices that don't deal with assistance in these areas. Answer (A) deals with military support; (B) is about construction projects; and (E) talks about currency, so none of these choices works. The quote doesn't mention military occupation, so (D) is a better answer than (C). See Chapter 19 for more information on the Marshall Plan.

3. **E.** First you have to figure out what the question wants you to do. You're supposed to figure out which explorer matches the activity conveyed in each Roman numeral and then find an answer that lists them in the proper order. The question tells you that the explorers are Spanish, so you can eliminate any answer choice that contains explorers from other nationalities without even reading the three activities. Because (C) and (D) include John Cabot and Jacques Cartier, you can cross these choices out. Now you're left with (A), (B), or (E). Amerigo Vespucci didn't make his way inland, so you can eliminate (A). Just based on I, you know that the answer has to be (E). Hernan Cortes terrorized the Aztecs, so he needs to be part of the correct answer choice. (Check out Chapter 3 if you didn't remember this info.)

At this point, don't spend time checking the rest of the answer. If you have time at the end, you can double-check.

4. **B.** This question may be a little confusing because many of the answers are buzzwords from the same era. Think about the economic climate in the U.S. in the late 1800s and remember that this was the era of government corruption and support for powerful corporations, holding companies, trusts, and monopolies. (See Chapter 12 for more.)

You can eliminate choices that don't fit in the era. Progressivism was an early-1900s movement and involved government intervention in the general welfare of Americans (see Chapter 14), so (D) is wrong. The New Freedom Policy was Richard Nixon's invention (see Chapter 21), so it's from the wrong era, too. "The Gospel of Wealth" and Social Darwinism were part of the late-1800s philosophy, but they don't apply directly to government policy, so cross out (A) and (E). Now you're left with laissez-faire politics, which means "to let things alone" and describes the hands-off political policy of the times.

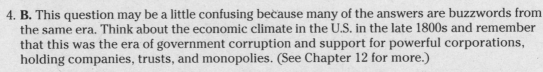

5. **E.** The SAT II uses EXCEPT questions a lot. (They're tricky and are easy to write.) Be careful with these. Rephrase them so you know exactly what you're looking for when you read the answer choices. In this case, you can reword the question as "Which of the answers is something that wouldn't result from a movement to the suburbs?"

In Chapter 19, you find that the 1950s witnessed a mass migration from the urban centers to the suburbs. The new suburbs offered privacy, security, and a new way of life that most Americans found better and more affordable than city living. One of the results was a big boom in automobile sales, *not* a decline.

6. **C.** To answer this question correctly, you need to have a little knowledge about domestic issues in 1917. Looking at the cartoon, you automatically know that it has something to do with a women's issue (otherwise men would be holding the signs) and President Wilson. The biggest issue for women in the early 1900s (and one that Wilson was initially opposed to) was the right to vote. (For more about women's suffrage, see Chapter 14.) Women were generally anti-war and pro-Prohibition, so (A) and (E) are wrong. Answer (D) is not the best answer because labor union strikes weren't specifically a women's issue, and (C) is just sort of silly.

7. **A.** Don't get thrown by the answer possibility of manifest destiny. Manifest destiny is the philosophy that resulted in the acquisition of Western territories, but it wasn't an official act that the question asks for. You can eliminate the Treaty of Versailles (Chapter 15), the Adams–Onis Treaty (Chapter 6), and popular sovereignty (Chapter 9) because they didn't bring in the specified territory. Under the Treaty of Guadulpe Hidalgo, the United States acquired Utah, California, Nevada, Arizona, and parts of Colorado, New Mexico, and Wyoming at the end of the Mexican War (Chapter 8).

8. **B.** You can eliminate (A) and (D) right off the bat because the SAT II won't test you on famous flappers, and no presidents were named Stanton, Anthony, or Mott.

Answers (B), (C), and (E) — women's rights, the abolition of slavery, and reform in mental hospitals, respectively — represent major social movements; therefore, they are more likely choices. Read Chapter 8 to find out more about these women's efforts for women's suffrage.

9. **E.** Court cases can be confusing. However, making yourself somewhat familiar with ten or so landmark Court cases is probably in your best interest. *McCulloch v. Maryland* (1819) is an important Marshall Court decision (see Chapter 6) because it dealt with a states' rights issue. But even if you don't remember its importance, you can deduce that the case had something to do with a state, particularly Maryland. Answers (D) and (E) deal with the rights of a state, so consider those choices first. Remember that Marshall believed in a strong federal government; therefore, (E) is the most likely answer because it deals with limiting states' rights.

Answer (B) is wrong because it confuses another Marshall Court decision, *Marbury v. Madison* with the *McColluch* case. The College Board likes to include bogus answer choices that are actually good answers to different questions that you should know. Make sure you clarify for yourself just what question you should be answering.

10. **D.** If you don't remember the Kitchen Cabinet (see Chapter 7), think about the characteristics of Andrew Jackson. He was a frontier boy who brought his friends with him to office. Options (B), about the spoils system, and (E), about his background, are true statements, but they don't address the topic of the question at all. Answer (A) just wastes your time, and (C) contradicts what you know about Jackson. Instead of using the official cabinet members for counsel, Jackson got political advice from his friends and allies, who he trusted more than the official cabinet.

11. **A.** Knowing the vocabulary in this question will certainly help you answer it, but if you don't, you can get some clues from the question and the answer choices.

If you don't know what an *encomienda* is, check out Chapter 3, but also consider that "conquests" has a negative connotation. All choices seem to deal with some aspect of stronger/weaker relationships. Which choices show a negative or overbearing relationship? Probably

(A), (B), and (C). When the conquistadors encountered native populations, they conquered them, placed them under Spanish rule, and justified their actions by telling themselves that it was for the good of those conquered. Sound familiar? Southern plantations owners in the Antebellum period treated African slave labor very similarly.

12. **D.** Unfortunately, nothing about the title of the book leads you to the correct answer, but the 1906 publication date reveals that the book came out during the Progressive Era, and you know that the author was a muckraker (see Chapter 14). Muckrakers investigated the social ills caused by big business and government, so you can eliminate (B) right away because muckraking Progressives weren't big advocates of unrestrained capitalism. Latin American immigration wasn't a big issue in 1906, like European immigration was, so (C) is a good choice to cross out. An author probably wouldn't use a book to expose corruption in local government, and the other possible choices are more specific (see Chapter 2 on eliminating answer choices), so you may eliminate (A). That leaves (D) and (E). Answer (D) is the one. Upton Sinclair's book exposed unsanitary conditions and abuses within the meat-packing industry and inspired two important pieces of legislation: the Pure Food and Drug Act and the Meat Inspection Act in 1906. Fellow muckraker Ida Tarbell exposed Standard Oil.

13. **B.** Don't let the choices confuse you. All the answers contain truth about one of the colonies; you just have to find the one that's true about the Massachusetts Bay Colony.

The Rhode Island Colony (A) was established after the Massachusetts Bay Colony. The Georgia Colony (C) provided a haven for debtors. The Pennsylvania Colony (D) was a refuge for Quakers. And the Maryland and Carolina colonies grew tobacco as a main crop (E), although tobacco wasn't the reason those colonies were established. So, answer (B) is correct; remember that the Puritans settled the Massachusetts Bay Colony/Boston area (check out Chapter 4).

14. **E.** The northern colonies were settled primarily by British *families* who sought a place where they could freely practice their religion, so you can rule out (A), (B), and (C). Quakers were men and women, so their settlement wasn't founded by mostly men; (D) isn't it. Answer (E) is the best answer; the founders of the Jamestown settlement were men who sought to improve their economic positions in the New World. (For more details on these settlements, read Chapters 3 and 4.)

15. **C.** Although all these actions or events probably compounded to anger the British Parliament, the Parliament instituted the Intolerable Acts of 1774 (also called the Coercive Acts) directly in response to the Boston Tea Party (see Chapter 5). In opposition to the Intolerable Acts, delegates of each of the colonies met at the First Continental Congress and took actions to prepare for a war against Great Britain.

16. **A.** During World War II, women began to enter the workforce in increasing numbers, and the trend continued in the decades after. So (A) is absolutely not true and, therefore, is the correct answer. For more details, see Chapter 20.

17. **D.** Graph questions usually aren't difficult to analyze, but they can be time-consuming. If you're spending too much time reading the graph, mark your test booklet and go back to the graph if you have time at the end of the section.

From the information in the graph, you can say that the percentage of white female-headed households remained pretty constant, so you can eliminate (A). Answer (B) takes a little more concentration. First, you need to remember that the Clinton administration began in 1993 and essentially ended in 2000. Second, you need to take a look at the percentage of black female-headed households in 1993, which is about 25 percent, and compare it to the percentage in 2000, which is about 23 percent. The difference is about 2 percent (25 – 23), so (B) is probably consistent with the data and should be eliminated.

That little bulge in the Asian line shows a slight increase between 1990 and 1992, so you can cross out (C). According to the data represented in this graph, the percentage of households headed by hispanic females has actually steadily increased since 1980, with only a short decline in the mid-1990s and in the early 2000s. Answer (D) looks like the one with inconsistent information (there were more female hispanic households in 2000 than there were in 1980), but check out (E), just in case. Choice (E) is kind of tricky, too. The percentage of black female household heads increased slowly but surely between 1975 and 1994; don't let that little bump in the line at about 1993 throw you off. The 1994 percentage is still higher than it was in 1984. Answer (D) is a better answer than (E) because the line actually shows a general increase rather than a decrease. If this graph question threw you, don't worry too much because only one or two graph-related questions are likely to appear on the test.

18. **C.** As Chapter 4 notes, Benjamin Franklin was a key figure in the Enlightenment. He was a writer, an inventor, and a deist. He was also an influential American politician and served as a delegate to the Constitutional Convention (see Chapter 5). In spite of all his accomplishments, Franklin never served as vice president, so (C) is your answer.

19. **E.** During the Cuban Missile Crisis of 1962, the Kennedy administration ordered thousands of U.S. troops to Florida in case the United States needed to invade Cuba. Soviet Premier Nikita Khrushchev agreed to dismantle the bases and remove missiles if Kennedy agreed not to invade Cuba. For more details, flip to Chapter 20.

20. **B.** As Chapter 17 reveals, Franklin Delano Roosevelt (FDR) was the first president to regularly use the radio as a means of communicating with the American people, and his signature method of communication was the "fireside chat." FDR gave newspaper interviews, but so did other presidents. The question asks you for a signature, or unique, method, so (A) is out. You can immediately eliminate (C) because FDR was physically disabled and liked to hide his disability from the American people as much as possible. Answer (D) isn't an option because television didn't make its widespread debut until after World War II. Finally, FDR didn't have a monthly schedule of state of the union speeches, so the answer is not (E).

21. **B.** Thomas Jefferson strongly believed in education for all citizens and would likely be quite happy today with K–12 public education and college education opportunities. Although Jefferson advocated an agrarian society, he was not a fan of big business, so the large, corporation-owned farms indicated in answer (C) would not have appealed to him. He also wasn't particularly fond of industry or a centralized government, so (D) and (E) are wrong. He tried to simplify the office of the presidency, so (A) isn't right. The best answer is (B). Jefferson thought that his founding of the University of Virginia (which was one of the first universities to offer tuition assistance to worthy applicants) was one of his greatest accomplishments. See Chapter 6.

22. **C.** Even though gay marriage was a hot button issue in 2004, as of 2004, no amendment was added to the Constitution that provided homosexuals with the legal right to marry other homosexuals, so (E) is wrong. The Constitution gives Congress (not the Supreme Court) the right to choose the president in the event of an electoral tie (see Chapter 22); you can eliminate (D). The Constitution does not allow Congress to reinstitute the draft without presidential approval, so cross out (A). The Jones-Shafroth Act of 1917 gave Puerto Ricans U. S. citizenship but not the right to participate in the electoral college (see Chapter 13), so (B) is wrong. The 6th Amendment guarantees the right to a speedy trial (see Chapter 5), so answer (C) is correct.

23. **A.** First, you need to know that the Union is synonymous with the North, and that "Confederacy" is the name for the South. Second, you need to realize that because you're looking for an answer that's *not* a Northern advantage, you're really looking for a choice that *is* a Southern advantage. After you establish those basic facts, refer to the table in Chapter 9 to review the advantages the South had over the North.

The South had two distinct advantages over the North: strong military leaders and military tradition and familiar turf. Answer (A) addresses the first advantage.

24. **C.** See Chapter 14 for a brief list of Theodore Roosevelt's environmental accomplishments during his presidency. And, in Chapter 17, you'll notice that the Civilian Conservation Corps was actually created under a different Roosevelt, Theodore's distant cousin, Franklin.

25. **C.** The Strategic Defense Initiative, SDI, also known as "Star Wars," was a military program Reagan proposed in the early 1980s. SDI proposed the use of satellites and lasers to create an invisible shield of sorts that would protect against any incoming nuclear missiles. The other answer options, SALT I (Chapter 21), the Nuclear Non-Proliferation Treaty (Chapter 20), SALT II (Chapter 21), and the Limited Nuclear Test-Ban Treaty (Chapter 20), represent diplomatic efforts during the Cold War to reduce and limit nuclear missiles and arms in the United States, the Soviet Union, and other countries around the world.

26. **D.** For more than 20 years, the United States completely ignored China, refusing to recognize a Communist government. If you didn't know that President Richard Nixon started the ball rolling on diplomatic relations between the two countries, read Chapter 21. Jimmy Carter established formal diplomatic relations with China in 1978.

27. **A.** As Chapter 4 tells you, although the New England climate and geography allowed only for small-scale agriculture, the New England coastal colonies excelled in shipbuilding, fishing, whaling, lumbering, and trade with Britain and the British West Indies. The climate of the Middle Colonies allowed for larger-scale agriculture, and the Southern Colonies had a climate and geography that encouraged large-scale, year-round agriculture and plantation life. All areas had similar governments, and most colonists were from Britain, so (B) and (C) aren't big factors. Religion and education had minor impacts on the way colonists in the different areas made a living, so (D) and (E) aren't right.

28. **C.** Did this question fool you? Sometimes charts seem so easy that you forget to read carefully. As you can see from this question, making quick assumptions can really throw you off. If a question about a graph seemingly produces no correct answer, you're probably missing something.

   Notice that the last line of the chart gives statistics for immigration from other countries. Now carefully read the title of the chart: "Immigrants Admitted by Top 15 Countries of Birth in Fiscal Year 1990." Have you caught on yet? The chart shows the exact numbers of immigrants that entered the United States in fiscal year 1990 from the top 15 countries. However, "other" includes dozens or maybe even hundreds of other countries from where immigrants originated. A country included in that figure may even have been responsible for the entrance of only one immigrant. Therefore, the information on the chart shows Haiti as the 15th ranked country overall, not the country from which the least number of immigrants hailed in fiscal year 1990.

29. **B.** You can read about the Sherman Antitrust Act in Chapter 12. The act was designed to break up existing monopolies and encourage competition within industry.

   The inclusion of the word "completely" in answer (A) should be a red flag to you. An answer is rarely correct if it contains a debatable word (see Chapter 2).

30. **D.** The best way to think about U.S. foreign affairs after World War II is to remember that nearly all of them involved a fight against Communism in one way or another. Because (D) deals with efforts to restrain Communism, it's the best answer. After all, this period was the Cold War! For more about the Truman Doctrine, see Chapter 19.

31. **C.** This cartoon came out in 1913 before federal laws existed to regulate child labor. (President Woodrow Wilson initially refused to support child labor laws and other reforms but changed his mind to win the election of 1916; see Chapter 14.) The cartoon depicts profit as a shrine where industry sacrifices children, so your answer must show that profit is more important than children are.

   Answer (E) goes too far. A correct SAT II answer will not contain outrageous statements, especially if a blander answer choice like (C) is available.

32. **E.** When Reagan entered office in 1981, interest rates were at an all-time high and inflation was nearly 10 percent per year. Chapter 22 outlines Reagan's bold economic plan, which included substantial tax cuts that were supposed to cause a trickle-down effect and a reduction in government spending for social programs. The federal budget deficit and national debt grew during Reagan's presidency.

33. **B.** Malcom X advocated that African Americans be self-reliant and independent, free themselves from whites (so (D) isn't right), and take pride in their race, so the best answer is (B). Although, he didn't advocate unwarranted violence, he did realize it was necessary for self-defense, so (C) isn't right. Martin Luther King Jr. headed the SCLC, and Malcolm X wasn't a Christian; eliminate (A). And, although Malcolm X became disillusioned with the Nation of Islam group, he embraced orthodox Islam during a visit to Mecca; (E) is also wrong. See Chapter 20 for more on Malcolm X.

34. **B.** This is an EXCEPT question, so you're looking for an answer that isn't true about both plans. FDR's New Deal of the 1930s (Chapter 17) and Lyndon B. Johnson's Great Society of the 1960s (Chapter 20) had many similarities in policy. However, although extensive landmark civil rights legislation occurred during the time of the Great Society, no such landmark legislation occurred during the New Deal.

35. **C.** You need to be clear on the vocabulary in this question (and you thought you only needed to know vocabulary for the SAT I!) "Augment" means "to increase," so you need to find the answer choice that gives the reason that Kennedy and Johnson would increase troops.

Eisenhower's Domino Theory stated that if a nation fell under Soviet influence, then all surrounding nations in that region would follow suit. In the 1950s and 1960s, U.S. presidents and leaders were afraid that if the United States didn't get involved when nations succumbed to Soviet control, the entire world would succumb to Communism, which gave them good reason to augment troops.

The Viet Cong were pro-Communism, so the administrations would not have believed in their cause. So you can eliminate (A). The Gulf of Tonkin Resolution, which allowed for an escalation of U.S. troops in Vietnam, may have been a result of belief in a Communist threat, but belief in the resolution itself didn't give these administrations a reason to increase troops; so (B) is wrong. The Tet Offensive was a military offensive launched by the Viet Cong in which many American troops perished; again, it's not something that a belief in would cause the administrations to build up troops. So, (D) is wrong. Détente was a relaxation of tensions between the United States and the Soviet Union, so it would have had the opposite effect of decreasing troops. Now you can cross off (E). So (C) is your answer. See Chapter 21 for more about the Vietnam War.

36. **D.** The Supreme Court cases *Brown v. Board of Education of Topeka* (1954; see Chapter 19) and *Plessy v. Ferguson* (1896; see Chapter 10) addressed the constitutionality of separate but equal facilities. In 1896, the Supreme Court ruled in *Plessy v. Ferguson* that separate but equal facilities were constitutional. In 1954, in *Brown v. Board of Education of Topeka,* the Court ruled that separate facilities were inherently unequal and that the segregation of public schools was unconstitutional.

Voting Rights were guaranteed through amendments to the Constitution and other pieces of legislation, not Supreme Court decisions, so you can cross out (E). The issues in (A), (B), and (C) were addressed by other Warren Supreme Court decisions (see Chapter 20).

37. **E.** France's goals in North America in the 1500s to the 1700s were similar to those of other colonizing nations and included trading with the Native Americans (A), finding a Northwest Passage to Asia (B), converting people to Christianity (C), and locating sources of riches (D). Britain used the colonies as a place to send its debtors (E), especially the colony of Georgia (see Chapter 4), but France did not. For more about France in the New World, see Chapter 3.

38. **B.** Jane Addams (see Chapter 12) was a social worker in the 1880s who felt that education and opportunity would help the impoverished more than the preaching of morality. In 1889, she and another social worker founded Hull House, a kind of welfare home for the poor.

39. **E.** Henry Ford's revolutionary assembly-line technique changed the face of American manufacturing (see Chapter 16). Its efficiency made the automobile accessible and affordable for many Americans, so you can immediately eliminate (B) and (D). Because people from most

classes could then afford an automobile, it no longer was a symbol of wealth and status, so (C) is wrong. In an assembly line, workers are responsible for one part of the process, so (A) is not correct. Answer (E) is the best and most logical answer.

40. **B.** George H. W. Bush, or "Bush Senior" as you may think of him, was president of the United States from 1989 to 1993. The United States' and United Nations' forces invaded Iraq in 1991 and, within a month and a half, the war was over. Keep this invasion of Iraq separate from George W. Bush's war with Iraq, which started in 2003. See Chapter 22 for details about both Bushes.

41. **C.** The Warren Court did make important rulings on the segregation of schools (A), defendants' rights to legal counsel (B), prayer in public schools (D), and interracial marriage (E). You can find information about important Warren Court decisions in Chapter 20, and Chapter 19 covers the *Brown v. Board of Education* decision about school desegregation. Although Earl Warren headed a commission to investigate the cause of the assassination of John F. Kennedy at the request of President Lyndon B. Johnson, the investigation was not a Supreme Court case.

42. **E.** The question asks you to evaluate the cartoon, so base your answer primarily on the cartoon's message. In the cartoon, Uncle Sam (the United States) contemplates choosing Cuba, Puerto Rico, the Philippines, or Hawaii (also known as the Sandwich Islands) for his dinner while President McKinley waits on him.

McKinley isn't making the decision, so you can eliminate (D). The nonviolent restaurant depiction doesn't indicate that the United States wants to go to war over the acquisitions, so you can eliminate (B). Uncle Sam is choosing, not protecting, so you can cross out (C). Now you're left with (A) and (E). Again, consider the intent of the cartoon. The cartoonist's point is not the United States' indecision but its desire to make the decision in the first place. The emphasis is on the country's penchant toward imperialism, so (E) is the best answer. (For more about imperialism in the late 1800s and early 1900s, see Chapter 13.)

43. **D.** The best strategy for a question like this one is to figure out what was going on during the time period in question. 1945 signified the end of World War II, and the late 1980s and early 1990s signified the collapse of the Soviet Union. What was going on during that period? Why the Cold War, of course. During the Cold War, the United States spent the largest portion of the federal budget on national defense and security (see Chapter 19). Just think of how the United States could have spent those trillions and trillions of dollars if there had never been a Cold War.

44. **A.** For more information about the civil rights movement, see Chapter 20. The King demonstrations in Birmingham, Alabama (B), the sit-in at Woolworth's Lunch Counter in Greensboro, South Carolina (C), the March on Washington (D), and the Freedom Rides (E) were events that led up to the passage of the Civil Rights Act in 1964. Choice (A), the Freedom Summer, was a name for the summer of 1964 *after* the Civil Rights Act was passed.

45. **C.** The Puritans in New England set up the first universities (see Chapter 4) and their primary concern was to prepare young men for the ministry.

46. **A.** Alexander Hamilton, as secretary of the treasury under Washington from 1789 to 1797, developed a program to organize the finances of and establish the credit of the new nation. Hamilton's financial get-in-shape program included debt payment, excise taxes on distilled liquor, and the establishment of a national bank of the United States. His program created a great deal of controversy between the Federalists and the Antifederalists and led to the formation of two distinct political parties: the Federalists and the Democratic Republicans. So, you can eliminate (B), (C), (D), and (E). You can read more about Hamilton in Chapter 5. Hamilton's financial program had nothing to do with the two-term precedent set by George Washington (choice A), which became law with the passage of the 22nd Amendment in 1951.

47. **C.** All the people in this question represent cultural icons of the 1950s. Jack Kerouac was an author and a leader of the Beat movement. Allan Ginsberg, a poet best known for his poem *Howl*, was also a leader of the Beat movement. Lucille Ball was a well-known actress on the hit television show *I Love Lucy*, which debuted in 1951. Elvis Presley and Chuck Berry were popular rock 'n' roll musicians in the 1950s. For more about 1950s culture, see Chapter 19.

48. **B.** The United States entered World War II as a direct result of the Japanese bombing of Pearl Harbor on December 7, 1941. Although the United States had been providing aid to the Allies, it took a direct hit on U.S. troops for the United States to get actively involved in the war. Beware of (E): Germany's unrestricted submarine warfare led to America's involvement in World War I, not World War II. Read Chapter 18 for a synopsis of the events of World War II.

49. **A.** Both Taft's policy of "dollar diplomacy" and Hay's Open Door policy sought to protect American economic interests abroad. (Check out Chapter 13 for more details.)

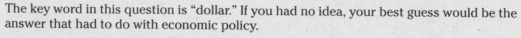

The key word in this question is "dollar." If you had no idea, your best guess would be the answer that had to do with economic policy.

In the Open Door policy, Hay proclaimed that all ports in China were open to U.S. business and that all nations would have equal trading rights in China. Taft's dollar diplomacy was a revision of his predecessor Theodore Roosevelt's "big stick" policies. Taft felt the United States would have more influence abroad with economic concerns than it would with military intervention.

50. **D.** Another trick question alert! Read the question carefully. It's asking you for what Jefferson did as *president*.

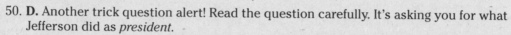

Considering that he served as president of the United States from 1801 to 1809, he obviously did not write the Declaration of Independence (which was officially approved on July 4, 1776) during his presidency. See Chapter 6 for more about Jefferson's administration.

51. **D.** The Compromise of 1820, also known as the Missouri Compromise (see Chapter 7), and the Compromise of 1850 (see Chapter 9) dealt directly with whether slavery would be extended to new states and territories, which influenced how slave states would be represented in Congress. So you can eliminate (B) and (C).

The Three-fifths Compromise (A) in the Constitution was important to the existence of slave states because it stated that ⅗ of the slave population would be counted toward representation in Congress (see Chapter 5). The Dred Scott decision (E) made slavery in the territories potentially legal, so this decision impacted the expansion of slave states and their level of representation in Congress (see Chapter 9). Although the Fugitive Slave Law mandated the return of escaped slaves, it did not specifically address the expansion of slave states or how they were represented in the Union, so (D) is right.

52. **B.** The official reason that the United States intervened in the Korean Conflict and the Vietnam War was to stop the spread of Communism (see Chapters 19 and 21 for more information). Answers (C) and (D) list characteristics of the Vietnam War but not the Korean Conflict. The United Nations was involved only in the Korean Conflict, so (E) is out. And both the Korean Conflict and the Vietnam War were limited wars, which meant that they did not resort to nuclear weapons and that superpowers used the conflicts to fight each other indirectly.

53. **D.** Although George Washington set the precedent for two terms in office (and most presidents voluntarily followed), the Constitution didn't require that limitation until Congress passed the 22nd Amendment in 1951 (see Chapter 5). The 18th and 19th Amendments sound familiar because they passed and repealed Prohibition, so you can eliminate (B) and (E). The 25th Amendment dealt with presidential and vice presidential succession in the event of the death of an executive, so (C) is wrong. The 10th Amendment (A) was one of the Bill of Rights, so it probably wouldn't deal with term limits.

54. **A.** As president, James Monroe was concerned that European powers would try to reassert colonial dominance over Latin American countries that had recently gained independence. In order to prevent this, he issued the Monroe Doctrine (see Chapter 6). Option (E) is wrong because the U.S. was more concerned about keeping Europe out of Latin American affairs than it was about intervening in Latin American affairs itself. The Roosevelt Corollary (see Chapter 13) gave the U.S. a more active role in Latin America.

55. **D.** One of the problems for the colonists in the American Revolution was that despite strong leadership, they did not have a well-trained military or even sufficient military equipment or supplies. The British troops were far better outfitted than the colonists. The Continental Army was comprised mostly of dedicated but inexperienced volunteers, many on a short-term basis. And, eventually, France, Holland, and Spain joined the American side, and Britain wasn't prepared to continue fighting. Thus, you can eliminate choices (A), (B), (C), and (E). See Chapter 5 for more on about why Americans succeeded in winning the American Revolution.

56. **E.** You can eliminate (B), (C) and (D) — the options that include Hawaii — because Spain never controlled Hawaii, which was an independent nation until 1898. Although the United States occupied Cuba until 1902, Cuba gained its status as an independent nation in the Spanish-American War. So, (A) is wrong. As a result of the Spanish-American War, Spain ceded Guam, the Philippines, and Puerto Rico to the United States, choice (E). See Chapter 13 for details.

57. **C.** The Indian Removal Act of 1830 gave President Jackson the authority to use force to move Native Americans to designated western lands (see Chapter 7). Jackson ordered the removal of the Cherokee tribe from Georgia to present-day Oklahoma.

    The Dawes Act of 1887 divided Native American reservation lands into 160-acre farms (A) and required Native Americans to assimilate to western culture (D). The federal "concentration" policy of 1851 broke up the large reservations created in the 1830s and created distinct reservations for each Native American tribe so the government could maintain better control over the tribes (E). The Bureau of Indian Affairs (B) was a corrupt and incompetent agency created in the 1800s to manage the reservations; see Chapter 11 for more information.

58. **C.** Abraham Lincoln was not a popular presidential candidate in the South in the election of 1860, partly because he was a Northern Republican but mostly because he opposed extending slavery to the territories and favored the eventual emancipation of all slaves in the United States. You can quickly eliminate (E) because Lincoln was a Republican, not a member of the Free-Soil Party. Lincoln wasn't an abolitionist who'd worked on the Underground Railroad, either, so you can cross out (D). Southerners wanted to secede from the Union, but the reason was primarily because Lincoln was elected president; you can eliminate (A). Finally, (B) is false because Southerners didn't support Lincoln's opponent Stephen Douglas, who ran on a platform that favored popular sovereignty; they supported the Southern Democratic candidate John Breckenridge, who supported the Dred Scott decision. See Chapter 9 for more details.

59. **C.** Andrew Jackson wasn't a big-business guy (see Chapter 7). He vetoed re-chartering the Second Bank of the United States because he thought the bank acted as a monopoly, and he feared too much concentration of economic power in one institution. Jackson, a westerner himself, favored Western interests and was suspicious of foreign interests, so (A) and (E) are out. Though Jackson was pretty upset about the election outcome in 1824, he had legitimate reasons for opposing the bank, and a national bank differed from any other banks, so you can eliminate (B) and (D).

60. **D.** You can probably best answer this question by process of elimination, based on a general knowledge of Jefferson's personality from Chapter 6.

    You can immediately eliminate (E); Lewis and Clark explored the Louisiana Purchase *after* the United States purchased it. Jefferson wasn't particularly an abolitionist, so you can cross out (B). Jefferson believed in an agrarian society, not an urban one, which eliminates (C). Now you have to choose between (A) and (D). A Napoleonic invasion from New

Orleans wasn't a big threat, but the French did have a lot of control over the Mississippi River, an important trade route. The purchase gave the U.S. control of the Mississippi, so (D) is the best answer.

61. **B.** This question really just tests a little geography and your ability to read a map. The only difficulty is the time you take to analyze each answer choice. In the early years of the transcontinental railroad lines, travel was pretty limited. All lines from Butte to Santa Fe went through either Chicago or California. All other answer choices are possible, so (B) is your answer. (We cover the railroad era in Chapter 11.)

The actual test will probably have only one map question. If you have a difficult time reading maps and you're running low on time, skip the map question and come back to it at the end, if you have time left.

62. **E.** One of the major and unanticipated consequences of Prohibition was a marked increase in organized crime, which led to the rise of several notorious gangsters. Bootleggers were highly successful in their efforts to smuggle liquor into the United States from other countries, especially nations in the West Indies and Canada, so you can eliminate (A). Answer (B) is also false; many places called speakeasies continued to sell alcohol in the United States throughout the years of Prohibition. Answer (C) is false because many Americans weren't thrilled with the new law. During Prohibition, a great grain surplus occurred — partially due to the fact that little was being used to distill alcohol — and the surplus resulted in very low grain prices during the 1920s, which was one of the many causes of the Great Depression. See Chapter 16.

63. **C.** This question may be tough because the topic is very specific, and the answer choices offer few clues for eliminating them. You can probably cross out (E) (a book about D-Day written in 1962 isn't particularly relevant for the SAT II), which means you can at least guess and mark an answer choice on your bubble sheet. All the other choices deal with concerns in 1962, so they'd be hard to eliminate unless you know the topic. As Chapter 20 reveals, Rachel Carson, an environmentalist, scientist, and prolific writer, published several books in her short lifetime, the most significant of which was *Silent Spring*. The bestselling *Silent Spring* alerted the American public to the dangers that insecticides, notably DDT, had on the environment and created widespread public concern and legislative environmental reform as a result.

64. **C.** Although knowing exactly what the two leaders may have been thinking as they rode toward the White House is impossible, the most comprehensive and plausible explanation is (C). Roosevelt's landslide victory over incumbent Hoover couldn't help but produce glee in Roosevelt and shame in Hoover. Answers (B), (D), and (E) address only one of the men, so they aren't comprehensive answer choices. Choice (A) makes too many assumptions about the thoughts of the two men. See Chapter 17 for more details about Hoover and Roosevelt.

65. **E.** As we explain in Chapter 11, Chinese immigrants, most of whom initially came to California during the Gold Rush, were responsible for rapidly completing the Central Pacific Railroad, which was built east from California.

Don't confuse the Central Pacific Railroad with the Union Pacific Railroad, which was built west from Iowa by a workforce largely comprised of Irish immigrants.

66. **B.** The only correct pairing of a president and his major piece of legislation is Harry S Truman and the Taft–Hartley Act of 1947 (see Chapter 19), which may throw you off a bit because you may associate the act with President Taft. Even if these legislative acts are unfamiliar to you, we bet that you can eliminate enough answers to be able to mark a guess on your answer sheet. Abraham Lincoln was assassinated in 1865, and the Sherman Antitrust Act was a response to corruption in the Second Industrial Revolution in the late 1800s, so you can eliminate (C). Now, just guess among the remaining choices. Look carefully at Andrew Jackson and the Fugitive Slave Law (A) and Theodore Roosevelt and the Chinese Exclusion Act (E). Both pieces of legislation occurred before the men became presidents. Answer (E) is tricky. Woodrow Wilson died in 1924, and the Smoot–Hawley Tariff was passed a few years later during Hoover's administration, so (D) doesn't work, either.

67. **D.** Chapter 8 tells you that Harriet Beecher Stowe, Frederick Douglass, William Lloyd Garrison, and Harriet Tubman were all well-known abolitionists. Frederick Douglass and Harriet Tubman were both former slaves. Harriet Beecher Stowe was a white abolitionist who worked on the Underground Railroad and authored the bestseller, *Uncle Tom's Cabin.* William Lloyd Garrison, a radical white abolitionist, was the publisher of *The Liberator,* an abolitionist newspaper.

68. **D.** Popular sovereignty was the principle that Congress wouldn't interfere with the issue of slavery in any new U.S. territories. Instead, the people of each territory would determine whether slavery would be permitted before they sought admission to the Union. This principle was a provision of the Compromise of 1850 (see Chapter 9).

69. **B.** Though shipbuilding was the predominate manufacturing activity in the New England Colonies, producing final goods was somewhat limited in the colonies. Britain operated the colonies on a mercantilist policy, which meant that Britain expected the colonies to provide raw materials to Britain and then purchase the finished products from Britain or other countries. By the mid-1750s, Britain had several pieces of legislation in place that prohibited the colonies from exporting certain manufactured goods overseas or to other colonies. For info on the incorrect choices, see Chapter 4.

70. **A.** Historians cite several economic, social, and political factors throughout the 1920s (and even before) that contributed to the Great Depression (see Chapter 17). The unequal distribution of wealth in the United States in the 1920s was the main reason. Crop surpluses, not shortfalls (B), caused *low* prices and devastation for farmers. High trade tariffs, stock market speculation, and an unsteady bank system were also contributing factors, so you can eliminate (C), (D), and (E) from the running.

71. **C.** The question states the problem as being a lack of men to hold manufacturing positions. You want to choose an answer choice that provides an adequate substitute for the lack of men. Foreign countries were at war, too, so (D) isn't an option. Child labor and general labor reforms had taken hold by World War II, so eliminate (A) and (B). Industry was fairly well mechanized at the turn of the century, so (E) isn't right. Women entered the workforce in record numbers to fill the vacancies left by men who were at war and to help fulfill the great labor demands of industry to meet war production needs. So, (C) is correct. See Chapter 18 for the scoop.

72. **E.** Herbert Hoover created the largely ineffective and unsuccessful Emergency Committee for Employment (E) in 1930 to coordinate private agencies to create employment opportunities for the unemployed in the early years of the Great Depression. The other four options represent programs Roosevelt created in his New Deal policy, which you can read about in Chapter 17.

73. **B.** Manifest destiny was the belief that the United States was destined to extend across the continent to the Pacific Coast (see Chapter 8) and didn't concern protective tariffs. The only regions that fit the definition of manifest destiny are Texas and California.

74. **D.** This quote comes from Thomas Paine's *Common Sense,* a widely distributed pamphlet that encouraged American independence from Britain (see Chapter 5). The quotation's tone and its reference to writing a constitution should tip you off that an American colonist wrote it. When you look at the answer options, you notice that four of the five options share a common theme: The American colonists perceived the Intolerable Acts (A), the Writs of Assistance (B), British mercantilist laws (C), and the Proclamation of 1763 (E) as hostile acts by Britain *against* the American colonies in the 1760s and 1770s. The only answer that fits the views of the colonial rebels is (D).

75. **D.** Again, get your clues from the picture. This cartoon portrays a personification of "War," who is standing on papers labeled "Peace Proposals" as he sharpens his large sword labeled "Renewed Efforts." A woman portrays the personification of "Peace" and is shirking in the distance. When this cartoon was published in January 1917, war seemed to be looming. Therefore, you can eliminate any answer choices that indicate that peace is possible, like (A), (B), and (C). Answer (E) is wrong because the cartoon's date is 1917 and the attack on Pearl Harbor was a World War II event, not a World War I event. For details on World War I, see Chapter 15.

76. **D.** This question is pretty tough because it really requires you to be familiar with activist organizations in the 1960s. Choices (A), (B), (C), and (E) all formed in the 1960s (see Chapter 20 for more about these organizations). However, Martin Luther King Jr. and several other African American ministers formed the Southern Christian Leadership Conference (SCLC) in 1957 to oppose policies of segregation and discrimination using King's method of nonviolent civil disobedience. The formation of the SCLC was what really started the ball rolling for the civil rights movement in the South. See Chapters 19 and 20 for more about civil rights.

77. **C.** Texas was briefly an independent nation before it obtained statehood in 1845, and Hawaii was a long-time monarchy that the United States acquired as a territory in 1898. All of the other territories were controlled by another country immediately before they became U.S. possessions. See Chapter 8 for more about Texas and Chapter 13 for more about Hawaii.

78. **A.** Since the Revolutionary War, the only time the U.S. Army has fought foreign troops in the continental United States was during the War of 1812 against Great Britain (see Chapter 6). In the French and Indian War (C), American colonists fought against the French on American soil, but this war occurred before the Revolutionary War, so it's incorrect. The Civil War (D) was fought on U.S. soil but not against foreign troops. World Wars I and II (answers B and E) were fought abroad.

79. **A.** The Declaration of Independence says nothing about the establishment of the Articles of Confederation (A). The Articles of Confederation was the framework for the new government that was adopted in 1781; eventually, the Constitution replaced the Articles of Confederation (see Chapter 5). All the other answer choices are elements of the Declaration of Independence.

80. **C.** A moral diplomacy policy defined Woodrow Wilson's preferred foreign policy during his administration. Wilson rejected Roosevelt's "big stick" diplomacy, under which America maintained status as a world power through aggressive involvement in foreign affairs, especially in the Western Hemisphere. The other answer choices fit the "big stick" description. See Chapter 13 for more information on Wilson and Roosevelt's policies on imperialism.

81. **D.** Baez, Mitchell, and Dylan were popular folk singers (see Chapter 20), so the answer is (D). You can eliminate jazz (E) because it was popular during the 1920s. Although rock and roll was still popular in the 1960s, it's emergence is associated with the 1950s, so you can eliminate (C). Motown music (A) and psychedelic rock (B) were popular in the 1960s, but Baez, Mitchell, and Dylan weren't part of those music movements.

82. **D.** The Populist Party emerged as a result of farmers who were discontent with the Democratic and Republican parties and eastern industrialists and bankers. The Populist Party's platform supported a graduated income tax that would replace the protective tariff (A), restrictions on immigration (B), free silver, direct election of senators (C), federal ownership of utilities (such as railroad, telephone, and telegraph; E), and voting by secret ballot. In the heated election of 1896, the Populist Party took a stance against the gold standard in favor of free silver, so (D) is the right answer. See Chapter 12.

83. **B.** This one may be tricky. Although several of the options represent goals or agendas of the women's movement of the 1960s and early 1970s, the question asks for the *legislative* goals of the movement.

The two primary legislative goals of the women's movement were to advocate for laws that would allow abortions and require equal pay and rights in the workplace. During the women's rights movement, women fought for dissemination of contraception (not federal research into new methods) and wider availability of women's health (and abortion) clinics. It wasn't illegal for women to run their own health clinics in the first place. (A). Women sought to gain admission to all-male colleges (and wanted men to be able to attend women's colleges) and achieved success in most cases without legislative measures (C). Many women (D) supported and revered Betty Freidan's *The Feminine Mystique* and the creation of the National Organization for Women (NOW) and advocated free love and bra-burning (E), but none of these required new laws. So, (B) is the correct answer. See Chapters 20 and 21.

84. **E.** This question may be tough, if you're not familiar with the vocabulary. A muckraker was a writer, usually a novelist or journalist, who exposed scandal, social injustice, and corruption in the hopes of encouraging reform. Upton Sinclair, author of *The Jungle,* and Ida Tarbell were well-known muckrakers (see Chapter 12). "Scalawags" were Southern white Republicans or moderates who favored Reconstruction (A); see Chapter 10. Persons who illegally smuggled liquor into the United States from other countries during Prohibition were called "bootleggers" (B); see Chapter 16. Former slaves who paid or gave a share of their crop to white landowners in exchange for a parcel of land to farm were known as "sharecroppers" (C); see Chapter 10. Finally, white opportunists from the North who relocated to the South during Reconstruction were known as "carpetbaggers" (D); see Chapter 10.

85. **A.** The transcendentalists believed in intuition, insight, absolute truth, and an emotional (as opposed to a rational or institutional) belief in God. Ralph Waldo Emerson and Henry David Thoreau are the two best-known transcendentalists (see Chapter 8 for more on this philosophy). You may be able to eliminate some of the answer choices by knowing that transcendentalism emerged in the 1830s. Thomas Paine wrote about 50 years before that, so (B) can't be right. And Twain (E) and Bellamy (D) are more modern writers, so they probably wouldn't be influenced by transcendentalism, either.

86. **D.** Southerners opposed protective tariffs because they limited Britain's demand for the South's cotton (see Chapter 7). The South favored less-stringent tariffs, so (A) is wrong. Tariffs increased the cost of the North's manufactured goods; the South produced primarily raw products. Eliminate (B). Answer (C) is wrong because the tariffs were imposed on foreign goods, so they had little effect on any minimal trade that the South had with the West. Southerners thought the tariffs were unfair because they favored Northern interests, so (E) is also out.

87. **C.** Characteristics of the Progressive Era (see Chapter 14) included a desire for reform in politics, business, and industry; social justice; poverty relief; conservation of natural resources; expansion of government regulation over the economy; and the expansion of democracy. Progressives sought to correct the social ills of the late 1800s. Although (E) may tempt you, the Progressive movement may have inspired unions to grow and strike in the late 1800s, but it didn't develop because labor unions grew and went on strike.

88. **C.** Samuel Adams founded the Committees of Correspondence in 1772 to establish networks of communication among the colonies in order to organize resistance to British policies. The other answer options are a series of British actions that angered the American Colonists and helped lead the colonists down the path to war. See Chapter 5.

89. **E.** The quotation doesn't mention anything about succession requirements, so cross out (B). Nor does it mention term limits; you know that mandated presidential term limits didn't appear until the 20th century after FDR, so (C) is wrong. The quotation doesn't mention qualifications for citizenship, so (D) is also incorrect. You're left with (A) and (E). The overall purpose of the excerpt is to provide the qualifications one must meet in order to serve as president of the United States. The excerpt states that the president must be a natural born citizen (one born in the United States). The only exception to this requirement dealt with citizens during the time of the newly established nation. Future qualifications mandated natural born citizenship, so (E) is the better answer of the two. See Chapter 5 for more about the creation of the Constitution.

90. **B.** The slogan "Fifty-four forty or fight" was James K. Polk's campaign slogan during the presidential election of 1844. For several years, Britain and the United States had jointly occupied the Oregon Territory peacefully. After the election, Polk decided to compromise with Great Britain and divide Oregon at the 49th parallel rather than demand that the border be at latitude coordinates 54-40 because he was already occupied in a border dispute with Mexico. Dividing Oregon at the 49th parallel created a straight-line border between the western United States and Canada. See Chapter 8.

Practice Test 2 Answer Sheet

Each question in this chapter is followed by five suggested answers designated (A), (B), (C), (D), and (E). Select the best answer for each question and fill in the proper oval on your answer sheet.

1. Ⓐ Ⓑ Ⓒ Ⓓ Ⓔ   46. Ⓐ Ⓑ Ⓒ Ⓓ Ⓔ
2. Ⓐ Ⓑ Ⓒ Ⓓ Ⓔ   47. Ⓐ Ⓑ Ⓒ Ⓓ Ⓔ
3. Ⓐ Ⓑ Ⓒ Ⓓ Ⓔ   48. Ⓐ Ⓑ Ⓒ Ⓓ Ⓔ
4. Ⓐ Ⓑ Ⓒ Ⓓ Ⓔ   49. Ⓐ Ⓑ Ⓒ Ⓓ Ⓔ
5. Ⓐ Ⓑ Ⓒ Ⓓ Ⓔ   50. Ⓐ Ⓑ Ⓒ Ⓓ Ⓔ
6. Ⓐ Ⓑ Ⓒ Ⓓ Ⓔ   51. Ⓐ Ⓑ Ⓒ Ⓓ Ⓔ
7. Ⓐ Ⓑ Ⓒ Ⓓ Ⓔ   52. Ⓐ Ⓑ Ⓒ Ⓓ Ⓔ
8. Ⓐ Ⓑ Ⓒ Ⓓ Ⓔ   53. Ⓐ Ⓑ Ⓒ Ⓓ Ⓔ
9. Ⓐ Ⓑ Ⓒ Ⓓ Ⓔ   54. Ⓐ Ⓑ Ⓒ Ⓓ Ⓔ
10. Ⓐ Ⓑ Ⓒ Ⓓ Ⓔ   55. Ⓐ Ⓑ Ⓒ Ⓓ Ⓔ
11. Ⓐ Ⓑ Ⓒ Ⓓ Ⓔ   56. Ⓐ Ⓑ Ⓒ Ⓓ Ⓔ
12. Ⓐ Ⓑ Ⓒ Ⓓ Ⓔ   57. Ⓐ Ⓑ Ⓒ Ⓓ Ⓔ
13. Ⓐ Ⓑ Ⓒ Ⓓ Ⓔ   58. Ⓐ Ⓑ Ⓒ Ⓓ Ⓔ
14. Ⓐ Ⓑ Ⓒ Ⓓ Ⓔ   59. Ⓐ Ⓑ Ⓒ Ⓓ Ⓔ
15. Ⓐ Ⓑ Ⓒ Ⓓ Ⓔ   60. Ⓐ Ⓑ Ⓒ Ⓓ Ⓔ
16. Ⓐ Ⓑ Ⓒ Ⓓ Ⓔ   61. Ⓐ Ⓑ Ⓒ Ⓓ Ⓔ
17. Ⓐ Ⓑ Ⓒ Ⓓ Ⓔ   62. Ⓐ Ⓑ Ⓒ Ⓓ Ⓔ
18. Ⓐ Ⓑ Ⓒ Ⓓ Ⓔ   63. Ⓐ Ⓑ Ⓒ Ⓓ Ⓔ
19. Ⓐ Ⓑ Ⓒ Ⓓ Ⓔ   64. Ⓐ Ⓑ Ⓒ Ⓓ Ⓔ
20. Ⓐ Ⓑ Ⓒ Ⓓ Ⓔ   65. Ⓐ Ⓑ Ⓒ Ⓓ Ⓔ
21. Ⓐ Ⓑ Ⓒ Ⓓ Ⓔ   66. Ⓐ Ⓑ Ⓒ Ⓓ Ⓔ
22. Ⓐ Ⓑ Ⓒ Ⓓ Ⓔ   67. Ⓐ Ⓑ Ⓒ Ⓓ Ⓔ
23. Ⓐ Ⓑ Ⓒ Ⓓ Ⓔ   68. Ⓐ Ⓑ Ⓒ Ⓓ Ⓔ
24. Ⓐ Ⓑ Ⓒ Ⓓ Ⓔ   69. Ⓐ Ⓑ Ⓒ Ⓓ Ⓔ
25. Ⓐ Ⓑ Ⓒ Ⓓ Ⓔ   70. Ⓐ Ⓑ Ⓒ Ⓓ Ⓔ
26. Ⓐ Ⓑ Ⓒ Ⓓ Ⓔ   71. Ⓐ Ⓑ Ⓒ Ⓓ Ⓔ
27. Ⓐ Ⓑ Ⓒ Ⓓ Ⓔ   72. Ⓐ Ⓑ Ⓒ Ⓓ Ⓔ
28. Ⓐ Ⓑ Ⓒ Ⓓ Ⓔ   73. Ⓐ Ⓑ Ⓒ Ⓓ Ⓔ
29. Ⓐ Ⓑ Ⓒ Ⓓ Ⓔ   74. Ⓐ Ⓑ Ⓒ Ⓓ Ⓔ
30. Ⓐ Ⓑ Ⓒ Ⓓ Ⓔ   75. Ⓐ Ⓑ Ⓒ Ⓓ Ⓔ
31. Ⓐ Ⓑ Ⓒ Ⓓ Ⓔ   76. Ⓐ Ⓑ Ⓒ Ⓓ Ⓔ
32. Ⓐ Ⓑ Ⓒ Ⓓ Ⓔ   77. Ⓐ Ⓑ Ⓒ Ⓓ Ⓔ
33. Ⓐ Ⓑ Ⓒ Ⓓ Ⓔ   78. Ⓐ Ⓑ Ⓒ Ⓓ Ⓔ
34. Ⓐ Ⓑ Ⓒ Ⓓ Ⓔ   79. Ⓐ Ⓑ Ⓒ Ⓓ Ⓔ
35. Ⓐ Ⓑ Ⓒ Ⓓ Ⓔ   80. Ⓐ Ⓑ Ⓒ Ⓓ Ⓔ
36. Ⓐ Ⓑ Ⓒ Ⓓ Ⓔ   81. Ⓐ Ⓑ Ⓒ Ⓓ Ⓔ
37. Ⓐ Ⓑ Ⓒ Ⓓ Ⓔ   82. Ⓐ Ⓑ Ⓒ Ⓓ Ⓔ
38. Ⓐ Ⓑ Ⓒ Ⓓ Ⓔ   83. Ⓐ Ⓑ Ⓒ Ⓓ Ⓔ
39. Ⓐ Ⓑ Ⓒ Ⓓ Ⓔ   84. Ⓐ Ⓑ Ⓒ Ⓓ Ⓔ
40. Ⓐ Ⓑ Ⓒ Ⓓ Ⓔ   85. Ⓐ Ⓑ Ⓒ Ⓓ Ⓔ
41. Ⓐ Ⓑ Ⓒ Ⓓ Ⓔ   86. Ⓐ Ⓑ Ⓒ Ⓓ Ⓔ
42. Ⓐ Ⓑ Ⓒ Ⓓ Ⓔ   87. Ⓐ Ⓑ Ⓒ Ⓓ Ⓔ
43. Ⓐ Ⓑ Ⓒ Ⓓ Ⓔ   88. Ⓐ Ⓑ Ⓒ Ⓓ Ⓔ
44. Ⓐ Ⓑ Ⓒ Ⓓ Ⓔ   89. Ⓐ Ⓑ Ⓒ Ⓓ Ⓔ
45. Ⓐ Ⓑ Ⓒ Ⓓ Ⓔ   90. Ⓐ Ⓑ Ⓒ Ⓓ Ⓔ

Chapter 25

Pulling It All Together, Part II: Practice Test 2

· ·

Are you ready for some more practice? The following exam consists of 90 questions. Remember, you have only 60 minutes to take the test, which gives you 45 seconds or less to answer each question. As you take the test, keep an eye on the time so you can get through as many questions as possible. At 30 minutes, you should be on about question 45.

Whatever you do, take the practice tests under actual exam conditions. Take the practice test seriously; doing so is a good way to prepare for the real thing!

- ✔ Set a timer or alarm for an hour and stop as soon as the timer or alarm goes off.

- ✔ Take the exam in a quiet place where you won't be interrupted: your bedroom, a library, or anywhere quiet.

- ✔ Remove all distractions; let your family know not to bother you, unplug the telephone, and so on.

- ✔ Use the answer grid we provide in this chapter, just like you would during the actual exam.

- ✔ If you need to use the bathroom, leave the clock running. The test proctor isn't going to stop the time during the actual test for you to make a bathroom run.

- ✔ If you finish early, go back and check the answers on the ones you weren't sure about.

- ✔ Try to take at least one practice exam at the same time of day that you'll be taking the real exam. This suggestion may sound weird, but it really can help you. Unfortunately, testing centers only offer many of these tests on weekend mornings, and that's probably when you normally sleep in. We know that getting up to take a test sounds like torture, but get up early one Saturday, eat a good breakfast, and take the practice test for an hour at the actual time you'll be taking the exam. Just look at it as good practice for the big day! Besides, you can go back to sleep after you're done.

When you finish the practice test, check your answers against the answer key at the end of this chapter. You can also figure out your score. After you do that, go through the explanations of *all* the answers in Chapter 26. Of course, you want to check the ones you got wrong, but going through all the explanations is worthwhile because you may discover something that'll help you out on test day!

Practice Test 2

1. The Monroe Doctrine

   (A) declared that the United States would develop economic interests abroad and limit military intervention altogether.

   (B) warned the nations of Europe against interfering in the Americas.

   (C) declared that the United States would assist any nation threatened by Communism.

   (D) stated that the United States, not Europe, would dominate Latin America.

   (E) declared that the United States would not seek territorial expansion abroad.

2. What was the African American style of music that emerged in the early 1960s and had widespread popularity with white audiences?

   (A) Jazz

   (B) Folk

   (C) Rock 'n' roll

   (D) Motown

   (E) Psychedelic rock

3. During his presidency, Theodore Roosevelt helped set aside over 150 million acres of land for national forests in order to

   (A) provide land for the United States Forest Service to use for mining and forestry.

   (B) later sell the land to big businesses at a large profit.

   (C) give to settlers under the Homestead Act.

   (D) lease out for farming and ranching.

   (E) conserve and protect the land and natural resources.

4. Brigham Young led which persecuted religious group from Illinois to the Great Salt Lake in Utah in the first half of the 19th century?

   (A) Transcendentalists

   (B) Puritans

   (C) Anglicans

   (D) Mormons

   (E) Quakers

5. All the following are true about the sharecropping system in the South in the post-Reconstruction period EXCEPT

   (A) Freedmen rented out parcels of land from plantation owners.

   (B) Poor whites rented out parcels of land from plantation owners.

   (C) The system was successful in that the sharecroppers usually made enough profit after a few years to purchase their own farmland.

   (D) The landowners provided the sharecroppers with the land, use of farming equipment, and shelter.

   (E) In exchange for what the landowner provided, the sharecroppers would usually give the landowner half of their crop.

Go on to next page

Courtesy of BoondocksNet.com

6. The artist of this 1919 cartoon is most likely trying to make which of the following statements?

   (A) Bolshevism is a far superior political system to capitalism.

   (B) It is up to Americans to destroy Bolshevism.

   (C) Education is the key to quelling the spread of Bolshevism.

   (D) Americanism is far superior to Bolshevism.

   (E) Bolshevism is just another bad political idea.

7. The role of the colonies in the British economic policy of mercantilism was

   (A) to manufacture all the goods needed in the colonies from raw materials purchased from Britain.

   (B) to provide raw materials for British factories to manufacture into finished goods and then purchase those finished goods from Britain.

   (C) to convert raw materials into manufactured goods in colonial factories and sell those goods to Britain.

   (D) to export raw goods to any nation as long as those nations pay a tariff to Britain.

   (E) to conduct free trade with France and Spain as long as the colonies paid a port tax to Britain.

8. Which of the following early 19th-century writers was best known for his colorful accounts about life on the American frontier?

   (A) James Fenimore Cooper

   (B) Herman Melville

   (C) Edgar Allan Poe

   (D) Washington Irving

   (E) Nathaniel Hawthorne

Go on to next page

9. The leading powers of Western Europe financed expeditions to the New World from the late 1400s to the early 1600s with all the following goals EXCEPT

  (A) to seek a western passage to Asia.

  (B) to convert the native populations to Christianity.

  (C) to trade and cooperate politically with the native populations.

  (D) to claim new lands for future trading posts and settlements.

  (E) to seek gold, silver, and other precious commodities.

10. All the following are true about the Lend-Lease Act of 1941 EXCEPT

  (A) It allowed the United States to lease weapons to Great Britain and the Soviet Union.

  (B) It helped United States' industries mobilize for war.

  (C) It allowed any nation vital to United States' security to borrow weapons.

  (D) It permitted United States' merchant ships to deliver weapons directly to Spain and Italy.

  (E) Roosevelt authorized over $50 billion in aid.

11. Which of the following United States' acquisitions is least likely to be considered an act of manifest destiny?

  (A) The acquisition of Maine under the Webster–Ashburton Treaty of 1820

  (B) The annexation of Texas in 1845

  (C) Acquisition of the Oregon Territory in 1846

  (D) The Gadsden Purchase in 1853

  (E) The Mexican Cession in 1848

12. During the colonial period, triangular trade routes among the colonies, Britain, Africa, and the West Indies led to

  (A) increased unemployment in the colonies.

  (B) an increased slave population in the colonies.

  (C) increased exports of cotton and tobacco from the West Indies to the colonies.

  (D) a decrease in the merchant population in the colonies.

  (E) increased pirate attacks on British merchant ships.

13. Which of the following is true about the political climate during the later half of the 19th century?

  (A) The government decreased the federal bureaucracy by eliminating unnecessary federal positions.

  (B) Democrats and Republicans had very different political agendas.

  (C) Many farmers joined the Populist Party to advocate for a silver standard and tougher government regulations on businesses.

  (D) Presidential administrations advocated Progressive reforms.

  (E) The federal government was concerned about regulating the transportation industry.

14. Which of the following groups was affected by the first U.S. anti-immigration measure targeted at a specific ethnicity?

  (A) Greeks

  (B) Armenians

  (C) Jews

  (D) Mexicans

  (E) Chinese

Go on to next page

15. The Native American tribes of North America were known for all the following EXCEPT

    (A) the use of animal products for food, clothing, shelter, and protection.

    (B) the use of plants for medicinal purposes.

    (C) generally nomadic living, moving when deemed necessary for survival.

    (D) invention of an accurate calendar and development of an extensive road system.

    (E) reliance on and respect for the environment.

16. Which of the following is NOT accurate regarding urban trends in the 1870s and 1880s?

    (A) The rise of tenements in slums and ghettos

    (B) A decrease in overall population in the cities

    (C) Mass migration of the wealthy to suburban developments

    (D) Increased immigrant populations in cities

    (E) Increase in public transportation infrastructure between cities and suburban areas

Go on to next page

Immigration to the U.S.
Fiscal Years 1820 to 2001

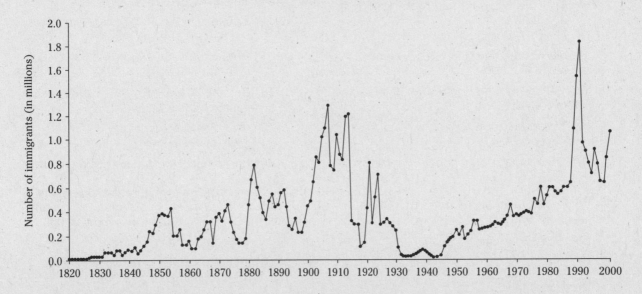

17. Which of the following statements is consistent with the data presented in this graph?

    (A) A substantial increase in immigration to the United States occurred during the Great Depression.

    (B) A steady decrease in immigration to the United States occurred during John F. Kennedy's presidency.

    (C) A marked increase in immigration to the United States occurred in the six years leading up to the Civil War.

    (D) Approximately 1.8 million immigrants came to the United States in 1990.

    (E) The smallest increase in immigration in a three-year period in the United States occurred from 1987 to 1990.

18. The system under which early colonists gained free passage to the colonies in exchange for several years of labor, often on a Southern plantation, was known as

    (A) sharecropping.

    (B) indentured servitude.

    (C) mercantilism.

    (D) the Enlightenment.

    (E) slavery.

19. Which late 19th-century author was best known for his satirical commentaries on society, poverty, class tensions, and race relations?

    (A) Mark Twain

    (B) Edward Bellamy

    (C) Langston Hughes

    (D) Ernest Hemingway

    (E) Henry James

Go on to next page

20. Which of the following was NOT a component of the Missouri Compromise?

    (A) Missouri was admitted to the Union as a slave state.

    (B) Slavery was prohibited in the remainder of the Louisiana territory lands north of 36°30'.

    (C) Maine was admitted to the Union as a free state.

    (D) Texas was admitted to the Union as a slave state.

    (E) The region south of 36° 30' latitude was open to slavery.

21. Which president is credited with bringing about the end of the Cold War?

    (A) Harry S Truman

    (B) Bill Clinton

    (C) Jimmy Carter

    (D) George W. Bush

    (E) Ronald Reagan

22. The main reason Britain imposed the Sugar Act (1764) and the Stamp Act (1765) on the colonists was

    (A) to retaliate against the colonists for the Boston Tea Party.

    (B) to stop all illegal smuggling of sugar and stamps by the colonists.

    (C) to raise funds to pay off the debts from the French and Indian War.

    (D) to lower tariffs to appease the colonists.

    (E) to prove to the colonists they were virtually represented in Parliament.

23. All the following characterized the years of Richard Nixon's presidency EXCEPT

    (A) the signing of the SALT I Treaty with the Soviet Union.

    (B) the Iran Hostage Crisis.

    (C) the Watergate scandal.

    (D) the Paris Accords, which ended U.S. involvement in Vietnam.

    (E) paving the way for diplomatic relations with China.

24. The French and Indian War was a source of increased tension between the colonies and Britain mostly because

    (A) Britain expected the colonies to share the costs of the war.

    (B) Britain refused to allow the colonists to fight in the war.

    (C) the war caused property damage in many of the colonies.

    (D) the colonists were angry about the Writs of Assistance.

    (E) the colonies had sided with the French.

25. Which of the following was most responsible for large numbers of families relocating to the Western frontier beginning in 1862?

    (A) The California Gold Rush

    (B) Plentiful rainfall in the West and drought in the East

    (C) The Homestead Act

    (D) The South Dakota Gold Rush

    (E) The completion of the transcontinental railroad

26. Which of the following ruled that separate accommodations for whites and blacks were legal so long as the accommodations were equal?

    (A) The 15th Amendment

    (B) Jim Crow laws

    (C) The grandfather clause

    (D) The 14th Amendment

    (E) *Plessy v. Ferguson*

27. With the election of Democratic Republican Thomas Jefferson in 1800, the 12-year Federalist era came to a close. Which of the following was NOT an achievement of the Federalists?

    (A) The enforcement of federal law during the Whiskey Rebellion

    (B) The creation of unopposed economic policies

    (C) The institution of a neutral foreign policy

    (D) The signing of the Treaty of Greenville with Native American tribes

    (E) The creation of a central banking system

Go on to next page

Courtesy of BoondocksNet.com

28. Which of the following describes the meaning that the artist of this cartoon most likely intended?

    (A) A federal income tax will eliminate the need for protective tariffs in the United States.

    (B) A federal income tax will not provide enough funds for the federal government.

    (C) A federal income tax will leave the United States poor.

    (D) The maximum tax rate for the new graduated federal income tax would not exceed 7 percent.

    (E) Income tax will be good because it will eliminate the need for the Ways and Means Committee.

29. The relatively easy takeover of Native American populations by European settlers in North America may be primarily attributed to

    (A) the rapid spread of European diseases that killed nearly all the native populations.

    (B) differences in language and a resulting inability to communicate.

    (C) a widespread famine in North America at the time of initial European settlement.

    (D) a lack of solidarity among Native American tribes.

    (E) the peaceful and passive nature of the Native American tribes.

30. Thomas Paine's "Common Sense" pamphlet, distributed in 1776, was significant because it

    (A) persuaded the colonists to start resisting the British.

    (B) inspired the Boston Tea Party.

    (C) convinced many American colonists that complete independence from Britain was the only acceptable solution.

    (D) called for continued economic and political dependence on Britain.

    (E) recommended a plan of reconciliation between the colonies and Britain.

Go on to next page ⟶

31. Which of the following was not part of American foreign policy following World War II?

    (A) The Marshall Plan

    (B) The Truman Doctrine

    (C) Isolationism

    (D) Containment

    (E) Deterrence

32. What do the following five people have in common: Betty Friedan, Jimi Hendrix, Bob Dylan, Cesar Chavez, and Ed Sullivan?

    (A) All represent politicians of the 1960s.

    (B) All represent artists of the 1960s.

    (C) All represent famous authors of the late 20th century.

    (D) All represent cultural icons from the 1960s.

    (E) All represent cultural icons of the 1970s.

33. In 1682, the Quakers first founded which economically prosperous colony on the principle of religious tolerance?

    (A) Georgia

    (B) Delaware

    (C) Pennsylvania

    (D) New Jersey

    (E) New York

34. John F. Kennedy's short term in office was marked by

    (A) his failure to push the majority of his reform legislation through Congress.

    (B) a successful invasion of Cuba in 1961.

    (C) passage of the Civil Rights Act.

    (D) appointment of the first African American justice to the Supreme Court.

    (E) creation of Medicare and Medicaid.

35. All the following motivated British settlers to settle the New World EXCEPT

    (A) King James's mandate that all citizens observe the religious practices of the Church of England.

    (B) steadily growing crime and poverty rates in Britain.

    (C) financial and employment opportunities.

    (D) religious persecution.

    (E) complete freedom from rule by the British Crown.

36. During the 1960s, the Chief Justice who delivered such landmark Supreme Court decisions as *Engel v. Vitale, Miranda v. Arizona,* and *Gideon v. Wainwright* was

    (A) John Marshall.

    (B) Earl Warren.

    (C) William Rehnquist.

    (D) Warren Burger.

    (E) Thurgood Marshall.

37. By July 1776, the colonists had many reasons for declaring complete independence from Britain. These reasons included all the following EXCEPT

    (A) colonists were inspired by Thomas Paine's pamphlet, "Common Sense."

    (B) the colonists thought that if they declared independence, Britain would grant it and end the war immediately.

    (C) colonists objected to taxation without representation.

    (D) the colonists hoped if they were independent they could receive military aid from France.

    (E) many colonists were convinced that the British government was despotic and must be overthrown.

Go on to next page

38. Which of the following 20th-century presidents is INCORRECTLY matched with a major scandal or crisis during his presidency?

    (A) John F. Kennedy, Bay of Pigs invasion

    (B) Ronald Reagan, Iran-Contra Affair

    (C) Richard Nixon, Watergate

    (D) William H. Taft, The Teapot Dome scandal

    (E) Jimmy Carter, Iran Hostage Crisis

Go on to next page

**Labor Force Participation Rates,
1970 to 2000**

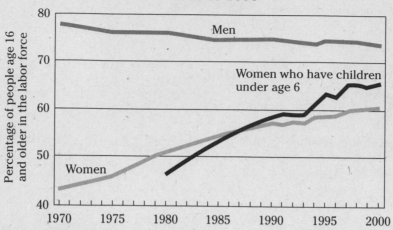

39. Which of the following is NOT a true representation of the data presented in the graph?

(A) In 2000, just over 60 percent of women worked.

(B) The gap between the percent of women working and the percent of men working is steadily closing.

(C) In 1980, fewer than 50 percent of women with children under age 6 worked.

(D) The number of men in the labor force has steadily declined since 1970.

(E) In 1987, 60 percent of women worked and 66 percent of women with children under age 6 worked.

40. Maine businessman Neal Dow was best known in the 1850s for

(A) founding a long-lasting Utopian community in New York.

(B) advocating insane asylums for the mentally ill.

(C) his work as an abolitionist.

(D) his reform of the state school system in Massachusetts.

(E) his extensive work for the temperance movement.

41. Which of the following forms of entertainment gained great popularity during the 1950s?

(A) Radio

(B) Television

(C) Music

(D) Motion pictures

(E) Theater

Go on to next page

42. All the following are factors that contributed to industrial growth in the United States in the second half of the 19th century EXCEPT

    (A) the development of electricity.

    (B) improved means of communication.

    (C) the rapidly expanding population.

    (D) the invention of the automobile.

    (E) improved means of transportation.

43. What was the primary motivation behind the United States' annexation of the Philippines in 1898?

    (A) U.S. business interests in Asian trade, raw materials, and investment opportunities

    (B) Education of the native peoples

    (C) Conversion of the native peoples to Christianity

    (D) Creation of an infrastructure

    (E) Implementation of sanitation programs and disease control

44. All the following characterize Dwight D. Eisenhower's presidency EXCEPT

    (A) massive growth of big business.

    (B) government spending to stimulate economic growth.

    (C) support of civil rights for African Americans.

    (D) cooperation with the Democrats in Congress.

    (E) extremely conservative social policies.

45. The Three-fifths Compromise in the Constitution stated that

    (A) Congress can pass a law that the president vetoes if three-fifths of Congress approves it.

    (B) five slaves would be counted as three free persons for the purposes of taxation and representation.

    (C) in order to become a state, a territory must have a population that is three-fifths white male.

    (D) three-fifths of the House of Representatives must pass a bill before it is sent to the Senate.

    (E) impeaching the president requires a three-fifths vote in favor in the House of Representatives.

46. Under his Great Society program, Lyndon B. Johnson passed all the following pieces of legislation EXCEPT

    (A) the Civil Rights Act.

    (B) the health Insurance Act for the Aged.

    (C) the Social Security Act.

    (D) the Voting Rights Act.

    (E) the Immigration Act.

47. Which of the following was NOT a decision of John Marshall's Supreme Court?

    (A) *McCulloch v. Maryland*

    (B) *Marbury v. Madison*

    (C) *Cohens v. Virginia*

    (D) *Dred Scott v. Sanford*

    (E) *Dartmouth College v. Woodward*

Go on to next page

48. The purpose of the North Atlantic Treaty Organization was to

    (A) establish a collective security alliance between the United States, Canada, and ten Western European nations.

    (B) ensure that the United States would provide military protection to any nation threatened by Communism.

    (C) establish a pact between the United States and the Soviet Union to agree not to wage war for 20 years.

    (D) provide financial assistance for war reconstruction to Europe.

    (E) construct an airlift to supply West Berlin during the Berlin Blockade.

49. "... We, therefore, the Representatives of the United States of America, in General Congress, Assembled, appealing to the Supreme Judge of the world for the rectitude of our intentions, do, in the Name, and by Authority of the good People of these Colonies, solemnly publish and declare, that these United Colonies are, and of Right ought to be Free and Independent States, that they are Absolved from all Allegiance to the British Crown, and that all political connection between them and the State of Great Britain, is and ought to be totally dissolved; and that as Free and Independent States, they have full Power to levy War, conclude Peace, contract Alliances, establish Commerce, and to do all other Acts and Things which Independent States may of right do. . . ."

This excerpt is from which of the following documents?

(A) The U.S. Constitution

(B) The Articles of Confederation

(C) The Declaration of Independence

(D) The Treaty of Paris of 1783

(E) "Common Sense"

Go on to next page

U.S. Population Trends, 1790–1980

Year	Total population in millions	Urban population by percentage	Rural population by percentage	Cities over 1,000,000	Cities of 100,000 to 1,000,000
1790	4	5.1	94.9	0	0
1850	23	15.3	84.7	0	6
1900	76	39.7	60.3	3	35
1950	151	64.0	36.0	5	101
1960	179	69.9	30.1	5	130
1970	203	73.5	26.5	6	147
1980	227	73.7	26.3	6	163

50. Referencing this chart, which of the following is NOT a true statement?

   (A) The rural population of the United States steadily decreased from 1790 to 1980.

   (B) The population of the United States increased by one million more people in the period 1950–1980 than in 1900–1950.

   (C) Overall population growth between 1850 and 1900 is less than the population growth between 1900 and 1950.

   (D) As the urban population of the United States decreased, the rural population of the United States increased between 1790 and 1980.

   (E) The U.S. population increased by approximately 24 million people between 1960 and 1970 and again between 1970 and 1980.

51. Which of the following is NOT a goal of a monopoly?

   (A) To set prices within an industry

   (B) To allow unlimited governmental regulation

   (C) To increase profits

   (D) To control production within an industry

   (E) To eliminate competition

52. Due to a severe famine in their country, nearly two million immigrants from which country entered the United States between 1847 and 1854?

   (A) Germany

   (B) Russia

   (C) Ireland

   (D) China

   (E) Greece

Go on to next page

53. At the onset of World War I, Congress passed the Selective Service Act, which required

    (A) all men and women ages 18 to 50 to register for military duty.

    (B) all white men to register for military duty.

    (C) the armed services to immediately hire willing men.

    (D) a long-term ramp-up of the military.

    (E) all men between the ages of 21 and 30 to register for military duty.

54. Andrew Jackson was known for his use of the spoils system. The spoils system is best described as

    (A) a system in which the president appoints only his close friends and allies to his cabinet.

    (B) a system in which the president removes all government-appointed officeholders of the opposite political party and replaces them with members of his own party.

    (C) a system in which the president works only with members of Congress who are in his political party.

    (D) a system in which the president vetoes the majority of legislation passed by Congress during his administration.

    (E) a system in which the president allows regional interests to dominate presidential legislation.

55. Which of the following movements or organizations of the 1960s sought peace, freedom, and respect for the earth and sought to reject materialism and societal constraints?

    (A) The Students for a Democratic Society

    (B) Free speech movement at the University of California at Berkeley

    (C) The hippie movement

    (D) The women's liberation movement

    (E) The United Farm Workers

56. Some historians argue that the Revolutionary War was a civil war. The best explanation for this rationale is that

    (A) Britain hired mercenaries to fight against the colonists.

    (B) few colonists remained loyal to the Crown.

    (C) many colonists remained loyal to the British Crown throughout the war.

    (D) the colonies received French help in fighting the British.

    (E) the colonists didn't declare independence for more than a year after the fighting started.

57. Woodrow Wilson's one major achievement at the Versailles peace conference was the approval of his plan for the League of Nations. This achievement was ironic because

    (A) he died before the League of Nations started.

    (B) his proposals for the treatment of Germany were strongly resisted by the other allied nations.

    (C) World War II began only 20 years later.

    (D) Congress never gave approval for the United States to join the League of Nations.

    (E) the Allied nations were bitter and resentful toward Germany.

58. The primary motivation behind the Spanish creation of the first American settlement at St. Augustine in present-day Florida was to

    (A) convert the natives in the St. Augustine region to Christianity.

    (B) build a fort in which they could protect their New World profits and riches and protect their entrance into the Caribbean from the corsairs.

    (C) set up a trading post for trade with Native Americans.

    (D) provide a place for religiously persecuted Spanish citizens to relocate.

    (E) provide a place for the Spanish to service and repair their ships and stock up with provisions before sailing back across the Atlantic to Spain.

Go on to next page

59. "This great Nation will endure as it has endured, will revive and will prosper. So, first of all, let me assert my firm belief that the only thing we have to fear is fear itself — nameless, unreasoning, unjustified terror that paralyzes needed efforts to convert retreat into advance. In every dark hour of our national life, a leadership of frankness and vigor has met with that understanding and support of the people themselves which is essential to victory. I am convinced that you will again give that support to leadership in these critical days. In such a spirit on my part and on yours, we face our common difficulties. They concern, thank God, only material things."

What are the critical days to which the speaker of this quote from the early 20th century refers?

(A) World War I

(B) The Stock Market Crash of 1929

(C) The Great Depression

(D) World War II

(E) The Cold War

60. What was the main reason why organized labor attempts in the 1830s through the 1850s were largely unsuccessful?

(A) Workers were not interested in labor unions.

(B) Workers didn't have time to make a stand for better hours and wages.

(C) Adults were afraid of losing their jobs to children.

(D) Workers did not want to jeopardize their jobs due to the high influx of immigrants.

(E) Wages, hours, and working conditions for workers were usually very good.

Go on to next page

Courtesy of BoondocksNet.com

61. Which of the following best summarizes the idea presented in this 1907 cartoon?

   (A) Children should be allowed to work in factories if their families need them to.

   (B) Children going to school instead of working represents a decline in civilization.

   (C) The United States is becoming a more civilized nation now that children have to go to school instead of work in the factories.

   (D) Children should not be required to attend school.

   (E) Georgia should be allowed to set its own child labor laws.

62. All the following characterized the Reagan administration EXCEPT

   (A) two economic recessions.

   (B) increased government involvement in social programs.

   (C) the Iran-Contra scandal.

   (D) increased defense spending.

   (E) supply-side economic policy.

63. Which of the following is NOT one of the points of the Compromise of 1850?

   (A) Congress would fortify the Fugitive Slave Law.

   (B) California would be admitted to the Union as a free state.

   (C) Texas would give up its claim to a portion of the New Mexico Territory in question and, in exchange, the United States would forgive Texas's war debt.

   (D) The New Mexico and Utah territories would have to allow slavery.

   (E) The slave trade would be abolished in Washington, D.C., but slavery would still be allowed.

Go on to next page

64. Which of the following is true about President Thomas Jefferson's administration?

    (A) It increased the size of the military.

    (B) It eliminated all federal whiskey taxes.

    (C) It instituted the First Bank of the United States.

    (D) It emphasized the rights of government over the rights of individuals.

    (E) It proposed lavish plans for the new federal capital.

65. The main opponent to the 15th Amendment to the Constitution, which passed in 1870 and guaranteed African American male suffrage, was which of the following groups?

    (A) The scalawags

    (B) The Radical Republicans

    (C) The carpetbaggers

    (D) The Freedman's Bureau

    (E) The Ku Klux Klan

66. The Neutrality Acts of 1935, 1937, and 1939 were controversial because

    (A) the acts did not distinguish between friendly and enemy nations, and enemy nations actually profited more from the first two acts.

    (B) the acts slanted toward supporting the Allied nations and not providing any support to the Axis powers.

    (C) the United States was selling weapons only to the Axis nations.

    (D) the people of the United States wanted to remain completely neutral.

    (E) United States' businesses and industries were not benefiting from the acts at all.

67. All the following represent prominent abolitionists of the antebellum era EXCEPT

    (A) Harriet Beecher Stowe.

    (B) William Lloyd Garrison.

    (C) Frederick Douglass.

    (D) James Henry Hammond.

    (E) Sojourner Truth.

68. Which of the following does not correctly match a late 19th-century invention with its inventor?

    (A) Telephone, Alexander Graham Bell

    (B) Automobile, Henry Ford

    (C) Inexpensive camera, George Eastman

    (D) Refrigerator car, Joel Tiffany

    (E) Light bulb, Thomas Edison

69. Thomas Jefferson's purchase of the Louisiana Territory in 1803 was significant for all the following reasons EXCEPT

    (A) it removed the last vestiges of French influence in North America.

    (B) it nearly doubled the size of the United States.

    (C) it provided the United States with ownership of land along the Pacific Coast.

    (D) it set a precedent for future territorial land purchases.

    (E) it gave the United States control of the Mississippi River.

70. What do Bill Clinton and Andrew Johnson have in common?

    (A) Both of their vice presidents resigned from office.

    (B) Both were involved in sexual scandals and subsequent coverups.

    (C) Both were impeached by the House of Representatives.

    (D) Both served two full terms in office.

    (E) Both served as vice presidents before they became president.

71. The founding fathers created the system of checks and balances because

    (A) they wanted to make it difficult to pass new laws and taxes.

    (B) they wanted to make sure the president held the ultimate power in government.

    (C) they wanted to create two distinct branches of government.

    (D) they feared tyranny in national government.

    (E) they wanted to give Congress the ultimate power in government.

Go on to next page

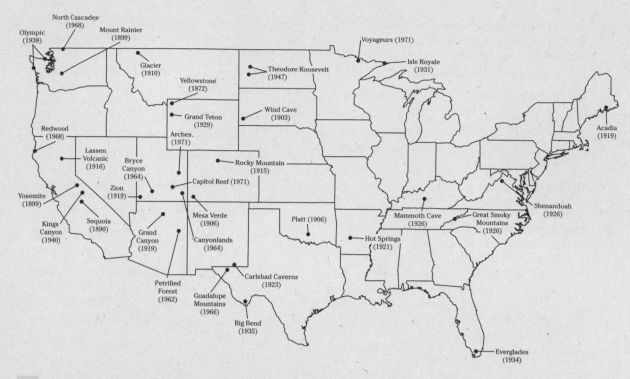

72. Which of the following statements is not supported by the map?

    (A) Yellowstone National Park was established first.

    (B) The largest numbers of national parks and forest areas are located west of the Rocky Mountains.

    (C) More national parks or forests are in Alaska than in any other state.

    (D) Most of the United States' national parks and forests were established prior to the end of World War II.

    (E) A greater number of national parks and forests are located along the eastern seaboard of the United States than are located in the state of California.

73. During his presidency, George Washington set an important precedent that was finally signed into law in 1951 with the 22nd Amendment. This precedent was

    (A) the chartering of the National Bank.

    (B) the creation of four presidential cabinet positions.

    (C) setting a two-term limit for the presidential office.

    (D) establishing the presidential "Farewell Address."

    (E) setting an official policy of neutrality toward all conflicts in Europe.

74. In Andrew Carnegie's essay "The Gospel of Wealth," he suggests that the wealthy should

    (A) continue to make as much money as possible without concern for the needs of others.

    (B) dedicate any wealth in excess of their own needs or their families' needs to philanthropic works.

    (C) give 5 percent of their annual incomes to charitable causes.

    (D) write books to share with the masses on how to become wealthy.

    (E) use their wealth to win power and influence in society.

Go on to next page

75. The creation of this agency during Franklin Roosevelt's Second New Deal allowed for the federal employment of artists, writers, musicians, and actors.

(A) The Public Works Administration

(B) The Civilian Conservation Corps

(C) The National Recovery Administration

(D) The Works Progress Administration

(E) The Agricultural Adjustment Administration

76. Which of the following pairings does NOT correctly match a colony with its colonial founder(s)?

(A) Puritans, Massachusetts Bay Colony

(B) William Penn, Pennsylvania

(C) Roger Williams, Rhode Island

(D) James, Duke of York, New York

(E) Pilgrims, Connecticut

77. One of the foreign policy successes of the Kennedy administration was the signing of the Limited Nuclear Test-Ban Treaty with the Soviet Union, which was significant because

(A) it limited the number of nuclear weapons that each country could test.

(B) it limited the number of nuclear weapons that other nations could possess.

(C) the Soviet Union agreed to a decrease in underground testing of nuclear weapons.

(D) it marked a beginning of détente between the United States and the Soviet Union.

(E) the United States agreed to a decrease of underground testing of nuclear weapons.

78. Political parties first appeared during Washington's administration for all the following reasons EXCEPT

(A) some leaders joined together to oppose the financial policies of Secretary of the Treasury Alexander Hamilton.

(B) the Federalists favored a loose interpretation of the Constitution.

(C) Britain possessed political parties, and the founding fathers wished to mimic the British system of government.

(D) the group called the Democratic Republicans favored a strict interpretation of the Constitution.

(E) the Federalists favored a strong centralized government, whereas the Democratic Republicans favored the rights of states and individuals.

79. Which of the following occurred as a result of the Red Scare in the 1920s?

(A) The U.S. implemented the Marshall Plan.

(B) The government arrested socialist presidential candidate Eugene Debs for violating the Espionage Act.

(C) The U.S and Western European nations formed an alliance to combat Communism.

(D) The U.S. decreased immigrant limits on those from Eastern European countries.

(E) The House Un-American Activities Committee banned many Hollywood screenwriters and filmmakers from making films.

80. Which of the following was NOT a significant effect of Lincoln's Emancipation Proclamation, which went into effect in 1863?

(A) It garnered support from Britain and France for the Union.

(B) It freed all the slaves in the United States.

(C) It allowed more than 200,000 African American men to enlist in the Union Army.

(D) It appeased the Radical Republicans in Congress.

(E) It freed all slaves in Southern states that were under rebel control.

Go on to next page

81. The Supreme Court under Chief Justice Earl Warren overturned an 1896 ruling on separate but equal facilities with which of the following decisions?

    (A) *Miranda v. Arizona*

    (B) *Roe v. Wade*

    (C) *Plessy v. Ferguson*

    (D) *Brown v. Board of Education of Topeka*

    (E) *Engel v. Vitale*

82. "It would be fatal for the nation to overlook the urgency of the moment and to underestimate the determination of the Negro. This sweltering summer of the Negro's legitimate discontent will not pass until there is an invigorating autumn of freedom and equality. Nineteen sixty-three is not an end, but a beginning. Those who hope that the Negro needed to blow off steam and will now be content will have a rude awakening if the nation returns to business as usual. There will be neither rest nor tranquility in America until the Negro is granted his citizenship rights."

    The speaker of this quotation was most likely advocating

    (A) the Immigration Act of 1965.

    (B) the Civil Rights Act of 1957.

    (C) the Voting Rights Act of 1965.

    (D) the Economic Opportunity Act of 1964.

    (E) the Civil Rights Act of 1964

Go on to next page

Courtesy of BoondocksNet.com

83. The artist of this October 1920 cartoon is making the point that

    (A) which political party will support women's suffrage in the 1920 election is not clear.

    (B) the Republicans are likely to get more women's votes.

    (C) which party the majority of women will vote for in the upcoming 1920 election is unclear.

    (D) the women's vote will go mostly toward the Democrats.

    (E) whether or not women will decide to vote in the 1920 election is unclear.

84. Franklin D. Roosevelt's "court-packing" scheme can best be described by which of the following?

    (A) FDR wanted Congress to pass legislation requiring term limits for Supreme Court justices.

    (B) FDR hoped to add up to six new justices to the Supreme Court in order to obtain a pro-New Deal majority in the Supreme Court.

    (C) FDR wanted to add 15 new justices to the Supreme Court.

    (D) FDR wanted to replace five of the current Supreme Court justices with ones he appointed.

    (E) FDR wanted to get rid of all the current justices and replace them with justices he appointed.

85. Why was the Bill of Rights amended to the Constitution in 1791?

    (A) To ensure that the rights of individuals and states wouldn't be commandeered by a strong central government

    (B) To ensure that states received more rights than the federal government

    (C) To provide universal suffrage

    (D) To ensure that the federal government received more rights than the states

    (E) To ratify into law liberties of individuals that could be violated by the federal government

Go on to next page

86. Which of the following statements is true about society and culture in the 1930s?

(A) Motion pictures were unpopular because most people didn't have any money during the Depression.

(B) Mark Rothko and Jackson Pollock were employed as actors by the Works Progress Administration.

(C) Newspaper circulation did not diminish during the Great Depression.

(D) Photographers couldn't find work anywhere.

(E) Ernest Hemingway and William Faulkner wrote about migrant farm workers in California in the 1930s.

87. All the following are true about slavery in the Southern colonies in the 1600s EXCEPT

(A) it provided a much-needed labor force for large labor-intensive plantations.

(B) it was legalized in 1660.

(C) it was an inexpensive source of labor.

(D) it contributed to the growth of the Southern agricultural economy.

(E) it increased class struggles between rich and poor whites in the South.

88. What was the primary advantage of the Lend-Lease Act of 1941 for the United States?

(A) U.S. ships were able to help the British track German submarines in the Atlantic.

(B) It secured United States' national security.

(C) It helped keep Britain from being taken over by Germany.

(D) It allowed U.S. industry to mobilize for war production.

(E) It helped keep the Soviet Union from being taken over by Germany.

89. Which of the following early 19th-century social reformers is INCORRECTLY matched with his or her cause?

(A) Elizabeth Cady Stanton, advocate for women's rights

(B) Susan B. Anthony, founder of the socially progressive Oneida Commune

(C) Dorothea Dix, developer of institutions for the mentally ill

(D) Harriet Tubman, leader in the Underground Railroad and abolitionist movement

(E) Horace Mann, educational reformer in the Massachusetts public schools

90. The role of the World War II propaganda piece *Rosie the Riveter* was

(A) to inspire men to sign up for the armed forces during World War II.

(B) to inspire women to stay at home to raise their families during World War II.

(C) to inspire women to join the workforce during World War II.

(D) to inspire minorities to seek factory work during World War II.

(E) to inspire women to sign up for the armed forces during World War II.

Answer Key for Practice Test 2

1. B	31. C	61. C
2. D	32. D	62. B
3. E	33. C	63. D
4. D	34. A	64. B
5. C	35. E	65. E
6. C	36. B	66. A
7. B	37. B	67. D
8. A	38. D	68. B
9. C	39. E	69. C
10. D	40. C	70. C
11. A	41. B	71. D
12. B	42. D	72. E
13. C	43. A	73. C
14. E	44. E	74. B
15. D	45. B	75. D
16. B	46. C	76. E
17. D	47. D	77. D
18. B	48. A	78. C
19. A	49. C	79. B
20. D	50. D	80. B
21. E	51. B	81. D
22. C	52. C	82. E
23. B	53. E	83. C
24. A	54. B	84. B
25. C	55. C	85. A
26. E	56. C	86. C
27. B	57. D	87. E
28. A	58. B	88. D
29. D	59. C	89. B
30. C	60. D	90. C

Scoring Practice Test 2

Okay, now you get to assess the damage. You want to first determine your raw score. Your *raw score* is based on the number of questions you answered correctly or incorrectly. Then use the raw score to determine your three-digit scaled score.

Calculating your raw score is somewhat complicated, but here's how you do it:

1. **Find the number of questions you answered correctly:** _____

2. **Find the number of questions you answered incorrectly:** _____

3. **Multiply the number you calculated in Step 2 by 0.25 (or ¼), which leaves you with:** _____

   (Remember, you lose only ¼ of a point for each wrong answer, and you aren't penalized for leaving answers blank.)

4. **Take the number you calculated in Step 3 and subtract it from your answer in Step 1:** _____

5. **Round your answer in Step 4 to the nearest whole number.** (Tip: 0.50 or greater round up, 0.49 or less, round down). The result is your raw score: _____

To figure out your approximate scaled score, find your raw score in Table 25-1.

Table 25-1		Score Conversion Chart			
Raw Scores	*Scaled Score*	*Raw Scores*	*Scaled Score*	*Raw Scores*	*Scaled Score*
82–90	800	50	620	19–20	440
79–81	790	49	610	17–18	430
77–78	780	47–48	600	15–16	420
75–76	770	45–46	590	13–14	410
73–74	760	44	580	11–12	400
72	750	42–43	570	9–10	390
70–71	740	40–41	560	7–8	380
69	730	39	550	5–6	370
67–68	720	37–38	540	3–4	360
66	710	35–36	530	2	350
64–65	700	33–34	520	0–1	340
62–63	690	31–32	510	−1	330
61	680	30	500	−2/−3	320
58–59	670	28–29	490	−4/−5	310
56–57	660	26–27	480	−6/−7	300
55	650	24–25	470	−8/−9	290
53–54	640	22–23	460	−10	280
51–52	630	21	450		

Chapter 26

Explaining the Answers to Practice Test 2

. . . .

*T*his chapter provides explanations for the answers to the second practice test in Chapter 25. We strongly suggest that you read through all the answer explanations, even the ones for questions you answered correctly. The explanations may convey information that you hadn't thought of before.

1. **B.** The Monroe Doctrine is an important U.S. history concept like manifest destiny. You're extremely likely to see a question about it on the SAT II U.S. History exam. You may remember from Chapter 6 that the doctrine was designed to keep European powers from meddling in the affairs of the Americas. If you don't remember, you can still eliminate answer choices just by knowing when James Monroe (who the doctrine was named after) was president.

   Monroe was president during the early 19th century when the United States was expanding. Communism wasn't an early 19th-century issue, so you can eliminate (C) immediately. Answer (A) contains one of those debatable words, "altogether," which should be a clue that it's probably wrong. An American president probably wouldn't issue a doctrine stating that the United States would not try to expand, so you can eliminate (E), too. A president also probably wouldn't state outright that his nation planned to dominate neighboring countries, like (D) states. The more diplomatic SAT II-type answer is (B).

2. **D.** This question mentions the early 1960s, so you can eliminate answer choices that aren't relevant to that decade. Jazz emerged in the 1920s (see Chapter 16), so you can cross off (A). Psychedelic rock came about a little later in the 1960s, so (E) is wrong. Out of the remaining choices — folk (B), rock 'n' roll (C), and Motown (D), the music style that was the domain of African American artists was Motown. See Chapter 20 for more on this topic.

3. **E.** As president from 1901 to 1909, Roosevelt removed millions of acres of federal land from sale, created five national parks and 18 national monuments, and increased the role of and strengthened the National Forest Service (see Chapter 14). Once you recall that Roosevelt was a nature lover, eliminating wrong answer choices is easy. A conservationist wouldn't want land used for mining and forestry, and the motivation of a conservationist isn't to make big profits, so eliminate (A) and (B). The Homestead Act was a 19th-century deal that wasn't relevant to the early 20th century, so (C) is wrong. You're left with (D) and (E). Option (E) is more in tune with Roosevelt's goals.

4. **D.** If you get your time period right, you should have no problem with this question.

   Puritans and Quakers were persecuted for their religious beliefs, but their problems occurred mostly during the 1600s, so you can eliminate (B) and (E). Anglicans weren't necessarily persecuted for their beliefs, plus you should associate this group with the Church of England; (C) is wrong. Transcendentalists (A) and Mormons (D) are correctly associated with the early 19th century, but only the Mormons were persecuted and forced to move West. See Chapter 8, if you need more information.

5. **C.** If you know that sharecropping was a very lucrative system for the plantation or large farm owners but not a successful system for the sharecroppers (see Chapter 10), you should be able to eliminate the wrong answers for this question.

You're looking for the answer choice that is *false* about sharecropping, so your answer will probably say that sharecropping was a good thing for the workers or a bad thing for the plantation owners — just the opposite of what you know to be true.

Choices (A), (B), (D), and (E) provide factual information about how sharecropping was supposed to work. Answer (C) puts a positive value judgment on the system that could be disputed and, therefore, (C) is the best choice for a false answer.

6. **C.** Observe the cartoon carefully. You probably noticed the big fly swatter marked "Education" first. You should also note that the fly represents Bolshevism. A fly is a pest, so you can assume that the creator of this cartoon is not pro-Bolshevism. Therefore, you can eliminate (A) about Bolshevism being superior to capitalism.

The fly is one of many emanating from a trash can marked "Civilization's Refuse Theories," so you may be tempted to pick (E), but (E) doesn't take into consideration the big "Education" fly swatter. The best answer is one that encompasses the whole of the cartoon.

Answer (E) isn't correct, so you're left with (B), (C), and (D). The cartoon contains nothing depicting America or Americanism, so you can eliminate (B) and (D). The only answer choice that mentions education is (C).

The SAT II uses Bolshevism and Communism interchangeably. For more about the Bolshevik Revolution and the Red Scare in America during the 1920s, see Chapter 16.

7. **B.** Under the theory of mercantilism, the colonies provided raw goods for British factories to manufacture into finished goods. Because Britain limited the goods that the colonists could manufacture themselves, the colonies needed to purchase most of their finished goods from Britain. The only choice that conveys the process correctly is (B). See Chapter 3.

8. **A.** This question is one of those rare SAT II questions where you have to know the information. The question doesn't give you much on which you can base eliminations.

All the answer choices listed are authors who wrote in the early to mid-19th century, so you can't eliminate based on time period. Herman Melville wrote *Moby Dick,* which wasn't about life on the frontier, and you may be familiar with the dark stories written by Edgar Allan Poe, which also don't fit into the American frontier category. Therefore, you may be able to eliminate (B) and (C). The only author listed who wrote prolifically about the frontier was Cooper. Chapter 8 features more detail about Cooper and these other stars of American literature.

9. **C.** Because the native populations of the Americas were not "civilized," were not Christian, spoke different languages, and were not nearly as technologically advanced, western Europeans felt they were inferior and had no intention of cooperating with them politically. All the other choices were goals of conquering nations. See Chapter 3.

10. **D.** Remember to rephrase the question before you look at the answer choices. In this case, you can reword it as "Which of the following is untrue about the Lend-Lease Act?" Even though EXCEPT questions are sometimes confusing, you can first look to see whether a wrong answer stands out.

In 1941, Spain and Italy weren't nations friendly to the United States, so (D) should raise your eyebrows a bit. Why would a World War II-era act permit sales of arms to unfriendly nations? Answer (D) is probably untrue and is probably the right answer, but look at the others to be sure. First note the name of the act. If you remember that the United States was on the side of Great Britain and the Soviet Union in World War II, then you can eliminate (A). An act advocating lending and leasing in 1941 seems like it'd benefit the United States' allies, so (A) is probably true, and therefore, incorrect. Answer (B) was an indirect result of the act, so (B) is also true and incorrect. Even if you don't remember anything about the Lend-Lease Act, helping out nations vital to U.S. security seems like a likely result of a World War II-era Lend-Lease Act, so you can cross out (C). Answer (E) is also true; under the Lend-Lease Act, Roosevelt eventually authorized more than $50 billion in aid to Great Britain, Russia, and other countries. So you can eliminate (E). Answer (D) is the correct answer because it's untrue for two reasons. Although U.S. ships did provide protection part way across the ocean to the foreign ships that carried the borrowed goods, they didn't actually deliver the goods themselves. Plus, neither Spain nor Italy were considered vital to U.S. security. Italy was involved with Hitler, and Spain had isolated itself from the rest of the world. See Chapter 18 for more about World War II.

11. **A.** Manifest destiny was the theory that America's destiny was to expand westward across the continent all the way to the Pacific Coast. Because you're looking for acts that did NOT acquire land in the United States toward the West Coast, you can eliminate any answers that brought these lands into America's possession. Answers (B) and (C) state Texas and Oregon outright. Acquisition of these two territories definitely demonstrated manifest destiny, so you can eliminate them. Now you're in good guessing range. If you realize that Mexico owned what became California, Nevada, and Utah (among other states), you can probably assume that the Mexican Cession brought these territories into the United States, so (E) is incorrect. You're down to two choices.

    If you remember that the Gadsden Purchase (see Chapter 9) included parts of Arizona and New Mexico, you can see America making its way across the continent with that purchase. So (D) is wrong. The Webster–Ashburton Treaty involved a dispute with Great Britain over the border of Maine and is not considered an act of manifest destiny because it didn't move American possession further west toward the Pacific Coast. You can refresh your memory on this topic by checking out Chapter 8.

12. **B.** The question tells you that the trade routes were among the colonies, Britain, Africa, and the West Indies. What do you immediately think of when you consider trade associated with Africa and the West Indies? These two countries were heavily involved in the slave trade. These routes brought slaves from Africa to the colonies and led to an increased slave population in the colonies. Trade wouldn't decrease employment, so (A) is wrong. The colonies produced cotton and tobacco, so they would not import it from the West Indies or any other place, so (C) isn't right. Answer (D) is counterintuitive because trade would mean more merchants. Answer (E) may have tripped you up a bit; pirate attacks did occur along the trade routes, but they didn't specifically concentrate on British ships or that particular route (see Chapter 3 for more about pirates in the New World). So (B) is the best answer. For details, see Chapter 4.

13. **C.** Politics in the Gilded Age were characterized by big bureaucracy (A), little definition between the platforms of the two political parties (B), and a hands-off policy toward industry (E). Progressive presidents didn't appear on the scene until Theodore Roosevelt's time, so (D) is wrong. Farmers were just one group who suffered from the political policies of the late 1800s, so many joined the Populist Party to try to bring about reforms that would help them out financially. For more, see Chapter 12.

14. **E.** The Chinese Exclusion Act of 1882 was the first piece of anti-immigration legislation based exclusively on nationality passed in the United States. The act completely banned Chinese immigration to the U.S. for ten years. You can eliminate (C) and (D) because a large wave of Jewish immigration occurred during the World War II era, not during the late 1800s. Mexican immigration wasn't widespread during the late 1800s, either. Between 1860 and 1890, ten million immigrants from Northern Europe entered the United States, but immigrants from other areas, such as Greece (A) and Armenia (B), weren't as common; therefore, these groups didn't pose a threat to Americans. When you think of the 1800s, consider the California Gold Rush that brought Asians to the United States and their efficient work on the railroad expansion, which threatened American workers. You can find more on this policy in Chapter 12.

15. **D.** The highly sophisticated native populations of *Mesoamerica* (like the Mayans, Aztecs, and Incas) are known for their invention of an accurate calendar (the Mayans and Aztecs) and the development of an extensive road system (the Incas). All the other answer choices portray characteristics of North American native peoples. See Chapter 3 for more info on Mesoamericans and North American peoples.

16. **B.** The mention of the 1870s and 1880s should immediately bring to mind the Second Industrial Revolution. Consider what industry meant for cities. Industry brought workers into the cities and caused people who could afford to to move away from the cities and escape the crowding. For this "NOT" question, you can eliminate answer choices that convey these trends.

Immigrants came to the United States in record numbers, so you can eliminate (D). Increased urban populations gave rise to tenements in slums and ghettos, so cross out (A). With the increase in urban population, the wealthy migrated to suburban developments, so (C) isn't right, either. As a result of the exodus of the wealthy from the cities, public transportation infrastructure developed between cities and suburban areas so that suburban dwellers could travel to their jobs in the cities; you can eliminate (E). Choice (B) is the answer that doesn't fit and, therefore, is the correct answer. To refresh your memory on the Second Industrial Revolution, take a peek at Chapter 12.

17. **D.** This question tests your graph-reading skills as well as your knowledge of when events occurred in history. You're likely to encounter one or two graph questions on the SAT II U.S. History test, and they're usually pretty easy.

The graph shows low immigration in the 1930s, which was the era of the Great Depression (see Chapter 17), so (A) can't be right. Immigration increased during the early 1960s, which was the time of Kennedy's presidency (see Chapter 20), so cross out (B). The graph shows a decrease in the years before the Civil War, which were the 1850s (see Chapter 9); (C) can't be right. And all you need to do is look at the data on the graph to know that (E) is wrong. The only correct answer choice is that approximately 1.8 million immigrants came to the United States in 1990.

18. **B.** You can eliminate (A) based on the time period; sharecropping evolved after the Civil War. The Enlightenment was a movement, not a practice to provide passage to the colonies, so you can cross out (D). Nor did mercantilism involve providing a way for Europeans to travel to the colonies, so you can eliminate (C). So (B) and (E) remain. Slavery provided no time in which forced labor would cease, so you can chuck (E). Choice (B) is the best answer. Indentured servitude was the system under which early colonists gained free passage to the colonies in exchange for several years of labor, often on a Southern plantation (see Chapter 4).

19. **A.** If you remember that Mark Twain was a late 19th-century author who was best known for satire, most notably in his novels, *The Adventures of Huckleberry Finn* and *The Adventures of Tom Sawyer*, you're home-free on this one. Otherwise, unless you know something about the remaining authors, you may not be able to guess correctly. If you can't eliminate any answer choices, skip this question. On the other hand, you may know from your literature classes that Hemingway and Hughes wrote in the 20th century. If so, you can eliminate these two choices and hazard a rational guess. You can brush up on literature of the Second Industrial Revolution era in Chapter 12.

20. **D.** To answer this question, you either need to know the elements of the Missouri Compromise or the chronology of states admitted to the Union. If you know that the compromise occurred in 1820 after Missouri applied for statehood and that Texas didn't enter the Union until 1845, you know that (D) is your answer. All other answer choices are provisions of the Missouri Compromise. See Chapter 7 for details.

21. **E.** The Cold War officially ended in the late 1980s at the end of the Ronald Reagan administration (see Chapter 22). You can eliminate (A) because the Cold War began after World War II during the Truman years. Knowing this fact at least lets you cross out one answer choice, which is good enough to merit a guess. The symbolic end of the Cold War was the

destruction of the Berlin Wall in 1989. Even though George H. W. Bush was in office at the time, it was Reagan's policies that led to the event, so (D) is wrong. The Cold War was still going strong during Carter's administration (C) and was over before Clinton's (B).

22. **C.** You can safely eliminate (B) — you don't often hear about colonial stamp smuggling rings. And you know these acts weren't something that made colonists happy, so (D) and (E) are out. The Boston Tea Party occurred later than the mid 1760s in response to the taxes Britain imposed, so (A) can't be right. The answer must be (C). Britain had to recoup its war losses somehow, and its members of government reasoned that because the colonists benefited the most from the land acquired from the British victory in the war, the colonists ought to pay for it. You can refresh your memory on the French and Indian War and the Sugar and Stamp Acts by reading Chapters 4 and 5.

23. **B.** If you remember that the Iran Hostage Crisis was a debacle during Jimmy Carter's presidency, you can immediately locate the answer to this question. Otherwise, you can begin by eliminating (C) because Watergate and Nixon are infamously linked. (Remember you're eliminating answers that *do* characterize Nixon's term.) You've eliminated one answer choice and can hazard a guess. You probably remember that Vietnam ended under Nixon, so you can cross out (D), too. During his presidency, Nixon signed the SALT I with the Soviet Union (A) and opened the door for diplomatic relations with China (E), so (B) must be the answer. For more on the Nixon and Carter presidencies, refer to Chapter 21.

24. **A.** If you answered 22 correctly, you're bound to get this one right, too.

Sometimes info in one question can help you answer another one, so don't be afraid to go back and change an answer if a later question gives you an "aha!" experience.

The French and Indian War was a source of increased tension between the colonies and Britain because the British expected the colonies to share the costs of the war. You can eliminate (B) and (E): The colonists did fight in the war on the British side. The Writs of Assistance came after the war, and the war was primarily fought in French territories, so (C) and (D) are also wrong, which leaves (A). See Chapters 4 and 5.

25. **C.** The California Gold Rush had pretty much waned by 1862 (think the '49ers), and it wasn't responsible for the migration of families, so you know that (A) is wrong. The Western frontier has never been known for plentiful rainfall, so you can safely eliminate (B). White settlers invaded South Dakota in search of gold, but that caused the Sioux War, not a mass migration, so (D) isn't right. And although the completion of the railroad seems like a logical reason for relocation to the West, the railroad wasn't completed until later that decade, so (E) is wrong. That leaves the Homestead Act of 1862, which provided plots of land to settlers for very cheap prices, if the settlers agreed to live on the land for at least five years. So (C) is your answer. Chapter 11 offers more information on settling the American West.

26. **E.** All these answer choices regard rights for African Americans, so eliminating answer choices for this question would be difficult unless you know that in 1896 in *Plessy v. Ferguson,* the Supreme Court ruled that segregation was legal, so long as separate accommodations for whites and blacks were equal. Jim Crow laws (B) included segregation laws, but they didn't hand down an official ruling. Refer to Chapter 10 for more on *Plessy v. Ferguson* and the other answer choices.

27. **B.** Federalists favored a strong central (federal) government, so you can start eliminating answer choices from there. Proponents of a strong central government favored a central banking system, so you can get rid of (E). George Washington's administration signed a treaty with Native Americans, so you can cross out (D). You know that tensions were tight between Federalists and Democratic Republicans, so Federalist economic policies were not popular with Democratic Republicans. Choice (B) is your answer. See Chapters 5 and 6 for more on the Federalists.

28. **A.** This pro-federal income tax cartoon from 1913 points out that the main argument of the Progressive federal income tax supporters is that a federal income tax would eliminate the need for protective tariffs in the United States. The "protection" pants ripped apart by the

Ways and Means Committee gives you this clue. You can't determine exact percentages from the cartoon, so eliminate (D). The Ways and Means Committee is still hanging on, so (E) isn't right. Choices (B) and (C) essentially say the same thing, and they can't both be right. Besides, neither choice addresses the protection issue raised by the pants. Option (A) is the best answer.

29. **D.** Had the Native American groups in North America been more united, they would have posed a serious threat to European settlement in North America. (See Chapter 3 for more details.) European diseases didn't wipe out Native American populations in North America, so (A) is wrong. Famine hurt the Europeans much more than it did the resourceful Native Americans, so (C) is wrong. Native Americans weren't particularly passive even among themselves, so cross out (E). Although differences in language (B) may have been one of the reasons for a lack of unity, that lack made them relatively easy targets for the Europeans.

30. **C.** If you know anything about "Common Sense," you know that you can eliminate (D) and (E). This 1776 piece was significant because it convinced many wishy-washy colonists that complete independence from Britain was the only acceptable solution. The Boston Tea Party had already occurred; therefore, you know that resistance to Britain had already occurred. Options (A) and (B) are out. See Chapter 5.

31. **C.** Answers (A), (B), (D), and (E) were all aggressive actions the United States took to check the expansion of Communism, which became a threat after World War II (see Chapter 19). Isolationism (C), America's attempt to stay out of world affairs for a while (a World War I issue), definitely wasn't the case after World War II.

32. **D.** If you can place at least one of these individuals in the proper decade, you're on your way.

Knowing that Ed Sullivan was the host of a very popular television show in the early days of television or that Jimi Hendrix is associated with the psychedelic rock movement of the 1960s helps you eliminate answers that don't deal with the 1960s. Cross out (C) and (E). You know that Hendrix wasn't a politician (A) and that Sullivan wasn't an artist (B). Bob Dylan was a part of the folk music movement, and Betty Friedan is best known for her landmark women's liberation work *The Feminine Mystique.* Cesar Chavez is known for leading the Mexican American civil rights movement. You can find more about cultural icons of the 1960s in Chapter 20.

33. **C.** Quaker William Penn received a charter for Pennsylvania from King Charles II. He founded the colony on the principle of religious tolerance. Penn established Delaware after Pennsylvania. You can read more about the Pennsylvania colony in Chapter 4.

34. **A.** Despite John F. Kennedy's status as a major icon among presidents, his administration didn't actually accomplish much. In fact, his short term in office was mostly marked by Kennedy's failure to push the majority of his reform legislation through Congress (A). The Bay of Pigs incident in Cuba (B) wasn't successful, and Lyndon B. Johnson, Kennedy's successor, pushed the Civil Rights Act through Congress (C), appointed Thurgood Marshall, the first African American justice to the Supreme Court (D), and created Medicare and Medicaid under the 1965 Health Insurance Act for the Aged (E); so you can eliminate (B), (C), (D), and (E). Chapter 20 discusses the JFK and LBJ administrations.

35. **E.** Colonists were subject to British rule, not free from it, so (E) must be the correct answer. Chapter 3 details the motivations for settlement of the New World, which include those mentioned in (A), (B), (C), and (D).

36. **B.** Earl Warren was the Chief Justice of the Supreme Court from 1953 to 1969 and delivered many landmark Court decisions having to do with civil liberties, such as *Engel v. Vitale, Miranda v. Arizona,* and *Gideon v. Wainwright.* You can eliminate (A) because John Marshall served on the Supreme Court in the early 1800s. William Rehnquist and Warren Burger were two conservative justices whom Richard Nixon appointed to the Court after the resignation of Warren in 1969, so you can eliminate (C) and (D). Thurgood Marshall was the first African American Supreme Court Justice (E), but he wasn't Chief Justice. Refresh your memory on Warren's decisions by referring to Chapter 20.

37. **B.** By July 1776, the colonists had many reasons for wanting to declare complete independence from Britain. Colonists were inspired by Thomas Paine's pamphlet "Common Sense" (A). The colonies were fed up with British taxes and having no say in the government (C). The colonists hoped that if they declared independence, then they'd receive military aid from France (D; which they eventually did). Additionally, Paine had convinced many that the British government was despotic (E). However, Britain had been too stubborn for the colonists to expect that Britain would grant their independence and end the war immediately. For details about the Revolutionary War, flip to Chapter 5.

38. **D.** If you know recent history, you can get this question correct. Richard Nixon is well known for his involvement in the Watergate scandal (C), and Jimmy Carter is best known for his involvement in the Iran Hostage Crisis (E; see Chapter 21). The Iran-Contra Affair occurred during Reagan's presidency (B; Chapter 22), and Kennedy was involved in the Bay of Pigs invasion (A; Chapter 20). Warren G. Harding, not William H. Taft, endured the Teapot Dome scandal (see Chapter 16), so (D) is your answer.

39. **E.** Okay. Here's just another test of your graph-reading skills. This time the question asks you to find the one incorrect answer of the five possibilities. Answering questions about graphs should be pretty easy because you usually don't have to know too many additional facts — the information is in the graph. In this case, you know that the graph will support four of the answer choices; you just need to find the one that isn't. Don't read too much into the information that the test presents!

The graph shows that in 2000, the percentage of working women was just over 60 percent; you can eliminate (A). The lines representing men and women are merging, so you can cross out (B). If you look at 1980 and just the line for women with small children, you see that you can eliminate (C). The line for men goes down; (D) is wrong. Choice (E) is correct. The year 1997 was when the percentages were 60 and 66.

40. **C.** This question is another one of those rare questions where you just need to know the information. You have very little else to go on to eliminate answer choices. Neal Dow is best known for his work for the temperance movement. In the 1850s, he lobbied the Maine state government to outlaw liquor manufacturing and sales. Many other prominent social reformers were around in the 1800s; for more details about 1800s social reform, go to Chapter 8.

41. **B.** Movies and radio were popular during the Great Depression of the 1930s (see Chapter 17), so you can eliminate (A) and (D) from contention. Music and theater have been popular forms of entertainment for centuries, so (C) and (E) are wrong. Television was the form of entertainment that gained greatest popularity during the 1950s. For more about television's popularity, turn to Chapter 19.

42. **D.** Although the automobile engine was under development in Europe in the late 1800s, the first gasoline-powered motor vehicle was built in the United States in 1903. During the second half of the 19th century, the development of electricity (A), improved means of communication (B; think telephones), a rapidly expanding population (C), and improved means of transportation (D; railroads) all contributed to rapid industrial growth in the United States. Look at Chapter 12 for more information on the new technologies of this industrial age.

43. **A.** The motivation behind the United States's annexation of the Philippines in 1898 wasn't primarily altruistic, so you can eliminate (B), (C), (D), and (E). The United States had extensive business interests in Asian trade, raw materials, and investment opportunities in the Philippines. Any plans to educate the Filipinos, convert them to Christianity, create infrastructure in the Philippines, or impose sanitation programs and control disease in the Philippines were secondary goals. Chapter 13 covers the annexation of the Philippines.

44. **E.** The public liked Eisenhower because he was a moderate and business-oriented president who labeled his government philosophy as "dynamic (or active) conservatism," so you can eliminate choices that align with this philosophy (A, B, C, and D). The presence of the word "extremely" to describe his conservatism in answer choice (E) doesn't fit with the term "dynamic." Look at Chapter 19 for more about Ike.

45. **B.** The Three-fifths Compromise in the Constitution stated that for the purposes of taxation and representation, five slaves would be counted as three free persons. This decision came about as the founding fathers drafted the Constitution. Southern states wanted each slave to count as a full member of the population for purposes of representation, but they didn't want slaves to be counted at all for purposes of taxation. The northern states obviously didn't like this plan very much and, thus, settled the matter with the Three-fifths Compromise, which we cover in Chapter 5.

46. **C.** The answer is (C) because Franklin D. Roosevelt created the Social Security Act during his second New Deal, which occurred 30 years earlier than Lyndon B. Johnson's Great Society program. Because LBJ's Great Society program managed to pass legislation on civil rights, medical care, voting rights, and immigration, you can eliminate the other options (A, B, D, and E). To read more about LBJ's Great Society programs, see Chapter 20; to find out more about FDR's New Deal, see Chapter 17.

47. **D.** John Marshall was the prolific Supreme Court Chief Justice who served from 1801 to 1835 and made numerous landmark decisions that heightened the prestige of the Supreme Court and continue to shape the U.S. judicial system today. *McCulloch v. Maryland* (A), *Marbury v. Madison* (B), *Cohens v. Virginia* (C), and *Dartmouth College v. Woodward* (E) were four such cases. The Court decided *Dred Scott v. Sanford* 22 years after Marshall left the Supreme Court; this case dealt with slavery issues, which weren't legally contended in Marshall's days. We cover the Marshall Court cases in Chapter 6 and the Dred Scott case in Chapter 9.

48. **A.** You can be pretty sure that (C) is incorrect; the U.S. government never forged such a pact with the Soviet Union. The other answer choices may be hard to eliminate, if you don't remember much about NATO. Look for clues in the name of the organization: Treaties form alliances, and a North Atlantic alliance involving the United States and Canada would make sense. Yup, (A) is the right answer. NATO formed in April 1949, a month before the Berlin Blockade ended, to create a collective security alliance between the United States, Canada, and ten Western European nations. You can read up on NATO in Chapter 19.

49. **C.** The first key to figuring out this quote is the following statement: "That these United Colonies are, and of Right ought to be Free and Independent States, that they are Absolved from all Allegiance to the British Crown, and that all political connection between them and the State of Great Britain, is and ought to be totally dissolved."

This section of the excerpt mentions colonies, so you know that the revolution hasn't taken place yet. Therefore, you can eliminate (A), (B), and (D) because they're all documents written after America had become a nation. *Common Sense* was a persuasive propaganda piece written by Thomas Paine. The first sentence of the quotation conveys that more than one person wrote the statement: "We, therefore, the Representatives of the United States of America, in General Congress, Assembled." This part makes it pretty clear that this quote is from the Declaration of Independence. Chapter 5 contains more information on the Declaration of Independence.

50. **D.** You need to read this question carefully. Because it's a "NOT" question, you need to look for the one wrong answer. Eliminate the answers that the chart supports. You can make a case for a steady decrease in rural population from 94.9 to 26.3 over the course of about 200 years, so (A) is wrong.

Evaluating (B) and (C) takes a while because you have to do some figuring. You may want to look at (D) and (E) first. If they seem wrong, go back to (B) and (C) to find the right answer; however, if you find the right answer in (D) and (E), you haven't wasted your time on (B) and (C).

As you read (D), you may notice that you already established that rural population decreased (not increased) from 1790 to 1980. From that information alone, you know that (D) isn't supported by the chart and is the right answer. You can go back and figure out (B), (C), and (E), if you want, but we don't advise you to spend that much time on any one question during the test.

51. **B.** Monopolies rose in popularity in the late 1800s, the era of big business and scant regulation. Price setting (A), increasing profits (C), controlling production within an industry (D), and eliminating competition (D) all characterize a monopoly. The only answer that doesn't fit is (B); monopolies aren't in favor of unlimited governmental regulation. See Chapter 12 for more about monopolies.

52. **C.** A severe potato famine in Ireland resulted in nearly two million Irish people immigrating to the United States between 1847 and 1854. Take a look at Chapter 8 for more about immigration trends in the United States from 1800 to the Civil War.

53. **E.** Selective service is also known as registering for military duty. You can eliminate (A) right away because women have never been required to register for military duty, and this would be especially unlikely given the mindset regarding women at the start of the 20th century. The armed services were already set up to take volunteers, so you can cross out (C). Option (D) can't be right, because selective service has a more specific purpose than a general ramp up. That leaves you with (B) and (E).

The ages listed in (E) may throw you off. Later requirements for registration set the minimum age at 18, but the World War I requirement was for men between the ages of 21 and 30.

The act didn't specify race (B), so, (E) is the answer. Check out Chapter 15 for more on World War I mobilization.

54. **B.** This question is tough because at first glance, all the choices seem to describe Jackson's practices, so you need to focus on what the spoils system was. Jackson removed all government-appointed officeholders of the opposite political party and replaced them with members of his own political party. Through the spoils system and the selection of his cabinet, Jackson managed to completely surround himself with supporters. See Chapter 7 for more on Jackson.

55. **C.** Choices (A), (B), (D), and (E) are movements with more specific purposes than the ones the question outlines. The primary motivation for people in organization (A) was the passage of civil rights and protesting the Vietnam War. The people involved in (B) supported the free speech movement. Supporters of (E) advocated for the migrant farm worker. The women's liberation movement (D), though important in the 1960s, was more of a 1970s phenomenon. The hippie movement (C) had a more general desire to promote peace, freedom, and respect for the earth and to reject materialism and societal constraints. Chapter 20 discusses youth counterculture and the hippies.

56. **C.** First, consider that a civil war is war within a nation. Second, eliminate answers that don't demonstrate how the Revolutionary War was a war among members of the same nation.

The use of mercenaries isn't relevant, so cross out (A). Nor is receiving help from other countries (D) or when the colonies actually declared their independence (E). Now you're left with (B) or (C), which are opposites. Ask yourself which one makes the war more like a war among those of the same nation. The more colonists that remained loyal to the Crown, the more the colonists were warring amongst each other, so the answer is (C). See Chapter 5 for more on the Revolutionary War.

57. **D.** You're looking for an answer that makes Wilson's achievement ironic. It wouldn't be ironic for him to propose something that other countries would reject (plus, the question says that the plan was approved), so you can cross out (B). Options (C) and (E) are irrelevant, so they're wrong. Answer (A) isn't true, so you can eliminate it, too. The irony of Wilson's plan is that the other nations approved the League of Nations, but the United States's Senate didn't allow the United States to join. See Chapter 15.

58. **B.** The Spaniards set up St. Augustine to protect their wealth from pirates, or corsairs, (see Chapter 3). If you don't remember this fact, you can at least eliminate (D) and probably (A) and (C), because Spaniards didn't use the New World as a means to escape religious persecution or as a place to become friendly with Native Americans. Their primary motivation was to gain riches. Although Spaniards probably did use the fort as a place to repair and load their ships (E), this use wasn't the primary reason that they choose to settle there.

59. **C.** We hope you recognized the quote "the only thing we have to fear is fear itself" from Franklin Delano Roosevelt's famous inaugural speech from March 1933. If not, then note from the last line that the common difficulties refer to material things. Roosevelt wasn't president during the stock market crash, and he issued this speech more than three years after that event, so (B) can't be right. The Cold War and World War II are from the wrong era, and World War I wasn't primarily a material difficulty. Eliminate (A), (D), and (E). The best answer is (C). See Chapter 17.

60. **D.** You know that you can eliminate (E) because it's untrue. Workers were interested in unions (A) and they wanted better hours and wages, so they would make time to stand up for them (B). Children didn't usually occupy the same positions that adults did, so adults weren't threatened by children (C). But another group did threaten workers during that time period — immigrants. Remembering that the 1830s to 1850s was a period of high immigration will be helpful for answering this question. Workers didn't want to jeopardize their jobs due to the possibility of losing their jobs to immigrants, who were often willing to work longer hours and for less pay; see Chapter 8.

61. **C.** The cartoon shows "Civilization" holding a spelling book and leading a child from the Georgia factories. The cartoon favors child labor laws. The only answer that incorporates all these ideas is (C).

62. **B.** Conservative social policies characterized the Reagan administration, so choose the answer that conveys the most liberal policy, which would be (B). The other choices are all part of the Reagan administration. Read up on Reagan in Chapter 22.

63. **D.** The Compromise of 1850 was another compromise regarding the issue of whether or not the U.S. government would admit new states as free or slave states. The compromise did not establish New Mexico and Utah as slave territories, but it did give the residents of the territories the right to decide the issue. The other answer choices are components of the plan. See Chapter 9.

64. **B.** Thomas Jefferson was concerned about the rights of the people and favored a limited federal government, so you can eliminate (A), (C), and (D) because each of these answers promotes a strong federal government. Jefferson didn't like lavish spending, so (E) is out of the question. The best answer is (B); to help out farmers, Jefferson eliminated the whiskey tax. See Chapter 6 for more about Jefferson's ideas.

65. **E.** If you know that the Ku Klux Klan was a vigilante group dominated by white Southerners against non-whites after the Civil War, you can guess that this group was the main opponent to the 15th Amendment. You can read more about the South during Reconstruction in Chapter 10.

66. **A.** The Neutrality Acts were controversial because enemy nations (Germany and Italy) actually profited more from the first two acts than did the friendly nations because the acts didn't distinguish between friendly and enemy nations. The acts were also controversial because many Americans believed that United States' arms and weapons trades would benefit U.S. industries and business so much that they would influence the government to enter World War II prematurely, so you can eliminate (E). Choice (B) doesn't make sense because Americans didn't want to support the Axis powers; they saw Germany as the aggressor. And (C) is too extreme to be true. Option (D) can't be right because the acts were designed to keep America neutral, so America's desire for neutrality wouldn't make them controversial. See Chapter 18.

67. **D.** Harriet Beecher Stowe (A), William Lloyd Garrison (B), Frederick Douglass (C), and Sojourner Truth (E) were all prominent abolitionists of the *antebellum* (that is, the pre-Civil War) era. James Henry Hammond (D) was the pro-slavery South Carolina Senator and plantation owner who developed the *mud-sill theory,* which stated his perception that African Americans were inferior, thus rationalizing slavery. If you know your abolitionists, you can answer this question by process of elimination. See Chapter 8.

68. **B.** Henry Ford is associated with the rise of the automobile, but he didn't actually invent it. Henry Ford developed the first "Ford" automobile and implemented the assembly-line procedure in his factories. Chapter 12 is where you can read about inventions of the Second Industrial Revolution. For more about the emergence of the automobile in American society, see Chapter 16.

69. **C.** Remember that the United States did not own Pacific Coast territory until the 1840s under manifest destiny (see Chapter 8), so the Louisiana Purchase did not pick up Pacific Coast territory. All the other answer choices convey significant results of the Louisiana Purchase. See Chapter 6 for more details.

70. **C.** Clinton didn't serve as vice president, so you can eliminate (E). Vice President Al Gore didn't resign, and Johnson didn't have a vice president, so (A) is wrong. Johnson served only one term, so you can eliminate (D). You're down to (B) and (C). You probably know that Clinton was involved in a sexual scandal, but because you haven't heard anything like that about Johnson, choose (C). During their presidencies, both Bill Clinton and Andrew Johnson were impeached by the House of Representatives. For more details about Johnson, see Chapter 10. For more about Clinton, see Chapter 22.

71. **D.** You can eliminate (C) because you know that the U.S. government has three branches. Answers (B) and (E) don't work because checks and balances ensure that no one branch has ultimate power. The founding fathers wouldn't have wanted to make the legislative process difficult, so (A) is out. The answer must be (D). The founding fathers created the system of checks and balances among the three branches of government because after living under the great big roof of the British Crown, they feared tyranny in national government. See Chapter 5.

72. **E.** You need to know a little about United States' geography to answer this question. For instance, if you don't know where the Rocky Mountains are located, knowing whether or not (B) is correct will be difficult. Looking at the map, clearly (E) is the only acceptable answer because the East Coast has one national park and forest (Acadia), and California has three (Redwood, Yosemite, and Sequoia).

73. **C.** Washington set the precedent for a two-term limit for presidential office (see Chapter 5). All presidents followed Washington's lead until Franklin D. Roosevelt in 1940. After Roosevelt, Congress decided to make Washington's precedent law. The 22nd Amendment, signed in 1951, prohibits any president from seeking more than two terms in office. If you didn't know this requirement, you could at least eliminate (D) because giving the Farewell Address is not a law.

74. **B.** If you remember that Andrew Carnegie was a devoted philanthropist (do-gooder), you can eliminate answer choices (A), (D), and (E).

When in doubt, eliminate choices that provide exact figures that could be debatable.

So, between (C) and (B), (B) is the better answer because (C) is debatable. In "The Gospel of Wealth," Andrew Carnegie suggested that the wealthy should dedicate any wealth in excess of their own needs or their families' needs to philanthropic works. Chapter 12 has more on Carnegie.

75. **D.** The creation of the Works Progress Administration (WPA) allowed artists to continue practicing their works and get paid for it. If you didn't know this fact, you could still eliminate (B) and (E) based on only the wording. The Civilian Conservation Corps and the Agricultural Adjustment Administration probably had little to do with the employment of artists. Check out Chapter 17 for more.

76. **E.** This question was a freebie. You remember the Pilgrims, right? They landed at Plymouth Rock, Massachusetts (near Boston; answer A), and had Thanksgiving with the Native Americans. The Pilgrims didn't land in or settle in Connecticut. See Chapters 3 and 4.

77. **D.** The Limited Nuclear Test-Ban Treaty with the Soviet Union (see Chapter 20) was significant because it marked a beginning of détente between the United States and the Soviet Union. Détente is the name for the general cooling off period of the Cold War between the

1960s and 1980s and is one of those United States' history vocabulary words that the test-makers love to use, so be on the lookout for it. The treaty didn't limit the number of nuclear weapons, so (A) and (B) are wrong. It also didn't limit underground testing, so (C) and (E) are wrong.

78. **C.** Political parties evolved during Washington's administration for several reasons: in opposition to Hamilton's financial policies (A), because the Federalists favored a loose interpretation of the Constitution (B), because the Democratic Republicans favored a strict interpretation of the Constitution (D), and because the Federalists favored a strong central-ized government, whereas the Democratic Republicans favored the rights of states and individuals (E). Therefore, by process of elimination, (C) is the answer. Knowing that the first parties evolved from differences over how much power the federal government should have will help you eliminate choices for this question. The founding fathers didn't intend to create political parties, and they certainly didn't devise them because Britain had political parties. See Chapter 5.

79. **B.** Two Red Scares occurred in the United States — one in the 1920s, and the other in the 1950s. Answers (A), (C), and (E) provide events from the second Red Scare (see Chapter 19), so you can eliminate them. In the 1920s, the U.S. increased immigration limits because it thought Eastern Europeans would bring Communism to the country, so (D) is wrong. Answer (B) is the one; Americans associated Socialism with Communism, so the government arrested Eugene Debs for an anti-war speech he made.

80. **B.** A common misconception about the Emancipation Proclamation is that it freed all the slaves in the United States; it didn't. It affected only the slave states that were still under the control of the Confederate forces. At the time Lincoln delivered the proclamation, some slave states were not under rebel control; therefore, they weren't subject to the proclamation. Refer to Chapter 9 for more details.

81. **D.** Don't read this question so quickly that you think you're looking for an 1896 case. The date appears in the question to trick you.

The Warren Court existed during the 1950s and 1960s. It overturned the 1896 *Plessy v. Ferguson* (C) ruling on separate but equal facilities. The Warren Court based its ruling on its *Brown v. Board of Education of Topeka* decision, which stated that separate was not equal and declared segregation unconstitutional (see Chapter 19). Both *Plessy v. Ferguson* and *Brown v. Board of Education of Topeka* are landmark civil rights cases that you should be comfortable with going into the SAT II U.S. History exam. You're probably familiar enough with the famous *Roe v. Wade* (A) and *Miranda v. Arizona* (B) cases to know that those cases didn't deal with separate but equal facilities. So even if you didn't know the answer, you could eliminate some choices and guess. *Engle v. Vitale* was a 1962 case about school prayer.

82. **E.** The first clue to answering this question is to note the year buried in the middle of the quote: "Nineteen sixty-three." Knowing that this quote is from 1963, you can automatically eliminate option (B), which is from 1957. Based on the content of the excerpt (about African Americans), you should be able to eliminate options (A), which is about immigration, and (D), which is about economics.

To choose between the Voting Rights Act of 1965 (C) and the Civil Rights Act of 1964 (E), look again at the last sentence of this quote from Martin Luther King Jr.'s March on Washington speech: "There will be neither rest nor tranquility in America until the Negro is granted his citizenship rights." The operative words are "citizenship rights," which equates with civil rights more than it does voting rights. The correct answer is (E). See Chapter 20 for more about Martin Luther King Jr.

83. **C.** The 1920 presidential election marked the first time that women voted. As the cartoon portrays, the American public is unsure which party the majority of women would vote for. You can rule out (B) and (D), because the point of the cartoon is that no one knew which party would benefit from women's votes. Answer (A) may tempt you, but Congress granted

women's suffrage with the 19th Amendment to the Constitution in 1919, not as a ballot measure in any election. Option (E) is illogical given the effort women made to obtain the right to vote.

84. **B.** Franklin D. Roosevelt's "court-packing" scheme was to add up to six new justices to the Supreme Court to obtain a pro-New Deal majority on the Supreme Court, although he claimed the purpose was to reduce the current Court justices' workload. If you aren't familiar with his scheme, you can derive clues from the term "court-packing." Answer (A), which is about Congress, doesn't refer to packing the court, so you can eliminate it and be in good guessing shape. Answers (C) and (E) seem pretty drastic, so you can cut those options. "Packing" seems to deal with adding rather than replacing, so (B) is better than (D). See Chapter 17.

85. **A.** The Bill of Rights is the first ten amendments to the Constitution. When you think about these amendments, you realize that they deal with rights for individuals more than they deal with the rights of governments. Therefore, you can eliminate (B) and (D). You also know that women didn't achieve suffrage until more than 100 years later, so (C) isn't right. Although most of the amendments cover the rights of individuals, the 10th Amendment addresses the rights of states, so (A) is a better answer than (E). For more information on the Bill of Rights, see Chapter 5.

86. **C.** During the Great Depression, newspapers were an inexpensive way for people to stay informed about what was going on domestically and abroad. In the 1930s, motion pictures (A) remained popular despite the cost because they were an escape from reality. Mark Rothko and Jackson Pollock (B) were artists, not actors, employed by the WPA. The WPA also employed photographers (D) to capture the problems of the Depression and to document New Deal projects. John Steinbeck — not Hemingway and Faulkner, as (E) suggests — wrote about migrant farm workers in California in the 1930s, best illustrated in his 1939 work *The Grapes of Wrath*. You can read about society and culture during the Great Depression in Chapter 17.

87. **E.** The advent of slavery in the Southern colonies actually helped alleviate class struggles between rich and poor whites in the South. Prior to the legalization of slavery in 1660, a substantial class conflict existed between the wealthy plantation owners and the growing class of freed indentured servants. Slavery helped reduce these class conflicts sizably. If you didn't know this fact, you could eliminate a few answer choices. You know that slavery provided the labor force for large plantations, so (A) is out. And you know that slavery cut labor costs for plantation owners, so cross out (C). Decreased labor costs promoted the growth of Southern agriculture, so (D) is wrong. You're left with (B) and (E), which gives you a good chance of guessing correctly. See Chapter 4.

88. **D.** Read this question carefully to note the act's primary advantage for the United States. The Lend-Lease Act allowed the United States to loan weaponry to countries that would "return" them after World War II (see Chapter 18). The increased production readied American industry when the United States finally entered the war a year later. Answers (A), (C), and (E) provide the benefits to other countries, not to the United States. The act didn't secure national security (B; remember Pearl Harbor), so (D) is the best answer.

89. **B.** Susan B. Anthony was a leading advocate for the women's suffrage movement in the 1800s. Along with Elizabeth Cady Stanton and Lucretia Mott, she organized the Seneca Falls Convention for women's rights, but she wasn't a member of the Oneida Commune. Other prominent leaders of 19th-century reform movements included Neal Dow, a temperance advocate (A); Dorothea Dix, who developed institutions for the mentally ill (C); Harriet Tubman, an abolitionist who worked on the Underground Railroad (D); and Horace Mann, who brought about educational reform (E). To read up on social reformers in the 19th century, see Chapter 8.

90. **C.** The U. S. government used the propaganda poster featuring *Rosie the Riveter* as a tool to inspire women to join the workforce during World War II. If you didn't know this tidbit, you can still eliminate answer choices based on what you know about World War II. First, the

fact that the poster features "Rosie" gives you a clue that the poster is meant to appeal to women, and a riveter works in a factory. You can probably eliminate (A), which is about men, and (D), which is about minorities. Option (B) deals with staying at home to raise families, which contradicts the riveter image, so you can eliminate it. You're left with (C) and (E) — and good guessing odds. You know that women had to enter the workforce because men were away fighting the war. As a result, many women took factory jobs, so (C) is the most logical answer. Check out Chapter 18 for more about mobilization on the home front during World War II.

Part VIII
The Part of Tens

The 5th Wave   By Rich Tennant

THE TAFT-HARTLEY ACT   THE MIRANDA DECISION

72 FLAVORS

THE SWEARING-IN OF   HOOVER IN THE ROSE GARDEN
PRESIDENT GARFIELD

In this part . . .

Time to relax and take a breather. This part is just for fun, though you may find some invaluable information on these pages. In the Part of Tens, you get to read up on ten influential American leaders and ten crucial presidencies. At a minimum, you can at least use what you discover in this part to impress your U.S. history teacher with your extensive knowledge. Think of this section as a cool-down for your U.S. history workout!

Chapter 27

Ten Influential American Leaders

You won't find any profiles on American presidents in this chapter — we saved that for Chapter 28! In this chapter, you find some exceedingly powerful as well as some very ordinary Americans who made a big difference and proved themselves to be influential leaders. They aren't necessarily the greatest American leaders of all time, but they each made an impact on the United States. You'll probably see at least one of these leaders mentioned on the SAT II, but the details we provide in this chapter are primarily for fun, so you don't need to know specifics for the exam.

Alexander Hamilton

Alexander Hamilton played many vital roles in the development of the United States after the Revolutionary War. He was a delegate from New York at the Constitutional Convention in Philadelphia in 1787 and a key figure in persuading New York to ratify the Constitution. Hamilton, along with John Jay and James Madison, is also known for writing the *Federalist Papers,* a series of articles designed to win support for the proposed Constitution.

During George Washington's presidency, Hamilton, a Federalist, served as secretary of the treasury. As secretary of the treasury, Hamilton was responsible for organizing the financial system of the new nation. Hamilton recommended a system for repaying foreign debts and assuming state debts incurred during the Revolutionary War through an excise tax on commodities and protective tariffs on manufactured goods. He also recommended that the federal government charter a national bank.

Although merchants, businessmen, and the wealthy applauded Hamilton's proposals, he also faced hostile opposition, especially from the Antifederalists. His proposal for a national bank was the most controversial of any of his ideas, and it increased the animosity between the Federalists and the Antifederalists. On July 11, 1804, Aaron Burr, Thomas Jefferson's vice president, fatally shot Hamilton in a duel. (See Chapter 5 for more about Hamilton.)

John Marshall

John Marshall is the man responsible for making the U.S. Supreme Court into an influential government force in the United States. Marshall served as Chief Justice of the Supreme Court from 1801 to 1835. During that time, Marshall, a stalwart Federalist, supported a loose interpretation of the Constitution and worked to strengthen the role of the federal government. In the early 1800s, his cases often triggered controversy because he favored a strong central government over states' rights and broadly interpreted the Constitution. Some of the cases he's most well known for are

- *Marbury v. Madison:* This Supreme Court decision, made in 1803, set the precedent of judicial review (meaning that the Court had the power to review the constitutionality of a law).

- *Dartmouth College v. Woodward:* This 1819 decision stated that states could not interfere with contracts.

- *McCulloch v. Maryland:* In 1819, this decision declared that states could not tax federal institutions and allowed the Second Bank of the U.S. to continue, both of which reinforced the supremacy of federal law over state law.

- *Gibbons v. Ogden:* In 1824, the Supreme Court decided that the federal government, not the states, regulated all interstate commerce.

Check out Chapter 6 for more details about Marshall's influence on the Supreme Court.

Frederick Douglass

Frederick Douglass was the most prominent African American abolitionist of the 19th century. Born to a slave and a white man in Maryland in 1818, Douglass learned to read from his master's wife when he was 12 years old. He was especially fond of speeches by Cicero, the great Roman orator. In 1836, his master lent him to a shipyard and allowed him to keep some of his wages. In Baltimore, Douglass joined a debate club for African Americans and, through the club, made contacts that allowed him to escape bondage in 1838. He ended up in New Bedford, Massachusetts, where he joined an African American church and became active in the abolitionist movement. (Flip to Chapter 8 for more about the abolitionist movement.)

In the years prior to the Civil War, Douglass published several newspapers, continued to work for the abolition of slavery, and wrote an autobiography, *The Narrative of the Life of Frederick Douglass, an American Slave*. His autobiography, published in 1845, became an instant bestseller. During and after the war, Douglass met with Presidents Abraham Lincoln and Andrew Johnson on various race issues. During Reconstruction, he served as the president of the Freedman's Savings Bank.

Susan B. Anthony

Susan B. Anthony was a leading figure in the women's suffrage movement of the mid- to late 1800s. Born a Quaker in Massachusetts in 1820, Anthony was a teacher for the first 15 years of her career and was very active in the temperance movement. In 1852, she befriended Elizabeth Cady Stanton (known for her organization of the 1848 Seneca Falls Convention for Women's Rights) and joined the women's rights movement. In 1845, Anthony moved with her family to Rochester, New York, where she became very active in the abolitionist movement. (See Chapter 8 for more about the beginnings of the women's rights movement.)

From 1852 until her death in 1906, Anthony, who never married, traveled around the nation canvassing for women's suffrage, women's rights, and temperance. She was president of the National American Woman Suffrage Association from 1892 to 1900, and, in 1900, persuaded the male-only University of Rochester to begin admitting women.

Jane Addams

Jane Addams, a social worker and reformer, founded Hull House in 1889 in Chicago. Hull House was a settlement house that provided welfare services and social reform services for Chicago's urban poor. Hull House had a kindergarten, a night school for adults, teen clubs, a book bindery, a public kitchen, a music school, a gymnasium, girls' clubs, drama clubs, an art gallery, a coffeehouse, a library, and offices for assistance with labor relations. The services of Hull House helped more than 2,000 people each week.

Addams felt that providing opportunities and education for the poor was far more important and effective than preaching morality to them. In her lifetime, Addams was an active member of the American Anti-imperialist League (a group that formed primarily to protest the annexation of the Philippines; see Chapter 13) and helped found the NAACP and the American Civil Liberties Union (ACLU). She was very active in the women's suffrage movement and an active pacifist. In 1931, she won the Nobel Peace Prize for her peace efforts during World War I.

Andrew Carnegie

Andrew Carnegie was born into a poor family in Scotland and immigrated to the United States with his father in 1848. As a boy, Carnegie worked long hours in factories to earn money to help support his family. His talent for business was recognized at the Pennsylvania Railway, and before long, he was the company's vice president.

In 1864, Carnegie bought his first business — a very successful foray into oil. But the iron and steel industry was where he made his fortune. When Carnegie retired, J. P. Morgan and his partner bought out Carnegie's holdings for more than $100 million and formed the United States Steel Corporation; $100 million is a lot of money now, but it was an astronomical sum then.

In the early 1900s, Carnegie turned to philanthropy. Using his massive wealth, he devoted his life to providing money for causes of social and educational advancement. He founded numerous public libraries and schools in Scotland and the U.S. He's also known for his essay, "The Gospel of Wealth," in which he argues that the wealthy should use their money to help society rather than frivolously spending it on themselves or letting the government cure societal ills. A multi-million dollar foundation in his name is still one of the leading philanthropic organizations in the U.S. today. See Chapter 12 for more about Carnegie.

Henry Ford

Henry Ford is best known as the founder of the Ford Motor Company and for introducing assembly-line production to American industry. Ford, the son of Irish immigrants, had a knack for mechanics and built his first internal combustion engine before he was 15. One of his first jobs was working as an engineer with Edison Illuminating Company. Throughout his 20s and early 30s, he continued to experiment with engines and mechanics on the side.

Due to the success of his engines and his first automobile called the Quadricycle, Ford and a group of investors founded the Ford Motor Company in 1903. In 1908, Ford introduced the Model T, the first basic and affordable automobile for the common man. By 1913, he introduced the assembly-line method of production to his automobile plants. Through this production method, his automobile factories became efficient and cost effective.

Although Ford adamantly opposed labor unions, he paid his workers very well. In the years from 1913 to 1919, Ford's workers earned $5 to $6 per day (a great wage at that time), participated in profit-sharing, and worked an eight-hour day. Although some of Ford's practices and beliefs were controversial (he was known to be friendly with Nazi Germany but no wrongdoing was ever proved), history recognizes him for making the automobile affordable for the middle class and for opening up the freedom of automobile travel to the nation. His contributions to the American automobile industry in the 1920s and 1930s changed the way America traveled forever. See Chapter 16 for more about the influence of automobiles in America.

Rosa Parks

The cold December day that Rosa Parks decided not to give up her bus seat for a white man instigated a series of events that would change American history forever. Parks was an active civil rights leader in Montgomery, Alabama, where Jim Crow laws still dominated the city in the 1950s. One city law required African American passengers on the city's buses to give up their seats for white passengers and move to the back of the bus. On December 1, 1955, Parks decided to make a change. When a white male passenger requested her seat, she refused to move and was arrested. However, her stand led African American leaders to quickly organize a bus boycott in Montgomery, which lasted over a year. Without its African American passengers, the bus company lost 60 percent of its revenue, and the decrease in traffic hurt merchants in the downtown area.

Parks knocked over the first in a series of dominoes. Late in 1956, the Supreme Court, under Chief Justice Earl Warren (who we cover later in this chapter), handed down a decision that declared segregation on any type of public transportation illegal. For more about the emergence of the civil rights movement in the 1950s, see Chapter 19.

Martin Luther King Jr.

Martin Luther King Jr., a Baptist reverend and Nobel Peace Prize winner, was the most prominent civil rights activist in U.S. history. During the late 1950s and 1960s, as the head of the Southern Christian Leadership Conference (SCLC), King used his influence and power to organize numerous non-violent protest demonstrations.

King first became well known as the organizer of the Montgomery bus boycotts in 1955 to 1956 (see the previous section). In the early 1960s, he helped organize numerous non-violent demonstrations throughout the South to fight for civil rights and voting rights for African Americans. To show support for President John F. Kennedy's proposed civil rights legislation, King helped organize the March on Washington in August 1963. There King made his most famous speech, the "I Have a Dream" speech. King is also known for organizing demonstrations in Birmingham and Selma, Alabama, which led to the Voting Rights Act in 1965. These demonstrations also helped increase public support for the civil rights movement nationwide.

Tragically, a white racist assassinated King in April 1968 while he was in Memphis, Tennessee. Angry African Americans rioted in more than 100 cities in the days following his death. See Chapter 20 for more about King.

Earl Warren

Earl Warren was the highly controversial Chief Justice of the Supreme Court from 1953 to 1969. Under Warren's direction, the Supreme Court issued decisions in many landmark cases during the 1950s and 1960s.

In 1953, President Dwight D. Eisenhower nominated Warren, who'd been governor of California since 1943, to be Chief Justice of the Supreme Court. During his term as Chief Justice, Warren oversaw historic decisions on civil rights, the separation of church and state, civil liberties, racial segregation, and police arrest procedure. His Court handled many famous cases. including *Brown v. Board of Education of Topeka, Kansas*, *Engel v. Vitale*, *Miranda v. Arizona*, *Gideon v. Wainwright*, *Loving v. Virginia*, and *Wesbery v. Sanders*. In late 1963, Warren also was appointed to head an investigation into the murder of John F. Kennedy and possible conspiracy theories.

Warren had a reputation for being liberal, and he believed that the role of the Constitution was to protect the people from a potentially unjust government. Because of his decisions on civil rights cases, people of the South widely disliked him. Today, Warren is celebrated as a protector of civil rights and civil liberties of the American people. See Chapter 20 for the scoop on the Warren Court's major decisions in the 1960s.

Chapter 28

Ten Crucial Presidencies

There are leaders, and then there are great leaders. In this chapter, we profile the great American presidents who had a vast historical impact on the United States. The following ten presidents were crucial to American history and are the ones you should be most familiar with in order to do well on the SAT II U.S. History test.

George Washington, 1789–1797

George Washington, the first Commander in Chief of the United States, led the Continental Army to victory during the Revolutionary War and was the nation's first choice to lead the new nation as its first president. During his two terms as president, Washington set many precedents that have shaped the office ever since.

Washington appointed capable men to serve on his presidential cabinet. He selected men who would do the best job, regardless of their political views. Throughout his time in office, Washington concentrated mostly on foreign affairs and matters of finance. Washington knew that the United States needed to remain neutral to maintain its independence and to develop a cohesive national unity, so he kept the U.S. from getting involved in the turmoil of Europe surrounding the French Revolution.

By serving only two terms in office, Washington set the most lasting legacy of his presidency: the two-term limit. No other president in U.S. history remained in office longer than two terms until Franklin D. Roosevelt ran for and won his third and fourth reelections in 1940 and 1944. In 1951, the two-term limit became law when Congress passed the 22nd Amendment to the Constitution. See Chapter 5 for more about Washington.

Thomas Jefferson, 1801–1809

One of Thomas Jefferson's most lasting presidential legacies is that the United States more than doubled in size with the purchase of the Louisiana Territory from France. As a strict interpreter of the Constitution, Jefferson felt uncomfortable with the Louisiana Purchase because he didn't believe that the Constitution gave him the authority to purchase territory to expand the nation. Nevertheless, he authorized many exploratory expeditions to this new territory, including the now-famous expedition led by Meriwether Lewis and William Clark.

The Louisiana Purchase was significant because it not only more than doubled the size of the nation, but it also gave the U.S. complete control of the Mississippi River, removed the French from North America, and established a precedent for the federal government to purchase future territory.

Throughout his presidency, Jefferson, a Democratic Republican, also continued George Washington's legacy of neutrality in regard to foreign affairs, continued to pay down the federal debt, reduced the size of the military, repealed the whiskey tax, repealed the Judiciary Act of 1801 (which had established new judiciary positions that President Adams filled before the end of his term to try to keep Jefferson from appointing judges while he was president), and repealed the Naturalization Act of 1798 (which had increased the amount of years immigrants had to live in the U.S. before they could become citizens and vote; the Federalists created this act primarily to keep immigrants from voting because immigrants tended to vote for Democratic Republicans.) See Chapter 6 for more details.

Andrew Jackson, 1829–1837

Nicknamed "Old Hickory," Andrew Jackson was the first American president who didn't hail from an aristocratic Massachusetts or Virginia family. Celebrated as the president of the common man, Jackson won the election of 1828, which was the first national election in which many states allowed men who didn't own property to vote.

Jackson, whose face now appears on the $20 bill, worked to abolish the Bank of the United States. He felt that the bank was unconstitutional and that it put too much power in the hands of wealthy merchants at the expense of farmers and laborers. In 1832, he vetoed the recharter of the bank, but the bank was merely replaced by a series of local and state banks that extended credit to and encouraged speculation for wealthy merchants, just like the Bank of the United States had.

Jackson was the first president to employ the spoils system, which meant that he gave official appointments to men who would help him politically rather than to those who would be qualified for the jobs. Friends and political allies, most from his home state of Tennessee, became Jackson's unofficial advisors, known as the "Kitchen Cabinet." Jackson used his presidential veto power more than all the previous presidents combined, which his opponents saw as anti-democratic. His opponents nicknamed him "King Andrew I."

Under Jackson, a major change in the political process occurred. By 1832, in all but one state, the people rather than state legislators chose the people from their state who would vote in the U.S. Electoral College. See Chapter 7 for more.

Abraham Lincoln, 1861–1865

Abraham Lincoln led the United States through the most divisive era in the history of the nation. He held the nation together and maintained his faith in democracy through four long, difficult years of the Civil War.

Lincoln was a great orator. His performances in the 1858 Lincoln–Douglas Debates were legendary, and his Gettysburg Address and inaugural addresses in 1861 and 1865 are among the greatest speeches given by U.S. presidents. In his rational and eloquent speeches, Lincoln appealed to both Northerners and Southerners in an attempt to bring unity to a fractured nation.

Throughout the Civil War, Lincoln proved to be an extremely adept politician, exemplifying superb leadership qualities. He maintained an expansive view of the powers that the president assumed during war and had more power than any of his predecessors. In fact, one of his administration's most lasting precedents was that the president could use the power of the executive office to its fullest during a time of national crisis. In addition to maintaining the union of the United States, Lincoln also gets credit for abolishing slavery in the states that seceded from the Union because of his Emancipation Proclamation, which took effect in 1863. See Chapter 9 for more on this legendary president.

Theodore Roosevelt, 1901–1909

When Theodore Roosevelt took office at the age of 42, he was the youngest person to serve as President of the United States. Roosevelt entered office after the assassination of President William McKinley and embraced the presidency with his signature enthusiasm, vigor, and confidence.

Known as a Progressive leader, Roosevelt believed that government should be honest, fair, and shouldn't favor any one group but that all people should receive fair treatment and a "square deal." Americans often referred to Roosevelt as the "Trust-buster" because of his efforts to curb the power and influence of trusts in American business. Almost as soon as he entered the White House, he aggressively enforced the Sherman Antitrust Act (an act designed to eliminate trusts, which form when a group of companies who control an industry agree not to lower prices in that industry). He endorsed many new consumer protection measures during his presidency, such as the Pure Food and Drug Act and the Meat Inspection Act.

History also remembers Roosevelt for his diplomatic skills. He earned a Nobel Peace Prize in 1906 for his efforts to end the Russo-Japanese War. In foreign affairs, Roosevelt felt the U.S. should "speak softly but carry a big stick." He exemplified this belief in his Roosevelt Corollary to the Monroe Doctrine, where he stated that the U.S. would act as the international police officer of the Western Hemisphere.

One of Roosevelt's lasting legacies is conservationism. During his presidency, he designated more than 200 million acres of land for national forests, mineral reserves, and waterpower sites. He also dedicated five new national parks, designated 18 new national monuments, and increased the role of the U.S. Forest Service. See Chapters 13 and 14 for more about Roosevelt.

Woodrow Wilson, 1913–1921

With a PhD in political science from Johns Hopkins University, Woodrow Wilson is the only U.S. President to earn a doctoral degree. Wilson is remembered for being a reformer. During his presidency, Congress passed women's suffrage with the adoption of the 19th Amendment to the Constitution. Prohibition also went into effect in 1920 with the passage of the 18th Amendment. Throughout his presidency, Wilson supported aid to farmers, lowered tariffs, improved the banking system, set limitations on corporate power, and increased protection for labor unions and workers.

But Wilson's most lasting legacy was his plan for peace following World War I. Wilson introduced his proposal for an international peacekeeping organization called the League of Nations in his Fourteen Points. Unfortunately, the bitter and war-torn European nations didn't adopt most of Wilson's Fourteen Points into the Treaty of Versailles, despite Wilson's extended negotiations. But they did embrace the creation of the League of Nations, which was the predecessor of the United Nations. (However, the U.S. Congress refused to sign the treaty or participate in the league.) For his peacekeeping efforts, Wilson won the Nobel Peace Prize in 1919. See Chapters 14 and 15 for more about Wilson.

Franklin D. Roosevelt, 1933–1945

History often credits Franklin Delano Roosevelt (FDR) with pulling the United States out of the Great Depression. He was also the only president to break the precedent of serving two terms. FDR easily won four consecutive terms in office, although he died only a few months into his last term. Additionally, Roosevelt helped a "new" Democratic Party emerge; for the first time, the Democratic Party earned support from African Americans, organized labor, farmers, and urban workers.

FDR was a great orator and a very likeable person. He enjoyed immense popularity during his presidency. He was the first president to regularly use radio to communicate with the American people and to build morale and support for his programs. During his presidency, FDR greatly expanded the role of the federal government and embarked on an ambitious program of government spending to bring about an economic recovery during the Depression. With his New Deal legislation, he provided opportunity, recovery, and hope to the millions of down-and-out Americans during the Great Depression. During World War II, he maintained strong diplomatic relations with America's allies abroad and maintained strong leadership throughout the war. See Chapters 17 and 18 for more about Roosevelt.

Harry S Truman, 1945–1953

Harry S Truman succeeded Franklin Delano Roosevelt near the end of World War II. Truman had an extremely eventful presidency. He was president until the end of World War II and, in an effort to end the war in the Pacific, he ordered the U.S. military to drop atomic bombs on Hiroshima and Nagasaki in Japan. He witnessed the formation of the United Nations and the beginning of the Cold War, and he was also president during much of the Korean War.

Truman was also the most recent president not to possess a college degree. As a result, people saw him as a champion of the common citizen. Internationally, Truman firmly supported the creation of the United Nations. He helped with the economic and social recovery of Europe after World War II with the Marshall Plan and the subsequent protection of Europe from Communism through the Truman Doctrine. Under the Truman Doctrine, the U.S. supported free peoples who were trying to resist takeovers by armed minorities or outside powers; the doctrine was specifically aimed at preventing Communist takeovers. So, Truman initiated the U.S.'s containment policy — a commitment to keep Communism from spreading to non-Communist nations. See Chapters 18 and 19 for more on Truman.

Richard Nixon, 1969–1974

Richard Nixon was the only person to be elected to two presidential terms and two vice-presidential terms. Unfortunately for him, his main claim to fame came from the dubious distinction that he's the only U.S. president to resign from office. Well, that and his notorious involvement in the Watergate scandal and the several schemes to cover it up. When the truth about the scandal came out, Nixon resigned because he knew the House of Representatives would likely impeach him and that the Senate would convict him. The Watergate scandal and Nixon's resignation had a major impact on the American people. Until Nixon, Americans, for the most part, trusted their leaders. After Nixon, many Americans viewed their leaders with a cautious skepticism.

Despite the scandal that ruined his presidency, Nixon accomplished quite a bit. During his six years as president, Nixon signed the Paris Accords to end U.S. involvement in the Vietnam War. His other accomplishments as president included ordering secret bombings of Cambodia in 1969 and 1970, nominating four new Supreme Court justices, traveling to China to open diplomatic relations, seeking better relations with the Soviet Union, and approving the establishment of the Environmental Protection Agency (EPA). See Chapter 21 for more about Nixon's administration.

Ronald Reagan, 1981–1989

Ronald Reagan was the first U.S. president who had been a former Hollywood film actor and the first president who had been divorced. His Hollywood background and skills as an orator were responsible for his nickname "The Great Communicator."

As president, Reagan was vehemently anti-Communist, conservative, friendly to big business, and tough on crime and drugs. Americans criticized his economic policy known as Reaganomics, which instated tax cuts, increased defense spending, and reduced spending on social programs. But history will most likely remember Reagan most for his contribution to ending the Cold War. Reagan advanced diplomatic relations with Soviet General Secretary Mikhail Gorbachev from 1985 to 1988 while increasing America's military buildup to produce a policy of "peace through strength." Reagan's Strategic Defense Initiative (SDI) sought to deploy a space-based defense system that Reagan initiated to protect the U.S. from nuclear weapon missile attack. Critics of the plan worried that it would just make the Soviet Union increase its military might. But at the end of his presidency, the power of the Soviet Union was breaking up, and many people attribute the leveling of the Berlin Wall, which occurred in 1989 shortly after his second term, to Reagan. The fall of the Berlin Wall was a symbol of the decline of Communism in Eastern Europe and the Soviet Union. See Chapter 22 for more on Reagan's presidency.

416 Part VIII: The Part of Tens

Index

continued

Fundamental Orders of
 Connecticut, 42
fundamentalism, 207

• G •

Gadsden Purchase, 115
gag rules, 112
Garfield, James A., 163
Garrison, William Lloyd, 111
gender discrimination, 273, 274,
 279
Germany
 aggression in Europe, 231–232
 beginnings of World War I, 193
 division of Berlin and, 255
 emergence of Hitler in, 230
 Hitler's defeat, 240–241
 invades France, 233
 invades Poland, 232
 Treaty of Versaille, 201
 U.S. enters World War I,
 194–195, 339, 355
Gettysburg Address, 126
GI Bill of Rights, 249
Gibbons v. Ogden, 87, 406
glasnost, 301
"Gospel of Wealth, The"
 (Carnegie), 146, 380, 399, 407
grandfather clause, 141
Grangers, 165
Grant, Ulysses S.
 Civil War general, 126, 127
 presidency, 138–139
graphs, questions using, 323,
 347–348
Great Awakening
 First, 47–48
 Second, 100
Great Britain
 battles of American Revolution,
 59–61
 Berlin Airlift, 255
 Churchill at Yalta Conference,
 241–242
 colonial revenue increases by,
 56–58
 explores New World, 33, 365,
 390
 French and Indian War, 53–54
 Lend-Lease Act with, 235–236
 mercantilism, 36, 50, 364, 390
 Oregon Treaty, 103
 Proclamation of 1763, 55–56
 settlements in America, 35–38,
 321, 347, 370, 394
 Treaty of Paris, 61
 War of 1812, 82–83, 340
 wars affecting colonies, 52
Great Compromise, 65–66
Great Depression. *See also* New
 Deal

effects of, 219–220
end of, 237–238
Hoover's relief efforts, 218–219
minorities during, 228
New Deal, 220–227
newspaper circulation in, 228,
 384, 401
questions, 217–218, 337, 355
Roosevelt's inaugural speech,
 220, 377, 398
stock market crash, 215–218
Great Migration, 186, 205,
 213–214
Great Society
 legislation of, 273
 questions, 329, 350, 373, 396
guessing on test, 15
Gulf of Tonkin Resolution, 284,
 285
Gulf War, 302, 303

• H •

Haitian Revolution, 70
Hamilton, Alexander
 constitutional contributions, 65,
 66, 67
 duel with Burr, 80
 economic policies of, 69, 71, 74,
 331, 351
 influence of, 405
Hammond, James Henry, 398
Harding, Warren G., 208–209
Harlem Renaissance, 214
Harper's Ferry, 120
Harrison, Benjamin, 163
Harrison, William Henry, 98
Hartford Convention, 84
Harvard College, 41
Hawaii, 173, 339, 356
Hayes, Rutherford B., 140,
 162–163
Hayne, Robert Y., 97
headright system, 44
health
 AIDS and Safe Sex, 299–300
 during World War I, 200
 medical insurance for elderly,
 274
 Spanish flu epidemic, 204
Hearst, William Randolph, 160,
 171
Hepburn Railroad Act, 188
hippie movement, 280, 376, 397
Hiss, Alger, 256
Hitler, Adolf, 230, 240–241
Holocaust, 241
Homestead Act, 144, 368, 393
Hoover, Herbert
 heads Food Administration, 196
 presidency, 210, 336, 354

relief efforts during Depression,
 218–219, 220
House of Representatives. *See
 also* United States Congress
 impeaches A. Johnson, 137
 impeaches Clinton, 304–305,
 379, 399
House on Un-American Activities
 Committee (HUAC), 256
Housing Act of 1949, 252
Hussein, Saddam, 311–302

• I •

"I have a dream" (King), 275
immigrants
 Chinese Exclusion Act of 1882,
 158, 365, 391
 deportation of Mexican
 American, 228
 discrimination against, 205–206
 headright system and, 44
 labor pool of new, 108, 336, 354,
 377, 398
 questions, 326, 349, 367, 392
 railroads built by, 336, 354
 reaction to Irish, 118, 375, 397
 reforming restrictions on, 274
impeachment
 Clinton, 304–305, 379, 399
 Johnson, A., 137, 379, 399
imperalism. *See* American
 imperalism
income tax reforms
 New Deal, 225
 Progressive Era, 184–185
 questions, 369, 393–394
indentured servants, 44, 367, 392
Indian Removal Act, 96, 332, 353
indigenous cultures, 27–28
individualism, 47
Industrial Revolution. *See also*
 Second Industrial Revolution
 First, 105–106
 Second, 151–168
industry. *See also* Second
 Industrial Revolution
 inventions of Second Industrial
 Revolution, 152–153
 mass-production techniques,
 211–212, 329, 350–351, 379,
 399
 New Deal for, 223
 questions on, 153
 reforms in food, 188, 321
 World War II's influence on, 238
influential leaders, 405–409
instructions
 Practice Test I, 317
 Practice Test II, 361
Internet, 304, 309

continued

continued

continued

continued